DEVELOPMENT MACROECONOMICS

DEVELOPMENT MACROECONOMICS

Pierre-Richard Agénor and Peter J. Montiel

PRINCETON UNIVERSITY PRESS   PRINCETON, NEW JERSEY

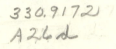

Copyright © 1996 by Princeton University Press
Published by Princeton University Press, 41 William Street,
Princeton, New Jersey 08540
In the United Kingdom: Princeton University Press, Chichester,
West Sussex

Library of Congress Cataloging-in-Publication Data
Agénor, Pierre-Richard.
    Development macroeconomics / Pierre-Richard Agénor and Peter J.
Montiel.
        p.   cm.
    Includes bibliographical references and index.
    ISBN 0-691-03413-3 (cloth : alk. paper)
    1. Developing countries–Economic conditions. 2. Development eco-
nomics. 3. Macroeconomics. I. Montiel, Peter. II. Title.
HC59.7.A7422   1996
330.9172'4—dc20   95-2853

This book has been composed in Times Roman

Princeton University Press books are printed on acid-free paper and meet
the guidelines for permanence and durability of the Committee on Production Guidelines for Book Longevity of the Council on Library Resources

Printed in the United States of America

10 9 8 7 6 5 4 3 2 1

TO OUR FATHERS,

The late Frédéric, and Pedro, ——————————————————

FOR THEIR SUPPORT AND GUIDANCE

Acknowledgments ‾‾‾‾‾‾‾‾‾‾‾‾‾‾‾‾‾‾‾‾‾‾‾‾‾‾‾‾‾‾‾‾‾‾‾‾‾

THIS BOOK is the product of many years of research in development macroeconomics conducted mostly in the stimulating environment provided by the Research Department of the International Monetary Fund. We owe thanks to many of our colleagues and co-authors in the Fund and elsewhere for commenting on successive chapter drafts and helping to clarify our thinking. We have greatly benefited from comments and discussions over the years with Joshua Aizenman, Carlos Asilis, David Bevan, Jagdeep Bhandari, Eduardo Borensztein, Paul Cashin, José De Gregorio, Sebastián Edwards, Robert Flood, Maxwell Fry, Linda Goldberg, Morris Goldstein, Nadeem Haque, Steven Kamin, Mohsin Khan, Saul Lizondo, Donald Mathieson, Jonathan Ostry, Carmen Reinhart, Julio Santaella, Mark Taylor, Murat Ucer, and Carlos Végh. We are particularly grateful to Joshua Aizenman for reading the complete typescript and suggesting several improvements to preliminary drafts. We would also like to express our appreciation to the publishers of the *Handbook of International Macroeconomics,* the *Journal of Development Economics,* the *Journal of Macroeconomics,* the *IMF Staff Papers,* and *Princeton Essays in International Finance* for permission to use material from our published articles.

Contents

List of Figures	xiv
List of Tables	xvii
Foreword	xxi
Introduction and Overview	3
Overview of the Book	4
Some Methodological Issues	8
One	
Scope of Development Macroeconomics	11
1.1 Monetarism, Structuralism, and Developing Nations	13
1.2 Economic Structure and Macroeconomic Analysis	16
1.2.1 Openness to Trade in Commodities and Assets	16
1.2.2 Long-Run Supply Behavior	22
1.2.3 Short-Run Supply Behavior	22
1.2.4 Financial Markets	23
1.2.5 Characteristics of the Government Budget	26
1.2.6 Characteristics of Private Behavior	29
1.2.7 Stability of Policy Regimes	30
1.3 Development Macroeconomics: Special Topics	32
PART I MACROECONOMIC RELATIONSHIPS AND MARKET STRUCTURE	35
Two	
Aggregate Accounts, Production, and Market Structure	37
2.1 A General Accounting Framework	38
2.1.1 The Nonfinancial Private Sector	38
2.1.2 The Public Sector	40
2.1.3 The Commercial Banking System	42
2.1.4 Aggregate Relationships	43
2.2 Production Structure in an Open Economy	44
2.2.1 The Mundell-Fleming Model	44
2.2.2 The "Dependent Economy" Model	48
2.2.3 A Model with Three Goods	52
2.3 The Structure of Labor Markets	55
2.3.1 Functioning of Labor Markets	55
2.3.2 Output and Unemployment	57

    2.3.3 Indexation and Wage Rigidity   60
    2.3.4 Labor Market Segmentation   62
  2.4 Informal Financial Markets   64
    2.4.1 Informal Loan Markets   65
    2.4.2 Parallel Markets for Foreign Exchange   67

Three
Behavioral Functions   73

  3.1 Consumption and Saving   73
    3.1.1 Consumption Smoothing   77
    3.1.2 Length of Planning Horizon
           and Liquidity Constraints   78
    3.1.3 Effects of Interest Rate Changes on Savings   79
    3.1.4 Public and Private Consumption   80
  3.2 Private Investment   81
    3.2.1 Specification Issues   81
    3.2.2 Determinants of Private Investment: The Evidence 84
  3.3 The Demand for Money   86
    3.3.1 Conventional Money Demand Models   87
    3.3.2 Currency Substitution and the Demand for Money 89
  3.4 Aggregate Supply Functions   96
    3.4.1 Cross-Regime Tests   97
    3.4.2 Within-Regime Tests   98
    3.4.3 An Assessment of the Evidence   101

PART II SHORT-RUN MACROECONOMIC POLICIES   103

Four
Fiscal Deficits, Public Solvency, and the Macroeconomy 105

  4.1 The Government Budget Constraint   106
    4.1.1 The Consolidated Budget Deficit   106
    4.1.2 The Measurement of Fiscal Deficits   109
    4.1.3 Seignorage and Inflationary Finance   111
  4.2 Policy Consistency and the Solvency Constraint   121
    4.2.1 The Intertemporal Solvency Constraint   122
    4.2.2 Financing Constraints and Policy Consistency 125
  4.3 Macroeconomic Effects of Fiscal Deficits   126
    4.3.1 Ricardian Equivalence   127
    4.3.2 Deficits, Inflation, and the "Tight Money" Paradox 128
    4.3.3 Deficits, Real Interest Rates, and Crowding Out 137
    4.3.4 Deficits, the Current Account,
           and the Real Exchange Rate   147

Five
Financial Markets, Capital Mobility, and Monetary Policy

Financial Markets, Capital Mobility, and Monetary Policy   151

5.1 *Financial Repression: Macroeconomic Effects*   152
5.2 *Financial Repression, the Inflation Tax,*
    and Capital Controls   153
    5.2.1 *Financial Repression and Inflationary Finance*   154
    5.2.2 *A General Public-Finance Approach*   157
5.3 *Capital Mobility: Empirical Evidence*   159
    5.3.1 *The Magnitude of Gross Flows*   160
    5.3.2 *Tests of Interest Parity Conditions*   161
    5.3.3 *Tests of Monetary Autonomy*   165
    5.3.4 *Saving-Investment Correlations*   166
    5.3.5 *Summary*   167
5.4 *Models of Informal Credit and Foreign Exchange Markets*   167
    5.4.1 *Models of Informal Credit Markets*   168
    5.4.2 *Models of Informal Currency Markets*   174
5.5 *Monetary Policy with Informal Financial Markets*   180
    5.5.1 *The Analytical Framework*   181
    5.5.2 *Changes in Monetary Policy Instruments*   185

Six
Exchange-Rate Management I: Credibility and Crises

Exchange-Rate Management I: Credibility and Crises   190

6.1 *Evidence on Exchange-Rate Regimes*   190
6.2 *Credibility and Exchange-Rate Management*   195
    6.2.1 *Time Inconsistency and Exchange-Rate Policy*   196
    6.2.2 *Credibility of a Fixed Exchange Rate*   200
    6.2.3 *Reputation, Signaling, and Exchange-Rate*
        Commitment   201
    6.2.4 *Credibility Effects of Monetary Unions*   203
6.3 *Speculative Attacks and Balance-of-Payments Crises*   207
    6.3.1 *A Model of Exchange Regime Collapse*   208
    6.3.2 *Extensions to the Basic Framework*   213
    6.3.3 *Evidence on Balance-of-Payments Crises*   218

Seven
Exchange-Rate Management II: Contractionary Devaluation and Real-Exchange-Rate Rules

Exchange-Rate Management II: Contractionary Devaluation and
Real-Exchange-Rate Rules   223

7.1 *Contractionary Devaluation*   224
    7.1.1 *Effects on Aggregate Demand*   224
    7.1.2 *Effects on Aggregate Supply*   240
    7.1.3 *Empirical Evidence*   248

7.2 Real-Exchange-Rate Targeting   255
    7.2.1 The Analytical Framework   256
    7.2.2 Targeting the Real Exchange Rate   258
    7.2.3 Effects of Macroeconomic Shocks   260

PART III ANALYSIS OF STABILIZATION PROGRAMS   263

Eight
An Overview of Stabilization Programs   265

8.1 Populism   267
    8.1.1 Chile under Allende (1970–73)   267
    8.1.2 Peru under García (1986–90)   269
8.2 Orthodox Money-Based Stabilization   270
    8.2.1 Chile (September 1973)   271
    8.2.2 Bolivia (August 29, 1985)   272
8.3 Exchange-Rate-Based (Southern Cone)
    Stabilization Programs   275
    8.3.1 Chile (February 1978)   275
    8.3.2 Uruguay (October 1978)   276
    8.3.3 Argentina (December 1978)   280
8.4 Heterodox Programs   282
    8.4.1 Argentina (June 14, 1985)   282
    8.4.2 Israel (July 1, 1985)   286
    8.4.3 Brazil (February 28, 1986)   290
    8.4.4 Mexico (December 1987)   293

Nine
Inflation and Short-Run Dynamics   298

9.1 Models of the Inflationary Process   298
    9.1.1 Inflation, Money, and Fiscal Deficits   299
    9.1.2 Food Supply, Distribution, and the Wage-Price Cycle   306
    9.1.3 A Structuralist-Monetarist Model   311
9.2 Dynamics of Monetary and Exchange-Rate Rules   314
    9.2.1 A One-Good Framework   314
    9.2.2 A Three-Good Model with Sticky Wages   327

Ten
Analytical Issues in Disinflation
Programs   338

10.1 Two Puzzles in Exchange-Rate-Based Programs   338
    10.1.1 The Boom-Recession Cycle   339
    10.1.2 The Behavior of Real Interest Rates   356

10.2 The Role of Credibility in Disinflation Programs 359
    10.2.1 Sources of Credibility Problems 360
    10.2.2 Enhancing the Credibility of Disinflation
           Programs 365
    10.2.3 Policy Lessons 378
10.3 Disinflation and Nominal Anchors 381
Appendix: Output Effects of Price Controls 385

Eleven
Stabilization Policies with Informal Financial Markets 389

11.1 An Integrated Analytical Framework 389
    11.1.1 Structure of the Model 390
    11.1.2 Effects of Interest Rate Liberalization 399
11.2 A General Equilibrium Simulation Model 403
    11.2.1 Structure of the Model 404
    11.2.2 Effects of Stabilization Policies 409
Appendix: Equations of the Simulation Model 416

PART IV GROWTH, DEBT, AND STRUCTURAL REFORMS 419

Twelve
Models of Stabilization and Growth 421

12.1 Bank-Fund Models 423
    12.1.1 The IMF Financial Programming Model 423
    12.1.2 The World Bank RMSM Model 425
    12.1.3 A Simple Bank-Fund Model of Stabilization
          and Growth 426
12.2 "Three-Gap" Models 427
12.3 Macroeconometric Models 431
    12.3.1 Structure of Production 432
    12.3.2 Aggregate Supply 433
    12.3.3 Aggregate Demand 434
12.4 Computable General Equilibrium Models 436
Appendix: The Khan-Knight Monetary Disequilibrium Model 439

Thirteen
The Debt Overhang, Investment, and Growth 442

13.1 Origins of the Debt Crisis 444
    13.1.1 Public Sector Solvency 444
    13.1.2 Application to the Debt Crisis 446
13.2 Policy Response and Macroeconomic Implications 450
13.3 Resolution of the Crisis: The Brady Plan 454
    13.3.1 Outline of the Plan 454
    13.3.2 Macroeconomic Effects: Conceptual Issues 456

13.3.3 An Overview of Some Early Brady Plan Deals 463
Appendix: Incentive Effects of a Debt Overhang 468

Fourteen
Trade, Financial, and Exchange-Rate Reforms 472

14.1 Monetary and Financial Liberalization 472
14.1.1 Monetary Reform 473
14.1.2 Financial Liberalization 477
14.2 Unification of Foreign Exchange Markets 479
14.2.1 Short-Run Dynamics of Unification 479
14.2.2 Longer-Run Effects of Unification 487
14.2.3 Evidence on Unification Attempts 489
14.3 Macroeconomic Effects of Trade Reforms 491
14.3.1 Trade Reforms: Some Recent Evidence 492
14.3.2 Trade Liberalization, Wage Rigidity,
and Employment 494
14.4 Sequencing and Speed of Reforms 499
14.4.1 Sequencing of Reforms 500
14.4.2 Adjustment Costs, Credibility, and the Speed
of Reform 505

PART V ENDOGENOUS GROWTH, POLITICAL
ECONOMY, AND LABOR MARKETS 509

Fifteen
Human Capital, Financial Intermediation, and Growth 511

15.1 The Neoclassical Growth Model 513
15.2 Endogenous Growth Theories: A Brief Overview 518
15.2.1 Externalities and Increasing Returns 519
15.2.2 Human Capital and Knowledge 520
15.2.3 Effects of Financial Intermediation 522
15.3 Empirical Evidence and Assessment 527

Sixteen
The Political Economy of Stabilization and Adjustment 533

16.1 Politics, Economic Policy, and Adjustment 533
16.1.1 The Political Economy of Structural Adjustment 534
16.1.2 Political Instability, Inflation, and Fiscal Deficits 536
16.2 Political Stabilization Cycles 536
16.2.1 "Opportunistic" Models 537
16.2.2 Models with Informational Asymmetries 543
16.3 Elections-Induced Economic Cycles: The Evidence 545
16.3.1 Informal Evidence 546
16.3.2 Econometric Evidence 547

Seventeen
Macroeconomic Adjustment with Segmented Labor Markets   556

17.1 A Partial-Equilibrium Framework   556
17.2 A Macroeconomic Model with Segmented Labor Markets   559
       17.2.1 Output and the Labor Market   559
       17.2.2 Consumption and the Market for Nontraded Goods   562
       17.2.3 The Government   563
       17.2.4 Labor Market Adjustment   563
17.3 Government Spending, Real Wages, and Employment   564
*17.4 Labor Heterogeneity, Minimum Wages,
       and Unemployment*   567

Epilogue   571

Notes   575

References   625

Index of Names   661

Index of Subjects   671

List of Figures

1.1	Distribution of World Output, 1993	12
1.2	World Commodity Prices	19
1.3	Developing Countries: Terms of Trade and Nonfuel Commodity Prices	20
1.4	Inflation and Seignorage in Industrial and Developing Countries	30
2.1	Internal and External Balance in the Mundell-Fleming Model	47
2.2	Classical Equilibrium in the Dependent-Economy Model	51
2.3	Effects of a Negative Terms-of-Trade Shock in the Three-Good Model	54
2.4	Output and Unemployment in Developing Countries	58
2.5	Real Wages and Unemployment in Developing Countries	61
2.6	Korea: Formal and Informal Interest Rates	66
2.7	Parallel Market Premiums in Developing Countries	69
2.8	Exchange Rate and Price Variability in Developing Countries	71
3.1	Foreign-Currency Deposits Held in Domestic Banks	90
3.2	Foreign-Currency Deposits Held Abroad	92
4.1	Mexico: Public Sector Fiscal Balance	109
4.2	Inflation and Revenue from Inflationary Finance	114
4.3	Inflation, Inflationary Finance, and Total Tax Revenue	117
4.4	Inflation and Fiscal Deficits	129
4.5	Steady-State Equilibrium with Constant Conventional Deficit	135
4.6	Dynamics with Constant Conventional Deficit	136
4.7	Fiscal Deficits and Real Interest Rates	138
4.8	Steady-State Equilibrium with Zero Capital Mobility	144
4.9	Permanent and Temporary Increases in Government Spending with Zero Capital Mobility	145
5.1	Seignorage, Reserve Ratio, and the Inflation Tax	155
5.2	Determination of Output and the Informal Interest Rate in van Wijnbergen's Model	172

5.3 Devaluation, Underinvoicing, and the Current Account 178

6.1 Credibility and Commitment: Alternative Equilibria 199

6.2 The Process of a Balance-of-Payments Crisis 212

7.1 Equilibrium under a Real-Exchange-Rate Rule 259

7.2 Effect of an Improvement in the Terms of Trade 261

8.1 Inflation and Price Controls in Brazil, 1984–90 294

9.1 Seignorage and Dual Inflation Equilibria 300

9.2 Fiscal Deficits and Inflation with Gradual Adjustment
of the Money Market 304

9.3 Equilibrium in the New Structuralist Model 308

9.4 The Wage-Price Cycle in the New Structuralist Model 310

9.5 Equilibrium with Money and Food Subsidies
in the New Structuralist Model 313

9.6 Steady-State Equilibrium in the One-Good Model 322

9.7 Reduction in the Devaluation Rate in the One-Good Model 324

10.1 Real Interest Rates in the Tablita Experiments 340

10.2 Real Interest Rates in Heterodox Experiments 341

10.3 Equilibrium and Adjustment in the Rodríguez Model 343

10.4 Dynamics of the Calvo-Végh "Temporariness" Model
with Imperfect Credibility 350

10.5 Price Controls under Competitive and Monopolistic Markets 386

11.1 Steady-State Equilibrium with Constant Reserves 402

11.2 Increase in Interest Rates on Bank Deposits 403

12.1 The Polak Model 425

12.2 The Three-Gap Model 430

12.3 Logical Structure of the Khan-Knight Model 440

13.1 Growth and Real Interest Rates in Highly
Indebted Developing Countries 447

14.1 Steady-State Equilibrium Prior to Reform 482

14.2 Dynamics upon Unification: Case I 484

14.3 Dynamics upon Unification: Case II 485

14.4 Chile: Trade Volumes and the Real Exchange Rate 495

15.1 Growth and Initial Per-Capita Income
in Developing Countries 518

15.2   Investment and Growth in Latin America   530

16.1   The Electoral Devaluation Cycle, Case I: $\alpha > 0$ 542

16.2   The Electoral Devaluation Cycle, Case II: $\alpha < 0$ 543

16.3   Government Spending and the Electoral Cycle
       in Latin America   548

17.1   Labor Mobility, Sectoral Wage Rigidity, and Adjustment   557

17.2   Efficiency Wages and Effort   561

17.3   Steady-State Equilibrium with Relative Wage Rigidity   566

17.4   Reduction in Government Spending on Nontraded Goods   567

List of Tables

1.1	Developing Countries: Trade Indicators	17
1.2	Developing Countries: Debt Indicators	21
1.3	Share of Private Investment in Total Investment in Developing Countries	24
1.4	Composition of Real Imports of Developing Countries	25
1.5	Monetization Ratios	27
1.6	Composition of Central Government Expenditure	28
1.7	Level and Composition of Tax Revenue	29
1.8	Macroeconomic Indicators, 1987–93	31
2.1	Developing Countries: Open Unemployment Rate	57
3.1	Overseas Foreign-Currency Deposits	91
4.1	Seignorage and the Inflation Tax	113
4.2	Inflation, Inflationary Finance, and Tax Revenue	118
4.3	Collection Lags by Major Revenue Categories	119
5.1	Effective Reserve Ratio and Seignorage	156
5.2	Estimates of the Capital Mobility Parameter for Developing Countries	164
5.3	Accounting Framework of van Wijnbergen's Model	171
6.1	Exchange-Rate Arrangements of Developing Countries, 1976–92	192
6.2	Geographical Distribution of Exchange-Rate Arrangements for Developing Countries, 1982–93	194
8.1	Incidence of High Inflation in Developing Countries, 1965–89	266
8.2	Chile: Macroeconomic Indicators, 1970–73	268
8.3	Peru: Macroeconomic Indicators, 1985–88	270
8.4	Chile: Macroeconomic Indicators, 1973–77	271
8.5	Bolivia: Macroeconomic Indicators, 1979–86	273
8.6	Chile: Macroeconomic Indicators, 1977–82	277

8.7   Uruguay: Macroeconomic Indicators, 1978–82   279

8.8   Argentina: Macroeconomic Indicators, 1976-82   281

8.9   Argentina: Macroeconomic Indicators, 1984–88   284

8.10   Israel: Macroeconomic Indicators, 1984–87   289

8.11   Brazil: Macroeconomic Indicators, 1985–87   292

8.12   Mexico: Macroeconomic Indicators, 1982–89   295

10.1   Intertemporal Elasticity of Substitution: Estimates
       for Developing Countries   353

11.1   Parameter Values for the Simulation Model   409

11.2   Simulation Results of Macroeconomic Shocks   411

13.1   Highly Indebted Countries: Share of Public and Publicly
       Guaranteed Debt in Total Debt   443

13.2   Highly Indebted Countries: Public Sector Deficit,
       1974–1982   447

13.3   Highly Indebted Countries: Ratio of Public Debt to GDP   448

13.4   Highly Indebted Countries: Actual and Sustainable Values
       of the Primary Surplus, 1982   449

13.5   Highly Indebted Countries: Responses to the Debt Crisis,
       1976–88   452

13.6   Highly Indebted Countries: Private Investment and Private
       External Assets, 1980–88   455

13.7   Heavily Indebted Countries: Debt Overhang Tax Rate   460

13.8   DDSR Operations under the Brady Plan, 1989–93   464

13.9   Brady Plan Countries: Changes in V_t from DDSR
       Operations   466

13.10 Brady Plan Countries: Debt Reduction in DDSR Operations   466

14.1   Trade Liberalization and Employment   492

14.2   Indicators of Trade Regimes Before and After Reform   494

15.1   Developing Countries: Growth Performance   512

15.2   Productivity and Growth in Developing Countries   515

15.3   Productivity and Growth in Latin America, 1940–80   516

15.4   Developing Countries: Decomposition
       of Trend Output Growth   517

15.5   Developing Countries: Growth Characteristics   528

16.1   Estimation Results: Government Expenditure:
       1972q1–1990q4   550

16.2   Estimation Results: Domestic Credit to the Government:
       1972q1–1990q4   552

16.3   Estimation Results: Wages and Transfers: 1972–90   553

THIS BOOK on "emerging market" macroeconomics could not be more timely. Around the world, from the transition economies of Europe, Russia, and China to the developing economies of Latin America and Africa, students want to understand, professors want to teach, and policy makers want to address the same kinds of macroeconomic issues. But all too often the answer to their problems is a homegrown refrain: "This country is different, professor. You don't understand."

True, developing economies have market structures and institutions that fundamentally affect the way macroeconomic policies work, and these may in fact make them different. Yet, giving in to the notion that they are different—worse, each uniquely different from any and all others!—throws overboard a vast amount of knowledge and experience that could be brought to bear on solving real problems. The very notion that each country is unique and thus so are its problems is, of course, ridiculous. Major inflation experiences have a vast amount in common, as do stabilization experiences or experiences of trade liberalization or currency overvaluation. In fact, how could one seriously address these problems without looking across the world and asking just how they presented themselves elsewhere? The battle cry "this country is different" is ultimately a scoundrel's plea for protecting outdated interpretations or politicized policy advice from intellectual import competition.

As a guide to the macroeconomics of developing economies, Agénor and Montiel's book uniquely fills the role of bringing together the useful knowledge and evidence of decades of research. It strikes a balance between the recognition that these countries are, in fact, different in interesting and important ways that are relevant to policy making and the recognition that in some deep ways the problems are about the same everywhere. In so doing, the book opens up this area of macroeconomics to an international competition of ideas and professional standards that will enable young researchers, who are willing and able to invest in the requisite skills, to break the control of established pundits who have all too long held a monopoly on interpreting events and mechanisms.

For the past decade, the World Bank and the International Monetary Fund have had the good fortune of having a number of great research directors—Anne Krueger, Stan Fischer, Larry Summers, and Michael Bruno at the Bank and Jacob Frenkel and Michael Mussa at the Fund. They and their colleagues have encouraged active, systematic, and modern research on the macroeconomic problems of developing countries and emerging market economies. The need to fill the vacuum was essential both to guide the institutions in their own policy thinking and to make them more effective partners in local dialogue. In doing so, the research departments of the Bank and the Fund have welcomed a talented group of researchers from around the world who have come as senior visitors or brand new staffers. In addition, there is increasingly more research being done in developing economies themselves; returning Ph.D.s as well as students who have not even gone abroad are joining the game. They use modern methods and models to test just what the relationships are, and how important, in fact, special institutions or features turn out to be. In the process, more often than not, they confirm the view that there are striking similarities across borders.

This book takes one step further the progress in cross-border research on developing economies. It systematically integrates the literature and in so doing opens it up to generations of students—both in developing economies and in advanced economies. In using the modern language of formal models, it immediately widens the applicability of an argument across countries, challenges researchers or students to identify their own local counterpart of a variable or structural feature, and highlights the need to adapt or change a particular piece of the model. It thus brings discipline to the question of whether and how a country might differ from a stylized case. Importantly, it shows how opening up, deregulating, or modernizing will change an economy's structural relations, and it specifies where the change will show up.

Of course, the basic question is whether developing economies really are different from the industrialized world. Agénor and Montiel accept the premise that there are at least four important ways in which developing economies differ from stylized advanced countries. First, there is a significant difference in the productive structure. Specifically, the terms of trade play a very important role. That is obvious for a country which is significantly involved in commodity production—Nigeria in oil or Chile in copper, for example. Favorable terms of trade shocks show up as a trade surplus, an income shock for businesses and households, and an improvement in the budget. In principle, the same is true for advanced economies; however, with the exception of oil, no commodity plays a significant enough role to deserve special attention. But maybe even that is wrong—the sharp decline in commodity prices of the past decade may well have played a large role in the relatively painless disinflation among rich countries.

The second special feature of developing economies is the segmentation of markets for capital, labor, and goods. In the capital market, financial repression is the counterpart of a search to control credit and the easily overplayed ability to finance deficits cheaply. In labor markets, the duality of formal and informal markets is a prominent element. In goods markets, protection and the resulting loss of thorough competition are a key feature of price formation. In foreign exchange markets, various forms of exchange control limit market integration and open up the possibility (and often the illusion) of a newfound degree of policy flexibility. These segmentation factors are, indeed, part of the reality of an emerging market. Yet, with the arrival of reform, openness, and deregulation, they are also all on the way out. Even so, there is good reason to pay attention to them, because it will take a while for them to disappear altogether, and the transition itself involves important policy issues. Removing capital controls, deregulating banks, or opening trade cannot be done just as an isolated step; it needs to be part of a more comprehensive macroeconomic package. Trade opening, for example, needs as a countermeasure a real depreciation. Without that, a Mexican- or Chilean-style payments crisis is just a few years off.

Third, the book highlights the open economy aspect of macroeconomics in ways that differ substantially from treatments in the texts written for advanced countries. In the latter, the open economy even today is relegated to a sideshow, despite the fact that it is a key part of what makes up the mechanism and the constraints under which policy operates. Thus, this book might be a more useful guide for students in, say, Spain or Italy than are their usual texts.

Finally, political economy is far more prominent in the macroeconomic operation of developing countries than in established industrial countries. If markets are segemented, the institutional counterpart of that segmentation is often a bureaucracy that benefits from the implicit regulatory power along with economic agents who, by way of factor prices or privileges, enjoy advantages from the status quo. Understanding that link between political economy and structure is the first step in engineering successful reform. It has been said of the Holy Roman Empire that more money was made in the few hundred years of its decline than in the thousands of years of its existence. In a compressed time frame, much the same is strikingly underway in the developing world and in the former socialist countries, as evidenced, for example, by the Mexican billionaires or the appearance of Russia's super rich. If there were nothing special about the macroeconomics of developing and emerging market economies and their transformation, these vast changes in wealth would not have come about.

Agénor and Montiel have done a great job in shaping this book. *Development Macroeconomics* fills an obvious gap, and it does so in a masterful way. Rather than focusing on formal, self-satisfied theory, the book is centered on the analytical foundations of policy formulation. That makes it especially effective as a teaching instrument and useful as a guide to policy makers and their advisors. For their work and effort, Agénor and Montiel deserve congratulations. They have created a wonderful book and will come away with the satisfaction and reward of great teachers.

Rudiger Dornbusch
Massachusetts Institute of Technology

DEVELOPMENT MACROECONOMICS

Introduction and Overview _____

ATTENTION to short-run macroeconomic issues in developing countries emerged largely in the context of the monetarist-structuralist debate about the sources of inflation in Latin America during the 1950s and 1960s.[1] Whereas the early literature in this area was essentially nontechnical, a growing analytical literature has developed since the early 1970s to address a succession of macroeconomic woes that have afflicted developing countries. This literature has reached a level of rigor and sophistication comparable to that which characterizes industrial-country macroeconomics. Much of it, however, is written at an advanced level and is scattered over a wide range of professional economic journals.

Partly as a result of this, the existing teaching material on developing economies has largely ignored these recent developments in macroeconomic analysis. Consequently, existing texts in development economics and macroeconomics do not meet the needs of those concerned with macroeconomic issues in developing nations. Economic growth, rather than short-run macroeconomic policy, remains the dominant concern in existing texts on development economics. Attention is often concentrated on the contribution of aggregate supply to economic growth, in terms of either the productive use of unlimited supply of labor or the removal of particular supply constraints, such as a shortage of domestic saving or foreign exchange.[2] Similarly, in standard textbooks in macroeconomics (or open-economy macroeconomics) the analysis is generally conducted in terms of advanced, industrialized economies. When issues relevant to developing countries are raised, there is often no attempt to adapt the theoretical framework to the particular conditions and structural characteristics of these countries.[3] A series of influential books by Lance Taylor (1979, 1983, 1991) does attempt to provide a systematic analytical treatment of developing-country macroeconomic issues. However, Taylor is more concerned in these books with presenting the "new structuralist" approach to macroeconomics as a challenge to the "orthodox" approach, rather than presenting a balanced overview of the field. Consequently, many of the areas in which "orthodox" thinking has provided much insight—and, ironically, even strengthened new structuralist arguments in some cases—tend to be ignored in these books, and the fundamental complementarities that often exist between rival schools of thought are lost.

This book attempts to present a more balanced approach to the macroeconomics of developing nations. It presents a coherent, rigorous, and comprehensive overview of the analytical literature in this area. It reviews attempts to formulate and adapt standard macroeconomic analysis to incorporate particular features and conditions found in developing economies, and uses a variety of models to examine macroeconomic policy issues of current concern to these countries. Empirical evidence on behavioral assumptions as well as on the effects of macroeconomic policies in developing countries is examined systematically, in light of the predictions of the analytical models. The book's level of rigor makes it suitable for teaching graduate students in development economics, macroeconomics, and international economics, or advanced undergraduates with a solid background in standard macroeconomics and international economics. It should also be of interest to policymakers—and their advisors—in developing countries. The book provides extensive references to the literature, with the objective of making this material more easily identifiable to students and researchers, and eventually of helping to establish development macroeconomics as a coherent and legitimate subfield of development economics and macroeconomics.

Overview of the Book

We set the stage by attempting to define the scope and objectives of development macroeconomics. Traditional approaches to development macroeconomics (as exemplified by the monetarist-structuralist debate of the 1950s and 1960s) are reviewed in Chapter 1. Our discussion emphasizes the need to take structural factors systematically into account in macroeconomic analysis. The chapter goes on to describe the structural features that, in our view, distinguish most developing countries from the textbook industrial-country model. Among the distinctive aspects of development macroeconomics are the usefulness of a three-good (exportables, importables, and nontradables) disaggregation of production and the roles of financial repression, informal markets, public sector production, imported intermediate goods, working capital, and labor market segmentation.

The rest of the book is organized into five parts. The first part focuses on macroeconomic relationships and differences in market structure between industrial and developing nations. Chapter 2 focuses on the accounting framework and some key aspects of macroeconomic modeling for developing countries. Essentially, macroeconomic modeling consists of giving economic content to a set of aggregate accounting relationships by adding behavioral equations and equilibrium conditions. The accounting relationships that are relevant for a particular case depend on the structure of the economy. Thus, this chapter describes a "benchmark" accounting framework that can be adapted for specific uses later in the book. Next the chapter turns to particular modeling issues, the first of which involves alternative choices of commodity disaggregation. The particular role played by the structural features of the labor market and the degree of development of the financial system are also reviewed.

Chapter 3 focuses on behavioral functions, exploring in particular how the specification of standard macroeconomic functions must be altered to reflect structural features that are either specific to or more pronounced in the developing world. This includes liquidity constraints in aggregate consumption, credit and foreign exchange rationing as well as debt overhang effects on production and private investment, and the effects of financial repression, currency substitution, and informal financial markets on money demand. In each case we present a critical overview of the recent empirical and analytical work.

The second part of the book focuses on fiscal, monetary, and exchange-rate policies in developing countries. Chapter 4 examines the nature and implications of fiscal rigidities and the effect of fiscal deficits on a variety of macroeconomic variables. An inadequate tax base and administrative difficulties in tax collection are key macroeconomic problems in the developing world and typically lead to inefficient systems of taxation in which high tax rates are levied on a narrow base. In addition, these structural features, coupled with political and other constraints on the level of government expenditures, result in heavy reliance on revenue from financial repression and multiple-currency practices, on the inflation tax, and on excessive debt financing, both external and (less familiarly) domestic. Actual or prospective fiscal insolvency has been at the heart of many macroeconomic problems in such countries, such as debt crises, capital flight, excessive domestic real interest rates, and hyperinflation. The chapter presents an overview of fiscal issues, summarizing key empirical facts and drawing on the analytical relationships among the various macroeconomic problems described above and fiscal rigidities.

Financial repression is a central macroeconomic phenomenon in many developing countries. Yet the theory of short-run macroeconomic management, as opposed to that of efficiency and growth issues, under financial repression is not well developed. In Chapter 5 we analyze the tools of monetary policy and the monetary transmission mechanism under financial repression in the context of an economy that is at least semiopen financially. We present empirical evidence on financial openness in developing countries, on government revenue from financial repression, and on the effects of financial repression on saving, investment, the degree of capital mobility, and the extent of capital flight. Alternative analytical approaches to modeling informal credit and foreign exchange markets at the macroeconomic level are also discussed, with an emphasis on the role of portfolio factors and expectations in the determination of informal interest rates and parallel exchange rates in these models.

Chapters 6 and 7 discuss various issues related to exchange-rate management in developing countries. The primary message of Chapter 6 is that exchange-rate systems in the developing world differ markedly from those in industrial countries. Fixed official rates are much more prevalent, but these are often accompanied by foreign exchange rationing and the emergence of parallel markets. Both of these phenomena have profound macroeconomic implications. The chapter also emphasizes the role of credibility—and the lack thereof—as well as the implications of inconsistencies between fiscal policy and exchange-rate policy for the balance of payments. In addition, the management of the official exchange rate raises a number of important macroeconomic issues, such as the possibility that devaluation may have contractionary effects on output or that targeting the real exchange rate may destabilize the price level. Chapter 7 provides an extensive review of the analytical issues involved in these controversies, as well as an overview of the empirical literature.

The third part of the book focuses more closely on short-run stabilization issues in light of the features of developing economies described previously. Because high inflation has been the central problem confronting many well-known stabilization episodes in the developing world, we begin Chapter 8 by reviewing attempts at stabilizing high inflation in developing countries. We classify stabilization attempts into the categories of money-based and exchange-rate-based programs, and we draw on the voluminous existing literature to summarize experience with alternative approaches to stabilization, including the literature on "heterodox" programs. Whereas Chapter 8 is mainly descriptive in nature, Chapters 9 and 10 are mainly analytical. Chapter 9 presents alternative models of the inflationary process, focusing on differences between "orthodox" and "new structuralist" approaches, and examines the macroeconomic dynamics associated with monetary and exchange rate policy rules in a context where international capital mobility is imperfect. Chapter 10 discusses two important sets of issues that have arisen in the context of exchange-rate-based disinflation programs (the behavior of output and real interest rates) and presents an extensive discussion of the role of credibility factors in disinflation programs. We examine, in particular, several alternative proposals to enhance the credibility of stabilization plans.

Chapter 11 examines (in a more detailed context than in Chapter 5) how informal financial markets affect the dynamic response of the economy to various types of stabilization policies. The issue is important because such markets are forward-looking and will thus bring to the present the effects of anticipated future policy changes. Thus, the consequences of credibility—or its absence—will often be transmitted through such markets in developing countries. A medium-size integrated analytical framework is developed that takes into account the two main types of informal financial markets. A more detailed, general equilibrium simulation model with informal credit and foreign currency markets is then described and used to study the results of alternative policy experiments.

Part 4 of the book focuses on medium-term issues in development macroeconomics. Chapter 12 provides a critical examination of alternative analytical treatments of growth and its relationship with short-run stabilization. The focus is on the two approaches to the growth issues developed at the International Monetary Fund and the World Bank, cum-two gap models and computable general equilibrium models, although conventional "Cowles Foundation" econometric models of developing countries are reviewed as well.

Chapter 13 concentrates on the recent growth problems of the heavily indebted developing nations, particularly on the relationship between the debt overhang, investment, and growth. As in previous chapters, the approach is both analytical and empirical. First we document the recent growth and investment experience (treating private and public investment separately) of these countries. We then consider analytical relationships among debt overhang, debt service, investment, and growth. Finally, we evaluate the existing empirical evidence on these relationships.

The fiscal, financial, and exchange-rate issues discussed in the first and second parts of the book have interacted to result in a heavily repressed and controlled macroeconomic environment in many developing countries. Yet the severe macroeconomic crises that afflicted many of these nations in the 1980s, together with the successful examples of liberalizing economies in East Asia, unleashed a wave of trade and financial reforms almost everywhere in the early 1990s. Chapter 14 documents the evidence on trade and financial liberalization and macroeconomic performance, and discusses problems of short-run macroeconomic management during the liberalization process. A key problem confronting recent programs of liberalization and structural change in developing countries is the relationship between structural reforms and stabilization policies. In particular, a central preoccupation has been the question of whether structural changes need to be preceded by macroeconomic stabilization or whether the two can proceed concurrently. In addition, the proper sequencing of the liberalization and reform measures themselves has been the subject of controversy. A detailed account of the debate in this area is provided, integrating analytical arguments and empirical evidence on alternative sequencing options.

Part 5 of the book discusses some areas of development macroeconomics that have been particularly active in recent years. Recent developments in the endogenous growth literature are considered in Chapter 15. The chapter begins by providing a brief overview of the growth experience in the developing world and an examination of the role of traditional neoclassi-cal theories of growth in explaining cross-country growth differences. The discussion is then extended to consider alternative channels for long-run growth—in particular, the roles of human capital and economies of scale. The importance of financial factors in the process of growth and develop-ment is also examined in detail.

Chapter 16 focuses on the role of political factors in the adoption and abandonment of stabilization and structural adjustment programs in devel-oping countries. It summarizes the major findings of existing research and attempts to examine empirically whether a regular "political business cy-cle" can be detected in the pattern of public spending in Colombia, Costa Rica, and Venezuela. It also provides an analytical framework for examin-ing the link between exchange-rate policy and electoral cycles—an issue that has not received much attention but may prove particularly relevant for some developing countries.

As discussed in Chapter 2, the analysis of labor markets in development economics has focused traditionally on issues such as the determinants of rural to urban migration, the growth of the urban labor force and the associ-ated rise in urban unemployment, and the effects of education on levels of earnings. The role that the structure of labor markets may play in determin-ing the long-run effects of trade reforms and structural adjustment policies has also been long recognized. In the past few years, however, there has been much interest in the role of labor markets in the context of short-run macroeconomic adjustment in developing countries. Chapter 17 examines the role of labor market segmentation and sectoral wage rigidity in the trans-mission of macroeconomic policy shocks.

Some Methodological Issues

Our attempt to provide coverage of both theory and policy at an accessible level has inevitably involved simplification of what are sometimes complex and controversial issues. As a result of sacrificing generality in the interest of clarity and analytical convenience, the conclusions may sometimes ap-pear less compelling than they would otherwise be. Proofs of complicated results are presented in some important cases; in other cases the general properties of relevant models are described and appropriate references to the literature are provided. The mathematical background required for this book includes standard algebra, differential equation systems, and basic dy-namic optimization techniques.

Many of the models developed in the book are not derived from "first principles" but are included because they have proved useful in understand-ing some key macroeconomic issues. As is well known, "ad hoc" macroeconomic models can be criticized on a number of grounds. First, such models yield results that may be sensitive to arbitrary assumptions about private sector behavior. Second, they are susceptible to the Lucas critique, according to which decision rules should be policy-invariant (Lucas, 1976). Third, without an explicit description of the preferences of different categories of agents and the budget constraints that they face, such models are, strictly speaking, unsuitable for making welfare comparisons. Fourth, they often ignore intertemporal restrictions implied by transversality conditions, that is, appropriate restrictions on the solution path associated with the optimization process. In contrast, models in which individual behavior is derived from an explicit intertemporal optimization problem serve a variety of purposes. First, optimizing models are suggestive of assumptions under which aggregate behavioral relations often postulated are consistent with individual maximizing behavior. Second, because they are built up on the basis of preferences that are invariant with respect to policy change, they provide vehicles for policy analysis that are less vulnerable to the Lucas critique. Third, they provide a natural setting in which welfare consequences of macroeconomic policies can be assessed.

However, optimizing models with "representative agents" are themselves subject to a number of criticisms. Heterogeneity and aggregation issues are often avoided in these models, leading in some circumstances to misleading results. Macroeconomic models based on "representative" firms and consumers, for instance, cannot adequately address issues that arise from imperfect information, where heterogeneity is crucial.[4] Money is often introduced into these optimizing models in rather ad hoc ways, so their immunity to the Lucas critique is not complete. Finally, the results and insights derived from ad hoc models can often be shown to carry through in more complex, optimizing models. Our overall strategy has therefore been to eschew, wherever possible, attempts to recast the existing developing-country macroeconomic literature in an optimizing framework, thereby avoiding overly complicated mathematical models in favor of simpler models with clear policy implications. In our analytical discussion of disinflation policies, however, we introduce a series of models with behavioral functions explicitly derived from an optimizing framework, thus showing how this type of analysis can be fruitfully applied to the case of developing countries.

In this context, an important methodological issue is the treatment of money. The very existence of money remains a vexing question in monetary economics, and it is not our purpose to get involved in this debate. Rather, in the models examined here, various "operational" assumptions are used to introduce money, in line with much of the recent literature in open-economy macroeconomics. In one approach that has been followed recently, money is introduced directly as an argument in the utility function, because agents are assumed to derive utility from holding cash balances in the same way that they derive utility from consuming real goods. A second approach views money as being necessary for transactions and held before purchases of consumption goods takes place; this leads to the popular "cash-in-advance" constraint (see Stockman, 1989). A third approach is to view money as facilitating transactions by reducing shopping time and thus acting as a substitute for leisure. This leads to the specification of a "transactions technology" directly in the private agents' budget constraint. Our preference is to adopt the transactions costs approach when using optimizing models because of the restrictive implications of the cash-in-advance constraint (it imposes, in particular, a zero-interest-rate elasticity of money demand). There are conditions under which choosing a particular operational formulation matters little (Feenstra, 1985), although, in general, alternative assumptions about the function of money do affect the predictions of macroeconomic models.

Despite our efforts, we have been unable to ensure that the notation used in the book is uniform and consistent. The same symbol sometimes carries different meanings. However, differences in notation never occur within a single chapter, and therefore there should be little possibility of confusion. Throughout the book, the derivative of a function of one variable is denoted with a prime, and (partial) derivatives of a function with several variables are indicated with subscripts. Finally, the derivative of a variable with respect to time is denoted by a dot over the variable.

One

Scope of Development Macroeconomics

In 1993 developing countries accounted for approximately one-third of world output (Figure 1.1), and 130 of the 177 countries monitored by the International Monetary Fund were classified in May 1994 as belonging to the developing world. Thus, although most of the world's production takes place in the industrial countries, country-specific macroeconomic policy formulation is usually carried out in a developing-country context. Despite this, much of modern macroeconomics has been developed to address circumstances and issues that arise in the context of industrial nations. The extent to which the analytical tools and models appropriate for the analysis of industrial-country macroeconomic problems are able to offer guidance for the formulation and conduct of macroeconomic policy in developing nations is thus an important issue for economists and policymakers alike.

The title of this book suggests that there is something intrinsically different about macroeconomics in developing nations. If the standard textbook treatment of macroeconomics developed for industrial countries were adequate to deal with macroeconomic phenomena in the developing world, there would be little justification for "development" macroeconomics. The title also suggests that macroeconomic phenomena in individual developing countries are sufficiently similar that it is meaningful to speak of a "development macroeconomics" rather than the macroeconomics of, say, Brazil, Bénin, or Nepal. We are aware that both implications are problematic; many economists subscribe to the notion that the standard tools and models of macroeconomics can be used in developing nations, and others would argue that Brazil, Bénin, and Nepal have so little in common that the very notion of a "development" macroeconomics lacks meaning.

These views are sufficiently compelling that the burden of proof falls on us. The view that development macroeconomics is distinctive may sound suspiciously like an old and discredited claim from the 1960s that modern neoclassical (micro) economics is not relevant to developing countries, because these countries are somehow "different" in unspecified ways or because these "traditional" societies are populated by nonoptimizing—and nonrational—economic agents. The perspective adopted in this book should not be confused with that view. We do not believe that economic agents in developing countries behave differently from those in industrial economies in ways that are inconsistent with the rational optimizing principles of neoclassical microeconomics; rather, we believe that they behave similarly to

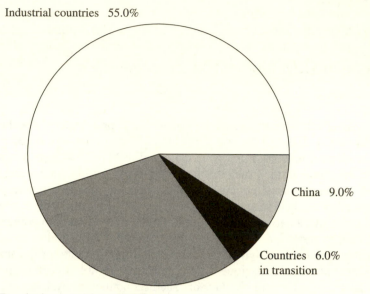

Figure 1.1   Distribution of World Output, 1993 (in percent of world GDP)

Source: International Monetary Fund, *World Economic Outlook* (May 1995, p. 71).

Notes: The GDP shares are based on the purchasing-power parity (PPP) valuation of country GDPs for 1993. The category "countries in transition" includes Mongolia, and countries of the former Soviet Union and central Europe.

their industrial-country counterparts, but operate in a different environment. Our perspective is that the standard analytical tools of modern macroeconomics are indeed of as much relevance to developing countries as they are to industrial countries, but that different models are needed to analyze familiar issues.

This is so because structural differences between developing and industrial nations make many popular industrial-country models less than ideally suited to the analysis of developing-country macroeconomic phenomena. These differences in macroeconomic environment can be identified explicitly. Moreover, the structural features that distinguish developing from industrial economies are sufficiently widespread throughout the developing world that it is indeed meaningful to speak of a distinct class of "development" macroeconomic models. The task of development macroeconomics is to uncover the implications of these differences in macroeconomic structure for macroeconomic behavior and policy.

In addition to differences in structure, a number of specific macroeconomic issues that have concerned economists and policymakers in developing nations have not received similar emphasis in the industrial world. Again, these issues have not been specific to single countries but have come up in different developing nations at various times and have therefore been of widespread interest in the developing world. In short, not only the nature of the models used, but also the purposes to which they have been applied, distinguish macroeconomics in developing countries from that in industrial countries.

The proof of this pudding, of course, will be in the eating. We intend to discharge the burden of making the case for a distinctive development macroeconomics throughout this book by demonstrating the empirical and analytical relevance of the structural features to which we have referred, as well as by discussing a number of macroeconomic issues specific to developing countries. In this chapter, however, we shall attempt to lay the groundwork for the perspective to be adopted by presenting an overview of important macroeconomic characteristics that are broadly shared among developing nations but that do not figure prominently in mainstream industrial-country macroeconomic models. We will also describe several issues that have been of particular interest in the developing-country context over the past two decades. Before doing so, however, we will describe some antecedents.

1.1 Monetarism, Structuralism, and Developing Nations

The relevance of industrial-country macroeconomic analysis to developing nations has been the subject of debate for some time, particularly in Latin America, where the contending parties have been dubbed "monetarist" or "orthodox" on the one hand and "structuralist" on the other. The former are associated with the view that mainstream macroeconomic orthodoxy is directly applicable to both long-run and short-run macroeconomic issues in developing countries. In particular, the monetarist school takes the view that long-run growth in developing countries is hampered by dirigiste policies that distort the allocation of resources. The long-run policy prescription is that growth can be promoted by giving full scope to market mechanisms via free trade and noninterventionist domestic policies. In the short run, the high inflation and balance-of-payments deficits that often afflict developing countries reflect excessive money growth fueled by large fiscal deficits.[1] The cure is orthodox medicine—tight fiscal policy coupled with "getting prices right," usually by devaluing and raising domestic interest rates. The orthodox view is often associated with Harberger (1963) and Sjaastad (1983). Its policy prescriptions lay behind the approach to macroeconomic adjustment followed by the "Chicago Boys" in Chile during the decade of the 1970s, as well as the Southern Cone stabilization programs of the late 1970s. More broadly, policies loosely based on this set of views have long been promoted by the international financial institutions, both in Latin America and elsewhere in the developing world.

The inception of the structuralist school is associated with work done for the Economic Commission on Latin America by Raúl Prebisch early in the postwar period.[2] An important tenet of the early structuralist school was that, due to lower income elasticities of demand for raw materials than for industrial goods, the primary-exporting countries in the developing-world "periphery" would face secularly deteriorating terms of trade relative to the manufactured goods–exporting industrial nation "center." The central policy recommendation for long-run growth that emerged from this prognosis was that production specialization along classical comparative-advantage lines was to be avoided. Policy intervention was required to change the structure of production in the periphery. Industrialization should be promoted in developing nations by protecting indigenous "infant industry" against competition from the "center" through the use of trade barriers and foreign exchange controls, as well as by providing special advantages to the industrial sector in the form of cheap imported inputs (secured through an overvalued exchange rate), cheap credit, and cheap labor (promoted by turning the internal terms of trade against agriculture). This "import substitution" strategy was adopted widely in the immediate postwar period not only in Latin America, but elsewhere in the developing world (see Cardoso and Helwege, 1992).

More recently, economists writing in the structuralist tradition have turned their attention to short-run macroeconomic stabilization. The best-known proponent of this "new structuralist" view of short-run development macroeconomics is Lance Taylor. In a recent essay (Taylor, 1990), he identifies the "new structuralist" view with a number of general hypotheses about development macroeconomics. These include the recognition that: (1) many agents possess significant market power; (2) macroeconomic causality in developing countries tends to run from "injections" such as investment, exports, and government spending, to "leakages" such as imports and saving; (3) money is often endogenous; (4) the structure of the financial system can affect macroeconomic outcomes in important ways; and (5) imported intermediate and capital goods, as well as direct complementarity between public and private investment, are empirically important.[3]

New structuralists question the wisdom and efficacy of orthodox short-run macroeconomic policy prescriptions, particularly "shock treatment" in the form of fiscal austerity coupled with devaluation and tight monetary policy. Their diagnosis of the source of inflation attributes an accommodative rather than a causal role to money growth. The source of inflation is slow relative productivity growth in agriculture (arising from poor land tenure patterns) combined with administered prices (arising from noncompetitive market structures and implying downward price rigidity) in industry, together with wage indexation (see Chapter 9). Monetary policy is perceived to be passive in the face of these underlying inflationary forces.

Moreover, in part because of the roles of working capital and imported inputs, and in part because substitution possibilities are more limited than assumed by the proponents of orthodox macroeconomic management, a policy package combining devaluation with tight fiscal and monetary policies will result in stagflation in the short run, with little or no improvement in the external accounts. The alternative new structuralist policy prescription is not always clear, but it would in all likelihood contain a greater element of gradualism, direct intervention, and emphasis on the medium-term resolution of structural problems than is contained in traditional stabilization programs.

The perspective adopted here draws, in effect, from both monetarist and structuralist analyses. Both approaches yield useful insights, and we believe that macroeconomic reality in the developing world indeed combines features of both. In particular, experience seems to suggest that outward orientation and reliance on market mechanisms are more successful in promoting long-run growth than inward orientation and dirigiste policies (see Chapter 15). At the same time, the central role of the fiscal deficit in fueling money creation and thus high steady-state inflation commands a wide consensus among contemporary macroeconomists. These are central tenets of "monetarist" orthodoxy. Nevertheless, agreement on these issues does not preclude accepting a number of points made by the new structuralists. For example, although inflation may be attributable to high fiscal deficits, the *persistence* of large public deficits itself needs to be explained, and the explanation may feature an important role for the continuing struggle over distributive shares emphasized by new structuralists.[4]

More important, the preceding comments pertain to long-run properties of the economy. In the framing of short-run macroeconomic policy, which has been the bread and butter of industrial-country macroeconomics since Keynes, structural features of the economy, as well as of the policy environment, come into their own. As is well known, the dynamics of macroeconomic adjustment to changes in any given set of policies will invariably depend on structural features of the economy as well as on the nature of the other policies pursued contemporaneously. In this sense, it becomes important to identify the macroeconomic characteristics of developing countries that are likely to govern the response of their economies to macroeconomic shocks and that must therefore figure prominently in macroeconomic models designed to be applied in a developing-country setting.

1.2 Economic Structure and Macroeconomic Analysis

What, then, are the macroeconomic features that tend to define development macroeconomics? The structural characteristics that differentiate a "representative" developing economy from the textbook industrial-country model cover a wide spectrum, spanning most of the standard components of a macroeconomic model. They include the nature of openness to trade with the rest of the world in both commodities and assets, the properties of the economy's long-run and short-run supply functions, the nature of financial markets, the characteristics of the government's budget and their implications for fiscal policy, the determinants of private-sector behavioral functions, and the stability of policy regimes.

1.2.1 Openness to Trade in Commodities and Assets

1. Developing economies tend to be open and to have little control over the prices of the goods they export and import.

A standard measure of openness is the trade share, that is, the sum of the shares of exports and imports in GDP. As indicated in Table 1.1, by this measure, developing nations tend to be substantially more open than the major industrial countries, with the mean value of the trade share amounting to 45 percent, compared with about 25 percent in the Group of Seven (G-7) countries.[5] Openness to this extent, of course, limits at the outset the applicability of the closed-economy textbook industrial-country model to the developing-country context. Very few developing nations (perhaps only India and Brazil, with trade shares close to 9 and 12 percent, respectively) can be even approximately described as closed economies by this measure.

The exogeneity of the terms of trade for developing economies is suggested both by their small share in the world economy and by the composition of their exports. In 1990 developing nations as a group accounted for only about one-quarter of world exports and imports. Moreover, in spite of a substantial increase in the share of manufactured goods in these countries' exports over the past two decades, in 1991 over half of the exports of low- and middle-income countries consisted of fuels, minerals, metals, and other primary commodities, compared with a world share of about one-quarter.[6] The share of primary commodities in the exports of a selected group of developing countries is given in Table 1.1. These are fairly homogeneous commodities, the prices of which are set in international markets. As indicated in the next column of the table, the markets for these products, as well as for the manufactured exports of developing countries, remain by and large in the industrial countries. On average,

TABLE 1.1
Developing Countries: Trade Indicators (in percent)

Country	Trade Ratio, 1980–89[a]	Export Share of Primary Commodities, 1991[b]	Share of Exports to Industrial Countries, 1991[c]
Developing countries	44.9	71	67.8
Africa			
Algeria	24.9	97	85.9
Côte d'Ivoire	40.6	90	59.3
Gabon	54.6	96	81.7
Ghana	20.6	99	82.0
Kenya	29.2	80	58.3
Mauritania	61.4	95	81.0
Morocco	28.1	49	80.3
Nigeria	21.4	99	89.7
Senegal	39.9	78	59.3
Tunisia	42.6	32	75.7
Zaire	25.3	—	93.8
Asia			
Bangladesh	13.4	30	75.8
India	8.5	27	54.4
Indonesia	26.0	59	65.1
Korea	38.6	7	64.2
Malaysia	62.4	—	50.9
Pakistan	18.5	27	56.0
Philippines	28.5	29	78.0
Singapore	191.5	26	47.6
Sri Lanka	35.6	35	69.4
Thailand	31.5	34	66.6
Western Hemisphere			
Barbados	62.5	—	38.5
Bolivia	29.5	95	47.9
Brazil	11.8	44	66.8
Chile	32.0	85	70.1
Colombia	17.9	67	79.0
Costa Rica	41.3	74	80.8
Ecuador	28.1	98	64.2
Haiti	22.3	58	99.0
Jamaica	60.9	44	87.0
Mexico	17.4	55	93.3
Venezuela	26.3	88	67.0
Middle East			
Egypt	33.2	60	37.3
Israel	45.9	12	75.5
Syria	23.9	77	46.9

Sources: [a]Montiel (1993); [b]World Bank, *World Development Report*, 1993; [c]International Monetary Fund, *Direction of Trade Statistics*, 1992.

two-thirds of the exports of the countries listed in the table went to industrial countries in 1991.

Of course, what matters for the purpose of determining the exogeneity of developing countries' terms of trade is the size of individual countries' exports and imports in particular markets. Very few developing countries account for a significant portion of the world market even for the commodities in which their exports are heavily specialized. For instance, only sixteen developing countries account for as much as 10 percent of the world market for commodity exports based on three-digit SITC classifications, according to the 1990 *Handbook of International Trade and Development Statistics,* prepared by the United Nations Commission on Trade and Development. Moreover, careful studies of this issue confirm that, with limited exceptions for particular goods, these countries have little individual influence over the prices at which they buy and sell (see Goldstein, 1986).

Exogenous terms of trade call into question the usefulness, for the analysis of many macroeconomic policy issues in developing nations, of the open-economy model most widely used in the industrial-country context. The Mundell-Fleming model, which has long been the workhorse open industrial-country model, assumes endogenous terms-of-trade determination, with the domestic economy completely specialized in the production of a good over which it exerts significant market power. The production structure most suitable for the analysis of developing-country macroeconomic phenomena is instead likely to be the Salter-Swan "dependent economy" model or (since terms-of-trade changes tend to be very important for such countries) a three-good model consisting of exportables, importables, and nontraded goods. Such a production structure permits a distinction to be drawn between the exogenous terms of trade and an endogenous real exchange rate, which is the central intratemporal macroeconomic relative price in these economies.

The importance for many developing nations of primary-commodity exports with exogenously determined prices accounts for a significant source of macroeconomic instability in these countries. Prices of primary commodities tend to fluctuate quite sharply, as illustrated for a selected group of such commodities in Figure 1.2. Consequently, developing countries have faced highly unstable terms of trade at various times over the past two decades.[7] As shown in the top panel of Figure 1.3, the past twenty years have been punctuated by several episodes of drastic changes in the terms of trade for developing countries as a group. The episodes in the top panel are dominated by changes in oil prices, but the bottom panel in Figure 1.3 shows that nonfuel commodities have themselves undergone sharp fluctuations in price during the 1970s and 1980s. Coupled with the relatively large share of exports and imports in domestic economic activity, such fluctuations in export prices represent substantial exogenous changes in national income from one year to the next.

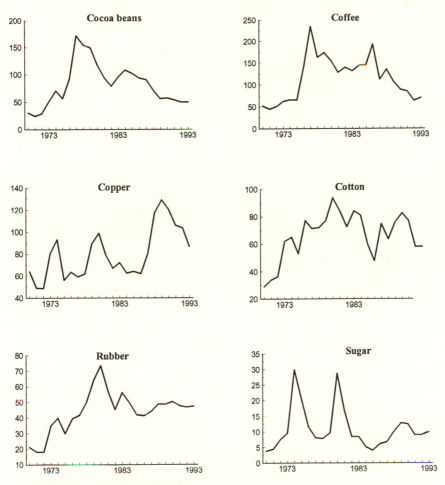

Figure 1.2   World Commodity Prices (U.S. cents per pound)

Source: International Financial Statistics.

2. In contrast to the major industrial countries, the vast majority of developing countries have not adopted flexible exchange rates. The nature of the "representative" exchange rate regime thus differs between industrial and developing countries.

Industrial countries are typically modeled as operating flexible exchange rates, whereas in developing countries officially determined rates, adjusted by a variety of alternative rules (loosely referred to as "managed" rates), predominate. A description of the nature of exchange rate regimes in individual developing countries is presented in Chapter 6. The prevalence of official parities implies that issues relating to the macroeconomic consequences of pegging, of altering the peg (typically in the form of a

Terms of trade

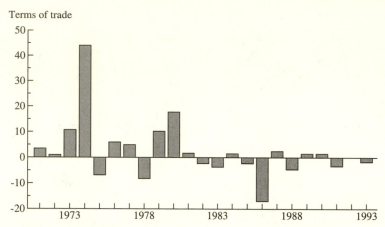

Nonfuel commodity prices

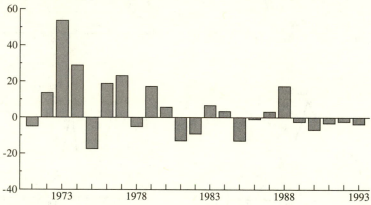

Figure 1.3 Developing Countries: Terms of Trade and Nonfuel Commodity Prices (annual change, in percent)

Source: International Financial Statistics.

devaluation), and of rules for moving the peg are of particular importance in developing countries. Moreover, this exchange regime is commonly supplemented by quantitative restrictions on foreign exchange availability, resulting in the emergence of free exchange markets in parallel with the official ones. The analysis of the aggregate implications of such informal, dual-exchange-rate regimes is an important topic in development macroeconomics.

3. Developing countries tend to be capital importers, and the servicing of external debt is a central policy issue in many of them.

Table 1.2 presents a set of external-debt indicators for a representative group of developing countries. It is important to note that the debt figures

TABLE 1.2
Developing Countries: Debt Indicators (in percent)

Country	Debt/GDP	Debt Service/ Exports	Share of Concessional Debt
Africa			
Algeria	74.9	18.4	22.8
Burundi	83.8	31.5	88.2
Cameroon	57.5	18.7	23.9
Côte d'Ivoire	222.6	43.4	12.5
Gabon	88.7	6.5	21.4
Ghana	66.9	26.9	56.9
Kenya	89.6	32.7	40.6
Lesotho	39.2	4.6	77.0
Morocco	80.0	27.8	25.9
Nigeria	108.8	25.2	3.1
Asia			
India	29.3	30.7	41.6
Indonesia	66.4	32.7	28.3
Korea	14.4	7.1	11.6
Malaysia	47.6	8.3	12.1
Pakistan	50.1	21.1	54.9
Philippines	70.2	23.2	25.9
Sri Lanka	72.6	13.9	73.3
Thailand	39.0	13.1	13.2
Western Hemisphere			
Argentina	49.2	48.4	0.9
Bolivia	85.3	34.0	42.1
Brazil	78.8	30.0	2.5
Chile	60.7	33.9	2.1
Colombia	43.5	35.2	5.6
Jamaica	134.9	29.4	27.4
Mexico	36.9	30.9	1.0
Peru	44.3	27.7	11.5
Venezuela	65.3	18.7	0.2

Source: World Bank, *World Development Report,* 1993.

appearing in this table refer to gross external debt. For many countries, the gross figure approximates the country's international net debtor position, but in the case of several countries that experienced one or more episodes of substantial capital flight, the gross debt figure may substantially overstate the economy's net debtor position. Even for those countries, however, a large stock of gross external debt presents important problems, essentially because the domestic sector that holds the external assets (generally the private sector) is not the same as the sector that holds the external liabilities (the government). The role of debt also varies across countries depending on whether debt has been acquired from private creditors on market terms or from bilateral and multilateral donors on concessional terms. As indicated in the last column of Table 1.2, substantial differences emerge in this regard among developing countries.

4. *The extent of external trade in assets tends to be more limited in developing than in industrial countries.*

Perfect capital mobility has become the standard textbook assumption for industrial countries. In developing countries capital controls are the rule, and although their effectiveness is questioned, the degree of capital mobility that characterizes these economies remains an unresolved issue. Thus, unlike standard macroeconomic modeling for industrial countries, in the developing-country case the assumption of perfect capital mobility may be inappropriate. Evidence on this issue is presented in Chapter 5 and used in Chapter 9 to formulate an appropriate framework for the analysis of stabilization policies in developing countries.

1.2.2 Long-Run Supply Behavior

5. *The large direct role that the state has played in production in many developing countries implies that the size and efficiency of the public capital stock figures prominently in the aggregate (or sectoral, under the three-good classification suggested earlier) production function(s).*

Nonfinancial public enterprises have been important economic actors in most of the developing world. Public capital represents a much larger share of the aggregate capital stock in such countries than in developed nations. Although reliable capital stock data are not available for such countries, evidence on the public/private composition of investment provided in Table 1.3 confirms the widespread importance of the public sector in capital accumulation. For the group of 47 countries considered by Pfeffermann and Madarassy (1993), the public sector accounted for about 43 percent of total investment over the period 1981–91. Given the important role that the public sector has played in the development process, the medium-term supply-side effects of government spending often cannot be ignored.

1.2.3 Short-Run Supply Behavior

6. *Imported intermediate goods play an important role in the aggregate (or, under the three-good structure, sectoral) production function(s) in developing countries.*

Imported intermediate goods play a prominent role in economic activity in the developing world. Such goods account for approximately half of all developing-country imports (Mirakhor and Montiel, 1987). In some countries the share of energy and non-energy intermediate imports can even exceed 70 percent (Table 1.4). As a result, the difference between the value of domestic production and domestic value added tends to be larger in developing than in industrial nations. Through the cost of imported intermediates, the exchange rate has an important influence on the position of the economy's short-run supply curve. The role of imported intermediate goods means not only that exchange-rate changes will have short-run supply effects, but also that, in the presence of foreign exchange rationing, the availability of foreign exchange may have a direct effect on the position of the economy's short-run supply curve.

7. Short-run supply functions in developing economies may be significantly affected by working-capital considerations.

Many analysts have claimed that costs of working capital tend to give interest rates and credit availability an important short-run supply-side role, though this has proven to be controversial and the evidence on the empirical importance of this phenomenon is mixed.[8] If empirically relevant, the role of working capital in the short-run supply curve would imply, for example, that contractionary monetary policy may have short-run stagflationary consequences.

8. Developing countries offer a rich variety of institutional features with regard to wage-setting behavior.

The nature of short-run wage-setting behavior represents one of the key differences between the major schools of modern macroeconomics, but most participants in these disputes acknowledge that country-specific institutional differences (such as the prevalence of staggered overlapping contracts in the United States or synchronized wage bargaining in Scandinavia) are important in determining the economy's short-run supply behavior. There is limited evidence on wage-setting behavior in developing countries, but extreme cases and interesting issues abound. The former include economywide backward indexation in Brazil, Chile, and Israel, as well as the growing perception that many developing countries are characterized by a high degree of real wage flexibility (see Horton et al., 1994).

1.2.4 Financial Markets

9. Financial markets in developing nations are characterized by the prevalence of rudimentary financial institutions in low-income countries and, regardless of the level of per-capita income, by "financial repression."

Developing-country financial markets are dominated by a single type of institution—the commercial bank—and secondary markets for securities as well as equity markets tend to be small or nonexistent. Thus, the menu of assets available to private savers is limited. Moreover, the commercial

TABLE 1.3

Share of Private Investment in Total Investment in Developing
Countries (in percent)

Country	1970–80	1981–85	1986–90	1991
Africa				
Côte d'Ivoire	—	—	43.4	44.4
Ghana	—	60.1	34.6	50.3
Kenya	58.8	58.3	58.3	58.5
Malawi	25.3	35.4	41.1	50.6
Mauritius	67.4	65.2	65.0	66.7
Morocco	53.2	48.4	57.5	—
Nigeria	—	26.8	27.9	—
Tunisia	43.2	45.6	50.2	46.2
Asia				
Bangladesh	—	43.1	48.1	48.3
India	56.8	49.7	52.0	—
Indonesia	—	52.8	59.1	61.1
Korea	63.0	74.9	78.8	75.8
Malaysia	65.1	52.0	61.2	67.9
Nepal	69.4	56.7	56.4	64.7
Pakistan	40.8	44.7	48.5	55.0
Philippines	71.7	73.9	82.1	70.9
Singapore	70.5	68.9	72.5	79.9
Sri Lanka	54.4	46.6	54.6	61.2
Thailand	72.4	64.7	76.1	77.2
Western Hemisphere				
Argentina	59.6	58.7	53.4	—
Bolivia	51.4	46.5	37.3	32.8
Chile	46.5	57.6	60.3	74.3
Colombia	65.9	53.4	52.5	49.0
Costa Rica	69.0	64.8	76.5	78.8
Ecuador	61.0	55.9	57.8	68.1
El Salvador	68.0	59.3	78.0	80.6
Guatemala	73.0	60.1	78.8	84.3
Mexico	62.2	60.2	74.2	76.6
Paraguay	73.9	77.9	75.2	84.4
Peru	—	67.3	79.0	87.8
Uruguay	66.4	61.0	64.9	65.0
Venezuela	—	63.2	49.2	46.1

Source: Pfeffermann and Madarassy (1993).

TABLE 1.4
Composition of Real Imports of Developing Countries (in percent of total)

| Country | Capital Goods | Consumer Goods | Intermediates | |
			Energy	Non-Energy
Argentina				
1976–81	25.4	10.8	16.1	47.7
1982–87	22.2	7.0	9.8	61.0
Brazil				
1976–81	15.1	4.4	42.9	37.6
1982–87	11.1	5.9	46.6	36.4
Chile				
1976–81	22.6	17.7	21.9	37.8
1982–86	21.7	14.8	18.7	44.8
Colombia				
1976–81	27.3	9.6	6.7	56.4
1982–87	26.5	7.9	4.6	61.0
Ecuador				
1976–81	39.0	10.6	2.3	48.1
1982–84	28.6	9.4	1.1	60.7
Indonesia				
1976–81	27.2	14.8	12.8	45.2
1982–87	27.7	5.8	14.8	51.7
Malaysia				
1976–81	20.7	16.1	16.1	47.1
1982–87	22.8	15.5	9.4	52.3
Mexico				
1976–81	30.9	7.6	2.8	58.7
1982–86	27.7	9.4	2.7	60.2
Peru				
1976–81	28.1	11.7	11.1	49.1
1982–84	27.6	16.7	2.1	53.5
Philippines				
1976–81	17.4	5.4	33.6	42.6
1982–86	14.1	6.9	28.7	50.3
Uruguay				
1976–81	19.1	10.5	34.0	36.4
1982–87	15.9	13.0	31.3	39.8
Venezuela				
1976–81	36.7	17.4	0.5	45.4
1982–87	28.5	18.8	1.5	51.2

Source: Adapted from Hentschel (1992, pp. 9–10).

banking sector is heavily regulated; it is often subjected to high reserve and liquidity ratios as well as legal ceilings on interest rates together with sectoral credit allocation quotas. Credit rationing in the developing world thus tends to be legally imposed rather than endogenously generated by information asymmetries, as is commonly taken to be the case in industrial countries.

The consequence of these restrictions is that the size of the commercial banking system is artificially curtailed. This phenomenon is suggested by the contrast shown in Table 1.5 between monetization ratios in industrial and developing countries. This index measures the size of the banking system by taking the ratio of its liabilities (either narrow or broad money) to GDP. As is evident from the table, in spite of the more limited range of financial assets available to savers in developing nations, monetization ratios are generally lower for such countries than for industrial countries. The differences are particularly pronounced when the broad money measure is used, since it contains interest-bearing assets such as time and saving deposits that bear the brunt of interest-rate ceilings in developing countries.

In response to this "financial repression," an informal financial sector often arises with market-determined loan interest rates, again operating in parallel with the official sector. The instruments of monetary policy and the nature of the monetary transmission mechanism in this setting tend to be quite different from their industrial-country counterparts, when such markets are large.

1.2.5 Characteristics of the Government Budget

10. Aspects of the government budget, and thus of fiscal policy, differ markedly between industrial and developing countries.

In many developing nations, the state plays a pervasive role in the economy. This role is exercised through the activities of not just the nonfinancial public sector (consisting of the central government, local governments, specialized agencies, and nonfinancial public enterprises), but also of financial institutions owned by the government. As will be shown in Chapter 4, the fiscal role of the latter has at times been important in several countries. Regarding the nonfinancial public sector itself, the government tends to play a more active role in production than is the case in most industrial nations, and the performance of public-sector enterprises is often central in determining the fiscal stance.

Unfortunately, systematic data on the size and performance of the consolidated nonfinancial public sector are not available for a large number of developing countries. Published information tends to refer to the finances of the central government only. Table 1.6 presents data on the level and composition of central government expenditure in both industrial and developing

TABLE 1.5

Monetization Ratios (percentage averages over 1980–91)

Country	Narrow Money Ratio	Broad Money Ratio
Industrial countries		
Belgium	20.7	46.2
Canada	13.3	46.4
France	27.2	69.8
Germany	18.2	59.2
Italy	38.9	65.6
Japan	29.1	100.9
United Kingdom	24.5	60.4
United States	15.9	59.4
Developing countries		
Africa		
Burundi	12.8	17.3
Cameroon	12.8	22.0
Gabon	12.1	19.9
Kenya	14.3	29.5
Lesotho	20.5	48.3
Madagascar	16.1	18.6
Morocco	34.7	46.9
Nigeria	16.8	28.6
Tunisia	27.8	46.9
Zambia	16.1	30.2
Asia		
India	15.8	42.9
Indonesia	10.9	26.7
Korea	9.7	36.7
Malaysia	19.8	63.6
Pakistan	27.9	41.0
Philippines	8.0	28.7
Singapore	24.1	79.2
Sri Lanka	12.5	30.7
Thailand	9.6	56.0
Western Hemisphere		
Argentina	6.7	20.1
Bolivia	8.8	18.1
Barbados	14.5	45.4
Chile	6.5	37.2
Colombia	11.9	20.2
Haiti	16.5	32.1
Jamaica	14.9	45.3
Mexico	8.3	25.8
Peru	10.6	20.8
Venezuela	19.0	37.9

Source: International Financial Statistics.

TABLE 1.6
Composition of Central Government Expenditure (percent of total expenditure)

	Industrial Countries	Developing Countries (by Region)				
		Africa	Asia	Europe	Middle East	Western Hemisphere
General services	8.1	18.5	17.9	16.9	13.3	16.1
Defense	7.3	8.9	13.0	13.6	26.7	7.5
Education	8.5	16.0	14.4	7.3	12.5	14.0
Health	9.6	5.5	5.2	6.3	4.9	8.3
Social security	37.7	8.3	7.1	23.1	13.2	18.8
Transport and communications	5.1	7.1	11.2	6.5	3.7	6.8
Other services	7.2	17.5	19.4	21.2	11.1	11.9
Other	16.6	18.3	11.8	5.2	14.6	16.6
In percent of GDP:						
Total expenditure	31.5	25.6	19.9	29.2	33.1	25.0

Source: Burgess and Stern (1993, p. 766).
Notes: All region averages are unweighted. Data refer mostly to 1987–88.

countries. There are two major observations: the central government absorbs a smaller fraction of output in developing than in industrial countries, and the composition of spending differs between the two groups of countries. Developing nations devote a substantially larger fraction of expenditures to general public services, defense, education, and other economic services (reflecting the role of government in production) than do industrial nations, whereas the latter spend somewhat more on health and substantially more on social security.

As for revenue, the main source of central government revenue is taxation, but the share of nontax revenue in total revenue is much higher in developing than in industrial countries (Table 1.7). The collection of tax revenue in developing countries is often hindered by limited administrative capacity and political constraints. One consequence of this is that direct taxation plays a much more limited role in developing than in industrial nations. Direct taxes, taxes on domestic goods and services, and taxes on foreign trade account for roughly equal shares of total tax revenue in developing countries, in contrast with industrial countries, where income taxes account for the largest share and taxes on foreign trade are negligible. Of direct taxes, the share of tax revenue raised from individual incomes is much larger than that from corporations in the developing world, whereas the reverse is true in the industrial world. Trade taxes consist primarily of import rather than export duties in developing countries and are used more extensively in the poorest countries.

The political and administrative constraints on tax collection in developing nations, coupled with the limited scope for the issuance of domestic

TABLE 1.7
Level and Composition of Tax Revenue

Country Group	Total Taxes	Income Taxes	Taxes on Goods and Services	Social Security	Taxes on Foreign Trade Import Duties	Export Duties	Other
In Percent of GDP							
Industrial countries	31.2	11.0	9.4	8.9	0.7	—	2.2
Developing countries	18.1	5.5	5.2	1.3	4.3	0.8	1.0
Africa	19.5	6.7	4.9	0.4	5.7	1.1	0.7
Asia	14.8	4.5	4.6	0.0	4.8	0.7	0.2
Europe	21.9	5.8	6.9	5.1	2.8	—	1.3
Middle East	14.7	4.8	2.3	1.2	4.1	0.1	2.2
Western Hemisphere	18.2	4.8	6.5	2.4	2.5	1.0	1.0
In Percent of Total Tax Revenue							
Industrial countries	100.0	35.8	29.3	28.4	2.7	0.1	3.7
Developing countries	100.0	28.9	30.4	6.2	24.3	5.1	5.1
Africa	100.0	32.3	25.8	2.3	28.4	7.2	4.0
Asia	100.0	27.4	34.8	0.2	30.9	4.1	2.6
Europe	100.0	25.2	34.5	18.0	16.7	—	5.6
Middle East	100.0	40.0	14.7	7.4	26.0	0.2	11.7
Western Hemisphere	100.0	24.2	36.5	12.0	15.8	5.5	6.0

Source: Burgess and Stern (1993, p. 773).
Notes: Regional averages are unweighted. Data refer mostly to 1987–88.

debt in many such countries, has led to greater reliance on seignorage, and therefore to higher levels of inflation, than in industrial countries. This is illustrated in Figure 1.4, which shows the relationship between the share of seignorage in GDP and the rate of inflation for a sample of industrial and developing nations. With few exceptions, industrial countries tend to raise less than 0.8 percent of GDP in seignorage revenue, whereas the vast majority of developing countries collect more than 1 percent of GDP in this fashion. As a result, inflation rates in developing countries tend to be higher than those that prevail in the industrial world.

1.2.6 Characteristics of Private Behavior

11. In large part because of the nature of the financial system, but also because of some of the other features mentioned previously, standard macroeconomic behavioral relationships tend to differ in the developing-country context. An important feature is the necessity to incorporate the implications of credit and foreign exchange rationing in private decision rules.

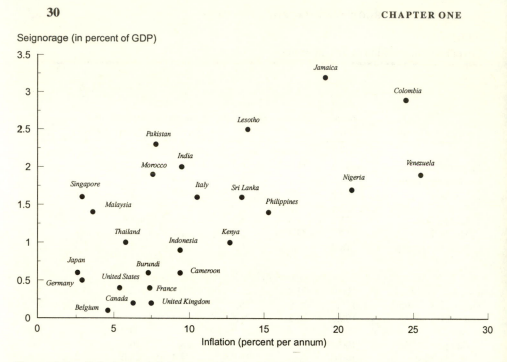

Figure 1.4   Inflation and Seignorage in Industrial and Developing Countries (averages over 1980–91)

Source: Author's calculations based on *International Financial Statistics.*

This affects, for instance, private consumption, investment, asset demand, export supply, and import demand functions. The incorporation of these phenomena has been treated in different ways: by including, for instance, quantity constraints in consumption and investment equations or by employing prices in informal credit and foreign exchange markets in addition to (or instead of) those prevailing in official markets in these demand functions. These issues are taken up in Chapter 3.

1.2.7 Stability of Policy Regimes

Overall, developing countries have tended to exhibit higher fiscal deficits, substantially higher rates of inflation, and higher average growth rates than the major industrial countries. However, because of the significantly higher rates of population growth in the developing world, per-capita growth rates have not been significantly different. A broad picture of macroeconomic performance for the two groups of countries, as well as for developing countries by region, is given in Table 1.8 for the period 1987–93. The data

TABLE 1.8

Macroeconomic Indicators, 1987–93 (in percent)

	1987	1988	1989	1990	1991	1992	1993
Fiscal Balance[a]							
G-7 countries	−3.4	−2.8	−2.4	−2.8	−3.2	−4.2	−4.3
Developing countries	−5.6	−5.9	−4.8	−4.4	−4.5	−3.9	−4.3
Africa	−7.2	−6.8	−6.4	−6.0	−6.0	−5.1	−6.2
Asia	−4.0	−2.4	−3.2	−4.4	−4.6	−4.2	−4.7
Middle East and Europe	−11.9	−9.1	−5.3	−5.8	−7.2	−5.6	−4.7
Western Hemisphere	−2.9	−4.4	−4.4	−2.3	−2.0	−2.0	−1.8
Broad Money Growth							
G-7 countries	7.0	7.9	8.5	7.7	3.8	2.7	3.3
Developing countries	45.1	66.9	81.0	77.5	54.0	71.9	68.7
Africa	18.3	23.3	16.5	17.0	26.7	31.9	22.9
Asia	25.6	23.8	23.0	20.7	21.7	20.6	18.5
Middle East and Europe	16.4	18.7	19.8	20.3	9.0	39.4	27.6
Western Hemisphere	131.5	288.0	456.7	443.1	224.1	289.4	299.2
Inflation[b]							
G-7 countries	2.9	3.3	4.5	5.0	4.4	3.1	2.8
Developing countries	35.1	53.7	61.9	65.4	35.7	38.7	45.9
Africa	16.8	21.3	21.9	16.9	32.2	40.2	31.7
Asia	9.2	13.8	11.5	7.6	8.5	7.4	9.5
Middle East and Europe	21.7	26.1	21.9	23.8	23.8	20.6	24.4
Western Hemisphere	124.6	245.0	363.3	478.9	135.8	169.9	236.5
GDP Growth							
G-7 countries	3.2	4.5	3.2	2.4	0.5	1.7	1.4
Developing countries	5.7	5.3	4.0	3.7	4.4	5.9	6.1
Africa	1.4	4.0	3.6	1.7	1.5	0.4	1.1
Asia	8.0	9.1	5.3	5.6	6.1	8.1	8.4
Middle East and Europe	5.9	0.3	3.7	4.2	1.9	7.5	4.7
Western Hemisphere	3.4	1.0	1.6	0.3	3.3	2.5	3.4

Source: International Monetary Fund, *World Economic Outlook.*

[a] Central government, in percent of GDP.

[b] Annual rate of change in consumer prices.

indicate that, although inflation performance differs markedly by region in the developing world, being particularly poor among Western Hemisphere countries, average inflation rates tend to exceed those of the major industrial countries in all regions.

High inflation has been a symptom of policy instability and has frequently been associated with policy uncertainty. In large parts of the developing world—particularly in Latin America and Africa—macroeconomic instability has been endemic. In part, this has been the result of indigenous factors. Political instability has characterized many developing countries from the time of their independence, and multiparty democracies with free elections have been rare. Up to the mid-1980s, for example, most of Latin America was ruled by military governments, and one-party rule continues to prevail in Africa. Changes in government not infrequently signal changes in ruling ideologies and correspondingly in economic policy regimes. In addition, however, external shocks in the form of substantial changes in the terms of trade or in international financial conditions have often triggered domestic macroeconomic instability.

Policy uncertainty has been an important factor in the macroeconomics of development, in many instances triggering currency substitution, capital flight, exchange-rate crises, and the collapse of private investment. Uncertainty regarding the policy environment—or the anticipation of future policy reversals—is a feature that frequently must be built into developing-country macroeconomic models and the design of macroeconomic reform programs.

1.3 Development Macroeconomics: Special Topics

As mentioned in the introduction, economists and policymakers in developing nations over the past two decades have been concerned with a number of issues that have not received similar attention in industrial countries. These issues have been of particular importance in the developing world precisely because they have arisen from features of these economies such as those mentioned in this chapter. Although all of these will be considered in some detail later in the book, they are listed here to complete our overview of development macroeconomics.

Exchange-Rate Management

The macroeconomic effects of devaluation have been rather controversial in the developing-country context, though this topic has ceased to preoccupy industrial-country macroeconomists over the past two decades. At issue is the "new structuralist" critique of the role of the exchange rate in orthodox stabilization. The macroeconomic consequences of alternative nominal exchange-rate rules and the role of the exchange rate as a nominal anchor in an open economy have also been important policy issues.

Stabilization of High Inflation

As indicated previously, high inflation has been more common in the developing world than in the industrial world over the past two decades. The developing world has also witnessed several alternative approaches to price-level stabilization, ranging from orthodox money-based programs relying on tight fiscal and monetary policies and exchange-rate policy geared to external balance, to "heterodox" programs based on tight aggregate demand policies supplemented by an exchange-rate freeze as well as some form of wage and price controls. The evaluation of this experience and its lessons for future stabilization efforts in the developing world and elsewhere has been an important topic of research.

Capital Flight

Several developing countries, particularly countries in Latin America during the late 1970s and early 1980s, have experienced sudden episodes of substantial capital outflows that have severely complicated macroeconomic management.[9] The causes of such outflows, their welfare implications, and appropriate policy responses have been subjects of attention in developing nations for a long time.

The Debt Crisis

The debt crisis was perhaps the dominant macroeconomic event of the 1980s for many highly indebted developing countries. Analysis of the causes of the crisis, its domestic consequences, and the nature of desirable policy responses—on the part of both the international community and domestic governments in the indebted countries—has generated an enormous literature. More recently, attention has shifted to understanding the implications of the Brady plan as a potential solution to the crisis for countries with substantial debt contracted on commercial terms.

The Macroeconomic Role of Informal Markets

The coexistence of regulated formal markets and informal markets for either goods and services or financial assets is not limited to the developing world, of course, but the importance of this phenomenon in developing countries has generated a large literature that examines the macroeconomic role of parallel foreign exchange markets as well as curb markets for loans. Among the issues that have been addressed are the use of the free exchange rate as an indicator of real exchange rate misalignment, and the roles of both the free exchange rate and the curb interest rate in transmitting the macroeconomic effects of changes in fiscal and monetary policies, as well as changes in official exchange rates and interest rates, to the real economy.

Trade and Financial Reform

In recent years a large number of developing countries have followed the lead of several East Asian developing countries in undertaking wide-ranging reforms to their trade and financial systems designed to enhance the role of financial intermediaries in channeling domestic saving, as well as to give the real economy a more outward orientation. Both the structural reforms themselves and the interpretation of the experience of the East Asian countries have proven controversial, and their relationship with macroeconomic stabilization has been a recurrent focus of attention.

Political Aspects of the Macroeconomy

In all countries, political factors play a pervasive role in economic life. The recent literature in macroeconomics has recognized the need to take these factors into account in attempting to understand many macroeconomic phenomena, such as inflation inertia, the setting of policy instruments, and the sustainability of reform programs. The interactions between the political objectives of policymakers and the design of economic policy is critically important in developing countries undergoing macroeconomic reform, and remains a major area of investigation.

The Functioning of Labor Markets

The role of labor markets has received much attention in the development literature (particularly in the analysis of rural to urban migration) and more recently in the literature on trade and structural reform. Macroeconomists have also begun to appreciate the role that the various types of labor market structures observed in developing nations may play in the analysis of the transmission mechanism of policy shocks. Particularly important phenomena are the existence of labor market segmentation, the role of government regulations (in setting, for instance, the minimum wages for different categories of workers or in designing unemployment benefit schemes), and the low degree of labor mobility across sectors in the short run.

———————

The view that will be advocated in this book, then, is as follows: Although economic agents in developing countries are no less likely to behave in neoclassical optimizing fashion than their industrial-country counterparts, and although the long-run determinants of growth and inflation are likely to be very similar in developing and in industrial economies (as emphasized by Latin American monetarists), structure matters, and it matters particularly for the issues of short-run stabilization that have long preoccupied macroeconomists. Developing economies share a number of features not often found in industrial-country macroeconomic models, so a somewhat different family of models is required for developing-country macroeconomic analysis. In addition, these features have given rise to a set of macroeconomic problems that are specific to developing countries and that have been of broad interest in the developing world. Both of these facts call for a specifically "development" macroeconomics.

Part I

MACROECONOMIC RELATIONSHIPS
AND MARKET STRUCTURE

Two

Aggregate Accounts, Production, and Market Structure

CHAPTER 1 described a set of macroeconomic characteristics that are particularly relevant for developing economies. Based on these, this chapter and the next provide an overview of some general analytical features of developing-country macroeconomic models. This chapter takes a model-based perspective, focusing on the general structure of macroeconomic models for developing countries, including the accounting framework, the level of commodity disaggregation, and the particular role of labor and informal financial markets. Chapter 3 will focus on specific components of macroeconomic models, examining evidence on the properties of private behavioral functions in developing nations.

This chapter is divided into four sections. Section 2.1 sets out a general accounting framework consisting essentially of budget constraints for each type of agent typically appearing in a developing-country macroeconomic model, and defines several concepts that will prove useful later on. In Section 2.2 we consider how economic structure can be imposed on these accounting relationships by reviewing three alternative approaches to commodity disaggregation in an open economy: the Mundell-Fleming model, the "dependent economy" model, and a three-good structure distinguishing exportables, importables, and nontraded goods. Almost all macroeconomic models for developing countries rely on some variant of one of these approaches. Each of these three production structures is analyzed in both classical and Keynesian modes.

Sections 2.3 and 2.4 look at two markets that share two important characteristics: they play central analytical roles in all macroeconomic models, and their functioning is widely accepted to depend on country-specific institutional factors, both in the industrial- and developing-country contexts. As emphasized in Section 2.2, labor markets play a key role in determining the properties of an economy's short-run aggregate supply function. Accordingly, in Section 2.3 we examine the structural features of labor markets in developing nations. We focus on the short-run implications of these features, emphasizing the role of wage rigidity and the nature of labor market segmentation. Section 2.4 discusses the role of informal financial markets. Informal markets in credit and foreign currencies are a widespread phenomenon in developing countries and constitute one of the most significant structural differences from financial systems in developed countries. In countries where such markets are large, accounting for their existence may prove crucial to understanding the transmission process of macroeconomic policy shocks. We review in this chapter the general characteristics of such markets, as well as their macroeconomic role. Analytical models of informal markets are discussed in Chapter 5. Chapter 11 will present more detailed macroeconomic models that integrate such markets simultaneously.

2.1 A General Accounting Framework

All macroeconomic models are based on an accounting framework that, in essence, describes the intratemporal budget constraints confronting all types of economic agents included in the model. The accounting framework does little more than specify the set of choices that can be made by each type of agent. The model is completed by adding decision rules governing such choices and equilibrium conditions reconciling the decisions made by different agents. In this section we describe a general accounting framework on which a large variety of particular developing-country macroeconomic models can be based. Our purpose is to adapt the standard industrial-country macroeconomic accounting framework to the developing-country characteristics described in Chapter 1.

The first step is to specify the list of agents involved. We shall discuss in turn the nonfinancial private sector, the nonfinancial public sector, the central bank, and the commercial banking system.

2.1.1 The Nonfinancial Private Sector

In describing the budget and balance sheet constraints faced by the nonfinancial private sector, a logical place to begin is the specification of the menu of assets available to private agents. This is, of course, a function of the degree of sophistication of the country's financial system. In several middle-income developing nations small equity markets have been in existence for some time, and in some countries government bonds are sold to the nonbank private sector and are traded in secondary markets. In the rest of the developing world, however, these phenomena are exceptional. Moreover, the analysis of macroeconomic models with these features is familiar from standard industrial-country applications. Thus, the portfolio choices that will be described here are those that are relevant for developing countries with less-developed financial systems.

The nonfinancial private sector holds both financial and real assets. Financial assets consist of currency issued by the central bank CU_t, deposits issued by the commercial banks D_t^P, [1] net foreign assets $E_t F_t^P$ (where E_t is the exchange rate expressed as the domestic-currency price of foreign currency and F_t^P is the foreign-currency value of these assets), and loans extended by households in informal markets L_t^h. Liabilities of the sector consist of credit from banks L_t^P and loans received through informal markets. The sector's real assets consist of inflation hedges (typically real estate or gold), with price q_t and quantity $\bar{H}$.[2] In the absence of equity markets, physical capital is treated in the same manner as human capital—that is, as a nonmarketable asset that generates income available to finance consumption—but does not represent a component of households' marketable portfolios. Under these conditions, the nonfinancial private sector's marketable net worth Ω_t^P is

$$\Omega_t^P = CU_t^P + D_t^P + E_t F_t^P + q_t \bar{H} - L_t^P. \tag{1}$$

Note that loans extended through the informal market do not affect net worth, since these loans are transacted entirely within the nonfinancial private sector and thus do not represent a claim by the sector on the rest of the economy.

Differentiating Equation (1) with respect to time yields

$$\dot{\Omega}_t^P = C\dot{U}_t^P + \dot{D}_t^P + \dot{E}_t F_t^P + E_t \dot{F}_t^P + \dot{q}_t \bar{H} - \dot{L}_t^P. \tag{2}$$

The change in the marketable net worth of the nonfinancial private sector consists of the purchase of financial assets (financial saving, denoted S_t^P) plus capital gains:

$$\dot{\Omega}_t^P = S_t^P + \dot{E}_t F_t^P + \dot{q}_t \bar{H}. \tag{3}$$

From Equations (2) and (3), S_t^P is given by[3]

$$S_t^P = C\dot{U}_t^P + \dot{D}_t^P + E_t \dot{F}_t^P - \dot{L}_t^P. \tag{4}$$

Finally, financial saving is the difference between disposable income and expenditure on consumption and investment:

$$S_t^P = Y_t + i_d D_t^P + i^* E_t F_t^P - i_c L_t^P - \tau_t^P - C_t^P - I_t^P. \tag{5}$$

Equation (5) indicates that disposable income consists of factor income Y_t plus net interest income (income from deposits and foreign assets minus interest payments on bank credit, where the respective interest rates are given by i_d, i^*, and i_c), minus net taxes τ_t^P.[4] Private consumption is C_t^P, and private investment is I_t^P.

2.1.2 The Public Sector

2.1.2.1 THE NONFINANCIAL PUBLIC SECTOR

The nonfinancial public sector is typically a substantial net financial debtor. Its debt is owed to the central bank (L_t^{bg}),[5] to commercial banks (L_t^{cg}), and to foreigners $(-E_t F_t^g)$.[6] The nonfinancial public sector's net worth, Ω_t^g, is thus given by

$$\Omega_t^g = E_t F_t^g - L_t^{bg} - L_t^{cg}. \tag{6}$$

The change in Ω_t^g over time obeys

$$\dot{\Omega}_t^g = \dot{E}_t F_t^g + E_t \dot{F}_t^g - \dot{L}_t^{bg} - \dot{L}_t^{cg}, \tag{7}$$

which consists of new borrowing by the nonfinancial public sector, $-S_t^g$, plus capital gains on net foreign assets:

$$\dot{\Omega}_t^g = S_t^g + \dot{E}_t F_t^g. \tag{8}$$

From Equations (7) and (8), S_t^g consists of

$$S_t^g = E_t \dot{F}_t^g - \dot{L}_t^{bg} - \dot{L}_t^{cg}. \tag{9}$$

Total new borrowing by the nonfinancial public sector must be equal to the overall fiscal deficit:

$$-S_t^g = C_t^g + I_t^g + i_b L_t^{bg} + i_c L_t^{cg} - i^* E_t F_t^g - \tau_t^p - \tau_t^g, \tag{10}$$

where τ_t^g represents transfers from the central bank to the nonfinancial public sector and i_b the interest rate paid on loans received from the central bank.

2.1.2.2 THE CENTRAL BANK

The central bank's balance sheet will play a central role in many of the models to be examined in this book. Under present assumptions, it is given by

$$\Omega_t^b = E_t R_t + (L_t^{bg} + L_t^{bc}) - M_t, \tag{11}$$

where R_t represents net foreign assets of the central bank, L_t^{bc} credit from the central bank to commercial banks, and M_t high-powered money (or the monetary base), defined as the sum of currency held by the nonfinancial private sector and reserves of the commercial banking system held in the vaults of the central bank, RR_t:

$$M_t = CU_t + RR_t. \tag{12}$$

As with the other sectors, the change in Ω_t^b can be written as

$$\dot{\Omega}_t^b = E_t \dot{R}_t + (\dot{L}_t^{bg} + \dot{L}_t^{bc}) - \dot{M}_t + \dot{E}_t R_t, \tag{13}$$

or

$$\dot{\Omega}_t^b = S_t^b + \dot{E}_t R_t, \tag{14}$$

where S_t^b is given by

$$S_t^b = E_t \dot{R}_t + (\dot{L}_t^{bg} + \dot{L}_t^{bc}) - \dot{M}_t. \tag{15}$$

S_t^b is referred to as the "quasi-fiscal" surplus (or, when negative, deficit).[7] It is the difference between the central bank's earnings and its expenditures. The former consist of interest earnings on net foreign exchange reserves, credit to commercial banks, and net credit to the nonfinancial public sector; the latter consist of transfers to the government τ_t^g and to commercial banks τ_t^c:

$$S_t^b = i^* E_t R_t + i_b (L_t^{bg} + L_t^{bc}) - \tau_t^g - \tau_t^c, \tag{16}$$

where, for simplicity, we assume that the central bank charges the same interest rate i_b on its loans to the government and to commercial banks.

Equation (15) can be rewritten in a useful way to derive the sources of base money growth:

$$\dot{M}_t = \dot{L}_t^{bg} + E_t \dot{R}_t - S_t^b + \dot{L}_t^{bc}. \tag{17}$$

Equation (17) indicates that the sources of base money growth consist of central bank financing of the nonfinancial public sector, balance-of-payments surpluses, quasi-fiscal deficits, and credit extended by the central bank to the private banking system.

2.1.2.3 THE CONSOLIDATED PUBLIC SECTOR

The consolidated public sector consists of the nonfinancial public sector and the central bank. Using Equations (6) and (11), the financial net worth of the consolidated public sector, Ω_t^{ps}, is given by

$$\Omega_t^{ps} = \Omega_t^g + \Omega_t^b = E_t(F_t^g + R_t) + (L_t^{bc} - L_t^{cg}) - M_t, \qquad (18)$$

which changes over time according to

$$\dot{\Omega}_t^{ps} = E_t(\dot{F}_t^g + \dot{R}_t) + (\dot{L}_t^{bc} - \dot{L}_t^{cg}) - \dot{M}_t + \dot{E}_t(F_t^g + R_t). \qquad (19)$$

Its financial saving consists of

$$S_t^{ps} = S_t^p + S_t^g = E_t(\dot{F}_t^g + \dot{R}_t) + (\dot{L}_t^{bc} - \dot{L}_t^{cg}) - \dot{M}_t, \qquad (20)$$

so that Equation (19) can alternatively be written as

$$\dot{\Omega}_t^{ps} = S_t^{ps} + \dot{E}_t(F_t^g + R_t). \qquad (21)$$

The overall financial surplus of the consolidated public sector is given by, from Equations (10) and (16):

$$S_t^{ps} = S_t^g + S_t^b = (\tau_t^p - C_t^g - I_t^g - \tau_t^c) + i_b L_t^{bc} + i^* E_t(F_t^g + R_t) - i_c L_t^{cg}. \qquad (22)$$

Other useful concepts of the overall public sector accounts are the primary surplus (consisting of the non-interest portion of the overall public sector surplus) and the operational surplus, which excludes the inflation component of nominal interest transactions and thus consists of the primary surplus plus real interest payments. These concepts will be examined in more detail in Chapter 4.

2.1.3 The Commercial Banking System

The commercial banks' financial net worth Ω_t^c is the difference between bank assets and liabilities that have already been identified:

$$\Omega_t^c = L_t^p + L_t^{cg} + RR_t - D_t^p - L_t^{bc}, \qquad (23)$$

which changes over time according to

$$\dot{\Omega}_t^c = \dot{L}_t^p + \dot{L}_t^{cg} + R\dot{R}_t - \dot{D}_t^p - \dot{L}_t^{bc}. \qquad (24)$$

Since commercial banks are assumed to hold neither foreign assets nor inflation hedges, the change in banks' net worth over time simply consists of

$$\dot{\Omega}_t^c = S_t^c = \dot{L}_t^p + \dot{L}_t^{cg} + R\dot{R}_t - \dot{D}_t^p - \dot{L}_t^{bc}, \qquad (25)$$

and S_t^c is constrained by

$$S_t^c = i_c(L_t^p + L_t^{cg}) + \tau_t^c - i_d D_t^p - i_b L_t^{bc}. \tag{26}$$

2.1.4 Aggregate Relationships

Summing Equations (1), (18), and (23), the economy's aggregate net worth Ω_t consists of its net international indebtedness (net claims on foreigners, F_t) plus its stock of inflation hedges:

$$\Omega_t = \Omega_t^p + \Omega_t^{ps} + \Omega_t^c = E_t(F_t^p + F_t^g + R_t) + q_t \bar{H} = E_t F_t + q_t \bar{H}, \tag{27}$$

which grows over time according to

$$\dot{\Omega}_t = E_t \dot{F}_t + \dot{E}_t F_t + \dot{q}_t \bar{H}. \tag{28}$$

Equation (28) can be derived by either differentiating Equation (27) or summing Equations (2), (19), and (24). From Equations (8), (21), and (25), it can also be written as

$$\dot{\Omega}_t = S_t^p + S_t^{ps} + S_t^c + \dot{E}_t F_t + \dot{q}_t \bar{H} = S_t + \dot{E}_t F_t + \dot{q}\bar{H}, \tag{29}$$

where S_t represents national financial saving. Equations (28) and (29) imply

$$S_t = E_t \dot{F}_t, \tag{30}$$

which indicates that national financial saving represents the net accumulation of claims on the rest of the world.

By summing Equations (5), (22), and (26), S_t can also be expressed as

$$S_t = Y_t + i^* E_t F_t - (C_t^p + C_t^g) - (I_t^p + I_t^g), \tag{31}$$

which indicates that national financial saving is the difference between gross national product, $GNP_t = Y_t + i^* E_t F_t$, and domestic absorption, $DA_t = (C_t^p + C_t^g) + (I_t^p + I_t^g)$, which is the current account of the balance of payments, CA_t. The negative of national financial saving as used here is what is commonly referred to as foreign saving (the current account deficit). Some familiar macroeconomic identities can be derived from Equation (31). First, defining total absorption by the nonfinancial public sector as $G_t = C_t^g + I_t^g$ and replacing S_t by CA_t yields the national income accounting identity:

$$GNP_t = C_t^p + I_t^p + G_t + CA_t. \tag{32}$$

Second, defining total national saving ST_t (the sum of aggregate financial and real saving) as the difference between national income and total consumption ($ST_t = GNP_t - C_t^p - C_t^g$) yields the flow-of-funds version of Equation (32):

$$CA_t = ST_t - (I_t^p + I_t^g), \tag{33}$$

which is the standard identity linking total saving ($ST_t - CA_t$) to total investment ($I_t^p + I_t^g$). Third, replacing S_t by its value in Equation (30), we have, after sectoral disaggregation:

$$E_t\dot{R}_t = (GNP_t - C_t^p - I_t^p - G_t) - E_t(\dot{F}_t^p + \dot{F}_t^g). \tag{34}$$

Equation (34) is the familiar balance-of-payments identity, expressed in domestic-currency terms. The left-hand side corresponds to reserve accumulation by the central bank (the overall balance of payments), and the first term on the right-hand side is the current account and the second is the capital account.

2.2 Production Structure in an Open Economy

To convert the set of identities described in the preceding section to a macroeconomic model, economic behavior and equilibrium conditions must be specified. First, however, the degree of sectoral disaggregation must be determined. As suggested in the introduction, open-economy macroeconomics offers three basic options. In this section we describe each of these in turn.

2.2.1 The Mundell-Fleming Model

The most common analytical framework adopted in modeling the production structure in open-economy models of industrial countries is the Mundell-Fleming framework.[8] This framework assumes that the economy specializes in the production of a single (composite) good, which is an imperfect substitute for the single (composite) good produced by the rest of the world. The law of one price holds for each individual good, so the domestic-currency price of the foreign good is equal to the foreign-currency (international) price (which we denote P^*) multiplied by the domestic-currency price of the foreign currency, E_t. Similarly, the foreign-currency price of the domestically produced good is its domestic-currency price, P_t, divided by the domestic-currency price of the foreign currency. Domestic residents demand both the domestic and foreign goods, as do foreign residents. Thus, the foreign good is the home economy's importable good, and the domestic good is its exportable good. The relative price of the foreign good in terms of the domestic good is referred to as the domestic economy's terms of trade or its real exchange rate. The two terms are interchangeable in the Mundell-Fleming model.

The key property of the Mundell-Fleming model is that the domestic economy's terms of trade are endogenous, because the home country is small in the market for its importable good but large—in the sense of possessing some degree of monopoly power—in the market for its exportable good. The latter implies that changes in domestic demand for the exportable good will affect its relative price or level of production. The mechanism through which it does so, and the extent to which equilibrium is restored through relative price or output adjustments, depends on the exchange-rate system and the short-run supply function for the exportable good. To illustrate the determination of the terms of trade, we examine a simple short-run Mundell-Fleming model that focuses only on the production side of the economy, that is, the goods and labor markets. We consider only the case of fixed exchange rates, since (as discussed in Chapter 6) this provides a closer approximation to the managed exchange-rate systems that tend to characterize developing countries.[9]

Let y_t represent output of the domestic good, a_t the level of domestic absorption, and b_t the trade balance, all measured in units of the domestic good. Also, let $z_t = E_t P^*/P_t$ denote the terms of trade. Since domestic and foreign goods are imperfect substitutes, the trade balance can be written as

$$b_t = b(\overset{+}{z}_t, \bar{a}_t, \ldots) \qquad -1 < b_a < 0, \tag{35}$$

where the sign of the derivative with respect to the terms of trade assumes that the Marshall-Lerner condition holds.[10] The equilibrium condition of the market for domestic goods is given by

$$y_t = a_t + b(z_t, a_t, \ldots). \tag{36}$$

The nature of the equilibrating mechanism depends on the supply side of the economy. In the short run, domestic output is determined by a production function that exhibits diminishing returns to labor:

$$y_t = y(\overset{+}{L}_t, \ldots), \qquad y_{LL} < 0, \tag{37}$$

where L_t is the level of employment. Let w_t denote the nominal wage, and ω_t the real wage in terms of the importable good. Then the real wage in terms of exportables is $w_t/P_t = (w_t/E_t P^*)(E_t P^*/P_t) = z_t \omega_t$, and labor demand L_t^d is given by the profit-maximizing condition

$$y_L(L_t, \ldots) = z_t\omega_t \Rightarrow L_t^d = L^d(z_t\omega_t, \ldots), \tag{38}$$

where $\partial L^d/\partial(z_t\omega_t) = -1/y_L < 0$. Finally, labor market equilibrium requires:

$$L^d(z_t\omega_t, \ldots) = \bar{L}, \tag{39}$$

where $\bar{L}$ is the exogenous supply of labor.

This model can be solved for z_t as a function of a_t under classical or Keynesian conditions. In the former case, the labor market clears, so Equation (39) can be used to replace L by $\bar{L}$ in Equation (37), leaving Equation (36) in the form

$$y(\bar{L}, \ldots) = a_t + b(z_t, a_t, \ldots), \tag{40}$$

which determines z_t implicitly as a function of a_t. The effect on z_t of an increase in a_t is given by $dz_t/da_t = -(1 + b_a)/b_z$, which has a negative sign because an increase in domestic absorption increases the domestic price level, so that the terms of trade improve.[11] In the Keynesian mode, ω_t is exogenous and the labor market-clearing Equation (39) does not hold. Solving (38) for the demand for labor L_t^d as a function of the product wage $z_t\omega_t$ (that is, $L(z_t\omega_t)$, where $L' = -1/y_L < 0$) and substituting the result in Equation (37) allows us to write (40) in the form

$$y[L(z_t\omega_t), \ldots] = a_t + b(z_t, a_t, \ldots), \tag{41}$$

which implies that, in this case, the relationship between z_t and a_t is $dz_t/da_t = (1 + b_a)/(\omega y_L L' - b_z) < 0$, since the numerator is positive and the denominator negative. A change in domestic absorption has a smaller effect on the terms of trade in the Keynesian case (the denominator of dz_t/da_t is larger in absolute value) because a change in z_t elicits a supply as well as a demand response in this case, so a given change in z_t is more effective in eliminating excess demand in the market for domestic goods.

The simultaneous determination of internal and external balance in this model is illustrated in Figure 2.1. The CC schedule depicts the set of combinations of z_t and a_t compatible with equilibrium in the market for home goods that prevails when the model operates in classical mode. The slope of CC reflects the dependence of the terms of trade on domestic spending in the Mundell-Fleming model, as derived above. The BB schedule depicts the set of combinations of z_t and a_t compatible with a given trade balance outcome, say a sustainable trade balance level b_0. It is derived from Equation (35). Its slope is positive and given by $-b_a/b_z$. Points above BB correspond to an improvement in the trade balance relative to b_0, and points below imply

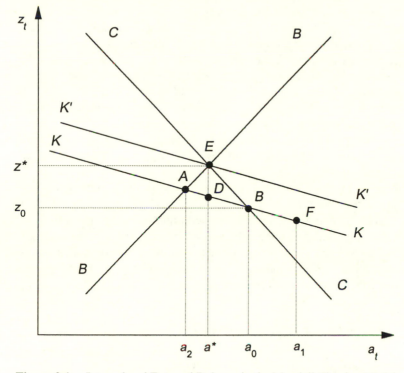

Figure 2.1   Internal and External Balance in the Mundell-Fleming Model

a deterioration relative to b_0. Equation (36) implies that the economy must always lie along CC, where the market for domestic goods clears. Given a level of absorption a_0, CC determines the value of z_t required to clear the market for domestic goods, and the negative slope of CC follows from the sign of dz_t/da_t, derived above. In the figure, the equilibrium value of the terms of trade corresponding to a_0 is z_0. The trade balance at point B corresponding to (a_0, z_0) exhibits a deficit in excess of b_0. Thus, in the classical case, B represents a point of internal, but not external, balance. The simultaneous achievement of external and internal balance, at point E, requires a reduction in domestic absorption from a_0 to a^*.

The commodity-market equilibrium schedule in the Keynesian mode is derived from Equation (41). Its position depends on the initial value of the real wage measured in terms of importables, ω_t. Graphically, a change in ω_t causes the commodity-market equilibrium locus to shift vertically. The shift is downward for an increase in ω_t and upward for a reduction in ω_t. In both cases the magnitude of the shift is less than proportional to the change in ω_t.[12] The Keynesian commodity-market equilibrium locus that passes through the initial point B is labeled KK. Since z_t is more responsive to

a_t in the classical than in the Keynesian mode, KK is depicted in the diagram as flatter than CC. In the Keynesian case internal balance may not hold at B since, although the goods market clears by assumption, the labor market equilibrium condition (39) may not hold.[13] Increasing absorption to a_1 would move the economy to F, achieving internal balance. However, this implies further departure from external balance. An adjustment of absorption to a^*, as in the classical case, would fail to restore external balance (since the terms of trade would not deteriorate sufficiently) and move the economy further away from internal balance. Finally, external balance could be restored at point A, but this would move the economy further away from internal balance.

What is required in the Keynesian model is the simultaneous adjustment of absorption and the real wage in terms of importables. In the classical model, the latter is achieved through nominal wage flexibility. In the Keynesian model, it must be achieved by an adjustment in the nominal exchange rate. A reduction of absorption from a_0 to a^*, coupled with a nominal exchange-rate depreciation sufficient to shift KK to $K'K'$ would simultaneously achieve external and internal equilibrium at point E.

2.2.2 The "Dependent Economy" Model

The endogeneity of the terms of trade in the Mundell-Fleming model is inconsistent with the evidence cited in Chapter 1 that developing countries tend to be small in the market for their exports, so that such countries in fact exert very little control over the world prices of their exports. If the terms of trade are instead taken as exogenous, but the Mundell-Fleming assumption of a single domestically produced good is retained, then domestic demand conditions would have no effect on either the price or output of the domestic good, since that good would effectively face an infinitely elastic world demand at a domestic-currency price determined by the law of one price. The only role for domestic demand in this case would be to determine the excess demand for the domestic good, and thus the trade balance.

This situation is unrealistic, because many domestic goods and services indeed cannot be sold abroad; transportation costs and commercial policies make such domestic goods uncompetitive in foreign markets. However, such goods and services may not be imported either, since trade barriers such as those mentioned may render their foreign equivalents uncompetitive in the domestic market. Goods and services of this type that can neither be sold nor bought abroad are referred to as nontraded. Nontraded goods are produced at home for sale at home.

The dependent-economy model due to Swan (1960) and Salter (1959) contains two domestic production sectors, one producing traded and the

other nontraded goods. The traded goods sector consists of both importables and exportables. They can be aggregated into a single sector because
the terms of trade are taken to be both exogenous, as suggested above, and
constant, so that exportables and importables can be treated as a single
Hicksian composite good. What matters for macroeconomic equilibrium is
the total value of domestic production and consumption of traded goods,
rather than exportables or importables separately. Domestic residents are
assumed to spend on both traded and nontraded goods.

As already indicated, in the dependent-economy model the terms of trade
are constant. The law of one price holds for traded goods, so in the small-
country case the domestic economy faces infinitely elastic world demand
for exportables and supply of importables at their respective world market prices. The key relative price in the dependent-economy model is the
real exchange rate, defined as the price of traded goods in terms of nontraded goods, or $z_t = P_T(t)/P_N(t)$, where $P_T(t)$ is the domestic-currency
price of traded goods—measured in terms of exportables, importables, or
any combination of these goods—and $P_N(t)$ is the price of nontraded goods.
Production in each sector is described by a linearly homogeneous sectoral
production function in capital and labor, but in the short run each sector's
capital stock is fixed. Labor, on the other hand, is homogeneous and intersectorally mobile. In the short run, supply of output in each sector depends
on employment in that sector:

$$y_h(t) = y_h[\overset{+}{L}_h(t), \dots], \qquad y_{hLL} < 0, \qquad h = N, T, \qquad (42)$$

where $y_T(t)$ and $y_N(t)$ denote, respectively, the value of domestic production of traded and nontraded goods, and $L_T(t)$ and $L_N(t)$ correspond to employment in each of the two sectors. Demand for labor from each sector is
inversely related to that sector's product wage:

$$L_T^d(t) = L_T(\bar{\omega}_t, \dots), \qquad L_N^d(t) = L_N(z_t^{-}\omega_t, \dots), \qquad (43)$$

where $\omega_t = w_t/P_T(t)$ is the real wage in terms of traded goods. Substituting
(43) in (42) yields the sectoral supply functions:

$$y_T^s(t) = y_T(\bar{\omega}_t, \dots), \qquad y_N^s(t) = y_N(z_t^{-}\omega_t, \dots). \qquad (44)$$

Domestic demand for traded and nontraded goods is taken to depend
on the relative prices of the two goods, given by the real exchange rate,
and on total domestic absorption measured in terms of traded goods, a_t,
given by

$$a_t = a_T(t) + z_t^{-1}a_N(t). \qquad (45)$$

Thus,[14]

$$a_T(t) = a_T(\bar{z}_t, \overset{+}{a}_t, \ldots), \qquad 0 < a_{Ta} < 1 \tag{46a}$$

$$a_N(t) = a_N(\overset{+}{z}_t, \overset{+}{a}_t, \ldots), \qquad 0 < a_{Na} = 1 - a_{Ta} < 1. \tag{46b}$$

The trade balance b_t is determined by the value of the domestic excess supply of traded goods:

$$b_t = y_T(\omega_t, \ldots) - a_T(z_t, a_t, \ldots). \tag{47}$$

Equilibrium in the nontraded goods market requires

$$y_N(z_t\omega_t, \ldots) = a_N(z_t, a_t, \ldots). \tag{48}$$

Finally, the labor market-clearing condition is given by

$$L_T(\omega_t, \ldots) + L_N(z_t\omega_t, \ldots) = \bar{L}. \tag{49}$$

Unlike the Mundell-Fleming model, the classical version of this model is not recursive. Rather than determining the real exchange rate first, and from that the real wage, the real exchange rate and the real wage must be solved together from conditions (48) and (49); that is, the equilibrium values of ω_t and z_t are those that simultaneously clear the labor and nontraded goods markets. The solution is portrayed graphically in Figure 2.2. The locus LL depicts the set of combinations of ω_t and z_t that satisfy the labor market equilibrium condition (49), and NN is the corresponding locus for the nontraded goods market (48). The slope of LL is $-(L_N' + L_T')/L_N' < -1$, and that of NN is $-y_N'L_N'/(y_N'L_N' - a_{Nz}) > -1$, which, though greater than -1, is negative.[15] The line CD, with slope -1, is inserted in the figure for reference. To the right (left) of LL, the real wage is too high (low), and excess supply (demand) prevails in the labor market. Similarly, below (above) NN the real exchange rate is excessively appreciated (depreciated), and excess supply (demand) prevails in the market for nontraded goods. The equilibrium combination of z_t and ω_t is given by (z^*, ω^*), where LL and NN intersect (point E).

Consider now the effects of an increase in absorption, a_t. The nontraded goods locus NN shifts down to a position like $N'N'$, since equilibrium in this market requires a more appreciated real exchange rate when aggregate spending is higher. The new equilibrium moves to B, with an appreciated real exchange rate and an increase in the real wage. Notice that, since B lies below CD, the proportional reduction in z_t exceeds the proportional increase in ω_t. This means that the product wage in the nontraded goods sector falls.

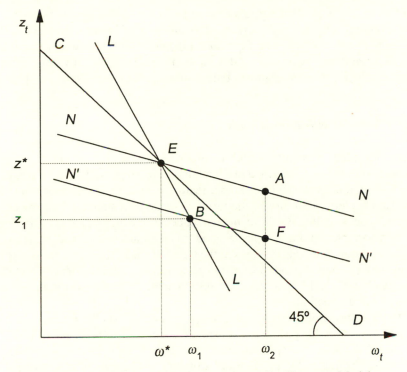

Figure 2.2   Classical Equilibrium in the Dependent-Economy Model

Thus, labor is released from the traded goods sector and absorbed by the nontraded goods sector. For this reason, and because the appreciation of the real exchange rate shifts demand towards the traded good, the trade balance deteriorates.

The graphical analysis of the determination of internal and external balance can be conducted in a manner similar to that of the Mundell-Fleming model by solving Equation (49) for ω_t in terms of z_t. The slope of this relationship is that of the LL locus in Figure 2.2; it is negative and greater than unity in absolute value. Substituting the resulting expression into Equations (47) and (48) yields a pair of equations that determine the trade surplus and the nontraded goods market equilibrium as functions of z_t and a_t, in the manner of Figure 2.1.

The Keynesian form of this model takes ω_t to be exogenous. In Figure 2.2, if the initial value of ω_t is ω_2, the market for nontraded goods will clear at point A and the labor market will be characterized by a situation of excess supply, since point A is to the right of LL. An increase in a_t would move the economy to point F, which would reduce the extent of excess supply in the labor market since the nontraded goods sector would expand, in this case not by drawing labor away from the traded goods sector but by absorbing unemployed workers. The analysis of internal and external balance in this case can use Equations (48) and (49) as they are, treating ω_t as given. Because a nominal devaluation would alter ω_t, it would cause shifts in the Keynesian version of both Equations (48) and (49) in z-a space.

2.2.3 A Model with Three Goods

The dependent-economy model incorporates an important developing-country stylized fact described in Chapter 1—the exogeneity in the terms of trade—but it does not capture another feature of such economies mentioned in that chapter: variability in the terms of trade as a source of macroeconomic shocks. It does not do so, of course, because to aggregate exportables and importables into a composite good means that the terms of trade are taken as fixed. Allowing changes in the terms of trade, then, requires disaggregating the traded goods sector into separate exportables (identified with the symbol X) and importables sectors (symbol I); that is, it requires the use of a three-good model.

In this subsection we examine a simple version of such a model, one in which the exportable good is not consumed at home. This assumption would represent a reasonable approximation to reality in an economy whose exports are dominated by a primary commodity. As suggested in Chapter 1, despite an increase in the relative importance of manufactured goods in recent years, this continues to be the case in many developing countries.

In the three-good model, production takes place in three sectors, with sectoral production functions given by

$$y_h(t) = y_h[(\overset{+}{L}_h(t), \ldots], \qquad h = X, I, N, \tag{50}$$

with $y_{hLL} < 0$. Labor demand is given by

$$L_X^d(t) = L_X(\omega_t \Theta_t^{-1}, \ldots), L_I^d(t) = L_I(\omega_t, \ldots), L_N^d(t) = L_N(z_t \omega_t, \ldots), \tag{51}$$

with $L_h' < 0$ for $h = X, I, N$. In this equation Θ_t denotes the terms of trade, given by $P_X(t)/P_I(t); z_t$ the real exchange rate measured in terms of importables, so that $z_t \equiv P_I(t)/P_N(t)$; and ω_t the real wage in terms of importables. $P_X(t), P_I(t)$, and $P_N(t)$ represent the domestic-currency prices of exportables, importables, and nontraded goods, respectively. The first two are given by the law of one price, so that $P_X(t) = E_t P_X^*$ and $P_I(t) = E_t P_I^*$. By contrast, $P_N(t)$ is determined domestically.

In general, changes in the terms of trade can be expected to have sectoral resource reallocation effects on the supply side of the economy, of the type already seen in our discussion of the dependent-economy model. In addition, however, because terms of trade changes affect a country's real income, they can be expected to have demand-side effects as well. To incorporate these effects in the simplest possible fashion, we shall assume that domestic absorption measured in terms of importables, denoted a_t, is given by

$$a_t = a(\overset{+}{\Theta}_t, \overset{+}{k}).\tag{52}$$

Thus, absorption depends positively on the terms of trade as well as on the shift parameter k. As in the previous section, sectoral supply functions can be derived by substituting the sectoral labor demand functions given in Equation (51) into the sectoral production functions in Equation (50). Equilibrium in the market for nontraded goods requires

$$y_N(z_t\omega_t, \ldots) = a_N(\overset{+}{z}_t, \overset{+}{a}_t, \ldots), \qquad 0 < a_{Na} < 1.\tag{53}$$

The trade surplus measured in units of importables b_t is given by the domestic excess supply of traded goods:

$$b_t = \Theta_t y_X(\omega_t\Theta_t^{-1}, \ldots) + y_I(\omega_t, \ldots) - a_I(z_t, a_t, \ldots).\tag{54}$$

Finally, the full employment condition is

$$L_X(\omega_t\Theta_t^{-1}, \ldots) + L_I(\omega_t, \ldots) + L_N(z_t\omega_t, \ldots) = \bar{L}.\tag{55}$$

Like the others, this model can be analyzed in the classical or Keynesian mode. For a given value of the terms of trade, the analysis exactly duplicates that of the dependent-economy model and will not be repeated here. What distinguishes this model from the previous ones, however, is its ability to handle changes in the terms of trade. Accordingly, the rest of this section examines the effects of terms-of-trade changes on the real exchange rate and the real wage in the three-good model. In the classical mode, these variables are determined simultaneously by Equations (53) and (55). The diagrammatic apparatus is presented in Figure 2.3, where the curves NN and LL depict Equations (53) and (55), respectively, and the determination of equilibrium at point E is exactly as in Figure 2.2.

Consider now a deterioration in the terms of trade brought about by a reduction in $P_X(t)$. In this case, Θ_t falls on impact. From Equation (52), absorption also falls. This means that the real exchange rate must depreciate to maintain equilibrium in the market for nontraded goods; that is, the NN locus shifts up in Figure 2.3, to $N'N'$. At the same time, the product wage rises in the exportables sector, inducing this sector to shed labor as it contracts production. To maintain full employment at a given value of ω_t,

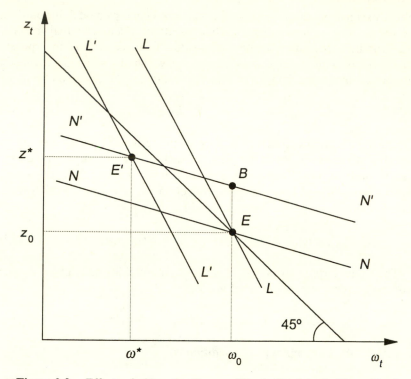

Figure 2.3   Effects of a Negative Terms-of-Trade Shock in the Three-Good Model

the excess labor must be absorbed by the nontraded goods sector. This can happen only if z_t falls, so LL shifts down. The outcome, as shown in Figure 2.3, is a new equilibrium with a depreciated real exchange rate and reduced real wage, at point E'.

In the Keynesian case, the real wage in terms of importables cannot change. Thus the new equilibrium is at point B, rather than E'. The situation is characterized by unemployed labor, since point B lies to the right of the labor market equilibrium locus $L'L'$. The real exchange rate depreciation in the Keynesian case is less than that in the classical case. To maintain full employment under Keynesian conditions requires a nominal devaluation that would reduce the real wage from ω_0 to ω^*, thus moving the economy from point B to point E' along $N'N'$.

An important application of the model described in this section is to the "Dutch disease" phenomenon, which refers to the macroeconomic implications of the existence of a booming sector.[16] A "boom" in the present context can be represented by the reverse of the shock just analyzed, that is, an increase in $P_X(t)$. In this case, the real exchange rate would *appreciate*

(z_t would fall), and as a consequence ω_t would rise. The result would be a *contraction* of output in the importables sector. Because this outcome arises in part due to the larger spending on nontradables induced by the favorable income effects associated with the terms of trade shock, it will be more pronounced the larger such effects are. In developing countries, the "Dutch disease" phenomenon has often been aggravated by expansionary macroeconomic policy responses to favorable terms-of-trade shocks. Such responses have proved difficult to reverse when the shocks that induced them proved to be transitory.

2.3 The Structure of Labor Markets

The study of labor markets in development economics focuses traditionally on medium- and long-run issues, such as the determinants of rural-to-urban migration, the growth in the urban labor force and the associated rise in unemployment, and the effects of education on levels of earnings. More recent work has recognized the crucial role that the structure of labor markets may play in determining the effects of trade reforms and structural adjustment policies.[17] However, labor markets also play an important role in the transmission of macroeconomic policy shocks. The different effects of policy and external shocks in the classical and Keynesian versions of the models analyzed in the previous sector, for instance, are entirely attributable to differing assumptions about the degree of nominal wage flexibility. More generally, the degree of wage inertia determines to a large extent the effect of fiscal, monetary, and exchange-rate policies on real output. In particular, as will be shown in Chapter 7, real wage resistance plays an important role in determining whether or not a nominal devaluation is contractionary. The purpose of this section is to examine the main empirical characteristics of labor markets in developing countries and highlight their macroeconomic implications, with a particular emphasis on the short-term determination of wages and the nature of labor market segmentation. We begin by outlining some structural features of these markets. We then examine the correlation among output, wages, and unemployment. We conclude by discussing the nature and sources of labor market segmentation in developing countries.

2.3.1 Functioning of Labor Markets

Labor markets in developing nations differ in important ways from those operating in industrial countries. Key structural differences are the importance of the agricultural sector in economic activity (which implies that employment tends to display a marked seasonal pattern), the importance of self-employment, and irregular work activities. These structural differences imply that standard labor market concepts used in the industrial world (such as employment and unemployment) do not necessarily have the same meaning here and must be interpreted with care.

Development economists typically distinguish three sectors in the labor market in developing countries (see Rosenzweig, 1988). The first is the rural sector, which is characterized by a large share of self-employed persons and unpaid family workers. The second segment is the informal urban sector, characterized by self-employed individuals or small, privately owned enterprises producing mainly services and other nontradables. Activities in this sector rely mostly on the provision of labor services by owners and their families, but occasionally also on paid labor without any formal employment contract. Job insecurity is pervasive, wages are highly flexible, and workers get very few benefits from their employers. Legal minimum wage laws do not apply or are not enforced, and labor unions play a very limited role. The third segment of the labor market is the formal urban sector, consisting of medium and large enterprises (including state-owned firms) that hire workers on the basis of formal contracts. Workers and employers are subject to various labor market regulations. Employers, in particular, must provide a variety of benefits (such as a pension plan, health insurance, and relative job security) to their workers.[18] Labor unions often play an important role in the determination of wages, and legal minimum wage laws exist—albeit enforced with varying stringency across professions and countries.

In many developing nations, agriculture still employs the great majority of the labor force in rural areas, and the "modern" sector is small. The functioning of rural and urban labor markets differs considerably in at least three respects (Rosenzweig, 1988). First, the heterogeneity and diversity of production in urban areas requires a wider variety of competence and skills among workers. Second, seasonal and climatic effects on production in urban areas are less pronounced than in rural areas. Third, urban production activities are more concentrated geographically than in rural agriculture.

As a result of the importance of the rural and urban informal sectors, the proportion of wage earners in total employment tends to be much lower than in the industrial world, although there are large variations across countries and regions. Wage employment accounts for about 10 percent of total employment in some low-income sub-Saharan African countries, but as much as 80 percent in some middle-income Latin American countries.[19] The share of informal sector employment in total urban employment is sizable in many developing countries—particularly in some parts of Asia, the Middle East, and sub-Saharan Africa—and may vary between 30 and 60 percent (Rosenzweig, 1988).

TABLE 2.1

Developing Countries: Open Unemployment Rate (period averages, in percent)

Country	1971–75	1976–80	1981–85	1986–90
Argentina	4.8	3.4	4.1	6.1
Brazil	3.2	6.3	6.7	3.8
Chile	8.0	12.8	14.3	6.8
Colombia	—	9.3	11.1	10.6
Jamaica	21.7	25.1	26.1	19.2
Korea	4.2	4.0	4.1	2.9
Mexico	7.1	6.4	5.1	3.5
Peru	4.3	6.3	9.1	—
Philippines	4.8	4.4	5.8	8.1
Singapore	—	3.7	3.1	3.7
Thailand	—	0.9	2.5	4.1
Uruguay	8.1	10.1	12.1	9.9
Venezuela	7.6	5.3	9.9	9.4

Source: International Labor Office, *Yearbook of Labor Statistics.*
Notes: Data refer to open urban unemployment rates.

2.3.2 Output and Unemployment

Available data on employment and unemployment in developing countries are not very reliable and often are not comparable across nations.[20] Another problem is that published measures of unemployment are based mostly on unemployed workers looking for jobs in the formal sector and do not include underemployed workers in the informal and rural sectors—the so-called disguised unemployment. The effective excess supply of labor may thus be understated. In addition, open unemployment may show a rising trend despite strong employment growth, as industrialization combined with migration from rural to urban sectors frequently means that previously underemployed workers are registered as openly unemployed while they are looking for industrial jobs. The available evidence suggests, in fact, that underemployment is far more pervasive than open unemployment. In some countries, open and disguised unemployment includes anywhere from 25 to 60 percent of the labor force (Turnham, 1993).

Table 2.1 presents data on open unemployment for a group of mostly upper-middle-income developing countries in Latin America and Asia. The data may be reasonably meaningful for these countries—despite the caveats indicated earlier—since in most cases between two-fifths and three-quarters of the labor force is in wage employment and a high proportion of the

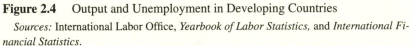

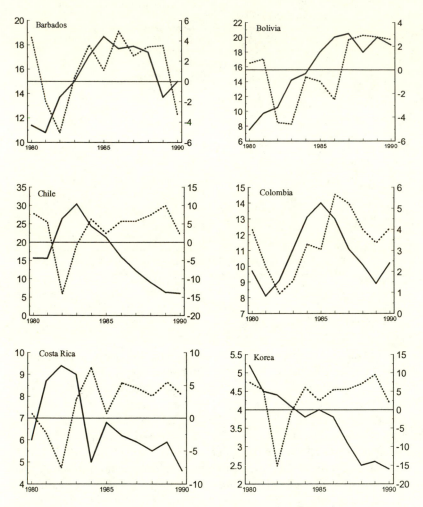

Figure 2.4   Output and Unemployment in Developing Countries

Sources: International Labor Office, *Yearbook of Labor Statistics,* and *International Financial Statistics.*

population live in urban areas. The data suggest a wide variety of unemployment patterns across countries during the past two decades. Figure 2.4 shows the behavior of output and the measured unemployment rate for several developing countries over the 1980s. The first observation is that the economic slowdown of the early 1980s translated into marked increases in the rate of unemployment in most of these countries. Second, although the data

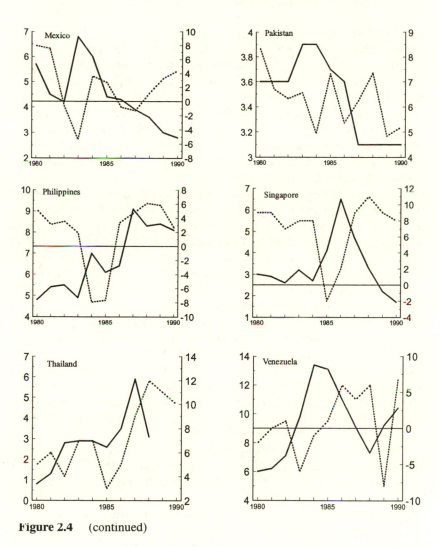

—— Unemployment rate, in percent (left scale)   ······ Real GDP growth, in percent (right scale)

Figure 2.4   (continued)

indicate in some cases a relatively close inverse correlation between the rate of output growth and the unemployment rate, the relationship is rather weak for others and seems to vary erratically over time. The absence of a stable "Okun's law" (as defined in Blanchard and Fischer, 1989, pp. 8–9) may be the result of spillover effects across different segments of the labor market, as discussed below.

2.3.3 Indexation and Wage Rigidity

From a macroeconomic perspective, a critical aspect of the functioning of labor markets is the degree of real wage rigidity. In developing countries, a variety of labor market regulations—minimum wages, indexation laws, employment-protecting measures such as labor tenure laws, restrictions on labor mobility, government-imposed taxes, and large and powerful trade unions—may inhibit real and nominal wage flexibility. Although the relative importance of these factors varies considerably across regions, countries, and over time,[21] an endemic feature has been implicit or explicit wage indexation. In high-inflation countries in particular, wage indexation is an essential feature of the labor market.

Indexation clauses, under normal circumstances, allow for adjustment of wages for productivity changes as well as past inflation. Procedures differ among countries and over time in three main respects: the interval between wage adjustments, the degree of indexation to inflation, and the nature of adjustments for productivity changes. In some countries, the law permits the productivity adjustment to be negotiated freely between workers and employers; in others, the adjustments are specified by the government. In Brazil, for instance, the frequency of wage adjustments has tended to increase with the rate of inflation; many economists view the frequency itself as one of the structural elements in the inflationary process (see Dornbusch et al., 1990; Simonsen, 1983; and Parkin, 1991). In some cases (again, notably Brazil) the degree of indexation to inflation is a function of the wage level, with overindexation at certain wage levels and underindexation at others. The average degree of indexation has also been used as a means of altering inflationary expectations and reducing the inertial element in inflation, as was the case in Argentina (see Chapter 8).

The manner in which indexation operates is important for the transmission of policy shocks to output, inflation, and unemployment. The traditional view of indexation suggests that it helps to insulate output and employment from monetary (demand) shocks, but not from real (supply) shocks.[22] A high degree of real wage rigidity would therefore insulate the real sector from aggregate demand shocks. However, a high degree of wage indexing at the sectoral level may also distort policy-induced price signals, such as a nominal devaluation, and may hamper the reallocation of resources. Moreover, for orthodox and new structuralist macroeconomists alike, indexed contracts are often viewed as the root cause of the stickiness of inflationary expectations and the inflation persistence observed in many Latin American countries.[23] Institutional reforms aimed at reducing the degree of indexation of wages may thus be a critical component for ensuring the credibility and ultimate success of disinflation programs (see Chapter 10).

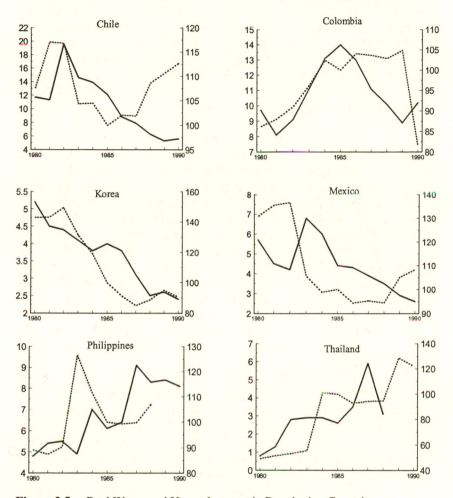

—— Unemployment rate, in percent (left scale)   ······· Real wages (1985 = 100), in percent (right scale)

Figure 2.5   Real Wages and Unemployment in Developing Countries

Sources: International Labor Office and *International Financial Statistics.*

Despite the widespread existence of wage indexation, however, real wages in many countries seem to be more flexible than is generally assumed. Horton et al. (1994), in particular, summarize the findings of a large World Bank study on labor markets and adjustment in developing countries that provides quantitative evidence supporting the existence of a relatively high degree of real wage flexibility in Latin America and Asia. At a less formal level, Figure 2.5, which presents data on real wages and unemployment for six countries (Chile, Colombia, Korea, Mexico, the Philippines, and Thailand), also suggests some degree of real wage flexibility in Chile, Colombia, Mexico, and Thailand. The persistence of unemployment in many cases, therefore, cannot be attributed to excessive real wage rigidity but may result from aggregate demand effects associated with declining real wages and output market imperfections. The first type of effect has been emphasized by new structuralist economists and is known as the Keynes-Kalecki effect (Taylor, 1991). It relies on the assumption that the propensity to save is considerably lower for wage earners than for profit recipients. To the extent that a fall in real wages is accompanied by a fall in the share of wages in national income, aggregate demand will also fall. Unemployment may therefore persist despite a substantial reduction in real wages. The second type of effect may occur as a result of imperfect competition in product markets, even if labor markets are competitive and real wages flexible (Layard et al., 1991). Unfortunately, empirical attempts at discriminating among these alternative hypotheses are scarce.

Although the prevalence of real wage rigidity may be questionable, there is a widespread consensus that nominal wage rigidity is a pervasive feature of the labor market in many developing countries. Nominal wage inertia results from a variety of factors, including lagged indexation, staggered and overlapping wage contracts, and slow adjustment in inflationary expectations. The existence of multiperiod labor contracts appears to be the prevalent source of nominal wage rigidity in middle-income developing nations, particularly in Latin America. For instance, the evidence provided by Reinhart and Reinhart (1991) for Colombia (where the average length of labor contracts in the private sector is estimated to be about two years) suggests that there is considerable inertia in the behavior of nominal wages and prices. Studies by Condon et al. (1990), Corbo (1985a), and Le Fort (1988) on Chile, and van Wijnbergen (1982) on Korea also support the view that nominal wages are sticky in the short run and that prices (in the nontraded goods sector) are determined as a markup over labor and imported input costs.[24] Additional evidence on this issue is discussed in the next chapter (Section 3.4). We will develop a formal specification of nominal wage contracts that captures both backward- and forward-looking indexation rules in the two-sector, short-run macroeconomic model presented in Chapter 9.

2.3.4 Labor Market Segmentation

Labor market dualism in developing countries may be related to the sector of employment or the production structure (agriculture and industry, or traditional and modern), the geographic location of activities (rural and urban, as indicated earlier), the legal nature of activities (formal and informal), or the composition of the labor force (skilled and unskilled workers). These disaggregations do not in general correspond to the distinctions discussed earlier between tradable and nontradable sectors or to the three-good production framework, but may prove useful for macroeconomic analysis. This is because a frequent implication of dualism is labor market segmentation, which can be defined as a situation where observationally identical workers receive different wages depending on their sector of employment. In particular, restrictions on occupational mobility between sectors—resulting from institutional barriers or other factors—may prevent workers in the "low-wage" segment from having full access to a job in the "high-wage" segment held by workers with similar qualifications, even if wages are fully flexible. If there were no barriers, workers in the low-wage sector would enter the high-wage sector and bid wages down in that sector, until sectoral earnings are equalized. Labor market segmentation may also be induced by the existence of sectoral wage rigidities, which lead to demand-constrained employment.

The best-known model of labor market segmentation in developing nations is the migration model of Harris and Todaro (1970). The main objective of the model is to explain the persistence of rural-to-urban migration, despite the existence of widespread urban unemployment in developing countries. A key element of the model is the equality of expected (rather than actual) wages as the basic equilibrium condition across the different segments of the labor market. Specifically, Harris and Todaro assume that rural workers, in deciding to migrate, compare the current wage in agriculture w_A to the expected urban wage w_U^a, which is calculated by multiplying the prevailing wage w_U—assumed fixed as a result of, say, a minimum wage law—by the urban employment ratio, which measures the probability of being hired. In equilibrium, the Harris-Todaro hypothesis yields

$$w_A = w_U^a = w_U \frac{L_U}{L_U + N_U}, \tag{56}$$

where L_U is urban employment and N_U the absolute number of workers unemployed in urban areas. The Harris-Todaro model has been extended in a variety of directions over the years (see Rozensweig, 1988). Particularly interesting developments have been the explanation of urban wage rigidity as a result of efficiency considerations rather than government regulations. According to these hypotheses, real wage cuts lower productivity because they directly reduce incentives to provide effort (Stiglitz, 1982), raise incentives to shirk, increase the quit rate (and thus turnover costs, as emphasized by Stiglitz, 1974), and reduce loyalty to the firm. For instance, workers' effort may depend positively on the wage paid in the current sector of employment (say, the urban sector), relative to the wage paid in other production sectors (the agricultural wage) or the reservation wage. In such conditions each firm will set its wage so as to minimize labor costs per efficiency unit, rather than labor costs per worker. The wage that minimizes labor costs per efficiency unit is known as the efficiency wage. The firm hires labor up to the point where its marginal revenue product is equal to the real wage it has set. A typical case, then, is that aggregate demand for labor, when each firm offers its efficiency wage, falls short of labor supply, so that involuntary unemployment emerges.[25] Efficiency wage theories are particularly useful for explaining why modern-sector firms pay more than the market-clearing wage in models with segmented labor markets. They predict the existence of noncompetitive wage differentials even in the absence of unions and other institutional constraints. We will examine in Chapter 17 how labor market segmentation and relative wage rigidity induced by efficiency considerations alter the transmission of macroeconomic policy shocks.

An additional implication of labor market segmentation is that it offers a particularly clear interpretation of the apparent instability (discussed earlier) of Okun's law in developing countries. Agénor and Aizenman (1994) provide an analytical framework, which is discussed in more detail in Chapter 17, that helps explain the mechanisms at work. Essentially, their analysis stresses the possibility that interactions between the formal and informal urban labor markets may be characterized by substitutability rather than complementarity in the short run, implying that the employment effects of macroeconomic policy shocks can be highly mitigated. In periods of weak output growth, for instance, skilled as well as unskilled workers laid off in the formal sector may seek employment in the informal sector, where wages and labor productivity tend to be lower. Unless skilled workers' reservation wage is higher than the going wage for unskilled workers in the informal sector—as a result, for instance, of generous unemployment benefits in the formal sector—fluctuations in aggregate demand will translate into changes in average productivity rather than a rise in open unemployment.

2.4 Informal Financial Markets

While the functioning of labor markets is a central determinant of aggregate an economy's short-run aggregate supply curve, the characteristics of financial markets exert an important influence on both aggregate demand and supply. A distinguishing feature of developing countries is the coexistence of formal and informal financial markets. In general, informal markets—whether they refer to credit, foreign exchange, or any other good or asset—are a widespread phenomenon in developing nations and often constitute a significant component of economic activity. They typically develop in response to a situation of excess demand in an official market, resulting from the existence of quantitative restrictions on transactions or from the imposition of price ceilings. They are often illegal but are tolerated in many countries.

Informal *financial* markets play a particularly important role in development macroeconomics, although (because of their very nature) they are difficult to monitor or quantify in any meaningful manner. Consequently, information on the size and nature of these markets is not very extensive or reliable. The existing evidence suggests, nevertheless, that in some countries the informal sector is at least as large as the official sector and may even be larger. As a result, these markets may play an important role in the process of transmission of macroeconomic policies. The purpose of this section is to review the scope, nature, and implications of informal financial markets in developing countries and to emphasize their short-term macroeoconomic implications.[26]

2.4.1 Informal Loan Markets

Informal credit markets consist of a variety of unregulated transactions, including the lending and borrowing activities of professional and non-professional moneylenders, private finance firms, indigenous bankers, rotating savings and credit associations, pawnshops, traders, landlords, and households. These transactions can be classified into the following four categories: (1) regular moneylending by individuals or institutions (such as pawnbrokers, indigenous bankers, or finance companies) whose principal activity consists of lending through the use of their own funds or intermediated funds; (2) occasional or intermittent lending by individuals, firms, and institutions with a surplus of funds; (3) tied credit, that is, lending by those whose main activity lies in markets other than the credit market but who tie credit to transactions in markets where their primary activities lie; and (4) group finance, or various forms of cooperative efforts aimed at generating loanable funds for individual credit needs. The importance of each activity varies considerably across countries. In India, for instance, tied credit accounts for a large fraction of total informal credit. Rotating savings and credit associations are very common in Asia and Africa but less so in Latin America. Group finance is used frequently in both urban and rural areas of developing countries.

Available information on informal loan markets, while fragmentary and relying on disparate and noncomparable sources across countries, reveals that informal credit markets are an important feature of developing-country financial markets. The estimates reported by Montiel et al. (1993) for a large group of developing countries suggest that the share of informal credit in total credit varies from about one-third to three-quarters. Informal credit accounts for about one-third to two-thirds of total credit in Bangladesh, about two-fifths in India and Sri Lanka, and two-thirds to

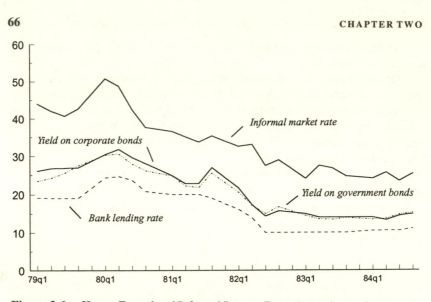

Figure 2.6   Korea: Formal and Informal Interest Rates (annual rates, in percent)
Source: Bank of Korea.

three-quarters in Nepal, Pakistan, Thailand, and Malaysia. In Taiwan the
ratio of financial loans to private enterprises from the informal credit market
to those from the regulated market averaged nearly 28 percent during the
period 1971–88.

Interest rates in informal credit markets are generally substantially higher
than those prevailing in official markets. Figure 2.6 presents some evidence
for Korea.[27] In the absence of organized securities markets and in the presence of financial repression, interest rates in the informal credit market may
represent the relevant opportunity cost of holding money for domestic residents. If so, informal loan rates may play the role in repressed economies
that market-determined interest rates or securities play in industrial countries, and thus would respond primarily to domestic money market conditions. Alternatively, in poor economies market-determined rates in informal
credit markets may respond primarily to arbitrage opportunities between
domestic lending and foreign lending (or the holding of foreign currency).
The evidence provided by Montiel et al. (1993) and the discussion in Chapter 5 suggest that foreign financial variables may indeed exert a significant
influence on informal interest rates.

The entire informal sector may not be affected by events (such as changes
in government credit policy) in the formal sector. Chandravarkar (1987)
makes a useful distinction between the "autonomous" informal sector,
which relates to indigenous activities (often based on social customs), and
the "reactive" part of the informal sector, which refers to activities that
emerge as a response to regulations, credit constraints, or other deficiencies

of the formal sector. It is the second component of the informal sector that would be more directly affected by credit policy and the level of financial repression, and therefore would interact with macroeconomic developments in the formal economy. For instance, an increase in the rate of inflation may raise both the supply of funds to and the demand for loans from the informal sector by reducing the real deposit interest rate in the formal sector and increasing the demand for foreign exchange or for real assets such as real estate and the accumulation of stocks of durable goods. The reactive component would also be more responsive to any changes in regulation or the extent of liberalization. The autonomous component, which relies more on exploiting asymmetric information advantages and low transactions costs, may exhibit less response to policy changes.

2.4.2 Parallel Markets for Foreign Exchange

Exchange and trade restrictions have been largely ineffective in preserving foreign reserves or in supporting an inadequate exchange rate in developing countries. Evasion has been endemic and illegal markets for foreign currencies have expanded, defeating the very purpose of controls. Although, as with informal credit markets, the nature of parallel currency markets precludes collection of detailed and reliable data, they appear to be a common phenomenon in the developing world, with well-documented qualitative features. In this subsection we examine the nature and scope of these markets and highlight their basic structural characteristics.

Parallel currency markets in developing countries have emerged primarily due to foreign trade restrictions and capital controls.[28] In the former case, the process starts with the government trying to impose regulations—such as licensing procedures, administrative allocations of foreign exchange, and prohibitions—on trade flows. The imposition of tariffs and quotas creates incentives to smuggle and falsify invoices (so as to lower the tariff duties) by creating excess demand for goods at illegal, pretax prices. Illegal trade creates a demand for illegal currency, which, in turn, stimulates its supply and leads to the creation and establishment of a parallel currency market if the central bank is unable to meet all the demand for foreign exchange at the official exchange rate.[29] Under capital controls the parallel market expands to become a major element in financing capital flight and portfolio transactions, foreign currency being a hedge against adverse political change and—in high-inflation economies—a hedge against the inflation tax (see Chapter 4).[30] Other factors that help explain the development of a parallel currency market in particular circumstances include private transfers in the context of an overvalued exchange rate and illegal activities. In Pakistan, for instance, the rapid expansion of the illegal market for foreign exchange in the late 1970s is often viewed as being primarily the result of the large influx of worker remittances from the Middle East. In some countries the development of the illegal market for dollars has been closely associated with drug-related activities (Grosse, 1982, and Melvin and Ladman, 1991).

Although illegal, parallel currency markets are often tolerated by governments in developing countries. The size of this market depends upon the range of transactions subject to exchange controls as well as the degree to which restrictions are enforced by the authorities. In countries where large and chronic balance-of-payments deficits force the central bank to ration foreign exchange allocated to the private sector (because government needs are large and must be satisfied in priority), parallel currency markets are typically well developed, with an exchange rate that is substantially more depreciated than the official rate. Figure 2.7 shows the evolution of the parallel market premium—the proportion by which the parallel rate exceeds the official rate—in a group of developing countries. The figure shows that the premium, which depends in the long run upon "structural" factors such as the penalty structure and the amount of resources devoted to apprehension and prosecution of offenders, displays large fluctuations in the short run, a phenomenon often seen as reflecting the asset-price characteristics of the parallel exchange rate. In periods characterized by uncertainty over macroeconomic policies or by unstable political and social conditions, parallel market rates tend to react rapidly to expected changes in future economic circumstances.[31]

Transactions in parallel currency markets usually take the form of operations in cash and checks. Sources of supply and demand vary from country to country and depend heavily on the nature and effectiveness of exchange restrictions imposed by the authorities. The illegal supply of foreign currency comes from five main sources: underinvoicing of exports, smuggling of exports, overinvoicing of imports, foreign tourists, and diversion of remittances through nonofficial channels.[32] Available estimates suggest that smuggling[33] and underinvoicing of exports, and overinvoicing of imports are the major sources of supply in most developing countries.[34] It should be noted, however, that the incentive for overinvoicing of imports exists only when the tariff rate on imported goods is sufficiently low relative to the parallel market premium. In a country with high tariff barriers, the price incentive is for *under*invoicing (smuggling *in*) of imports rather than overinvoicing—the one exception being, of course, the case of capital goods imports, on which tariffs are generally lower than average, or even zero. Consequently, it appears that the single major source of foreign-currency supply from illegal trade results from underinvoicing of exports. When there is a tax on exports, underinvoicing allows the exporter to avoid the tax and to sell the illegally acquired foreign exchange at a premium; when there is a subsidy on exports that is less than the parallel market premium, the sale of foreign exchange in the parallel market will more than compensate for the loss of the subsidy. Thus, for given taxes, the higher the

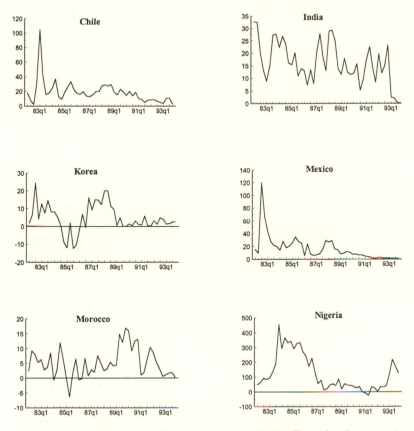

Figure 2.7   Parallel Market Premiums in Developing Countries (in percent)

Sources: International Financial Statistics and *World Currency Yearbook.*

parallel market premium is, the higher will be the propensity to underin-voice exports.

The demand for foreign currency in the parallel market results generally from four main components: imports (legal and illegal), residents traveling abroad, portfolio diversification, and the purposes of capital flight. The demand for foreign currency to finance legal imports stems from the existence of rationing in the official market for foreign exchange. Demand also results from the desire to finance illegal imports of goods that are either prohibited or highly taxed and thus smuggled into the country. The inherent confidentiality of transactions in the parallel market provides an incentive for agents to use it to conceal illicit activities. The portfolio motive is particularly acute in high-inflation economies and in countries where considerable uncertainty over economic policies prevails, because foreign-currency holdings represent an efficient hedge against inflationary bursts. Finally, the capital flight motive derives from the existence of restrictions on private capital outflows. Attempts at circumventing official regulations are funded through the parallel market. Portfolio and capital flight motives are, of course, often related, as shown by the experience of some major Latin American countries.

The existence of a large parallel currency market has important macroeconomic implications.[35] First, it entails a variety of costs for the government: a cost of enforcement, incurred in attempting to counteract parallel market activities and to prosecute and punish offenders; a loss of tariff revenue (due to smuggling and underinvoicing) and revenue from income taxes and domestic indirect taxes; and a reduced flow of foreign exchange to the central bank, which lowers the capacity to import through the official market and service the external debt. To the extent that parallel markets encourage rent-seeking activities (such as corruption of government officials), they also lead to a suboptimal allocation of scarce resources.

Second, the existence of a large parallel market in foreign exchange weakens the effectiveness of capital controls imposed by the central bank. Formally, it has effects similar to an increase in capital mobility—which may help accelerate capital flight—and may lead to an increase in the degree of substitution between domestic and foreign currencies. The potential for currency substitution—defined as the ability of domestic residents to switch between domestic and foreign money (see Chapter 3)—becomes an effective way of avoiding the inflation tax on holdings of domestic cash balances. The shift from domestic to foreign money results, therefore, in a loss of seignorage for the government, which, for a given real fiscal deficit, may call for a higher inflation rate.

Third, parallel exchange rates may have a large impact on domestic prices. Since trade takes place at both the official exchange rate (through official channels) and the parallel market rate (through smuggling), the domestic price of tradable goods will reflect both exchange rates. However, in most countries where foreign exchange rationing prevails, the officially fixed exchange rate is not relevant for the determination of market prices of tradable goods. It measures only the rents captured by those (usually the government and a small group of "privileged" importers) to whom foreign exchange is made available at the official rate. If domestic prices of tradables are based on the marginal cost of foreign exchange—or its implicit resale value, that is, the parallel market rate—the aggregate price level will reflect to a large extent the behavior of the unofficial exchange rate. Indeed, it has been noted that in several African countries (Ghana and Uganda, in particular), prices of tradable goods have tended to more closely reflect the prevailing exchange rate in the parallel market than that in the official market (Roberts, 1989). To the extent that parallel exchange rates—being very sensitive to actual and anticipated changes in economic conditions— are more volatile than official exchange rates, domestic prices are likely

Consumer price index

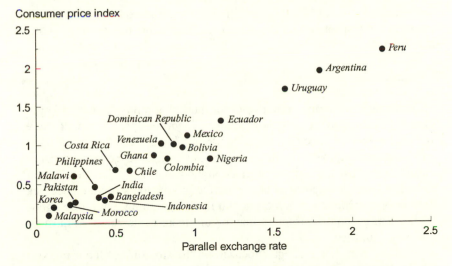

Figure 2.8   Exchange Rate and Price Variability in Developing Countries (period averages, January 1980–March 1993)

Sources: International Financial Statistics and *World Currency Yearbook.*

Notes: Variables are the consumer price index and the end-of-period U.S. dollar–domestic-currency parallel exchange rate. Variablity is measured by the coefficient of variation of each variable.

to display a significant degree of instability, which may adversely affect economic decision making. Figure 2.8 shows that, indeed, countries with the highest degree of parallel exchange variability also tend to exhibit a greater degree of price variability. This positive relationship cannot, of course, be construed as evidence of a causal link, but it is consistent with the view that domestic price setters take into account (directly or indirectly) the behavior of the marginal cost of foreign exchange when setting their prices.

Fourth, since there are two prices at which foreign exchange can be bought and sold, exports whose proceeds are repatriated at the official exchange rate are taxed relative to other exports. Consequently, the parallel market premium may be seen as an implicit tax on exports. In countries where the central bank is a net buyer of foreign exchange, implicit taxes on exports may account for a large share of public resources. This view suggests the existence of a potential trade-off between the premium and the rate of inflation in financing a given real fiscal deficit. We will examine in Chapter 14 the implications of this trade-off for exchange market unification strategies.

Finally, the parallel market for foreign exchange can be expected to play an important role in the transmission mechanism of short-term macroeconomic policies. The analytical models developed in Chapters 5 and 11 will examine the channels through which the parallel exchange rate and the informal interest rate affect the effectiveness of short-run macroeconomic policies.

This chapter has laid the groundwork for those that follow by covering preliminary material in the form of accounting identities, production structure, and characteristics of key aggregate markets. The first part described a general accounting framework and derived some key macroeconomic accounting relationships that will be used throughout the book. The second part provided a simple exposition of alternative production structure specifications in open-economy macroeconomic models, arguing that a three-good, "dependent economy" structure may be of greatest relevance for most developing countries.

The third part of the chapter focused on the structure of labor markets. While a large portion of the development literature focuses on issues such as internal and external migration, and the extent and measurement of surplus labor, there has been only a limited amount of research on the short-run behavior of labor markets in developing countries and their macroeconomic implications. The evidence reviewed here suggests that labor markets in developing countries are characterized by nominal, rather than real, wage rigidity. The evidence on aggregate supply behavior described in the next chapter supports this conclusion. We also emphasized an important source of labor market distortions in developing countries: the existence of labor market segmentation and noncompetitive wages, which may explain the absence of a close relationship in the short run between changes in output and the unemployment rate. These issues are discussed further in Chapter 17.

The final part focused on informal financial markets, which are a phenomenon of particular relevance in many developing countries. The available evidence suggests that the volume of transactions in such markets often represents a substantial fraction of total transactions in credit and foreign exchange. We discussed the main characteristics and macroeconomic roles of informal markets for credit and foreign exchange. Both of these markets arise due to restrictions placed on official transactions, usually in the form of price ceilings. They play important macroeconomic roles because of their flexibility and their forward-looking nature. We will examine in Chapters 5 and 11 analytical models that capture the channels through which informal credit and foreign exchange markets may alter the transmission of macroeconomic policy shocks.

Three

Behavioral Functions

THE formulation of a complete macroeconomic framework suitable for policy analysis requires not only a description of the basic accounting identities or equilibrium conditions that must hold at the level of the aggregate economy, but also the specification of private agents' behavioral functions. A large literature aimed at formulating and estimating models of private agents' behavior in developing countries has emerged over the years. While the focus of the early literature—in this area as well as in many others—was the application of standard concepts and specifications used in the industrial world, more recent studies have been characterized by a systematic account (at the analytical as well as the empirical level) of some of the specific structural features of developing countries.

This chapter examines the specification of and empirical evidence on aggregate behavioral functions in developing nations. The first part analyzes the formulation of consumption and savings functions, focusing in particular on the role of liquidity and credit constraints and the effect of interest rates on saving decisions. The second part discusses the determinants of private investment, emphasizing the role of credit rationing, macroeconomic instability, uncertainty and irreversibility effects, and the relation between private capital formation and public investment. The third part examines the determinants of the demand for money. It distinguishes between conventional models, which emphasize the substitution effects between money and real goods, and more recent models that stress the role of currency substitution factors and financial innovation in the determination of the demand for real money balances.

3.1 Consumption and Saving

As in industrial countries, private consumption represents by far the largest component of aggregate demand in developing nations. Analytically, consumption occupies a strategic role in macroeconomic models, whether of industrial or developing countries. The effects of fiscal policy on aggregate demand, for instance, depend critically on the properties of the consumption function in any macroeconomic model. In developing nations the behavior of private consumption has also received attention because, in spite of the role of external resources, the bulk of domestic investment in almost all of these countries continues to be financed by domestic saving, an important determinant of which is private consumption. Moreover, since the current account deficit of the balance of payments is definitionally equal to the difference between domestic investment and domestic saving (see Chapter 2), private consumption behavior is central to the external adjustment process as well.

The standard model of household consumption widely used for industrial countries postulates a representative household devising a consumption plan that maximizes utility over its lifetime, subject to an intertemporal budget constraint.[1] With additively separable utility and no uncertainty, the household maximizes lifetime utility V as given by

$$V = \sum_{t=0}^{T} \frac{1}{(1 + \alpha)^t} u(c_t),$$
(1)

where $u()$ is a concave period utility function, c_t is real consumption in period t, and α is a constant rate of time preference. Assuming a constant real interest rate ρ, the function V is maximized by choosing a path of consumption $\{c_t\}_{t=0}^T$ subject to

$$\sum_{t=0}^{T} \frac{c_t}{(1 + \rho)^t} \leq a_0 + \sum_{t=0}^{T} \frac{y_t}{(1 + \rho)^t},$$
(2)

where a_0 is the household's initial wealth and y_t denotes disposable factor income in period t. The first-order condition for an optimum is given by the Euler equation

$$u'(c_{t+1}) = \frac{1 + \alpha}{1 + \rho} u'(c_t), \quad t = 1, \ldots, T - 1.$$
(3)

Condition (3) states that the allocation of consumption across periods must be such that an extra unit of consumption would make the same contribution to lifetime utility no matter to what period it is allotted.[2] The consumption path that solves the household's optimizing problem is that satisfying Equation (3), and for which (2) holds as an equality, so no income is wasted. Heuristically, condition (3) determines the shape of the consumption path (the rate of growth of consumption) while Equation (2), written as an equality, determines the height of the consumption path (the initial level of consumption).

The key property of this model of consumption is its implication that households will tend to smooth consumption; that is, consumption will not necessarily be tied to current income, as in the simple Keynesian consumption function (KCF). With diminishing marginal utility ($u'' < 0$) and fluctuating income, tying consumption too closely to current income would violate the Euler equation (3), since adjacent periods of high and low consumption would produce ratios of marginal utilities $u'(c_{t+1})/u'(c_t)$ that would exceed or fall short of $(1 + \alpha)/(1 + \rho)$. The model also predicts that the effect of changes in income on current consumption depends on when such changes take place and how long they are expected to last, since these characteristics will determine the impact of the income change on the lifetime resources of the household. Finally, the model makes no prediction about the effects of changes in the interest rate on the consumption behavior of households that are net savers in the current period. For such households the substitution effect (arising from consumption "tilting" toward the future, based on Equation (3)) would tend to depress current consumption while the income effect (arising from an easing of the intertemporal budget constraint (2)) would tend to increase it. The net effect on consumption of a change in ρ would depend on the relative strength of these two effects, which in turn depends on properties of the utility function.

The application of this theory in the context of developing countries raises four issues. The first issue stems from whether households can effectively smooth consumption. This depends on access to unconstrained borrowing and lending, which may be inhibited by the possible existence of liquidity constraints preventing households from moving resources across periods. The second issue relates to the effective length of planning horizons. Even if households are able to smooth consumption over time, they may not choose to do so over sufficiently long periods to make much difference. The extent to which the model described above departs from the simple KCF thus depends on the length of the planning horizon, with greater differences for longer horizons. The relevance of Ricardian equivalence in particular applications, for instance, depends on the length of consumers' planning horizon (see below). The third issue relates to the empirical determination of the effects of interest rate changes on consumption. To test the theory, it is necessary to distinguish between the effect of higher interest rates on the *level* of current consumption, about which the theory makes no prediction, and the effect on the *growth* of consumption, which should be positively related to the interest rate. Finally, the question arises as to the effects of fiscal policy on private consumption. These effects depend not just on the issues already listed, but also on the possibility that public consumption may be an argument in the instantaneous utility function $u()$ and, in the extreme, may be a close substitute for private consumption, so that "direct crowding out" of private by public consumption occurs.

Surveys by Gersovitz (1988) and Deaton (1989) suggest a number of reasons that household consumption behavior in developing countries may differ from that in industrial countries. First, households in developing countries tend to have different demographic structures from those in industrial countries. The individual household tends to be larger and more generations tend to live together, sharing resources. This has several implications for consumption behavior. First, if resources are shared among the several generations within the household, there is no need for "hump" saving to finance retirement, since household income will tend to be sustained as a new working generation replaces the old. Second, with resources pooled among household members, the household provides insurance for individuals against certain types of risk (such as health risk) that may only be imperfectly insured against in the market, and that would otherwise have provided a motive for precautionary household saving. Third, the relationship between generations in a single household makes more plausible the intergenerational altruism required to extend the household planning horizon beyond the lifetime of the current working generation; that is, developing-country households may provide a closer approximation to the "dynastic" household of Barro (1974).

A second source of differences in consumption behavior between developed and developing countries relates to the observation that household incomes in the developing world may be more uncertain than those in industrial nations, for several reasons. These include the greater share of agricultural incomes in developing countries as well as macroeconomic instability arising from both external shocks (for instance, the variability in the terms of trade described in Chapter 1) and domestic macroeconomic policy shocks. This sort of uncertainty affects the entire household and cannot be diversified away by risk pooling within the household. Thus, as emphasized in particular by Deaton (1989), a precautionary saving motive may be more important in developing countries.[3]

A third source of differences may result from the widely observed phenomenon that many households in developing countries operate at near-subsistence income levels. This may strengthen the motive for consumption smoothing, since the consequences of a bad income draw in a given period would be catastrophic under such circumstances. Finally, differences in consumption behavior may also be the consequence of developing-country households' need to cope with the implications of financial repression (see Chapter 1). Thus, while their motive to smooth consumption may be strong, households may be restricted in their ability to transfer resources across time, both by an inability to borrow against future earnings and by very low real returns on current saving. To see how these factors play out in practice, we now examine the evidence on the behavior of private consumption in developing countries, focusing on the issues raised previously.

3.1.1 Consumption Smoothing

As indicated above, given that the utility function is concave, consumption smoothing will be observed if households both plan consumption over multiple periods and have the means to transfer resources across periods. Thus, evidence that households smooth consumption suggests that both factors are present. This evidence takes several forms in developing countries.

First, since the alternative to smoothing consumption is to consume out of current income, evidence of consumption smoothing comes from tests of the permanent income hypothesis (PIH). A large number of such tests have been conducted for developing nations. These tests effectively consist of estimating the regression

$$c_t = a_0 + a_1 y_{pt} + a_2(y_t - y_{pt}) + u_t, \tag{4}$$

where c_t is real per-capita consumption, y_{pt} real per-capita permanent income, y_t current per-capita real income, and u_t a disturbance term. Under the PIH, consumption is equal to permanent income, so $a_1 = 1$ while $a_0 = a_2 = 0$. Under the KCF, in which consumption depends on current income and the permanent/transitory distinction is irrelevant, $a_1 = a_2$ and $a_0 > 0$. Equations of this type have been estimated at various times for developing countries—for instance, by Bhalla (1980) and Wolpin (1982) for rural households in India, by Musgrove (1979) for urban households in three South American countries, and more recently by Gan and Soon (1994) for Malaysia and Singapore. Overall, the results indicate that income decomposition matters; that is, the propensity to consume out of permanent income exceeds the propensity to consume out of current income. These results are thus consistent with the consumption-smoothing hypothesis.[4] At the same time, however, the elasticity of consumption with respect to permanent income is not typically found to be unity, nor is the propensity to consume out of transitory income found to be zero. Thus, while evidence of this type supports consumption smoothing, the strict form of the PIH is not often supported by the data in developing nations.[5]

A second type of evidence emerges from cross-country studies of saving behavior. If "hump" saving over the life cycle is indeed important, the theory suggests that countries experiencing rapid growth in per-capita incomes should exhibit relatively high saving rates, since young cohorts engaging in "hump" saving will be more affluent than older cohorts with lower saving rates, and thus will account for a larger share of aggregate income. For a similar reason, countries with a larger share of the population in the peak earning years should exhibit larger saving rates. The cross-sectional evidence for developing countries is broadly consistent with these predictions—see, for instance, Fry (1988), Aghevli et al. (1990), and Schmidt-Hebbel et al.

(1992)—suggesting that consumption smoothing over the life cycle may indeed be important in these countries.[6] Several authors have also produced time series evidence supportive of this mechanism, such as Lahiri (1989), who studied saving behavior in eight Asian developing countries.

A very different type of evidence has to do with responses to income shocks. As already suggested, changes in the terms of trade, typically emanating from changes in the prices of primary export commodities, have been quite large in many developing countries at various times. Because of the public sector's role in export production, these shocks are not always transmitted to household incomes. In cases where they have been, however, the response of household consumption is informative with respect to the prevalence of consumption smoothing. For example, Bevan et al. (1993) analyzed the effects of the 1976–79 coffee boom on farmers in Kenya. Unlike the situation in neighboring Tanzania, the increase in international coffee prices was passed on to small growers in Kenya, who thus experienced a windfall in income. The evidence reported by Bevan et al. indicates that this windfall, understood to be temporary because it was known to be caused by a frost in Brazil, was largely saved, as would be expected if peasant households sought to smooth consumption.

3.1.2 Length of Planning Horizon and Liquidity Constraints

The evidence suggesting that consumption smoothing takes place in developing countries implies that, on average, planning horizons extend beyond a single period and that at least some households are able to move resources intertemporally. More direct evidence on the length of planning horizons and the prevalence of liquidity constraints is also available. Haque (1988), for instance, devised an empirical test of the Yaari-Blanchard proposition according to which the probability of dynastic extinction drives a wedge between the effective planning horizons of the public and private sectors (see Blanchard and Fischer, 1989, pp. 115–26) and tested it for a group of sixteen developing countries. In fifteen of the sixteen cases no such wedge could be detected, suggesting that the planning horizon of private households was effectively infinite. A similar result was derived by Leiderman and Razin (1988) for the case of Israel. This conclusion was reinforced by Haque and Montiel (1989), who generalized Haque's procedure to measure independently the length of household planning horizons and the share of total consumption attributable to liquidity-constrained "rule of thumb" consumers spending only out of current income. In a different sixteen-country sample from that of Haque, they were unable to reject the null hypothesis of infinite horizons in any country. Overall, then, the direct evidence on the length of household planning horizons in developing nations does not appear to be inconsistent with Deaton's suggestion that the "dynastic family" construct may be more relevant in the developing world than in industrial countries.

By contrast, the measured incidence of liquidity constraints appears to be substantially greater in developing countries. Corbo and Schmidt-Hebbel (1991) found that variables measuring liquidity constraints added significantly to the explanatory power of an equation explaining aggregate consumption for thirteen developing countries that already included determinants suggested by the consumption-smoothing theory. This result suggests the existence of two groups of consumers: those who smooth consumption over time and those whose consumption is limited by current resources.[7] The panel study by Schmidt-Hebbel et al. (1992) found an important role for similar variables in explaining household saving rates. The authors interpreted this evidence as strongly suggestive of the presence of liquidity constraints. Haque and Montiel (1989) derived point estimates of the share of total consumption accounted for by households that simply spend their current incomes. For fourteen of their sixteen countries the estimated share exceeded 20 percent, and several cases exceeded 50 percent. These values are substantially larger than the typical estimate of 0.1 for the United States. The country-specific estimates derived by Haque and Montiel are of the same order of magnitude as regional estimates derived by Rossi (1988) using an Euler equation approach (see below). For low-income countries Rossi's estimates were in the range 0.7–0.8; for middle-income countries values were in the broader but still relatively high range of 0.2–0.8.

3.1.3 Effects of Interest Rate Changes on Savings

As indicated earlier, the theory of consumption described in this section is compatible with either positive or negative effects of changes in interest rates on saving, depending on the strength of income and substitution effects. Nevertheless, the issue is important in developing countries, because one argument frequently adduced in support of either raising controlled interest rates in repressed financial systems or liberalizing the financial system in the context of stabilization and adjustment programs is that higher real interest rates will stimulate domestic saving.[8]

The traditional empirical approach to this issue has been the estimation of structural saving equations, in which the saving rate is regressed on a set of variables loosely motivated by the theory described above. While some authors have found evidence of positive interest rate effects on saving in developing countries using this approach, estimated effects tend to be small.[9] Fry (1988), for example, estimated the effects of several variables on national saving rates using a pooled cross-section time series sample of fourteen

Asian developing countries over the period 1961–83. He found that a 1 percent point increase in the real deposit rate increased the saving rate by about
0.1 percent.[10] In contrast, several studies—see Giovaninni (1985) as well
as Schmidt-Hebbel et al. (1992)—have failed to detect a statistically significant positive interest rate effect.

In addition to the standard Lucas critique problems faced by such specifications, in the developing-country context they are also complicated by the
common lack of data permitting national saving rates to be disaggregated
into private and public components, so such estimation is often based on national, rather than private, saving. This makes the results difficult to interpret. An alternative is to estimate the intertemporal elasticity of substitution
directly. If the instantaneous utility function exhibits constant relative risk
aversion, the Euler equation (3) will relate the rate of growth of consumption to the difference between the real interest rate and the (constant) rate of
time preference, with a factor of proportionality equal to the intertemporal
elasticity of substitution. Estimation of the Euler equation can thus yield an
estimate of the intertemporal elasticity of substitution. A negative interest
rate effect on consumption requires that this elasticity be sufficiently large
to generate a substitution effect that dominates the positive income effect of
higher interest rates on net savers. This approach has the virtues that it estimates a "deep" parameter directly and that it relies on consumption data,
which are available separately for the private sector.

Giovaninni (1985) estimated Euler equations for eighteen developing
countries, finding a statistically significant intertemporal elasticity of substitution (averaging about 0.5) in only five cases. Rossi (1988) modified
Giovaninni's procedure to allow for liquidity constraints and direct substitutability between private and public consumption. His generalized specification yielded larger estimates of the intertemporal elasticity of substitution
for developing-country regions than had been found by Giovaninni for individual countries, but Rossi concluded that these were still too small to
alter the implication that changes in real interest rates would have but weak
effects on consumption.

3.1.4 Public and Private Consumption

The final issue to be addressed in this section is the possibility that public
consumption could be a direct substitute for private consumption in developing countries. While McDonald (1983) provided some early evidence
consistent with this view, subsequent work has failed to corroborated the hypothesis that public consumption directly affects private consumption levels; for example see Haque (1988) and Rossi (1988). In fact, a recent study
by Karras (1994) covering a large number of developing countries suggests

that private and public consumption expenditure appear to be complementary rather than substitutes.

3.2 Private Investment

Private investment plays an important role in developing nations for the same reason that it does in industrial countries: investment determines the rate of accumulation of physical capital and is thus an important factor in the growth of productive capacity. Moreover, because investment is a forward-looking activity with irreversible aspects, it tends to be a volatile component of aggregate demand. In the developing world, the association of capacity growth with physical capital accumulation has, if anything, traditionally been viewed as closer than in industrial countries.[11] Interest in the behavior and determinants of private investment in developing nations has recently increased as a response to the collapse of private capital formation in many heavily indebted countries during, and in the aftermath of, the international debt crisis.[12]

3.2.1 Specification Issues

Empirical investment functions for industrial countries have relied on either a "stock" or a "flow" approach (see Abel, 1990). Under the stock approach (also referred to as the neoclassical or "flexible accelerator" approach), installed capital is assumed to be available at price $p_K(t)$. Given a discount rate α and rate of depreciation δ, the rental price of capital is given by $\sigma_t = (\alpha + \delta)p_K(t)$. Let $\pi(K)$ denote the flow profit function, given by

$$\pi(K_t) = P_t F[K_t, L(w_t/P_t, K_t)] - w_t L(w_t/P_t, K_t), \tag{5}$$

where P_t is the price of output, w_t the nominal wage, and $L()$ the level of employment, derived from profit maximization conditioned on the existing capital stock. Then the optimal capital stock K^* will satisfy

$$\pi'(K^*) = \sigma_t. \tag{6}$$

Given an initial capital stock K_0, net investment represents a gradual adjustment of the actual to the desired capital stock, and gross investment is derived by adding to this an amount of replacement investment that is proportional to the initial capital stock. The flow model, by contrast, postulates the existence of a convex function $h(I_t)$ that measures the total cost (in units of output) of achieving the level of gross investment I_t. If the firm's objective is to maximize the present value $V(K_t)$ (using the discount rate α) of its profits $\pi(K_t)$ net of the costs of investment $P_t h(I_t)$, then at each moment the rate of investment must satisfy

$$h'(I^*) = q_t/P_t, \tag{7}$$

where $q_t = dV(K_t)/dK_t$ is the marginal value of installed capital at time t, and q_t/P_t is the marginal value of "Tobin's q," the ratio of the value of installed capital to its replacement cost.

The determinants of investment in these specifications include, in the stock version, expected future values of aggregate demand, the user cost of capital (with the simple version above typically modified to reflect tax policies that affect investment), and the wage rate, as well as the initial capital stock. These interact in nonlinear forms suggested by the model. In the flow version, what matters is the marginal value of Tobin's q and the parameters of the adjustment-cost function.

In spite of the importance attached to investment in developing countries, relatively little empirical work has been done on the determinants of private investment in such countries. This may be attributable to a scarcity of data or to an overemphasis on public investment, given the large role of nonfinancial public enterprises in many developing countries. An additional obstacle is the need to reformulate investment theories developed for industrial countries to fit the circumstances typical of developing nations.[13]

Modification of standard industrial-country investment theory is required for several reasons. First, the influence of financial variables on investment behavior makes the specification of investment functions heavily dependent on the institutional environment in the financial system. The typical absence of equity markets and prevalence of financial repression in the developing world imply that neither Tobin's q nor standard neoclassical "flexible accelerator" investment functions can be applied uncritically in developing countries. Credit rationing or the cost of funds in informal financial markets may influence the behavior of private investment in many such countries.

Second, given the importance of imported capital goods in the developing world, foreign exchange rationing and the cost of foreign exchange in unofficial "free" markets may also be important determinants of private investment behavior. Third, the role of imported intermediate goods in developing nations suggests that the specification of relative factor prices in empirical investment functions cannot be restricted to the wage rate and the user cost of capital, but must also take into account the domestic-currency price, as well as the availability, of such goods.

The importance of accounting for the role of imported capital goods in explaining investment behavior is demonstrated by Servén (1990b), who studies the effect of a real exchange-rate devaluation on capital formation.[14]

Servén shows that the long-run effect of a real devaluation on private capital formation is, in general, ambiguous. Whether the total capital stock rises or falls depends in particular on the effect of the real depreciation on the import content of capital goods. In the long run, the capital stock is likely to rise in the traded goods sector and fall in the nontraded goods sector. However, despite this long-run ambiguity, an anticipated real-exchange-rate appreciation provides the incentive for an intertemporal reallocation of investment over time. When a real depreciation is expected, an investment boom is likely to develop if the import content of capital goods is high relative to the degree of capital mobility, because the expected depreciation induces a switch toward foreign goods. The boom is subsequently followed by a slump when the depreciation is effectively implemented, because the exchange-rate change is equivalent to the removal of a subsidy on investment. With high capital mobility, the anticipated depreciation promotes flight into foreign assets, and the opposite pattern occurs.

A fourth factor that underlines the need to reformulate investment theories in the developing-country context results from the existence of a debt overhang in many countries, which has often been cited as a factor inhibiting private investment. The possibility that confiscatory future taxation will be used to finance future debt service may need to be reflected in the specification of private investment behavior.[15]

Fifth, the large role of the public capital stock suggests the need to incorporate complementarity-substitutability relationships between public and private capital into private investment decisions. The relationship between public and private investment takes on greater importance in the developing world than in industrial countries because of the larger role played by the government in the overall process of capital formation. Whether, on balance, public sector investment raises or lowers private investment is uncertain a priori. On the one hand, public sector investment can crowd out private investment expenditure if it uses scarce physical and financial resources that would otherwise be available to the private sector. The financing of public sector investment, whether through taxes, issuance of debt instruments, or inflation, can reduce the resources available to the private sector and thus depress private investment activity.[16] Moreover, the public sector may produce marketable output that competes with private output. On the other hand, public investment to maintain or expand infrastructure and the provision of public goods is likely to be complementary to private investment. Public investment of this type can enhance the prospects for private investment by raising the productivity of capital. There is no a priori reason to believe that public and private capital formation are necessarily substitutes or complements. Moreover, public investment may stimulate private output by increasing the demand for inputs and other services, and may augment overall resource availability by expanding aggregate output and saving. The net effect of public investment on private investment will depend on the relative impacts of these various effects.

Finally, macroeconomic instability, often induced by political factors, has been identified in Chapter 1 as an important feature of the macroeconomic environment faced by developing countries, and the resulting uncertainty may have a large influence on private investment.[17] The tendency to delay irreversible investment in the face of uncertainty has also been much emphasized in the recent analytical literature on capital formation, and has been shown to exist even when investors are risk-neutral agents (Pindyck, 1991). When the future is uncertain, delay involves trading off the returns from investing now against the gains from being able to make a more informed decision in the future.[18]

Of course, the empirical relevance of phenomena such as these will differ across countries and at different points in time. However, existing studies of private investment in developing countries have not always taken them into account, even where they seem clearly relevant; and to the extent they have done so, it has often been undertaken in an ad hoc fashion, by adding new variables to a regression that specifies investment as a linear function of explanatory variables suggested by the theories described above, rather than by reformulating the theory and estimating the revised model of investment.

3.2.2 Determinants of Private Investment: The Evidence

A comprehensive survey of empirical investment functions for developing countries has recently been provided by Chhibber and Dailami (1993) and Rama (1993). Rama, in particular, examined thirty-one studies conducted over the period 1972–92. The results of these studies must be interpreted with care. All of them are vulnerable to the Lucas critique. Moreover, many of them employ ad hoc investment functions not derived from a specific model, and the treatment of expectations is often rudimentary. Empirical problems also abound. In several cases the dependent variable is total, rather than private, investment. Data are typically annual, and the available time series are often very short (20–25 years), so degrees of freedom tend to be scarce. In response, several studies pool data from a large number of countries. Finally, the estimating techniques do not always handle simultaneity problems, which are bound to be severe in this instance, and issues of spurious correlation are addressed only in the most recent studies.

Nevertheless, with the results of the existing studies taken at face value and given other evidence not reviewed by Rama, the following tentative conclusions seem to emerge. First, aggregate demand plays an important role driving private investment. Its coefficient is almost always positive and significant in empirical investment functions. This is consistent with the standard industrial-country "flexible accelerator" specification. Second, relative factor prices (the user cost of capital, the wage rate, and the price of imported inputs) enter the stock version of the theoretical investment function discussed above. Rama emphasizes that the form of the theoretical investment function—and thus the way in which relative factor prices enter—depends on demand conditions facing the firm in this specification,[19] but whatever the nature of such conditions, factor prices matter. Yet most of the developing-country empirical work he examined neglected this variable or misspecified it. Where properly specified, the coefficients of factor prices tended to have the right sign in estimated regressions but were not always statistically significant (see, for instance, Shafik, 1992). This implies that little information is available at present on the effects of financial variables on private capital formation through the user cost of capital in developing countries—a key link between financial markets and real economic activity in industrial-country macroeconomic models.

Third, a link between the financial system and private investment behavior is established in the studies surveyed by Rama through a credit variable, which is typically included in investment functions for developing countries to capture the effect of financial repression. This variable, included in various forms in twenty-one of the thirty-one papers surveyed, almost always turned out to have a statistically significant coefficient with the expected sign (see, for instance, Leff and Sato, 1988). A more recent study by Oshikoya (1994) suggests that credit availability also has a large effect on private investment in Africa. However, in such cases causation may not be one-directional, since actual credit flows may reflect the demand for credit by investing firms rather than a rationed supply.

Fourth, indicators of foreign exchange availability (such as the stock of foreign exchange reserves or dummies for import controls) were included in some of the empirical investment functions, and where present they tended to behave as expected. Again, however, the interpretation of these variables is problematic. As Rama points out, they could simply proxy for sound and sustainable domestic policies. Fifth, regarding the public capital stock, eleven of the papers examined by Rama addressed the issue of substitutability-complementarity with private capital, and seven of these found a positive role for the public capital stock. While early studies, such as those of Sundararajan and Thakur (1980) and Wai and Wong (1982), attempting to gauge the effect of total public sector investment on private capital formation typically produced results that were not conclusive,[20] more recent studies by Cardoso (1993), Bleaney and Greenaway (1993a), Oshikoya (1994), Ramírez (1994), and Shafik (1992) have identified a positive effect of public investment on private capital formation. In addition, when a distinction is made between infrastructural and other types of public investment, more significant results are obtained. Blejer and Khan

(1984), for instance, using a pooled sample of twenty-four developing countries for the period 1971–79, show that $1 increase in real infrastructural public investment would increase real private investment by about $0.25. An equivalent increase in other forms of public investment, on the other hand, would reduce real private investment by nearly $0.30. These results are consistent with the hypothesis that infrastructural investment is complementary to private investment, while increases in other types of government investment tend to crowd out the private sector.[21]

Finally, several papers have included indicators of macroeconomic instability of various types, finding significant negative effects on private investment. Rodrik (1991), for instance, provides evidence suggesting that uncertainty on the part of economic agents regarding the government's future intentions affects investment behavior in developing countries. Similar results have been obtained by Aizenman and Marion (1993), using a sample of forty developing countries and data covering the period 1970–85. Larraín and Vergara (1993) have argued that real exchange-rate variability (a popular measure of macroeconomic instability) has an adverse effect on private capital formation. Evidence on the effect of external shocks and the debt overhang on private investment has also been found. Cardoso (1993) and Bleaney and Greenaway (1993a) have shown that fluctuations in the terms of trade (through their effects on real income and the profitability of the export sector) also affect private investment. Cardoso (1993), Fitzgerald et al. (1994), Greene and Villanueva (1991), Oshikoya (1994), and Schmidt-Hebbel and Muller (1992) have found a significant negative effect of the debt/output ratio on investment, providing support for debt overhang effects.[22] The evidence provided by Cohen (1993) suggests, however, that the stock of debt itself does not appear to have had a significant influence on investment in the 1980s, but that debt service may have crowded out investment. According to Cohen's calculations, a transfer of 1 percent of output to external creditors by rescheduling countries during the 1980s reduced investment by 0.3 percent of output.

3.3 The Demand for Money

The specification of the demand for real money balances plays an important role in macroeconomic analysis for both theoretical and empirical purposes. At the analytical level, the money demand function is a key element in the formulation of many macroeconomic theories. From an operational point of view, the determination of a stable relationship between real balances and other macroeconomic variables is an essential requirement for the formulation of quantitative monetary targets. The transmission mechanism of monetary policy shocks (and, more generally, macroeconomic management) depends on the variables that determine the demand for money balances.

The estimation of the demand for money in developing countries has generated a voluminous literature over the years, which has by and large followed advances in econometric and statistical methods—particularly the development of cointegration techniques and the estimation of long-run relationships in economics (see Harvey, 1990). We begin this section by discussing the existing evidence relating to the conventional specification of money demand models in developing countries, and we evaluate some of the more recent and more sophisticated econometric studies. We then discuss the phenomenon of currency substitution and its effects on the demand for domestic real money balances. Because of the breadth of the existing literature on money demand in developing nations, we do not attempt to provide a comprehensive survey of existing studies. Rather, we focus our attention on general methodological issues that arise in this particular context, and we illustrate the discussion with some specific references.

3.3.1 Conventional Money Demand Models

Conventional models of money demand in developing countries typically include only real income as a scale variable and the rate of inflation as an opportunity cost variable. Domestic interest rates are excluded either because alternative financial assets are assumed not to be available, so that the choice of asset holdings is limited to either money or real assets, such as commodity inventories or consumer durable goods, or because government regulations associated with financial repression imply that such rates tend to display little variation over time, so that their potential effect is difficult to determine econometrically (Khan, 1980).

Early studies that attempted to introduce nominal interest rates in money demand functions met with little success. For instance, in the results reported by Fair (1987) for seven developing countries, the interest rate variable was significant and correctly signed in only one case. However, some recent studies have found a significant effect of interest rates on money demand in upper-middle-income developing nations—mostly in Asia and Latin America—particularly in those countries where the financial system has reached a relatively high degree of diversification and financial markets have begun to operate with relative freedom from government intervention and regulations. For instance, Arrau et al. (1995), José Rossi (1989) (for Brazil), and Reinhart and Végh (1994) (for Argentina, Chile, and Uruguay) report statistically significant effects of interest rate variables on the demand for real money balances. In a recent study of the demand for money in Morocco, Hoffman and Tahiri (1994) have argued that a foreign interest rate can also serve as the relevant opportunity cost of holding domestic monetary assets.

A general limitation of most conventional money demand studies in developing countries results from their ignoring the fact that when informal credit markets are large, the relevant opportunity cost of holding cash balances is the interest rate in the informal financial sector and not the official interest rate. This neglect may explain why early studies using official interest rates were not very successful.[23] In addition, it suggests that more recent studies using official interest rates may not provide relevant estimates of the interest rate elasticity of money demand. Van Wijnbergen (1982), for instance, showed that the informal-market interest rate had a significant effect on the demand for time deposits in Korea. However, the lack of adequate time series information on informal interest rates in most countries where curb markets for credit are large has prevented a systematic use of these data in the estimation of money demand models.

Excluding interest rates and assuming a partial adjustment mechanism of actual to desired levels, the conventional money demand function can be expressed as:[24]

$$\ln m_t = \lambda a_0 + \lambda a_1 \ln y_t - \lambda a_2 \pi^a_{t+k} + (1 - \lambda) \ln m_{t-1} + u_t, \qquad (8)$$

where m_t denotes real money balances, y_t real income, π^a_{t+k} the expected inflation rate for period $t + k$, u_t a disturbance term, and $0 < \lambda < 1$ the speed of adjustment.

Estimation of Equation (8) raises a host of econometric issues related to simultaneity, the choice of proxy variables for expectations, and so on.[25] Most studies of the conventional demand-for-money function in developing countries suggest that the expected inflation rate (often proxied by the actual inflation rate and measured in terms of consumer prices) is highly significant. This result stresses the importance of the substitution effects between real assets and real money balances.

In line with recent developments in econometric techniques, many recent studies of the demand for money in developing countries, based on the conventional specification described earlier as well as several variants of it, have used a two-step estimation approach (see Harvey, 1990). Essentially, the first step consists of estimating the long-run determinants of the demand for money using cointegration techniques. In the second step, the "general-to-specific" approach to modeling dynamic time series is used to specify the short-run dynamics of money demand. This approach generates an error correction model that distinguishes between short-run disequilibrium and long-run equilibrium properties of the demand function for real money balances. The two-step approach has been followed by Asilis et al. (1993) for Bolivia, Domowitz and Elbadawi (1987) for Sudan, and Ahumada (1992) for Argentina, as well as many others. This literature provides a much richer specification of the short-run dynamics than the simple partial adjustment framework used earlier, and typically yields regression equations that provide better predictions of the short-run behavior of real money holdings.[26] However, the long-run parameter estimates derived from this approach do not seem to vary significantly from those derived by less sophisticated techniques. In addition, problems are often encountered in explaining economically the excessively long lags that appear in estimated money demand equations.

Recent approaches to the study of the demand for money in developing countries have also aimed at integrating additional explanatory variables in the conventional specification. Several authors have attempted to capture the role of financial innovation, for instance, Arrau et al. (1995) and Tseng and Corker (1991). The effect of inflation variability on money demand has also been the subject of recent research (Deutsch and Zilberfarb, 1994). But the issue that has captured the most attention, at the theoretical as well as the empirical level, has been the demand for domestic- versus foreign-currency holdings.

3.3.2 Currency Substitution and the Demand for Money

Currency substitution—the process whereby foreign currency substitutes for domestic money as a store of value, unit of account, and medium of exchange—has become a pervasive phenomenon in many developing countries.[27] This phenomenon has been observed in countries that differ considerably in levels of financial development, in the degree of integration with the rest of the world, and in types of exchange rate regimes and practices. In some cases, particularly where high and variable inflation rates and uncertainty about domestic policies have prevailed for a substantial period of time, a large proportion of domestic sales and contracts are transacted in foreign currency.[28]

The degree of currency substitution depends on a variety of factors. The transactions motive may be particularly important in small, very open economies. More generally, in countries where inflation is high and where opportunities for portfolio diversification are limited or ceilings on domestic interest rates are present, assets denominated in domestic currency lose their capacity to provide an efficient hedge over time. If transactions costs incurred in switching from domestic-currency assets to foreign-currency assets are low, the degree of currency substitution tends to be high. Uncertainty about social and political developments, fear of expropriation of assets denominated in domestic currency, and the potential need to leave the country also tend to encourage holdings of foreign currency.[29] As indicated in the previous chapter, the existence of informal currency markets facilitates transactions in foreign exchange and may reinforce the substitution process between domestic- and foreign-currency assets.

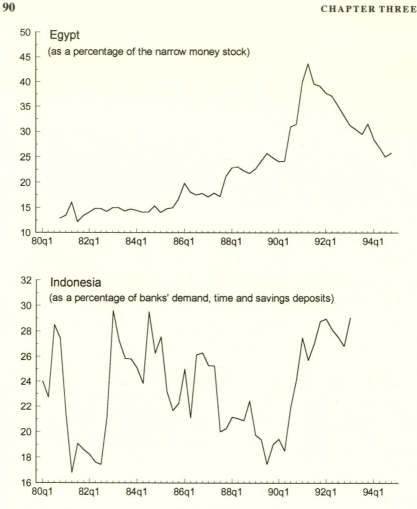

Figure 3.1   Foreign-Currency Deposits Held in Domestic Banks

Source: *International Financial Statistics*

3.3.2.1 DOMESTIC- AND FOREIGN-CURRENCY DEPOSITS

Foreign currency in developing countries is held either in the form of cash
"under the mattress," as deposits in the domestic banking system, or as
deposits in banks abroad. Estimates of the stock of foreign currency held by
private citizens are extremely difficult to obtain, although some tentative estimates have been developed in particular cases (see, for instance, Melvin,
1988). Information on foreign-currency denominated deposits in domestic
banks is much easier to obtain—available data are generally reported in *International Financial Statistics*—since such deposits are being allowed by a
growing number of developing countries. Figure 3.1 shows the evolution of

TABLE 3.1

Overseas Foreign-Currency Deposits (averages over 1981–90)

		As a Percentage of:		
Region	*Amount (US$ billions)*	*Reserves (excluding gold)*	*Exports*	*Imports*
Developing countries	269.7	121.3	42.0	42.7
Africa	20.5	204.8	31.8	31.5
Asia	39.4	40.6	14.4	13.8
Europe	5.7	53.8	8.3	7.5
Middle East	70.8	121.5	50.3	62.4
Western Hemisphere	133.4	385.9	129.8	153.3

Source: International Financial Statistics.

Note: Figures for the Middle East region refer only to the period 1981–87.

such deposits, a large proportion of which are held in the form of interest-bearing time deposits, in Egypt and Indonesia during the 1980s. Other countries where bank deposits in foreign currency can be legally held by individuals include Bolivia, Lebanon (where the share of foreign-currency deposits in the domestic banking system averaged 63 percent of the broad money stock between 1989 and 1993), Mexico, and Singapore.[30]

Since the early 1980s the International Monetary Fund has also been collecting and publishing data on foreign-currency deposits held abroad by residents of a large number of developing countries.[31] Table 3.1 shows average magnitude of these deposits for various regional groupings of developing countries for the period 1981–90, and their evolution over time is shown in Figure 3.2. The data indicate that foreign-currency deposits held overseas averaged about US$270 billion for all developing countries during the 1980s, with nearly half this amount held by residents of Latin America. The Middle East region accounted for about US$70 billion, followed by Asia (US$40 billion) and Africa (US$20 billion).

These figures, while large in absolute terms, are even more striking when expressed as a proportion of foreign-exchange reserves and trade flows. For developing countries as a whole, foreign-currency deposits held abroad represented over 120 percent of official foreign-exchange reserves; for Latin America they amounted to nearly four times the level of official reserves. The proportions for Africa (205 percent) and the Middle East (121 percent) are also sizable. The corresponding figure for Asia (41 percent) appears quite modest by comparison. As a proportion of exports and imports, for all developing countries foreign-currency deposits held abroad amounted to about 42 percent. Again, the picture for Latin America, where such deposits amounted to 130 percent of exports and 153 percent of imports, is quite dramatic. The corresponding ratios for the other regional groupings are

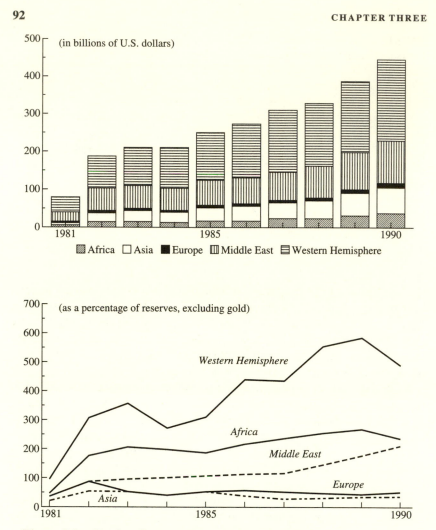

Figure 3.2   Foreign-Currency Deposits Held Abroad

Source: International Financial Statistics

much smaller, but by no means insignificant. For example, in the case of Africa the reserves-to-import ratio averaged only about 15 percent, while the ratio of foreign-currency deposits to imports was over 30 percent.

The growth of foreign-currency deposits held abroad was very rapid in the 1980s (Figure 3.2). The upper panel of the figure indicates that for developing countries as a whole, these deposits rose from about US$80 billion in 1981 to US$450 billion by the end of 1990—an annual average rate of increase of nearly 50 percent. For Latin America the annual average growth rate was over 70 percent, while that for African countries was around 60 percent. The ratio of foreign-currency deposits to foreign-exchange reserves has remained relatively stable (see lower panel of Figure 3.2), except for Latin America, a phenomenon that stems largely from the acceleration of capital flight during the 1980s.

Both the short- and long-run consequences of an increase in the holdings of foreign currency are well recognized (Agénor and Khan, 1992).[32] In the short run, a rise in foreign-currency deposits held abroad—which is equivalent to a capital outflow—can have potentially destabilizing effects on domestic interest rates, the exchange rate, and international reserves. Such an outflow may create a shortage of liquidity in the domestic banking system, which in turn would exert upward pressure on domestic interest rates. The outflow would also tend to depreciate the domestic currency under a floating exchange-rate regime. If the government is committed to defending a particular exchange rate, it would deplete its reserves. Furthermore, when a country faces the possibility of a balance-of-payments crisis and immediate corrective policy action is not taken, residents of the country, foreseeing an eventual devaluation and higher inflation or the imposition of exchange controls, are likely to increase transfers abroad. Consequently, at the very time that foreign-exchange resources are required by the country, funds are shifted abroad, accelerating the erosion of official reserves and precipitating the crisis (see Chapter 6). If the buildup of foreign-currency deposits abroad is permanent, that is, if the resources are effectively lost by the home country, there are several additional long-term effects. First, there is a reduction in available resources to finance domestic investment, leading in the short run to a reduction in activity and in the long run to a decline in the rate of capital formation, thus adversely affecting the country's growth rate.[33] Second, the shift to foreign-currency deposits abroad reduces the government's ability to tax all the income earned by its residents, mainly because governments have difficulty taxing wealth held abroad as well as income generated from that wealth. Third, as government revenues fall with the erosion of the tax base, there is an increased need to borrow from abroad (thereby increasing the foreign debt burden) or greater recourse to domestic monetary financing, which raises the long-run inflation rate.

To summarize, the degree of currency substitution has important implications for many developing countries. Formulating an accurate measure of foreign-currency holdings would require adding information on foreign-currency deposits held abroad by domestic residents to data on foreign-currency deposits held in domestic banks, as well as data on foreign-currency notes in circulation. The last component, however, is almost impossible to estimate with any degree of accuracy. Existing data on total foreign-currency deposits thus provide only a lower bound on the amount of foreign-money balances held by residents of developing countries.

3.3.2.2 CURRENCY SUBSTITUTION: EMPIRICAL EVIDENCE

A large number of empirical studies of currency substitution in developing countries have been conducted over the past few years in order to isolate the factors that give rise to this phenomenon.[34] In many of these studies, the presence of currency substitution is gauged without any attempt to explicitly account for the existence of foreign-currency holdings, in part because of the difficulties (alluded to above) involved in comprehensively estimating existing stocks of such assets. To capture the effect of currency substitution, researchers usually introduce into an otherwise conventional money demand equation the interest rate differential between domestic and foreign interest rates or, when information on market-determined domestic interest rates is not available, only the expected rate of depreciation of the exchange rate. Typically, the expected rate of exchange-rate depreciation is proxied by the actual rate of depreciation of the (official or parallel) exchange rate, but several alternative measures have also been used in the literature. Blejer (1978), for instance, measures the expected rate of depreciation of the domestic currency by using deviations from purchasing power parity, with foreign prices valued at the parallel market rate. In his study on Argentina and Mexico, Ramírez-Rojas (1985) uses the differential between the domestic and foreign inflation rates to approximate the expected rate of change of the exchange rate. For Mexico he also uses the three-month future price of the U.S. dollar in pesos, while for Uruguay he uses the differential between the domestic interest rate paid on deposits denominated in domestic currency and the domestic interest rate paid on foreign-currency deposits. Phylaktis and Taylor (1993), using a sample of five Latin American countries during the 1970s and 1980s, tested for the presence of currency substitution effects by using the rate of depreciation of the black market rate augmented with the foreign inflation rate as an explanatory variable. The evidence based on this approach seems to support the existence of significant currency substitution effects in many developing countries.[35]

Some studies have also attempted to use data on domestic foreign-currency deposits. A typical regression equation takes the form[36]

$$M_t/e_tF_t = h(\bar{\hat{e}}_t^a, \ldots),$$ (9)

where M_t and F_t measure domestic and foreign currency holdings, e_t is the exchange rate, and $\hat{e}_t^a$ is its expected rate of depreciation. Equation (9) relates the currency ratio inversely to the expected rate of depreciation of the (official or parallel) exchange rate, as well as to other variables, such as lagged values of the currency ratio. Inclusion of the inflation rate, which measures the rate of return on real assets, as an additional regressor is typically avoided due to the high degree of collinearity between inflation and the rate of depreciation of the parallel or official exchange rate. The domestic-foreign interest rate differential is sometimes included in studies dealing with countries for which data on domestic market-determined rates are available—although the foreign interest rate may not be an adequate measure of the opportunity cost of domestic-currency-denominated assets if restrictions exist on capital movements. In many cases, however, Equation (9) is estimated with the rate of depreciation of the official or parallel exchange rate as the key explanatory variable. Estimation results obtained with various forms of Equation (9) using a conventional, partial adjustment formulation have been reported by a number of authors, for instance, Calomiris and Domowitz (1989), El-Erian (1988), Melvin (1988), and Ortíz (1983).[37] As pointed out by Calvo and Végh (1992), strictly speaking, equations such as (9) test for the existence of a dollarization phenomenon rather than currency substitution per se, since they do not capture the role of foreign-currency holdings as a medium of exchange.

In some studies, data on foreign-currency deposits held domestically are supplemented by available information on monetary assets held overseas. Savastano (1992), for instance, uses data on foreign-currency deposits both at home and abroad in the United States in his study of currency substitution in Latin America. In their study of dollarization in Argentina, Kamin and Ericsson (1993) use an estimate of the stock of dollars circulating in that country (calculated by using recorded bilateral currency flows compiled by the U.S. Treasury) in addition to data on dollar deposits.[38] Agénor and Khan (1992), in contrast, use only data on deposits held abroad by residents of developing countries and estimate a dynamic, forward-looking model of currency substitution. The Agénor-Khan model, which incorporates the assumption of rational expectations, is developed in two steps. The desired composition of currency holdings is first derived from an optimizing model of household behavior. Actual currency holdings are then determined in a multiperiod, costs-of-adjustment framework. The complete solution of the model leads to an empirical specification that incorporates both backward- and forward-looking elements. One of the appealing features of the empirical implementation of the model is that it does not require information on the domestic interest rate. In most studies the lack of a suitable domestic interest rate series has inhibited the estimation of currency substitution models relying on relative rates of return between domestic and foreign currencies based on interest rates. The approach taken by Agénor and Khan circumvents this particular problem. The model is estimated using quarterly data for a group of ten developing countries (Bangladesh, Brazil, Ecuador, Indonesia, Malaysia, Mexico, Morocco, Nigeria, Pakistan, and the Philippines) by an errors-in-variables procedure. The results tend to support the theoretical specification, indicating that the foreign interest rate and the expected rate of depreciation of the parallel market exchange rate are important factors in the choice between domestic money balances and overseas foreign-currency deposits.[39]

3.4 Aggregate Supply Functions

For the past two decades the specification of the economy's short-run supply function has been one of the most contentious issues in industrial-country macroeconomics. For most of that time controversy has involved the relative merits of "new classical" macroeconomics, featuring the Lucas "surprise" supply function, versus Keynesian "sticky wage" formulations as empirical approximations to the economy's short-run supply behavior. At issue, of course, was the power of systematic aggregate demand policies to affect the deviation of economic activity from its full-capacity level. In this section we review the evidence on this issue for developing countries.

The degree of stickiness of wages and prices is widely considered to depend on the institutional structure of labor markets. The prevalence of staggered, overlapping multiperiod wage contracts as noted by Taylor (1980) is conducive to stickiness of the average nominal wage. Observers such as Corden (1989) have taken the view that the less-organized labor markets in developing countries make Keynesian nominal wage stickiness less likely to be observed in such countries than in industrial countries with long traditions of organized union activity. Thus, it may be more feasible to characterize labor markets in developing countries as auction markets. If so, then the Lucas "surprise" short-run aggregate supply function, which postulates a positive relation between output and unexpected movements in prices, may be of particular relevance for developing countries. This is because the Lucas model of aggregate supply behavior requires, in addition to wage-price flexibility, the key assumption embodied in Lucas's "island" parable that workers not be able to infer the aggregate price level based on contemporaneously available information (see Hoover, 1988). While this assumption may be difficult to maintain in industrial countries, where aggregate macroeconomic information is widely and cheaply accessible, it may be more tenable in the case of developing nations, where aggregate data are scarce, imperfect, and often available only after long lags.

The policy ineffectiveness proposition associated with new classical macroeconomics requires, along with the Lucas supply function, the use of rational expectations on the part of economic agents.[40] The relevance of this mechanism for the formation of expectations has been questioned for developing countries, based in part on the scarcity of information alluded to above. However, this argument may simply imply a larger variance of forecast errors in the context of developing economies, rather than the persistence of systematic bias in such errors. In any event, it is clear that, whether because of differences in labor market structure or in the mechanisms used for the formation of expectations, little can be inferred about the relevance for developing countries of the policy neutrality proposition associated with new classical macroeconomics and the Lucas supply function from industrial countries' experience.

Tests of the neutrality proposition for developing countries have taken two forms. Cross-regime tests have examined the empirical plausibility of the "surprise" supply function itself using cross-sectional evidence, following the approach of Lucas (1973). Within-regime tests have used time series data for individual countries and have examined the power of anticipated aggregate demand policy to affect the deviation of actual real output from its capacity level, following Barro (1978).

3.4.1 Cross-Regime Tests

The existing evidence of the first type, including that of Lucas (1973), typically includes substantial numbers of developing countries. Cross-regime tests rely on an implication of Lucas's "island" parable: If agents know the true distribution of relative prices and the average price level, but are able to observe only their own selling price (and not the average price level) when formulating supply decisions, they face an inference problem, since their supply choice depends on the unobservable relative price of what they sell. Their optimal forecast of the aggregate price level will be a weighted average of the price they observe and the mean of the aggregate price level distribution, with the weight attached to the observed own selling price equal to the ratio of the true variance of relative prices to the sum of the true variances of relative prices and the average price level. Thus, the more variable the history of nominal demand in the economy, the more agents will interpret an observed increase in their own selling prices as a change in the aggregate price level rather than in relative prices, and the smaller will be their supply response. The "surprise" supply function is written as

$$y_t = \bar{y}_t + \gamma(p_t - p_t^a) + \lambda(L)y_{t-1} \qquad (10)$$

where y_t denotes actual output, $\bar{y}_t$ "normal" output, p_t the actual price level, and p_t^a the expected price level (with all variables expressed in logarithms). The parameter γ is a decreasing function of the variance of aggregate demand. Thus, the prediction is that in more unstable aggregate demand regimes, the short-run aggregate supply function will be steeper in the price-output space.

Lucas (1973) found this prediction corroborated in a sample of eighteen countries—of which six were developing countries—and noted in particular the small size of γ in Argentina and Paraguay, which provided his only two volatile observations. Alberro (1981) extended Lucas's sample to forty-nine countries, confirming his results. Alberro's sample consisted of twenty-nine developing countries, including all six countries that provided the volatile-demand observations. Both Lucas and Alberro judged conformity

of the data with the hypothesis being tested by examining simple correlations. Williams and Baumann (1986) tested the statistical significance of
this correlation in Alberro's sample using nonparametric methods and found
that the measured correlation was indeed significantly different from zero.
Another extension in sample size, by Ram (1984), included fifty-eight developing countries among the seventy-nine countries in the sample. Ram's
results also supported the predictions of Lucas's model.

Cross-regime tests of the Lucas supply function have also been conducted
using samples consisting solely of developing countries. Jung (1985) refined Lucas's test by noting that the slope of the aggregate supply curve
in Lucas's model depends not just on the variance of nominal income, but
also on the variance of relative prices as well as on the responsiveness of
supply to unanticipated changes in relative prices. Cross-regime tests thus
need to examine the partial correlation between nominal income variance
and the slope of the supply curve, not the simple correlation measured by
most authors. Jung conducted this test for two separate samples, consisting
of nineteen industrialized countries and twenty-seven developing nations.
He found a negative partial correlation for both groups, a result consistent
with Lucas's formulation, but the relationship was statistically weaker for
developing than for industrial countries.

Overall, the cross-regime evidence for developing countries appears to
be consistent with the predictions of the Lucas supply function. These tests,
however, can provide only weak support for the model, since they do not
discriminate among competing hypotheses. In particular, it is not clear that
a Keynesian short-run supply specification would be inconsistent with the
pattern of correlations described above. If high and variable inflation induced a shortening of contract length or more extensive indexation, for
instance, the slope of the Phillips curve would be expected to increase, generating a similar pattern of correlations. To obtain more definitive results,
it is necessary to use a test that can discriminate between these competing
models of short-run supply behavior.

3.4.2 Within-Regime Tests

An alternative approach to the empirical testing of the Lucas supply function satisfies this criterion. This test is based on estimating the reduced-
form output equation emerging from a model that incorporates the function
as its description of short-run supply behavior, following Barro (1978).
Adding to the supply function (10) an aggregate demand function in
the form

$$y_t = \alpha(m_t - p_t) + \mathbf{Z}_t, \tag{11}$$

where m_t is the logarithm of the nominal money supply and $\mathbf{Z}_t$ is a vector of other variables that affect aggregate demand, yields a quasi reduced-form equation for y in the form

$$y_t = \bar{y}_t + a_1(m_t - m_t^a) + a_2(\mathbf{Z}_t - \mathbf{Z}_t^a) + a_3(L)y_{t-1}, \qquad (12)$$

where m_t^a and $\mathbf{Z}_t^a$ denote the expected values of m_t and $\mathbf{Z}_t$, respectively. This equation has the implication that only unanticipated changes in m_t and $\mathbf{Z}_t$ can cause y_t to deviate from its full-capacity level, in contrast to the "sticky wage" Keynesian formulation, in which the distinction between anticipated and unanticipated changes in aggregate demand is not relevant. The policy ineffectiveness proposition follows from (12) since systematic aggregate demand policy, such as would emerge from a feedback rule, would be foreseen by economic agents who know the rule and thus would be incapable of generating unanticipated changes in m_t or $\mathbf{Z}_t$. A test of the model against the Keynesian alternative thus involves estimating (12) and determining whether the decomposition of changes in aggregate demand into its anticipated and unanticipated components matters, that is, whether anticipated changes in m_t and $\mathbf{Z}_t$ add explanatory power to the regression (12) after the unanticipated components have been included. Because these tests require the specification of anticipated changes in m_t and $\mathbf{Z}_t$, the rule governing the behavior of these variables must be estimated jointly with (12). Because m_t is a policy variable, and to the extent that policy variables are included in $\mathbf{Z}_t$, these rules imply stable policy regimes, and these tests are therefore within-regime tests of the "surprise" supply function.

The prediction that anticipated demand changes should not matter is a consequence of the supply function. However, the particular variables that enter the reduced-form output equation on which the empirical tests are based, and the form in which they do so, depend on the full specification of the model. Thus, tests of this sort represent joint tests of the "surprise" supply function and the assumed expectations mechanism, conditional on the appropriate specification of the rest of the model, as well as the prediction equations for m_t and $\mathbf{Z}_t$.

Within-regime tests such as those just described have been implemented for many developing nations. However, much of the work in this area has focused on Latin American countries. An early test by Barro (1979a) found a link between money growth and output in Mexico. However, in contrast to Barro's earlier results for the United States, the distinction between anticipated and unanticipated money growth was not important, since reduced-form output equations in m_t performed as well as those in $(m_t - m_t^a)$. Barro was unable to find strong links between money growth and output in either Brazil or Colombia. Hanson (1980), by contrast, found statistically significant, though small,[41] effects of unanticipated money growth on output in

Brazil, Chile, Colombia, Mexico, and Peru, but he found that different processes explained money growth in different countries. He did not test for the importance of the anticipated/unanticipated distinction. The results of Edwards (1983), however, were more in keeping with those of Barro. After taking into account the role of fiscal deficits in causing money growth, which he argued to be particularly important in developing countries, he found significant effects of money growth (anticipated or not) in only three of nine Latin American countries, and for two of those it was not possible to distinguish between the roles of anticipated and unanticipated variables. Canarella and Pollard (1989), using a sample of sixteen Latin American nations, found in most cases a significant effect of unanticipated money growth on real output, as well as a negative effect on the price level. In addition, they found a significant negative relationship between unanticipated money growth and its predictability, supporting the Lucas hypothesis.

Sheehey (1986) also considered a sample of sixteen Latin American countries and used a more comprehensive set of predictors for monetary policy than previous authors had. His results were not supportive of the Lucas supply function. Unanticipated money helped to explain real output movements in three countries, while anticipated money did so in four. Moreover, Sheehey found only a weak negative association between the variance of unanticipated money growth (as a measure of aggregate demand volatility) and the effect of unanticipated money on output, thus raising questions about the strength of the cross-regime evidence as well.

Sheehey compared regressions using unanticipated money with those using anticipated money, rather than including both in the same equation and using tests of exclusion restrictions, as suggested above and as done in two other papers. Choudhary and Parai (1991) used a sample of thirteen Latin American countries and estimated reduced-form output equations including contemporaneous and lagged terms in both unanticipated and anticipated money. They then tested exclusion restrictions on the anticipated money terms, finding that the null hypothesis that anticipated money had no effect could be rejected at the 5 percent level for eleven of their thirteen countries, and at the 10 percent level for all the countries. Chopra (1985) proceeded somewhat differently. Rather than estimating a reduced-form output equation, he estimated a reduced-form price level equation using aggregate demand (nominal GDP) as the policy variable, following the original approach of Lucas (1973). He showed that in a Keynesian formulation, this equation would both contain lagged prices and impose equal coefficients on anticipated and unanticipated aggregate demand components, whereas the Lucas formulation would exclude lagged prices and require a unitary coefficient on anticipated movements in aggregate demand. Chopra tested these restrictions using a sample of thirteen countries, four of which were in Latin America. He found that the restrictions imposed by the Lucas formulation were consistent with the estimated parameters in only three cases. In six other cases these restrictions were rejected in favor of the Keynesian alternative. For the remaining countries the results were ambiguous, in that either lagged inflation mattered or the coefficient of anticipated demand was less than 1, but not both.

3.4.3 An Assessment of the Evidence

How is all of this evidence to be interpreted? Although the cross-regime tests support the Lucas supply function in developing countries, such tests do not necessarily discriminate against a Keynesian alternative. The within-regime tests that can potentially be used for that purpose have not always been applied in that way. Where they have, the weight of the evidence for developing countries seems to suggest, contrary to Corden's (1989) conjecture, that the Keynesian alternative is not easily rejected in developing countries. However, the evidence is weak, for two reasons. First, the geographic coverage of this research has been quite limited. With the exception of the paper by Chopra (1985), all of the work described here has focused on Latin America.[42] Obviously, short-run supply behavior may be quite different elsewhere, since labor market institutions may display more uniformity within regions than across different regions. Second, and more important, the existing within-regime tests have often represented an uncritical application to developing countries of reduced-form output equations derived from simple "representative" industrial-country macroeconomic models. If the relevant developing-country model is different, then the reduced-form output equation will be misspecified and the statistical tests will be biased in unknown directions.

For instance, if capital mobility is high, neither anticipated nor unanticipated money should enter a reduced-form output regression in a "new classical" open-economy model, whereas fiscal policy and foreign interest rates should.[43] Indeed, the failure of several of the studies cited here to find a significant role for unanticipated money, sometimes interpreted by their authors as inconsistent with the "surprise" supply function or as resulting from an inappropriate prediction equation for money growth, may simply reflect high capital mobility.[44] An appropriate test requires respecifying the relevant macroeconomic model from which the reduced-form output equation is derived, to avoid misspecification in the latter. "New classical" macroeconomic models for developing countries incorporating rationed intermediate goods (Agénor, 1990a; Chopra and Montiel, 1986) and adopting a "dependent-economy" production structure (Montiel, 1987) yield reduced-form output equations that are quite different from those estimated in the existing literature. The conclusion that Keynesian features are indeed relevant in many developing countries could be defended more confidently if such models were generalized to yield reduced-form output equations nesting both classical and Keynesian hypotheses, which would permit tests of exclusion restrictions to discriminate between them.

————————

The specification of aggregate behavioral functions is a critical component of any macroeconomic model. In this chapter we have examined the formulation of such functions in four critical areas: consumption and saving, investment, money demand, and the short-run supply of output. We began in each case by explaining how structural features of developing countries may lead to behavioral equations that differ substantially from those commonly adopted in industrial countries. Liquidity constraints, for instance, seem to play a more important role in the developing world. Private investment in developing countries depends more on factors such as the degree of credit rationing or the availability of bank financing, foreign exchange availability, and the level of public investment in infrastructure. Cost-of-capital variables usually enter investment equations with the correct sign but are typically not statistically significant. Thus, interest rates may influence private investment only indirectly, through their effect on the real return on financial assets and thus on the volume of financial saving. Finally, given the degree of diversification of the financial system in many developing countries, the main determinants of the demand for domestic currency are the inflation rate, which captures substitution effects between money and real goods, and the rate of depreciation of the (official or parallel) exchange rate, which captures currency substitution effects.

A general and important methodological implication of the preceding discussion is that estimating appropriate, reduced-form behavioral functions requires explicit and careful derivation of the theory underlying the specification chosen. Too often in the past, econometric studies have consisted of adding variables in regression equations without a clear underlying analytical framework. For instance, the specification of "new classical" reduced-form output equations for developing countries incorporating rationed intermediate goods (an important feature of many developing countries) differ substantially from standard models not only in the set of variables introduced in the estimating equation, but also in the particular form in which those variables enter the regression. Whether it should be the anticipated or unanticipated components of a variable that should appear cannot be an arbitrary decision, but should result from an explicit structural framework. We will provide other examples of this methodological principle in our discussion of the empirical work aimed at measuring the effect of devaluation on output (Chapter 7), and the determinants of long-run growth (Chapter 15).

Part II

SHORT-RUN MACROECONOMIC POLICIES

Four

Fiscal Deficits, Public Solvency, and the Macroeconomy

THE assessment of the macroeconomic effects of public sector deficits has been the subject of an extensive literature, both in developed and developing countries. The relationship between fiscal deficits, money growth, and inflation, in particular, has long been a central element in the "orthodox" view of the inflationary process, as mentioned in Chapter 1. More recently, attention has focused on the role of alternative financing options in the behavior of real interest rates and the sustainability of fiscal deficits, the impact of public sector imbalances on the current account and the real exchange rate, the role of expectations about future fiscal and monetary policies in price dynamics, and the extent to which bonds are considered "net wealth" by private agents—the so-called Ricardian equivalence proposition. Although many of these issues are common to developed and developing countries, structural differences between these two groups—most importantly, as discussed in Chapter 1, differences in the structure of public finance, the degree of diversification of the financial system, and the nature of the institutional arrangements that prevail between the central bank and the fiscal authorities—have important implications for the terms of the debate and the importance of specific factors in almost every respect.

This chapter discusses the measurement, sustainability, and macroeconomic effects of fiscal deficits in developing countries.[1] The government budget constraint is presented in Section 4.1, and alternative deficit concepts are derived. Our discussion of measurement issues focuses on the evaluation of quasi-fiscal deficits, a common phenomenon in many developing nations. Section 4.2 discusses the factors determining the sustainability of fiscal deficits (or, more generally, the solvency of the public sector) and the overall consistency of stabilization programs. The macroeconomic effects of fiscal deficits are the subject of Section 4.3. We first examine the theoretical applicability of the Ricardian equivalence proposition and review the empirical evidence related to developing countries. The linkage between fiscal deficits, monetary policy, and inflation is then explored, using a closed-economy model in which the government faces a solvency constraint and must adjust the overall policy stance at a well-defined date in the future. The impact of public sector deficits on real interest rates and private investment (through crowding-out effects) is also examined, using an optimizing model of a small open economy with zero capital mobility. The last part of Section

4.3 focuses on the relation between fiscal deficits, the current account, and the real exchange rate.

4.1 The Government Budget Constraint

When fiscal revenues fall short of current and capital expenditure (including interest payments on the public debt), the government incurs a deficit that may be financed in a variety of ways. The government budget constraint provides the linkage between taxes, expenditure, and alternative sources of financing of public imbalances. It is an essential tool for understanding the relationship between monetary and fiscal policies, and more generally the macroeconomic effects of fiscal deficits. We begin by providing a detailed derivation of this constraint, and we then examine some measurement issues that often arise in developing countries. We focus in particular on issues related to the measurement of so-called quasi-fiscal deficits. We then examine the role of seignorage and the inflation tax as sources of deficit finance.

4.1.1 The Consolidated Budget Deficit

Consider a small open economy operating under a predetermined exchange-rate regime. The central bank provides loans only to the general government, which includes local and central governments. In general, the government can finance its budget deficit by either issuing domestic bonds, borrowing abroad, or borrowing from the central bank. The consolidated budget identity of the general government can thus be written as

$$\dot{L}_t + \dot{B}_t + E_t \dot{F}_t^g = P_t(g_t - \tau_t) + i_t B_t + i_t^* E_t F_t^g + i_c L_t, \tag{1}$$

where L_t is the nominal stock of credit allocated by the central bank, B_t the stock of domestic-currency-denominated interest-bearing public debt, F_t^g the stock of foreign-currency-denominated interest-bearing public debt, g_t real public spending on goods and services (including current and capital expenditure), τ_t real tax revenue (net of transfer payments), i_t the domestic interest rate, i_t^* the foreign interest rate, $0 \leq i_c \leq i_t$ the interest rate paid by the government on central bank loans, E_t the nominal exchange rate, and P_t the domestic price level.[2] Equation (1) abstracts from the existence of nontax revenue and foreign grants, although these components may be sizable in some developing nations. As documented in Chapter 1, the proportion of nontax revenue in total fiscal resources is much larger in developing countries than in industrial countries.[3] More specifically, Burgess and Stern (1993) estimate that nontax revenue accounted in 1987–88 for over 50 percent of total revenue for the Middle East, 22 percent of total revenue in Asia, 16 percent in Africa, and 15 percent in the Western Hemisphere.[4] For simplicity, we will nevertheless exclude nontax revenue and foreign grants in the discussion that follows.[5]

The right-hand side of Equation (1) shows the components of the general government deficit (expenditure, taxes, and interest due on domestic and foreign debt), and the left-hand side identifies the sources of financing of the fiscal imbalance. The government budget constraint thus indicates that the fiscal deficit is financed by an increase in interest-bearing domestic and external debt, or credit from the central bank.

The central bank balance sheet in this economy is given by

$$M_t = L_t + E_t R_t - \Omega_t, \tag{2}$$

where M_t is the nominal stock of base money (currency held by the public and reserves held by commercial banks), R_t the stock of foreign exchange reserves, and Ω_t the central bank's accumulated profits or, equivalently, its net worth. Equation (2) can be generalized to Equation (11) of Chapter 2 by including central bank loans to commercial banks. Profits of the central bank consist of the interest received on its loans to the government, its interest earnings on foreign reserves, and capital gains resulting from the revaluation of reserves $\dot{E}_t R_t$. In the absence of operating costs, the counterpart of these profits is an increase in the central bank's net worth, the nominal value of which is also affected by capital gains arising from exchange rate depreciation:[6]

$$\dot{\Omega}_t = i_t^* E_t R_t + i_c L_t + \dot{E}_t R_t, \tag{3}$$

where, for simplicity, the interest rate earned on reserves is assumed to be the same as that paid on the government's foreign debt.

As in Chapter 2, obtaining the overall public sector deficit requires consolidating the general government budget constraint with that of the central bank. To do so, central bank profits need to be subtracted from the general government deficit, and the increase in its net worth must be deducted from the general government's increase in liabilities. Thus, from Equations (1) and (3),

$$\dot{L}_t + \dot{B}_t + E_t \dot{F}_t^g - \dot{\Omega}_t = P_t(g_t - \tau_t) + i_t B_t + i_t^* E_t(B_t^g - R_t) - \dot{E}_t R_t. \tag{4}$$

From Equation (2), $\dot{L}_t = \dot{M}_t - E_t \dot{R}_t - \dot{E}_t R_t + \dot{\Omega}_t$. Substituting this result in Equation (4) yields

$$\dot{M}_t + \dot{B}_t + E_t(\dot{F}_t^g - \dot{R}_t) = P_t(g_t - \tau_t) + i_t B_t + i_t^* E_t(F_t^g - R_t).$$

Defining net public foreign debt as $F_t^* = F_t^g - R_t$ yields[7]

$$\dot{M}_t + \dot{B}_t + E_t\dot{F}_t^* = P_t(g_t - \tau_t) + i_t B_t + i_t^* E_t F_t^*. \tag{5}$$

On the basis of Equation (5), several commonly used budget concepts can be derived.[8] The first concept refers to the primary (noninterest) fiscal deficit. Measured in real terms, it is given by

$$d_t \equiv \frac{D_t}{P_t} \equiv (g_t - \tau_t). \tag{6a}$$

The primary deficit is important for evaluating the sustainability of government deficits and the consistency among macroeconomic policy targets, as discussed below.

The second, most commonly used concept is that of the conventional fiscal deficit, which is equal to the primary deficit augmented by interest payments on the domestic and foreign debt of the public sector. Measured in real terms, the conventional fiscal deficit is defined as

$$d_t \equiv g_t + i_t\left(\frac{B_t}{P_t}\right) + i_t^*\left(\frac{E_t}{P_t}\right)F_t^* - \tau_t. \tag{6b}$$

Finally, the (inflation-corrected) operational fiscal deficit can be defined as

$$d_t \equiv g_t + (i_t - \pi_t)\left(\frac{B_t}{P_t}\right) + i_t^*\left(\frac{E_t}{P_t}\right)F_t^* - \tau_t, \tag{6c}$$

where π_t denotes the domestic inflation rate.[9]

The operational deficit deducts from the real conventional deficit the inflation component of interest payments on domestic debt. The rationale for this adjustment is the presumption that inflation-induced interest payments are tantamount to amortization payments in their economic impact; that is, they do not represent "new" income to asset holders and are willingly reinvested in government bonds, and therefore do not affect real aggregate expenditure. The operational deficit can be thought of as providing an approximate measure of the size of the deficit the government would face at a zero inflation rate.

In practice, the difference between alternative measures of fiscal balance can be substantial. Figure 4.1 displays the behavior of the primary and operational fiscal balances for Mexico over the period 1965–91. While the two measures correlate well until the beginning of the 1980s, sharp divergences emerged subsequently. In 1988, for instance, the primary fiscal balance in-

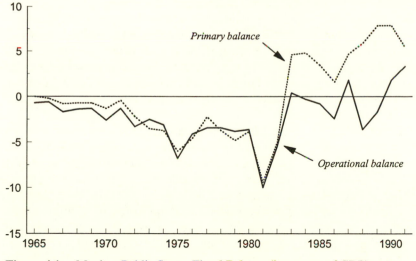

Figure 4.1   Mexico: Public Sector Fiscal Balance (in percent of GDP)

Source: International Monetary Fund, Occasional Paper No. 99 (September 1992, p. 4).

dicated a surplus of 5.9 percent of GDP. By contrast, the operational balance indicated a deficit of 3.6 percent, and the conventional balance (which is not shown in the figure) showed a deficit of 12.4 percent. In Ghana, in 1981, the conventional deficit amounted to 6.4 percent of GDP, the primary deficit to 4.3 percent, and the operational balance to a surplus of 5.5 percent (Blejer and Cheasty, 1991, p. 1656).

4.1.2 The Measurement of Fiscal Deficits

The measurement of fiscal deficits in developing nations raises a host of conceptual and practical issues, which are compounded by the lack of uniformity among countries.[10] For instance, the conventional deficit can be measured on a cash basis or an accruals (or payment order) basis. In the first case, the deficit is simply the difference between total cash-flow expenditure and fiscal revenue. In the second case, the deficit records accrued income and spending flows, regardless of whether they involve cash payments or not. Accumulation of arrears on payments or revenue is reflected by higher deficits when measured on an accrual basis compared with a cash-based measure. Another important measurement problem arises in countries where controls on interest rates or key public and private prices are pervasive. To the extent that expenditure is measured at official prices, the deficit may be largely underestimated. The appropriate solution in this case is to determine, for valuation purposes, an adequate "shadow" price for the goods or services whose prices are subject to government regulations. But this is often a daunting task, fraught with empirical and conceptual difficulties. For instance, in the presence of an informal credit market, the valuation of interest payments on the domestic debt at the (lower) controlled rate would make the deficit appear lower than if the market-determined interest rate were used. To the extent, however, that the informal interest rate incorporates a large risk premium due to a high probability of default of private borrowers, the deficit would be grossly overestimated if the risk of default on the public debt is low.

Determining the appropriate—that is, economically meaningful—degree of coverage of the "consolidated public sector," accounting for some of the operations performed by different public entities, can also be extremely difficult in practice. In that regard, a particularly important issue for developing nations relates to the treatment of central bank operations. In many countries, central banks perform a variety of "quasi-fiscal" operations, such as the implicit levy of taxes (either through the exchange-rate system,[11] or through the imposition of unremunerated reserve requirements, as discussed in Chapter 5), the management of government subsidy programs, debt service and transfers, the provision of preferential credit, and emergency loans to the financial system or other industries experiencing liquidity or solvency problems. Significant central bank losses related to these quasi-fiscal operations are common in developing countries, particularly in Latin America. In 1990 central bank losses amounted to 2.2 percent of GDP in Chile, 5 percent in Jamaica, and 3.6 percent in Uruguay. In the same year the nonfinancial public sector balance registered a surplus of 3.8 percent in Chile and 0.5 percent in Uruguay, and a deficit of 1.3 percent in Jamaica. Operations performed by public financial intermediaries other than the central bank may also account for sizable quasi-fiscal deficits.

Quasi-fiscal deficits in developing countries may exceed conventional fiscal deficits in overall size. In Argentina, for instance, quasi-fiscal deficits were roughly as large as conventional deficits during 1982–85, reaching 25 percent of GDP in 1982 and 18 percent in 1984 (Easterly and Schmidt-Hebbel, 1994). In Chile, during the same period, the quasi-fiscal deficit was more than double the size of the conventionally measured deficit (Blejer and Cheasty, 1991). To the extent that these quasi-fiscal operations are similar to other budgetary activities, they should be included in a comprehensive measure of the public sector balance. The use of the consolidated nonfinancial public sector deficit, to the extent that it excludes the losses and gains of the central bank and other important public financial intermediaries from quasi-fiscal operations, may thus provide a distorted picture of the fiscal stance.

In practice, separating monetary and quasi-fiscal operations of central banks raises difficult methodological questions, such as the appropriate treatment of capital gains or losses resulting from valuation changes—

arising, for instance, from the effect of exchange-rate fluctuations on the domestic-currency value of net foreign assets—or the proper way to estimate quasi-fiscal activities performed outside the central bank's profit-and-loss account. In some countries, exchange-rate or loan guarantees provided by the central bank remain completely off its balance sheet. In addition, governments and central banks typically use different accounting systems: government accounts are on a cash basis, whereas central bank accounts are on an accrual basis. The current budgetary practice, as pointed out by Robinson and Stella (1993) and Blejer and Cheasty (1991, pp. 1661–63), is such that when a central bank operates profitably, it generally transfers a substantial portion of its profits to the government. However, when it operates at a loss, the central bank generally runs down its reserves (or prints money) rather than receiving a transfer from the government to cover all or part of the loss. Such an asymmetric accounting treatment may seriously bias the accuracy of a country's measured fiscal deficit when central bank losses are large. Symmetry needs to be restored and the full amount of the central bank loss must be included in the government accounts in order for the size of the fiscal deficit to be accurately assessed.

4.1.3 Seignorage and Inflationary Finance

> A government can live for a long time ... by printing paper money. That is to say, it can by this means secure the command over real resources, resources just as real as those obtained by taxation. The method is condemned, but its efficacy, up to a point, must be admitted ... so long as the public use money at all, the government can continue to raise resources by inflation .... What is raised by printing notes is just as much taken from the public as is a beer duty or an income tax. What a government spends the public pays for. There is no such thing as an uncovered deficit (John Maynard Keynes).[12]

Seignorage is an important implicit tax levied by the government. Broadly defined, it consists of the amount of real resources appropriated by the government by means of base money creation. With the base money stock denoted M_t and the price level P_t, seignorage revenue S_{rev} can be defined as

$$S_{rev} = \dot{M}_t/P_t = \mu_t m_t = \dot{m}_t + \pi_t m_t, \qquad (6)$$

where $\mu_t \equiv \dot{M}_t/M_t$ denotes the rate of growth of the monetary base and m_t real money balances. The first expression in Equation (6) defines seignorage as the change in the nominal money stock divided by the price level. The second expression defines total seignorage as the product of the rate of nominal money growth and real balances held by the public. By analogy with the public finance literature, μ_t is often referred to as the tax rate and m_t, which is equal to the demand for cash balances under the assumption of money market equilibrium, as the tax base. The third expression in Equation (6) expresses the value of resources extracted by the government as the sum of the increase in the real stock of money $\dot{m}_t$ and the change in the real money stock that would have occurred with a constant nominal stock because of inflation, $\pi_t m_t$. The last expression represents the inflation tax, I_{tax}:

$$I_{\text{tax}} = \pi_t m_t, \tag{7}$$

so that

$$S_{\text{rev}} = I_{\text{tax}} + \dot{m}_t, \tag{6'}$$

which implies that in a stationary state (with $\dot{m}_t = 0$), seignorage is equal to the inflation tax.[13] To the extent that money creation causes inflation, thereby affecting the real value of nominal assets, seignorage can be viewed as a tax on private agents' domestic-currency holdings.

Table 4.1 presents data on seignorage, the inflation tax, and the level of inflation for a large group of developed and developing countries during the 1980s.[14] The table shows considerable differences across nations in the use of seignorage. In recent years seignorage has been a negligible source of revenue in all industrial countries except Italy. In developing countries, by contrast, seignorage accounts for a substantially higher share of government tax and nontax revenue, particularly in India, Pakistan, and almost all Latin American countries. Seignorage and the inflation tax also amount to a large fraction of output.

4.1.3.1 THE OPTIMAL INFLATION TAX

While the inflation tax has long been recognized as an important source of government revenue (as suggested by the preceding quotation by John Maynard Keynes), Phelps (1973) was the first to emphasize that the inflation rate can be determined *optimally* by policymakers in a public finance context. To show how his analysis proceeds, consider an economy in which there are no commercial banks, so that base money consists only of real cash balances held by private agents. Suppose that the economy is in a steady-state equilibrium, where the rate of output growth is zero, expectations are fulfilled, and the inflation rate is constant at π^s.[15] From Equation (7), inflation tax revenue is thus equal to

$$I_{\text{tax}} = \pi^s m_t. \tag{8}$$

TABLE 4.1

Seignorage and the Inflation Tax (percentage averages over 1980–91)

Country	Inflation	Seignorage Percent of Government Revenue	Seignorage Percent of GDP	Inflation Tax (percent of GDP)
Industrial Countries				
Belgium	4.6	0.3	0.1	1.1
Canada	6.3	1.1	0.2	0.8
France	7.4	0.9	0.4	1.8
Germany	2.9	1.6	0.5	0.5
Italy	10.5	5.9	1.6	4.0
Japan	2.6	5.4	0.6	0.8
United Kingdom	7.5	0.6	0.2	1.7
United States	5.4	1.8	0.4	0.9
Developing Countries				
Africa				
Burundi	7.3	4.5	0.6	0.9
Cameroon	9.4	3.0	0.6	1.2
Gabon	6.6	1.6	0.2	0.6
Kenya	12.7	4.6	1.0	1.8
Lesotho	13.9	7.3	2.5	2.9
Morocco	7.6	5.8	1.9	2.6
Nigeria	20.9	6.9	1.7	3.4
Somalia	48.6	—	2.1	12.4
Asia				
India	9.5	14.7	2.0	1.5
Indonesia	9.4	4.5	0.9	1.0
Malaysia	3.6	4.8	1.4	0.7
Pakistan	7.8	13.4	2.3	2.2
Philippines	15.3	10.0	1.4	1.2
Singapore	2.9	5.2	1.6	0.7
Sri Lanka	13.5	8.1	1.6	1.7
Thailand	5.8	5.9	1.0	0.6
Latin America				
Bolivia	1,155.8	111.6	5.0	91.5
Brazil	547.9	11.0	3.8	14.2
Chile	21.8	40.9	10.7	1.5
Colombia	24.5	24.8	2.9	3.0
Jamaica	19.1	10.0	3.2	3.0
Mexico	61.7	25.0	3.8	4.7
Peru	1,058.7	65.3	6.9	110.4
Venezuela	25.5	7.9	1.9	4.0

Source: Authors' calculations based on *International Financial Statistics.*

Notes: Seignorage is measured in terms of the increase in the base money stock as a percentage of total government revenue or GDP. Inflation is measured as the annual rate of change in consumer prices. The inflation tax is measured as $\pi_t M_{t-1}/GDP$.

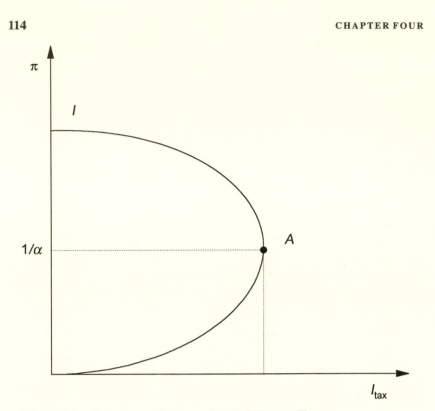

Figure 4.2   Inflation and Revenue from Inflationary Finance

Suppose that the money demand function follows the Cagan specification (see Blanchard and Fischer, 1989, pp. 195–96), so that real money balances vary inversely with the expected—and actual, in this case—inflation rate:

$$m_t = m_0 e^{-\alpha \pi^s}, \quad \alpha > 0 \tag{9}$$

where m_0 denotes a constant. Combining Equations (8) and (9) and setting, for simplicity, $m_0 \equiv 1$ yields

$$I_{\text{tax}} = \pi^s e^{-\alpha \pi^s}. \tag{10}$$

The right-hand side of Equation (10) is depicted in Figure 4.2 as curve I, which defines the inflation tax Laffer curve. When $\pi^s = 0$, the revenue from the inflation tax is also zero. With an increase in the inflation rate, revenue rises (at a decreasing rate) at first and begins falling (at an increasing rate) beyond a certain point. Maximum revenue is reached when $dI_{\text{tax}}/d\pi^s = 0$, or, equivalently, when the absolute value of the elasticity of the demand for real money balances is unity (point A). For any given level of inflation tax revenue lower than that corresponding to point A, there are two equilibrium levels of inflation. The unique revenue-maximizing rate of inflation is thus equal to

$$\pi_{\text{tax}}^s = \alpha^{-1}, \tag{11}$$

which is the inverse of the semielasticity of the demand for money. Given a specific assumption about the formation of inflationary expectations, the parameter α can easily be estimated for individual countries (see, for instance, Rodríguez, 1991).

The analysis of the optimal inflation tax has been extended in a variety of directions. It has been recognized, for instance, that governments levy the inflation tax not only on currency holdings by the public, but also on non-interest-bearing required reserves that they impose on commercial banks. We will examine in Chapter 5 the link between reserve requirements and the inflation tax. Along different lines, Cox (1983) determines the revenue-maximizing rate of inflation (and the welfare cost associated with deficit finance) in a model where government bonds and privately issued bonds are imperfect substitutes. His analysis shows that traditional formulations (which view private debt and public debt as perfect substitutes) may considerably underestimate the revenue-maximizing rate of inflation. Fischer (1983) examines how optimal inflation tax considerations affect the choice between exchange rate regimes. The link between the inflation tax and currency substitution, which plays a pervasive role in many developing countries, has also been explored.[16] Végh (1989a) examines whether the use of inflationary finance is optimal in the presence of currency substitution. He shows, in particular, that the higher the degree of currency substitution, the higher the optimal inflation tax is for a given level of government spending. In addition to examining whether or not recourse to the inflation tax is optimal in the presence of currency substitution, some authors have studied the effect of currency substitution on the level (and variability) of inflation tax revenue. Khan and Ramírez-Rojas (1986), for instance, show that the revenue-maximizing rate of inflation is lower in the presence of currency substitution, because the elasticity of the demand for domestic real money balances is higher in this case—since the foreign currency also provides liquidity services. However, the conventional argument that a high degree of currency substitution reduces the yield of the inflation tax—since agents are able to reallocate the composition of their portfolios away from domestic-currency holdings—does not always hold. Brock (1984), in particular, has shown that when a reserve requirement is imposed on capital inflows—in addition to domestic deposits—inflation tax revenue may in fact increase when the economy becomes more open to world capital markets. Significant developments in the analysis of the optimal inflation tax have also focused on the introduction of collection lags and collection costs.

4.1.3.2 COLLECTION LAGS AND THE OLIVERA-TANZI EFFECT

An important element that ought to be considered in the debate over the optimal use of inflationary finance relates to the effects of inflation on the tax system—in particular, the link between inflation and the collection lag in conventional tax revenue. This factor, which has been emphasized by Olivera (1967) and more forcefully by Tanzi (1978), has become known as the Olivera-Tanzi effect. It plays an important role in the analysis of fiscal, monetary, and inflation dynamics in developing countries.[17]

Taxes are collected with lags in almost all countries. In industrial nations, average collection lags—which measure the time between the moment taxes due are calculated and the moment they are actually paid to the fiscal authority—vary from one month in some cases and for particular sources of taxation (such as income taxes that are withheld at the source) to 6–10 months in other cases (such as indirect taxes). In developing countries, by contrast, average collection lags may be substantially higher. The share of revenue generated by taxes collected with progressive rates and withheld at the source is small, and taxes (such as import duties and excises) are often levied at specific rates. In such conditions an increase in the inflation rate will bring a fall in real conventional tax revenue, the extent of which will depend on the average collection lag and the prevalent tax burden, that is, the initial ratio of taxes to aggregate output. Formally, let n denote the average lag in collection of conventional taxes measured in months, and let π_M denote the monthly inflation rate. The real value of conventional tax revenue at a level of inflation equal to π^s on an annual basis is given by (Tanzi, 1978, p. 426)

$$\text{Tax}(\pi^s) = \frac{\text{Tax}(0)}{(1 + \pi_M)^n} = \frac{\text{Tax}(0)}{(1 + \pi^s)^{n/12}}, \tag{12}$$

where $\text{Tax}(0)$ denotes the real value of conventional taxes at a zero inflation rate.[18]

Total government revenue T is therefore equal to

$$T = \pi^s e^{-\alpha\pi^s} + \frac{\text{Tax}(0)}{(1 + \pi^s)^{n/12}}. \tag{13}$$

Setting the derivative of Equation (13) with respect to π^s equal to zero gives the value of the inflation rate that maximizes total real revenue, $\tilde{\pi}$:

$$dT/d\pi = (1 - \alpha)e^{-\alpha\tilde{\pi}} - \left(\frac{n}{12}\right)\frac{\text{Tax}(0)}{(1 + \tilde{\pi})\left(1 + \dfrac{n}{12}\right)} = 0, \tag{14}$$

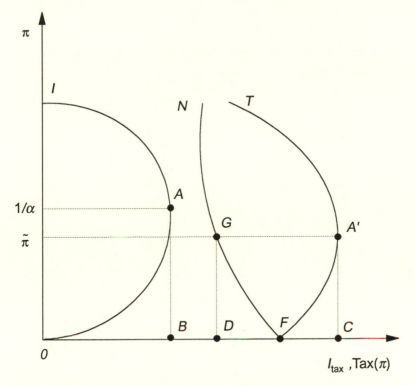

Figure 4.3   Inflation, Inflationary Finance, and Total Tax Revenue
Source: Adapted from Tanzi (1978, p. 435).

which is a nonlinear equation in $\tilde{\pi}$. A graphical determination of the solution is depicted in Figure 4.3. Curve I represents, as before, the inflation tax Laffer curve. Curve N represents revenue from conventional taxes, which depends negatively on inflation and is maximized at a zero inflation rate (point F). Curve T represents the horizontal sum of curves I and N and gives total revenue. As the figure shows, the total revenue-maximizing rate of inflation $\tilde{\pi}$ is lower than the rate that maximizes revenue from the issuance of money, $1/\alpha$ (see Equation (11)). At that level of inflation, revenue from the inflation tax is equal to OB (which is equal to DC) and conventional tax revenue is equal to BC (which is equal to OD). Since revenue from conventional taxes falls by DF as a result of higher inflation, the *net* contribution of the inflation tax to total revenue is only FC, which is lower than the gross contribution OB. In fact, the fall in conventional revenue resulting from an increase in inflation may be large enough to outweigh the increase in revenue from the inflation tax, yielding an overall *decline* in total real revenue. The simulation results provided by Tanzi (1978, 1988) show that

TABLE 4.2

Inflation, Inflationary Finance, and Tax Revenue (ratio of total tax revenue to gross domestic product)

Annual Inflation Rate (percent)	Revenue from Inflationary Finance	Total Tax Revenue		
		$n = 2$	$n = 4$	$n = 6$
5.0	0.9	20.8	20.6	20.5
10.0	1.8	21.5	21.2	20.9
15.0	2.6	22.1	21.7	21.2
20.0	3.3	22.7	22.1	21.5
25.0	3.9	23.2	22.5	21.8
30.0	4.4	23.6	22.8	22.0
35.0	4.9	24.0	23.0	22.1
40.0	5.4	24.3	23.2	22.3
45.0	5.7	24.5	23.4	22.3
50.0	6.1	24.8	23.5	22.4*
60.0	6.6	25.1	23.7*	22.4
70.0	7.0	25.3*	23.7	22.3
80.0	7.2	25.3	23.6	22.1
90.0	7.3	25.3	23.5	21.8
100.0	7.4	25.2	23.2	21.5
120.0	7.2	24.8	22.6	20.7
140.0	6.9	24.2	21.8	19.8
160.0	6.5	23.5	21.0	18.9
180.0	6.0	22.8	20.1	17.9
200.0	5.4	22.1	19.3	17.0
250.0	4.1	20.3	17.3	14.8
300.0	3.0	18.9	15.6	13.0
350.0	2.1	17.7	14.2	11.5
400.0	1.5	16.8	13.2	10.4
450.0	1.0	16.1	12.3	9.5
500.0	0.7	15.5	11.7	8.8

Source: Adapted from Tanzi (1978, pp. 446 and 448).

Notes: n denotes the collection lag, in months. The calculations reported assume that $\alpha = 1$ and that the ratio of money to GDP and the ratio of total tax revenue to GDP (both at a zero inflation rate) are equal to 20 percent. An asterisk denotes the highest value of the ratio of total revenue to GDP.

this outcome is entirely plausible, under reasonable parameter configurations. Some of Tanzi's results are shown in Table 4.2. When the collection lag is two months, the total-revenue-maximizing rate of inflation is equal to 70 percent. When the collection lag rises to six months, the revenue-maximizing inflation rate drops to 50 percent. In that case, inflating at a rate of 70 percent would increase revenue from the inflation tax (from 6.1 percent of GDP to 7 percent), but total tax revenue would fall.[19]

TABLE 4.3
Collection Lags by Major Revenue Categories (in months)

Revenue Component	Collection Lag
Current revenue	6.5
Tax revenue	6.0
Taxes on income and profits	6.3
Individual income	(7.2)
Profits and capital gains	(13.7)
Domestic taxes on goods and services	9.4
General sales, turnover or value added	(5.4)
Excises	(8.3)
Other	(17.7)
Taxes on international trade and transactions	4.0
Import duties	(8.0)
Other taxes on goods and services	3.9
Nontax revenue	11.7

Source: Adapted from Choudhry (1991, p. 9).

Notes: These estimates were obtained using pooled time series cross-section annual data over the period 1970–88 for a sample of eighteen developing countries.

To gauge the potential relevance of the Olivera-Tanzi effect, Table 4.3 reports estimates of collection lags for different components of fiscal revenue that are derived from a sample of eighteen developing countries. The average collection lag appears to be about six months for total revenue but varies widely among the different categories of revenue. The lag is higher than average for income taxes, taxes on domestic goods and services, import duties, and nontax revenue (such as transfers from public enterprises). In addition, although individual-country estimates are not reported here, these lags appear to vary considerably across countries. In several cases, the econometric estimates indicate that the erosion of fiscal revenue would have substantially offset the resources generated by an increase in the yield of the inflation tax, and would have resulted in a fall in net revenue. Thus, in countries where collection lags are high, raising the inflation tax may be counterproductive, as a result of the Olivera-Tanzi effect.[20]

The conventional inflation tax Laffer curve depicted in Figure 4.2 appears to be well supported by the empirical evidence on countries with moderate inflation. Easterly and Schmidt-Hebbel (1994) have drawn attention to the fact that conventional estimates of revenue-maximizing inflation rates may be biased—upward in high-inflation countries, downward in low-inflation countries—by misspecification of the demand function for real money balances as being of constant semielasticity with respect to inflation, when in fact the semielasticity may fall as inflation rises. More generally, the available evidence suggests that, at least in high-inflation countries, the rate of inflation has been higher than the rate that maximizes steady-state revenue from the inflation tax. The public finance motive for inflationary finance does not seem to explain cases of chronic high-inflation countries, although the evidence suggests that the acceleration of inflation in Latin America after the outbreak of the debt crisis in 1982 appeared to have emanated from the need to finance external and internal obligations with internal resources (see Chapter 13).[21] Thus, if imperfect information or lags in the adjustment of inflationary expectations are ruled out, an alternative explanation for the existence of chronically high inflation must be found. The lack of credibility and the time inconsistency problem faced by policymakers may provide such a rationale, which is discussed at length in Chapter 10.

4.1.3.3 COLLECTION COSTS AND TAX SYSTEM EFFICIENCY

The use of inflationary finance for financing government spending and fiscal deficits has been justified by a variety of arguments. The early debate on the desirability of inflationary finance focused on the welfare cost of alternative options for financing public expenditure; see Bailey (1956) and Auhernheimer (1974). However, as pointed out by Aghevli (1977), if alternative revenue sources are not readily available, a comparative analysis is of little relevance. In most developing economies, the tax base is inadequate, the share of small-income earners is disproportionately large, and evasion is endemic, preventing the imposition of a high tax burden on the population. Tax administration is weak, inefficient, and often subject to a large degree of corruption (Goode, 1984). In such conditions the appropriate comparison is between the total cost of inflationary finance—taking into account the distortions introduced into the tax system itself by inflation, as emphasized by Tanzi (1978)—and the benefits, in terms of additional consumption in the future, derived from a higher level of government expenditure.

The effect of the efficiency of the tax system on the optimal inflation tax rate can be illustrated using a simple framework. Suppose that the government faces the budget constraint

$$\bar{g} - e\iota y_t = \pi_t m_t,$$

where $\bar{g}$ denotes government spending, $0 < \iota < 1$ the conventional income tax rate, $0 < e < 1$ a coefficient that reflects the efficiency of the tax system—that is, the fraction of tax liabilities actually collected—and y_t the tax base. The wedge $(1 - e)\iota$ represents unit collection costs, which are wasted by the inefficiencies of the tax system. The government's objective is to maximize potential revenue ιy_t with respect to the conventional tax rate and the inflation rate, subject to the budget constraint given above. Given this objective, as shown by De Gregorio (1993), a reduction in the efficiency of the tax system (a fall in e) leads in general to an increase in the optimal inflation rate and a fall in the inflation tax base. The effect on the optimal tax rate is ambiguous, but the share of income tax revenues falls as the share of revenue from the inflation tax in total resources increases. Thus, even when the optimal conventional tax rate increases, it will not outweigh the effects of the fall in efficiency on the revenue collected from the income tax.

The trade-off between explicit direct taxation and the inflation tax has been shown to persist in more general settings, notably by Aizenman (1987) and Végh (1989b). Both authors argue that a decline in the efficiency of the tax system raises the inflation rate.[22] Végh, in particular, examines the relationship between government spending and inflationary finance in a model where alternative, conventional taxes (such as the consumption tax) are subject to increasing marginal collection costs. As a result, the inflation tax is shown to depend positively on the level of government spending. An improvement in the efficiency of tax collection would therefore reduce the government's reliance on the inflation tax as a source of revenue.

More recent work has attempted to identify the effect of political factors on the efficiency of the tax system, in addition to institutional constraints, such as the degree of competence of public administration. In most developing nations, high-income earners have considerable political power, making it difficult for the government to enforce tax laws. A formal analysis of the relationship between tax system efficiency—measured by the extent to which seignorage is used as a source of fiscal revenue—political instability, and economic structure has been provided by Cukierman, et al. (1992). Their analysis indicates that the efficiency of the tax system in developing countries is highly correlated with the composition of output (countries with a large agricultural sector, for instance, tend to rely more on seignorage than countries with large mining and manufacturing sectors) and with the degree of instability and polarization of the political system. The degree of openness to foreign trade and the rate of urbanization also have significant effects on tax system efficiency. Thus, in addition to structural and administrative factors, countries that are more politically unstable tend to rely more on the inflation tax as a source of government revenue.

4.2 Policy Consistency and the Solvency Constraint

The flow budget identity of the government derived earlier, while useful for assessing the fiscal stance at any given moment in time, does not highlight the dynamic nature of the financing constraint that the public sector typically faces. Governments cannot indefinitely accumulate domestic and foreign debt. They therefore face an *intertemporal* budget constraint, which also imposes restrictions on the paths followed by different components of the budget identity. In addition, the flow budget constraint imposes consistency requirements on the overall formulation of macroeconomic policy targets that must be taken into account in the design of stabilization programs. The first part of this section examines how the solvency constraint can be derived to evaluate the sustainability of fiscal policy. The second part analyzes the requirements imposed by financing constraints on the formulation of macroeconomic policy objectives.

4.2.1 The Intertemporal Solvency Constraint

As shown in Equation (5), the consolidated public sector deficit can be defined in real terms as

$$\frac{\dot{M_t}}{P_t} + \frac{\dot{B_t}}{P_t} + \left(\frac{E_t}{P_t}\right)\dot{F_t^*} = g_t + i_t\left(\frac{B_t}{P_t}\right) + i_t^*\left(\frac{E_t}{P_t}\right)F_t^* - \tau_t. \tag{15}$$

Equation (15) can be rewritten in terms of the behavior over time of stocks and flows per unit of output, which yields

$$\frac{\dot{M_t}}{P_t y_t} + \dot{b_t} + z_t\dot{f_t^*} = g_t - \tau_t + (i_t - \pi_t - n_t)b_t + (i_t^* + \epsilon_t - \pi_t - n_t)z_t f_t^*, \tag{16}$$

where lower-case letters represent the corresponding upper-case quantities expressed as a proportion of nominal output (that is, $b_t \equiv B_t/P_t y_t$, for example), n_t the rate of growth of real output, $z_t = E_t/P_t$ the real exchange rate, and ϵ_t the devaluation rate. The quantity $M_t/P_t y_t$ is seignorage as a fraction of output.[23]

Let $d_t' \equiv (g_t - \tau_t)/y_t$ measure the primary public sector deficit as a fraction of output, and let seignorage as a share of output be equal to $s_t \equiv \dot{M_t}/P_t y_t$. Total public debt as a fraction of output can be defined as $\Delta_t \equiv b_t + z_t f_t^*$.

Using the identity $(z_t\dot{f_t^*}) \equiv \dot{f_t^*}z_t + \hat{z_t}f_t^*z_t$—where $\hat{z_t}$ denotes the rate of depreciation of the real exchange rate—Equation (16) can be written as

$$\dot{\Delta_t} = (\rho_t - n_t)\Delta_t + d_t' + (i_t^* + \hat{z_t} - \rho_t)z_t f_t^* - s, \tag{17}$$

where ρ_t is the domestic real interest rate. Defining the augmented primary deficit as

$$d_t \equiv d_t' + (i_t^* + \hat{z_t} - \rho_t)z_t f_t^* \tag{18}$$

yields

$$\dot{\Delta_t} = (\rho_t - n_t)\Delta_t + d_t - s_t, \tag{19}$$

which indicates that the difference between the (augmented) primary deficit plus interest payments on the existing debt and seignorage revenue must be financed by domestic or foreign borrowing.

Integrating forward Equation (19) yields the public sector's intertemporal budget identity:

$$\Delta_t = \mathbb{E}_t \int_t^\infty (s_k - d_k) \exp\left[-\int_t^k (\rho_h - n_h)dh\right]dk$$
$$+ \lim_{k \to \infty} \mathbb{E}_t \Delta_t \exp\left[-\int_t^k (\rho_h - n_h)dh\right], \tag{20}$$

where $\mathbb{E}_t$ denotes the expectations operator, conditional on information available at period t. The government is solvent if the expected present value of the future resources available to it for debt service is at least equal to the face value of its initial stock of debt. Under these circumstances, the government will be able to service its debt on market terms. Solvency thus requires that the government's prospective fiscal plans satisfy the present-value budget constraint

$$\Delta_t \le \mathbb{E}_t \int_t^\infty (s_k - d_k) \exp\left[-\int_t^k (\rho_h - n_h)dh\right]dk, \tag{21}$$

or, equivalently,

$$\Delta_t \le PV(s, t, \rho - n) - PV(d, t, \rho - n), \tag{21'}$$

where

$$PV(x, t, \rho - n) \equiv \mathbb{E}_t \int_t^\infty x_k \exp\left[-\int_t^k (\rho_h - n_h)dh\right]dk$$

denotes the present value at time t of flow x, discounted at the instantaneous rate of discount $(\rho_h - n_h)$. Equation (21') indicates that public debt must be (at most) equal to the present value as of time t of seignorage revenue minus the present value as of time t of future (augmented) primary deficits. These conditions imply the transversality condition

$$\lim_{k \to \infty} \mathbb{E}_t \Delta_t \exp\left[-\int_t^k (\rho_h - n_h)dh\right] \le 0. \tag{22}$$

Equation (22) indicates that, as of time t, the expectation of the present value of the consolidated (domestic and foreign) future public debt cannot be positive in the limit.

Equation (22) implies that, ultimately, the debt/output ratio must grow at a rate *below* the real interest rate minus the rate of growth of output.

This restriction rules out an indefinite Ponzi game: the government cannot pay forever the interest on its outstanding domestic and foreign debt simply by borrowing more. At some point the debt must be serviced by reducing primary deficits or by increasing seignorage revenue.

The solvency restriction—or, equivalently, the government's intertemporal budget constraint—ensures only that the existing debt is ultimately serviced (by current and future primary surpluses or by current and future seignorage); it does not imply that the debt is actually paid off (Buiter, 1989). A logical implication of the foregoing analysis is that solvency is ensured even if the debt/output ratio grows at a positive rate, as long as this rate remains below the long-run value of the difference between the real interest rate and the real growth rate. A government may thus be solvent despite the fact that its real outstanding debt and even its debt/output ratio are growing without bound. If the real interest rate remains below the growth rate of output forever ($\rho_t < n_t$, for all t), condition (22) will not be binding: the government will be able in each period to service the existing debt by further borrowing, engaging in an "honest" Ponzi scheme. We will, however, assume that this condition does not hold for an indefinite period of time, thus excluding Ponzi games.[24] Solvency requires, eventually, positive values for $s_t - d_t$, the difference between seignorage revenue and the augmented primary deficit. Although running a conventional surplus is not necessary to ensure solvency, positive operational surpluses are eventually required in the absence of seignorage revenue. More generally, to ensure solvency requires reducing the augmented primary deficit (by reducing government expenditure, increasing net current revenue, or shifting the composition of the public debt between internal and external debt) or increasing the present value of future seignorage.

For different paths of $\rho_t - n_t$ and for a given present value of seignorage revenue, the size of the primary surplus required to stabilize the debt/output ratio can in principle be calculated. Alternatively, by treating debt and primary surpluses as exogenous, the level of seignorage revenue required for ensuring solvency can be calculated for different values of $\rho_t - n_t$. Depending on the assumed form of the money demand function, such an option also has implications for the inflation rate. In practice, however, the use of the solvency constraint to determine a sustainable path of fiscal policy is fraught with difficulties, which result in particular from the uncertainty about future revenue and expenditure flows. As a result, few attempts have been made to evaluate the sustainability of fiscal deficits in light of the solvency constraint. Among the few developing-country studies available are those of Buiter and Patel (1992) for India, and Haque and Montiel (1994) for Pakistan. In Chapter 13 we will make use of the solvency constraint in discussing the debt crisis and the policy choices that it imposed on some of the highly indebted developing countries.

Perhaps more important, solvency is a weak criterion with which to evaluate the sustainability of fiscal policy (Buiter, 1985). Several alternative fiscal policy rules can be consistent with a given intertemporal constraint, but not all of them are necessarily sustainable in the long run.[25] As discussed below, the sustainability of alternative fiscal strategies must be evaluated in the context of the overall macroeconomic policy mix, taking into account all macroeconomic targets.

4.2.2 Financing Constraints and Policy Consistency

Macroeconomic programs typically consist of specifying targets for inflation, output growth, domestic and foreign borrowing, and the overall balance of payments. The existence of such targets imposes restrictions on the use of alternative sources of financing of the public sector deficit. The government budget constraint thus determines a "financeable" or sustainable level of the fiscal deficit given the authorities' policy targets. If the actual deficit exceeds its sustainable level, one or all macroeconomic targets must be abandoned, or fiscal policy adjustment must take place. For instance, for a given size of the fiscal deficit, the government budget constraint allows the derivation of an "equilibrium" inflation rate for which no fiscal adjustment is required. However, given a fixed exchange-rate regime, limited foreign reserves determine the path of central bank credit to the government and, through the budget constraint, the size of the primary deficit. Ignoring the consistency requirement between fiscal policy, inflation, and credit growth implied by a fixed exchange rate would lead, as discussed in Chapter 7, to recurrent speculative attacks and eventually to a collapse of the exchange-rate regime.

A convenient accounting framework for the analysis of consistency requirements between fiscal deficits, inflation, output growth, and the balance of payments in a small open economy is provided by the government budget identity derived above.[26] The essential analytical tool is provided by Equation (17). For instance, whether a given fiscal policy path is sustainable can be determined by projecting the future course of the debt/output ratio for given predictions about the evolution of money demand (using one of the alternative specifications discussed in Chapter 3), the desired inflation rate, the real interest rate, and the growth rate of the economy. If the analysis shows the debt/output ratio to be rising continually, eventually violating the solvency constraint, fiscal adjustment or adjustment in other targets is required.

If the policy target is to maintain a fixed debt/output ratio for both internal and external debt, real debt cannot grow faster than real output. Using Equation (17) together with an inflation target (and therefore a given level of revenue from money creation) yields the primary deficit plus interest payments on domestic and foreign debt. Given the level of the primary deficit, it is possible to determine the inflation rate at which revenue from the inflation tax covers the difference between the government's financing needs and its issuance of interest-bearing debt. A similar strategy would lead to the determination of the appropriate path of foreign and domestic borrowing, given primary deficit and inflation targets. Whatever the "closure rule" chosen, the resulting path of policy variables will depend on assumptions about the behavior of the predetermined variables (domestic output growth, the real exchange rate, foreign inflation, and foreign real interest rates), as well as the estimated form of the demand for real money balances.

Consistency checks among the different objectives of macroeconomic policy and their financing implications are an essential aspect of the design of macroeconomic reform programs. However, the fact that a given path of fiscal policy is sustainable, given other macroeconomic targets, does not imply that it is necessarily the optimal choice (Fischer and Easterly, 1990). For instance, a financeable fiscal deficit may be large enough to crowd out private investment. Reducing the debt/output ratio would be an appropriate policy choice in such conditions since it would "crowd in" private capital expenditure and allow the economy to sustain a higher growth rate of output.

4.3 Macroeconomic Effects of Fiscal Deficits

A key starting point for understanding the macroeconomic effects of government fiscal deficits is the economy's aggregate resource or saving-investment constraint discussed in Chapter 2, which shows how conventional public deficits $(I_t^g - S_t^g)$ are financed by surpluses from the private sector $(S_t^p - I_t^p)$ and the rest of the world, CA_t, where CA_t is the current account deficit:[27]

$$D_t \equiv (I_t^g - S_t^g) = (S_t^p - I_t^p) + CA_t. \tag{23}$$

The nature of the effects of large public deficits on the macroeconomy thus depends on the components of this equation that actually adjust. Adjustment depends on the scope for domestic and foreign financing, the degree of diversification of financial markets (which determines to some extent the choice between money or bond financing), and the composition of the deficit. As discussed below, expectations about future government policies also play a critical role in the transmission of fiscal deficits.

We begin by discussing an issue central to the subsequent analysis, the relevance of Ricardian equivalence in the context of developing countries. We then focus on the link between fiscal deficits and inflation, a relation that, as mentioned before, has often been viewed as a key mechanism in the inflationary process in developing countries. Next we turn to the relationship between fiscal deficits, real interest rates, and their potential crowding-out effect on private expenditure. Finally, we discuss the link between public sector deficits, the current account, and the real exchange rate.

4.3.1 Ricardian Equivalence

The Ricardian equivalence proposition states that deficits and taxes are equivalent in their effect on consumption (Barro, 1974). Lump-sum changes in taxes have no effect on consumer spending, and a reduction in taxes leads to an equivalent increase in saving. The reason is that a consumer endowed with perfect foresight recognizes that the increase in government debt resulting from an increase in government spending or a reduction in taxes will ultimately be paid off by increased taxes, the present value of which is exactly equal to the present value of the reduction in taxes. Taking the implied increase in future taxes into account, the consumer saves today the amount necessary to pay them tomorrow. Ricardian equivalence implies, in particular, that fiscal deficits have no effect on aggregate saving or investment or consequently, through the economywide saving-investment identity presented above, on the current account of the balance of payments.

The conditions required for Ricardian equivalence to hold are the existence of infinite planning horizons, certainty about future tax burdens, perfect capital markets (or the absence of borrowing constraints), rational expectations, and nondistortionary taxes. The restrictive nature of these assumptions has been demonstrated by various authors. In particular, the debt neutrality proposition has been shown to break down if agents have finite horizons, capital markets are imperfect, or uncertainty and distributional effects play a pervasive role in individuals' consumption and savings decisions.[28]

The available evidence for developing and industrial countries has failed so far to provide much support for the Ricardian equivalence hypothesis. The evidence from industrial countries appears to be largely inconclusive (Seater, 1993). In developing countries where financial systems are underdeveloped, capital markets are highly distorted or subject to financial repression, and private agents are subject to considerable uncertainty regarding the incidence of taxes, many of the considerations necessary for debt neutrality to hold are unlikely to be valid. As alluded to in Chapter 3, the empirical evidence has indeed failed to provide much support for the Ricardian equivalence proposition. Haque and Montiel (1989) reject the null hypothesis of debt neutrality for fifteen out of a group of sixteen developing countries. Veidyanathan (1993), using a group of almost sixty countries and annual data covering three decades, Corbo and Schmidt-Hebbel (1991), and the empirical studies reviewed by Easterly and Schmidt-Hebbel (1994) for the most part also fail to detect any significant effects of public deficits on private consumption.[29] Both Haque and Montiel and Veidyanathan suggest that consumers in developing countries are subject to liquidity and borrowing constraints.

4.3.2 Deficits, Inflation, and the "Tight Money" Paradox

Milton Friedman's famous statement that inflation is always and everywhere a monetary phenomenon is correct. However, governments do not print money at a rapid rate out of a clear blue sky. They generally print money to cover their budget deficit. Rapid money growth is conceivable without an underlying fiscal imbalance, but it is unlikely. Thus rapid inflation is almost always a fiscal phenomenon (Fischer and Easterly, 1990, pp. 138–39).

The relationship between fiscal deficits and inflation has been the focus of considerable attention in development macroeconomics. We will examine below some of the empirical and analytical issues that arise in this context—in particular, the role of policy expectations and financing constraints. Chapter 8 will examine the role of fiscal adjustment in several recent stabilization experiments, and Chapter 9 will examine further the link between fiscal deficits and money growth in the inflationary process.

One common explanation for the inflationary consequences of public fiscal deficits in developing nations is the lack of sufficiently developed domestic capital markets that can absorb newly issued government debt (Shahin, 1992). Moreover, in some countries the central bank is under the direct control of the central government and often passively finances public deficits through money creation. At the level of any particular country, however, there may be no clear short-term link between fiscal deficits and inflation. The correlation may even be negative during extended periods of time. The emergence of a positive correlation in the long run is also not a clear-cut phenomenon. Figure 4.4 displays the relation between fiscal deficits and inflation over the period 1970–88 for a large group of developing countries. A positive correlation is discernible, although it appears weak. This, however, may be the result of the existence of a nonlinear relationship between fiscal deficits and inflation, or of other factors—such as the behavior of world prices or supply-side shocks—that are not accounted for. Econometric studies are thus more suited to examine this long-run relationship. For instance, Haan and Zelhorst (1990) investigated the relationship between government deficits and money growth in seventeen developing countries over the period 1961–85. Their results provide strong support

Fiscal deficit (percent of GDP)

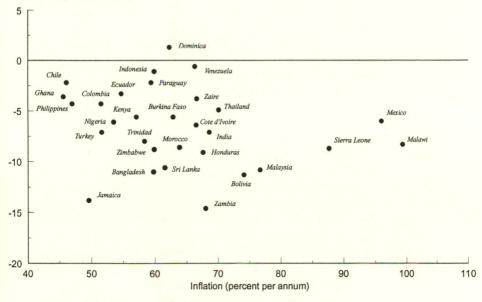

Figure 4.4   Inflation and Fiscal Deficits, Consolidated Public Sector: Period Averages over 1970–88

Source: Easterly and Schmidt-Hebbel (1994) and *International Financial Statistics.*

for a positive long-run relationship between budget deficits and inflation in high-inflation countries.

Various arguments have been proposed to explain the absence of a close correlation between budget deficits and inflation in the short run. First, an increase in fiscal deficits may be financed by issuing bonds rather than money; although such a policy is not sustainable as a result of the government's solvency constraint (as discussed above), it may imply a weak relation in the short run between deficits and inflation. Second, a change in the composition of the sources of deficit financing over time (in particular, a substitution of domestic financing for foreign financing) may lead to higher inflation without substantial changes in the level of the consolidated public sector deficit. Third, the correlation may be low if the money demand function is unstable, if expectations are slow to adjust, or if inertial forces (such as the existence of staggered wage contracts) prevent the economy from adjusting rapidly to changes in inflationary pressures.

A fourth and particularly appealing argument relies on the existence of strong expectational effects linked to perceptions about future government policy. Private agents in an economy with high fiscal deficits may at different times form different expectations about how the deficit will eventually be closed. For instance, if the public believes at a given moment that the government will attempt to reduce its fiscal deficit through inflation (thus eroding the value of the public debt), current inflation—which reflects expectations of future price increases—will rise. If, at a later time, the public starts believing that the government will eventually introduce an effective fiscal adjustment program to lower the deficit, inflationary expectations will adjust downward and current inflation—reflecting, again, expectations about the future behavior of prices—will fall (Drazen and Helpman, 1990).

A particularly well-known example of the role of expectations about future policy is provided by the "monetarist arithmetic," or the so-called tight money paradox. In a seminal contribution, Sargent and Wallace (1981) have shown that when a financing constraint forces the government to finance its budget deficit through the inflation tax, any attempt to lower the inflation rate today, even if successful, will require a higher inflation rate tomorrow. For a given level of government spending and "conventional" taxes, the reduction in revenue from money creation raises the level of government borrowing. If a solvency constraint (of the "no Ponzi game" type discussed previously) imposes an upper limit on public debt, the government will eventually return to a rate of money growth high enough to finance not only the same primary deficit that prevailed before the initial policy change, but also the higher interest payments due to the additional debt accumulated as a result of the policy change. Solvency and macroeconomic consistency thus impose constraints on policy options in attempts to reduce the inflation rate. In the discussion that follows we present the Sargent-Wallace result, following Liviatan (1984, 1986).[30]

4.3.2.1 THE ANALYTICAL FRAMEWORK

Consider a closed economy with a zero rate of population growth ($n = 0$) and in which the representative household's flow budget constraint is given by

$$\dot{m}_t + \dot{b}_t = (1 - \iota)(\bar{y} + \tau_t + \rho b_t) - c_t - \pi_t m_t, \qquad (24)$$

where m_t denotes real money balances, b_t the stock of government-indexed bonds held by the public, $\bar{y}$ exogenous output, τ_t net lump-sum transfers from the government, c_t consumption expenditure, π_t the inflation rate, and ρ the constant real interest rate.[31] $0 < \iota < 1$ is the proportional income tax rate, which, for simplicity, is assumed to be levied on all components of gross income. Real wealth a_t can be defined as

$$a_t = m_t + b_t + (1 - \iota) \int_t^\infty (\bar{y} + \tau_t) e^{-(1-\iota)\rho s} ds.$$

Assuming that transfers are constant over time ($\tau_t = \bar{\tau}$) yields

$$a_t = m_t + b_t + (\bar{y} + \bar{\tau})/\rho. \qquad (25)$$

The demand functions for goods and money are defined as[32]

$$c_t = \kappa a_t, \quad \kappa > 0 \qquad (26a)$$

$$m_t = (\alpha - \kappa)a_t/i_t, \quad \alpha > \kappa, \qquad (26b)$$

where $i_t \equiv (1 - \iota)\rho + \pi_t$ denotes the net nominal interest rate and α the rate of time preference, which is assumed here to equal the after-tax real interest rate ($\alpha = (1 - \iota)\rho$).

The equilibrium condition in the goods market is given by

$$c_t = \bar{y} - \bar{g}, \qquad (27)$$

where g, noninterest government spending, is assumed constant over time. The government budget constraint can be written as

$$\dot{m}_t + \dot{b}_t = \bar{g} - \iota\bar{y} + (1 - \iota)(\bar{\tau} + \rho b_t) - \pi_t m_t. \qquad (28)$$

Finally, the dynamics of the real money stock are given by

$$\dot{m}_t = (\mu - \pi_t)m_t, \qquad (29)$$

where $\mu \equiv \dot{M}_t/M_t$ denotes the rate of growth of the nominal money stock.

In the steady state $\dot{m}_t = \dot{b}_t = 0$, so that using Equations (24) to (29) yields, with $\rho = \alpha/(1 - \iota)$,

$$c^* = \bar{y} - \bar{g}, \qquad (30a)$$

$$m^* = \frac{\alpha - \kappa}{(1 - \iota)\rho + \mu}\left\{m^* + b^* + \rho^{-1}(\bar{y} + \bar{\tau})\right\}, \qquad (30b)$$

$$\bar{g} - \iota\bar{y} + (1 - \iota)(\bar{\tau} + \rho b^*) = \mu m^*, \qquad (30c)$$

and $\pi^* = \mu$. There are only two independent equations in this system, which can be used to determine the steady-state values of the inflation rate (or, equivalently, the rate of growth of the nominal money stock) and real money balances for a given level of the stock of bonds, or the solutions for real money holdings and bonds for a given inflation rate. Whatever the "closure rule" chosen, however, it is useful to note for what follows that consumption and the real interest rate are independent of the rate of growth of the nominal money stock across steady states. This is implied for the real interest rate by the assumption that $\rho = \alpha/(1 - \iota)$ and for consumption by the market-clearing condition requiring that $c_t = \bar{y} - \bar{g}$.

4.3.2.2 CONSTANT PRIMARY DEFICIT

Consider a temporary reduction in the rate of money growth μ during the time interval $(0, T)$, with the primary government deficit held constant at $\bar{d}$, which is equal to

$$\bar{d} = \bar{g} - \iota\bar{y} + (1 - \iota)\bar{\tau}. \tag{31}$$

After T, the stock of real government bonds is assumed to remain constant at the level it attained at period T. Therefore, during the interval $(0, T)$ μ is exogenous and b_t endogenous, while for $t \geq T$ the stock of bonds remains constant at the level b_T^+, and μ becomes endogenous.[33]

Examining the effects of this policy rule on the dynamics of inflation and real money balances proceeds in two stages. First, substituting Equation (29) in (28) yields

$$\dot{b}_t = (1 - \iota)\rho b_t - \mu m_t - z_b, \tag{32}$$

where $z_b = (1 - \iota)(\bar{y} + \bar{\tau}) - c_t$. Since output and public spending are constant, private consumption is also constant—at $(\bar{y} - \bar{g})$, from (27)—along the equilibrium path. Hence z_b is also constant.

Since, from Equation (29), $\pi_t m_t = \mu m_t - \dot{m}_t$, Equations (26a) and (26b) imply, given the definition of the nominal interest rate,

$$\dot{m}_t = [\mu + (1 - \iota)\rho]m_t + z_m, \quad z_m \equiv -\left(\frac{\alpha - \kappa}{\kappa}\right)(\bar{y} - \bar{g}), \tag{33}$$

where z_m is also constant. From Equation (26a), a constant level of consumption implies that real wealth must be constant along the equilibrium path, so that $\dot{m}_t + \dot{b}_t = 0$. This condition can be verified by adding Equations (32) and (33), using (25) and (26a).

Suppose that, starting at a steady state where $\mu = \mu^h$, the monetary authority reduces the rate of money growth unexpectedly at time $t = 0$ to a value $\mu^s < \mu^h$ over the interval $(0, T)$. Although the price level is fully flexible, real money balances will not jump at $t = 0$ because m_0 is determined, from Equations (26a) and (26b), by the requirement that consumption remain constant and by the fact that b_0 cannot jump on impact.[34] It follows from Equation (33) that a reduction in the rate of growth of the nominal money stock implies $\dot{m}_0 < 0$, so that real money balances will be declining over time. Solving Equation (33) yields

$$m_t = \bar{m}(\mu^s) + [m_0 - \bar{m}(\mu^s)]\exp[(\mu^s + (1 - \iota)\rho)t], \qquad (34)$$

where $m_0 < \bar{m}(\mu^s) = -z_m/[\mu^s + (1 - \iota)\rho]$. Equation (34) indicates that real money balances will be declining at an increasing rate over the interval $(0, T)$. From Equations (26) and (27),

$$\pi_t = \left(\frac{\alpha - \kappa}{\kappa}\right)(\bar{y} - \bar{g})m_t^{-1} - (1 - \iota)\rho, \quad 0 < t < T, \qquad (35)$$

implying that the inflation rate increases continuously over the interval $(0, T)$.

The solution for $t \geq T$ is obtained as follows. During the interval $(0, T)$, b_t must be rising since $\dot{m}_t < 0$ and $\dot{m}_t + \dot{b}_t = 0$. Since the latter condition must continue to hold for $t \geq T$ and the stock of bonds must remain constant at b_T^+ for $t \geq T$, we must have $\dot{m}_t = 0$ for $t \geq T$. Real money balances must therefore remain constant at, say, m_T^+ for $t \geq T$. The condition $\dot{m}_t = 0$ for $t \geq T$ is satisfied by adjusting discontinuously the rate of money growth μ at T so as to satisify Equation (33):

$$\dot{m}_T = 0 = [\tilde{\mu} + (1 - \iota)\rho]m_T^+ + z_m. \qquad (36)$$

Since $\dot{m}_t < 0$ for $0 \leq t < T$, Equation (36) implies that $\tilde{\mu}$ must be raised above μ^s. Moreover, since $m_T^+ < m_0$, it follows that

$$\mu^s < \mu^h < \tilde{\mu}, \qquad (37)$$

which indicates that the reduction in the money growth rate during the interval $(0, T)$ below its initial value must be followed at T by an increase beyond the initial value.

It can also be shown using Equation (35) that in the postadjustment steady state inflation remains constant at π_T^+ and that

$$\pi_T^+ > \pi_0, \quad t \geq T, \qquad (38)$$

which indicates that the steady-state inflation rate that prevails beyond T is higher than in the initial steady state. The increase in the inflation rate occurs during the interval $(0, T)$, since no jump can occur at time T as a result of perfect foresight.

The thrust of the analysis is thus that a temporary reduction in the rate of money growth raises the inflation rate both during and after the policy change. Intuitively, a temporary reduction in nominal money growth is offset by an increase in bond finance. Thus, after the temporary policy is removed, higher interest payments require that seignorage revenue be higher to finance the deficit, and this, in turn, requires a higher inflation rate. The expectation of higher inflation in the future implies higher inflation even while the contractionary policy is in place, because otherwise pure level jumps would give rise to arbitrage profits.

4.3.2.3 CONSTANT CONVENTIONAL DEFICIT

Consider now what happens if it is the deficit inclusive of interest payments—that is, the conventional deficit—that remains fixed, rather than the primary deficit. Using Equation (30c), Equation (31) is therefore replaced by

$$\bar{d} = \bar{g} - \iota\bar{y} + (1 - \iota)(\tau_t + \rho b_t). \tag{31$'$}$$

For Equation (31$'$) to hold continuously with b_t endogenous, we assume that the government makes compensatory adjustments in transfer payments to households, τ_t. Since public spending and output are constant, the financing rule implies that $\tau_t + \rho b_t$ is constant at, say, k. We will also assume in the following analysis that the rate of population growth n is positive (and constant), instead of zero.[35]
   Equations (25)–(27) and (29) now yield, using (31$'$),

$$\dot{b}_t = -nb_t - \mu m_t + z_b', \quad z_b' \equiv (1 - \iota)(\bar{y} + k) - (\bar{y} - \bar{g}), \tag{39}$$

and Equation (33) is unchanged. For μ given, Equations (33) and (39) form a differential Equation system in b_t and m_t whose steady-state equilibrium is a saddlepoint. The slope of the saddlepath coincides in the present case with the slope of the $[\dot{m}_t = 0]$ curve, as shown in Figure 4.5. The steady state is reached at point E, for a given value of $\mu = \mu^h$. Real balances may now jump on impact since endogenous transfers ensure that wealth, and therefore consumption, remains constant initially. Varying μ and maintaining $\dot{m}_t = \dot{b}_t = 0$ permits the derivation of alternative long-run equilibrium values of real money balances and the stock of bonds. Alternatively, for a given value of b_t, treating m_t and μ as endogenous allows us to derive the steady-state relation between real holdings of money and bonds. This relationship is given by

$$m_t = (nb_t - z_b' - z_m)/(1 - \iota)\rho. \tag{40}$$

Equation (40) is represented by curve MM in Figure 4.6. The initial long-run equilibrium with $\mu = \mu^h$ obtains at E in the figure.

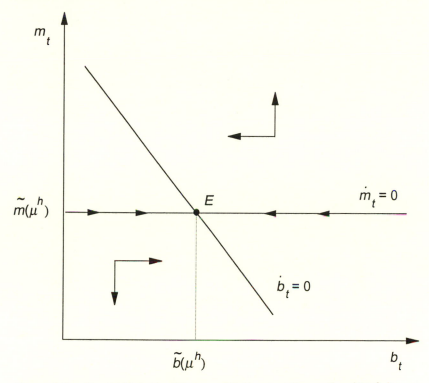

Figure 4.5   Steady-State Equilibrium with Constant Conventional Deficit
Source: Adapted from Liviatan (1984, p. 13).

Consider now, as before, a reduction of the money growth rate from μ^h to μ^s over the interval $(0, T)$. The new steady-state solution associated with Equations (33) and (39) with $\mu = \mu^s$ obtains at point E', which is also located on *MM*. On impact, real money balances increase, in association with a fall in both the price level and the initial steady-state inflation rate, and the system jumps from point E to point A. The economy then follows a divergent path over $(0, T)$, moving over time from point A to point B located on curve *MM*, which is reached exactly at period T. If at that moment the policymaker raises the rate of growth of the money stock to some value $\mu^c > \mu^s$ and freezes the stock of bonds at b_T^+, point B will represent a steady-state equilibrium.[36] During the transition period, real balances fall while the stock of bonds and the inflation rate rise. However, at point B real balances remain above their original equilibrium level $\tilde{m}(\mu^h)$, implying that the inflation rate will remain permanently below its initial steady-state level. Consequently, a *temporary* reduction in the money growth rate leads to a *permanent* reduction in the inflation rate. Essentially, the difference from the previous case results from the fact that when the primary deficit is held

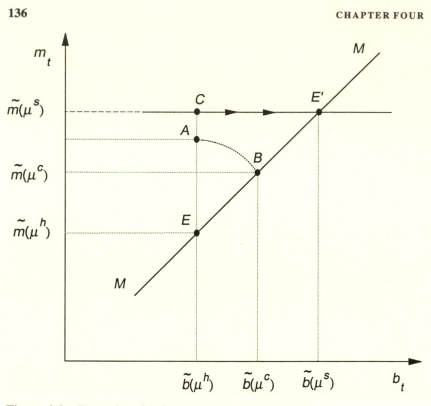

Figure 4.6   Dynamics with Constant Conventional Deficit
Source: Adapted from Liviatan (1984, p. 14).

constant, the increase in interest payments on the public debt is financed by the inflation tax and is therefore inflationary. By contrast, when the overall deficit is held constant, the increase in interest payments on government debt is financed by a rise in taxes, which leads to a lower reliance on the inflation tax.

In the preceding framework, defining "tight" monetary policy as a reduction in the rate of growth of the nominal money stock leads to a system that is dynamically unstable during the interval $(0, T)$. The solvency constraint eventually requires a freeze of the stock of government bonds. Consequently, for $t \geq T$, the economy is "stuck" with a smaller stock of money, a larger stock of bonds, and a permanently higher rate of inflation. Liviatan (1986) shows that this dynamic instability disappears if a "tight monetary policy" is defined as a reduction in the *share* of money financing of the government deficit over the interval $(0, T)$. In this formulation, the ratio of money financing to bond financing γ is exogenous, while the rate of growth of the nominal money stock μ_t is endogenous. Monetary tightening is now defined as a temporary reduction in γ. Liviatan shows that the modified model is saddlepath stable, provided that the initial share of money financing is not too small. He also shows that with a constant primary deficit, a temporary monetary tightening leads to an immediate but temporary increase in inflation, whereas a permanent tightening leads to an immediate and permanent increase in inflation. The first result differs from the Sargent-Wallace paradox derived earlier, where tighter money was defined as a reduction in the money growth rate. However, the result regarding conventional deficits derived above persists: if the deficit is defined as including interest payments on the public debt, the Sargent-Wallace paradox is reversed.

A further generalization can be obtained if the deficit target is written as

$$\bar{d} = \bar{g} - \iota y_t + (1 - \iota)\tau_t + \Theta \rho b_t,$$

where $0 \leq \Theta \leq 1$. The case of constant primary deficit thus obtains for $\Theta = 0$, while the constant overall deficit case obtains for $\Theta = 1$. Assuming that the composition of deficit finance γ is again the policy parameter, Liviatan (1988b) demonstrates that a policy trade-off emerges in the choice of the optimal combination (γ, Θ). In particular, he shows that there exists a value Θ^* such that for $\Theta < \Theta^*$ an increase in the money-to-bond ratio is deflationary, while for $\Theta > \Theta^*$ an increase in γ is inflationary. At any given level of inflation there exists a trade-off between γ and Θ, which is negative when $\Theta < \Theta^*$ and positive when $\Theta > \Theta^*$.

The lack of a close correlation between fiscal deficits and inflation may be compounded by the existence of uncertainty about the type of policy instruments that policymakers are expected to use to close the budget deficit. Suppose that the government increases public spending today and finances the resulting budget deficit by issuing bonds. As argued above, this policy is not sustainable and requires future measures to close the deficit and satisfy the intertemporal government budget constraint. However, the public is not sure whether the government will opt to increase taxes or use money financing—or a combination of the two options. Kawai and Maccini (1990) have examined the effects of this type of uncertainty in a closed economy.[37] Their analysis shows that if "pure" money finance is anticipated to be used in the future, then inflation usually displays a strong, positive correlation with fiscal deficits. But if tax finance is anticipated to be used, then inflation and deficits may be positively or negatively correlated.

4.3.3 Deficits, Real Interest Rates, and Crowding Out

In countries where the financial system is relatively developed and interest rates are market determined, the reliance on domestic debt financing of government fiscal deficits may exert a large effect on real interest rates.

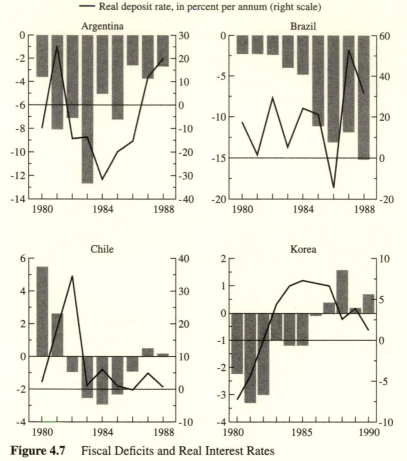

■ Government fiscal deficit, percent of GDP (left scale)

— Real deposit rate, in percent per annum (right scale)

Figure 4.7   Fiscal Deficits and Real Interest Rates

Source: Adapted from Liviatan (1984, p. 14).

In Colombia, for instance, large public deficits during the period 1983–86 seem to have been the primary factor behind the sharp increase in real interest rates during that period (Easterly and Schmidt-Hebbel, 1994). The evidence pertaining to highly indebted developing countries also suggests that in recent years a substantial proportion of fiscal deficits has been financed by domestic borrowing (Guidotti and Kumar, 1991). The rise in domestic public debt has increased the risk of default and reduced private sector confidence in the sustainability of the fiscal stance, leading to very high real interest rates and further fiscal deterioration—a potentially destabilizing mechanism (Fishlow and Morley, 1987). However, the evidence displayed in Figure 4.7 for eight middle-income developing countries is

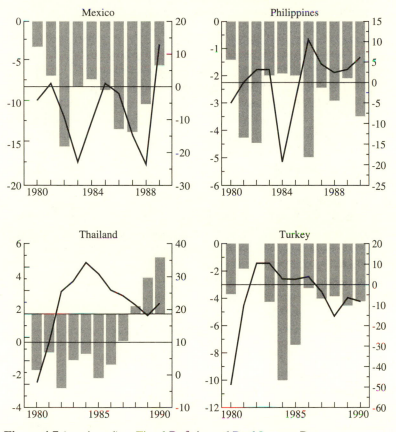

Figure 4.7 (continued)   Fiscal Deficits and Real Interest Rates
Source: International Financial Statistics.

not entirely conclusive, although in some countries the inverse relationship between real interest rates and fiscal deficits seems to hold reasonably
well—particularly in Brazil, Korea, and Thailand.

The weak association between fiscal deficits and real interest rates may
result from central bank regulations that prevent a complete adjustment of
nominal interest rates to market levels. Impediments to nominal interest rate
flexibility are, indeed, a common feature in developing countries. It may
also result from expectations about future, rather than current, fiscal policy.
We present in the following discussion a simple macroeconomic model that
allows us to capture the dynamics of real interest rates induced by policy
expectations.

4.3.3.1 EXPECTATIONS, DEFICITS, AND REAL INTEREST RATES

Consider a small open economy in which there are only three categories of agents: households, the government, and the central bank. Domestic production consists of a tradable consumption good and is assumed fixed at $\bar{y}$ during the time frame of the analysis. Purchasing power parity holds continuously and world prices are normalized to unity, implying that the domestic price level is equal to the nominal exchange rate, which is devalued at a constant, predetermined rate ϵ_t by the central bank. Households hold two categories of assets in their portfolios: domestic money and a government-indexed bond. Domestic money bears no interest, but the transactions technology is such that holding cash balances reduces liquidity costs associated with purchases of consumption goods. Capital is perfectly immobile internationally.[38] The government consumes final goods, collects income taxes, and pays interest on the outstanding stock of bonds. It finances its fiscal deficit by issuing bonds or by borrowing from the central bank. Finally, agents are endowed with perfect foresight.

The representative household maximizes discounted utility over an infinite horizon:

$$\int_0^\infty u(c_t)e^{-\alpha t}dt, \quad u(c_t) \equiv \ln c_t, \tag{41}$$

where $\alpha > 0$ denotes the rate of time preference (assumed constant) and c_t consumption. The instantaneous utility function is assumed to be logarithmic and satisfies the usual conditions.[39]

Real financial wealth of the representative household a_t is given by

$$a_t = m_t + b_t, \tag{42}$$

where m_t denotes real money balances and b_t the real stock of government-indexed bonds. The flow budget constraint gives the actual change in real wealth as the difference between ex ante savings and capital losses on real money balances:

$$\dot{a}_t = (1 - \iota)(\bar{y} + \tau_t + \rho_t b_t) - \left[1 + v\left(\frac{m_t}{c_t}\right)\right]c_t - \epsilon_t m_t, \tag{43}$$

where ρ_t denotes the real interest rate, τ_t lump-sum transfers from the government, and $0 < \iota < 1$ the proportional income tax rate. For simplicity, taxes are levied on gross income at a uniform rate. The function $v()$ characterizes transactions costs associated with purchases of consumption goods. Holding money reduces transactions costs ($v' < 0$) but entails diminishing returns ($v'' > 0$).[40]

Using (42), Equation (43) can be written as

$$\dot{a}_t = (1 - \iota)\rho_t a_t + (1 - \iota)(\bar{y} + \tau_t) - \left[1 + v\left(\frac{m_t}{c_t}\right)\right]c_t - i_t m_t, \qquad (43')$$

where $i_t = (1 - \iota)\rho_t + \epsilon_t$ denotes the net nominal interest rate.

Households treat ρ_t, ϵ_t, and τ_t as given and maximize (41) subject to (43') by choosing a sequence $\{c_t, m_t, b_t\}_{t=0}^{\infty}$. The Hamiltonian for this problem can be written as[41]

$$H = \ln c_t + \lambda_t \left\{ (1 - \iota)\rho_t a_t + (1 - \iota)(\bar{y} + \tau_t) - \left[1 + v\left(\frac{m_t}{c_t}\right)\right]c_t - i_t m_t \right\},$$

where λ_t, the costate variable associated with the flow budget constraint, can be interpreted as measuring the marginal utility of wealth. The required optimality conditions are given by

$$1/c_t = \lambda_t \left\{ \left[1 + v\left(\frac{m_t}{c_t}\right)\right] - m_t c_t^{-1} v'\left(\frac{m_t}{c_t}\right) \right\}, \qquad (44a)$$

$$-v'\left(\frac{m_t}{c_t}\right) = i_t, \qquad (44b)$$

$$\dot{\lambda}_t = \alpha\lambda_t - \frac{\partial H}{\partial a_t} = [\alpha - (1 - \iota)\rho_t]\lambda_t, \qquad (44c)$$

together with the transversality condition $\lim_{t\to\infty}(a_t e^{-\alpha t}) = 0$.

Equation (44a) indicates that consumption is inversely related to the marginal utility of wealth and the marginal transactions costs associated with purchases of goods and liquidity services. Equation (44b) states that at the optimum the gain resulting from a reduction in transactions costs derived from higher real money balances must be equal to the nominal interest rate, which represents the opportunity cost of holding money to facilitate purchases. Finally, Equation (44c) shows that the dynamics of the costate variable are determined by the difference between the rate of time preference and the after-tax real interest rate.

Equation (44b) can be written as

$$m_t = m(i_t)c_t, \quad m' = -1/v'' < 0, \qquad (45)$$

which relates the demand for money inversely to the nominal interest rate and positively to the level of transactions. Substituting Equations (44b) and (45) in (44a) yields

$$1/c_t = \lambda_t\{1 + v(i_t) + i_t m(i_t)\} = \lambda_t \overset{+}{\mathbf{p}}(i_t), \qquad (46)$$

where $\mathbf{p}()$ measures the effective price of the consumption good. This price is equal to the direct price of the good (unity) plus the transactions costs associated with purchasing the good and the opportunity cost of holding domestic money balances to facilitate purchases. For a given level of the marginal value of wealth, a rise in the nominal interest rate raises transactions costs as well as the opportunity cost of the existing stock of real money holdings, thus increasing the marginal cost of purchases. The effective price is thus an increasing function of the opportunity cost of holding money.

The nominal money stock must satisfy

$$M_t = D_t + E_t R_t, \tag{47}$$

where D_t measures the stock of domestic credit—extended by the central bank to the government—and R_t the foreign-currency value of net foreign assets held by the central bank. Changes in the real credit stock d_t are given by

$$\dot{d}_t = (\mu_t - \epsilon_t)d_t, \tag{48}$$

where μ_t denotes the rate of nominal credit growth. Assuming for simplicity that net foreign assets and loans to the government do not bear interest, net profits of the central banks consist only of capital gains on reserves $\dot{E}_t R_t$, which are transferred to the government. In real terms, the government budget constraint is thus given by

$$\dot{d}_t + \dot{b}_t = \bar{g} - \iota\bar{y} + (1 - \iota)(\tau_t + \rho_t b_t) - \epsilon_t m_t, \tag{49}$$

where $\bar{g}$ denotes noninterest public spending, assumed constant.

Combining Equations (43'), (47), (48), and (49) gives the overall budget constraint of the economy, which determines the evolution of the balance of payments:

$$\dot{R}_t = \bar{y} - \bar{g} - \left[1 + v\left(\frac{m_t}{c_t}\right)\right]c_t. \tag{50}$$

From Equation (46) we have

$$c_t = c(\bar{\lambda}_t, \bar{i}_t). \tag{51}$$

Using Equations (45) and (51), the equilibrium condition of the money market can be written as

$$m_t = m[i_t]c(\lambda_t, i_t),$$

which can be solved for the equilibrium real interest rate:

$$\rho_t = [i(\bar{\lambda}_t, \bar{m}_t) - \epsilon_t]/(1 - \iota). \tag{52}$$

Equation (52) indicates that an increase in the marginal value of wealth reduces consumption and requires a fall in the real interest rate to maintain equilibrium of the money market. A rise in the real money stock, resulting from either an expansion of domestic credit or an accumulation of net foreign assets, also lowers the real interest rate. Finally, an increase in the devaluation rate requires a compensating reduction in the real interest rate.

Substituting Equation (52) in (51) yields

$$c_t = c(\bar{\lambda}_t, \overset{+}{m}_t). \tag{51'}$$

An increase in the real money stock raises aggregate consumption since it reduces real and nominal interest rates, thus stimulating private expenditure. An increase in the marginal value of wealth affects consumption both directly and indirectly. For a given level of the real interest rate, it lowers private spending directly. As a result, however, the real interest rate must fall to maintain equilibrium in the money market, thus lowering the opportunity cost (or the effective price) of consumption and stimulating spending. The net effect of an increase in the marginal value of wealth on private consumption is assumed in Equation (51') to be negative.

Suppose that the central bank decides to expand nominal credit so as to compensate the government for the loss in the real value of the outstanding credit stock due to inflation ($\mu_t = \epsilon_t$). As a result, $\dot{d}_t = 0$. To ensure long-run solvency and eliminate Ponzi games, let us further assume that the government forgoes the issuance of bonds to finance its fiscal deficit ($\dot{b}_t = 0$) and instead adjusts the level of net transfers to households to balance the budget. Equation (49) therefore becomes

$$\tau_t = (1 - \iota)^{-1}(\iota\bar{y} - \bar{g} + \epsilon_t R_t), \tag{49'}$$

where for simplicity the constant real stocks of domestic credit and bonds are normalized to zero. Seignorage revenue is thus equal to $\epsilon_t R_t$.

Define gross consumption, that is, expenditure inclusive of transactions costs, as $\mathbf{c}() = [1 + v()]c()$, with $\mathbf{c}_\lambda < 0$ and $\mathbf{c}_m > 0$.[42] Substituting this expression together with Equations (51') and (52) in (44c) and (50) yields a differential equation system in λ_t and R_t. Alternatively, the system can be expressed in terms of ρ_t and R_t.[43] Using a linear approximation in the neighborhood of the steady state yields

$$\begin{bmatrix} \dot{\rho}_t \\ \dot{R}_t \end{bmatrix} = \begin{bmatrix} h_\rho^{-1}[h_R\mathbf{c}_\rho - h(\tilde{\rho}, \tilde{R})(1 - \iota)] & h_\rho^{-1}h_R\mathbf{c}_m \\ -\mathbf{c}_\rho & -\mathbf{c}_m \end{bmatrix} \begin{bmatrix} \rho_t - \tilde{\rho} \\ R_t - \tilde{R} \end{bmatrix} \tag{53}$$

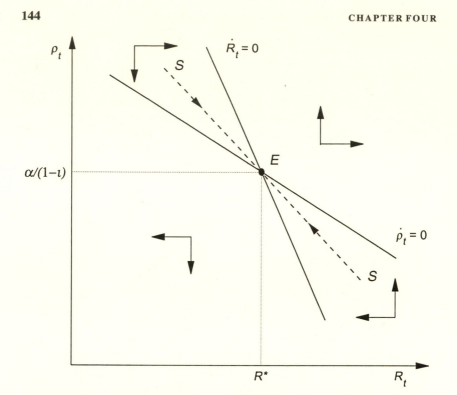

Figure 4.8   Steady-State Equilibrium with Zero Capital Mobility

where $\tilde{\rho}$ and $\tilde{R}$ denote steady-state values. Given the solution of this system, the behavior of consumption, the marginal value of wealth and the path of real transfers over time can be calculated. We assume in what follows that the condition for the system (53) to be saddlepath stable holds, that is, that the determinant of the coefficient matrix is negative. As shown in Figure 4.8, this condition requires that the slope of the $[\dot{R}_t = 0]$ locus be steeper than the slope of the $[\dot{\rho}_t = 0]$ locus. The saddlepath SS has a negative slope, and the steady-state equilibrium obtains at point E. As indicated by Equation (44c), the real after-tax interest rate must be equal to the rate of time preference at point E.

Suppose that the economy is initially in a steady-state equilibrium, and consider a fiscal policy shock brought about by a permanent, unanticipated increase in government spending. The increase in public expenditure generates on impact an excess demand for goods, which—domestic production being constant—requires a concomitant fall in private consumption. For this to occur, the marginal utility of wealth must rise. As a result of lower private expenditure, the real interest rate must also fall to maintain equilibrium in the money market. Over time, the reduction in the effective

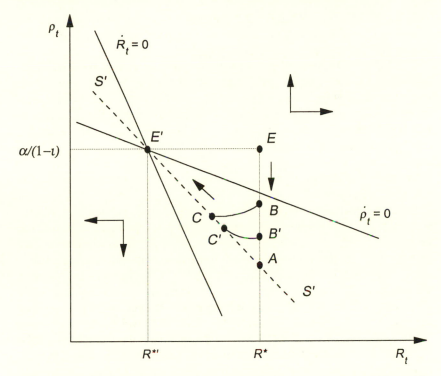

Figure 4.9 Permanent and Temporary Increases in Government Spending with Zero Capital Mobility

price of consumption brought about by the initial fall in interest rates raises consumption, which in turn leads to a gradual increase in the real interest rate, until it returns to its initial steady-state value. Foreign reserves fall throughout the transition period. The adjustment process is shown in Figure 4.9. The increase in public expenditure shifts both curves $[\dot{\rho}_t = 0]$ and $[\dot{R}_t = 0]$ to the left. The real interest rate jumps downward from point E to point A located on the new saddlepath $S'S'$, and begins rising along $S'S'$ toward the new steady state, point E'.

Consider now the case where the increase in government spending is announced at $t = 0$ to occur at period T in the future. Qualitatively, the long-run effects are similar to those described above. In the short run, however, the dynamics of the real interest rate will depend on the horizon T. If the horizon is very distant in the future, the real interest rate will jump downward to a point such as B, and will continue to fall along the divergent path BC during the interval $(0, T)$. The economy will reach the new saddlepath $S'S'$ (at point C) exactly at the moment the increase in public expenditure is implemented. By contrast, if the horizon is short, the real interest rate will begin rising immediately after the initial downward drop to point B', along the divergent path $B'C'$. The new saddlepath will be reached exactly at period T, as before.

The thrust of the preceding analysis is that real interest rates will tend to fluctuate in reaction not only to actual fiscal policy shocks, but also to expected changes in the fiscal stance. For instance, to the extent that agents correctly anticipate an increase in, say, public spending, the real interest rate will begin adjusting immediately, with little effect occurring when the policy measure is effectively implemented. The correlation between fiscal deficits and real interest rates can therefore be weak in the short run. This expectational effect provides an important element for understanding the data shown in Figure 4.7.

Expectations may be related not only to perceived changes in policy instruments *per se*, but also and more generally to the financing mix that the government may choose in the future. For instance, the government may initially raise the level of public expenditure and finance the ensuing deficit by issuing bonds during an interval of time $(0, T)$. At the same time, it may announce its intention to either reduce net transfers to households or scale down expenditure on final goods to balance the budget, in such a way that the real stock of bonds is maintained constant at a level b_T^+ beyond period T. A formal analysis of the effect of an alternative policy sequence on the behavior of real interest rates is provided by Kawai and Maccini (1990) in a model where inflation is endogenously determined. In their framework, the government runs a fiscal deficit (brought about by a tax cut or an increase in government spending) using bond finance for a transitory period, and closes it at a given date in the future by either raising taxes or using money finance.[44] When agents anticipate the latter option to be used, the expected inflation rate will rise and translate into an immediate increase in nominal interest rates. This induces asset holders to reduce their money balances and shift into bonds, thereby reducing the real interest rate. Thus, although current deficits and nominal interest rates are positively correlated, there is an inverse relation between current public deficits and real interest rates. Depending on the state of policy expectations, larger fiscal deficits may paradoxically lower real interest rates. Furthermore, to the extent that uncertainty about the financing option that the government will use in the future to close the fiscal gap varies over time, the correlation between current deficits and interest rates can be subject to large fluctuations.

4.3.3.2 DEFICITS, INVESTMENT, AND CROWDING OUT

In countries where interest rates are relatively flexible, large public deficits financed by borrowing from domestic credit markets will exert upward pressure on real interest rates and thus reduce private investment and output. In financially repressed economies where the structure of interest rates is determined by government fiat, excessive domestic borrowing may also lead to crowding out of private sector expenditure, by entailing a direct reduction of the amount of credit allocated by the banking system (see Chapter 3). In addition, in the presence of an informal credit market, tighter restrictions on the availability of official loans may lead to a higher informal interest rate, which may in turn lead to an increase in prices if financial costs have a large effect on pricing decisions.[45] Large fiscal deficits may thus have, in addition to an inflationary impact, a negative output effect. The adverse effect of large fiscal deficits may, however, be mitigated if they reflect predominantly an increase in public investment and if, as discussed in Chapter 3, private and public investment are complementary rather than substitutes. Thus, in general, whether fiscal deficits have a negative effect on private investment, output, and growth depends to a large extent on the sources of the deficit and the composition of government expenditure.

4.3.4 Deficits, the Current Account, and the Real Exchange Rate

The relation between fiscal deficits and the current account can be understood by looking at the financing identity derived in Equation (23) and assuming for a moment that net private saving is given. In such conditions, if the opportunity to borrow internally is limited, a close correlation may exist between fiscal deficits and current account deficits.[46] The implication is that a reduction in the availability of external financing—as happened in the aftermath of the debt crisis for a large number of developing countries—requires either fiscal adjustment or an increase in inflation and seignorage revenue (see Chapter 13).[47]

Several analytical models have attempted to link fiscal deficits, external deficits, and the real exchange rate. Carlos Rodríguez (1991), for instance, develops an analytical framework that captures several mechanisms through which fiscal policies affect private spending and the accumulation of foreign assets. The external deficit determines the real exchange rate that is consistent with the clearing of the market for nontraded goods. An important implication of such models is that the effect of deficits—or, more generally, fiscal policy—on the current account and the real exchange rate depends not only on the level but also on the composition of public expenditure (see Montiel, 1986; Khan and Lizondo, 1987).[48]

An alternative way to view the link between fiscal deficits and the current account is through expectations about future policy, as emphasized in the previous subsections on real interest rates and the tight money paradox. Suppose the government runs a bond-financed fiscal deficit for a limited period of time. The dynamics of the economy during the transition period depend on whether the public expects the government to switch in the future to a tax finance regime or to a money finance regime (Kawai and Maccini, 1991). If tax finance is expected to be used to close the deficits in the future, then current fiscal deficits will be associated with a current account deficit. On the contrary, if money finance—or seignorage—is primarily anticipated to be used, then fiscal deficits may be associated with current account surpluses. "Twin deficits" therefore arise only when private agents anticipate that the government will raise taxes in the future to eliminate current fiscal deficits.

The available empirical evidence seems to suggest the existence of a positive relation between large fiscal deficits and large external imbalances (Easterly and Schmidt-Hebbel, 1994). In a recent study, Khan and Kumar (1994) have provided an econometric analysis of the role of public deficits, together with other domestic and external variables, in the determination of the current account for non-oil developing countries. The study combines annual data for forty-two countries and covers the period of the 1970s and 1980s. For the group of countries considered as a whole, Khan and Kumar show that fiscal deficits have a highly significant effect on the behavior of the current account. When regional groupings are considered, the strongest effect is obtained for Africa and the Middle East, while no significant effect seems to exist for Latin America.[49] When countries are disaggregated according to the composition of their exports, the effect of public fiscal imbalances on the current account deficit appears to be largest for those countries with the most diversified export base. Thus, the empirical evidence seems to suggest that fiscal deficits are often associated with a deterioration in the current account of the balance of payments.

The purpose of this chapter has been to examine the macroeconomic effects of government fiscal deficits. We first provided a description of alternative concepts of fiscal deficits. We noted that the definition of the public sector and the type of operations included in the measurement of fiscal deficits have important implications for the design, implementation, and monitoring of macroeconomic reform programs. We have also taken the view that a central bank's quasi-fiscal revenue and expenditure activities, in contrast to its purely monetary operations, should be incorporated in the government's accounts—and, consequently, in measures of the government's fiscal deficit—not only when they affect the central bank's profit-and-loss account, but also when such activities (related, for instance, to exchange rate or loan guarantees) fall outside the profit-and-loss account.

The public finance approach to the determination of inflation emphasizes the revenue collection aspects of money creation, particularly in countries where the tax system is deemed inefficient. The optimal inflation tax rate, in the simplest case, was shown to be inversely related to the inflation elasticity of real money balances. However, operating at that level of inflation may be neither possible nor desirable. In developing countries where the share of revenue generated by taxes collected with progressive rates and withheld at the source is small, and where taxes levied at specific rates are important, inflation can substantially reduce the real value of tax revenue. Whether or not inflation results from the government's optimal choice regarding the combination of taxes remains a source of controversy at the empirical level. On balance, however, analysis of recent hyperinflation cases suggests that these episodes often reflect a desperate attempt to continue spending rather than a rational decision about the optimal combination of taxes.

We then examined the sustainability of fiscal deficits and the consistency requirements that must be imposed on alternative financing options in the context of a macroeconomic adjustment program. The role of foreign borrowing in financing public sector deficits was highlighted through the government budget constraint.[50] Excessive reliance on foreign borrowing for financing large public deficits may lead to a debt crisis, as occurred in the early 1980s (see Chapter 13). Ensuring the sustainability of fiscal imbalances necessitates fixing the deficit at a level that does not require more financing than is compatible with sustainable external and internal borrowing and with existing targets for inflation and output growth. Government solvency obtains when the present value of the government's present and future net liabilities is zero. In practice, however, evaluating whether the solvency constraint is satisfied or not is a task fraught with difficulties.

Finally, we discussed the effects of fiscal deficits on a variety of macroeconomic variables. There is little theoretical and empirical support for the Ricardian equivalence proposition in developing countries. Large public sector imbalances may lead to high domestic real interest rates or to a reduction in bank credit to the private sector (a common occurrence in financially repressed economies), thus crowding out private investment. It may even be inflationary, if the informal loan market interest rate rises to eliminate excess demand for loans, and if financial costs affect pricing decisions. The relationship between fiscal deficits, real interest rates, inflation, and the current account, although discernible in the medium and the long run—particularly in high-inflation countries—can appear relatively weak in the short run. A particularly important reason may be the changing state of expectations about future government financing policies. There appears to be a strong positive correlation in the medium term between fiscal deficits and inflation as well as fiscal and current account imbalances.

The broad message of this chapter is that adequate fiscal policy is crucial to the achievement of macroeconomic stability. Excessive fiscal deficits may lead to inflation, exchange-rate crises and balance-of-payments difficulties, real exchange-rate appreciation, external debt crises, and high real interest rates. Although fiscal policy must confront a number of objectives (such as economic efficiency and equity) in addition to macroeconomic stabilization, tax reform has become a short-term objective rather than a long-term one, because it is now perceived as essential for a stable macroeconomic environment. Chapters 9 and 10 will further examine the link between fiscal deficits, money growth, and inflation, and the role of fiscal adjustment in enhancing the credibility of disinflation programs.

Five

Financial Markets, Capital Mobility, and Monetary Policy

A KEY economic feature that differentiates developed and developing countries is the structure of their financial systems.[1] The menu of assets available to private savers in developing countries from the formal financial system is often limited to cash, demand deposits, time deposits, and sometimes government securities acquired in a primary market. In addition to being limited in scope, the financial system is often also limited in size and geographic distribution. Many private individuals thus have limited access to commercial banks, which are by far the dominant organized financial institutions—often operating under oligopolistic market structures and a high degree of concentration. Other specialized institutions exist, but they typically conduct a very small portion of total financial intermediation in the economy. Secondary securities and equities markets are either nonexistent or very limited in scope, so that bank credit and internally generated funds provide the bulk of financing for private firms.[2] Commercial banks often operate under a large array of government-imposed restrictions. These include binding legal ceilings on lending rates, high reserve ratios and liquidity requirements,[3] and restrictions on their portfolio composition designed to direct resources toward favored sectors. In addition to these legal restrictions on banks, domestic agents are often enjoined from lending or borrowing abroad, and the central bank does not make foreign exchange available for that purpose. Restrictions on the degree of capital mobility affect the links between prices of domestic and foreign assets. More generally, informal modes of financial intermediation tend to arise in response to government regulations. As emphasized in Chapter 1, the paucity of assets, the weak degree of institutional diversification, the existence of extensive government interventions, and the emergence of an informal financial sector make the nature of financial markets and their macroeconomic role potentially very different in developing nations.

This chapter examines the nature and implications of differences in the financial structure between developed and developing countries. The first part defines the concept of financial repression and reviews some of its macroeconomic implications. We then present a public-finance view of the trade-offs between conventional taxes, the degree of financial repression, capital controls, and the inflation tax as alternative financing options for budget deficits. The third part examines the link between domestic and external financial markets in developing countries, reviewing the existing evidence on the degree to which these countries are integrated with world capital markets. The fourth section discusses alternative models of informal credit markets and parallel foreign exchange markets. The last part of the chapter examines the transmission mechanism of monetary policy instruments in a context where both types of informal markets coexist, as a result of financial repression and capital controls.

5.1 Financial Repression: Macroeconomic Effects

The term "financial repression" is due to analysts who take their lead from McKinnon (1973) and Shaw (1973). These authors presented the first systematic attempts at taking into account some of the specific characteristics of financial markets in developing countries. According to McKinnon (1973), the financial system in most developing countries is "repressed" (kept small) by a series of government interventions that have the effect of keeping very low (and often at negative levels) interest rates that domestic banks can offer to savers. To a large extent, the motivation for this set of interventions is a fiscal one; the government wants to actively promote development but lacks the direct fiscal means to do so, because of either a lack of political will or administrative constraints. It uses the financial system to fund development spending in two ways. First, by imposing large reserve and liquidity requirements on banks, it creates a captive demand for its own non-interest-bearing and interest-bearing instruments, respectively. Thus, it can finance its own high-priority spending by issuing debt. Second, by keeping interest rates low through the imposition of ceilings on lending rates, it creates an excess demand for credit. It then requires the banking system to set aside a fixed fraction of the credit available to priority sectors. This system has implications both for economic efficiency and for the distribution of income.

The combination of low rates of return on assets and high reserve requirements implies that even a competitive banking system will be forced to offer low interest rates on its liabilities. In many developing countries the combination of low nominal deposit interest rates and moderate to high inflation has often resulted in negative rates of return on domestic financial assets, with an adverse effect on saving and the financial intermediation process. If the rate of return available in the domestic formal financial system represents the relevant intertemporal relative price in the economy, whether saving falls or rises will depend on the familiar trade-off between income and substitution effects in consumption. Regardless of the direction of the effect on saving, however, interest rate ceilings introduce a wedge between the social and private rates of return on asset accumulation, thereby distorting intertemporal choices in the economy. Moreover, the portfolio effects of such ceilings are conducive to financial disintermediation, as savers are induced to switch from the acquisition of claims on the banking system to accumulation of real assets, assets traded in informal markets, and foreign assets. A standard response on the part of policymakers in developing nations has been to declare illegal the holding of both foreign assets and assets in the informal sector. As discussed in Chapter 2, these restrictions have met with limited success. Informal financial markets thrive in many developing countries, and capital controls have proven rather porous.[4] Even so, the demand for real assets has been artificially stimulated, and such assets as gold and real estate play important roles in the financial decisions of households in many such countries.

The induced incentive to hold real assets, however, does not imply the achievement of high levels of investment. The reason is that while the notional demand for investment may be high, many prospective investors will be unable to secure financing. Their own prospective savings may be inadequate to finance large projects; the formal financial system may not have the resources available, due to government absorption of a large part of the small pool of savings intermediated through commercial banks and other financial institutions; and the high potential costs of doing business in informal markets, as well as the costs of evading capital controls, may render financing through these channels uneconomical. Finally, in the absence of rationing through the price system, there is no assurance that those investment projects that *are* financed through the formal financial system will necessarily yield higher returns than those that are not.

The consequences of financial repression for the distribution of income arise because this system transfers resources from actual and potential savers, as well as from excluded borrowers, to favored borrowers who are able to acquire resources at the contracted interest rates. The most important of the latter, of course, is the public sector itself. In addition, however, enterprises in priority sectors and well-connected individuals will tend to benefit from privileged access.[5] Benefits also accrue to the beneficiaries of the additional public spending made possible by this source of financing for the public sector, as well as to potential taxpayers who would be affected by the replacement of the "financial repression tax" with more conventional taxes.

5.2 Financial Repression, the Inflation Tax, and Capital Controls

In the previous section we discussed the nature of financial repression and its association with capital controls, but we did not provide a general rationale for their existence. Why do countries choose to repress their financial systems and impose impediments to capital mobility, in view of the inefficiencies that the use of such policy instruments typically entail? We adopt the view here that accounting for the fiscal aspects of such measures is essential to understanding governments' motivations in adopting them. Specifically, we view the determination of the degree of financial repression and the intensity of capital controls as a fiscal issue involving a choice between alternative taxation instruments subject to appropriate constraints. We begin by considering the optimal choice between financial repression and the inflation tax in a model where the policymaker's objective is to maximize seignorage, given the portfolio structure of private agents. We then consider a more general framework in which conventional taxes and capital controls are used as additional taxation instruments by the government.

5.2.1 Financial Repression and Inflationary Finance

The tradeoff between the inflation tax (discussed in Chapter 4) and the degree of financial repression can be illustrated in a simple framework adapted from Brock (1989).[6] Consider a closed economy in which private agents hold cash balances and bank deposits, with the former asset bearing a zero rate of interest. Output is taken as given and is normalized at zero for simplicity. Banks are subject to a fractional reserve requirement on deposits. Asset demand functions for cash m_t and bank deposits d_t can be written in general form as[7]

$$m_t = m[\bar{i}_t, i_t \overset{+}{-} i_d(t)], \tag{1a}$$

$$d_t = d[\overset{+}{i}_t, i_t \overset{-}{-} i_d(t)], \tag{1b}$$

where i_t denotes the nominal lending rate and $i_d(t)$ the deposit rate. If banks face no operating costs, the zero-profit condition yields

$$i_t = i_d(t)/(1 - \mu), \qquad 0 < \mu < 1, \tag{2}$$

where μ denotes the required reserve ratio. For simplicity, assume that the asset demand functions take the form

$$\ln m_t = \alpha_0 - \alpha i_t, \quad \ln d_t = \beta_0 - \beta[i_t - i_d(t)] = \beta_0 - \beta \mu i_t. \tag{3}$$

Assume that the real interest rate is constant and set equal to zero. Thus, $i_t = \pi_t$, where π_t denotes the (actual and expected) inflation rate. The policymaker's objective is to maximize inflation tax revenues, which are given by

$$S_t = \pi_t(m_t + \mu d_t), \tag{4}$$

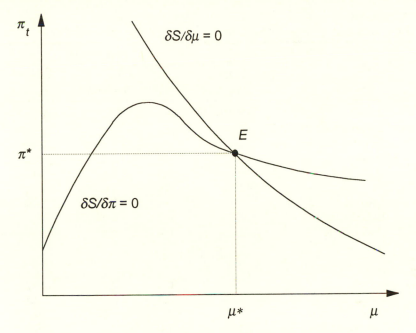

Figure 5.1   Seignorage, Reserve Ratio, and the Inflation Tax

with respect to the inflation rate and the reserve ratio μ.[8] Solving this maximization problem yields

$$\partial S_t/\partial \mu = 0 \Rightarrow \mu \pi_t = 1/\beta, \tag{5a}$$

$$\partial S_t/\partial \pi_t = 0 \Rightarrow \pi_t = \frac{1}{\alpha} + \frac{\beta \mu d_t}{\alpha m_t}\left(\frac{1}{\beta} - \pi_t \mu\right). \tag{5b}$$

Equation (5b) indicates that when the reserve ratio is zero, the revenue-maximizing inflation rate is equal to $1/\alpha$, as derived in Chapter 4. If both instruments are used, however, the optimal inflation rate may be either higher or lower than $1/\alpha$. Figure 5.1 shows graphically the determination of the optimal values of both policy instruments, which are obtained at the intersection of the two curves defined by Equations (5a) and (5b). Since, in general, $\mu^* > 0$, there exists an optimal degree of financial repression, which is traded off (within a given range) with the optimal inflation tax in order to raise the demand for money—the inflation tax base.

In practice, reserve requirements that are unremunerated or remunerated at a fixed rate may represent a large share of the revenue from seignorage. Table 5.1 presents data on effective reserve requirements on bank deposits in developed and developing countries, as well as a decomposition

TABLE 5.1
Effective Reserve Ratio and Seignorage (percentage averages over 1980–91)

Country	Effective Reserve Ratio on Bank Deposits	Seignorage		
		Total	Currency Component	Reserve Component
Industrial Countries				
Belgium	0.6	0.1	0.1	—
Canada	2.9	0.2	0.2	—
France	2.5	0.4	0.2	0.2
Germany	6.0	0.5	0.4	0.1
Italy	12.7	1.6	0.6	1.0
Japan	1.9	0.6	0.5	0.1
United Kingdom	1.5	0.2	0.2	—
United States	2.2	0.4	0.3	0.1
Developing Countries				
Africa				
Burundi	7.4	0.6	0.4	0.2
Cameroon	3.6	0.4	0.3	0.1
Gabon	3.2	0.3	0.2	0.1
Kenya	7.7	1.0	0.7	0.3
Lesotho	25.4	2.5	0.6	1.9
Morocco	3.3	1.9	1.4	0.5
Nigeria	11.7	1.7	1.1	0.6
Somalia	18.2	5.0	3.3	1.7
Asia				
India	9.5	2.0	1.2	0.8
Indonesia	7.6	0.9	0.6	0.3
Malaysia	5.8	1.4	0.8	0.6
Pakistan	6.0	2.3	1.8	0.5
Philippines	10.0	1.4	0.8	0.6
Singapore	6.2	1.6	0.9	0.7
Sri Lanka	10.3	1.6	0.9	0.7
Thailand	3.3	1.0	0.7	0.3
Latin America				
Bolivia	13.1	5.0	3.3	1.7
Brazil	19.7	—	—	—
Chile	84.5	10.7	0.7	10.0
Colombia	23.1	2.2	0.8	1.4
Jamaica	18.0	3.2	1.0	2.2
Mexico	23.8	3.8	1.4	2.4
Peru	27.8	6.8	2.7	4.1
Venezuela	17.4	1.9	0.5	1.4

Source: Calculations based on *International Financial Statistics.*

of revenue from seignorage.[9] The table indicates first that reserve requirements on bank deposits are typically much higher in developing countries than in industrial countries, and that among the countries of the former group the highest ratios are observed in Latin America. Second, it shows that seignorage levied on required reserves represents a large component of total seignorage revenue in many developing countries, not only in Latin America (Chile, Colombia, Jamaica, and Venezuela) but also in Africa (Lesotho and Somalia).

Another source of revenue from financial repression is the implicit subsidy from which the government benefits by obtaining access to bank financing at below-market interest rates, and the implicit tax—collected through the banking system—on private sector bank deposits that are remunerated at below-market interest rates. This source of the financial repression tax may be complementary to the inflation tax rather than substitutable, as discussed in the case of reserve requirements. This may occur, in particular, if the menu of financial assets available to portfolio holders is limited, and if real interest rates are sufficiently negative to increase the demand for real money balances, that is, the inflation tax base (Giovannini and de Melo, 1993).

5.2.2 A General Public-Finance Approach

Financial repression of the domestic financial system in developing countries is almost always accompanied by controls on international capital movements, in order to prevent restrictions on domestic financial intermediaries from being bypassed by recourse to foreign intermediaries. To the extent that the imposition of restrictions on capital mobility forces agents to hold more domestic-currency balances than they would prefer to hold (thus raising the base of the inflation tax), capital controls may be viewed as imposing a tax on asset holders, whose costs and benefits must be traded off with other taxes, explicit and implicit. A unifying framework for understanding the use of financial repression, capital controls, and the inflation tax in developing countries would thus require a model in which policymakers are faced with some type of constraints on the use of regular taxes. Although, to our knowledge, such a comprehensive framework has not yet been developed, here we sketch its basic elements and highlight its most probable implications.

The point of departure would be a portfolio structure similar to that described above, with the addition of imperfectly substitutable foreign bonds. In such a setting, capital controls could be modeled as an explicit tax on foreign interest income or as a tax on purchases of foreign assets.[10] The key aspect of the taxation system that needs to be taken into account is the existence of collection and enforcement costs, which, as for instance in Aizenman (1987) and Végh (1989b), can be assumed to be an increasing and convex function of the level of revenue. By contrast, other forms of taxation at the disposal of the government—financial repression and the inflation tax, which are implicit taxes, and capital controls—have low collection costs. The government's problem would then consist of maximizing either inflation tax revenue, an overall revenue target—in order to finance, say, a "minimum" level of public expenditure—or, as in the normative models of Aizenman (1987) and Végh (1989b), the representative consumer's indirect utility subject to its budget constraint. A likely outcome, suggested by results obtained in the existing literature dealing with some aspects of the general framework described above, may be that capital controls, financial repression, and the inflation tax must be used concurrently with regular taxes when collection or enforcement costs on the latter source of revenue are sufficiently large. An increase in collection costs may also reduce the use of regular taxes relative to other tax instruments, while an increase in the deficit target (resulting from, say, a rise in government spending) may lead to a more intensive use of all taxation instruments. The first prediction would accord well with the intuitive idea that in an optimal tax structure, the highest tax rates are imposed on activities that carry the lowest collection costs.

The unified public-finance framework highlighted in the foregoing discussion helps emphasize the fiscal considerations underlying the simultaneous existence of conventional taxes, financial repression, capital controls, and the inflation tax. Of course, reserve requirements are often changed as a result of purely monetary considerations (to reduce, for instance, excess liquidity in the economy), while capital controls are often imposed to prevent speculative attacks and the eventual collapse of a fixed exchange rate (see Chapter 6). Nevertheless, in a long-run context the fiscal view may be the most sensible approach to understanding the setting of these policy instruments in developing countries. One of the important implications of this approach is that the decision to impose a high degree of financial repression, far from being an aberration, may be the outcome of an optimally determined taxation structure. In such conditions, successful financial liberalization requires the simultaneous implementation of appropriate fiscal reforms—an issue to which we will return in Chapter 14.

Giovannini and de Melo (1993), using data on twenty-four developing countries over the period 1972–87, have provided evidence on the revenue generated by controls on capital flows and financial repression of the domestic financial system. Capital controls coupled with restrictions on domestic interest rates yield a positive differential between domestic and world interest rates, thus providing an implicit subsidy for the government on domestic debt financing. Specifically, the authors estimate government revenue from financial repression and capital controls as the spread between the foreign and the domestic cost of funds (which can be viewed as measuring the capital controls/financial repression tax rate), times the domestic stock of central government debt.[11] Their results suggest that the capital controls/financial repression tax rate varies considerably across developing countries, from about 4 percent in Thailand and 6 percent in Korea, to 25 percent in Costa Rica, 45 percent in Mexico, and 55 percent in Turkey. Government revenue from this source also differs widely across countries, as a result of substantial differences in the size of the domestic government debt. On average, revenue from repression of the financial system and capital controls amounts to 2 percent of GDP and 9 percent of government revenue in developing countries.[12]

5.3 Capital Mobility: Empirical Evidence

Financial repression tends to induce disintermediation, which can take the form of the emergence of a domestic informal credit market or financial intermediation through external financial markets. As suggested in the previous section, the factors that induce governments to adopt a policy of financial repression will lead them to seek to avoid the latter through the imposition of capital controls, and indeed such controls have long been prevalent in the developing world. However, their effectiveness has often been questioned. At one extreme, if such controls are effective and the economy is completely closed, external financial intermediation is ruled out. Taking a simple portfolio approach, in this case the marginal cost of funds in the economy becomes the interest rate in the informal credit market, which, since it corresponds to a nontraded asset, is endogenously determined within the domestic economy. Thus, the marginal cost of funds in the economy can be influenced by domestic monetary, fiscal, and other shocks. At the other extreme, if controls are completely ineffective and perfect capital mobility prevails (meaning that nonmonetary domestic financial assets are perfect substitutes for their foreign counterparts and that portfolio adjustment is instantaneous, possibly despite the presence of formal capital controls), the interest rate in the informal credit market must be equal to the uncovered-parity foreign rate, that is, the exogenous foreign interest rate plus the expected rate of depreciation of the domestic currency. The marginal cost of funds in the economy would then be given by the uncovered parity rate and would be unaffected by domestic phenomena—except to the extent that these affect the expected rate of depreciation of the domestic currency.

Which of these situations is relevant in the developing world? The degree of financial openness is bound to differ both across countries and over time, of course, but surprisingly little empirical work has been undertaken to explore this issue for individual cases. Developing countries tend to be treated, in both policy and analytical work, as either completely closed to capital flows (except perhaps for non-market-based lending from official sources or bank lending to their public sectors) or as completely integrated with world financial markets, with domestic interest rates determined by uncovered interest parity. The justification for the former view is that the vast majority of these countries maintain formal legal restrictions on capital movements. According to the International Monetary Fund's 1993 *Annual Report on Exchange Arrangements and Exchange Restrictions*, out of 157 member developing countries, 130 were classified as maintaining formal restrictions on payments for capital transactions. Yet, in spite of such controls, evidence of various types suggests that many developing countries are far from being financially closed. This section reviews the available evidence on this issue, which takes the form of indications of the size of gross capital flows, tests of interest parity conditions, tests of the effectiveness of sterilization, and some limited evidence on saving-investment correlations.

5.3.1 The Magnitude of Gross Flows

To the extent that the size of capital flows is indicative of the degree of financial integration, evidence on past episodes of substantial capital movements in and out of developing countries can be brought to bear on the issue. In Latin America, for instance, the recent past has witnessed several episodes in which capital flows in both directions have been large enough to become a source of major policy concern. These include the periods of substantial external debt accumulation during 1974–82, the large short-term capital inflows associated with the Southern Cone stabilization programs in 1978–82, the gross private capital outflows associated with the "capital flight" phenomenon that afflicted several Latin American countries during the first half of the 1980s, and, more recently, a widespread resurgence of capital inflows, primarily to the private sector (see Calvo et al., 1993). Each of these events has generated a substantial literature documenting the extent to which these economies have been financially linked to the world capital market.

One way to summarize the implications of the capital flow episodes is to measure, at a point in time, the gross stocks of financial claims between developing countries and external financial markets to which they have given rise. For the group of fifteen heavily indebted developing countries, the stock of gross external debt as of 1988 amounted to about 75 percent of GDP (see Montiel, 1992). For the same year Rojas-Suárez (1990) estimated that the total external claims of a very similar group of developing countries, overwhelmingly acquired in the form of private capital flight, amounted to about two-thirds of their external debt, or about half of GDP. Rojas-Suárez found a high correlation between the stock of flight capital and a measure of default risk, corroborating the findings of others—Cuddington (1986) and Dooley (1988), for instance, who have linked private capital outflows from developing nations to portfolio considerations. Thus the gross-flow evidence, which unfortunately is available only for the major indebted developing countries, indicates that these countries have exhibited a substantial amount of at least de facto financial openness.

5.3.2 Tests of Interest Parity Conditions

Tests of interest parity conditions are the most common approach to the measurement of financial integration for industrial countries. In brief, if i_t denotes the domestic interest rate on an asset of a given type, i_t^* the interest rate on the corresponding foreign asset, and ϵ_t the expected rate of depreciation of the domestic currency, then the differential return d_t between holding the domestic and foreign assets, without hedging the exchange risk in forward markets, is given by

$$d_t = i_t - i_t^* - \epsilon_t.$$

Under perfect capital mobility, expected returns on domestic and foreign assets should be equalized, so d_t should be zero.[13] However, d_t is not directly observable, since it depends on the unobserved expectation ϵ_t. If that expectation is formed rationally, then uncovered interest parity implies that $E(d_t/\Omega_t) = 0$, where Ω_t is the information set used in forecasting ϵ_t. Thus, d_t should not be correlated with any information contained in Ω_t. Joint tests of uncovered interest parity and rational expectations thus entail testing whether d_t is correlated with variables in Ω_t. A large number of such tests have been conducted for industrial countries.

Few such tests have been conducted for developing countries, however. Lizondo (1983) conducted tests of both covered and uncovered interest parity for Mexico, using monthly data over the period 1977–80. Based on standard tests, he was able to reject the joint hypothesis of uncovered interest parity and rational expectations, using either the one-month forward rate or the one-month interest differential as the predictor of the future spot rate. However, because of the "peso problem," he did not interpret these rejections as necessarily invalidating this hypothesis for Mexico during this period.[14] In testing covered parity, Lizondo followed the methodology of Frenkel and Levich (1975), computing neutral bands around the covered parity interest rate based on estimated transactions costs and tabulating the number of observations of domestic interest rates lying outside those bands during the period. He found that percentage to be extremely high, ranging from 75 percent for one-month Treasury bills to 96 percent for three-month time deposits. Lizondo was able to account for this rejection of covered parity in terms of legal regulations consisting of prior deposit restrictions on forward transactions and taxes on foreign exchange capital gains. The upshot is that, though unexploited profit opportunities were apparently absent, domestic rates could depart substantially from their covered parity in Mexico during the period under study. More recently, however, Khor and Rojas-Suárez (1991) found that, during 1987 to 1990, yields on dollar-indexed Mexican government bonds were cointegrated with yields to maturity on Mexican public external debt traded in the secondary market. This suggests that Mexico's degree of integration with external financial markets may have increased in recent years.

Results similar to those of Lizondo for Mexico were obtained by Phylaktis (1988) for Argentina during 1971–84. Using the methodology of Dooley and Isard (1980), she was able to account for 83 percent of the quarterly variance of the differential between the three-month domestic deposit rate and its uncovered-parity counterpart (using the United States as the reference country) through the use of standard portfolio variables and step dummies for capital controls. The implication is that, while foreign financial variables influenced domestic rates in Argentina during the 1970s and early 1980s (that is, the economy was financially open), foreign and domestic assets were imperfect substitutes, and certain types of capital controls proved to be effective in increasing the differential between foreign and domestic rates of return.

In a departure from the standard methodology, Edwards and Khan (1985) postulated that the actual domestic interest rate in a developing country could be expressed as a weighted average of the external (uncovered parity) rate and the domestic interest rate that would prevail in a financially closed economy. The latter was expressed as a function of the excess money supply and the expected rate of inflation. When the determinants of the closed-economy interest rate are substituted into the weighted-average expression for the domestic interest rate, the result is a reduced-form interest "parity" condition that expresses the domestic interest rate as a function not only of the external rate, but also of domestic monetary conditions. This approach in effect uses domestic monetary variables to explain the "risk premium." Estimating a reduced form of this type makes it possible to detect any influence of these variables on the domestic interest rate. If uncovered parity holds continuously, such variables should have no explanatory power in the reduced form. By contrast, if the economy is completely closed, the uncovered-parity variable should not enter. Edwards and Khan estimated their model using quarterly data for Colombia (1968–82) and Singapore (1976–83). They found that, for Colombia, both external and domestic variables mattered, making this economy "semi-open"; for Singapore, only the foreign interest rate helped to explain the domestic interest rate, as would have been expected under strong financial integration with international capital markets.

One reason interest parity tests have not been widely applied to developing countries is that, under financial repression, published interest rates for the formal financial system do not refer to assets with market-determined rates of return. Moreover, as noted in Chapter 2, data on market-determined interest rates in informal credit markets are rarely available. In these circumstances, inferences about the extent to which market-clearing interest rates in the domestic financial system are affected by world financial conditions become difficult to draw.

Recently, Haque and Montiel (1991) adapted the methodology of Edwards and Khan to allow testing of uncovered interest parity under such circumstances. Retaining the assumption that the (unobserved) domestic market-clearing interest rate is a stable weighted average of the autarky rate and uncovered parity, they were able to estimate the relevant weights by substituting the resulting expression for the market-clearing rate into the money-demand function and estimating the resulting nonlinear function of observable variables. In this estimation, the weight corresponding to the uncovered parity emerges as the coefficient of this variable in the estimate of the money-demand function. This coefficient, which is bounded between 0 and 1, indicates the degree of financial integration, with values approaching unity being indicative of perfect financial integration. Haque and Montiel's results for fifteen developing countries during the period 1969–87 are reported in Table 5.2. In ten of the fifteen cases reported, the weight of the uncovered parity rate could not be statistically distinguished from the perfect-capital-mobility value of unity. For four countries in the sample (Brazil, Jordan, Malta, and Turkey) an intermediate degree of financial integration prevailed during this period. The financial autarky value of zero failed to be rejected in only one case (that of India). Overall, these results are consistent with a substantial degree of integration with external financial markets for the countries considered.

The Edwards-Khan and Haque-Montiel methodology was applied to Korea and Taiwan by Reisen and Yeches (1993) and to Thailand by Robinson (1991). The former used quarterly data for the decade of the 1980s and direct observations on the curb market interest rate in these countries, finding a weight of 0.594 on the uncovered parity rate in Korea and 0.533 in Taiwan during this period, both distinguishable from zero and unity. This places these countries among the intermediate group. Kalman filter estimates suggested that the degree of integration peaked for Korea during the period 1981–84, but was relatively constant for Taiwan over the decade. Robinson's findings for Thailand were similar, with a weight for the uncovered parity rate of 0.590 during 1978–90.

Tests for changes in the degree of financial integration due to domestic financial liberalization in Pacific Basin countries were also conducted by

TABLE 5.2
Estimates of the Capital Mobility Parameter
for Developing Countries

Country	Estimate
Brazil	0.723^a
Guatemala	0.708^b
India	0.158^c
Indonesia	0.865^b
Jordan	0.500^a
Kenya	0.600^b
Malaysia	0.638^b
Malta	0.411^a
Morocco	0.877^b
Philippines	0.577^b
Sri Lanka	0.638^b
Tunisia	0.833^b
Turkey	0.525^a
Uruguay	0.890^b
Zambia	1.019^b

Source: Haque and Montiel (1991).
Notes:
[a] Significantly different from both 0 and 1.
[b] Significantly different from 0 but not from 1.
[c] Significantly different from 1 but not from 0.

Faruquee (1991). Using monthly observations, he constructed time series on the differentials between money-market interest rates in Korea, Malaysia, Singapore, and Thailand and the three-month Japanese yen LIBOR rate during the period from September 1978 to December 1990. Mean differentials were large and positive for Korea and Thailand, but not for Singapore and Malaysia. In all four countries both the mean and variance of the differentials decreased in the second half of the sample period. Time series modeling of the differentials revealed a statistically significant positive constant for Korea and Thailand only; the Korean differentials exhibited a significant negative trend over the period. Mean-reverting behavior was weak in all four countries. Because the residuals from the ARMA estimates exhibited smaller variability in the second half of the period, Faruquee reestimated the time series models using an autoregressive conditional heteroscedasticity (ARCH) approach and found that the variance of shocks to the ARMA residuals declined monotonically for Singapore, but not for the remaining countries.[15] In all cases, however, the variance of shocks was smaller in 1990 than it had been in 1980, leading Faruquee to conclude that the degree of financial integration increased in these countries over the 1980s.

5.3.3 Tests of Monetary Autonomy

Under perfect capital mobility, the "offset coefficient" that relates changes in the stock of domestic assets of the central bank to changes in reserve flows normally takes a value of -1, since any expansion of the domestic assets of the central bank will give rise to an offsetting capital outflow, leaving the stock of money unchanged and implying a loss of monetary autonomy (see Kreinin and Officer, 1978). A separate strand of investigation of the capital mobility issue in developing countries tests for this loss of monetary autonomy.

Cumby and Obstfeld (1983), using a structural model of the Mexican financial sector, found that, during the decade of the 1970s, perfect capital mobility did not hold between Mexico and the United States. Slow portfolio adjustment and imperfect asset substitutability permitted Mexico to retain at least some short-run monetary autonomy during that period. Within a quarter, only 30-50 percent of a domestic credit increase was found to leak abroad via capital outflows. The estimates of the portfolio balance model obtained by Kamas (1986) for Mexico also indicate no loss of monetary control during the 1970s. Rennhack and Mondino (1988) applied the Cumby-Obstfeld model to Colombia, using quarterly data drawn from 1975 to 1985, with very similar results: the within-quarter offset coefficient amounted to about 40 percent, and monetary autonomy was at least partially retained even in the long run. The same approach yielded very different results in the case of Malaysia during 1978–81, where Bini Smaghi (1982) found a 70 percent offset to changes in the stock of domestic credit in the first month. The econometric results obtained by Kamas (1986) also suggest a high offset to monetary policy through reserve flows in Venezuela.

An implication of maintaining some scope for independent monetary policy is, of course, that policy-induced changes in domestic financial aggregates will affect macroeconomic variables other than the capital account. Thus the identification of domestic macroeconomic effects arising from monetary policy shocks under fixed exchange rates provides an indirect confirmation of the retention of at least some degree of monetary autonomy. Boschen and Newman (1989), for instance, found that real interest rates in Argentina were significantly affected by unanticipated monetary growth during the period from the mid-1970s to the early 1980s, with little evidence of a role for foreign interest rates.

A recent approach aimed at assessing the degree of monetary autonomy without relying on structural estimates of offset coefficients is based on causality tests. In the absence of monetary autonomy under fixed exchange rates (that is, under perfect financial integration), domestic financial aggregates such as money or credit should not Granger-cause movements in nominal income. Montiel (1989) and Dowla and Chowdhury (1991) have tested this hypothesis for a number of developing nations.[16] The former used

annual data for twelve countries during 1962–86 and relied on vector autore-
gressions including broad money, domestic credit, international reserves,
and nominal income. Money or credit was found to Granger-cause nominal income in Bolivia, Chile, Ghana, Indonesia, Mexico, Morocco, Peru
and Sierra Leone, but not in India, Pakistan, Turkey, or Sudan. Dowla and
Chowdhury used quarterly data for thirteen countries over sample periods
of varying length during 1957–89. They found that some domestic financial
aggregate (narrow money, broad money, or domestic credit) Granger-caused
domestic real output in Greece, Côte d'Ivoire, Jordan, Korea, Malawi, Mexico, Singapore, and Tunisia, but not in Bangladesh, India, Israel, Malaysia,
or Pakistan.

5.3.4 Saving-Investment Correlations

An influential paper by Feldstein and Horioka (1980) argued that the degree
of capital mobility among industrial countries could be tested by examining
the degree of correlation between saving and investment rates, with the reasoning that under perfect capital mobility domestic saving and investment
rates should be uncorrelated. Several investigators who have constructed
such tests—Dooley et al. (1987) and Summers (1988)—included a number
of developing countries in their cross-section samples and considered the
effect of including such countries on their results. Surprisingly, these authors concurred in finding that the inclusion of developing nations *reduced*
the strength of the saving-investment correlation in their samples. This was
unexpected, since these countries were perceived ex ante as less integrated
with world capital markets than industrial countries.

A recent study focusing specifically on developing countries is due to
Wong (1990), who looked at a cross-section sample of forty-five developing countries using annual data averaged over the period 1975–81. Wong's
results were consistent with those cited above. For his full sample, the saving ratio was found to have no statistically significant effect on the investment ratio. When five extreme observations were excluded, the regression
coefficient on the saving rate took on a value of about 0.6, statistically different from both the autarky value of unity and the perfect integration value
of zero, but still substantially below what other investigators had found for
industrial countries.

An attempt was recently made by Montiel (1994) to integrate the disparate tests of capital mobility described above into a comprehensive
overview of the empirical evidence on capital mobility in developing countries. For a large sample of countries, Montiel used gross-flow data, tests
of uncovered interest arbitrage, saving-investment correlations, and Euler
equation tests to assess the country-specific degree of financial integration.
His evidence supports the thrust of the existing literature: while the degree

of financial integration differs markedly across developing countries, financial links with the world capital markets can be documented widely for such countries.

5.3.5 Summary

To summarize, the existing evidence for developing countries suggests that few, if any, of these countries can be considered to be financially closed. Even in the case of India, where the Haque-Montiel methodology is unable to reject the null hypothesis of financial autarky, some contrary evidence exists in the form of a similar inability to reject the proposition that the major financial aggregates do not Granger-cause real output. Elsewhere the evidence of financial openness is stronger. For countries such as Argentina, Colombia, Indonesia, Korea, Mexico, Morocco, and Thailand, tests of arbitrage relationships indicate that external interest rates play an important, but not necessarily exclusive, role in affecting domestic interest rates, suggesting that, while these economies should be regarded as financially open, perfect capital mobility has not held. Other evidence of various types is consistent with this conclusion for these countries. For example, gross flows have been large (in the form of both debt and capital flight) in Argentina, Colombia, and Mexico, yet independent evidence exists suggesting that all these countries have maintained some degree of monetary autonomy. Similarly, although arbitrage tests cannot rule out perfect capital mobility in Indonesia and Morocco, domestic financial aggregates are found to Granger-cause domestic activity in both countries. Brazil, Jordan, Malta, and Turkey may also be in this group. At the other extreme, the evidence suggests that Guatemala, Malaysia, and Singapore may represent instances of perfect capital mobility. Arbitrage tests are consistent with this conclusion, and tests of monetary autonomy do not provide contrary evidence for either Guatemala or Malaysia.

When the degree of financial repression is high, informal credit markets tend to develop. Similarly, when the intensity of capital controls is high, parallel markets for foreign exchange also tend to emerge. We now turn to the implications of the existence of such markets for the conduct of monetary policy.

5.4 Models of Informal Credit and Foreign Exchange Markets

As indicated in Chapter 2, informal markets in credit and foreign exchange play an important role in many developing countries. Failure to integrate these markets in a systematic and consistent framework may therefore result in misleading analysis of the effects of macroeconomic policy decisions.

The purpose of this section is to present and discuss a variety of macroeconomic models that have attempted to account explicitly for the existence of informal financial markets. Until recently, the approach followed in the literature has been to consider separately both types of markets. We will organize the discussion here along similar lines, beginning with models that account for informal credit markets and continuing with models integrating parallel markets for foreign exchange. The next section presents a model that integrates both types of markets.

5.4.1 Models of Informal Credit Markets

The macroeconomic implications of financial dualism induced by government regulations on interest rates have been highlighted in a series of contributions by new structuralist economists, most notably van Wijnbergen (1983a, 1983b) and Taylor (1983, 1990). A key insight of these contributions is that, in the presence of informal credit markets, "orthodox" monetary policy prescriptions may lead to results that differ significantly from those anticipated.

5.4.1.1 STAGFLATIONARY EFFECTS OF MONETARY POLICY

The "new structuralist critique" of orthodox monetary policy (Taylor, 1983) is based on the view that, in developing countries with a poorly articulated financial intermediation system, credit plays a predominant role as a source of funds for firms, both for short-term working capital purposes (such as financing of stocks of raw materials, semifinished goods, intermediate imports, and advance payments to workers) and for long-term fixed capital formation. With rationing in the official credit market and thriving unorganized loan markets, the transmission channel between monetary instruments and the supply side of the economy via credit financing of working capital requirements provides a critical link for gauging the effects of stabilization policy. Financing through the informal loan market implies that the cost of credit (the informal interest rate) is a component of input costs. Mark-up pricing rules will thus lead to an immediate cost-push effect of high informal interest rates on prices. Furthermore, a high cost of credit will not only lead to an increase in prices, but will also lead to a reduction in real output as real input costs have gone up. This transmission channel, from tight credit ceilings on commercial bank credit via the informal loan market and high costs of financing working capital into the supply side of the economy, gives a stagflationary bias to restrictive monetary policies. Essentially, this link adds an adverse supply-shock aspect to policies of monetary restraint, on top of their more traditional demand-reducing effects. Restrictive monetary policies lead to expensive credit, which leads to an increase in input costs; this in turn leads to higher prices and less output than would obtain without the supply-side credit channel. This effect has become known as the Cavallo-Patman effect (Cavallo, 1981; Taylor, 1991).

If credit extended through the official and parallel markets has a short-term maturity, the stagflationary impact of a tight credit policy via the credit–working capital link will work itself quickly through the system. On the contrary, the demand-restraining impact typically works only gradually: first aggregate demand—or, rather, investment, since consumer credit is often limited in developing countries—will fall, which will reduce output and raise unemployment over time. This in turn will, after further lags, ease real wage pressure and thus inflation. The response to a one-shot tightening of monetary policy might therefore be an initial acceleration of the inflation rate, after which demand effects would take over, effecting a slowdown in the rate of inflation, as shown in the simulation results performed by van Wijnbergen (1985) with an econometric model for South Korea. Both effects have a negative impact on output.

5.4.1.2 INTEREST RATE POLICY AND OUTPUT

Another area in which the "new structuralist critique" has stirred controversy is interest rate policy. McKinnon (1973) and Shaw (1973) have been the most prominent advocates of high interest rates in developing countries—a policy that has been characterized as an essential element of "orthodox" macroeconomic thinking. The McKinnon-Shaw argument is that a rise in interest rates on savings and time deposits will increase the saving rate in developing countries and, in standard neoclassical fashion, raise the rate of economic growth. The increase in interest rates will lead to an inflow of deposits into commercial banks, raising their capacity to lend and finance investment.[17,18] By contrast, van Wijnbergen (1983*b*) has argued that, if informal loan markets are prevalent, a rise in official interest rates may lead to a *reduction* in financial intermediation and have an adverse effect on output in the short and medium run. Essentially, this is because informal credit markets are more "efficient" at providing financial intermediation than the official commercial banking system, because operators in the informal markets are able to evade government banking regulations.

van Wijnbergen's critique of high-interest-rate policies can be illustrated with a simple macroeconomic framework. Consider a closed economy in which there are four categories of agents: households, firms, commercial banks, and the central bank. As a result of financial repression, an informal credit market coexists with the official market, allowing households to channel funds directly to firms. Commercial banks lend only to firms and do not operate in the informal market. The central bank sets interest rates as well as reserve requirements on commercial banks' loans, and does not provide direct credit to banks or the public. Households allocate their wealth among cash holdings, time deposits, and loans to the informal credit market, taking into account their level of income and the rates of return on alternative assets. The rate of return on currency is the negative of the expected inflation rate, $-\pi^a$ (which is assumed constant); the rate of return on bank deposits is the real deposit rate $i_d - \pi^a$; and the rate of return on informal market loans is the real parallel interest rate, $i_L(t) - \pi^a$. Assuming, for simplicity, unit wealth elasticities, portfolio allocation can be described by the following equations:

$$CU_t/A_t = h^C[-\overset{+}{\pi}{}^a, i_d \overset{-}{-} \pi^a, i_L(t) \overset{-}{-} \pi^a, \overset{+}{y}_t], \tag{6a}$$

$$D_t^p/A_t = h^D[-\overset{-}{\pi}{}^a, i_d \overset{+}{-} \pi^a, i_L(t) \overset{-}{-} \pi^a, \overset{+}{y}_t], \tag{6b}$$

$$L_t^p/A_t = h^L[-\overset{-}{\pi}{}^a, i_d \overset{-}{-} \pi^a, i_L(t) \overset{+}{-} \pi^a, \bar{y}_t] \tag{6c}$$

$$h_k^C() + h_k^D() + h_k^L() = 0, \quad k = 1, \dots 4 \tag{6d}$$

$$h^C() + h^D() + h^L() = 1, \tag{6e}$$

where CU_t denotes currency holdings, D_t^p households' deposits in the banking system, L_t^p loans to the informal market, y_t real income, and A_t nominal wealth, defined as

$$A_t = CU_t + D_t^p + L_t^p. \tag{7}$$

Equations $(6a)$–$(6c)$ assume that assets are gross substitutes, being positive functions of their own rate of return and negative functions of the rate of return on alternative assets. The negative income elasticity of the supply of parallel market loans results from the assumption of a positive relationship between income and both currency and time deposits—an assumption that appears to be reasonably well supported by the available empirical evidence—and from constraint $(6d)$. Equation $(6e)$ is the adding-up portfolio constraint.

Since the central bank does not provide credit to commercial banks, households' deposits are the only source of funds for the banking system. These deposits—whose actual stock is determined by the demand side of the market—earn a nominal interest rate equal to i_d and are subject to a reserve requirement ratio equal to μ. The credit supply function by commercial banks is therefore equal to[19]

$$L_t^s = (1 - \mu)D_t^p, \quad 0 < \mu < 1. \tag{8}$$

TABLE 5.3
Accounting Framework of van Wijnbergen's Model

	Demand			
Assets	Households	Banks	Firms	Supply
Currency	$h^c()A_t$	μD_t^p	D_t^f	$= M_t$
Bank deposits	$h^D()A_t$	$-D_t^s$	—	< 0
Credit	$h^L()A_t$	$(1-\mu)D_t^p$	$-D_t^f$	$= 0$

Source: Adapted from van Wijnbergen (1983b, p. 437).

Commercial banks lend only to firms, whose demand for credit is for the purpose of financing cash holdings related to working capital needs. These needs are assumed to depend positively on the real product wage, ω_t, and the level of output:

$$D_t^f = f(\overset{+}{\omega}_t, \overset{+}{y}_t). \tag{9}$$

Firms absorb all credit provided by commercial banks. Excess demand is satisfied in the informal market, at a rate of interest substantially higher than the official rate.[20] Table 5.3 provides a synoptic view of the model. As usual, the monetary base M_t is simply the sum of cash in circulation and banks' reserves held in the central bank. The total amount of loans to firms (which is equal to $L_t^p + L_t^s$ in equilibrium) is implicitly held as high-powered money.

There are two market-clearing conditions in this model. The first relates to the equilibrium between supply and demand for high-powered money, and the second to the equilibrium condition for the informal credit market. These conditions are not independent by Walras's law, and consequently we need to focus on only one of them.[21] Using the informal credit market equilibrium condition yields, using Equation (6c),

$$h^L[-\pi^a, i_d - \pi^a, i_L(t) - \pi^a, y_t]A_t = f(\omega_t, y_t) - L_t^s,$$

or, using Equations (6b) and (8),

$$h^L()A_t = f(\omega_t, y_t) - (1-\mu)h^D()A_t. \tag{10}$$

Differentiating Equation (10) and using (6d) implies

$$di_L(t)/dy_t|_{LL} = [f_y - (h_y^L + (1-\mu)h_y^D)A_t]/[h_L^L + (1-\mu)h_L^D]A_t > 0, \tag{11}$$

which determines the slope of the credit market equilibrium locus denoted *LL* in Figure 5.2.

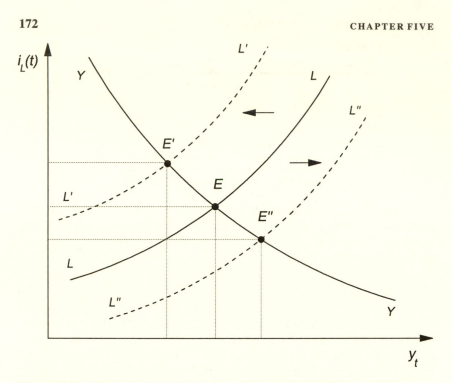

Figure 5.2 Determination of Output and the Informal Interest Rate in van Wijnbergen's Model

To close the model, assume that output is demand determined and depends only on the real interest rate in the informal loan market:

$$y_t = -\alpha[i_L(t) - \pi^a], \tag{12}$$

which yields

$$di_L(t)/dy_t|_{YY} = -1/\alpha < 0. \tag{13}$$

Equation (13) determines the slope of the commodity market equilibrium locus denoted YY in Figure 5.2.

Curves LL and YY show combinations of the informal interest rate and real output that simultaneously yield equilibrium in the informal credit market and the goods market. The equilibrium position of the economy obtains at point E, where the two curves intersect.

Consider now what happens when, as advocated by McKinnon-Shaw followers, the official interest rate on bank deposits is raised by the central bank. An increase in i_d does not change the position of the YY curve, since aggregate demand is independent of the deposit rate.[22] It leads, however, to a portfolio reallocation since it changes the real rate of return on bank deposits and therefore the relative attractiveness of alternative assets. Specifically, households will attempt to reduce their holdings of currency and the supply of informal market loans, and increase their holdings of bank deposits. The net effect of the change in deposit rates on the position of the LL curve is given by

$$di_L(t)/di_d|_{LL, y_t = \bar{y}} = [\mu h_d^L - (1 - \mu)h_d^C]/(h_L^C + \mu h_L^D) \gtreqless 0, \qquad (14)$$

which is, in general, ambiguous. The net impact of the change in the interest rate on time deposits depends on the relative elasticities of demand for the two alternative assets—cash holdings and informal market loans—to changes in i_d. This condition can be written as

$$\text{sg}\{di_L(t)/di_d|_{LL, y_t = \bar{y}}\} = \text{sg}\{\mu h_d^L - (1 - \mu)h_d^C\}.$$

Consider first the case where, as a result of the rise in deposit rates, households shift away mainly from informal market loans, so that $h_d^L/h_d^C > (1 - \mu)/\mu$. The consequence of this shift is a *decline* in the overall supply of funds to firms. This is because the informal credit market was providing "one-for-one" financial intermediation (since loans provided through the parallel market are not subject to reserve requirements), while funds deposited in commercial banks lead only to partial intermediation, as a result of financial regulations. Consequently, the informal interest rate rises and economic activity falls, moving the economy from the initial equilibrium position at point E in Figure 5.2 to point E'.[23]

Assume now that the rise in deposit rates leads households to shift to bank deposits and away mainly from cash holdings, $h_d^L/h_d^C < (1 - \mu)/\mu$. This shift entails an *increase* in real lending by commercial banks to firms—despite a partial accumulation of required reserves. The reduction in excess demand in the official market leads to a fall in interest rates in the informal credit market and an increase in output. The equilibrium position of the economy moves from point E to point E'' in Figure 5.2.[24]

The foregoing analysis can be extended to show that high-interest-rate policies can have an adverse effect on growth, essentially because of their "disintermediation effect" (see van Wijnbergen, 1983a, 1983b).[25] The thrust of the analysis, therefore, is that an increase in deposit rates may lead to results that are opposite to those expected. The financial structure is a critical factor in accounting for this effect. In the presence of informal credit markets, and given central bank regulations on reserve requirements, it is crucial to gauge the pattern of substitution among the different assets. Financial liberalization may therefore entail considerable risks, particularly in developing countries where there is little empirical evidence on portfolio demand functions.

5.4.2 Models of Informal Currency Markets

While the macroeconomic implications of informal credit markets were first emphasized by new structuralist economists, the analysis of parallel markets for foreign exchange has long been a subject of interest for orthodox economists. Various aspects of these markets have been highlighted over the years. The early literature, which evolved essentially from the theory of international trade, emphasized the effect of taxes and smuggling activities on illegal transactions in foreign exchange. More recently, the emphasis has been on the portfolio balance approach, which stresses the role of asset composition in the determination of supply and demand for foreign exchange in the official and parallel markets.[26] This section reviews these alternative approaches and highlights their major implications for short-term monetary and financial management.

5.4.2.1 ILLEGAL TRADE AND PARALLEL MARKETS

The parallel market for foreign exchange in "real trade" models is specified as reflecting, on the demand side, foreign currency needed to import illegal goods and, on the supply side, foreign currency receipts obtained from illegal sources—such as smuggling and underinvoicing of exports, or the resale of officially allocated foreign exchange (see, in particular, Pitt, 1984). These models typically neglect interactions of the parallel market for foreign exchange with the rest of the economy and follow early partial-equilibrium analyses of a consumption commodity market subject to price controls and rationing (Michaely, 1954).

The implications of this class of models can be readily explored in the framework developed by Macedo (1987), who considers a small open economy in which risk-averse domestic importers and exporters face given world prices. In each period both categories of agents must choose the quantities of goods to be transacted through official channels and the quantities to smuggle inside the country (for importers) or outside (for exporters). The government operates a customs agency whose purpose is to catch and prosecute offenders. As a result of prohibitive administrative costs, the agency cannot prevent smuggling, but the detection technology available is such that the probability of catching smugglers is an increasing function of the smuggling ratio—that is, the ratio of quantities transacted illegally to quantities legally transacted. Offenders, when caught, are subject to a penalty that consists of confiscating a proportion of the value of smuggled goods.

Consider first the representative importer. By transacting through the official market, the importer can obtain foreign exchange at the fixed official exchange rate, but must pay an ad valorem tariff. If he elects to transact through the parallel market, he must acquire foreign exchange at a more depreciated exchange rate and face a probability π of being caught by the customs agency, in which case a proportion Θ of smuggled goods is confiscated. The rational importer determines first the optimal amounts of the good to be imported legally and illegally so as to maximize profits, for given values of the tariff rate τ_m, the parallel market premium ρ, and the price mark-up charged to domestic consumers. The domestic price mark-up is a weighted average of the parallel market premium and the tariff rate, with the weight on the latter falling monotonically as the equilibrium smuggling ratio increases.[27] A necessary condition for the existence of a solution with smuggling is $\pi\tau_m > \rho$. Put differently, an importer will engage in smuggling activities only if the tariff is so high that it pays to purchase foreign exchange in the parallel market at a premium, given the possibility of getting caught by the customs enforcement agency.

Conceptually, risk-averse exporters face a problem similar to that faced by importers: they must determine the proportions of exports to sell abroad through legal and illegal channels, taking into account the possibility of being caught—and thus subject to a penalty—the cost of producing export goods, and the export tax rate τ_x. Like the importer, a rational exporter determines the levels of legal exports and smuggled exports so as to maximize profits. The resulting domestic price of exports is a weighted average of the export tariff rate, and the product of the probability of getting caught and the parallel market premium. A necessary condition for a well-defined solution is now $\pi\tau_x < \rho$, that is, that the tax rate on exports weighted by the probability of getting caught be smaller than the foreign exchange premium in the parallel market.

Flow equilibrium of the parallel market for foreign exchange is obtained by equating aggregate flow supply and demand, derived by summing individual supply and demand resulting from smuggling operations by (identical) exporters and importers. The equilibrium value of the parallel exchange rate is the value that equates total demand and total supply. First-order optimization conditions for importers and exporters determine the long-run relation between the premium and smuggling ratios. Since there are no capital flows between the economy and the rest of the world, current account equilibrium in the long run imposes two additional conditions. The value of legal exports must be equal to the value of legal imports, and the value of illegal exports must be equal to the value of illegal imports. These equations form a system that allows the simultaneous determination of smuggling ratios and the parallel market premium in the long run. The latter solution can be written as

$$\rho^* = \rho(\overset{+}{\tau}_m, \bar{\tau}_x; \pi, \Theta). \tag{15}$$

Equation (15) indicates that in the long-run equilibrium, where legal exports equal legal imports and successfully smuggled exports pay for planned smuggled imports, the premium is determined by the structure of tariffs, penalties, and the risk of getting caught. It can be used to analyze the effects of commercial policies and customs enforcement rules on the long-run value of the parallel market premium. An increase in the import tariff rate τ_m, for instance, raises the demand for illegal foreign exchange, raising the premium. A fall in the export tariff rate τ_x reduces the premium in the long run. The implications of changes in the other parameters of the model—the probability of getting caught and the penalty rate—can similarly be examined (see Macedo, 1987).

The foregoing discussion suggests that real trade models provide an adequate framework for an analysis of the impact of trade restrictions, as opposed to direct exchange controls, on parallel market exchange rates. The basic limitation of these models is that the only purpose of parallel market transactions in foreign exchange is to allow smuggling to take place. This approach thus assumes away the portfolio motive, which often plays an important role in the determination of the parallel market demand for foreign currency (see below). Moreover, there is no mechanism that provides a satisfactory explanation of the short-run behavior of the premium, which is taken as given by exporters and importers in most models. The approach can, however, be extended in this respect. Macedo (1987), for instance, extends the model discussed above and shows that whereas the premium is determined in the long run by the structure of trade taxes, it is given in the short run by the requirement of portfolio balance. The next part of this section focuses precisely on these portfolio effects.

5.4.2.2 PORTFOLIO AND CURRENCY SUBSTITUTION MODELS

The portfolio-balance model of the parallel market for foreign exchange was developed most notably by Dornbusch et al. (1983). It stresses the role of portfolio composition in the determination of parallel exchange rates, in contrast to the flow approach, which characterizes real trade models. The general assumption underlying this class of models is that foreign exchange is a financial asset held by agents as part of a diversified portfolio, both as a hedge and as a refuge for funds. Loss of confidence in domestic-currency-denominated assets, low real domestic interest rates, uncertainty about inflation, taxation, and the political environment may lead to abrupt changes in the demand for foreign currency. Forward-looking expectations play a key role in determining short-term supply and demand shifts and in accounting for exchange-rate volatility. Although the partial equilibrium formulation of Dornbusch et al. (1983) assumes the existence of domestic and foreign interest-bearing assets, the essential features of the approach are best highlighted in a "currency substitution" framework.[28] We will illustrate the properties of this class of models by providing an overview of a model developed by Kamin (1993).[29]

Kamin's model incorporates interactions of the parallel market for foreign exchange with the production sphere of the economy, thus providing an endogenous determination of output and the real exchange rate. The domestic money stock is also determined endogenously in this model, and depends on changes in central bank reserves—which are equal to the reported current account—and the rate of growth of domestic credit. The unreported current account determines the change in the stock of foreign currency held in private agents' portfolios. The flow supply of foreign exchange in the parallel market is assumed to derive from underinvoicing of exports. The propensity to underinvoice, in turn, depends positively on the level of the premium. As in real trade models, the probability of detection is assumed to rise as fraudulent transactions increase, and this translates into a rising—but at a decreasing rate—marginal underinvoicing share.

The properties of Kamin's model can be illustrated by examining the short-run behavior of the parallel exchange rate in response to an official devaluation. Consider first the case where the devaluation is unexpected. The parity change causes a decline in the flow supply of foreign currency to the private sector (since the premium falls) at the initial parallel rate. For current account balance to be maintained, a depreciation of the parallel rate is required.[30] At the moment the devaluation occurs, the parallel rate depreciates sharply. Subsequently, current account losses of foreign currency drive the unofficial exchange rate up still further until it reaches a new long-run equilibrium, at the same moment foreign-currency holdings reach their new steady-state level. If the devaluation is anticipated (because it is announced at period t_0 that it will occur at T, for instance), the parallel exchange rate also jumps upward—although the size of the jump is now smaller—and foreign-currency holdings begin rising. After the initial jump, the parallel rate continues to depreciate while private agents accumulate foreign currency in their portfolios, until the economy reaches its new equilibrium path, at the instant the devaluation actually occurs. From this point on, the parallel rate continues to depreciate while foreign-currency holdings decline, since the unofficial current account deteriorates following the devaluation. At the date of the announcement of the future devaluation, the underinvoicing share jumps upward and keeps growing as

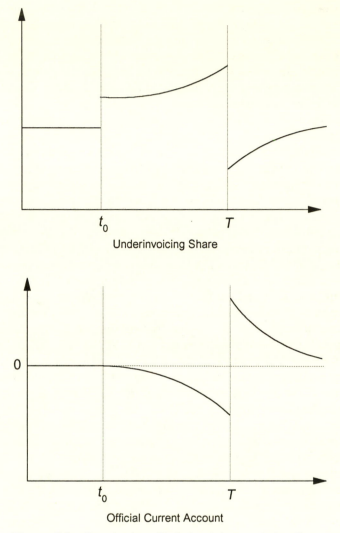

Underinvoicing Share

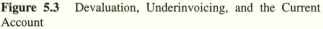

Official Current Account

Figure 5.3   Devaluation, Underinvoicing, and the Current Account

Source: Kamin (1993, p. 160).

the parallel market rate depreciates. When the devaluation is effectively implemented, the premium and the underinvoicing share fall sharply, but then recover partially, since the parallel market rate continues to depreciate, until it reaches its new steady-state level. The behavior of the underinvoicing share and the official current account in Kamin's model are represented in Figure 5.3.

The long-run impact of a once-and-for-all official devaluation on the parallel exchange rate is ambiguous in Kamin's model. In general, it depends on the degree to which fraudulent transactions react to changes in the premium, the rationing scheme imposed by the central bank, and the elasticity of export volumes to changes in relative prices. The greater the response of the underinvoicing share to the change in the parallel market premium, the lower is the central bank's propensity to resell official remittances of foreign exchange; or the smaller the response of exports, the more likely it is that the parallel market rate will depreciate in response to a parity change.[31] The parallel rate depreciation, however, will typically fall short of the official devaluation, implying that the premium is likely to fall.

Kamin's analysis provides a useful framework for interpreting some apparently puzzling facts surrounding a large number of devaluation episodes of the past three decades in developing countries. The empirical evidence gathered by Kamin (1988) suggests that prior to an official devaluation, measured growth rates of exports and imports seemed to decelerate abruptly, while the officially measured current account balance and official foreign reserves appeared to deteriorate. In the periods following the official parity change, exports rebounded strongly and the current account improved while imports continued to fall, albeit at a slower pace, recovering only in the second year after the devaluation. The behavior of the current account thus differed from what a J curve theory would predict.[32] Within Kamin's (1993) framework, however, the puzzle can readily be explained. His analysis suggests that expansionary fiscal and monetary policies in the periods preceding the devaluation led to an appreciation of the real (official) exchange rate and increases in the parallel market premium, leading in turn to a reduction in the volume of exports, an increase in underinvoicing, and a deterioration of the officially recorded current account.[33] The fall in officially remitted exports led to growing reserve losses, forcing the monetary authorities to tighten foreign exchange allocations to imports. To the extent that agents became convinced that the continuing deterioration of external accounts would prompt a devaluation of the official exchange rate, portfolio shifts away from domestic assets may have induced a speculative rise in the parallel market premium, exacerbating the rate of reserve loss in a self-fulfilling manner, and reinforcing further the need for official exchange-rate adjustment.[34] Following the devaluation, the parallel market premium fell on impact, reducing the propensity to underinvoice and leading to a sharp increase in officially measured exports. The gradual recovery of reserves allowed the authorities to increase sales of foreign exchange, leading to a recovery in imports.

Several attempts have been made to assess empirically the effect of a devaluation on the parallel market premium. The evidence in general supports the presumption that parallel market rates depreciate, but less than proportionally, in response to a devaluation of the official exchange rate, so that the premium falls initially. The evidence also suggests that this reduction will only be temporary if fiscal and credit policies are maintained on an expansionary course, implying that a devaluation, by itself, cannot permanently lower the premium. These facts have been well documented in studies by Edwards (1989a), Edwards and Montiel (1989), and Kamin (1993), on a large sample of devaluation episodes in developing countries.

5.5 Monetary Policy with Informal Financial Markets

Although informal markets for credit and foreign exchange have generally been modeled separately, in reality such markets tend to coexist in many developing countries. Moreover, the evidence on capital mobility reviewed in Section 5.3 suggests that assets in the informal credit market and foreign financial assets are probably best modeled as imperfect substitutes, and that in the typical situation the quantity of foreign assets in the portfolios of domestic private agents can change, albeit not instantaneously. Thus, a full description of the financial system in a "representative" developing economy needs to consider not just interactions between formal and informal financial markets, but also those between informal credit and foreign exchange markets. How does monetary policy work in such a setting? This section explores these issues using a simple open-economy, portfolio-balance framework incorporating the features described in previous sections of this chapter.[35] Specifically, the domestic financial system is repressed in the sense described in Section 5.1 and coexists with an informal credit market. There are no markets in which private agents can trade domestic securities or equity. Capital controls are in place, but the private sector has been able to evade these sufficiently well in the past to acquire foreign-currency-denominated assets, which are traded among private agents in a free exchange market and which are imperfect substitutes for domestic assets. As a result (and in accordance with the evidence reviewed in Section 5.3), movements in foreign interest rates influence domestic financial markets.

The monetary authorities possess four direct policy instruments in this setting: the level of administered bank interest rates, the required reserve ratio, the amount of credit extended by the central bank to the commercial banking system, and intervention in the parallel exchange market.[36] In addition to the conventional channel of transmission of monetary policy through changes in market-determined (in this case, curb market) interest rates, other mechanisms of transmission also play important roles. These include the wealth effects induced by changes in the degree of financial repression, and effects that operate through the exchange-rate premium in the parallel foreign exchange market.

The economy considered is assumed to be a small open one with four types of agents: households, the government, the central bank, and the rest of the banking system. The authorities maintain an official exchange rate for current international transactions but prohibit private capital movements. Private households have access to four assets: bank deposits, curb market loans, foreign assets, and bank credit (which is, of course, a liability for households). Bank credit and curb market loans are taken to be perfect substitutes in household portfolios. This implies that bank credit and curb loans can be treated as a single asset, and that all rationing-induced "spillover" effects of changes in the stock of bank credit are concentrated in the curb loan market.

5.5.1 The Analytical Framework

Households' financial portfolios are taken to consist of bank deposits D_t^p, curb market loans, bank credit L_t^p, and foreign assets F_t^p.[37] The value of households' financial portfolios A_t is given by

$$A_t = D_t^p + s_t F_t^p - L_t^p,$$

where s_t is the domestic-currency price of foreign exchange traded in the parallel market. Portfolio balance requires:

$$D_t^p/P_t = h^D[\bar{i_L}(t), \overset{0}{a_t}; \overset{+}{i_d}, \bar{s^a}], \tag{16a}$$

$$-L_t^p/P_t = h^L[\bar{i_L}(t), \dot{a_t}; \bar{i_d}, \bar{s^a}], \quad 0 < h_2^L < 1 \tag{16b}$$

$$s_t F_t^p/P_t = h^F[\bar{i_L}(t), \dot{a_t}; \bar{i_d}, \overset{+}{s^a}], \quad 0 < h_2^F < 1 \tag{16c}$$

where $i_L(t)$ and i_d are, respectively, the interest rate on curb market loans and the (controlled) interest rate on bank deposits; $\hat{s}^a$ is the expected (exogenous) rate of depreciation of the parallel market exchange rate; P_t is the domestic price level; and a_t is real private wealth. The signs of the first three partial derivatives of each function reflect the assumption that all assets are gross substitutes.[38] The partial derivatives in Equations (16) satisfy the standard constraints:

$$h_k^D() + h_k^L() + h_k^F() = 0, \quad k = 1, 3, 4$$

$$h_2^L() + h_2^F() = 1.$$

Private absorption c_t depends on the real loan interest rate and the level of household resources:

$$c_t = c(i_L \overset{-}{-} \pi^a, \overset{+}{a}_t), \tag{17}$$

where π^a denotes the anticipated inflation rate, which is also taken as given in the following analysis. Household resources consist of real financial wealth a_t and real factor income. However, real output is taken as constant in this full-employment model, so the (unchanging) level of real factor income is omitted from the function $c()$.

The implicit taxes and subsidies imposed on households by financial repression are taken into account as follows. Let i_c denote the controlled interest rate on bank credit. Individuals with access to such credit receive a subsidy of $(i_L(t) - i_c)L_t^p$, that is, the differential between the curb market rate and the bank lending rate times the amount of bank credit extended to individuals with privileged access to the official credit market. The present value of this subsidy is given by $(i_L(t) - i_c)L_t^p/i_L(t)$, and this represents a net addition to household financial wealth.[39] An index Θ_t of the degree of financial repression is given by

$$\Theta_t = [i_L(t) - i_c]/i_L(t), \tag{18}$$

that is, Θ_t is the present value of the subsidy, per unit of bank credit, implied by the prevailing interest rate ceilings. The present value of the tax on households as depositors is given by $(\tilde{i}_d - i_d)D_t^p/\tilde{i}_d$, where $\tilde{i}_d$ is the deposit interest rate corresponding to a loan interest rate of i_L under the banks' zero-profit condition (see Equation (22) below). This condition can be used to show that $(\tilde{i}_d - i_d)/\tilde{i}_d = \Theta_t$, so the degree of financial repression can be written equivalently as a function of banks' lending or borrowing rates, and the present value of the tax on depositors can be expressed compactly as $\Theta_t D_t^p$.

Taking these taxes and subsidies into account, households' real financial wealth can be expressed as

$$a_t = (D_t^p + s_t F_t^p - L_t^p + \Theta_t L_t^p - \Theta_t D_t^p)/P_t$$
$$= [(1 - \Theta_t)(D_t^p - L_t^p) + s_t F_t^p]/P_t. \tag{19}$$

Thus, the wealth effects of financial repression depend on whether households are net creditors $(D_t^p - L_t^p > 0)$ or debtors $(D_t^p - L_t^p < 0)$ of the banking system. When $D_t^p - L_t^p > 0$, an increase in the degree of financial repression Θ_t reduces household wealth, since the implicit tax imposed on households by interest rate ceilings on deposits exceeds the subsidy received by favored borrowers.

Banks' assets consist of reserves held at the central bank RR_t and credit extended to households L_t^p. Their liabilities are the deposits held by the public, and credit received from the central bank L^{cb}. The balance sheet of the banking system is therefore given by

$$RR_t + L_t^p = D_t^p + L^{cb}. \tag{20}$$

Banks hold no excess reserves. Given a required reserve ratio of μ, reserve holdings are thus given by

$$RR_t = \mu D_t^p, \qquad 0 < \mu < 1. \tag{21}$$

Reserves at the central bank pay no interest, but credit extended to the banking system by the central bank carries an interest charge that, for convenience, is set equal to the interest rate that banks charge their customers, i_c. Under these conditions, the zero-profit condition for the banking system is given by

$$i_c = i_d/(1 - \mu). \tag{22}$$

The central bank pegs the official exchange rate at a value $\bar{E}$. All international commercial transactions are settled at this rate. With the central bank's stock of foreign exchange reserves (measured in foreign currency) denoted as R_t and the trade balance—measured in units of the domestic good and taken to be an increasing function of the real exchange rate, $z_t = \bar{E}/P_t$—as $T(z_t)$, the stock of foreign exchange reserves evolves according to[40]

$$\bar{E}\dot{R}_t = P_t T(\overset{+}{z}_t). \tag{23}$$

The central bank's assets include both foreign exchange reserves and credit to the banking system, while its liabilities consist of reserves held by the banking system. Thus the central bank's balance sheet is

$$\bar{E}R_t + L^{cb} = RR_t. \tag{24}$$

Since the central bank's loans to the banking system earn interest, this income must be allocated in some way. It is assumed to be transferred to the government, which then uses it to purchase domestic goods. Since this section is concerned with monetary rather than fiscal policy, there is no other role for the government than to dispose of these funds. Letting $\bar{g}$ denote real government spending on domestic goods, the government budget constraint implies

$$P_t\bar{g} = i_c L^{cb}. \tag{25}$$

The model is closed by the condition that the market for domestic goods must clear. With $\bar{y}$ denoting domestic real output, this condition is

$$\bar{y} - c[i_L(t) - \pi^a, a_t] + \bar{g} + T(z_t) = 0. \tag{26}$$

To explore how monetary policy works in this framework, it is useful to summarize the model in a more compact form. Let $F_t = R_t + F_t^p$ be the economy's total net foreign assets, and $\rho_t = s_t/\bar{E}$ (1 plus) the parallel market premium. Using this notation, and with some substitutions, the equilibrium conditions in the informal loan and foreign exchange markets can be rewritten as

$$H[i_L(t), z_t(F_t + (\rho_t - 1)F_t^p); i_d, \hat{\rho}^a] + z_t l^{cb} + (1 - \mu)h^D[i_L(t); i_d, \hat{\rho}^a] = 0, \tag{27}$$

$$z_t \rho_t F_t^p - h^F[i_L(t), z_t(F_t + (\rho_t - 1)F_t^p); i_d, \hat{\rho}^a] = 0, \tag{28}$$

where $l^{cb} = L^{cb}/\bar{E}$, and $\hat{\rho}^a$ (which is equal to $-\hat{s}^a$ here, since the official exchange rate is fixed) denotes the expected rate of change of the parallel market premium.

Next, by using Equations (20) and (24) in (19), real household financial wealth becomes

$$a_t = [\bar{E}(F_t^p + R_t) + \Theta_t(L_t^{cb} - RR_t)]/P_t.$$

Thus, the wealth effects of financial repression depend on the excess of central bank lending to the banking system over reserves held by commercial banks. Intuitively, this is because credit to households L_t^p can exceed deposits D_t^p only if the resources made available to banks by the central bank L^{cb} exceed the resources extracted by the central bank RR_t. Using Equations (25) and (16) and letting $\tilde{a}_t = A_t/\bar{E}$, we can rewrite the preceding equation as

$$a_t = z_t \tilde{a}_t = z_t[F_t + (\rho_t - 1)F_t^p] + \Theta_t\{z_t l^{cb} - \mu h^D[i_L(t); i_d, \hat{\rho}^a]\}. \tag{29}$$

With this notation, the commodity market equilibrium equation (26) becomes

$$\bar{y} - c[i_L(t) + \hat{z}^a, z_t \tilde{a}_t] + i_c z_t l^{cb} + T(z_t) = 0, \tag{30}$$

where use is also made of the government budget constraint (25). $\hat{z}^a$ denotes the expected rate of depreciation of the real exchange rate (which is equal to the negative of the expected inflation rate here) and is also taken to be exogenous in what follows.

Equations (27) to (30), together with the balance-of-payments equation (23) and the definition of the financial repression index Θ_t given in (18), are the compact representation of the model. The monetary policy variables are the administered interest rate on deposits i_d, the required reserve ratio, central bank lending to the banking system l^{cb}, and central bank intervention in the free market. The last value is captured by the stock of foreign exchange available to the private sector F_t^p, which can be altered by the central bank subject to the condition $dR_t = -dF_t^p$, since the economy's net international indebtedness F_t is a state variable in the system. When the central bank sells foreign exchange in the parallel market, it may do so at either the parallel rate or the official rate. In the latter case, households will reap a windfall.[41] The endogenous variables in the system are the curb loan interest rate $i_L(t)$, the degree of financial repression Θ_t, the balance of payments R_t, the real exchange rate z_t, and the premium ρ_t. The effects of the monetary policy instruments on aggregate demand are captured by their effects on the official real exchange rate z_t, since $z_t = \bar{E}/P_t$ and changes in P_t reflect shifts in aggregate demand, given the full-employment assumption.

5.5.2 Changes in Monetary Policy Instruments

Under the assumption of perfect foresight, analyzing the effects of changes in monetary policy instruments on aggregate demand in the economy described above would require solving the model forward in conventional fashion, since in this case the entire future paths of the endogenous expectational variables (the real exchange rate and the parallel market premium) must be known for their initial values to be determined. Since the concern here is only with understanding how monetary policy works in the environment described, this process is rendered more transparent if we sever the links with the future by taking expectations to be static and focus on the interactions between the real and monetary sectors under this simpler assumption.[42] We now proceed by examining how each of the monetary policy variables in turn affects aggregate demand.

5.5.2.1 CREDIT EXPANSION

Consider first an expansion of credit to the banking system (an increase in l^{cb}). An increase in credit provided to households by the banking system creates an excess supply of loans in the curb market, since some borrowers previously active in that market can now be supplied by the banking system. The loan interest rate falls, and as households switch out of the informal loan market and into foreign assets, the premium rises. This combination influences private demand through the standard interest rate effects described in Section 5.4 as well as through wealth effects, partly associated with changes in the premium (see below). When the disposition of central bank revenue is accounted for, a third effect is added in the form of changes in government consumption.

The interest rate effect arises from the direct influence exerted by the curb market rate on private spending—which is unambiguously positive, since the informal interest rate falls. The wealth effect arises from two sources. First, the increase in the value of the private sector's holdings of foreign assets (induced by the increase in the premium) raises real wealth. Second, the reduction in the informal market interest rate reduces the degree of financial repression, reinforcing the positive effect of the increase in the premium on real private wealth.

However, the base of the financial repression tax will also be affected in this case, both because of the expansion of credit, which reduces the base, and because of the higher demand for deposits resulting from the reduction in the curb market interest rate, which increases it. The base for the financial repression tax may rise or fall in this case, depending on the properties of the asset demand functions and the required reserve ratio. An increase, for instance, in the base of the financial repression tax will exert a negative wealth effect, the size of which will be smaller the smaller the initial degree of financial repression.

Finally, an increase in central bank credit to commercial banks increases revenues for the public sector due to the interest charges on the larger stock of credit extended by the central bank, and since this additional revenue (amounting to $i_c dl^{cb}$) is spent by the government on home goods, demand increases for this reason as well.

5.5.2.2 CHANGES IN THE ADMINISTERED INTEREST RATE

An increase in the administered interest rate on deposits has, in principle, an ambiguous overall effect on demand. On impact, an increase in i_d will result in an excess supply of foreign exchange, as funds are attracted into the domestic financial system and away from the holding of foreign assets. However, the net asset demand for curb market loans may rise or fall. Although bank lending will rise as deposits increase, household lending will fall as asset holders shift funds away from the loan market and into deposits. Since banks hold reserves while private lending agents operating in the informal market do not, each unit moved by households from the loan market into the domestic financial system reduces the net supply of loans.[43] However, to the extent that funds attracted to banks come out of foreign-currency holdings instead, the supply of loans rises. Thus the key to the impact effect of changes in i_d is, as in the simple model examined above, whether households primarily move funds out of the loan market or out of foreign-currency assets, that is, whether loans or foreign-currency holdings are better substitutes for deposits.

In the "dollarization" case (in which foreign currency and domestic money are close substitutes), the expansion of deposits would be primarily at the expense of foreign currency, rather than loans, and in this case an increase in i_d is likely to result in an incipient excess supply of loans in the informal credit market, causing interest rates there to fall. Regardless of whether the curb market interest rate rises or falls, however, the effect on the premium will be negative, which has an adverse wealth effect on demand for goods that is ignored in models that fail to integrate the parallel foreign exchange market with the informal credit market. At the same time, since the degree of financial repression falls regardless of whether the curb market interest rate rises or falls, there is also a positive effect on wealth, which renders the overall contribution of the wealth effect ambiguous. The fiscal effect, nevertheless, is always positive, since central bank (and thus government) income increases when administered interest rates are raised. Thus, the partial-equilibrium effects of an increase in i_d on aggregate demand are ambiguous, even in the "dollarization" case in which the curb market interest rate falls.[44]

5.5.2.3 CHANGE IN THE REQUIRED RESERVE RATIO

Because banks are forced to contract lending to households, an increase in the required reserve ratio μ creates an excess demand for curb market loans and thus raises the portfolio-equilibrium loan interest rate, exerting a negative effect on demand through this channel. The premium on foreign assets falls as individuals attempt to switch out of such assets into lending on the informal credit market. Although the interest rate on bank credit must rise in this case, as a consequence of the zero-profit condition (22), the proportionate increase in the loan interest rate can be shown to exceed that of the interest rate on bank credit for small initial values of the required reserve ratio, so that the degree of financial repression increases in this case. The wealth effect arising from the increase in the degree of financial repression and the reduction of the premium is also negative. However, as a result of the increase in the rate charged by the central bank on its loans (which reflects the rise in the commercial banks' lending rate), fiscal revenue and government spending increase, partially offsetting the negative demand effects described above.

5.5.2.4 INTERVENTION IN THE PARALLEL FOREIGN EXCHANGE MARKET

The monetary authorities can bring about an increase in private sector holdings of foreign assets by selling some of their foreign exchange reserves in the free exchange market. The effect of an increase in this stock (through central bank intervention in the parallel market) is to create an incipient excess supply of foreign exchange as households seek to restore their desired portfolio composition. Consequently, a reduction in the premium is required to restore equilibrium. Since this reduces the value of asset holders' portfolios, the scale effect causes the asset demand for loans to decrease, putting upward pressure on the curb market interest rate.[45] The combination of an increase in the degree of financial repression and a reduction in the premium exerts a negative wealth effect. The extent to which the negative wealth effect is offset by the reduction in the base of the financial repression tax created by higher interest rates depends, as in other cases, on the initial degree of financial repression and the elasticity of the demand for bank deposits with respect to the interest rate in the informal credit market.

This chapter has examined the role of financial repression and capital mobility in the transmission of monetary policy in developing countries. The first section showed that financial repression entails a variety of macroeconomic implications. In particular, it was argued that financial repression has negative effects on the efficiency of the intermediation process between savers and borrowers, and affects the distribution of income because it transfers resources from savers to favored borrowers who acquire resources at official interest rates—the public sector, enterprises in priority sectors, and other well-connected individuals.

The second part of the chapter attempted to explain why, given well-known efficiency costs, a government chooses to repress its financial system and impose capital controls. The proposed approach dwells on the fiscal view of inflation. We described a unified public finance framework that emphasizes the fiscal considerations underlying the simultaneous existence of regular taxes, financial repression, capital controls, and the inflation tax. An important implication of our analysis is that financial repression, while commonly viewed as an "irrational" policy, may in fact be the optimal response of a government facing a spending target or a financing constraint while being unable to raise revenue—because of a weak fiscal administration—through conventional taxes.

Section 5.3 provided an empirical overview of existing studies on capital mobility in developing countries. The evidence suggests that, in spite of the prevalence of capital controls, few if any of these countries can be considered to be financially closed. Thus the assumption of imperfect capital mobility, rather than that of financial autarky, seems broadly applicable to developing countries. Indeed, for some countries the extreme assumption of perfect capital mobility may be viewed as a reasonable analytical simplification.

In Section 5.4 we described macroeconomic models that deal, respectively, with parallel credit markets and informal foreign exchange markets. We discussed, in particular, the new structuralist view according to which the pattern of asset substitution plays a key role in understanding the short-run effects of interest rate liberalization on output and prices. Portfolio models that deal with parallel currency markets were shown to lead to some fairly general and important implications for macroeconomic policy. In a fixed-exchange-rate regime, an expansionary fiscal and credit policy generates a depreciation of the parallel exchange rate, a rise in prices, an appreciation of the official real exchange rate, and a decline in the relative price of exports surrendered via the official market relative to those transiting through the parallel market. As a result, the proportion of export proceeds repatriated at the official exchange rate falls, and foreign reserves decline. Eventually, the central bank will "run out" of reserves. At this point, the inconsistency between expansive macroeconomic policies and a pegged official exchange rate will become unsustainable. A balance-of-payments crisis may ensue (see Chapter 6), and corrective measures will need to be implemented—for instance, in the form of a parity change. This process may lead, in fact, to recurrent periods of speculative attacks and devaluation crises.

The last part of the chapter examined the mechanism of transmission of monetary policy in a context where informal markets in credit and foreign exchange have both emerged as a result of financial repression and capital controls. The analysis showed that both the instruments of monetary policy and the channels through which their effects are transmitted to aggregate demand differ substantially from the standard textbook industrial-country *IS-LM* representation. Though interest rate effects play an important role in both contexts, in many developing countries those effects operate through informal markets that are not directly subject to the actions of the central bank. Open-market operations in this context are not a tool of monetary policy, since the central bank does not hold curb market loans in its portfolio. Instead, this market is influenced only indirectly by the central bank through the formal banking system and the free foreign exchange market. More generally, the banking system plays a central role in the transmission of the effects of changes in monetary policy instruments, since of the four instruments examined, three (changes in administered interest rates, reserve requirements, and central bank credit) are mediated in the first instance by the banking system.

In addition to the nature of the interest rate effects and the role of the banking system, the transmission mechanism described here contains some unconventional elements, in the form of wealth and fiscal effects. The former arise from changes in the value of stocks of foreign exchange as well as in the value of the implicit taxes and subsidies associated with financial repression, while the latter involve the disposition of the income generated by the operations of the central bank.

Six

Exchange-Rate Management I: Credibility and Crises

THE ROLE of exchange-rate policy in macroeconomic adjustment has been the subject of renewed controversy in the past few years. The traditional arguments involved in choosing between fixed and flexible exchange-rate regimes have been reexamined in light of the credibility and reputational effects that formal arrangements may provide. The sources and implications of inconsistencies that may arise between the exchange-rate regime and other macroeconomic policy instruments have also been the subject of considerable attention. Theoretical and empirical studies have emphasized the perverse effect that devaluations may exert on output, even when they lead to an improvement in the trade balance. Finally, the focus on competitiveness and the adoption of real exchange-rate targets in several countries has raised a variety of questions related to the broader macroeconomic implications of such policy choices.

This chapter and the next discuss some conceptual issues associated with exchange-rate policy in developing countries.[1] The first part of this chapter provides an overview of the evolution of exchange-rate regimes in developing countries over the past two decades and discusses some of the factors leading to the adoption of a particular type of exchange-rate arrangement. The second part examines the role played by credibility considerations in the adoption of an exchange-rate regime and the decision to adhere to a monetary union. The third part discusses how macroeconomic policy inconsistencies may lead to recurrent speculative attacks and ultimately to the collapse of a fixed exchange rate, and reviews some recent experiences in Latin America.

6.1 Evidence on Exchange-Rate Regimes

Since the collapse of the Bretton Woods system in the early 1970s, the process of exchange-rate determination in developing countries has been fundamentally different from that in industrial countries. For most of the two decades since that time, the major industrial countries have followed a policy of managed floating, in which their exchange rates were determined largely by market forces, albeit with frequent central bank intervention. By

contrast, the vast majority of countries in the developing world did not abandon the policy of determining an official exchange rate for their currencies
when the Bretton Woods system collapsed. Rather than allowing the foreign exchange values of their currencies to be determined endogenously by
market forces, the exchange rate has remained a policy instrument in most
developing nations.

In practice, the maintenance of an official exchange-rate parity has not
implied uniformity of exchange-rate arrangements in developing countries.
Indeed, a wide array of exchange-rate arrangements has existed in these
countries, although some systematic patterns have emerged both across
countries and over time.

Among countries that have maintained an official parity, a basic distinction is between those that have defended a fixed peg and those that have
permitted the exchange rate to crawl over time. The former approach includes the use of pegs to a single currency and to alternative baskets of
currencies (either preexisting baskets such as the SDR or tailor-made ones,
typically relying on partner-country trade weights). Such pegs have been
literally fixed for long periods of time or periodically adjusted. In cases in
which the exchange rate has been allowed to depreciate, again the crawl
has been against either a single currency or a basket, and the rate of crawl
has either followed a well-defined (nondiscretionary) feedback rule or been
discretionary. In cases where a rule was in place, it has sometimes been
made known to the public and sometimes not, while in cases where discretion has been used, the future path of the exchange rate has at times been
preannounced and at times not.

Perhaps the central uniformity with regard to exchange-rate arrangements is that full convertibility has rarely been achieved in the developing
world. As indicated in Chapter 5, capital controls have been pervasive,
and current account convertibility has often been abandoned in periods of
balance-of-payments difficulties. Thus, the official parity has frequently
been maintained with the assistance of a large array of exchange controls.
One implication of this, as suggested in Chapter 2, is that the official parity typically coexists with a parallel market in which foreign exchange is
traded at prices that vary substantially from the official parity.

A second important observation is that the forms of exchange-rate arrangements in developing countries have tended to evolve systematically
over time. This evolution is summarized in broad terms in Table 6.1. Immediately after the collapse of the Bretton Woods system, most developing
nations continued to peg against a single currency. In 1976 more than 60
percent of all developing IMF member countries did so (Table 6.1). Among
single-currency peggers, over two-thirds were pegged to the U.S. dollar.
Roughly a quarter of developing countries pegged against a composite
of currencies, so that in total almost nine out of ten developing countries

TABLE 6.1

Exchange-Rate Arrangements of Developing Countries, 1976–92 (percentage of total number of countries)

Classification	1976	1979	1983	1992
Pegged arrangements	86.0	75.2	71.7	60.5
To a single currency	62.6	52.1	43.5	35.5
U.S. dollar	43.0	35.0	29.0	20.2
French franc	12.1	12.0	10.5	11.3
Pound sterling	2.8	2.6	0.8	—
Other currency	4.7	2.5	3.2	4.0
To composite	23.4	23.1	28.2	25.0
SDR	10.3	11.1	11.3	4.0
Other (currency basket)	13.1	12.0	16.9	21.0
Flexible arrangements	14.0	24.8	28.2	39.5
Adjusting to indicators	5.6	3.4	4.0	3.2
Other[a]	8.4	21.4	24.2	36.3
Total	100.0	100.0	100.0	100.0
Number of countries	107	117	124	124

Sources: IMF, *Annual Report* (1982); IMF, *Report on Exchange Arrangements and Exchange Restrictions* (1983); and *International Financial Statistics* (September 1993).

Notes: Data are based on midyear classifications, except for 1989, which is based on year-end classifications. Democratic Kampuchea, for which no information is available, is excluded.

[a] Includes the following categories: (1) flexibility limited vis-à-vis single currency, (2) managed floating, and (3) independently floating.

maintained pegged arrangements. The major shift over time was away from pegging to the U.S. dollar primarily to what the IMF describes as "flexible arrangements," which consist predominantly of various forms of crawl but also include limited instances of flexible (that is, market-determined) rates. As recently as 1992, however, fully 60 percent of developing countries continued to peg, either to a single currency or to a composite. While flexible arrangements have become more common, characterizing about two-fifths of all developing countries in 1992, floating rates remain the exception. According to the IMF, about one-fifth (25 of 124) developing countries can be considered to have adopted this form of exchange-rate regime by 1992.

The third pertinent observation is that systematic patterns of exchange-rate arrangements are also observable across regions in the developing world. Table 6.2 examines the geographical distribution of exchange-rate regimes for developing countries during the period 1983–93.[2] Fixed exchange rates, whether pegged to a single currency or to a composite, have been dominant in Africa. This is partly due to the fourteen member countries of the CFA Franc Zone, which maintained a fixed parity against the French franc from 1948 to early 1994.[3] In addition, however, a large number of non–Franc Zone members have also chosen to peg the values of their currencies, either against the dollar or against a basket. As of March 1993, twenty-nine out of forty-four African member countries of the IMF continued to peg against a single currency or a basket, while ten countries were considered by the Fund to be independently floating. At the other extreme, Asian countries adopted much more active exchange-rate policies during the 1980s. Table 6.2 lists no Asian countries pegged to a single currency or following a nondiscretionary crawl, three pegged to a basket, and twelve pursuing discretionary crawls. These reflect active use of the official exchange rate as a policy instrument to achieve external objectives. Nondiscretionary crawls (or crawling according to a set of rules) were much more prevalent among Western Hemisphere countries during the period under consideration. In fact, developing countries in the Western Hemisphere fell neatly into two categories of exchange-rate regime during the past decade: they either pegged to the U.S. dollar or adopted a discretionary crawl.

Several explanations can be offered for the pattern of exchange-rate arrangements described above. As already mentioned, the near absence of free floating is an important difference between developing and industrial countries. This phenomenon may reflect the limited level of financial development achieved by developing countries and the large role of the public sector as a supplier of foreign exchange in many such countries. The tax levied on the domestic financial system by financial repression and the widespread restrictions on private financial activity would limit the number of private agents available to constitute a competitive foreign exchange market, and the important role of the public sector as a supplier of foreign exchange may limit the credibility of a "clean" float. The move among developing countries from pegging to a single currency to the use of basket pegs is likely to have been an indirect result of the adoption of floating rates among industrial countries. Moving to basket pegs may be the outcome of an attempt to dampen the impact of external sources of real exchange instability arising from large fluctuations among the real exchange rates of industrial countries in the post–Bretton Woods period.[4] The switch from pegging to crawling, however, undoubtedly reflects an attempt to avoid a domestic source of instability: the periodic overvaluations and exchange-rate crises associated with a fixed peg in a context of high inflation. As will be discussed in Chapter 13, the post–debt crisis years 1982-89 witnessed an increased reliance on the inflation tax among heavily indebted countries, and many such countries—particularly in the Western Hemisphere—abandoned a U.S. dollar peg in favor of a crawl. Finally, regional variations in currency pegs may reflect geographical differences in trading patterns, while the reliance on discretionary crawls in Asia may, at least in part, reflect the export promotion policy associated with outward-oriented development strategies adopted by several East Asian countries.

TABLE 6.2
Geographical Distribution of Exchange-Rate Arrangements for Developing Countries, 1982–93

Exchange-Rate Arrangement	Africa	Asia	Europe	Middle East	Western Hemisphere
Pegged					
U.S. dollar	Ethiopia, Liberia, Sudan			Bahrain, Saudi Arabia	Bahamas, Barbados, El Salvador, Guatemala, Haiti, Honduras, Nicaragua, Panama, Paraguay, Suriname, Venezuela, Trinidad and Tobago
French franc	Burkina Faso, Cameroon, Central African Republic, Congo, Côte d'Ivoire, Gabon, Mali, Niger, Senegal				
SDR	Burundi, Togo, Rwanda	Myanmar		Jordan	
Basket of currencies	Algeria, Kenya, Malawi, Mauritania, Mauritius, Tanzania, Zimbabwe	Fiji, Nepal	Hungary, Malta, Romania	Cyprus, Kuwait	
Crawling peg	Madagascar		Turkey, Yugoslavia		Argentina, Brazil, Chile, Colombia, Costa Rica, Ecuador, Jamaica, Mexico, Peru, Uruguay
Managed floating	Morocco, Tunisia	Bangladesh, China, India, Indonesia, Korea, Malaysia, Pakistan, the Philippines, Singapore, Sri Lanka, Thailand, Western Samoa			
Independent floating	Gambia, Ghana, Nigeria, Zaire, South Africa				

Sources: See Table 6.1.

What is clear from the foregoing discussion is that the official exchange rate continues to represent an important tool of macroeconomic policy in the developing world. The macroeconomic effects of adopting a fixed peg, of adjusting it, or of operating under alternative crawling exchange-rate regimes continue to be important policy issues in these countries.

6.2 Credibility and Exchange-Rate Management

Policymakers in developing countries typically face a dilemma when using the exchange rate as a policy instrument. Although a nominal depreciation may improve the trade balance and the balance of payments, it is usually associated with a rise in the price level, which may turn into inflation and ultimately erode external competitiveness. Conversely, keeping the exchange rate fixed to stabilize prices in the presence of a large current account deficit is often not a viable option if the country faces a shortage of foreign exchange reserves or an external borrowing constraint. Nevertheless, as argued in the previous section, the exchange rate continues to be used as a policy instrument in developing countries, many of which are moving away from pegging to a single currency to more flexible exchange-rate arrangements, such as composite pegs.[5]

Despite this notable evolution toward the discretionary use of the exchange rate as a policy tool, a variety of arguments have recently been proposed in favor of adopting a fixed-exchange-rate regime.[6] The debate has recently focused on the role of the exchange rate as an anchor for the domestic price level and on the "credibility effect" that a fixed rate may attach to a disinflation program when the commitment to defend the parity is clearly established.[7] Without central bank credibility, private agents will continue to expect a high inflation rate, and this will increase the cost of any attempt to stabilize domestic prices. Establishing credibility means convincing the public that the central bank will not deviate from its exchange rate or money supply target in order to secure short-term benefits associated with surprise inflation. This requires that the public be convinced that the authorities have some incentive to refrain from introducing monetary surprises.[8] It has been argued that by acting as a constraint on macroeconomic policies, a fixed exchange rate may enhance the credibility of the central bank's commitment to maintaining a low and stable rate of money growth.

This section examines recent arguments favoring a fixed-exchange-rate regime that are based on inflation problems caused by policymakers' lack of credibility. We first present a simple model that allows us to establish the basic time inconsistency proposition, and to determine the degree of credibility of a fixed exchange rate by examining how the policymaker is induced to behave under alternative policy rules. We then focus on how the "devaluation bias" generated by the time inconsistency problem faced by the policymaker can be alleviated by building up "reputation" or by the need to signal policy commitment. Finally, we examine the costs and benefits of joining an international monetary arrangement in which the country surrenders the power to alter the exchange rate.[9]

6.2.1 Time Inconsistency and Exchange-Rate Policy

Consider a small open economy producing traded and nontraded goods. The economy's exchange rate is determined by a policymaker whose preferences relate to external competitiveness and price stability. The foreign-currency price of traded goods is determined on world markets. Agents in the nontraded goods sector set their prices so as to protect their position relative to the traded goods sector, and to respond to domestic demand shocks. Prices in the nontraded goods sector are set *before* the policymaker sets the exchange rate.[10] The domestic rate of inflation, π, is given by

$$\pi = \delta\pi_N + (1 - \delta)(\epsilon + \pi_T^*), \quad 0 < \delta < 1, \tag{1}$$

where ϵ denotes the rate of devaluation of the nominal exchange rate, π_N the rate of increase in the price of nontradables, π_T^* the rate of increase in the price of tradables, and $1 - \delta$ the degree of openness. The government's loss function, L^g, depends on deviations of the rate of depreciation of the real exchange rate from a target rate Θ, and the inflation rate:

$$L^g = -\alpha\left[(\epsilon + \pi_T^* - \pi_N) - \Theta\right] + \lambda\pi^2/2, \quad \alpha, \lambda \geq 0. \tag{2}$$

The stated objective reflects the assumption that the authorities would welcome an improvement in competitiveness, which results from a depreciation of the real exchange rate. The rate of change of the real exchange rate enters the loss function linearly, because the authorities are assumed to attach a negative weight to a real appreciation relative to their target.[11] The government's objective is to minimize its loss function given by (2).

Agents in the nontraded goods sector change prices in reaction to fluctuations in the (expected) domestic price of tradable goods, and to an exogenous demand disturbance to their sector d_N, which occurs at the beginning of the period and becomes known immediately. Their loss function is therefore taken to be

$$L^p = [\pi_N - (\epsilon^a + \pi_T^*) - \Phi d_N]^2/2, \quad \Phi \geq 0, \tag{3}$$

where ϵ^a denotes the expected rate of depreciation of the exchange rate. The price setters' objective is to minimize L^p.

When the authorities decide whether or not to devalue the exchange rate, they know prices set in the nontraded goods sector. Substituting (1) in (2) and setting $\pi_T^* = 0$ for simplicity, the optimal rate of adjustment of the nominal exchange rate, conditional on π_N, is given by[12]

$$\epsilon = \frac{\delta}{1 - \delta} \left[\frac{\alpha}{\lambda\delta(1 - \delta)} - \pi_N \right]. \tag{4}$$

From (3), the optimal rate of inflation in the nontradable goods sector from the perspective of agents in that sector is

$$\pi_N = \Phi d_N + \epsilon^a. \tag{5}$$

In a discretionary regime (defined as one in which the private sector and the policymaker take each other's behavior as given when making their own decisions) the equilibrium values of the nontradable inflation rate and the rate of devaluation ($\tilde{\pi}_N$, $\tilde{\epsilon}$) are found by imposing rational expectations ($\epsilon^a = \epsilon$) on the part of agents in the nontraded goods sector and solving Equations (4) and (5) simultaneously. This yields

$$\tilde{\pi}_N = (\kappa + \Phi d_N)/\Omega \geq 0, \tag{6a}$$

$$\tilde{\epsilon} = (\kappa - \upsilon\Phi d_N)/\Omega \gtrless 0, \tag{6b}$$

where $\upsilon = \delta/(1 - \delta)$, $\Omega = \upsilon/\delta \geq 1$, and $\kappa = \alpha\upsilon/\lambda\delta(1 - \delta) > 0$.

Equations (6a) and (6b) indicate that, in the absence of demand shocks, the optimal discretionary policy requires a positive rate of devaluation and results in a positive rate of inflation in the nontradable sector. When demand shocks are present, that is, $d_N \neq 0$, whether the rate of devaluation $\tilde{\epsilon}$ is positive or negative depends on the relative importance of the real-exchange-rate target and the inflation objective in the government's loss function. When the latter predominates—that is, when λ is "high," when α is "low," or more generally, when $\alpha/\lambda < \delta(1 - \delta)\Phi d_N$—the optimal policy may call for an appreciation of the nominal exchange rate.

Substituting (6a) and (6b) in (1)–(3) yields the solutions for the inflation rate and the policymaker's loss function under discretion:

$$\tilde{\pi} = \kappa/\Omega, \tag{7a}$$

$$\tilde{L}^g = \alpha(\Phi d_N + \Theta) + \lambda(\kappa/\Omega)^2/2. \tag{7b}$$

Equation (7a) indicates that the economy's inflation rate is independent of the demand shock and increasing with the relative weight attached to competitiveness in the policymaker's loss function, α/λ. Inflation is positive because, if it were zero, the policymaker would always have an incentive to devalue. This is because, from (2), at zero inflation the gain from enhanced competitiveness outweighs the loss from higher inflation. Knowing this, private agents would adjust π_N upward (see Equation (5)), which implies that overall inflation must be positive. Thus, the policymaker incurs a net loss unless d_N takes on a large negative value—which simultaneously improves competitiveness and reduces the rate of increase in nontradable prices.

Consider now the case in which the government is able to commit to a predetermined exchange rate. Formally, this means that in minimizing its loss function, it takes into account the effect of its announced policy on private sector behavior, on the assumption that the private sector believes that the government will not renege. Rather than solving (3) for a given value of π_N, the government substitutes (5) into (3) and minimizes with respect to $\epsilon(= \epsilon^a)$. In this case the government will announce and maintain a fixed exchange rate—or a rate of devaluation $\epsilon = 0$.[13] If the private sector believes the announcement and acts on that basis, Equation (5) yields $\overline{\pi}_N = \Phi d_N$, which in turn implies $\overline{\pi} = \delta\Phi d_N$ and

$$\overline{L}^g = \alpha(\Phi d_N + \Theta) + \lambda\overline{\pi}^2/2, \tag{8}$$

or, if $d_N \equiv 0$,

$$\overline{L}^g = \alpha\Theta. \tag{8'}$$

From (7b) and (8), $\overline{L}^g \leq \tilde{L}^g$. Thus, the no-devaluation equilibrium gives a value of the loss function that is *less* than that obtained under the non-cooperative, discretionary regime when $d_N \equiv 0$. This reflects the fact that the policymaker is not able to achieve the gain in competitiveness sought in the discretionary regime, because price setters simply increase nontradable prices accordingly. Thus, a binding commitment entails a gain in the form of a lower inflation rate with no loss in competitiveness.[14]

Consider now the case where the government announces at the beginning of the period its intention to maintain the exchange rate fixed (that is, $\epsilon = 0$), but decides to deviate from this policy and to implement a discretionary change once price decisions have been made. If price setters believe the zero-devaluation announcement, they will choose $\ddot{\pi}_N = \Phi d_N$. Substituting this result in (4), the optimal rate of devaluation chosen by the policymaker becomes

$$\ddot{\epsilon} = \kappa - \upsilon\Phi d_N. \tag{9}$$

The minimized value of the policymaker's loss function under this "cheating" regime is

$$\ddot{L}^g = -\alpha[\kappa - \Phi d_N/(1 - \delta) - \Theta] + \lambda\ddot{\pi}^2/2, \tag{10}$$

where $\ddot{\pi} = (1 - \delta)\kappa$.

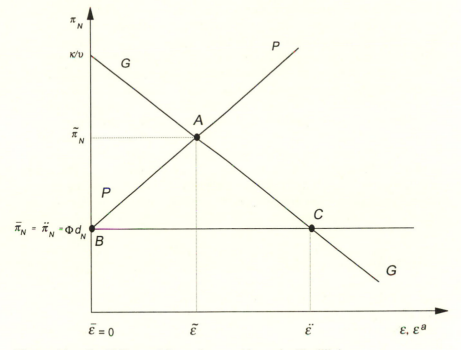

Figure 6.1   Credibility and Commitment: Alternative Equilibria

Source: Agénor (1994c, p. 7).

For $d_N \equiv 0$, it can be verified that $\ddot{L}^g < \bar{L}^g < \tilde{L}^g$.[15] The discretionary solution produces the largest loss for the authorities, resulting in a positive rate
of devaluation and inflation. Because the loss is lower when the government
succeeds in "fooling" the private sector than when it commits itself without
reneging, there is an incentive to deviate from the fixed-exchange-rate target
if price setters can be made to believe that the current parity will be adhered
to, so that, for $d_N \equiv 0$, $\ddot{\epsilon} = \kappa > \tilde{\epsilon} = \kappa/\Omega > \bar{\epsilon} = 0$. However, although the
rate of depreciation is *higher* under cheating than under discretion, the over-
all inflation rate is the same under both regimes ($\tilde{\pi} = \ddot{\pi}$), since, for $d_N \equiv 0$,
$\ddot{\pi}_N = 0$ and $\tilde{\pi}_N = \kappa/\Omega > 0$. The rate of inflation in the nontradable sector
is *lower* when price setters are fooled than in the discretionary regime. More-
over, under discretion, the rate of depreciation of the real exchange rate is zero
($\tilde{\epsilon} - \tilde{\pi}_N = 0$). The authorities are incapable of altering the real exchange rate
by a nominal devaluation. By contrast, if the private sector can be success-
fully misled by the fixed-exchange-rate announcement, $\ddot{\epsilon} - \ddot{\pi}_N = \kappa$. Such
a strategy, however, entails reputational costs, an issue we examine below.

The three different solutions are represented in Figure 6.1.[16] In the
π_N–ϵ space, the locus PP reflects the reaction function of the private sector (given by Equation (4)) and has a positive slope, while GG depicts the

policymaker's reaction function under discretion (given by Equation (5)) and has a negative slope. The noncooperative equilibrium is located at the intersection of curves GG and PP, that is, at point A. The precommitment solution obtains at point B, while the "cheating" solution obtains at point C. The discretionary solution is characterized by a "devaluation bias." Private agents know that once they set prices of nontradables, the policymaker has the incentive to devalue so as to depreciate the real exchange rate and improve the balance of payments. They therefore set prices at a higher level, to the point where they believe the authorities are unwilling to trade off a higher inflation rate for a more depreciated real exchange rate. The precommitment solution, although not the best possible, provides a better outcome than the discretionary alternative. This provides an argument in favor of a fixed exchange rate—assuming the commitment can be made binding and perceived as such by price setters.[17]

6.2.2 Credibility of a Fixed Exchange Rate

Precommitment to a preannounced zero-devaluation rule can be successful only if the authorities incur some penalty if they deviate from the rule. One form that this penalty can take is that if the government were to depart from the preannounced rule, the public would not believe its announcements in the following period(s), and the economy would revert to the discretionary equilibrium. In such a context, a zero-devaluation rule—that is, a fixed-exchange-rate target—is credible if the temptation to deviate from the rule is less than the discounted value of the "punishment" associated with reversion to the discretionary equilibrium. Following Barro and Gordon (1983) and Horn and Persson (1988), the degree of credibility of a fixed exchange rate, C, can be defined as the difference between the present value of the punishment ($\overline{L}^g - \tilde{L}^g$) and the temptation ($\ddot{L}^g - \overline{L}^g$):

$$C = (\ddot{L}^g - \overline{L}^g) - \gamma(\overline{L}^g - \tilde{L}^g)/(1 - \gamma), \qquad (11)$$

where γ is a discount rate.

Substituting Equations (7b), (8), and (10) in (11) and setting $d_N \equiv 0$, it can be shown that a necessary condition for the degree of credibility of a fixed exchange rate to be positive is

$$\tilde{\pi} \geq 2\alpha(1 - \gamma)/\lambda(1 - \delta) > \overline{\pi} = 0. \qquad (12)$$

Equation (12) indicates that a fixed exchange rate can be credible only if the inflation rate that would obtain in a discretionary regime is high enough to "discourage" any attempt to devalue. Using (7a), it can be shown that (12) requires, in turn, $\gamma \geq 0.5$. A fixed exchange rate, under perfect information about the policymaker's preferences, is the optimal strategy, provided that the future costs of higher inflation are not sufficiently discounted so as to fall short of the current gain from a depreciation of the real exchange rate resulting from a devaluation. Credibility requires that the short-term benefits from a nominal devaluation be forgone in order to secure the gain from low inflation over the long term.[18]

6.2.3 Reputation, Signaling, and Exchange-Rate Commitment

We now consider how reputational factors and signaling considerations may help mitigate the time inconsistency problem faced by the policymaker in choosing an exchange-rate policy.[19]

Following Rogoff (1989), let us assume that there is a continuum of types of policymakers that differ with respect to the cost incurred from reneging on a fixed-exchange-rate commitment. As time proceeds, private beliefs are updated on the basis of observed exchange-rate policy: the longer the policymaker sticks to a fixed exchange rate, the lower is the expected rate of devaluation. But if the policymaker deviates even once from the fixed-exchange-rate target, private agents will raise devaluation expectations (to the discretionary level) for the indefinite future. A sequential process of this type leads agents to revise continually upward the threshold level of cost below which they assume the government has an incentive to renege—provided, of course, that no devaluation occurs. As a result, devaluation expectations tend to fall over time. Although agents may never discover the "true" value of the cost attached to reneging by the policymaker, the behavior of expectations creates an incentive to commit to a fixed-exchange-rate rule. "Reputation" is thus viewed as a mechanism leading to a progressively lower expected rate of depreciation.[20] In this context, a government facing a relatively low cost of reneging may be tempted to devalue very early in its term in office. But if the policymaker's horizon is long enough (or if the discount rate is high enough), the temptation to devalue is lowered because of the costs resulting from high devaluation expectations.

The implication of the preceding analysis is that even policymakers who are concerned with a balance-of-payments target may tend, at the start of their term in office, to act as if they are not in order to maintain the impression (among private agents) that inflation is their primary target and thereby lower expectations. Policymakers of this type may, nevertheless, devalue near the end of their term in an attempt to improve competitiveness and raise output. A nominal devaluation will "work," in this context, as long as the policymaker has a reputation of being a "pegger" or as long as the cost of reneging on the exchange-rate commitment is not too large. The critical element on which this result rests is the public's lack of information about the policymaker: even if the authorities are committed to maintaining a fixed exchange rate, private agents cannot know this with certainty. Complete credibility in this context is impossible to achieve. This line of reasoning also suggests, however, that reputational factors can help mitigate the time inconsistency problem. A government that is more concerned about a balance-of-payments target retains an incentive to avoid the discretionary outcome early in its term of office because doing so secures more favorable price behavior on the part of private agents.

Consider now a situation in which there are only two types of policymakers, who differ in the relative weights they attach to the "internal" target (inflation) and the "external" target (the real exchange rate). Policymakers of the first type, labeled D-policymakers ("devaluers"), attach a value both to low inflation and to a more depreciated real exchange rate. The second type, labeled P-policymakers ("peggers"), attach a lower weight to the real exchange rate in its loss function. Price setters do not know the type of government currently in office, but they have a prior probability that it is type P. As time proceeds, private agents observe the exchange-rate policy and revise their assessment of the policymaker's type.

In the presence of imperfect information about policymakers' preferences, as shown by Vickers (1986), a policymaker who cares more about inflation can signal this preference to the private sector by inducing a temporary recession. Policymakers with relatively greater concern about output and employment are unwilling to bear this cost, so the signal successfully conveys the policymaker's preference for low inflation. In the context of the above framework, Vickers's analysis suggests that even a government concerned more about inflation (that is, a P-type policymaker) may have an incentive to devalue by less than it would otherwise find optimal, in order to signal its preferences to the public. One way for the P-type government to reveal its identity might be to select an exchange-rate policy that the D-type policymaker would not find optimal to replicate. Such a policy would not, of course, be without cost for the P-type policymaker, but could be a credible signaling device under some circumstances.

Assume, for simplicity, that the policy horizon is limited to two periods. The precise conditions under which the P-government will depart from the optimal, perfect-information response in the first period in order to successfully reveal its type can readily be established (see Agénor, 1994c). Through devaluing by less than it would find otherwise optimal, an anti-inflation government is able to signal immediately and unambiguously its commitment to price stability to private agents, and is able to secure the gain from lower inflation expectations in the second period.

The above result provides an interesting argument in support of an exchange-rate freeze in stabilization programs, of the type that has been observed recently in many Latin American countries and Israel (see Chapter 8). Fixing the exchange rate (or, more generally, lowering the rate of depreciation of the exchange rate) may prove successful in signaling the anti-inflationary commitment of the policymaker, and will therefore enhance the credibility of a stabilization program. Indeed, an extension of the argument suggests that it may ultimately be beneficial for a government to *revalue* its currency to convey unambiguous information about its policy preferences. Chile, for instance, revalued its currency twice in 1977, in an attempt to demonstrate the government's resolve to fight inflation.

There are, however, situations in which signaling considerations either are not important for or are incapable of mitigating the time inconsistency problem faced by policymakers operating under a fixed-exchange-rate regime. For instance, both types of policymakers may have a high rate of time preference, in which case the optimal solutions obtained under perfect information and uncertain preferences may not be very different from each other. Intuitively, this is because D-type policymakers have a reduced incentive to masquerade as P-type. If price setters understand that the future is heavily discounted, P-policymakers need not send an overly "strong" signal to distinguish themselves from D-type policymakers. Another situation, which is often relevant for developing countries, may be that, when implementing a disinflation program, a country is faced with a large current account deficit and a financing constraint. If the deficit is unsustainable and perceived as such by private agents, a "high" rate of depreciation will appear inevitable and will undermine any signaling attempt. Finally, there are other ways for a P-type government to send signals that would enable the public to clearly identify its preferences: such signals may be sent via the removal of capital controls, a drastic cut in the budget deficit, or the appointment of a "conservative" central banker. The benefits and costs of alternative signaling strategies are further discussed in Chapter 10, in the context of disinflation programs.

6.2.4 Credibility Effects of Monetary Unions

An alternative way to attach credibility to a fixed-exchange-rate regime (and signal the policymaker's commitment to low inflation) would be for the authorities to surrender the power to alter the exchange rate. This could be achieved, for instance, by forming a monetary union under which a group of countries adopt a common currency and fix their parity against a major currency; for developing countries, the CFA Franc Zone, the Common Monetary Area (which comprises South Africa, Lesotho, Namibia, and Swaziland), and the East Caribbean Currency Area provide examples of such an arrangement.[21] One way for a government to establish credibility for an anti-inflationary policy is to appoint a "conservative" central banker, one highly averse to inflation (Rogoff, 1985). It has been argued that membership in a monetary union plays an equivalent role: it allows member countries, in effect, to appoint a "strong" central banker, establishing credibility by linking a country's monetary policy to the anti-inflationary preferences of the dominant central bank. By "tying their hands" when joining a fixed-exchange-rate arrangement, therefore, "weak" policymakers can combat inflationary expectations more effectively (Giavazzi and Pagano, 1988). In these circumstances it may be desirable for the authorities to adopt an institutional arrangement that imposes large—political or otherwise—costs on reneging on such precommitment. The important general point emphasized in this line of reasoning is that, to be credible, such monetary arrangements must be based on institutional features that make it costly to alter the exchange rate.

There are, however, costs associated with forgoing the use of the exchange rate as a policy instrument, particularly in the presence of large external shocks. The credibility of a country's commitment to the "rules of the game" of a monetary union, and thus the extent to which membership in a union can overcome time inconsistency problems, must depend on the nature of such costs. We briefly examine these issues by extending the model developed previously so as to capture the institutional and macroeconomic constraints imposed by an international monetary arrangement.

Suppose that a country must decide whether or not to keep its exchange rate fixed within the framework of a monetary union with its major trading partner.[22] Suppose, moreover, that inflation in the partner country is positive (that is, $\pi_T^* > 0$). Both the policymaker and private agents learn about changes in foreign prices immediately after their occurrence, and make their decisions afterward. For simplicity, let $d_N \equiv 0$. The discretionary solution is now given by

$$\tilde{\pi}_N = \kappa/\Omega \geq 0, \tag{13a}$$

$$\tilde{\epsilon} = (\kappa/\Omega) - \pi_T^* \gtrless 0, \tag{13b}$$

which yields an overall inflation rate equal to

$$\tilde{\pi} = \tilde{\pi}_N = \kappa/\Omega \tag{14}$$

and a constant real exchange rate ($\tilde{\epsilon} + \pi_T^* - \tilde{\pi}_N = 0$). The associated loss for the policymaker is

$$\tilde{L}^g = \lambda(\kappa/\Omega)^2/2. \tag{15}$$

If the authorities decide to keep the nominal exchange rate fixed, and if their commitment to such a policy is assumed by price setters ($\bar{\epsilon} = 0, \bar{\pi}_N = \bar{\pi} = \pi_T^*$, so that $\bar{\epsilon} + \pi_T^* - \bar{\pi} = 0$), the loss function is equal to

$$\bar{L}^g = \lambda(\pi_T^*)^2/2. \tag{16}$$

A comparison of Equations (15) and (16) shows that the loss under a (credible) commitment to maintain the exchange rate fixed is higher than under discretion when $\pi_T^* > \kappa/\Omega$—in which case the government may decide to renege on its commitment to a fixed parity. When the foreign price shock is small, its direct inflationary impact is limited, and the rate of appreciation of the nominal exchange rate required to offset its impact in the discretionary regime is also small. If the commitment to the fixed exchange rate is credibly enforced, the rate of appreciation of the real exchange rate is the same under both regimes. But the overall effect on inflation under precommitment is π_T^* (since prices of nontradables are adjusted upward), while under discretion it is κ/Ω.

The analysis suggests that, for a policymaker concerned with both inflation and competitiveness, the desirability of "tying one's hands" as a solution to the time inconsistency problem depends on what one's hands are tied to. When union members have stable, low inflation rates, precommitment to a fixed exchange rate may help demonstrate domestic resolve to maintaining financial discipline. But when the economy is subject to large nominal shocks, the credibility gain may be outweighed by the cost of lost autonomy.

In practice, exchange-rate arrangements involving a peg typically incorporate an "escape clause" or a contingency mechanism that allows members to deviate from the declared parity under exceptional circumstances.[23] To examine this issue in the present setting, suppose that π_T^* is now a random variable that follows a uniform distribution over the interval (0, c) and is realized *after* private agents make their price decisions. Suppose also that the domestic country maintains a fixed parity when foreign price shocks are "small" but is allowed to alter the fixed exchange rate discretionarily if the foreign price shock is "large." The probability that the contingency mechanism will be invoked is therefore $q = \text{Prob}(\pi_T^* \geq \mu)$, where $0 \leq q \leq 1$, and $\mu \leq c$ denotes a given threshold. Under the assumption regarding the distribution of π_T^*, this probability is given by

$$q = \text{Prob}(\pi_T^* \geq \mu) = \int_\mu^c (1/c)\,d\pi_T^* = (c - \mu)/c. \tag{17}$$

Price setters form expectations prior to the realization of the foreign price shock. If they are aware of the policy rule followed by the authorities, the expected rate of depreciation of the exchange rate will be given by

$$\epsilon^a = qE(\epsilon|\pi_T^* \geq \mu) + (1 - q) \cdot 0,$$

or[24]

$$\epsilon^a = q(\kappa - \Omega\overline{\pi}_T^*)/(1 + vq), \tag{18}$$

where $\overline{\pi}_T^* = E(\pi_T^*|\pi_T^* \geq \mu) = (c + \mu)/2$. Suppose that, for the sake of argument, $\overline{\pi}_T^* \leq \kappa/\Omega$ so that $\epsilon^a \geq 0$. Equation (18) indicates that when $q = 0$ the expected rate of depreciation is also zero. By contrast, when $q = 1$ the expected rate of depreciation is $\epsilon^a = \kappa/\Omega - \overline{\pi}_T^*$, a solution that can be interpreted as the rate that would prevail in the purely discretionary regime examined above with a stochastic foreign inflation rate.[25] In general, as long as there is a positive probability less than 1 that the contingency mechanism will be invoked, the expected rate of depreciation is lower than under pure discretion since $q < 1$. The discretionary exchange-rate policy when the escape clause is activated is given by[26]

$$\tilde{\epsilon} = (\kappa + \Omega vq\overline{\pi}_T^*)/(1 + vq) - \Omega\pi_T^*, \tag{19}$$

which is lower than the value that would prevail under pure discretion (obtained by setting $q = 1$ in Equation (19)), since devaluation expectations are lower. An implication of Equation (19) is that the higher q is—or, equivalently, the lower μ is—the more effective the contingency mechanism will be in mitigating the devaluation bias of the discretionary regime ($\partial\tilde{\epsilon}/\partial q < 0$). A high value of q does, however, generate real costs in circumstances in which foreign price shocks turn out to be "small." To illustrate this result, note that in a purely discretionary regime, the *actual* (ex post) change in the real exchange rate is given by, using (18) and (19) with $q = 1$ and noting that $\tilde{\pi}_N = \epsilon^a + \pi_T^*$,

$$\tilde{\epsilon} + \pi_T^* - \tilde{\pi}_N = -\Omega(\pi_T^* - \overline{\pi}_T^*), \tag{20}$$

which essentially reflects unanticipated changes in the foreign inflation rate. By contrast, in a regime where the possibility to invoke an escape mechanism exists, the actual rate of depreciation of the real exchange rate is determined by the size of the foreign price shock. If the realized value of π_T^* is sufficiently large to trigger the contingency mechanism, Equations (18) and (19) imply

$$\tilde{\epsilon} + \pi_T^* - \tilde{\pi}_N = [\kappa(1 - q) + q\Omega^2\overline{\pi}_T^*]/(1 + vq) - \Omega\pi_T^*, \tag{21}$$

which indicates (by comparison with (20)) that the real rate of depreciation is lower than under pure discretion. However, if π_T^* turns out to be "small," the authorities will maintain the nominal exchange rate fixed. The change in the real exchange rate will in this case be given by $(\pi_T^* - \tilde{\pi}_N)$, that is, $-\epsilon^a$. Equation (18) indicates therefore that in "normal circumstances," a high probability of using the contingency mechanism may have a negative effect on competitiveness, since nontradable prices are set at a level that may be higher than they would be if instead $\epsilon^a = 0$. This suggests, therefore, that if escape mechanisms are to be considered as part of an exchange-rate arrangement, q should not be "too high"; that is, the threshold above which a discretionary adjustment of the exchange rate is allowed should not be excessively low.

6.3 Speculative Attacks and Balance-of-Payments Crises

A fundamental proposition of open-economy macroeconomics is that the viability of a fixed-exchange-rate regime requires maintaining long-run consistency between monetary, fiscal, and exchange-rate policies. "Excessive" domestic credit growth leads to a gradual loss of foreign reserves and ultimately to an abandonment of the fixed exchange rate, once the central bank becomes incapable of defending the parity any longer. Over the past decade a large formal literature has focused on the short- and long-run consequences of incompatible macroeconomic policies for the balance of payments of a small open economy in which agents are able to anticipate future decisions by policymakers. In a pioneering paper, Krugman (1979) showed that under a fixed-exchange-rate regime, domestic credit creation in excess of money demand growth may lead to a sudden speculative attack against the currency that forces the abandonment of the fixed exchange rate and the adoption of a flexible-rate regime. Moreover, this attack will always occur *before* the central bank would have run out of reserves in the absence of speculation, and will take place at a well-defined date.

This section examines the implications of the literature on balance-of-payments crises for understanding the collapse of exchange-rate regimes in developing countries.[27] We first set out a single-good, full-employment, small open-economy model that specifies the basic theoretical framework used for analyzing balance-of-payments crises. We then summarize some important extensions of this framework, namely, the nature of the postcollapse exchange-rate regime, the output and current account implications of an anticipated exchange-rate crisis, and the role of external borrowing and capital controls. Finally, we briefly review recent exchange-rate crises in Argentina, Brazil, Chile, and Mexico.

6.3.1 A Model of Exchange Regime Collapse

Consider a small open economy whose residents consume a single, tradable good. Domestic supply of the good is exogenous, and its foreign-currency price is fixed (at, say, unity). The domestic price level is equal, as a result of purchasing power parity, to the nominal exchange rate. Agents hold three categories of assets: domestic money (which is not held abroad), and domestic and foreign bonds, which are perfectly substitutable. There are no private banks, so that the money stock is equal to the sum of domestic credit issued by the central bank and the domestic-currency value of foreign reserves held by the central bank. Foreign reserves earn no interest, and domestic credit expands at a constant growth rate. Finally, agents are endowed with perfect foresight.

The model is defined by the following set of equations:

$$m_t - p_t = \bar{y} - \alpha i_t, \quad \alpha > 0, \tag{22}$$

$$m_t = \gamma D_t + (1 - \gamma)R_t, \quad 0 < \gamma < 1, \tag{23}$$

$$\dot{D}_t = \mu, \quad \mu > 0, \tag{24}$$

$$p_t = e_t, \tag{25}$$

$$i_t = i^* + \dot{e}_t. \tag{26}$$

All variables, except interest rates, are measured in logarithms. m_t denotes the nominal money stock, D_t domestic credit, R_t the domestic-currency value of foreign reserves held by the central bank, e_t the spot exchange rate, p_t the price level, $\bar{y}$ exogenous output, i^* the foreign interest rate (assumed constant), and i_t the domestic interest rate.

Equation (22) relates the real demand for money positively to income and negatively to the domestic interest rate. Equation (23) is a log-linear approximation to the identity defining the money stock as the stock of reserves and domestic credit, which grows at the rate μ (Equation 24). Equations (25) and (26) define, respectively, purchasing power parity and uncovered interest parity.

Setting $\delta = \bar{y} - \alpha i^*$ and combining Equations (22), (25), and (26) yields

$$m_t - e_t = \delta - \alpha \dot{e}_t, \quad \delta > 0. \tag{27}$$

Under a fixed-exchange-rate regime, $e_t = \bar{e}$ and $\dot{e}_t = 0$, so that

$$m_t - \bar{e} = \delta, \tag{27'}$$

which indicates that the central bank accommodates any change in domestic money demand through the purchase or sale of foreign reserves to the public.[28] Using Equations (23) and (27') yields

$$R_t = (\delta + \bar{e} - \gamma D_t)/(1 - \gamma), \tag{28}$$

and, using (27),

$$\dot{R}_t = -\mu/\Theta, \qquad \Theta \equiv (1 - \gamma)/\gamma. \tag{29}$$

Equation (29) indicates that if domestic credit expansion is excessive (that is, if it exceeds the rate of growth of the demand for money, which depends on δ as shown in Equation (27') and is assumed here to be zero), reserves are run down at a rate proportional to the rate of credit expansion. Any finite stock of foreign reserves will therefore be depleted in a finite period of time.

Suppose that the central bank announces at time t that it will stop defending the current fixed exchange rate after reserves reach a lower bound, $\bar{R}$, at which point it will withdraw from the foreign exchange market and allow the exchange rate to float freely thereafter. With a positive rate of domestic credit growth, rational agents will anticipate that, without speculation, reserves will eventually fall to the lower bound, and will therefore foresee the ultimate collapse of the system. To avoid losses arising from an abrupt depreciation of the exchange rate at the time of collapse, speculators will force a crisis *before* the lower bound on reserves is reached. The issue is thus to determine the exact moment at which the fixed-exchange-rate regime is abandoned or, equivalently, the time of transition to a floating-rate regime.

The length of the transition period can be calculated by using a process of backward induction, which has been formalized by Flood and Garber (1984). In equilibrium, under perfect foresight, agents can never expect a discrete jump in the level of the exchange rate, since a jump would provide them with profitable arbitrage opportunities. As a consequence, arbitrage in the foreign exchange market requires the exchange rate that prevails immediately after the attack to equal the fixed rate prevailing at the time of the attack. Formally, the time of collapse is found at the point where the "shadow floating rate," which reflects market fundamentals, is equal to the prevailing fixed rate. The shadow floating rate is the exchange rate that would prevail with the current credit stock if reserves had fallen to the minimum level and the exchange rate were allowed to float freely. As long as the fixed exchange rate is more depreciated than the shadow floating rate, the fixed-rate regime is viable; beyond that point, the fixed rate is not sustainable. The reason is that if the shadow floating rate falls below the prevailing fixed rate, speculators would not profit from driving the government's stock of reserves to its lower bound and precipitating the adoption of a floating-rate regime, since they would experience an instantaneous capital loss on their purchases of foreign currency. On the other hand, if the shadow floating rate is above the fixed rate, speculators would experience an instantaneous capital gain. Neither anticipated capital gains nor losses at an infinite rate are compatible with a perfect-foresight equilibrium. Speculators will compete with each other to eliminate such opportunities. This type of behavior leads to an equilibrium attack, which incorporates the arbitrage condition that the preattack fixed rate should equal the postattack floating rate.

A first step, therefore, is to find the solution for the shadow floating exchange rate, which can be written as

$$e_t = \kappa_0 + \kappa_1 m_t, \tag{30}$$

where κ_0 and κ_1 are as-yet-undetermined coefficients and, from (23), $m_t = \gamma D_t + (1 - \gamma)\overline{R}$ when reserves reach their lower level.[29]

Taking the rate of change of Equation (30) and noting from Equation (23) that under a floating-rate regime $\dot{m}_t = \gamma \dot{D}_t$ yields

$$\dot{e}_t = \kappa_1 \gamma \mu. \tag{31}$$

In the postcollapse regime, therefore, the exchange rate depreciates steadily and proportionally to the rate of growth of domestic credit. Substituting (31) in (27) yields, with $\delta = 0$ for simplicity,

$$e_t = m_t + \alpha \kappa_1 \gamma \mu. \tag{32}$$

Comparing Equations (32) and (30) yields

$$\kappa_0 = \alpha \gamma \mu, \quad \kappa_1 = 1.$$

From Equation (24), $D_t = D_0 + \mu t$. Using the definition of m_t given above and substituting in Equation (32) yields

$$e_t = \gamma(D_0 + \alpha\mu) + (1 - \gamma)\overline{R} + \gamma \mu t. \tag{33}$$

The fixed-exchange-rate regime collapses when the prevailing parity, $\overline{e}$, equals the shadow floating rate, e_t. From (33) the exact time of collapse, t_c, is obtained by setting $\overline{e} = e_t$, so that

$$t_c = [\overline{e} - \gamma D_0 - (1 - \gamma)\overline{R}]/\gamma\mu - \alpha,$$

or, since from Equations (23) and (27') $\bar{e} = \gamma D_0 + (1 - \gamma)R_0$,

$$t_c = \Theta(R_0 - \overline{R})/\mu - \alpha, \tag{34}$$

where R_0 denotes the initial stock of reserves.

Equation (34) indicates that the higher the initial stock of reserves, the lower the critical level, or the lower the rate of credit expansion, the longer it will take before the collapse occurs. With no "speculative" demand for money, $\alpha = 0$, and the collapse occurs when reserves are run down to the minimum level. The interest rate (semi-) elasticity of money demand determines the size of the downward shift in money balances and reserves that takes place when the fixed-exchange-rate regime collapses and the nominal interest rate jumps to reflect an expected depreciation of the domestic currency. The larger α is, the earlier the crisis.[30]

The analysis implies, therefore, that the speculative attack always occurs before the central bank would have reached the minimum level of reserves in the absence of speculation. Using Equation (28) with $\delta = 0$ yields the stock of reserves just before the attack (that is, at t_c^-):[31]

$$R_{t_c^-} \equiv \lim_{t \to t^-} R_{t_c} = (\bar{e} - \gamma D_{t_c^-})/(1 - \gamma),$$

where $D_{t_c^-} = D_0 + \mu t_c^-$, so that

$$R_{t_c^-} = [\bar{e} - \gamma(D_0 + \mu t_c^-)]/(1 - \gamma). \tag{35}$$

Using Equation (34) yields

$$\bar{e} - \gamma D_0 = \gamma\mu(t_c^- + \alpha) + (1 - \gamma)\overline{R}. \tag{36}$$

Finally, combining (35) and (36) yields

$$R_{t_c^-} = \overline{R} + \mu\alpha/\Theta. \tag{37}$$

Figure 6.2 illustrates the process of a balance-of-payments crisis, under the assumption that the minimum level of reserves is zero.[32] The top panel of the figure portrays the behavior of reserves, domestic credit, and the money stock before and after the regime change, and the bottom panel displays the behavior of the exchange rate. Prior to the collapse at t_c, the money stock is constant, but its composition varies since domestic credit rises at the rate μ and reserves decline at the rate μ/Θ. An instant before the regime shift, a speculative attack occurs, and both reserves and the money stock fall by

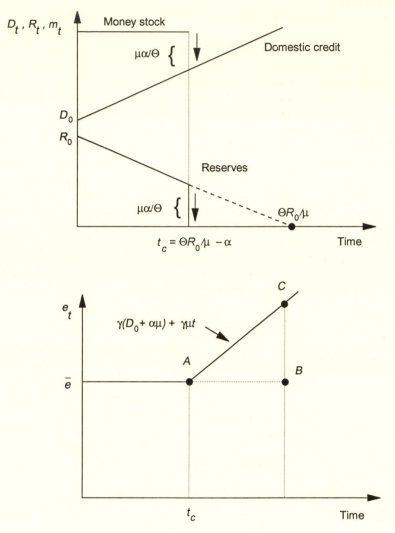

Figure 6.2   The Process of a Balance-of-Payments Crisis

Source: Agénor and Flood (1994, p. 230).

$\mu\alpha/\Theta$. Since $\overline{R} = 0$, the money stock is equal to domestic credit in the post-collapse regime. As shown in the bottom panel of Figure 6.2, the exchange rate remains constant at $\overline{e}$ until the collapse occurs. The path continuing through AB and then taking a discrete exchange-rate jump BC corresponds to the "natural collapse" scenario ($\alpha = 0$). With speculation, the transition occurs earlier, at A, preventing a discrete change in the exchange rate from occurring. Speculators, who foresee reserves running down to their critical level, avoid losses that would result from the discrete exchange-rate change by attacking the currency at the point where the transition to the float is smooth, that is, where the shadow floating exchange rate equals the prevailing fixed rate.[33]

6.3.2 Extensions to the Basic Framework

The literature on balance-of-payments crises has refined and extended the basic theory presented above in a variety of directions. This subsection examines some of the areas in which this literature has developed. It first considers alternative assumptions regarding the postcollapse exchange-rate regime, focusing on the case of a (perfectly anticipated) temporary post-collapse period of floating followed by repegging. We then discuss the real effects of an exchange-rate collapse, and the role of foreign borrowing and the imposition of capital controls as policy measures aimed at postponing (or preventing) the occurrence of a balance-of-payments crisis.

6.3.2.1 ALTERNATIVE POSTCOLLAPSE REGIMES

The focus of the early theoretical literature on balance-of-payments crises has been on the transition from a fixed exchange rate to a postcollapse floating rate. Various alternative scenarios are, however, suggested by actual experience. Following the breakdown of the fixed-rate system, the central bank can devalue the currency, implement a dual-exchange-rate arrangement, or adopt a crawling peg regime. In general, the timing of a crisis depends on the particular exchange-rate arrangement that agents expect the central bank to adopt after a run on its reserve stock has forced the abandonment of the initial fixed rate. We will examine, for illustrative purposes, the case in which, after allowing the currency to float for a certain period of time, the central bank returns to the foreign exchange market and fixes the exchange rate at a new, more depreciated level (Obstfeld, 1984).

Suppose that the length of the transitory period of floating, denoted by T, and the level $\bar{e}_H > \bar{e}$ to which the exchange rate will be pegged at the end of the transition are known with certainty.[34] The time t_c at which the speculative attack occurs is calculated, as before, by a process of backward induction. However, this principle now imposes two restrictions rather than one. First, as before, the initial fixed rate $\bar{e}$ must coincide with the relevant shadow floating rate, that is, $\bar{e} = e_{t_c}$. Second, at time $t_c + T$, the preannounced new fixed rate $\bar{e}_H$ must also coincide with the interim floating rate, $\bar{e}_H = e_{t_c + T}$.[35] The last requirement acts as a terminal condition on the exchange-rate differential equation.

In the foregoing discussion, when the central bank's policy was assumed to involve abandonment of the fixed rate and adoption of a permanent float thereafter, the shadow floating rate was given by Equation (32). Now, under a transitory floating regime, the shadow rate is given by

$$e_t = \kappa_0 + \kappa_1 m_t + C \exp(t/\alpha), \quad t_c \leq t \leq t_c + T \qquad (38)$$

where C is an undetermined constant.[36] The complete solution must therefore specify values for both t_c and C. These values are obtained by imposing $\bar{e} = e_{t_c}$ and $\bar{e}_H = e_{t_c+T}$ on Equation (38).[37] The solutions for t_c and C are

$$t_c = (\bar{e} - \alpha\gamma\mu - \gamma D_0 - \Omega)/\gamma\mu, \qquad (39a)$$

$$C = \Omega \exp(-t_c/\alpha), \qquad (39b)$$

where $\Omega = [(\bar{e}_H - \bar{e}) - \gamma\mu T]/[\exp(T/\alpha) - 1]$.

Equation (39a) indicates that the collapse time is linked to the magnitude of the expected devaluation $(\bar{e}_H - \bar{e})$ and the length of the transitional float.[38] Crises occur earlier the greater the anticipated devaluation: Equation (39a) shows that the higher the anticipated postdevaluation exchange rate, the sooner the speculative attack occurs $(\partial t_c/\partial \bar{e}_H < 0)$.[39] The relationship between the collapse time and the length of the floating-rate interval depends, in general, on the parameters of the model; it is negative for small T and positive for large T. If the transitional float is sufficiently brief, however, a speculative attack on the domestic currency will occur as soon as the private agents realize that the current exchange rate cannot be enforced indefinitely.

6.3.2.2 REAL EFFECTS OF AN ANTICIPATED COLLAPSE

Existing evidence suggests that balance-of-payments crises are often associated with large current account movements during the periods preceding, as well as during the periods following, such crises. Typically, large external deficits tend to emerge as agents adjust their consumption pattern, in addition to adjusting the composition of their holdings of financial assets, in anticipation of a crisis. As suggested by the experience of Argentina, Chile, and Mexico reviewed below, for instance, movements in the real exchange rate and the current account can be quite dramatic. Such movements may provide an explanation of why speculative attacks are often preceded by a period during which official foreign reserves are lost at accelerating rates.

A convenient framework for examining the real effects of exchange-rate crises was developed by Willman (1988), who assumes that domestic output is demand determined, positively related to the real exchange rate, and inversely related to the real interest rate.[40] The trade balance depends positively on the real exchange rate but is negatively related to aggregate demand. Prices are set as a mark-up over wages and imported input costs. In one variant of the model, nominal wages are determined through forward-looking contracts.[41] Under perfect foresight, an anticipated future collapse will affect wages immediately and, therefore, prices, the real exchange rate, output, and the trade balance. At the moment the collapse occurs, inflation jumps up, the rate of depreciation of the real exchange rate jumps down, and the real interest rate falls. As a result, output increases while the trade balance deteriorates. But since wage contracts are forward looking, antici-pated future increases in prices are discounted back to the present and affect current wages. Consequently, prices start adjusting before the collapse oc-curs. The real interest rate falls gradually and experiences a downward jump at the moment the collapse takes place, as indicated above. The decline in the (ex post) real interest rate has an expansionary effect on domestic ac-tivity before the collapse occurs. However, output also depends on the real exchange rate. The steady rise in domestic prices results in an apprecia-tion of the domestic currency, which has an adverse effect on economic activity and may outweigh the positive output effect resulting from a lower real interest rate. If relative price effects are strong, the net impact of an anticipated collapse on output may well be negative. The continuous loss of competitiveness, unless it is associated with a fall in aggregate demand (and thus downward pressure on the demand for imports), implies that the trade balance deteriorates in the periods preceding the collapse of the fixed-exchange-rate regime. The trade deficit increases further at the moment the crisis occurs and, in association with a gradual depreciation of the real ex-change rate, returns afterward to its steady-state level. The gradual appreci-ation of the real exchange rate until the time of collapse and the subsequent depreciation predicted by Willman's model account fairly well for the real-exchange-rate movements observed during crisis episodes in countries such as Argentina in the early 1980s, as discussed below.

The role of intertemporal substitution effects in understanding the real effects of exchange-rate crises has recently been clarified by Kimbrough (1992), who uses an optimizing framework in which money reduces trans-actions costs. Kimbrough shows that the effects of an anticipated specula-tive attack on the behavior of the current account depend crucially on the difference between the interest elasticity of the demand for money and the intertemporal elasticity of substitution in consumption. If the latter exceeds the former, an anticipated speculative attack raises consumption and real balances at the moment agents realize that the fixed exchange rate will even-tually collapse, and leads to a continued deterioration of the current account until the attack actually takes place. By contrast, if the interest elasticity of the demand for money exceeds the intertemporal elasticity of substitution in consumption, the outcome is an initial reduction in consumption and real money balances, and an immediate and continued improvement in the current account until the time of the speculative attack and the collapse of the fixed exchange rate. An implication of Kimbrough's analysis is that anticipated speculative attacks may not be associated with similar real effects in all countries and at all times. Nevertheless, as discussed below for the case of several Latin American countries, speculative attacks and impending balance-of-payments crises have often been associated in practice with large current account deficits.

6.3.2.3 BORROWING, CONTROLS, AND THE POSTPONEMENT OF A CRISIS

Countries facing balance-of-payments difficulties often have recourse to external borrowing to supplement the amount of reserves available to defend the official parity, or impose restrictions on capital outflows in an attempt to limit losses of foreign exchange reserves. In the basic model developed above, it is assumed that there is a critical level, known by everyone, below which foreign reserves are not allowed to be depleted. However, such a binding threshold may not exist. A central bank facing a perfect capital market can, at least in principle, increase foreign reserves at its disposal by short-term borrowing. Negative (net) reserves are therefore also feasible.

In fact, perfect access to international capital markets implies that, at any given time, central bank reserves can become negative without violating the government's intertemporal solvency constraint. Unlimited access to borrowing could therefore postpone or avoid a regime collapse. The rate of growth of domestic credit cannot, however, be *permanently* maintained above the world interest rate, because it would lead to a violation of the government budget constraint (Obstfeld, 1986c). In this sense, an overexpansionary credit policy would still ultimately lead to the collapse of a fixed-exchange-rate regime.[42] Moreover, even with perfect capital markets, the timing of borrowing matters considerably for the nature of speculative attacks. Suppose that the interest cost of servicing foreign debt exceeds the interest rate paid on reserves. If borrowing occurs just before the fixed exchange rate would have collapsed without borrowing, the crisis is likely to be postponed. If borrowing occurs long enough before the exchange-rate regime would have collapsed in the absence of borrowing, the crisis would occur earlier. The reason the collapse is brought forward is, of course, related to the servicing cost of foreign indebtedness on the public sector deficit, which raises the rate of growth of domestic credit (Buiter, 1987).

In practice, most developing countries face borrowing constraints on international capital markets. The existence of limited access to external financing has important implications for the behavior of inflation in an economy where agents are subject to an intertemporal budget constraint. Consider, for instance, a country that has no opportunity to borrow externally and in which the central bank transfers its net profits to the government. If a speculative attack occurs, the central bank will lose its stock of reserves, and its postcollapse profits from interest earnings on those reserves will drop to zero. As a consequence, net income of the government will fall and the budget deficit will deteriorate. If the deficit is financed by increased domestic credit—a typical situation for a developing country with limited access to domestic and external borrowing—the postcollapse inflation rate will exceed the rate that prevailed in the precollapse fixed-exchange-rate regime, raising inflation tax revenue so as to compensate for the fall in interest income (van Wijnbergen, 1991).

As indicated earlier, capital controls have often been used to limit losses of foreign exchange reserves and postpone a regime collapse. Such controls have been imposed either permanently or temporarily after the central bank had experienced significant losses, or at times when the domestic currency came under heavy pressure on foreign exchange markets.[43] With permanent controls, as shown by Agénor and Flood (1994), the higher the degree of capital controls, the longer it will take for the fixed exchange rate to collapse. This is because controls dampen the size of the expected future jump in the domestic nominal interest rate and the associated shift in the demand for money.

The effect of temporary capital controls on the timing of a balance-of-payments crisis has been studied most recently by Bacchetta (1990), who showed that temporary restrictions on capital movements may have pronounced real effects. In a perfect-foresight world, agents will anticipate the introduction of controls as soon as they realize the fundamental inconsistency between the fiscal policy and the fixed exchange rate. However, it is now critical to distinguish the case in which the timing of the policy change is perfectly anticipated and the case in which it is not. If controls take agents by surprise, capital outflows will increasingly be replaced by higher imports once such controls are put in place, leading eventually to a deterioration in the current account until a "natural" collapse occurs. The accelerated rate of depletion of foreign reserves through the current account will therefore precipitate the crisis, defeating the initial objective of controls. If capital controls are preannounced—or if agents are able to "guess" correctly the exact time at which controls will be introduced—a speculative attack may occur just *before* the controls are imposed, as agents attempt to readjust their portfolios and evade restrictions. Such an attack will, again, defeat the very purpose of capital controls and may in fact precipitate the regime collapse (Dellas and Stockman, 1993).

There are many other directions in which the theory of balance-of-payments crises has been extended, particularly in the areas of uncertainty (over the critical threshold of reserves, for instance, or the credit policy rule) and regime switches (see Agénor and Flood, 1994). The introduction of uncertainty on domestic credit growth provides a channel through which the sharp increases in domestic nominal interest rates that typically precede an exchange-rate crisis can be explained.[44] But beyond being consistent with rising interest rates prior to the crisis, the introduction of uncertainty in collapse models has several additional implications. First, the transition to a floating-rate regime becomes stochastic, implying that the collapse time is a random variable that cannot be determined explicitly, as before. Second, there will, in general, always be a nonzero probability of a speculative attack in the next period, a possibility that in turn produces a forward discount on the domestic currency—the so-called "peso problem" (Krasker, 1980) mentioned in Chapter 5. Available evidence indeed suggests that the forward premium—or, as an alternative indicator of exchange-rate expectations in developing countries, the parallel market premium—in foreign exchange markets tends to increase well before the regime shift. Third, the degree of uncertainty about the central bank's credit policy plays an important role in the speed at which reserves of the central bank are depleted (Claessens, 1991). In a stochastic setting, reserve losses exceed increases in domestic credit because of a rising probability of regime collapse, so that reserve depletion accelerates on the way to the regime change. As indicated above, such a pattern has often been observed in actual crises.

Finally, early models of balance-of-payments crises have been generally limited to the consideration of an exogenous rate of credit growth that has been, often implicitly, taken to reflect "fiscal constraints." The apparently ineluctable nature of a regime collapse that such an assumption entails runs into a conceptual difficulty—namely, why is it that policymakers do not attempt to prevent the crisis by adjusting their fiscal and credit policies? For instance, there is nothing in the basic model developed above that requires the central bank to float the currency and abandon the prevailing fixed exchange rate at the moment reserves hit their critical lower bound. Instead, the central bank could choose to change its credit policy rule (before reserves are exhausted) to make it consistent with a fixed-exchange-rate target. Some recent models of balance-of-payments crises have indeed considered endogenous changes of this type in monetary policy. Drazen and Helpman (1988) and Edwards and Montiel (1989), in particular, have emphasized that the assumption that the authorities choose to adjust the exchange rate instead of altering the underlying macroeconomic policy mix can provide only a temporary solution. Ultimately, if the new exchange-rate regime is inconsistent with the underlying fiscal policy process, there will be a need for a new policy regime.

6.3.3 Evidence on Balance-of-Payments Crises

We now briefly review recent experiences with exchange-rate and balance-of-payments crises in four developing countries: Argentina, Brazil, Chile, and Mexico. In many regards, the experience of these countries appears to be fairly representative of the main characteristics of these phenomena.

The Argentine experience in the early 1980s has been well documented by several authors, including Connolly (1986) and Cumby and van Wijnbergen (1989). As discussed in more detail in Chapter 8, in December 1978 the Argentine authorities adopted a stabilization program aimed at containing soaring inflation (in excess of 300 percent annually) and an enormous public sector deficit. A key aspect of the program was the setting of the exchange rate, which was adjusted based on a preannounced declining rate of crawl. Following a period of relative success, a series of bank failures in early 1980 touched off a financial crisis. The rate of increase of credit to the financial sector increased sharply in early 1980, undermining confidence in the exchange-rate regime. Large and increasing reserve losses coincided with the increase in domestic credit. The loss in confidence was reflected in a sharp increase in interest rates on peso deposits relative to foreign rates adjusted for the announced rate of devaluation. At the same time, the period prior to the collapse was marked by a steep rise in the parallel market premium (beginning in early 1981), very high inflation rates, and a sustained appreciation of the real exchange rate. The current account balance moved from a surplus of $1.9 billion in 1978 to deficits of $0.5 billion in 1979 and $4.8 billion in 1980. The crawling peg policy was abandoned in June 1981 and was followed by the temporary adoption of a dual-exchange-rate regime.

The Brazilian cruzado crisis occurred in October 1986, some eight months after the Cruzado Plan was launched in February of that year (see chapter 8). The plan attempted to fix all prices, including the nominal exchange rate. As in other instances, however, domestic credit increased rapidly throughout the precollapse period. Through 1986 domestic credit expanded by more than 40 percent while central bank foreign reserves again declined at an increasing rate. Net foreign reserves declined by some $5.8 billion during 1986. The Cruzado Plan was abandoned in October 1986 with devaluation of the cruzado. The parallel market premium increased steadily from around 30 percent in March 1986 to more than 100 percent in the month preceding the devaluation.

The Chilean peso crisis occurred in June 1982 and, as in the case of Argentina, appears to have been precipitated by a series of banking failures (see Velasco, 1987). The central bank responded to the failures with sharp increases in the rate of domestic credit creation, which reached nearly 100 percent in the last quarter of 1981. The acceleration of domestic credit expansion coincided with an appreciating real exchange rate and increasing foreign reserve losses by the central bank for some months prior to the actual exchange-rate collapse on June 15, 1982. The eroding confidence in the exchange-rate regime was reflected in a continually widening spread between spot and forward rates for the Chilean peso as well as a rising parallel market premium prior to the day of collapse.

The crisis of the Mexican peso that occurred in February 1982 was accompanied by a devaluation of 28 percent against the U.S. dollar (see Goldberg, 1994). Again, the turbulence in the foreign exchange market was preceded by sharp increases in the rate of central bank credit creation and reserve losses for some months prior to the collapse. Quarterly reserve losses of the central bank were estimated to amount to 39 billion pesos, 44 billion pesos, and 140 billion pesos, respectively, in the last three quarters of 1981. At the same time, the percentage spread between the spot and forward peso rates began to widen appreciably during the final quarter of 1981, with the widest spread, not surprisingly, occurring immediately prior to the collapse. The gradual acceleration in the domestic inflation rate (which rose on a month-to-month basis from 1.4 percent in June 1981 to 1.9 percent in November of that year and to 4.9 percent in January 1982) led to a steady appreciation of the real exchange rate and a deterioration of the current account deficit, which reached $16 billion in 1981, compared with $10.7 billion in 1980. On February 12, 1982, the Mexican authorities abandoned the quasi-fixed-exchange-rate system and allowed the exchange rate to float freely. Continuing capital outflows, however, led to a 67 percent depreciation of the peso vis-à-vis the U.S. dollar by the end of February 1982. In August 1982, with the central bank virtually out of reserves, a dual-exchange-rate regime was put in place.

This brief review of recent empirical evidence suggests the existence of strong similarities in the processes leading to exchange rate crises in developing countries. First, in the periods leading to a crisis, domestic inflation is high—and sometimes rising—while international reserves tend to fall at an increasing rate, reflecting the overexpansionary credit policy, rising current account deficits, and heightened perceptions of the ultimate collapse of the regime. Second, anticipations of a crisis translate into a forward premium or a parallel market premium that may rise to very high levels in the periods immediately preceding the regime collapse. Domestic interest rates, as a result, tend to rise substantially in the periods immediately preceding the exchange-rate crisis. Third, there are important real effects associated with balance-of-payments crises. The real exchange rate tends to appreciate (and the current account to deteriorate) during the transition period. The behavior of the real exchange rate (as well as the behavior of interest rates) tends to affect domestic output. The theoretical analysis developed in the preceding sections provides a rationale for these effects.

Two important policy issues relevant to countries adopting fixed-exchange-rate regimes were examined in this chapter. The first issue relates to the time inconsistency problem that typically emerges in the conduct of exchange-rate policy in small, open developing countries. The analysis was based on a simple model in which the interactions between price-setting behavior in the nontraded goods sector and concerns over the behavior of the real exchange rate create a temptation for policymakers to pursue an active exchange-rate policy. In this setting, inflation arises because price setters rationally fear that the authorities will try to devalue in order to depreciate the real exchange rate. The analysis also showed that a binding commitment to a fixed exchange rate, if feasible, would result in lower inflation with no loss in competitiveness. If commitment is not feasible—or not credible—the outcome is biased toward an inflationary process resulting from exchange-rate devaluations, even in the absence of shocks. The incentive structure under a pegged arrangement thus may not be conducive to the adoption of an immutably fixed exchange rate (with attendant financial discipline) but rather to periodic devaluations.

The degree of credibility of a fixed exchange rate was analyzed under the general assumption that a no-devaluation rule is credible only if it is rational for the public to believe that the authorities have the incentive to adhere to it. Credibility can be achieved if policymakers worry enough about their reputation and balance future losses of credibility against a short-term improvement in competitiveness. Alternatively, when the preferences of the policymaker are uncertain, eschewing devaluation may provide a valuable signal to the private sector, thus increasing the incentives for the authorities to adhere to an announced exchange-rate target. We also discussed the rationale for joining an international monetary arrangement in which exchange rates are permanently fixed. It was argued that an exchange-rate union can be viewed as a mechanism that enhances the pegging policymaker's credibility by raising the cost of inflationary policies. Governments can make binding commitments to the rules in the zone while they cannot precommit to macroeconomic rules outside the system because of the significant costs associated with dropping out. There are, however, costs associated with alternative strategies aimed at establishing the credibility of a fixed exchange rate. Little evidence is available on the balance between these costs and benefits.

The second substantive issue discussed in this chapter relates to the causes and consequences of speculative attacks in foreign exchange markets and balance-of-payments crises—phenomena that have occurred repeatedly in many developing countries, particularly in Latin America. A simple analytical model was developed to describe the process leading to such crises. The analysis showed that under perfect foresight about the policy rule pursued by the monetary authorities, an exchange-rate regime shift from a fixed to a floating rate will be preceded by a speculative attack on the currency. Moreover, the timing of such attacks is entirely predictable: intertemporal arbitrage ensures that the regime shift occurs smoothly. Its timing depends on the stock of foreign reserves committed by the central bank to the defense of the official parity, as well as the critical level of reserves that triggers the abandonment of the declared parity. The basic analytical framework was then extended to examine the implications of alternative assumptions about the postcollapse regime, the real effects associated with anticipated exchange-rate crises, and the role of capital controls and foreign borrowing in delaying or avoiding such crises.

The literature on speculative attacks provides important lessons for macroeconomic policy under a fixed-exchange-rate regime. Balance-of-payments crises, rather than being erratic events resulting from exogenous shocks, may be the equilibrium outcome of maximizing behavior by rational agents faced with a fundamental inconsistency between monetary and exchange-rate policies. In the periods preceding an eventual collapse, speculative attacks are likely to occur repeatedly, reflecting alternate periods of confidence and distrust in the ability of the central bank to defend the official parity, and changes in the degree of uncertainty regarding actual and future central bank policies. Measures such as foreign borrowing and capital controls may temporarily enhance the viability of a fixed exchange rate, but will not prevent the ultimate collapse of the system if a consistent—and sustainable, in light of the intertemporal budget constraint faced by the government—macroeconomic policy mix is not adopted.[45] The more delayed fundamental policy adjustments are, the higher will be the potential costs of a regime collapse.

Seven

Exchange-Rate Management II: Contractionary Devaluation and Real-Exchange-Rate Rules

AS INDICATED in the previous chapter, few developing countries have opted for flexible-exchange-rate arrangements in the aftermath of the collapse of the Bretton Woods regime. The majority of developing countries either maintain a fixed parity against a single currency or an announced basket of currencies, or manage their official exchange rate actively in accordance with an unannounced rule or through the discretion of their monetary authorities. However, because the exchange rate occupies such a central macroeconomic role, the circumstances under which a pegged rate should be adjusted, on the one hand, and the principles that should govern the behavior of a managed peg, on the other, continue to be subjects of much controversy. In this chapter we shall examine, in particular, the controversies surrounding the macroeconomic effects of devaluation and of purchasing-power-parity (PPP)–based rules for exchange-rate management.

Regarding the former, devaluation controversies have a long lineage in macroeconomics, centering in the case of industrial countries on whether an exchange-rate devaluation would improve the trade balance (Alexander, 1952). This issue has also arisen in the context of developing countries, where "elasticity pessimism" continues to be debated. In recent years, however, following the publication of an influential paper by Krugman and Taylor (1978), controversy has centered on the effects of devaluation on real output. At issue is whether a nominal devaluation, whether successful in improving the trade balance or not, would tend to have contractionary effects on economic activity. Krugman and Taylor described a number of channels through which contractionary effects could arise, setting off the "contractionary devaluation" debate.

In the case of actively managed exchange rates, a popular rule has been to depreciate continuously the official rate in order to offset any differential between the domestic and foreign inflation rates. Such rules thus fix the real exchange rate and cause the nominal exchange rate to track its PPP level, and so are referred to as PPP-based rules or fixed-real-exchange-rate rules.[1] Because PPP-based rules effectively index the nominal exchange rate to the domestic price level, they remove an important nominal anchor from the domestic economy. As such, their impact on price-level stability (and even determinacy) has been called into question.

The issues of contractionary devaluation and real-exchange-rate targeting are examined in the two parts of this chapter. In Section 7.1 the likelihood that a devaluation will have a contractionary effect on real output in a fixed-exchange-rate system is analyzed by considering both the demand and supply channels through which devaluation would affect activity. Section 7.2 examines the response of the domestic rate of inflation to real shocks in a context in which a managed exchange rate follows a PPP-based rule.[2]

7.1 Contractionary Devaluation

Consider a small open economy that operates under a fixed-exchange-rate system. We adopt a "dependent economy" framework in which traded and nontraded goods are produced using homogeneous, intersectorally mobile labor; sector-specific capital; and imported inputs. Production costs may also be affected by the need to finance working capital. Wage determination is crucial for the issue discussed here, and we shall allow for a variety of mechanisms to determine the nominal wage. Households hold money, capital, and foreign securities and issue debt to each other. This analytical framework is quite general, and consistent with the setup considered in various other places in this book. The first two parts of this section consider the separate effects of a nominal devaluation on aggregate demand for, and supply of, domestic output, and the last part reviews the empirical evidence on the contractionary effects of devaluation in developing countries.

7.1.1 Effects on Aggregate Demand

In a small open economy producing traded and nontraded goods, the demand curve facing the traded goods sector is given by the law of one price:

$$P_T = \bar{E} P_T^*,$$

where P_T is the domestic-currency price of traded goods, $\bar{E}$ is the nominal exchange rate (units of domestic currency per unit of foreign currency), and P_T^* is the foreign-currency price of traded goods, which we take to be unity. Aggregate real demand for nontraded goods, which we denote $d_N(t)$, consists of the sum of domestic consumption $c_N(t)$, investment $I_N(t)$, and government demand g_N for such goods:

$$d_N(t) = c_N(t) + I_N(t) + g_N.$$

This part of Section 7.1 examines the effects of devaluation on the components of this equation. Consumption and investment demand are treated separately, and government demand is incorporated in the discussion of the government budget constraint in the subsection on consumption (under the heading "Effects Through Changes in Real Tax Revenue"). Finally, we consider the impact on the domestic interest rate, which affects both consumption and investment.

7.1.1.1 CONSUMPTION

In this subsection we examine the effects of devaluation on consumption demand for nontraded goods. We will consider a fairly general ad hoc specification of household behavior, in which demand for nontraded goods depends on the real exchange rate $z_t = P_T(t)/P_N(t)$, where $P_N(t)$ is the domestic-currency price of nontraded goods; on real factor income received by households (y_t) net of real taxes paid by them (tax$_t$); on real household financial wealth (a_t); and on the real interest rate $i_t - \pi^a$, where i_t is the domestic nominal interest rate and π^a the expected inflation rate. Possible distributional effects on aggregate consumption are captured by a shift parameter, denoted k. Consumption demand for nontraded goods thus takes the general form[3]

$$c_N(t) = c_N[z_t, \ y_t - \text{tax}_t, \ i_t - \pi^a, \ a_t; \ k]. \tag{1}$$

We now examine the effects of devaluation on each of the arguments of $c_N(t)$.

Relative Price Effects

A nominal devaluation brings about changes in relative prices that affect the demand for domestically produced goods. Within the "dependent economy" framework adopted in this chapter, it is necessary to distinguish the relative price effect on the demand for traded goods and for nontraded goods. The *total* (domestic and foreign) demand for domestically produced traded goods is perfectly elastic and therefore is not affected by relative price changes. Although the domestic demand for these goods is affected by relative prices, an important effect for balance-of-payments purposes, it is the total demand that is relevant for output and employment in this sector. But changes in relative prices that affect the domestic demand for nontraded goods will affect the total demand for these goods, since both demands are the same by definition. A devaluation therefore will have a relative price effect on the demand for domestically produced goods through its effect on the demand for nontraded goods. A real depreciation of the domestic currency (that is, an increase in the relative price of traded to nontraded goods), with real income held constant, will increase the demand for nontraded goods, and vice versa. This implies a positive partial derivative c_{Nz} in Equation (1). This substitution effect, present in most models, is excluded in Krugman and Taylor (1978) by the assumption that consumers demand only nontraded goods.

Real-Income Effects

Devaluations also produce changes in real income that affect the demand for domestically produced goods. These real-income changes can be decomposed into those resulting from changes in relative prices at the initial level of output and those resulting from changes in output at the new relative prices. Because we are discussing effects on the demand for domestic output, we will be interested primarily in the change in real income at the initial level of output, which provides the impact effect. Effects occurring through the endogenous change in output (that is, Keynesian multiplier effects) are omitted here, since the purpose of the analysis is precisely to investigate the factors that determine the qualitative direction of such changes.

To analyze the income effect, we need some definitions. The price level will be denoted by P, with

$$P_t = \bar{E}^{\delta} P_N(t)^{1-\delta}, \quad 0 < \delta < 1, \tag{2}$$

where δ is the share of traded goods in consumption.[4] Real income is equal to

$$y_t = y_N(t)z_t^{-\delta} + y_T(t)z_t^{1-\delta}, \tag{3}$$

where $y_N(t)$ is the production of nontraded goods and $y_T(t)$ is the production of traded goods.

The effect of a real devaluation on real income for a given level of output is ambiguous. Differentiating Equation (3) with respect to z_t, with $y_N(t)$ and $y_T(t)$ kept constant, yields

$$\frac{dy_t}{dz_t} = z_t^{-1}(\alpha - \delta)[y_N(t)z_t^{-\delta} + y_T(t)z_t^{1-\delta}], \tag{4}$$

where α is the share of traded goods in total output:

$$\alpha = z_t y_T(t)/[z_t y_T(t) + y_N(t)]. \tag{5}$$

Equation (4) shows that the impact effect on real income depends on whether traded goods have a higher share in consumption or in income. Clearly, a variety of results are possible. Assume, for instance, that there is no expenditure on investment goods, so that consumption and expenditure are the same, and suppose that there is no public sector expenditure, so that $c_N(t) = y_N(t)$. In this case the net effect on real income depends on whether consumption of traded goods is higher or lower than $y_T(t)$—that is, on whether there is a trade deficit or a trade surplus. If there is a deficit, $\delta > \alpha$, and real income declines with a real devaluation. The reason is that the goods whose relative price has increased (traded goods) have a higher weight in consumption than in income. Introducing investment and public expenditure naturally complicates these simple results.

For models with traded and nontraded goods, besides the ambiguous effect on real income derived here for given levels of output, the demand for nontraded goods may also increase because of a higher level of output of traded goods. In general, the production of traded goods will increase as long as the price of its input does not rise by the full amount of the devaluation. As shown later, whether the latter condition holds will depend on the degree of wage indexation, the stance of inflationary expectations, and on other factors.

Effects Through Imported Inputs

The presence of imported inputs is an additional factor that may have a negative effect on the demand for domestically produced goods after a devaluation. The reason is that, under certain conditions, imported inputs make it more likely that the real income effect of a devaluation, discussed previously, will be negative.

The modification that imported inputs introduce in the previous analysis is that they must be subtracted from domestic output to obtain national income. A real devaluation therefore affects real income not only through the channels mentioned previously, but also through changes in the real value of imported inputs.

There are two opposing effects of a real devaluation on the real value of imported inputs. On the one hand, a real devaluation increases the relative price of imported inputs in terms of the basket of consumption, thereby increasing the real value of the initial volume of imported inputs. On the other hand, if the price of labor does not increase by the full amount of the devaluation, the relative price of imported inputs increases, and domestic producers have an incentive to substitute labor for imported inputs, thus reducing the volume of imported inputs. Clearly, the net effect of these two opposing forces depends, among other things, on the degree of factor substitutability in production and on the extent to which a devaluation is transmitted to wages.

Assuming that traded goods are produced with a fixed amount of specific capital and with labor, and that nontraded goods are produced with an imported input and labor according to a CES production function with elasticity of substitution σ, Lizondo and Montiel (1989) show that the effect of a real devaluation on real income identified in (4) is modified in the presence of imported inputs by the inclusion of an additional term given by

$$z^{-\delta} J_N [\sigma - (1 - \delta)], \tag{6}$$

where J_N is the volume of imported intermediate goods used in the nontradable sector. The presence of imported inputs will thus contribute to a reduction in real income when $(1 - \delta) > \sigma$. It is clear that the net effect is ambiguous, and a variety of results are possible. For example, if there is no substitution in production (as in Krugman and Taylor, 1978), $\sigma = 0$ and the net effect is necessarily negative.

In summary, the net effect on real income due to the presence of imported inputs is ambiguous. It is more likely to be negative the lower the elasticity of substitution between imported inputs and primary factors, and the higher the share of nontraded goods in the price index.

Income Redistribution Effects

Another factor frequently mentioned as a possible cause for a decline in the demand for domestically produced goods after a devaluation is the redistribution of income from sectors with high propensity to spend on goods of this type to sectors with a lower propensity. Alexander (1952) recognized the possibility that redistribution of income may affect expenditure, and included it as one of the direct effects of devaluation on absorption. He discussed redistribution of income in two directions, both associated with an increase in the price level: first, from wages to profits because of lags in the adjustment of wages to higher prices, and second, from the private to the public sector because of the existing structure of taxation. If profit recipients have a lower marginal propensity to spend than the private sector, absorption will decline for a given level of real income. Note, however, that whereas Alexander was interested in the effects on the trade balance and therefore examined the behavior of total expenditure, the focus here is on the demand for domestic output.

Of the two types of redistribution mentioned above, we will examine here the shift of income from wages to profits, leaving the shift from the private to the public sector to be discussed later. The redistribution from wages to profits has been examined formally by Díaz Alejandro (1963) and Krugman and Taylor (1978), and in both models the only impact effect of a devaluation is to redistribute a given level of real income from wages to profits because of an increase in prices, with nominal wages kept constant. Both show that this may cause a reduction in the demand for domestic output if the marginal propensity to spend on home goods is lower for profit recipients than for wage earners.

However, this is not the only type of income redistribution effect between workers and owners of capital that can be associated with a devaluation. For example, in a model with traded and nontraded goods, flexible wages, and sector-specific capital, a real devaluation would reduce real profits in the nontraded goods sector, increase real profits in the traded goods sector, and have an ambiguous effect on real wages. Real wages would increase in terms of nontraded goods but would decline in terms of traded goods. Sectoral considerations may therefore become important, and it is not clear a priori what the effect of this type of redistribution would be on the demand for the domestically produced good. Cooper (1971) mentioned the possibility of redistribution from the factors engaged in purely domestic industries to the factors engaged in export- and import-competing industries, and he recognized that, although in some cases this may have reduced demand, under different circumstances this may induce a spending boom. Furthermore, in the longer run, when all factors of production are mobile, the redistribution of income may depend on technological considerations. For instance, in a Heckscher-Ohlin world, real wages and profits in terms of either of the two goods depend, with intersectorally mobile labor and capital, on factor intensities. A real devaluation will increase real payments to factors used intensively by the traded goods sector and will reduce real payments to the other factor. All these considerations imply that the pattern of redistribution may change through time as the economy adjusts to the new situation after a devaluation. It seems natural to think of the redistribution of income as a dynamic process encompassing the various situations mentioned above. First, nominal wages are fixed for some period after a devaluation, then wages adjust to the new price level and workers move among occupations while capital remains sector specific, and, finally, capital also moves to the sectors with higher returns.

Besides the theoretical issues mentioned above, there remains the question of how important the effect on the demand for domestic output of redistribution from wages to profits is likely to be. Alexander (1952) emphasized that what is important is the marginal propensity to spend, so that even if profit recipients have a lower marginal propensity to consume than wage earners, higher profits may stimulate investment, and the redistribution of income may therefore result in increased absorption. Díaz Alejandro (1963), however, argued that investment expenditure is even more biased toward traded goods than consumption expenditure, and because investment expenditure is undertaken by profit recipients, the demand for domestically produced goods is likely to decline. Even if this proposition about the relative marginal propensities to spend on domestic output by workers and owners of capital is accepted, the next question is how important is the redistribution of income that will lead to a change in the pattern of aggregate expenditure. On this issue the evidence does not provide firm support for the hypothesis of redistribution against labor. Using data from thirty-one devaluation episodes, Edwards (1989*b*) showed that in fifteen cases there was no significant change in income distribution, whereas in eight cases the share of labor in GDP declined significantly, and in seven other instances it increased significantly.

Effects Through Changes in Real Tax Revenue

To the extent that devaluation affects the real tax burden on the private sector, thus redistributing income from the private to the public sector, changes in real tax revenue represent a separate channel through which a contractionary effect on economic activity may result. This effect may operate through the demand for domestic output or through its supply, and in the former case through private consumption expenditure or through private investment. Up to the present, only the effect of devaluation on the real tax burden faced by consumers has figured prominently in the literature, and here we shall focus on this effect.

As discussed in Chapter 1, many governments in developing countries derive a substantial proportion of their revenues from import and export taxes. Thus, as argued by Krugman and Taylor (1978), a nominal devaluation that succeeds in depreciating the real exchange rate will increase the real tax burden on the private sector by increasing the real value of trade taxes, for given levels of imports and exports.[5] This effect depends, however, on the presence of ad valorem rather than specific taxes on foreign trade. To the extent that nominal devaluation results in increases in the domestic price level, the presence of specific taxes would reverse the effect emphasized by Krugman and Taylor, since the real value of nonindexed specific taxes would fall as a consequence of the increase in the general price level brought about by a nominal devaluation.

The latter is, of course, simply a specific instance of the Olivera-Tanzi effect discussed in Chapter 4, which surprisingly has played only a limited role in the literature on contractionary devaluation. This effect is present when lags in tax collection or delays in adjusting the nominal value of specific taxes cause the real value of tax collections to fall during periods of rising prices. To the extent that nominal devaluations are associated with at least temporary bursts of inflation, the Olivera-Tanzi effect should be expected to be operative during the immediate postdevaluation period when prices are rising. Because the real tax burden would fall as a consequence of this effect, devaluation would exert an *expansionary* short-run effect on aggregate demand through this channel.

A third channel through which devaluation may affect aggregate demand by its effects on the real tax burden borne by households is that of discretionary tax changes caused by the effect of an exchange-rate adjustment on government finances. To clarify this point, let us suppose that, other than trade taxes, all taxes are levied on households in lump-sum fashion. To incorporate the two channels discussed above, let us write the government's real tax receipts, denoted tax_t, as

$$\text{tax}_t = \text{tax}(\overset{+}{z}_t, \ \bar{\pi}_t; \ \overset{+}{\tau}),$$

where τ is a parameter that captures the effects of discretionary taxes and π_t is the inflation rate. The first two terms in the function tax( ) capture the trade tax and Olivera-Tanzi effects. The government's budget constraint takes the form

$$\text{tax}(z_t, \ \pi_t; \ \tau) \equiv z_t^{1-\delta} g_T + z_t^{-\delta} g_N + i^* z_t^{1-\delta} F_t^g - z_t^{1-\delta}(\dot{L}_t^g/\bar{E} + \dot{F}_t^g), \quad (7)$$

where g_T and g_N denote government spending on traded and nontraded goods, respectively; i^* the foreign nominal interest rate; F_t^g net public external debt; and L_t^g the stock of net government liabilities to the central bank.[6]

The first point to be made from identity (7) is that, in the Krugman-Taylor case, the increase in the real value of trade taxes attendant on a real devaluation cannot be the end of the story. As identity (7) makes clear, this increase in tax( ) must be offset somewhere else within the government budget, since identity (7) must hold at all times. The effect of an increase in real trade taxes on aggregate demand will depend on the nature of this offset. If, for example, the offset takes the form of a *reduction* in discretionary taxes τ, leaving real tax receipts tax( ) unchanged, the contractionary effect on aggregate demand will disappear altogether. Other possible offsets will differ in their consequences for aggregate demand, in ways that are explored below.

A nominal devaluation that results in a real depreciation may potentially affect each of the entries on the right-hand side of identity (7). Among these, several authors have noted the importance of the existence of a stock of foreign-currency-denominated external debt in affecting the possible contractionary effects of a nominal devaluation (see Gylfason and Risager, 1984; van Wijnbergen, 1986; and Edwards, 1989b. In all of these cases, however, the external debt has been treated as if it were owed by the *private* sector.[7] As discussed in Chapter 13, most external debt in developing countries is typically owed by the public sector. Indeed, currency substitution and capital flight have probably made the private sector in many developing countries a net *creditor* in foreign-currency terms. The sectoral allocation of debt can be ignored, and all debt treated as private debt, only in the case of complete Ricardian equivalence, which is discussed below. For the moment, we examine the implications of public external debt in the absence of Ricardian equivalence.[8]

If the public sector is a net external debtor, a real devaluation will increase the real value of interest payments abroad. As identity (7) indicates, the government can finance such increased debt service payments by increased taxation, reduced spending, or increased borrowing from the central bank or from abroad. The effects on aggregate demand will depend on the mode of financing. If the government chooses to increase discretionary taxes, the effects on aggregate demand would be contractionary because private disposable income would fall. This is implicitly the effect captured by van Wijnbergen (1986), Edwards (1989b), and Gylfason and Risager (1984) in treating all debt as private debt and in deducting interest payments from private disposable income. The effect on private consumption would be similar to that of an increase in discretionary taxes arising from any other cause. As a second alternative, increased real debt service payments could be financed by a reduction in government spending on goods and services. If this takes the form of reduced spending on *nontraded* goods, the contractionary effects on aggregate demand would *exceed* those associated with tax financing unless the propensity to spend out of taxes approached unity. In contrast, if spending reductions fall on *traded* goods, the contractionary effects would be nil, since the small-country assumption ensures that government demand would be replaced by external demand. Finally, the increased real debt service payments could be financed by borrowing, either from the central bank or from abroad. In this case, with the exchange rate fixed at its new level, contractionary effects would again fail to appear because the counterpart to the increased flow of credit to the government would simply consist of an outflow of foreign reserves in the former case, and of increased government external debt in the latter, with no impact on aggregate demand in either case.

In addition to the effect on real interest payments, devaluation would affect the real value of government expenditures on goods and services. Because the real value of spending on traded goods rises while that on nontraded goods falls, the total effect depends on the composition of government spending between traded and nontraded goods. Should the net effect be an increase in real spending, the same financing options as before would present themselves. This would be the case if government spending were heavily weighted toward traded goods. In the alternative case, a *reduction* in discretionary taxes may ensue, for instance, with corresponding expansionary effects on aggregate demand.

Finally, the effect of a devaluation on discretionary taxes will also depend on the monetary policy regime in effect. This channel is captured by the last term on the right-hand side of identity (7). If the central bank pegs the flow of credit to the government in *nominal* terms, the rise in prices that attends a nominal devaluation will reduce $\dot{L}^g/P$ and call for an adjustment in the government budget, possibly through a discretionary tax increase. If the flow $\dot{L}^g$ is adjusted to accommodate the price increase, however, no further changes in the budget will emanate from this source. The last option we consider is that in which real valuation gains on the central bank's stock of foreign exchange reserves are passed along to the government. In this case $\dot{L}_t^g/P_t$ could *increase*, and the financing options would include an expansionary tax reduction.

Wealth Effects

Because an increase in wealth can be expected to increase household consumption, a devaluation can also affect the demand for domestically produced goods through its effects on real wealth. If the level of domestic expenditure depends on real wealth, and private sector asset holdings are not indexed to the domestic price level, a devaluation changes the real value of existing wealth and thus affects the demand for home goods.

Nominal wealth is often taken to coincide with the nominal stock of money, thus converting the wealth effect into a real cash balance effect. Alexander (1952) emphasized this channel when analyzing the consequences a devaluation would have for absorption. He noted that a devaluation would increase the price level and thus reduce the real stock of money. This reduction would in turn have two types of effects, both tending to reduce absorption: a direct effect, when individuals reduce their expenditures in order to replenish their real money holdings to the desired level; and an indirect effect, when individuals try to shift their portfolios from other assets into money, thus driving up the domestic interest rate in the absence of perfect capital mobility. We will be concerned in the present disscussion only with the direct effect, since the other effect is included in our discussion of the interest rate at the end of this section.

The real-cash-balance effect has been widely recognized and incorporated in the literature on contractionary devaluation. For instance, Gylfason and Schmid (1983), Hanson (1983), Islam (1984), Gylfason and Radetzki (1991), Buffie (1986*a*), and Edwards (1989*b*) take this effect into account by including real cash balances directly as an argument in the expenditure function or indirectly through the use of a hoarding function. In all these cases a devaluation, by increasing the price level in the presence of a given initial nominal stock of money, reduces real cash balances, thereby exerting a contractionary effect on demand.

This unambiguous result must be modified if the private sector holds other types of assets whose nominal value increases with a devaluation. For instance, assume that the private sector holds foreign-currency-denominated assets in an amount F_t^p. Then real wealth would be equal to

$$a_t = (M_t/P_t) + (\bar{E}F_t^p/P_t) = z_t^{1-\delta}[(M_t/\bar{E}) + F_t^p]. \tag{8}$$

The percentage change in real wealth from a nominal devaluation would then be equal to

$$\hat{a}_t = (1 - \delta)\hat{z}_t - \lambda\epsilon_t, \tag{9}$$

where λ is the share of domestic money in private sector wealth and ϵ_t the devaluation rate. Because $\hat{z}_t$ is bounded above by ϵ_t (unless the price of nontraded goods declines with a devaluation, which we do not consider), Equation (9) has the following implications. If domestic money is the only asset in the portfolio of the private sector, $\lambda = 1$, a devaluation necessarily has a negative effect on real wealth and on demand. This was the case considered above. Alternatively, if the private sector also holds assets denominated in foreign currency, the result is ambiguous. The source of the ambiguity is that, although the real value of the stock of domestic money declines because of the increase in the price level, the real value of the stock of foreign assets increases as long as the domestic price level does not rise by the full amount of the devaluation. The effect on the demand for domestic goods may thus be positive or negative. It is more likely to be negative the higher the share of traded goods in the price index δ, the lower the real depreciation $\hat{z}$, and the higher the share of domestic money in private sector wealth λ. The possibility of the private sector holding foreign assets, although incorporated in several other aspects of analyses of devaluations (see, in particular, Chapter 5), has not received sufficient attention in the literature on contractionary devaluation.[9]

This framework is also useful for examining the effects of external debt. The presence of private sector external debt reduces the net foreign asset position of the private sector F_t^p, thus increasing the share of domestic money in wealth λ, and therefore increasing the likelihood that a devaluation will have a negative effect on real wealth. If the level of external debt is so high as to result in a negative net foreign asset position of the private sector, λ will be greater than unity, and a devaluation will necessarily have a negative effect on real wealth and, consequently, a negative effect through the wealth channel on the demand for domestic goods. Thus, the presence of private sector external debt introduces another channel through which a devaluation can exert contractionary effects.

7.1.1.2 INVESTMENT

The effects of a devaluation on private demand for nontraded goods also depend on investment demand for this category of goods emanating from both the traded and nontraded goods sectors. For simplicity, suppose that the capital stock in each sector consists of traded and nontraded goods combined in fixed proportions. A unit of capital in the traded goods sector consists of γ_N^T units of nontraded goods and γ_T^T units of traded goods, whereas in the nontraded goods sector capital consists of γ_N^N nontraded goods and γ_T^N traded goods. Then the prices of a unit of capital in the traded goods sector (P_{KT}) and in the nontraded goods sector (P_{KN}) are given by

$$P_{KT}(t) = \gamma_N^T P_N(t) + \gamma_T^T \bar{E}, \tag{10a}$$

$$P_{KN}(t) = \gamma_N^N P_N(t) + \gamma_T^N \bar{E}. \tag{10b}$$

Suppose, as indicated above, that output in each sector is produced by using capital, labor, and imported inputs. The marginal product of capital in the two sectors is therefore given by[10]

$$MP_K^T = F_K^T(w_t/\bar{E};\ \bar{K}_T), \tag{11a}$$

$$MP_K^N = F_K^N[w_t/P_N(t),\ \bar{z}_t;\ \bar{K}_N], \tag{11b}$$

where w_t denotes the nominal exchange rate.

In the short run, the capital stock is fixed. By the first-order conditions for profit maximization, an increase in the product wage will reduce demand for labor. The ensuing increase in the capital intensity of production will cause the marginal product of capital to fall. A similar effect results from an increase in the real cost of imported inputs, z_t. Note that this variable does not enter Equation (11a), since the price of imported inputs in terms of traded goods is not affected by devaluation.

Because the demand for investment goods is inherently forward looking, today's demand for investment in each sector will depend on the anticipated future paths of w_t, $\bar{E}$, $P_N(t)$, and the nominal interest rate i_t. Under rational expectations, these paths can be generated only by the full solution of a model. Because we do not present such a solution here, we will examine the issues involved under the assumption that all relative prices are expected to remain at their postdevaluation levels. Under this assumption, the sectoral net investment functions can be expressed as

$$\hat{K}^T = q_T \left\{ \frac{\bar{E} M P_K^T / P_{KT}(t)}{i_t + \eta - \pi_{KT}} - 1 \right\}, \quad q_T(0) = 0,\ q_T' > 0$$

$$= q_T \left\{ \frac{\bar{E} F_K^T(w_t/\bar{E};\ K_T) P_{KT}(t)}{i_t + \eta - \pi_{KT}} - 1 \right\}, \tag{12a}$$

$$\hat{K}^N = q_N \left\{ \frac{P_N(t) M P_K^N / P_{KN}(t)}{i_t + \eta - \pi_{KN}} - 1 \right\}, \quad q_N(0) = 0,\ q_N' > 0$$

$$= q_N \left\{ \frac{P_N(t) F_K^N[w_t/P_N(t),\ z_t;\ K_N] P_{KN}(t)}{i_t + \eta - \pi_{KN}} - 1 \right\}, \tag{12b}$$

where π_{KJ} denotes the rate of increase in the price of capital in sector J.

Net investment demand in each sector depends on the ratio of the marginal product of capital to the real interest rate. Gross investment demand is the sum of net investment and replacement investment, where depletion is assumed to take place at the uniform rate $\mu > 0$ in both sectors. Equations (12) can now be combined with replacement investment to yield the total investment demand for nontraded goods:

$$I_N(t) = I_N^T(t) + I_N^N(t) \tag{13}$$

$$= \gamma_N^T q_T \left\{ \frac{\bar{E} F_K^T(w_t/\bar{E}; K_T) P_{KT}(t)}{i_t + \eta - \pi_{KT}} - 1 \right\} K_T + \mu(\gamma_N^T K_T + \gamma_N^N K_N)$$

$$+ \gamma_N^N q_N \left\{ \frac{P_N(t) F_K^N[w_t/P_N(t), z_t; K_N] P_{KN}(t)}{i_t + \eta - \pi_{KN}} - 1 \right\} K_N.$$

The effects of a real devaluation on the investment demand for nontraded goods can now be examined.

Both Branson (1986) and Buffie (1986b) have emphasized that, since a substantial portion of any new investment in developing countries is likely to consist of imported capital goods, a real depreciation will raise the price of capital in terms of home goods, discouraging new investment and exerting a contractionary effect on aggregate demand. As is evident from Equation (13), this analysis is valid only in the case of investment demand that originates in the nontraded goods sector. The situation is precisely the opposite in the traded goods sector, where a real depreciation *lowers* the real supply price of capital measured in terms of output. In this sector, therefore, this effect operates to stimulate investment, so the net effect on investment demand for nontraded goods of changes in the supply price of capital is ambiguous in principle.

A second channel through which devaluation affects the investment demand for nontraded goods operates through real profits. The analysis of this channel has to be model specific to a greater extent than the previous one because it will depend, for instance, on the extent to which product markets are assumed to clear, that is, on whether firms operate on their factor demand curves. The exposition above assumes that they do. In this case the return to capital is its marginal product, which depends on the initial stock of capital, on the product wage, and, in the case of the nontraded goods sector, on the real exchange rate, which determines the price of imported inputs. The effects of changes in product wages on profits, and therefore on investment spending, were emphasized by van Wijnbergen (1986), Branson (1986), and Risager (1988). Both van Wijnbergen and Branson contrasted the case of fixed nominal wages with that in which there is some degree of wage indexation. By contrast, Risager examined the effect on investment of holding the nominal wage constant over some fixed initial contract length and then restoring the initial real wage.

The basic result of these studies is that a devaluation may raise or lower the product wage on impact depending on the nature and degree of wage indexation. With rigid nominal wages, the product wage would fall on impact, and investment would increase in the short run, even if the original product wage were expected to be restored in the future (Risager, 1988). With indexation that gives significant weight to imports, however, the product wage could rise, thereby dampening investment. A common result in "dependent economy" models with some nominal wage flexibility, however, is that a nominal devaluation results in a *reduction* in the product wage in the traded goods sector and an *increase* in the product wage in the nontraded goods sector (see, for instance, Montiel, 1987). In this case, investment would be stimulated in the former and discouraged in the latter, with ambiguous effects on total investment demand for nontraded goods.

In the presence of imported inputs, a third channel will be operative. The marginal product of capital in the nontraded goods sector will be affected by a real devaluation through the higher real costs of such inputs (van Wijnbergen, 1986; Branson, 1986). The effect is unambiguously contractionary, since the depressing effect on profits in the nontraded goods sector is not offset by positive effects on profits in the sector producing traded goods.

As a final point, note that, in the case of a real depreciation that lowers the product wage in the traded goods sector and raises it in the nontraded goods sector, the three effects analyzed above (that is, the effects on the real cost of capital, the product wage, and the cost of imported inputs) together tend to increase investment in the traded goods sector and to decrease it in the nontraded goods sector. If these effects are sufficiently strong, total investment demand for nontraded goods must increase when capital is sector specific. In this case, an increase in investment demand in the traded goods sector can be met only through new production. It cannot be offset by negative *gross* investment in the nontraded goods sector. Thus, whenever a devaluation has a disparate effect on sectoral investment incentives sufficient to increase investment in the traded goods sector by more than the initial level of gross investment in the nontraded goods sector, total investment must rise, no matter how adverse the incentives for investment in the nontraded goods sector may be.

7.1.1.3 NOMINAL INTEREST RATES

An increase in the real interest rate can be expected to reduce private consumption of nontraded goods as well as investment spending on nontraded goods by both the traded and nontraded goods sectors. Although the expected-inflation component of the real interest rate is treated as exogenous here, in this subsection we examine the effects of devaluation on the nominal interest rate. To analyze those effects, it is useful to distinguish between the current effect of an anticipated (future) devaluation and the contemporaneous effect of a previously unanticipated devaluation. Both shocks will be analyzed here. The effect of a devaluation on the nominal interest rate will depend, of course, fundamentally on the characteristics of the economy's financial structure, and many of the diverse results derived in the literature can be traced to different assumptions about these characteristics. We begin by describing a fairly general framework (consistent with that described in Chapters 2 and 5) from which various special cases can be derived.

Suppose that domestic residents can hold financial assets in the form of money, domestic interest-bearing assets, and interest-bearing claims on foreigners (denominated in foreign exchange). Assume further that the domestic interest-bearing assets take the form of loans extended by households to other entities in the private sector (other households and firms). The effects of a devaluation on the nominal interest rate charged on these loans, whether it is a previously unanticipated current devaluation or an anticipated future devaluation, depend critically on the degree of capital mobility (that is, on the extent to which domestic loans are regarded by households as perfect substitutes for foreign assets) and on the severity of portfolio adjustment costs. We will assume that portfolio adjustment is costless and distinguish two cases, based on whether domestic loans and foreign assets are perfect or imperfect substitutes.[11]

If loans and foreign assets are imperfect substitutes, equilibrium in the loan market may be given by the fairly general formulation[12]

$$
h\left(\overset{-}{i_t}, \overset{+}{i^* + \epsilon^a}, \overset{+}{y_t}, \frac{M_t + \bar{E}F_t^p}{P_t}; x_t\right) = 0, \tag{14}
$$

where $h()$ is the real excess demand function for loans; i_t the nominal interest rate on loans; $i^* + \epsilon^a$ the nominal rate of return on foreign assets, consisting of the foreign nominal interest rate i^* plus the expected rate of depreciation of the domestic currency ϵ^a; y_t real income; $(M_t + \bar{E}F_t^p)/P_t$ real household financial wealth; and x_t a vector of additional variables that have been included in the real loan excess demand function in the contractionary devaluation literature (see below). An increase in i_t has a negative own-price effect on excess loan demand, whereas an increase in $i^* + \epsilon^a$ raises excess demand for loans as borrowers switch to domestic sources of finance while lenders seek to place more of their funds in foreign assets. An increase in domestic real income causes lenders to increase their demand for money, which they finance in part by reducing their supply of loans, thereby increasing excess demand in the loan market. Finally, other things being equal, an increase in private financial wealth both reduces borrowers' need for outside financing and provides lenders with surplus funds, which they can place in both loans and foreign assets after satisfying their own demands for money. This effect reduces excess demand in the loan market.

Now consider the effect of a devaluation on the nominal interest rate i_t at a given initial level of real income y_t and price of nontraded goods $P_N(t)$, with $\epsilon^a = 0$. In the case of a previously unanticipated devaluation, the effect on the domestic interest rate will depend, as can be seen from Equation (14), on the composition of household financial wealth. Whether the real excess demand for loans rises or falls depends on whether real household financial wealth increases or decreases. The devaluation will lower the real money stock but will raise the real value of foreign assets. If a large share of household financial wealth is devoted to the holding of cash balances, and if traded goods have a large weight in private consumption (so that the price level P_t registers a strong increase), the former effect will dominate; real private financial wealth will fall, the real excess demand for loans will increase, and the domestic interest rate will rise. This result will be reversed, however, if foreign assets dominate households' balance sheets or if traded goods carry a small weight in domestic consumption (or both). In van Wijnbergen's (1986) model, for example, households hold no foreign assets; thus, a nominal devaluation raises the domestic interest rate. In contrast, Buffie (1984a) derived opposite conclusions precisely because he assumed that households hold a substantial portion of their wealth in assets denominated in foreign exchange.

When the partial derivative h_i, evaluated at $i_t = i^* + \epsilon^a$, approaches negative infinity, domestic loans and foreign assets become perfect substitutes in private portfolios. In this case, Equation (14) is replaced by

$$i_t = i^* + \epsilon^a, \tag{15}$$

so that uncovered interest parity holds continuously. Under these conditions, a previously unanticipated current devaluation will have no effect on the domestic nominal interest rate. This is the assumption that appears in the models of Turnovsky (1981), Burton (1983), and Montiel (1991a).

The effects of an anticipated future devaluation are straightforward. In the case of imperfect substitutability, this is represented by an increase in ϵ^a in Equation (14), with the level of the exchange rate held constant. The domestic nominal interest rate thus rises. If the own-price effect h_i exceeds the cross-price effect $h_{i^*+\epsilon^a}$, the increase will be lower than the anticipated devaluation. In the case of perfect substitutability, however, the domestic interest rate will rise by the full amount of the anticipated devaluation, as indicated in Equation (15).

The literature on contractionary devaluation has placed a substantial emphasis on the importance of "working capital" in developing countries as a source of loan demand, following a key tenet of the new structuralist school (see Chapter 5). This introduces effects of a previously unanticipated current devaluation that were not included in the preceding analysis. These effects can be captured by defining the variable x_t in Equation (14) as

$$x_t = x[\overset{+}{w_t}, \overset{\pm}{\bar{E}}, \overset{-}{P_N}(t)]. \tag{16}$$

The variable x_t now becomes an index of real working capital requirements, which are taken to depend on the wage bill and on purchases of imported inputs (see the last part of subsection 7.1.1.1). An increase in x_t increases the demand for loans, an effect that explains the positive sign of h_x in Equation (14). Real working capital requirements are assumed to increase when the nominal wage or the domestic-currency price of traded goods (or both) increases, and they are assumed to fall when the price of nontraded goods rises. The positive sign of $x_{\bar{E}}$ is in keeping with the standard assumption in the literature on contractionary devaluation. Note, however, that this sign places restrictions on the share of imported inputs in variable costs and on the elasticity of substitution between labor and imported inputs.

Because a previously unanticipated current devaluation is represented by an increase in $\bar{E}$ and is also likely to increase nominal wages, the real excess demand for loans will rise, putting upward pressure on the domestic interest rate. Thus, taking working capital into account may cause the impact on nominal interest rates to be positive even if foreign assets figure prominently in private sector balance sheets. Working capital considerations, therefore, do enhance the likelihood that devaluation will be contractionary. Note, however, that these considerations become irrelevant if domestic loans and foreign assets are perfect substitutes—in which case Equation (15) applies—and do not affect the analysis of an anticipated future devaluation.

7.1.2 Effects on Aggregate Supply

In addition to affecting demand, as described in the previous discussion, a devaluation also affects the supply of domestically produced goods. The production cost of those goods in domestic currency is likely to increase as the prices of the factors of production rise in response to a devaluation. This can be thought of as an upward shift in the supply curve for those goods, which, together with a downward-sloping demand curve, would result in a lower level of output and a lower real depreciation than otherwise would be the case. A devaluation may cause an upward shift in the supply curve through three separate channels: increases in nominal wages, the use of imported inputs, and increases in the cost of working capital.

7.1.2.1 EFFECTS ON THE NOMINAL WAGE

In this subsection we will examine the effect of a devaluation on the nominal wage in the context of a general model from which specific results appearing in the literature can be derived as special cases. We assume again a "dependent economy" setup, take capital to be sector specific and fixed in the short run, and allow both sectors to employ imported inputs. With all variables in logarithms, the aggregate demand for labor is

$$
\begin{aligned}
n_t^d &= n_0 - d_1(w_t - \bar{e}) - d_2(w_t - p_N(t)) - d_3(\bar{e} - p_N(t)) \\
&= n_0 - (d_1 + d_2)(w_t - \bar{e}) - (d_2 + d_3)z_t,
\end{aligned}
\tag{17}
$$

where n_0, d_1, d_2, and d_3 are positive parameters. An increase in the product wage measured in terms of traded goods reduces the demand for labor in the traded goods sector both by reducing output in that sector and by encouraging the substitution of imported inputs for labor. The magnitude of d_1 depends on the share of labor employed in the traded goods sector, on the labor intensity of production in that sector, and on the elasticity of substitution between labor and imported inputs in the production of traded goods. The sign and magnitude of d_2 are determined similarly except, of course, that the nontraded goods sector is involved. Finally, d_3 captures the effect on the demand for labor in the nontraded goods sector of an increase in the price of imported inputs. The demand for labor falls because of a decrease in the level of output, but it increases as labor is substituted for imported inputs. The negative sign in Equation (17) will hold when substitution elasticities are sufficiently small that the former effect dominates the latter. The magnitude of d_3 depends on this substitution elasticity, on the labor intensity of output in nontraded goods, and on the share of the labor force employed in that sector.

Turning to aggregate supply, we assume the current nominal wage to be given by

$$
\begin{aligned}
w_t &= \bar{w} + s_1(n_t - n_0) + s_2 p^a + s_3(p_t - p^a) \\
&= \bar{w} + s_1(n_t - n_0) + s_3\bar{e} - s_3(1 - \delta)\bar{e} + (s_2 - s_3)[e^a - (1 - \delta)z^a],
\end{aligned}
\tag{18}
$$

where $\bar{w}$, s_1, s_2, and s_3 are positive parameters, all variables are again in logarithms, and expectations of current values are formed one period ago. In the contract described by Equation (18), the current nominal wage w_t consists of an exogenous component $\bar{w}$ (taken hereafter to be zero, for simplicity) plus an endogenous component that depends on the level of employment n_t relative to its "natural" or full-employment level n_0, on price expectations for the contract period formed when the contract was signed, and on the degree of indexation (s_3) to unanticipated price shocks ($p - p^a$).

When alternative restrictions are imposed, various special cases can be derived from Equation (18):

Exogenous nominal wages follow from $s_1 = s_2 = s_3 = 0$.

Predetermined nominal wages with Fischer-type contracts (see Blanchard and Fischer, 1989, pp. 415–16) are implied by $s_2 = 1$ and $s_1 = s_3 = 0$.

Wage indexation to the current price level in its simplest form can be imposed by setting $s_1 = 0$ and $s_2 = s_3$. As a special case, fixed real wages follow from $s_1 = 0$ and $s_2 = s_3 = 1$.

The simple Phillips curve, without expectations, is derived with $s_2 = s_3 = 0$. If employment was dated one period ago, the nominal wage would be predetermined. If, as in Equation (18), the *current* value of employment matters, then the nominal wage is endogenous.

A neoclassical labor market model can be produced by setting $s_2 = s_3 = 1$.

Finally, the Friedman-Phelps version of the Phillips curve (see Blanchard and Fischer, 1989, pp. 572–73) emerges from $s_2 = 1$ and $s_3 = 0$.

In this subsection, we will impose only the restrictions that $s_2 = 1$ and $s_3 < 1$, so that perfectly anticipated inflation has no effect on workers' real wage demands and the degree of indexation to current prices is only partial. Substituting Equation (17) in Equation (18) and simplifying, the equilibrium nominal wage implied by this more general model is

$$
\begin{aligned}
w_t = e^a &- \frac{1 - \delta + s_1(d_2 + d_3)}{1 + s_1(d_1 + d_2)} z^a + \frac{s_3 + s_1(d_1 + d_2)}{1 + s_1(d_1 + d_2)}(\bar{e} - e^a) \\
&- \frac{s_3(1 - \delta) + s_1(d_2 + d_3)}{1 + s_1(d_1 + d_2)}(z_t - z^a).
\end{aligned}
\tag{19}
$$

This formulation immediately leads to several important observations. First, in assessing the effects on the nominal wage of an exchange-rate depreciation, the extent to which a nominal depreciation translates into a real depreciation is crucial. The equilibrium nominal wage after a devaluation is determined simultaneously with the equilibrium real exchange rate as shown in Equation (19). The second observation is that, in the absence of perfect indexation (that is, as long as $s_3 < 1$), it is important to distinguish, in assessing the effects of devaluation on the nominal wage, whether a current devaluation was previously anticipated or not. If, as seems likely, the effect on the *real* exchange rate of an anticipated devaluation is smaller than that of an unanticipated devaluation, the impact of an anticipated devaluation on the nominal wage will exceed that of an unanticipated parity change.[13]

The third important observation, however, is that in neither case must the nominal wage necessarily increase. This highlights the importance of an integrated treatment of the labor market in assessing the likelihood that devaluation can be contractionary. To clarify this point, we adopt the working assumption that the price of nontraded goods is constant on impact. This simplifies Equation (19), which can now be written as

$$w_t = \frac{\delta + s_1(d_1 - d_3)}{1 + s_1(d_1 + d_2)}e^a + \frac{s_3\delta + s_1(d_1 - d_3)}{1 + s_1(d_1 + d_2)}(\bar{e} - e^a). \tag{20}$$

Note that if $d_3 > d_1$, the effects of both an anticipated and an unanticipated devaluation could be negative. To see how this possibility can arise, note from Equation (17) that if $d_3 > d_1$, an increase in the nominal exchange rate E will *lower* the demand for labor, given wages and the price of nontraded goods. The reason is that an increase in demand in the traded goods sector is offset by reduced demand in the nontraded goods sector. The latter, in turn, arises from the effect of an increase in the price of imported inputs, which reduces the level of output and therefore the demand for labor in that sector. This effect will be dominant if the share of labor in the nontraded goods sector is large, if that sector is relatively intensive in its use of imported inputs, and if the elasticity of substitution of labor for imported inputs in that sector is small. Note that, regardless of whether d_3 exceeds d_1 or not, the presence of imported inputs in the nontraded goods sector tends to dampen the increase in the nominal wage that would tend to accompany a devaluation. This effect acts as an offset to the contractionary effect of a devaluation on the supply of nontraded goods that operates through the imported input channel (see the next subsection).

As a final observation, note from Equation (19) that if $d_1 > d_3$, then as long as a nominal depreciation (whether anticipated or unanticipated) results in a less-than-proportional real depreciation ($0 < dz/de < 1$), the increase in the nominal wage will be no greater than the increase in the price of traded goods and no less than the increase in the price of nontraded goods. That is, the product wage will fall in the traded goods sector and rise in the nontraded goods sector.[14]

7.1.2.2 IMPORTED INPUTS

In the event of a devaluation, the price of imported inputs increases by the same percentage as the exchange rate, driving up the costs of production of domestically produced goods. The magnitude of this increase in costs depends on technological factors and on the extent to which the price of other factors of production responds to the devaluation. To illustrate these relationships, we will use a specific example.

Assume an economy that produces and consumes traded and nontraded goods. Nontraded goods are produced with imported inputs and "value added," according to a CES production function with elasticity of substitution σ. Value added, in turn, is produced with a fixed amount of specific capital and with labor according to a Cobb-Douglas production function. The share of labor in value added is denoted by γ. Nominal wages are assumed to be determined exogenously and to increase by a given amount as a result of the devaluation. The return on capital, in contrast, is endogenous and varies so as to clear the market for that factor.

In analyzing the effect of a devaluation on the supply of nontraded goods, we investigate the increase in costs, or supply price, for a given level of output. This is the upward shift in the supply curve of those goods. The percentage increase in the supply price is

$$\pi_N = \vartheta_J\epsilon + \vartheta_w\omega + \vartheta_k\hat{\rho}, \tag{21}$$

where ϵ is the percentage of the nominal devaluation, ω is the exogenous increase in nominal wages, and $\hat{\rho}$ is the endogenous increase in the return of capital. Because labor and capital are combined according to a Cobb-Douglas production function, we have, since the capital stock is constant,

$$\hat{\rho} = \omega + \hat{n}.$$

Cost minimization for a given level of production implies

$$\hat{n} = \sigma\vartheta_J\{\vartheta_w + \vartheta_J[\sigma(1 - \gamma) + \gamma]\}^{-1}(\epsilon - \omega),$$

and therefore

$$\hat{\rho} = \omega + \sigma\vartheta_J\{\vartheta_w + \vartheta_J[\sigma(1 - \gamma) + \gamma]\}^{-1}(\epsilon - \omega). \tag{22}$$

Equation (22) is useful for examining the effect of the devaluation and the adjustment of wages on the return to capital. If wages increase by the full amount of the devaluation ($\omega = \epsilon$), the return to capital will also increase by the same amount. The reason is simple. At the initial rate of return of capital, there is an incentive to substitute value added for imported inputs, and within value added to substitute capital for labor. The amount of capital is constant, however, and thus its rate of return increases—until the initial ratio of nominal wages to the rate of return of capital is restored, so that the initial desired capital/labor ratio is also restored. At the end, $\hat{\rho} = \omega = \epsilon$, and the same combination of inputs is used to produce the given level of output. A $\hat{\rho}$ different from ω would not be an equilibrium value. For example, assume that $\hat{\rho} < \omega$. Then the desired capital-labor combination would be higher, which together with a fixed capital stock implies lower employment, which in turn implies lower value added. For a given level of output, this implies a higher level of imported inputs. But this change in the use of factors is inconsistent with the change in factor prices. Since the rate of return of capital increased by less than the nominal wage, the price of value added increased by less than the price of imported inputs, so we should expect a decline (instead of an increase) in the intensity of the use of imported inputs.

If wages do not increase by the full amount of the devaluation, Equation (22) indicates that the return on capital increases by more than nominal wages. The reason is that if the rate of return on capital increases only by the same amount as nominal wages, producers will want to use the same capital/labor ratio. Because the capital stock is fixed, this implies a constant level of employment. But because the price of value added would decline relative to the price of imported inputs, there would be an excess demand for capital and labor. These excess demands are satisfied by an increase in the use of labor and a further increase in the return to capital.

Using Equation (22) to replace $\hat{\rho}$ in Equation (21), and remembering that $\gamma\vartheta_k = (1 - \gamma)\vartheta_w$ because capital and labor are combined according to a Cobb-Douglas function to produce value added, yields

$$\pi_N = \epsilon - \gamma(1 - \vartheta_J)\{\gamma(1 - \vartheta_J) + \vartheta_J[\sigma(1 - \gamma) + \gamma]\}^{-1}(\epsilon - \omega). \quad (23)$$

Therefore, if wages increase by the full amount of the devaluation, the supply curve shifts upward by the same percentage as the exchange rate. If wages do not increase by the full amount of the devaluation, the supply curve shifts upward by less than the exchange rate, but by more than the increase in wages, since in this case the return to capital increases more than wages, as discussed above. In this case it is also clear from Equation (23) that the increase in the supply price will be larger the larger is the share of imported inputs in total costs and, for a given share of imported inputs, the larger is the share of capital in value added. The increase in the supply price will also be larger the smaller is the elasticity of substitution between imported inputs and value added.

Equation (23) assumes that value added is produced by capital and labor according to a Cobb-Douglas production function. Therefore, it is assumed that the elasticity of substitution between labor and capital is equal to unity. If instead a CES function were assumed for the production of value added, when $\omega < \epsilon$ the increase in the supply price would be larger the lower the elasticity of substitution between labor and capital. The reason is that the lower this elasticity, the higher must be the increase in the return to capital needed to induce producers to increase the employment of labor necessary to compensate for a lower use of imported inputs.

The use of imported inputs in the production of traded goods does not offer new insights because the price of this type of input moves together with the price of output. Even if we assume the same structure of production as the one assumed above for nontraded goods, the level of output will depend on the product wage, or the ratio of nominal wages to the exchange rate.

Consequently, if wages increase by less than the full amount of the devaluation, output of traded goods will increase (if working capital considerations are ignored), and vice versa.

7.1.2.3 EFFECTS THROUGH COSTS OF WORKING CAPITAL

Several authors of the new structuralist school, notably Taylor (1983) and van Wijnbergen (1983a), have emphasized that a nominal devaluation could exert contractionary effects on the supply of domestic output by increasing the cost of working capital, that is, by financing labor costs and purchases of imported inputs. To examine how this effect could operate, consider first the nontraded goods sector. The need to finance working capital arises from an asynchrony between payments and receipts—much the same as the motivation sometimes used in justifying households' demand for money (see Blanchard and Fischer, 1989, chapter 4). Suppose that, in the nontraded goods sector, to finance a real wage bill $\omega_N(t)n_N(t)$—where $\omega_N(t) \equiv w_t/P_N(t)$ is the product wage in that sector—and a real imported input bill $z_t J_N(t)$ the firm is led to hold real stocks of loans outstanding in the amount of $h^n[i_t, \omega_N(t)n_N(t)]$ for real wages and $h^J[i_t, z_t J_N(t)]$ for imported inputs.[15] The representative firm's profits are thus given by

$$
\begin{aligned}
\Pi_N = {} & P_N(t)y_N[n_N(t), J_N(t)] - w_t n_N(t) - \bar{E}J_N(t) \\
& - i_t P_N(t)h^n[i_t, \omega_N(t)n_N(t)] - i_t P_N(t)h^J[i_t, z_t J_N(t)],
\end{aligned}
\tag{24}
$$

and the first-order conditions for profit maximization are

$$
\frac{dy_N}{dn_N} = \omega_N(t)\left\{1 + i_t h^n_{\omega_N n_N}[i_t, \omega_N(t)n_N(t)]\right\},
\tag{25a}
$$

$$
\frac{dy_N}{dJ_N} = z_t\left\{1 + i_t h^J_{z J_N}[i_t, z_t J_N(t)]\right\}.
\tag{25b}
$$

These equations can be solved for labor and imported input demand functions:

$$
n_N^d(t) = n_N^d[\omega_N^-(t), \overset{\pm}{z_t}, \bar{i}_t],
\tag{26a}
$$

$$
J_N^d(t) = J_N^d[\omega_N^-(t), \overset{\pm}{z_t}, \bar{i}_t].
\tag{26b}
$$

Substituting these equations in the short-run production function for nontraded goods yields the short-run supply function for nontraded goods:

$$y_N^s(t) = y_N^s[\omega_N^-(t), \bar{z}_t, \bar{i}_t]. \tag{27a}$$

Repeating this exercise for the traded goods sector yields a traded-goods supply function:

$$y_T = y_T^s[\omega_T^-(t), \bar{i}_t], \tag{27b}$$

where $\omega_T(t) \equiv w_t/\bar{E}$.

The presence of the costs of financing working capital has two important supply consequences that affect the likelihood of contractionary devaluation. The first of these is the Cavallo-Patman effect discussed in Chapter 5: an increase in loan interest rates adds to the costs of financing working capital and shifts the output supply curve upward. This effect is captured in the negative sign of the partial derivative of i_t in Equations (27). The magnitude of the effect depends on the properties of the functions h^n and h^J.[16] There are several important aspects of this effect, as applied to the contractionary devaluation issue:

> The Cavallo-Patman effect will appear in conjunction with a previously unanticipated current devaluation only if capital mobility is imperfect. If domestic and foreign interest-bearing assets are perfect substitutes, the domestic nominal interest rate will not be affected by a devaluation of this type, and no Cavallo-Patman effect will materialize.
>
> If domestic interest rates *do* rise, then the Cavallo-Patman effect represents the only channel through which devaluation may exert contractionary effects in the traded goods sector.
>
> Finally, the Cavallo-Patman effect represents a second channel, in addition to the effects of interest rate changes on aggregate demand, through which an anticipated future devaluation could affect current output. In the case where domestic and foreign interest-bearing assets are imperfect substitutes, an anticipated future devaluation would *stimulate* current production in the traded goods sector by lowering the expected real interest rate (measured in terms of traded goods). Whether current output of nontraded goods rises or falls will depend on whether the anticipated devaluation lowers or raises the expected real interest rate in terms of nontraded goods.

The second important consequence of the financing of working capital is the effect of working capital costs on the *elasticities* of the sectoral short-run supply curves given by Equations (27a) and (27b).[17] This effect is captured by the cross–partial derivatives of these supply equations. The presence of working capital costs is likely to *reduce* short-run supply elasticities in both sectors because of the increase in marginal costs associated with the need to finance additional working capital. In the presence of a real exchange-rate depreciation, this reduction in supply elasticities will be unfavorable with respect to economic expansion in response to devaluation in the traded goods sector, but the reduction may be either favorable or unfavorable with respect to activity in the nontraded goods sector, depending on whether demand for such goods contracts or expands in response to devaluation.

7.1.3 Empirical Evidence

Four alternative empirical approaches have been followed in the literature to analyze the contractionary effects of devaluation. The first, factual approach examines changes in output performance at the time of devaluation and is usually referred to as the "before-after" methodology. The second procedure, known as the "comparison" or "control group" approach, involves comparing output growth in devaluing countries with performance in a group of nondevaluing countries. The third strategy applies econometric methods to time series data in order to quantify the impact of exchange-rate changes on real output. A fourth, somewhat less direct approach to the problem uses simulation models or reduced-form equations to analyze the effects of exchange-rate variables on output.

7.1.3.1 BEFORE-AFTER APPROACH

One of the first studies using the before-after approach was Díaz Alejandro's (1965) analysis of the experience of Argentina over the period 1955–61. He argued that the 1959 devaluation of the peso was contractionary because it induced a shift in income distribution toward high savers, which, in turn, depressed consumption and real absorption.

In an important contribution, Cooper (1971) surveyed twenty-four devaluation episodes involving nineteen different developing countries that took place between 1959 and 1966 and assessed statistically the extent of the response of the balance of trade and payments, inflation, and the elements of aggregate demand. While his results showed that the trade balance (measured in foreign currency) and the balance of payments did improve in most cases, he also found evidence of contractionary effects following a devaluation. Cooper's study suffers, however, from two major weaknesses. First, he examined only the short-run or impact effects of a devaluation (that is, effects that take place within a year), although in most cases a devaluation can hardly be expected to have its principal—let alone its sole—effect in the following year. Second, the before-after approach he used was based on a strict ceteris paribus assumption, which makes it an unreliable inference technique. This type of approach does not yield an estimate of the independent effect of a currency depreciation on output when other determinants (domestic as well as external factors) of the outcome are changing between the predevaluation period and the postdevaluation period.

In a comprehensive study using the before-after approach, Killick et al. (1992) reviewed the results of 266 IMF-supported programs implemented during the 1980s—many of which incorporated nominal devaluation as a key policy measure. Their analysis suggests that although in the very short term programs have no discernible effect on output growth, over the longer term (after three or four years) growth rates tend to improve. However, these programs were also associated with a substantial fall in the share of investment in output. Killick et al. nevertheless attributed the positive-output effect to an increase in the marginal productivity of capital, rather than exchange-rate adjustment per se.

7.1.3.2 CONTROL GROUP APPROACH

The control group methodology in principle overcomes the inability of the before-after approach to distinguish between the effect of devaluation per se and the effect of other factors on output. The basic assumption is that devaluing and nondevaluing countries face the same external environment. Therefore, by comparing before-after changes in output growth in devaluing countries to those observed in the control group of nondevaluing countries, the effect of the external environment (or factors unrelated to devaluation per se) will cancel out—so that the difference in group performance reflects only the effect of exchange-rate changes.

Recent studies applying the control group approach to the specific question of devaluation in developing countries include those of Kamin (1988) and Edwards (1989b). Kamin's research exploits data for a set of 50 to 90 devaluations out of a sample of 107 devaluations that took place between 1953 and 1983. He performs formal statistical tests for the significance of changes over time for each economic indicator considered—for both the devaluing country's performance and the comparison group's performance—and for the difference between the two. Among other counterintuitive results,[18] Kamin finds that a contraction in economic activity, in the sense of an actual decline in output *levels,* is not typical for devaluations; the growth rate remains in general positive. Second, a sharp and significant decline in output *growth* is registered by the devaluing countries, but it occurs in the year preceding the devaluation. This lower rate appears to be maintained virtually unchanged through the year following the devaluation. Growth in subsequent years turns upward and also improves relative to the comparison group. In sum, the results offer little evidence that devaluations are followed by significant contractions in output; recessions prior to devaluation appear to be more typical.

A somewhat different perspective is provided by Edwards (1989b, pp. 320–24), who analyzes the evolution of a number of key variables during the three years preceding and the three years following eighteen devaluation episodes that took place between 1962 and 1982 in Latin America. Like Kamin, he constructs a control group consisting of twenty-four developing nations that maintained a fixed nominal exchange rate over the same period, and compares its behavior with that of the devaluing countries. Nonparametric statistical tests (variants of the Mann-Whitney U tests for differences in means) are used in these comparisons. His results suggest that the observed decline in output growth in periods surrounding devaluations may not, in fact, be a consequence of exchange-rate changes but rather may reflect the imposition of trade and capital restrictions that have often accompanied devaluations in Latin American countries. The point is indeed important; devaluations in developing countries are almost always one of several components of a stabilization package. It is thus difficult to separate the effect of the devaluation itself from that of the macroeconomic and structural policies implemented alongside a nominal parity change.

Several studies based on the control group approach have also examined the impact of devaluation on output in the broader context of stabilization programs supported by the IMF. In an initial study, Donovan (1981) examined twelve IMF-supported devaluations between 1970 and 1976, comparing the performance of the devaluing economies with that of all non-oil-exporting developing countries. Among other results, he found that meaningful reductions in GDP growth were registered only for those programs specifically aimed at import restraint. However, in a subsequent study (Donovan, 1982), where the sample of IMF-supported programs was extended to seventy-eight (covering the period 1971–80), he found that the rate of economic growth fell by more than the average decline experienced by non-oil developing countries in the one-year comparisons, but by less in the three-year comparisons.

Gylfason (1987) also used a comparison group approach in his study of thirty–two IMF-supported programs implemented during 1977–79. He found that differences in output growth between countries with IMF programs and the reference group of nonprogram countries were not statistically significant. Khan (1990) recently conducted a comprehensive evaluation of the effects of IMF-supported programs on the balance of payments, the current account, inflation, and growth in a group of sixty-nine developing countries over the period 1973–88. Using regression analysis to isolate the impact of policy variables on macroeconomic aggregates, and performing two-year comparisons (that is, using averages of target variables over periods t and $t + 1$), he finds that real-exchange-rate changes have a negative effect on the rate of growth of output, but the coefficient is small and not highly significant in statistical terms. Qualitatively similar results were obtained by Doroodian (1993) in a study covering forty-three countries during the period 1977–83.

7.1.3.3 ECONOMETRIC MODELS

Little econometric evidence on the relationship between devaluation and real economic activity in developing countries has been produced so far. Sheehey (1986) employs a Lucas-type supply function (see Chapter 3) and uses cross-country data for sixteen Latin American countries to estimate the impact on short-run output growth of unanticipated inflation, changes in the relative cost of foreign exchange, and business cycle fluctuations in the industrial countries. His results appear to support the contractionary devaluation hypothesis for Latin America, as well as suggesting a strong impact of external economic activity on real growth rates.

A well-known study is by Edwards (1986), who uses data on twelve developing countries for 1965–80, and estimates a model of real output behavior. His results indicate that real-exchange-rate changes have a small contractionary effect in the short run. In the medium run, however, the perverse effect is completely reversed. In the long run devaluations are neutral. In subsequent work, Edwards (1989*b*) developed a multisector macroeconomic model of a dependent economy with imported intermediate goods, foreign debt, and wage indexation to analyze the way in which devaluations affect aggregate output and employment. The regression results (based on a sample of twelve developing countries, with annual data covering the period 1965–84) corroborate his earlier findings that devaluations have a short-run contractionary effect on real output. The long-run neutrality result, however, was found to hold only in two cases.

Edwards' econometric tests, however, make no distinction between anticipated and unanticipated changes in the behavior of key macroeconomic variables, a dichotomy that plays a crucial role in the model developed by Agénor (1991). The impact of a real-exchange-rate devaluation on real output is, in Agénor's model, quite different from the results obtained in the literature examined above. In models where the distinction between anticipated and unanticipated movements plays no role (as in Hanson, 1983; Schmid, 1982; and Gylfason and Schmid, 1983), the impact of a devaluation is theoretically ambiguous.[19] This result derives from two conflicting factors: on the one hand, a devaluation generates an expansionary effect through aggregate demand (via substitution effects between imported goods and domestic goods, as well as its effect on exports); on the other hand, it has, through its effect on the cost of imported intermediate inputs, a negative impact on aggregate supply. As a consequence, a devaluation can be contractionary even if the net effect on aggregate demand is expansionary. By contrast, in the rational-expectations model developed by Agénor (1991), the distinction between expected and unexpected changes in the real exchange rate plays a crucial role. An anticipated depreciation of the real exchange rate, which can be seen as an adverse "supply shock," translates into a rise in the expected price level. Workers thus increase their nominal wage demands. As a result, the demand for both labor and imported inputs falls, and, consequently, output also falls. By contrast, an unanticipated devaluation has no effect on price expectations or the real wage.[20] It gives rise, however, to an unanticipated increase in domestic demand as the relative price of domestic output (unexpectedly) falls. In turn, this implies an unanticipated increase in prices, which stimulates aggregate supply. Econometric tests of the model, performed with a cross-section of annual data covering twenty-three countries and the period 1976–87, show that an anticipated depreciation of the real exchange rate has a negative effect on economic activity, while an unanticipated depreciation has a positive impact on output. Moreover, contrary to the results produced by Edwards (1986), the contractionary effect of anticipated depreciations remains significant even after a year.

The evidence provided by econometric studies, although broadly supportive of the contractionary hypothesis, is subject to several methodological limitations. As Kamin (1988) argues, time series regression analysis of exchange-rate effects on output may not be appropriate for characterizing devaluation episodes. First, they do not tell us what happened during a specific devaluation episode. Real exchange rates move more or less continuously over time; they merely show more exceptional movement during devaluations. Second, not only are devaluations typically associated with other stabilization policies, but they are large, isolated events that occur only sporadically; and their influence, particularly with regard to expectations, may differ qualitatively from slower, more routine exchange-rate adjustments. Finally, annual models may not use the proper time frame to examine the *long-run* effects of devaluations. As discussed earlier, some recent studies based on factual approaches have examined the long-term impact of currency changes within a three-year period.

7.1.3.4 MACRO-SIMULATION STUDIES

Evidence from macroeconomic models on the output effect of devaluation on real income is provided by Branson (1986), Gylfason and Schmid (1983), Gylfason and Risager (1984), Kamas (1992), Meller and Solimano (1987), and Solimano (1986). Gylfason and Schmid (1983), for instance, construct a log-linear macro model of an open economy with intermediate goods. In their model, a devaluation exerts some of the conflicting effects reviewed earlier: on the one hand, it generates an expansionary effect through aggregate demand; on the other, a devaluation has, through its effect on the cost of imported intermediate inputs, a negative effect on aggregate supply. The empirical relevance of the model is evaluated for a sample of ten industrial and middle-income developing countries using a calibration procedure to estimate the key parameters of the model for each country. Their results show that a devaluation is expansionary (it raises real income) in eight out of ten countries in the sample. The exception, among developing countries, is Brazil, where the Marshall-Lerner condition is not satisfied. The expansionary impact, through expenditure-switching effects, of a devaluation seems therefore generally to dominate contractionary effects. By contrast, Gylfason and Risager (1984) develop a model that stresses the effects of exchange-rate changes on interest payments on external debt. Also using a calibration procedure, they show that while a devaluation is likely to be expansionary in developed economies, it is generally contractionary in developing countries. A similar result is obtained by Gylfason and Radetzki (1991) for a larger group of developing countries, in a model emphasizing the role of wage indexation in transmitting exchange-rate changes to domestic prices.

In addition to multicountry simulation studies, several authors have constructed country-specific models to analyze the effectiveness of exchange-rate changes on output. Solimano (1986), for instance, using a computable macroeconomic model for Chile, shows a currency devaluation to be contractionary in the short to medium run. His analysis focuses on three factors: the structure of the trade sector in terms of the response of trade flows to changes in relative prices, the relative intensity of domestic value added with respect to imported inputs in production across export- and import-competing industries, and the degree of wage indexing. A stagflationary effect of devaluation is also obtained by Branson (1986) for Kenya, using a two-sector model with sticky prices, wage indexing, and imported intermediate goods. Roca and Priale (1987) have examined within a detailed macroeconomic framework the experience of Peru during 1977–78 and 1980–82, a period during which the Peruvian authorities attempted to reduce the current account deficit by depreciating the real exchange rate through large nominal devaluations. Because a large portion of loans to the business sector were contracted in U.S. dollars, the successive devaluations not only increased the price of imported inputs, but resulted also (as discussed previously) in a rise in the real cost of credit, pushing up the cost of working capital for highly indebted firms and generating a strong stagflationary effect.

Finally, Kamas (1992) estimates a small macroeconomic model for Colombia in which traditional and nontraditional exports are distinguished, and models the supply side in a more detailed manner than most previous econometric and simulation studies. Her analysis indicates that a nominal devaluation is more likely to be contractionary the lower the elasticity of substitution between capital and labor, the lower the elasticity of substitution between imported inputs and domestic value added, and the higher the degree of wage indexation. In particular, if the short-run elasticity of substitution between capital and labor is smaller than the long-run elasticity and if wages adjust rapidly, devaluation may be contractionary in the short run, even if the long-run effects on output are expansionary. Thus, previous studies, such as those of Branson (1986) and Gylfason and Schmid (1983) discussed earlier, in which the elasticity of substitution between capital and labor is assumed to be unity (as a result of Cobb-Douglas production functions) may have overestimated the expansionary impact of devaluation.

The foregoing review of empirical work suggests that, so far, evidence concerning the contractionary effect of devaluation on real output is mixed. Part of the diversity of the results may be attributable to the variety of research methodologies employed in the literature. Each method is subject to a number of inherent limitations. As mentioned earlier, studies using the before-after approach do not take into account the behavior of other variables such as monetary and fiscal policies, external disturbances, and structural changes. In addition, focusing on "before" and "after" makes it harder to detect causality among variables. While the control group approach copes with some of the problems of the before-after methodology, it also has limitations (see Goldstein and Montiel, 1986). The crucial problem is that devaluing countries do differ systematically from nondevaluing countries prior to a devaluation episode, and this matters considerably in evaluating the impact of a currency change on output. In principle, this problem can be dealt with—see, for instance, Gylfason (1987) and Khan (1990) in a different context—but considerable difficulties arise in practice. Studies using a simulation approach have a major advantage in that they usually provide considerable information on the transmission of exchange-rate changes to output, in contrast to factual approaches. Although most of the studies available so far use imputed parameter values, opening to question the reliability of results derived from a set of "guesstimates" and coefficients that are not consistently estimated in an integrated framework, this approach may continue to yield important insight.

Econometric studies available so far are also subject to a number of limitations. The specification of the output equation is often arbitrary (a strategy that raises well-known simultaneity and specification bias problems) and does not always provide a rigorous basis for distinguishing anticipated and unanticipated movements in variables. This distinction may, however, be a critical one. The results obtained by Agénor (1991), for instance, illustrate the point that the arbitrary procedure of simply adding expected/unexpected components, without explicit formulation of the underlying macroeconomic framework, may lead to an inappropriate specification of the output equation to be estimated. Moreover, existing studies have considered only some of the mechanisms that can explain a contractionary effect of devaluation;

several other links were discussed in the first part of this chapter, and their empirical implications need to be investigated.

7.2 Real-Exchange-Rate Targeting

While the contractionary devaluation debate has a long history, the analysis of the consequences for macroeconomic stability of PPP-based rules for managing officially determined exchange rates has only recently begun to receive attention. Dornbusch (1982) argued, using a Taylor-type overlapping-contracts framework (see Taylor, 1980), that the adoption of PPP-based rules would tend to stabilize output and the trade balance at the expense not only of increased price level instability, but also of increased persistence in the response to shocks of both output and prices. In the presence of imported inputs, Dornbusch (1982) also argued that such rules may not even succeed in stabilizing output in the short run, while continuing to destabilize prices. If output is destabilized, however, persistence would tend to be reduced.[21]

In the models analyzed by Dornbusch, the authorities are assumed to control both the nominal exchange rate and the stock of money, each of which can be separately indexed to the domestic price level. As long as the money stock is not perfectly indexed to the price level, shocks to the system may generate large and persistent movements in prices, but the steady-state price level would remain determinate. By contrast, Adams and Gros (1986) treat the money supply as endogenously determined (through the balance of payments). They work through a series of models that incorporate varying assumptions about the structure of production, the degree of capital mobility, and other structural features, finding that the adoption of PPP-based exchange-rate rules renders the rate of inflation a random walk. Although they concur with Dornbusch that control of the money supply (through sterilization) would tend to stabilize the price level, they find that it results in the destabilization of other key macroeconomic variables, such as the current account.

An important feature of the models analyzed by Adams and Gros is the absence of a wealth effect on consumption. A third strand of this literature, following Lizondo (1991b), incorporates such effects and shows that in its presence the inflation rate remains determinate under real-exchange-rate targeting, even with a domestic credit target rendering the money supply endogenous through the balance of payments. In essence, the inflation tax replaces the real exchange rate as a key endogenous variable ensuring the simultaneous attainment of internal and external balance. In this section we describe a model of this type, due to Montiel and Ostry (1991), which describes how the rate of inflation responds to a variety of domestic and external shocks under real-exchange-rate targeting.

7.2.1 The Analytical Framework

As in the first part of this chapter, we analyze the case of a small open economy in which competitive firms combine homogeneous labor (available in fixed supply) and sector-specific capital to produce nontraded goods and traded goods, using a standard concave technology. However, to allow the consideration of terms-of-trade shocks, we now adopt the three-good framework described in Chapter 2, separating traded goods into exportables and importables, supposing the former to be produced (but not consumed) at home and the latter to be produced abroad. All prices are flexible, ensuring that full employment is continuously maintained. The income generated from production of the two goods is received by consumers, who use it to buy home goods and importables. Households allocate a constant fraction of their total expenditures to each of the two goods in every period, as they would do, for example, if they possessed Cobb-Douglas utility functions.

The real value of aggregate household expenditures depends on the real value of factor income net of taxes, the real interest rate, and real financial wealth. Real factor income consists of the real value of output of exportables and home goods measured in terms of the consumption basket. It is an increasing function of the terms of trade (the price of exports relative to imports), so we can write it as $y_t = y(\Theta_t)$, where Θ_t denotes the terms of trade and $y' > 0$. Finally, real household financial wealth in terms of importables, which we denote a_t, consists of real money balances m_t plus the real value of foreign securities F_t^p, minus the real value of loans extended by the banking system to households L_t^p.

Measured in terms of the consumption bundle, real financial wealth can be expressed as $z_t^\delta a_t$, where z_t is the relative price of importables in terms of nontraded goods (or the importables' real exchange rate) and δ is the share of nontradables in the consumption basket, so that z_t^δ is the relative price of importables in terms of the consumption basket. To render the money supply endogenous in the short run, we assume that capital is perfectly mobile, which ensures that nominal interest rate parity is continuously maintained. Under fixed nominal exchange rates, this implies that the domestic nominal interest rate, which is equal to the real rate ρ plus the rate of inflation π_t, is equal to the foreign interest rate. The domestic real interest rate is given by $i^* + \delta \hat{z}_t$, where $\hat{z}_t$ is the expected and actual rate of change of the real exchange rate and i^* is the (constant) foreign interest rate. The latter is both a nominal and a real interest rate, since we will assume that foreign inflation is zero. The domestic real interest rate differs from i^*, because real interest rate parity need not hold even under perfect capital mobility when the real exchange rate is permitted to vary.

The equilibrium of the economy can be analyzed from two relationships, describing private wealth accumulation and equilibrium in the market for nontraded goods. Private wealth accumulation measured in terms of importables is equal to real factor income net of real lump-sum taxes $y_t - \tau_t$, less household consumption spending c_t, plus real interest earnings on existing holdings of nonmonetary financial assets, less the revenue from the inflation tax that accrues to the central bank:[22]

$$\dot{a}_t = y_t - \tau_t - c[y_t - \tau_t; \; i^* + \delta\hat{z}_t; \; z^\delta a_t] + i^* a_t$$
$$- (i^* + \epsilon_t)m^d(i^* + \epsilon_t; \; y_t), \tag{28}$$

where $m^d()$ is the real demand for money, which depends on the nominal interest rate ($i^* + \epsilon_t$, where ϵ_t is the devaluation rate) and real income. If the nominal exchange rate is literally fixed, rather than following a crawling peg, ϵ_t is equal to zero in Equation (28).

The government is assumed to consume the same two goods as the private sector and to finance its expenditures by levying taxes, through the receipt of transfers from the central bank, and by borrowing. The government budget must satisfy the standard intertemporal solvency constraint (see Chapter 4). We will ensure that it does so in a particularly simple way. As we shall see, the shocks to be considered will in the first instance affect the government budget through transfers from the central bank. We will assume that a change in the level of these transfers gives rise to one-for-one changes in government spending on importable goods, thereby keeping the government's budget in balance. In this case, the current account of the balance of payments will be equal to private saving, since there is no investment in this economy and central bank profits are assumed to be transferred to the government, which spends them on imports (that is, government saving is zero). Under fixed exchange rates, private saving will be equal to asset accumulation $\dot{a}_t$. For this reason, we will refer to Equation (28) as the *external balance* condition.

Because prices are flexible, the nontraded goods market must clear continuously:

$$y_N^s(\Theta_t, z_t) = \delta z_t^{1-\delta} c[y_t - \tau_t, i^* + \delta\hat{z}_t, z_t^\delta a_t] + g_N, \tag{29}$$

where $y_N^s()$ denotes the supply function for nontraded goods and g_N is the exogenous level of government consumption of such goods. Equation (29) is the *internal balance* condition. Equations (28) and (29) together determine the paths of the real exchange rate and real wealth at each instant. The economy approaches a long-run equilibrium in which both z_t and a_t reach a constant value. Since the real exchange rate is constant in the fixed-exchange-rate steady state, the domestic inflation rate must equal the world inflation rate, which in this case is zero. Since $\hat{z}_t$ and $\dot{a}_t$ are both zero, under nominal exchange rate targeting the conditions for internal and external balance given by Equations (28) and (29) jointly determine the steady-state equilibrium values of the real exchange rate and real wealth. These values will change in response to changes in the various exogenous variables of the system, including the terms of trade, world interest rates, and fiscal policy instruments.

7.2.2 Targeting the Real Exchange Rate

Suppose now that the authorities choose as their real-exchange-rate target that value of z_t that corresponds to the steady-state equilibrium under fixed exchange rates. The conditions that describe the equilibrium in this case are the same ones that prevail under nominal-exchange-rate targeting, but their interpretation is quite different. In particular, since the authorities are now committed to adjusting the nominal exchange rate to prevent the real exchange rate from deviating from its targeted level, the domestic price level is no longer tied to the world level through the fixed nominal exchange rate. In Equation (28), ϵ_t is no longer zero, as in the previous subsection, but must now be replaced by the domestic inflation rate π_t, which remains a separate endogenous variable.[23] At the same time, z_t becomes a constant—which can be set, for simplicity, equal to unity. In this case, both $\hat{z}_t$ and z_t disappear from Equations (28) and (29). Moreover, although *nominal* private wealth is predetermined, *real* wealth can change in the short run, through changes in the domestic price level. Thus, a_t becomes an endogenous variable, and internal balance is maintained not by changes in the relative price z_t, but rather by changes in the aggregate price level, manifest through a_t. This means that, as long as the exogenous and policy variables that affect the market for nontraded goods do not change, the condition $\dot{a}_t = 0$ must hold continuously, not just in the steady state, to maintain the market for nontraded goods in equilibrium. Under these circumstances, Equations (28) and (29) become

$$y(\Theta_t) - \tau_t - c[y(\Theta_t) - \tau_t; \ i^*, a_t]$$
$$+ i^* a_t - (i^* + \pi_t) m^d [i^* + \pi_t, \ y(\Theta_t)] = 0, \tag{30}$$

$$y_N(\Theta_t) = \delta c[y(\Theta_t) - \tau_t, \ i^*, \ a_t] + \bar{g}_N. \tag{31}$$

These equations imply that any *nominal* wealth accumulation by the private sector must be offset by a price level increase. In other words, the domestic rate of inflation must satisfy (30). The implication is that changes induced by shocks in the equilibrium value of real wealth required to maintain internal balance through (31) must be offset by adjustments in the inflation rate in Equation (30), since π_t is the only other endogenous variable

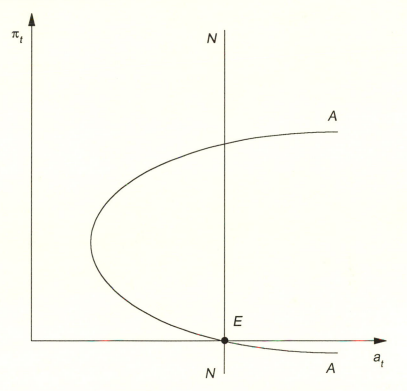

Figure 7.1   Equilibrium under a Real-Exchange-Rate Rule
Source: Montiel and Ostry (1991, p. 881).

appearing in that equation. In short, real shocks will have consequences for the equilibrium domestic inflation rate under real-exchange-rate targeting.

Consider, for instance, a shock that raises the domestic price level, thereby lowering the real value of the private sector's holdings of financial wealth a_t. From Equation (28), this will reduce consumption and increase private saving, causing $\dot{a}_t$ to become incipiently positive. This in turn would cause private consumption to increase over time, leading to an incipient excess demand for nontraded goods (Equation (29)). In order to maintain equilibrium in the home goods market in the face of this incipient demand pressure, domestic prices must rise sufficiently rapidly to maintain real wealth continuously at its new equilibrium level. As in Lizondo (1991b), the inflation tax $\pi_t m^d()$ must be high enough to induce private agents to willingly hold the stock of real wealth necessary to clear the market for nontraded goods, given the real exchange rate target and the values of the exogenous variables and policy instruments.

The determination of equilibrium is illustrated in Figure 7.1. The initial level of the real exchange rate is assumed to satisfy Equations (28) and (29)

with $\hat{z}_t$ and a_t both zero. On the assumption that world inflation is zero, domestic inflation is also zero. On the vertical axis, we plot the domestic rate
of inflation, π_t, and on the horizontal axis we plot the level of real wealth.
Equation (31) is represented by the NN locus, which shows that, given the
real-exchange-rate target, there is only one level of real assets that will clear
the market for home goods. The condition for zero real private wealth accumulation (Equation (30)) is labeled AA in the figure. The "C" shape of this
locus reflects the fact that, for plausible money demand functions, a rise in
the inflation rate will increase the inflation tax $\pi_t m^d()$ for low rates of inflation but will reduce it once inflation becomes sufficiently high (see Chapter
4). Thus, if we consider a slightly smaller level of wealth than is consistent
with Equation (30), so that $\dot{a}_t > 0$, an increase in the inflation rate will be
required to reduce $\dot{a}_t$ at low rates of inflation (so that AA will be negatively
sloped), but a reduction in inflation will be required for values of π_t that
are sufficiently high (so that the AA locus would slope upward in this case).
We assume that the government, upon adopting the real-exchange-rate target, remains at the low-inflation equilibrium, denoted by point E in Figure
7.1, which corresponds to the position of long-run equilibrium under fixed
exchange rates.

7.2.3 Effects of Macroeconomic Shocks

The question of interest, of course, is how the economy will respond to
shocks under the new policy regime. Consider first the effects of an improvement in the terms of trade (an increase in Θ_t). This raises both the
level of real factor income and that of consumption but, under the assumption that the marginal propensity to save is positive,[24] leads to an increase in
private saving and hence to an incipient accumulation of wealth, the elimination of which requires a rise in a_t (which increases consumption) to satisfy
the condition $\dot{a}_t = 0$. Thus, in Figure 7.2, the AA curve shifts to the right
in response to an improvement in the terms of trade.

To determine the new equilibrium value of real wealth, we turn to the
equilibrium condition in the market for nontraded goods (Equation (31)).
An improvement in the terms of trade raises the real product wage in the
home goods sector and thereby causes a reduction in the supply of nontradable goods.[25] In addition, real factor income rises, which increases the
demand for home goods. Thus, both the supply and the demand effects lead
to an incipient excess demand in the home goods market, which requires
a reduction in real wealth—brought about by a discrete rise in the nominal exchange rate—to restore market equilibrium. For this reason, the NN
schedule shifts leftward in Figure 7.2, to $N'N'$.

It is clear from Figure 7.2 that, at the original level of inflation, real private wealth would be increasing. The fact that $\dot{a}_t$ is incipiently positive gen-

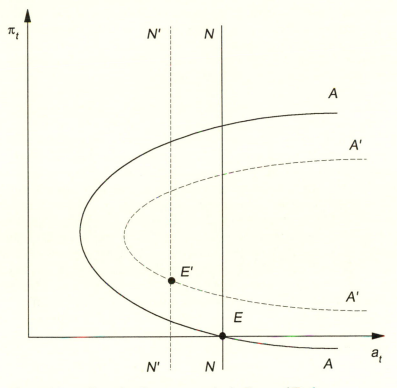

Figure 7.2   Effect of an Improvement in the Terms of Trade

Source: Montiel and Ostry (1991, p. 886).

erates excess demand pressures in the home goods market, putting upward pressure on domestic prices. Equilibrium is reestablished only once inflation and, hence, the inflation tax have increased to a level sufficient to induce the private sector to hold the new equilibrium value of a_t, which is determined in the home goods market—given the new value of Θ_t. The new steady-state position of the economy is at point E'.

Note that a policy of fixing the nominal credit stock would have no effect on domestic inflation. The reason is that control of the credit stock does not give the authorities a handle on private spending under perfect capital mobility. With domestic credit and foreign assets being perfect substitutes, a reduction, say, in the stock of credit would immediately be offset by the private sector through a reduction, on a one-for-one basis, of its rate of accumulation of foreign assets, all other aspects of its behavior remaining unchanged. The economy's equilibrium would therefore also be unchanged, except that some of the claims on foreigners previously acquired by the private sector with domestic credit financing would now be acquired directly by the central bank. The income of neither sector would be affected, because the central bank would now simply collect directly from foreigners the interest income that was previously passed on to it by the private sector. Thus, the pursuit of a nominal credit target would affect only the capital account of the balance of payments, and would leave the rate of inflation unchanged.[26]

Balance-of-payments adjustment typically requires an adjustment in the exchange rate. However, the role of exchange-rate policy in economic adjustment has been the subject of considerable debate in recent years. Two areas where controversy has been particularly intense were examined in this chapter: the effects of devaluation on output and real-exchange-rate rules. The first part of the chapter focused on the contractionary devaluation controversy. The conventional view suggests that, by inducing a reallocation of resources from the nontradable goods sector to the tradable goods sector and changes in the composition of expenditure between domestic and foreign goods, a parity change would typically lead to an expansion in output. The analysis showed, however, that there are a variety of macroeconomic channels through which an exchange-rate adjustment may exert adverse output effects. We provided a comprehensive review of the different mechanisms at work, distinguishing demand and supply-side effects. We also reviewed the evidence in this area and suggested that a number of existing studies are plagued by severe methodological problems.

The second part of the chapter focused on the macroeconomic effects of PPP-based exchange-rate rules. The analysis of such rules in the context of a simple macroeconomic model suggests that the adjustment to real shocks that would otherwise take place through changes in the real exchange rate come about, instead, through movements in the rate of inflation. In the face of permanent real disturbances, avoiding these destabilizing effects on the price level requires moving the real-exchange-rate target in line with movements in the equilibrium real exchange rate. Undoubtedly, countries that follow real-exchange-rate rules attempt to manage the exchange rate so as to keep target—and equilibrium—real rates from deviating too far from each other. However, given the detailed knowledge of the economic structure that is required, managing the real-exchange-rate target in this way must be regarded more as an art than a science. Precisely for this reason, developing countries where real-exchange-rate rules have been adopted have also tended to experience higher and more variable inflation rates than those that have operated under fixed or crawling peg regimes (see Aghevli et al., 1991). The advisability of adopting such rules will differ across countries depending on both the frequency and magnitude of permanent real shocks such as those considered here, as well as on the prospects for identifying the effects of such shocks on the underlying equilibrium real exchange rate.

Part III

ANALYSIS OF STABILIZATION PROGRAMS

Eight

An Overview of Stabilization Programs

As INDICATED in Chapter 2, high levels of inflation are much more common among developing countries than in the industrial world. Although developing countries in Latin America have been particularly prone to the high-inflation syndrome, the rest of the developing world has not been immune. Not only are annual rates of inflation above 10 percent per year common among developing nations, but sustained inflation rates in excess of 25 percent per year have periodically appeared in developing countries in Africa and Asia, as well as in the Western Hemisphere.

Table 8.1 summarizes the major inflation episodes in developing countries during the period 1965–89. Years in which the rate of change in domestic prices for a country exceeded 25 percent are cited in the table, and countries are listed by geographic region. Instances of high inflation are found in Africa, Asia, and the Middle East, as well as in the Western Hemisphere. However, the table also makes clear that, while for many developing countries episodes of high inflation are of short duration (they are often associated with large changes in the terms of trade or political instability), a small group of countries appear to have suffered from "chronic" high inflation (an expression apparently first used by Pazos, 1972) during this period.[1] This group includes Argentina, Bolivia, Brazil, Chile, Ecuador, Ghana, Guyana, Israel, Mexico, Paraguay, Peru, Turkey, Uruguay, and Zaire. The majority of these countries are in South America, but the experience of chronic high inflation is not limited to the Western Hemisphere.

A variety of approaches have been used in attempting to stabilize high inflation in the developing world. These approaches can broadly be classified as populist, orthodox (money-based and exchange-rate-based), and heterodox. Populist programs have focused on direct intervention in the wage-price process through the implementation of wage and price controls, not necessarily accompanied by adjustments in underlying fiscal imbalances. Orthodox programs, by contrast, have been concerned exclusively with getting the "fundamentals" right. Such programs feature an intended fiscal adjustment, and come in two varieties. Money-based programs rely on restrictions on the rate of monetary expansion to provide a nominal anchor for the economy while using the exchange rate to maintain external balance. Exchange-rate-based programs, by contrast, rely on exchange-rate pegging to provide the nominal anchor. Orthodox programs also differ with regard

TABLE 8.1
Incidence of High Inflation in Developing Countries, 1965–89

Country	Year(s)	Country	Year(s)
		Africa	
Botswana	1979	Seychelles	1976–77
Burkina Faso	1977	Sierra Leone	1984–88
Gambia	1975, 1977, 1979	Tanzania	1985–88
Ghana	1975–84, 1986–88	Togo	1974
Liberia	1975	Uganda	1975, 1977–89
Madagascar	1981–82	Zaire	1965, 1967–68, 1976–89
Mauritius	1974	Zambia	1986–87
Nigeria	1974, 1987, 1989		
		Asia	
Indonesia	1967–68, 1973–74, 1979	Pakistan	1974, 1977
Korea	1974–75	Philippines	1984
Malaysia	1975	Solomon Islands	1985
Maldives	1981	Sri Lanka	1983
Myanmar	1982		
		Middle East	
Iran	1974	Saudi Arabia	1974–75, 1979–80
Israel	1972, 1974–75, 1977–86	Turkey	1974, 1978–88
Kuwait	1974, 1979–80	UAR	1974
Oman	1973–74, 1979–80	Yemen	1974
		Western Hemisphere	
Argentina	1971–89	Guatemala	1986
Barbados	1979	Guyana	1974, 1987–90
Bolivia	1973–74, 1980, 1982–86	Haiti	1973
Brazil	1965–68, 1974, 1976–89	Jamaica	1978, 1984–85
Chile	1965–70, 1972–80, 1983, 1985	Mexico	1977, 1980–86
Colombia	1976–77, 1986	Nicaragua	1979–80, 1984–87
Costa Rica	1981–82	Peru	1976–90
Dominican Republic	1985, 1988–89	Suriname	1974
Ecuador	1974, 1983–85, 1987–89	Trinidad	1974
El Salvador	1986	Uruguay	1965–68, 1972–81, 1983–89
Grenada	1978	Venezuela	1984, 1987, 1989

Source: International Financial Statistics.

Notes: High inflation is defined here as a change in the GDP deflator in excess of 25 percent during the year(s) in question.

to their speed of implementation. In the "cold turkey" or "shock therapy" approach, the desired fiscal adjustment is implemented in one-step fashion, whereas "gradualist" programs aim to place the fiscal deficit on a declining path. The most recent approach to stabilization is the "heterodox" option, which combines several features of the other approaches: fiscal correction, an exchange-rate freeze or a preannounced exchange-rate path, and incomes policies in the form of either explicit wage-price controls or a "social contract."

This chapter presents an overview of experience with the stabilization of high inflation in the developing world.[2] Each of the approaches to stabilization is considered in turn. Section 8.1 describes the experience with populist programs. The next two sections consider orthodox programs, first money-based and then exchange-rate-based versions. Heterodox programs are taken up in Section 8.4. The chapter concludes with a tentative summary of the lessons learned from the experience of stabilization in developing countries.

8.1 Populism

Populist stabilization programs have been a recurrent feature of the macroeconomic experience of developing countries. While macroeconomic programs with a populist flavor can be identified at various times in various countries throughout the developing world, the best-known instances of populism have been in Latin America.[3] Strictly speaking, populism did not evolve as an approach to the stabilization of high inflation. Populist programs, rather, were aimed at a broader range of macroeconomic problems, including stagnant production, unequal income distribution, and external crises, in addition to high inflation. Nevertheless, such programs have embodied a distinctive approach to inflation stabilization that makes this class of macroeconomic programs worthy of consideration here. Specifically, the populist programs to be discussed in this chapter have attempted to combine rapid growth with low inflation by simultaneously pursuing stimulative aggregate demand policies and restraining wage and price increases through administrative controls.

The populist diagnosis leading to this policy prescription is based on the view that the economy possesses a substantial amount of unutilized productive capacity, due both to deficient aggregate demand and to monopoly power in the manufacturing sector. Deficient demand is seen as arising from overly restrictive aggregate demand policies as well as from an unequal distribution of income that depresses the incomes of wage earners, who are assumed to possess larger marginal propensities to consume than do capitalists. The remedy is to adopt expansionary fiscal policies (directed primarily at the needs of the poor) and to raise wages. Although per-unit profits may be depressed by the increase in labor costs, price increases are not considered necessary, since total profits would be increased by the expansion in output. To ensure that prices do not rise due to the exercise of monopoly power, administrative controls are the favored policy tool.

8.1.1 Chile under Allende (1970–1973)

The populist program of the Unidad Popular government led by Salvador Allende, which assumed power in Chile in 1970, contained the following features:

TABLE 8.2

Chile: Macroeconomic Indicators, 1970–73 (in percent, unless otherwise indicated)

	1970	1971	1972	1973
Inflation rate	34.9	34.5	216.7	605.9
Growth of real GDP	2.1	9.0	−1.2	−5.6
Government revenue[a]	23.7	20.4	18.2	20.2
Government spending[a]	26.4	31.1	31.2	44.9
Fiscal deficit[a]	2.7	10.7	13.0	24.7
Real wage (1970q3 = 100)	98.4	115.1	103.5	70.3

Source: Dornbusch and Edwards (1990, p. 260).

[a] In percent of GDP.

A large number of farms were appropriated under the previously existing Agrarian Reform Law. Soon after, large copper mines were nationalized. Large blocks of shares were purchased by the government in large manufacturing firms, and this operation was financed through central bank credit.

The crawling peg system that had been used by the previous government was abandoned, in favor of a fixed exchange rate.

Average public sector wages were raised by 48 percent in real terms in 1971. Since these were used as benchmarks in other sectors of the economy, private sector wages increased in that year as well, by an average of almost 40 percent.

Large increases in government spending were undertaken, directed at construction, farming, and social security. The surge in public spending was also financed with central bank credit.

A generalized system of price controls was implemented.

These policies provided a massive jolt to the Chilean economy in 1971 (Table 8.2). Real GDP grew by 9 percent, unemployment fell below 4 percent, and the real wage grew by 17 percent. The share of labor in total income increased from 52 percent in 1970 to almost 62 percent in 1971. In spite of this, the rate of inflation in 1971 remained at about the same level reached in 1970. However, the fiscal deficit increased from 3 percent of GDP in 1970 to 11 percent in 1971, and the annualized rate of growth of the money supply reached 100 percent in the fourth quarter of 1970. Moreover, the stock of foreign exchange reserves was cut in half. The government nationalized a large number of firms plagued by labor disputes.

The Chilean economy was evidently overheated by the end of 1971, and inflation was simply kept repressed by price controls. To evade such controls, a substantial underground economy emerged, which reduced tax revenue for the government. Fiscal problems were further aggravated by losses suffered by nationalized enterprises. The rate of inflation exceeded 200 percent in 1972, and the currency became seriously overvalued. Capital flight contributed to draining the stock of international reserves. An attempt to stabilize, combining a large devaluation with increases in the prices of the products sold by public sector enterprises and administative directives to increase production, was implemented in August 1972. However, in the same month the government acceded to an agreement with the national federation of labor in which nominal wages would be raised in October to compensate for cumulative inflation up to that point, with more frequent wage adjustments to be granted in the future.

By 1973 the fiscal deficit amounted to 25 percent of GDP, the informal economy was pervasive, and foreign exchange reserves neared depletion. Inflation soared and real activity was declining. The political unrest fueled by economic dislocation resulted eventually in the coup that toppled the government in September 1973.

8.1.2 Peru under García (1986–90)

The García administration, which took office in Peru in July 1985, inherited an economy characterized by high inflation, substantial unemployment and idle capacity, depressed real wages, and depleted foreign exchange reserves. The government adopted the achievement of rapid, sustained growth as its primary objective. Its macroeconomic program combined the following elements:

Multiple fixed exchange rates would replace an actively managed single rate.
External debt service would be limited to a fraction of exports determined so as to be compatible with sustained growth. The government announced that this fraction initially would be set at 10 percent.
Aggregate demand would be stimulated by real wage increases.
Firms' costs would be reduced by lowering interest rates and indirect taxes.
Incomes policies would be used to contain inflation.

As in Chile, the initial results of this strategy were quite favorable (Table 8.3). Real GDP expanded by more than 9 percent in 1986 and by a further 8 percent in 1987. The rate of inflation was cut by more than half from 1985 to 1986. Employment and real wages both increased, the latter by about 30 percent.

As in Chile, however, foreign exchange reserves began to be depleted early on. As repressed inflation squeezed profit margins, subsidies made up the difference, putting pressure on the government budget. In spite of adjustments, public sector prices remained low in real terms, and this combined with reductions in real tax revenue and central bank losses in the

TABLE 8.3
Peru: Macroeconomic Indicators, 1985–88 (in percent, unless otherwise indicated)

	1985	1986	1987	1988	1989
Inflation rate	158.3	62.9	114.5	1,722.3	2.775.3
Growth of real GDP	2.3	9.2	8.5	−7.9	−11.3
Nonfinancial public sector deficit[a]	2.7	5.2	6.6	7.5	5.6
Monetary base	531.3	68.8	111.0	438.5	1,783.5
Current account deficit[a]	0.3	6.0	7.2	7.4	1.0
Real wage (1970 = 100)	64.0	83.0	90.0	71.0	38.0

Sources: Cardoso and Helwege (1992, p. 209); and Cáceres and Paredes (1991, p. 85).
[a] In percent of GDP.

operation of the multiple-exchange-rate system[4] to cause the overall public sector deficit to exceed 6.5 percent of GDP in 1987 (Table 8.3). High fiscal deficits and increases in subsidized prices fueled inflation, which reached 114 percent in 1987 and finally exploded in early 1988. The overvaluation of the exchange rate, together with controlled domestic interest rates, contributed to massive capital flight, and international reserves were rapidly depleted. A large devaluation in late 1987 helped to attenuate these problems, but contributed to an acceleration of inflation late in the year and in early 1988. By the end of 1988, inflation ran at an annual rate of 6,000 percent. Economic chaos led to a change in government with the election of Alberto Fujimori in April 1989.

8.2 Orthodox Money-Based Stabilization

The distinguishing characteristic of the orthodox approach to stabilization is its emphasis on demand management without the use of direct wage-price controls or guidelines. The sine qua non of orthodox stabilization is fiscal adjustment. It is important to recall (see Equation (17) in Section 2.1) that central bank credit to the public sector is only one source of base money creation in developing countries, although in practice it is often the most important one. The balance of payments and credit extended to the private sector are alternative sources of money creation, so a fiscal adjustment that limits the public sector's call on central bank resources does not necessarily imply that the money stock will stop growing. In other words, fiscal adjustment does not, by itself, imply the use of money as a nominal anchor, and a program that seeks to reduce the fiscal deficit may or may not be accompanied by money growth targets. Consequently, in this section we shall refer to programs that feature fiscal adjustment as their centerpiece as orthodox programs, whether or not they are accompanied by separate targets for the rate of growth of money. While fiscal adjustment may not be sufficient to determine a money growth target, however, it is necessary for the sustained achievement of money growth rates compatible with low inflation and public sector solvency, as shown in Chapter 4. Thus, programs that rely on a money growth target as a nominal anchor typically feature fiscal adjustment. We refer to these as orthodox money-based programs. The other type of orthodox program, to be considered in the next section, couples fiscal adjustment with a targeted path for the exchange rate, with no explicit target for the growth rate of the money supply. These programs are termed orthodox exchange-rate-based programs.

Orthodox money-based stabilization programs have been widely applied in the developing world.[5] The two best-known recent applications, however, have been in Latin America—under the Pinochet government in Chile (1973) and, more recently, in Bolivia (1986). The outcomes of these episodes will be examined in this section.

8.2.1 Chile (September 1973)

The military government of Augusto Pinochet, which took power after the Allende government was deposed in Chile, immediately launched an orthodox attack on inflation, coupled with structural measures. The public sector deficit was cut from nearly 25 percent of GDP in 1973 to only 2.6 percent by 1975 (Table 8.4). Exchange-rate policy was directed at maintaining the economy's external competitiveness, rather than providing a nominal anchor. The rate of devaluation exceeded the inflation rate throughout the 1973–75 period, and the real effective exchange rate was significantly more depreciated on average during these years than it had been during the Allende period. Moreover, the government's free-market orientation precluded any direct intervention in the wage-price process such as would be entailed

TABLE 8.4
Chile: Macroeconomic Indicators, 1973–77 (in percent, unless otherwise indicated)

	1973	1974	1975	1976	1977
Inflation rate	441.0	497.8	379.2	232.8	113.8
Growth rate (per capita)	−7.1	−0.7	−14.4	1.8	8.0
Rate of devaluation	455.0	649.5	490.3	165.8	64.9
Fiscal deficit[a]	24.7	10.5	2.6	2.3	1.8
Real wage (1970 = 100)	80.0	64.8	62.1	63.0	71.1
Real effective exchange rate (1975q3 = 100)	107.2	93.5	100.2	87.1	84.4
Terms of trade	84.7	88.5	55.4	59.3	54.1

Source: Kiguel and Liviatan (1988, p. 289).
[a] In percent of GDP.

by wage and price controls. Structural measures included a tariff liberalization intended to result in a 10 percent uniform tariff by 1979.

The results of the fiscal contraction were dramatic. Real GDP fell drastically in 1975, while the unemployment rate increased to almost 17 percent of the labor force, from 4.5 percent in 1974. Over the same period, the real wage contracted by almost a quarter. Unfortunately, success on the inflation front was muted. The annual inflation rate actually increased to almost 500 percent in 1974 (see Table 8.4), before starting to decrease, but the short-run response of inflation was sluggish. By 1977, after four years of severe fiscal austerity, the rate of inflation remained in the triple-digit range. A deceleration in the rate of inflation was indeed achieved, but price stability was far from attained. The program's primary success was in the external sector, where the current account deficit was eliminated in the first year. Although a deficit was again registered in the current account in 1975, this had much to do with a severe deterioration in the terms of trade, and the current account returned to surplus again in 1976.

The key feature of the Chilean experience is that even a sharp and seemingly credible fiscal correction did not succeed in bringing inflation down quickly and painlessly to international levels—or, for that matter, to levels deemed acceptable by the Chilean authorities. While a substantial external correction was achieved, output costs were large and inflation gains relatively small. This pattern has often been repeated when orthodox money-based stabilization has been attempted in other high-inflation circumstances, such as Mexico in 1983 or Brazil in 1983–84.[6] It seems to matter for the outcome of orthodox stabilization, however, whether the initial condition is one of merely high inflation, as in the cases discussed here, or near-hyperinflation. The distinguishing feature of the latter is that the domestic currency is widely replaced by foreign currency as the unit of account, in the sense that domestic prices become formally or informally indexed to a market-determined exchange rate. In such cases, rapid price stabilization can be achieved with minimal output costs by stabilizing the exchange rate. The experience of Bolivia in the mid-1980s illustrates this case.

8.2.2 Bolivia (August 29, 1985)

Unlike many of its neighbors, Bolivia did not have a history of chronic high inflation before the decade of the 1980s.[7] The country is a major mineral exporter, and favorable terms-of-trade movements during the early 1970s led the government to embark on a substantial public investment program financed by external borrowing. The latter part of the 1970s and the early 1980s were marked by extreme political instability in Bolivia, with a succession of coups and military governments. The economic dislocations asso-

TABLE 8.5

Bolivia: Macroeconomic Indicators, 1979–86 (in percent, unless otherwise indicated)

	1979	1980	1981	1982	1983	1984	1985	1986
Inflation rate	—	47.2	28.6	133.3	269.0	1,281.4	11,750	276.3
GDP growth rate	—	1.2	−0.4	−5.6	−7.2	−2.4	−4.0	−2.9
Government [a]								
Expenditure	14.3	16.0	15.1	26.9	20.1	33.2	6.1	7.7
Revenue	9.4	9.6	9.4	4.6	2.6	2.6	1.3	10.3
Deficit	4.9	6.4	5.7	22.3	17.5	30.6	4.8	−2.6
Terms of trade (1980 = 100)	—	100.0	99.7	98.1	99.3	104.1	104.3	81.9

Sources: Fiscal data are from Sachs (1986). All other data are from Kiguel and Liviatan (1988, p. 275).

[a] Central government, in percent of GDP.

ciated with political instability, together with less-than-satisfactory performance of the nonfinancial public enterprises created (or expanded) earlier in the decade, resulted in several years that were characterized by high fiscal deficits, external crises, and mounting inflation during the late 1970s and early 1980s. Bolivia's failure to service its external debt led to a cutoff of capital inflows in 1982, at a time when the fiscal deficit had reached enormous proportions (Table 8.5). The switch in the mode of financing of this deficit, from external borrowing to domestic monetary financing, set off an explosive inflation. The inflationary process was magnified when a civilian government assumed power in late 1982 and faced stepped-up social demands from its labor constituency while lacking the political means to raise sufficient revenue to finance the satisfaction of these demands in a noninflationary manner. This situation culminated in hyperinflation (in the classic Cagan sense) by the end of 1984.

A key feature of hyperinflation in Bolivia was the nature of the wage-price system just prior to stabilization. As inflation accelerated, the frequency of wage adjustment increased, so that by the time of stabilization, wages were being set on a weekly or biweekly basis (see Sachs, 1986). Moreover, rather than allow the exchange rate to float when foreign exchange reserves were exhausted, the government decided to ration foreign exchange. This led to the emergence of a substantial informal market, and the parallel market price of the U.S. dollar became the marginal cost of foreign exchange, determining the prices of traded goods. With more frequent wage and price adjustments, changes in the parallel exchange rate began to govern wage- and price-setting behavior, since this was by far the most frequently observed price index available.[8] Since the parallel exchange rate was depreciating rapidly, the U.S. dollar quickly became the preferred store of value, and monetary velocity increased sharply; the domestic currency ceased to serve as a unit of account or store of value and became little more than a means of exchange. Thus, the Bolivian economy had become effectively dollarized by 1985.

A drastic stabilization program was launched in August 1985 by a new civilian government that took office after the early elections held the previous month. The program included the following features:

A fiscal adjustment, reducing the deficit to 6.3 percent of GDP, with external financing amounting to 5.3 percent of GDP. The fiscal adjustment was to be secured by raising public sector prices to world levels, implementing a wage freeze for public sector employees together with employment reductions in the public sector, effecting both tax reform and tax increases (including a new value-added tax and increased taxes on the state petroleum enterprise), and replacing quotas and nontariff barriers with a system of uniform tariffs as part of a trade reform.

Unification of the dual-exchange-rate regime, together with the adoption of free convertibility on the current and capital accounts. The unified exchange rate was allowed to float, although a maximum value for the peso that would trigger central bank sales of domestic currency was established.

Elimination of all existing price controls, as well as restrictions on private wage determination.

In addition to trade liberalization, other structural reforms were undertaken. These included the decentralization of public enterprises and the elimination of interest rate restrictions on the banking system.

Finally, the government undertook to reschedule its external debt to both private and public creditors, as well as to negotiate a new standby agreement with the IMF and normalize its previously disrupted financial relationship with the World Bank. An agreement with the IMF and a Paris Club rescheduling were both achieved in June 1986.

The official exchange rate underwent a one-time step depreciation when the float was announced, and together with the increase in public sector prices this triggered a sharp price increase during the first week of the program. After a week and a half, however, the price level stabilized. The fiscal measures adopted with the program gave the treasury a cash surplus for the rest of 1985. The economy was gradually remonetized through capital inflows during the remainder of the year. Nominal interest rates declined slowly, remaining relatively high for over a year, especially in view of the success achieved on the inflation front. The monthly loan rate, which had reached 45 percent in August, fell to 21 percent in December and continued to fall gradually thereafter, reaching the single-digit range in June 1986. An interpretation of the output costs of stabilization is complicated both by the structural measures that accompanied the program (in particular, the streamlining of public sector enterprises) and by the fact that very severe terms-of-trade shocks were experienced by Bolivia during the last half of 1985.

8.3 Exchange-Rate-Based (Southern Cone) Stabilization Programs

The failure of orthodox stabilization to bring inflation down quickly in chronic high-inflation countries led to the adoption of an alternative approach to stabilization in the Southern Cone countries of Latin America (Argentina, Chile, and Uruguay) during the late 1970s. The intellectual foundation for this approach was the monetary approach to the balance of payments (MABP), which was popular in academic thinking at that time.[9] An important tenet of the monetary approach was the belief that purchasing-power parity (PPP) held more or less continuously. Under continuous PPP, the domestic price level would be determined by the exchange rate, and inflation stabilization thus required slowing the rate of depreciation of the exchange rate. With the exchange rate assigned to the task of securing price stability, external balance would be achieved by restrictive aggregate demand policy. Output growth was taken to depend on domestic supply conditions, and could therefore be promoted by undertaking market-oriented structural reforms. The complete package, therefore, included a predetermined exchange-rate path, and fiscal and structural adjustment. Trade liberalization, in particular, had an important role to play, because the adoption of low and uniform tariffs not only would promote economic growth, but would support the price stability objective through the influence of the law of one price.[10]

8.3.1 Chile (February 1978)

Disappointment with the slow reduction of inflation despite the stabilization efforts undertaken during the early years of the Pinochet regime induced Chile to adopt this approach in early 1978. The restrictive fiscal policy followed earlier would continue to be vigorously pursued, but active exchange-rate management geared to an external objective was abandoned in favor of a succession of "tablitas" (schedules of preannounced exchange-rate changes), which would determine the path of the exchange rate in advance, thus using the exchange rate as a nominal anchor for domestic prices. The rate of devaluation was set below the previous month's inflation rate and was put on a declining trajectory converging to zero in June 1979, at which time the rate would be fixed. Ironically, wage indexation, which had existed in Chile since at least 1974, was strengthened by law in 1979.

The rapid convergence of domestic variables to their international counterparts envisioned in the MABP did not come to pass in Chile after 1978. As shown in Table 8.6, domestic interest rates indeed fell, but they remained substantially in excess of devaluation-adjusted foreign rates, despite enormous capital inflows through 1982. The domestic inflation rate came down as well, but also remained above international inflation plus the rate of devaluation. As a result, the real effective exchange rate appreciated strongly in spite of the depreciation of the U.S. dollar, with the cumulative appreciation amounting to about 30 percent from early 1978 to mid-1982. The depreciation of the dollar, however, pulled the peso along in 1979, and together with a strong fiscal contraction during that year resulted in a short-run improvement in the trade balance. This was reversed in 1980, and the trade deficit grew through the third quarter of 1981. Real GDP growth remained strong through late 1981.

The turning point for Chile came in the third quarter of 1981. A sharp contraction in domestic credit during the first quarter of the year succeeded in sterilizing capital inflows and contracting the monetary base. By the third quarter, net capital inflows began to fall rapidly. Corbo (1985b) attributes the cessation of capital inflows to a combination of factors, including the perception of increased credit risk in Chile (due to persistent current account deficits, stagnant investment, and the incipient international debt crisis) and the completion of stock portfolio adjustments after the adoption of the tablita. Nominal interest rates increased in Chile during 1981, and with slower inflation during the year, ex post real interest rates rose markedly. A financial crisis in the second half of the year led to a large central bank bailout financed through credit expansion. By the fourth quarter of 1981, real output growth turned negative (Table 8.6).

On June 14, 1981, the exchange-rate policy was finally modified. The peso was devalued against the dollar by 18 percent and then set to depreciate by 0.8 percent per month against a basket. Wage indexation was suspended. However, these measures were judged insufficient, and capital flight led to the adoption of a floating exchange rate two months later. Continued depreciation despite central bank intervention led to the imposition of restrictions on foreign exchange transactions, and eventually the replacement of the float by a PPP-based exchange-rate rule starting from an initially heavily depreciated level. The adoption of this rule, of course, signifies the abandonment of the attempt to use the exchange rate as a nominal anchor.

8.3.2 Uruguay (October 1978)

Uruguay is one of the chronic high-inflation countries identified in Table 8.1. In addition to high inflation, the country suffered from a prolonged period of

TABLE 8.6

Chile: Macroeconomic Indicators, 1977–82 (in percent, unless otherwise indicated)

Quarter	Inflation Rate	Growth Rate	Devaluation Rate	Fiscal Deficit[a]	Nominal Lending Rate	Real Effective Exchange Rate[b]	Real Wage[b]	Trade Balance[c]
1977								
1	90.4	11.9	24.5		265.0	—		152
2	74.7	9.6	56.8		148.0	—		39
3	53.5	6.1	92.4		107.5	—		−135
4	49.9	7.8	76.7	−1.1	132.1	—	108.8	29
1978								
1	33.0	3.6	36.5		101.3	100.0		141
2	34.7	6.4	26.7		79.8	102.1		−154
3	33.4	8.9	15.1		73.9	106.0		−103
4	27.2	7.3	9.2	−0.2	89.6	107.0	100.0	−122
1979								
1	25.4	10.4	19.6		67.6	105.4		129
2	34.6	8.2	45.7		60.5	102.4		6
3	51.8	8.8	0.0		59.6	104.4		1
4	41.1	6.4	0.0		60.8	98.4	108.3	−72
1980								
1	29.5	6.7	0.0	4.9	61.9	92.9		217
2	33.3	5.7	0.0		43.6	88.2		70
3	28.1	3.6	0.0		41.0	87.0		−243
4	34.4	7.7	0.0	5.5	42.0	83.0	118.1	−348
1981								
1	18.4	8.5	0.0		52.3	76.9		−242
2	11.7	8.9	0.0		50.7	71.7		−437
3	9.3	7.4	0.0		51.0	68.9		−556
4	6.7	−2.8	0.0	2.4	54.1	71.4	128.8	−383
1982								
1	2.9	−9.5	0.0		55.2	71.2		19
2	−0.8	−1.5	101.4		47.7	70.0		181
3	26.1	−4.7	343.2		64.2	87.6		247
4	55.8	−14.3	40.8	−2.3	88.4	100.5	128.3	254

Source: Végh (1992, pp. 680–81).

[a] In percent of GDP.

[b] 1978 = 100.

[c] In millions of U.S. dollars.

stagnation from the mid-1950s to the early 1970s.[11] A combined internal-external crisis with common symptoms (low growth, high inflation, large fiscal deficit, declining foreign exchange reserves) triggered a major reform effort in 1974, led by the new finance minister Végh Villegas.

Between 1974 and 1978 Uruguay carried out an orthodox adjustment program, coupled with structural reform. The fiscal deficit was reduced from 4.5 percent of GDP in 1974 to 1.3 percent in 1978. A crawling peg, which had replaced the fixed exchange rate in 1972, was used to achieve a real depreciation of over 20 percent during the same period, and the real wage fell by a comparable magnitude. The Uruguayan structural reforms were unusual in that they were led by capital account liberalization. A crawling peg exchange-rate regime had been adopted in 1972, but strong restrictions were in place for both current and capital account transactions. The latter were almost completely eliminated in 1974. Domestic financial liberalization followed, with interest rate ceilings raised in the same year and eliminated completely by September 1976; guidelines for credit allocations were removed in 1975, and barriers to entry into banking were eliminated in 1977. Domestically, price controls were progressively lifted beginning in 1974. Finally, trade liberalization was also undertaken, in the form of reductions in export tariffs on traditional exports and fiscal incentives for nontraditional exports. Import quotas were removed in 1975, but protection otherwise remained high.

In spite of adverse terms-of-trade movements, the combination of orthodox adjustment and structural reform led to improved growth performance during this period, led by an upsurge in investment (which increased from 8.5 percent of GDP in 1974 to 16 percent by 1978).[12] The inflation rate fell, but as in other instances of orthodox stabilization, progress was slow, with the annual rate decreasing from 77 percent in 1974 to about 44 percent in 1978.

In October 1978 the government undertook a concerted attack on inflation. The crawling peg was abandoned in favor of a succession of tablitas that would determine the path of the exchange rate six to nine months in advance. In addition, commercial policy began to be used as an anti-inflationary tool. All import tariffs and surcharges were to be consolidated into a uniform 35 percent tariff by 1985, using equal arithmetic cuts, and financial incentives to nontraditional exports were removed. The understanding was that the tablita would remain in place while tariffs were being reduced. At the same time, fiscal adjustment continued, with the general government deficit replaced by a surplus in the course of 1979 (Table 8.7).

The tablita implied a decline in the rate of devaluation throughout 1979 and into the first quarter of 1980. However, the immediate "convergence" results predicted by the MABP were not achieved. Deposit rates in domestic currency exceeded dollar deposit rates by more than the rate of devaluation,

TABLE 8.7

Uruguay: Macroeconomic Indicators, 1978–82 (in percent, unless otherwise indicated)

Quarter	Inflation Rate	Growth Rate	Devaluation Rate	Fiscal Deficit[a]	Nominal Lending Rate	Real Effective Exchange Rate [b]	Real Wage[b]	Trade Balance [c]
1978								
1	23.7	1.5	0.0		76.7	95.3		26.7
2	52.5	10.6	44.4		73.1	93.4		16.4
3	47.6	6.9	49.3		74.9	100.0		−34.1
4	49.4	8.5	34.1	−0.8	71.3	101.9	100	−30.0
1979								
1	68.9	11.9	28.2		69.5	98.2		−15.3
2	73.2	5.5	23.8		61.9	92.4		−37.8
3	90.0	7.9	17.2		62.5	87.3		−103.9
4	86.9	4.3	11.4	0.2	68.3	78.0	96.9	−157.9
1980								
1	66.7	6.3	9.5		67.1	70.8		−198.5
2	41.8	1.3	16.9		68.3	69.3		−139.4
3	57.4	4.9	24.2		65.4	68.1		−79.8
4	34.6	6.1	23.8	0.2	65.4	68.3	97.3	−13.9
1981								
1	25.1	4.9	17.4		63.6	64.4		−98.5
2	29.7	5.0	11.8		57.4	58.9		−57.4
3	40.4	1.8	18.5		58.5	54.5		−77.4
4	25.2	−4.4	15.0	−1.4	59.6	54.9	104.5	−45.2
1982								
1	7.7	−7.5	15.0		49.1	62.2		−64.9
2	11.4	−9.0	17.5		54.6	53.7		−50.7
3	22.7	−17.9	26.6		66.0	51.8		20.1
4	18.8	−8.5	4,098.1	−9.0	76.1	63.3	104.2	85.8

Source: Végh (1992, pp. 682–83).

[a] In percent of GDP.

[b] 1978 = 100.

[c] In millions of U.S. dollars.

and this margin proved relatively stable over time. The short-run inflation outcome was poor, as the rate of inflation accelerated during 1979. The result was a real-exchange-rate appreciation amounting to over 20 percent over the course of the year. The combination of real appreciation and poor terms of trade associated with the second international oil price shock resulted in a deterioration in the trade balance during 1979 and into 1980 (Table 8.7), although foreign exchange reserves increased due to substantial capital inflows. Real output growth remained relatively robust, led by a boom in private consumption.

After 1979, the domestic inflation rate indeed began to fall but, as indicated in Table 8.7, convergence remained slow and inflation continued to exceed the tablita into the first quarter of 1982. The growing overvaluation of the exchange rate and trade deficits led to the expectation of devaluation, which, coupled with signs of fiscal deterioration in 1981, reversed capital inflows in early 1982. Increased social security payments and government salaries, together with reduced labor taxes, resulted in a sharp increase in the fiscal deficit in 1982, which, added to the cumulative appreciation of the peso since 1979, sealed the fate of the tablita experiment in Uruguay as capital outflows depleted foreign exchange reserves. The tablita was abandoned in November of 1982.

8.3.3 Argentina (December 1978)

In Argentina a military government deposed the Peronist administration in 1976.[13] The Argentine economy was suffering at the time from low growth, high inflation, and large external imbalances. The economy was also highly regulated and distorted. Deposits in the financial system were effectively nationalized by a system of 100 percent required reserves, interest rate controls, and directed credit. Informal financial arrangements flourished. Prices and wages were administratively controlled. The commercial system was riddled with quantitative restrictions and disparate tariff rates. Exchange controls were in place, and multiple exchange rates existed.

The new government, under finance minister Martínez de Hoz, undertook to liberalize and stabilize the economy. In 1976 and 1977 prices (but not wages) were gradually decontrolled, and discrete wage adjustments were granted at given intervals. Bank deposits were decentralized in June 1977, and interest rates were freed to be determined by the market. A uniform 45 percent required reserve ratio was adopted, but banks were compensated by the payment of interest on reserves. Over the course of the year, exchange rates were unified. Restrictions on capital movements were liberalized, and most capital controls were eliminated between 1977 and 1979. Quotas and prior deposit requirements on imports were gradually removed. A series of tax reforms were implemented, including inflation adjustments for tax payments, simplification of income taxes, and generalization of the value-added tax.

On December 20, 1978, the government announced a new set of measures to combat inflation. These consisted of two key elements:

> A tablita was announced to fix the evolution of the exchange rate until the end of August 1979. Later announcements determined the exchange-rate schedule

TABLE 8.8
Argentina: Macroeconomic Indicators, 1976–82 (in percent, unless otherwise indicated)

	1976	1977	1978	1979	1980	1981	1982
Inflation	443.2	176.2	175.5	159.5	100.8	104.5	165.4
Unemployment rate	4.7	3.1	3.2	2.5	5.1	4.7	5.2
Public sector deficit [a]	12.9	11.9	10.1	9.0	11.3	16.4	17.2
Real exchange rate (1975 = 100) [b]	—	99.5	72.5	57.8	38.5	47.8	63.0
Real wage (1976 = 100)	100.0	101.0	98.2	112.1	124.6	114.2	99.4
Nominal lending rate [c]	—	37.8	24.6	23.5	18.8	27.9	27.6
Current account [d]	651	1,126	1,856	−513	−4,774	−4,712	−2,477

Source: Fernández (1985).

[a] In percent of GDP.

[b] The real exchange rate is defined as the export price index over the index of prices of nontradables.

[c] Thirty-day lending rate.

[d] In millions of U.S. dollars.

for December and for all of 1980, but no definite commitment was made as to how long this system would last. Throughout, the rate of devaluation was set on a declining trend.

A schedule of gradual tariff reductions was announced for the next five years. Average tariffs were to fall from 34 percent in 1980 to 16 percent in 1986, and export taxes were to be eliminated by 1986.

The tablita succeeded in dampening inflation, which decreased gradually from 175 percent in 1978 to a little over 100 percent in 1980. This occurred in spite of the very limited fiscal adjustment that took place in 1978 and 1979 (Table 8.8). However, interest rate convergence did not occur, as the spread between domestic nominal interest rates and foreign devaluation-adjusted rates remained substantial throughout 1979 and 1980 (see Fernández, 1985). During the period immediately following the implementation of the tablita, capital inflows reached such a magnitude that they created a monetary control problem. However, the speed of convergence of the inflation rate to the preannounced rate of devaluation proved to be very slow, and the resulting real-exchange-rate appreciation and deterioration in the external accounts (Table 8.8) fueled expectations of devaluation. These were aggravated by a financial crisis at the beginning of 1980 and a relaxation in that year of what little fiscal discipline had been achieved previously. The result was massive capital outflows in 1980. These were financed by public external borrowing, and Argentina's external debt rose substantially during the period 1979–81. Expectations of devaluation were borne out in 1981, when the tablita was abandoned and a succession of step devaluations implemented.

8.4 Heterodox Programs

Heterodox stabilization programs have been based on the premise that inflation has a strong inertial component, so that even if the "fundamentals" are corrected, inflation would continue at high rates. If so, the restrictive aggregate demand policies associated with correction of the fiscal and monetary fundamentals would result in a deep and perhaps prolonged recession. The emergence of such a recession would not only itself entail economic and political costs (as would the persistence of inflation), but would also call into question the authorities' commitment to persevere in the anti-inflation effort. Inertia may arise from two sources: the existence of explicit or implicit backward-looking indexation in nominal variables (that is, the nominal wage, the exchange rate, and monetary aggregates) and an initial lack of credibility.

Heterodox programs were undertaken by several developing nations in the mid- to late 1980s. The best known of these programs—those in Argentina in June 1985, Israel in July 1985, Brazil in February 1986, and Mexico in December 1987—will be examined in this section. While there were important differences among these countries, the similarities are striking. These are all middle-income developing countries that, with the exception of Argentina, had enjoyed considerable economic success during the 1960s and 1970s. In each of them, the stabilization effort was launched under what amounted to a new political regime that took power after a period of economic and political crisis.[14] Not all of these countries had suffered from chronic high inflation, but in all of them inflation accelerated in the first half of the decade and had reached triple-digit levels by the time the attempted stabilization was undertaken. All of these countries experienced disappointing growth performance during the early 1980s (although Brazil's experience was erratic in that regard), and they all confronted severe external imbalances associated with the international debt crisis.

All four of the programs to be examined enjoyed initial success, in that they achieved a substantial reduction in inflation without severe costs in terms of reduced economic activity. Yet only the Israeli and Mexican programs are currently considered to have achieved enduring success.[15]

8.4.1 Argentina (June 14, 1985)

As mentioned in the introduction to this chapter, Argentina has been one of the chronic high-inflation countries in Latin America. The inflationary problem was aggravated in the early 1980s by the collapse of the Martínez de Hoz experiment and the international debt crisis. When President Raúl Alfonsín was elected in the fall of 1983 the rate of inflation averaged 250 percent per year. By early June 1985 the monthly rate of inflation exceeded 30 percent, signifying the failure of the gradualist orthodox stabilization program that the new government had attempted to implement during 1984. The atmosphere of crisis associated with such elevated inflation rates led to the implementation of the Austral plan in June of that year. Its key features were the following:

A sharp devaluation coupled with an upward adjustment of public sector prices, plus higher taxes on exports and tariffs on imports. These measures were carried out before the program was implemented, and were intended both to "get prices right" and to contribute to fiscal adjustment.[16]

The imposition of wage-price controls of indefinite duration.

A commitment by the government not to borrow from the central bank. A reduced fiscal deficit—targeted at 2.5 percent of GDP for the second half of 1985, which implied a primary surplus—was to be financed externally.

The introduction of a new currency, the Austral, pegged to the U.S. dollar (at 0.8 Australs per dollar). Currency and demand deposits were converted on June 14 at a rate of 1,000 pesos for one Austral.

Deferred payments embodied in outstanding nominal loan contracts denominated in pesos were converted to Australs at a rate that depreciated by 29 percent per month (an amount roughly equal to the difference between the preprogram monthly peso inflation rate and the postprogram expected Austral inflation rate), to avoid the redistributions to creditors associated with a sharp and unanticipated halting of inflation.[17]

Controlled interest rates for deposits and loans, which had been at 28 and 30 percent per month, respectively, were set at 4 and 6 percent. The reduction in nominal interest rates was expected to contribute to the fiscal adjustment, since an important part of the overall deficit of the public sector consisted of the "quasi-fiscal" deficit of the central bank, incurred as a result of the payment of interest on (a high level of) required reserves.

A process of renegotiation of Argentina's external debt was begun.

In addition to the adjustment of public sector prices, the increase in trade taxes, and the reduced "quasi-fiscal" deficit, the fiscal adjustment counted on a reversal of the Olivera-Tanzi effect (see Chapter 4). No major cuts in public sector employment or in spending on social programs were contemplated, so the bulk of the fiscal adjustment was expected to be contributed by the revenue side. The expectation was that the overall public sector deficit, which amounted to almost 13 percent of GDP in 1984 and 12 percent of GDP in early 1985, would decline to 2 percent by 1986. No target for the rate of growth of the money supply was announced.

The effect on the inflation rate was immediate and sharp (Table 8.9). In the nine months after June, inflation in consumer prices averaged 3 percent per month. Real activity, which had been declining during the first half of the

TABLE 8.9
Argentina: Macroeconomic Indicators, 1984–88 (in percent, unless otherwise indicated)

Quarter	Inflation Rate	Growth Rate	Devaluation Rate	Fiscal Deficit[a]	Nominal Lending Rate	Real Effective Exchange Rate [b]	Real Wage[b]	Trade Balance [c]
1984								
1	508.6	1.9	291.7	11.7	339.6	109.3		1,379
2	650.7	4.2	501.2	9.7	618.1	97.7		1,462
3	827.4	1.1	929.8	7.0	708.0	91.7		886
4	810.0	2.7	1,337.4	9.4	1,808.0	98.8	129.1	255
1985								
1	1,004.4	−1.1	1,252.1	10.3	1,267.5	100.0		900
2	1,687.8	−4.6	2,875.7	7.5	3,141.0	109.8		1,712
3	258.5	−8.8	0.0	3.9	139.5	121.5		1,411
4	31.6	−3.1	0.0	2.4	93.2	116.7	100.0	855
1986								
1	40.4	0.7	0.0	5.5	83.6	116.4		649
2	63.9	6.2	53.1	2.3	68.9	111.6		888
3	113.0	11.6	107.3	1.8	110.1	109.3		632
4	107.2	4.4	91.5	9.2	167.6	109.5	109.3	277
1987								
1	113.9	3.5	124.1	6.4	135.7	116.0		343
2	88.9	3.5	87.0	8.5	162.6	117.0		470
3	215.7	1.3	357.5	10.0	365.9	116.2		123
4	336.1	1.8	313.2	7.5	306.6	134.6	102.2	81
1988								
1	179.9	2.9	291.5	10.4	391.6	137.2		641
2	480.0	−0.4	638.2	5.7	607.7	138.6		1,013
3	954.8	−5.5	258.0	3.8	520.1	131.2		1,335
4	220.2	−6.7	56.2	6.3	201.8	121.1	97.3	1,253

Source: Végh (1992, pp. 684–85).
[a] In percent of GDP.
[b] 1985q1 = 100.
[c] 1980 = 100.

year, continued to do so in the third quarter, but recovered in the last quarter, during which industrial production reached a peak for the year. Demand appeared to have been led by consumption and exports. The fiscal deficit was sharply reduced in the second half of 1985 and first three quarters of 1986 (see Canavese and Di Tella, 1988). The real money supply grew sharply in the second half of 1985, due to both the accumulation of foreign exchange reserves and credit extended by the central bank to the private banking system. The increase in foreign exchange reserves arose from a sizable trade surplus in the second half of 1985 and capital inflows. Nevertheless, immediately after the stabilization, real interest rates were extremely high, with the lending rate averaging over 90 percent per year in the last quarter of 1985.[18]

In January 1986 the authorities moved to the "flexibilization" stage of the program, announcing a modification in the system of wage-price controls. Wage increases of up to 5 percent were permitted for the first quarter, with an additional 5 percent possible where justified by productivity increases. Although inflation had been sharply reduced on impact by the Austral program, it had not been completely eradicated. With a cumulative increase in consumer prices of 24 percent from July 1985 to March 1986 with the exchange rate and public sector prices remaining frozen, pressure increased for adjustments in the latter.[19] In addition, the large trade surplus that had emerged in 1985 withered away during 1986, suggesting a loss of competitiveness. In response, a new, more flexible incomes policy was announced on April 4, 1986. A nominal devaluation of 4 percent was accompanied by increases in public sector prices. These were to be followed by successive minidevaluations and adjustments in subsequent months to prevent their real erosion. Price controls were lifted on all but the largest enterprises, which would negotiate price increases with the government based on the behavior of costs.

Inflation increased in 1986, with the monthly rate of change of the consumer price index averaging 4.5 percent during the second quarter. After an increase of 6.8 percent during the month of July, the premium in the free exchange market, which had become negligible, shot up by 30 percent. Money expansion remained fairly high, and although the treasury did not borrow from the central bank, the bank financed both the servicing of external debt by some public enterprises and lending by public financial institutions to provincial governments, feeding a sustained rapid increase in the money supply. In August the rate of inflation reached 8.8 percent.

The government responded by increasing the rate of nominal devaluation and raising controlled interest rates. This was followed in September by an attempt to control the slide of the currency. The government announced that rates of devaluation and of adjustment in public sector prices would be slowed in the future, and tighter control would be exercised over the prices set by large industrial enterprises. Quarterly wage guidelines remained in place. In addition, the rate of credit expansion to the private sector, which had fueled rapid growth in the money supply, would be contained. Tighter monetary policy was in effect from October 1986 to February 1987. Real interest rates rose rapidly, reaching 4 percent per month in December. Industrial production slowed, and in response tax receipts fell. The fiscal deficit increased in the fourth quarter, as real erosion in public sector prices reinforced the effects of reduced tax revenues. While there was still no direct financing by the central bank, the government began to make use of some previously blocked deposits in public financial institutions.

In February 1987 a new wage-price freeze was announced, together with a preannounced crawling peg for the exchange rate. However, increases in public sector wages and prices were announced in May, after the appointment of a union leader as secretary of labor. Fiscal management was further complicated by adverse movements in export prices, which the government tried to offset by cutting export taxes, with negative effects on revenues. The government's accommodative stance vis-à-vis workers and exporters was compounded by an accommodative stance by the central bank vis-à-vis financial institutions, and large rediscounts were offered at this time with dubious repayment prospects (Heymann, 1989). Large public sector deficits and renewed loose monetary management reignited inflation. By August 1987 inflation in consumer prices had reached 13 percent per month, and by October the rate was 20 percent.

Yet another stabilization attempt was made in October, featuring a wage-price freeze, but with the intention to address the budget deficit through increased taxation and some privatization of public enterprises. Some trade liberalization measures were also contemplated. As is evident from Table 8.9, these fiscal measures met with limited success, since the deficit exceeded 10 percent of GDP in the first quarter of 1988. Although a transitory reduction in inflation was achieved, vigorous inflation returned when controls were relaxed in January 1988. By April of that year, the monthly inflation rate stood at 17 percent.

8.4.2 Israel (July 1, 1985)

Unlike Argentina, Israel had not had a long history of high inflation. Triple-digit inflation appeared in Israel only at the end of the 1970s and has been attributed by Fischer (1987) to the receipt of large-scale U.S. military aid, the adoption of a crawling peg, and financial liberalization, which permitted greater access to foreign currency and foreign exchange–linked deposits.[20] The Israeli experience during the early 1980s was in many ways similar to that of Argentina: the economy experienced a period of high inflation, slow growth, and successive external crises. The monthly inflation rate in consumer prices averaged over 8 percent during 1980–84, but it increased to 15 percent in 1984 and remained at 14 percent during the first half of 1985. As in Argentina, high inflation accompanied a substantial fiscal deficit, with the overall public sector deficit amounting to over 10 percent of GDP during 1980–84 and 13 percent in 1985. The Israeli economy was highly indexed. Foreign exchange-linked (PATAM) deposit accounts squeezed out accounts denominated in domestic currency during the early 1980s, effectively indexing the money supply. Wage indexation was long established and widespread. The exchange rate was also effectively indexed through a PPP-based rule for the crawling peg.[21] As in Argentina, the authorities responded to the acceleration of inflation in 1984 and the first half of 1985 with a heterodox program announced in midyear.

Several observers have emphasized that the Israeli economic stabilization program (ESP) began from a particularly favorable set of conditions, primarily due to actions taken before the plan, but also because of favorable external developments. First, an ongoing military crisis in Lebanon had led to the accession to power after elections in September 1984 of a coalition government representing the major parties. The National Unity government faced no major parliamentary opposition to the ESP. Second, during a succession of pre-ESP "package deals," the new Israeli government had succeeded in securing a substantial real devaluation of the shekel, as well as a reduction of the real wage in terms of tradables (see Liviatan, 1988a).[22] This, together with a reduced level of domestic demand due to tightened monetary policy and a refurbished tax system, undoubtedly contributed to the favorable state of the trade balance prior to the implementation of the ESP.[23] It also represented a favorable constellation of relative prices from the point of view of maintaining the credibility of the exchange rate as a nominal anchor once the ESP was launched, since expectations of imminent devaluation would be forestalled in the event of some mild slippage of wages and prices.

Credibility of the exchange rate was also augmented by the receipt of $1.5 billion in grants from the United States over 1985–86, conditional on the adoption of a stabilization program. This inflow of external resources amounted to over 3 percent of GDP. In addition to U.S. assistance, depreciation of the dollar helped maintain the competitiveness of the new shekel, and favorable movements in Israel's terms of trade during the early part of the program eased the external constraints on the economy.

The components of the ESP announced on July 1 were the following:

A sharp reduction in the fiscal deficit below its 1984 level. The projected cut amounted to 7.5 percent of GDP. Four-fifths of the adjustment was to come from reduced subsidies and additional direct and indirect taxes, with the remainder coming from reduced government consumption. In addition, the implications of the fiscal adjustment for reductions in monetary financing were magnified by the external aid from the United States.

The Israeli shekel was devalued by 19 percent when the program was announced. It was then frozen, at 1.5 new shekels to the dollar (with a band of 2 percent), conditional on agreement with the labor federation (Histadrut) on the suspension of COLA adjustments and a predetermined path for the nominal wage.[24]

A wage agreement was negotiated later in the month. As the combination of devaluation and cuts in subsidies resulted in a large one-time increase in the general price level, the agreement provided for compensation of 14 percent of the July wage on August 1, a one-time 12 percent increase on September 1, and wage increases of 4, 4, and 3.5 percent to take effect on January 1, February 1, and March 1, respectively.[25] In addition, a COLA of 80 percent of the previous month's increase in the consumer price index was to be renewed in December, with a 4 percent threshold. The wage agreement was also accompanied by a freeze and subsequent control of the prices of most commodities (covering about 90 percent of all goods and services).

The expansion of credit to the private sector was to be restricted by the Bank of Israel, by increasing reserve requirements and the discount rate. Note that, although as in Argentina the money supply remained unrestricted, unlike the case in that country an attempt was made to control money growth through the expansion of credit to the private sector. A related monetary measure was a ban on converting shekels into new foreign-currency-indexed deposits.

The program also included a structural component—the lifting of some restrictions on the trading of domestic government debt. The intent was to foster the development of a secondary market in government debt, improving future monetary control by enhancing the scope for open market operations.

The stabilization program brought the monthly inflation rate from 14 percent to 2.5 percent on impact, and to the 1 to 2 percent range by the end of 1985.[26] As in Argentina, negative impact effects on real activity appear to have been slight. Industrial production regained its early 1985 level by the first quarter of 1986, and while the unemployment rate increased in the third quarter, by the fourth quarter it was approximately at the pre-ESP level. A substantial fiscal correction was achieved. Over the first year of the program, the fiscal deficit fell by 9 percent of GDP. By the fourth quarter of 1986 the public sector deficit had been eliminated. Real public sector spending declined over the third and fourth quarters of 1985, but the fiscal correction in the second half of the year relied primarily on increased revenues. On the external side, the trade surplus that had emerged before the program increased in magnitude and, coupled with the external assistance mentioned earlier, resulted in a current account surplus. This was supported, as in the case of Argentina, by the cessation of capital outflows and substantial inflows on capital account. As a result, reserve accumulation made an important contribution to money growth. As in Argentina, real interest rates were high immediately after the program was implemented. Monthly nominal bank lending rates, which were over 20 percent before the program, declined gradually—to 16 percent in August, 12 percent in September, 9 percent in October, 7 percent in November, and 5.5 percent in December.[27]

The unfreezing of prices began in early 1986. By January 1987 controls remained in place for about 46 percent of all goods and services (compared with about 20–25 percent during normal times).[28] Fiscal policy remained restrictive, as the overall public sector deficit remained on a declining trend

TABLE 8.10
Israel: Macroeconomic Indicators, 1984–87 (in percent, unless otherwise indicated)

Quarter	Quarterly Rate of Inflation	Quarterly Rate of Depreciation	Tax Revenue[a]	Fiscal Deficit[a]	Nominal Lending Rate[b]	Real Wage[c]	Trade Balance[d]
1984							
1	42.4	42.2	41.6	—	452.4	113.9	−2,367
2	56.2	54.2	40.0	—	710.7	124.8	−3,045
3	58.8	69.8	41.3	—	1,062.0	131.0	−3,367
4	54.2	59.1	36.6	—	1,067.1	120.3	−1,306
1985							
1	33.9	33.4	45.1	12.0	499.8	124.7	−1,496
2	46.5	47.1	44.3	12.0	715.3	118.6	−2,593
3	36.5	17.7	47.9	5.0	612.2	101.3	−1,963
4	6.5	1.0	48.1	4.0	186.3	100.2	−1,709
1986							
1	1.8	0.0	55.5	3.0	78.9	114.7	−1,828
2	6.7	0.1	52.1	1.0	51.7	120.0	−2,595
3	3.0	−0.1	51.6	3.0	53.4	120.7	−2,530
4	6.9	0.0	49.5	0.0	57.0	120.7	−2,492
1987							
1	4.5	—	52.2	0.0	67.8	—	−2,955

Sources: Data on inflation, depreciation, tax revenue, the trade balance, and the real wage are from Cukierman (1988). Data on the fiscal deficit are from Liviatan (1988[a]). The nominal lending rate is taken from Végh (1992, p. 688).

[a] In percent of GDP.
[b] Annual.
[c] 1978 = 100.
[d] In millions of U.S. dollars.

(Table 8.10). On the other hand, the money supply increased rapidly during the year, and by December 1986 the real supply of M1 was at two and a half times its June 1985 level. Although largely fueled by capital inflows, a rapid expansion took place in credit to the private sector after the first half of the year, partly in response to political pressures created by high real interest rates during the early stages of the program. The year as a whole was characterized by a substantial increase in real wages, some real appreciation of the shekel, a decline in real interest rates, and an increase in real aggregate demand, led by private consumption. The real wage increase reflected nominal wage hikes in excess of the agreed guidelines. Higher private consumption and the real appreciation of the shekel contributed to a deterioration of the current account. Real GDP rose slightly during the year in spite of the increase in demand, but remained sluggish in comparison to previous experience. In August pegging to the dollar was replaced by pegging to a five-currency trade-weighted basket, with the intention of bringing the rate of inflation closer to the OECD rate during a period of dollar depreciation and thus reducing the rate of increase of import prices.

However, in January 1987 the shekel was devalued by 10 percent against the basket, to correct the real appreciation accumulated during the previous year. A fresh agreement was signed with employers and workers in which workers agreed to waive half of the COLA to which they were normally entitled, as a result of the devaluation. Increases in labor costs to employers were avoided by cutting their contributions for social insurance. In spite of the devaluation, average price increases in the first quarter were lower than those in the last quarter of 1986 (Table 8.10), and the inflation rate was stable for the rest of the year. Growth in real GDP accelerated in 1987 (to over 5 percent per year, compared with 3.5 percent in 1986), but since demand expansion slowed, there was no significant worsening of the economy's external performance.[29]

After the January 1987 devaluation, the shekel was kept fixed vis-à-vis the currency basket for almost two years—until the end of 1988. Overall, the rates of inflation attained by Israel's ESP during the second half of 1985 proved to be durable, and the annual inflation rate settled in the vicinity of 20 percent, even after the gradual removal of the administrative price controls associated with the ESP. Continued fiscal restraint, use of the exchange rate as a nominal anchor, and periodic tripartite negotiations among the government, the labor federation, and employers all were basic features of the program after the initial "emergency period." By February 1989 the agreement with the labor federation stipulated a COLA adjustment every six months (rather than every three months, as had been done previously) of the excess of the cumulative inflation rate over 3 percent. The lengthening of this period of adjustment attests to the success of the program in stabilizing nominal variables.

While the ESP was successful in stabilizing inflation in the short run without large output costs, and in doing so while preserving external balance, growth performance after stabilization has been disappointing. The years 1985–86 produced GDP growth of about 3.5 percent, somewhat higher than the 1980–84 average of 2.4 percent. As already indicated, moreover, growth was rapid in 1987. The year 1988, however, proved to be a recession year, with growth of only 1.6 percent, and by the end of the year the unemployment rate was at 8 percent. Growth performance since that time has not been impressive, and Israel has not regained the vigorous growth rates that the economy achieved prior to the troubled 1980s.[30]

8.4.3 Brazil (February 28, 1986)

Brazil's economy had undergone double-digit rates of inflation for extended periods of time prior to the 1980s. However, cumulative annual inflation rates reached triple digits in the 1980s, and increased rapidly during the early part of the decade. After exceeding 200 percent in 1983, the annual inflation rate approached 300 percent by February 1986. The escalation of inflation during this period has been associated with the second oil shock, with a large devaluation in 1983—associated with a shortening of the wage indexation interval—following the onset of the debt crisis with adverse supply shocks, and with adjustments to public sector prices (see Cardoso and Dornbusch, 1987; Dornbusch and Simonsen, 1988). Growth performance had been irregular over the first half of the 1980s, and as a major commercial debtor, Brazil faced severe external problems as well.

The Cruzado Plan launched at the end of February 1986 sought to achieve a quick break in inflation without the costs associated with orthodox programs. The authorities took the position, however, that due to measures previously enacted, no additional fiscal adjustment was required; rather, the program should focus on breaking inertial inflation. The previous measures consisted of the following:

In December 1985 the congress approved a set of tax changes that were expected to reduce the fiscal deficit in 1986.[31]

The Banco do Brasil, which was the banking agent of the treasury, was no longer granted automatic access to central bank funds. Instead, such access became contingent on specific, previously defined resources.

The Cruzado Plan itself contained the following features:

A new currency, the cruzado, was introduced to replace the cruzeiro (at the rate of 1,000 cruzeiros per cruzado), and its exchange rate was fixed at 13.84 cruzados to the U.S. dollar indefinitely.

Prices were frozen at their levels of February 27, 1986, and most forms of indexation were abolished.

Wages in individual contracts subject to periodic adjustments (which typically occurred at six-month intervals) were converted from cruzeiros to cruzados on the basis of their average real value over the last six months plus a bonus of 8 percent (16 percent for the minimum wage). The intent was to avoid freezing in place an arbitrary relative wage structure arising simply from the lack of synchronization of wage adjustments. Wages were to be increased by the cumulative increase in the consumer price index, whenever that increase reached 20 percent. Although wages were not frozen, wage negotiations could only take place annually (and thus would not take place for another year). At the time of annual wage bargaining, workers would be automatically entitled to recoup 60 percent of past inflation, with any additional increases subject to negotiation.

As in Argentina, a system was devised to convert deferred payments in cruzeiros to cruzados. For this purpose, the cruzeiro was assumed to depreciate against the cruzado at a monthly rate of 14.4 percent.

Interest rates were frozen at the levels prevailing on February 28, 1986.

TABLE 8.11
Brazil: Macroeconomic Indicators, 1985–87 (in percent, unless indicated otherwise)

Month	Monthly Inflation Rate	Industrial Production Index	Unemployment Rate	Growth in M4	Monthly Deposit Rate	Nominal Wage	Trade Balance[a]
1985							
3	12.8	103.0	6.5	—	13.3	6.3	897
4	8.8	92.7	6.1	13.8	12.4	14.5	1,078
5	6.8	104.5	5.9	13.2	10.6	24.1	1,238
6	7.7	107.9	5.6	13.9	9.8	9.5	1,230
7	9.3	119.1	5.4	11.4	8.1	12.4	1,228
8	12.1	121.4	5.3	10.1	8.7	8.4	1,097
9	12.0	119.3	5.4	10.3	9.7	3.6	1,305
10	9.6	130.3	4.7	12.1	9.6	19.4	1,114
11	11.1	118.0	3.9	10.6	11.7	21.0	1,078
12	13.4	108.6	3.5	17.2	13.9	7.0	1,210
1986							
1	16.2	111.5	4.2	12.5	16.8	19.8	701
2	14.4	104.7	4.4	16.4	14.9	12.9	628
3	−0.1	107.3	4.4	12.3	1.2	11.9	1,136
4	0.8	111.6	4.2	1.2	1.2	0.9	1,292
5	1.4	116.5	4.1	3.2	1.2	2.5	1,341
6	1.3	123.0	3.8	3.6	1.7	0.6	1,071
7	1.2	133.3	3.6	0.7	1.7	3.6	1,034
8	1.7	132.2	3.5	5.3	1.9	3.1	1,029
9	1.7	138.5	3.2	5.5	2.0	2.4	824
10	1.9	144.5	3.0	3.9	2.3	3.6	186
11	3.3	128.0	2.6	2.4	3.2	6.5	132
12	7.3	116.2	2.2	6.9	2.8	4.5	161
1987							
1	16.8	118.1	3.2	2.1	17.4	5.8	129
2	13.9	117.5	3.4	15.9	20.2	11.1	303
3	14.4	122.1	3.3	12.7	15.0	—	206
4	21.0	—	—	10.3	17.6	—	520

Source: Modiano (1988).
[a] In millions of U.S. dollars.

This program encountered spectacular success in the short run. As with the Argentine and Israeli programs, inflation was stopped virtually in its tracks, and cumulative inflation was zero from February to June (Table 8.11). Moreover, unlike the experiences in Argentina and Israel, industrial production increased rapidly in the first two quarters after implementation. Fiscal performance, however, did not turn out as expected. The authorities had expected the tax measures of December 1985 to close a budget deficit of 6 percent of GDP, but a lowered income tax withholding schedule and increased reliance on taxation of financial assets that were no longer widely held undermined that hope. Moreover, the price freeze increased the financial difficulties of public enterprises. Public sector wages and subsidies also increased in excess of what was anticipated. Monetary expansion was rapid, as even the broad money aggregate M4 increased by one-fifth in the four months after the program was announced.[32]

Signs of overheating appeared early in Brazil. The trade surplus disappeared, and unlike the experience of Argentina and Israel, wage-price controls appear to have resulted in shortages.[33] By the end of 1986 the parallel market premium stood at more than 100 percent and short-term nominal interest rates at 150 percent (see Cardoso and Dornbusch, 1987). A fiscal adjustment package announced after elections in November 1986 relied heavily on excise tax increases on a few goods, rather than expenditure cuts or income tax increases, with the primary result that the price-level effects of these measures further undermined the credibility of the program.[34] Monthly inflation reached 3.3 percent in November of that year (Table 8.11). Indexation was reintroduced for the exchange rate and financial instruments, and the 20 percent threshold for wage adjustment was reached in December. By January 1987 the monthly inflation rate hit 17 percent, and price controls were lifted in February. Over the next three years, Brazil repeated the experience of the Cruzado Plan several times. A succession of programs (known as the Bresser and Verano plans) based on wage and price controls managed to halt inflation briefly, but the ongoing fiscal problem inevitably led to the return of virulent inflation (Figure 8.1).

8.4.4 Mexico (December 1987)

Prior to the mid-1970s Mexico had enjoyed several decades of price stability and per-capita growth averaging 3 percent per year. Mexico's financial stability was indicated by its maintaining a fixed exchange rate against the U.S. dollar for the entire period from 1954 to 1976. Ironically, this picture was changed by the discovery of substantial reserves of oil. The period 1979–81 was characterized by expansionary fiscal policy, an upturn in the inflation rate from the 20 percent range (where it had settled after the regime change of 1976) to the 30 percent range, an overvalued real exchange rate, and negative domestic real interest rates. The overvaluation and low nominal returns on domestic financial assets led to massive capital flight during that period, which was financed by foreign borrowing.[35] Mexico's external difficulties led it to suspend amortization of external debt in August 1982, triggering the international debt crisis. The crisis led to an inflationary explosion in Mexico, and by 1983 the annual inflation rate had reached 120 percent.

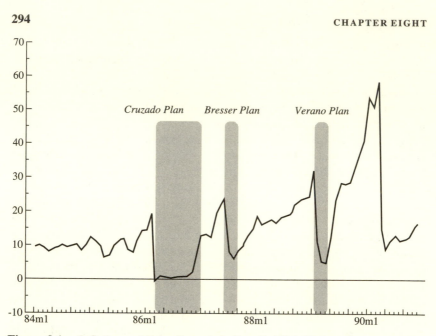

Figure 8.1   Inflation and Price Controls in Brazil, 1984–90 (month-to-month percentage changes in consumer prices)

Source: International Financial Statistics.

Notes: Shaded areas indicate periods during which price controls were in effect.

The administration of de la Madrid, which took office in 1982, sought to stabilize inflation and improve debt servicing capacity through fiscal adjustment. This process was rendered more difficult by continuously declining oil prices during that period, culminating in a near collapse in 1986. Over the period 1982 to 1987 noninterest outlays were reduced by almost 10 percent of GDP, with substantial reductions in public investment. However, an increase in interest payments implied that the total decrease in expenditures amounted to 2 percent of GDP. Overall, the primary budget deficit underwent a remarkable adjustment. The primary deficit had amounted to 8.5 percent of GDP in 1981, but by 1987 the fiscal balance had turned into a surplus of nearly 5 percent of GDP, representing a fiscal adjustment of 13 percent of GDP over the six-year period. Fiscal adjustment was accompanied by active exchange-rate management, and a cumulative real-exchange-rate depreciation of about 15 percent was achieved between 1982 and 1985, accompanied by sharply reduced real wages (Table 8.12). Thus, Mexico followed a determined orthodox adjustment program under the administration of de la Madrid.

The results, unfortunately, were disappointing. The combination of fiscal austerity and adverse movements in the terms of trade resulted in a reduction in per-capita real incomes of 13–15 percent over this period. The inflation

TABLE 8.12
Mexico: Macroeconomic Indicators, 1982–89 (in percent, unless otherwise indicated)

	1982	1983	1984	1985	1986	1987	1988	1989
Inflation rate	58.9	101.9	65.5	57.7	86.2	131.8	114.2	20.0
GDP growth	0.6	−5.3	3.7	2.8	2.0	1.4	1.1	12.9
Rate of devaluation	130.2	112.9	39.7	53.2	137.9	123.5	64.7	8.2
Operational deficit[a]	8.3	1.3	0.6	1.0	1.8	−2.0	4.5	1.7
Primary deficit[a]	7.4	−4.3	−4.8	−3.3	−2.2	−5.0	−5.9	−8.3
Real exchange rate[b]	115.2	123.7	102.5	98.5	145.1	157.5	130.3	118.4
Real wage[b]	105.7	72.7	67.2	70.0	64.7	63.0	62.0	63.3
Terms of trade[b]	103.2	96.5	97.2	96.3	63.8	—	—	—
Trade balance (US$ millions)	6,795	13,762	12,941	8,451	4,599	8,433	1,754	−663

Source: Kiguel and Liviatan (1992*b*).

[a] In percent of GDP.
[b] 1980 = 100.

rate was reduced over the three-year period to 1986, but was still at the very high level (relative to historical standards for Mexico) of 86 percent. Even worse, the collapse of oil prices in that year was associated with a sharp acceleration of inflation, and by 1987 the annual rate stood at 180 percent, after six years of fiscal austerity.

The performance of the economy during 1986–87 prompted the authorities to pursue a different course, and in December 1987 the Pact for Economic Solidarity was announced. "El Pacto" was a heterodox program with the following features:

Further fiscal adjustment. The primary surplus was to be increased by an additional 3 percent of GDP, with adjustment roughly shared equally between expenditure cuts and revenue increases.

A fixed exchange rate during 1988, after an initial step devaluation.

A temporary freeze (through the end of February) on wages, public sector prices, and the prices of commodities in a basket of basic goods and services. The freeze followed some substantial initial adjustments and was agreed in tripartite bargaining among the government and representatives of labor and business. After February 1988 wages and prices would be adjusted in line with projected inflation, with further adjustments made only if cumulative inflation after the end of February exceeded adjustments of wages and controlled prices by more than 5 percent.

Trade liberalization. This process, already under way, was to be strengthened, with a reduction in maximum tariffs from 45 to 20 percent and the almost complete removal of all import licensing procedures.

The program succeeded in stopping inflation quickly. The monthly rate of inflation fell from 15 percent in January (reflecting price increases during the month of December) to less than 1 percent over the rest of the year. An improvement in the primary surplus was achieved (raising it from 5 percent of GDP in 1987 to almost 6 percent in 1988), although high domestic real interest rates caused the operational balance to deteriorate (Table 8.12). Real growth, which had been very rapid in the second half of 1987, slowed somewhat in 1988 but remained positive and gathered steam in 1989. The maintenance of the exchange-rate freeze for the rest of the year, coupled with nonzero inflation, resulted in a real-exchange-rate appreciation of about 20 percent over the course of 1988. Coupled with a drop in the price of oil, this resulted in a deterioration in the trade balance in the first year of the program. In early 1989 the exchange-rate freeze was replaced by a system of constant absolute increases in the peso price of the U.S. dollar, leading to a gradual decrease in the rate of depreciation of the peso. While this policy was successful in stabilizing the real exchange rate, the appreciation was not reversed (Table 8.12). Fiscal adjustment has been sustained in Mexico, and after the signing of a Brady Plan agreement with the country's external creditors in 1989 (see Chapter 13) and the announcement that previously nationalized banks would be privatized, domestic interest rates began to drop, permitting the operational deficit to reflect the improvement previously achieved in the primary balance. At the same time, capital inflows became positive and large, permitting Mexico to continue financing a negative trade balance while accumulating foreign exchange reserves. Progress on the inflation front has proven to be durable, with annual inflation stabilizing in the 20 percent range in the period 1989–91.

The following lessons can be learned from the experience of inflation stabilization in developing countries.

Fiscal adjustment is necessary. In the absence of a permanent fiscal adjustment, inflation does not stay permanently low. This conclusion emerges clearly from the populist experiences of Chile and Peru; from the experience of Argentina under a variety of approaches to stabilization, including both the exchange-rate-based orthodox programs and heterodox programs reviewed here; and from the experience of Brazil under heterodox adjustment. A corollary of this observation is, of course, that setting price-based nominal anchors such as exchange-rate freezes and wage and price controls is not sufficient for inflation stabilization. The experience with populism sends this message clearly.

The costs of orthodox stabilization depend on the nature of ongoing inflation. Under chronic high inflation, nominal contracts will continue to exist, albeit of shortened duration relative to a situation of price stability. If such contracts possess a backward-looking element, or if the stabilization program lacks credibility, nominal contracts will impart inertia to the wage-price process. Such inertia will cease to exist under hyperinflation, when the domestic currency ceases to function as the unit of account and wages and prices are changed frequently with reference to a freely determined exchange rate. In the presence of inertia, adherence to noninflationary fiscal targets under a money-based program will generate a recession on impact and an improvement in the current account, with slow convergence of inflation to its targeted level, as in Chile during the mid-1970s. Under an exchange-rate-based program, the real exchange rate will appreciate and the current account may or may not improve, but inflation convergence will continue to be slow (the Southern Cone experience). When inertia is absent, which is typically the case under hyperinflation, quick inflation convergence with minimal output costs may be possible with a credible fiscal program.

Heterodox elements (an exchange-rate freeze accompanied by incomes policies) can be useful supplements to a credible fiscal program in stabilizing chronic inflation, but they are dangerous to use. With sufficient commitment to a permanent fiscal adjustment, a suspension of indexation and the adoption of incomes policies can help establish low inflation rapidly while avoiding the short-run damage to economic activity associated with orthodox adjustment under these circumstances, as demonstrated by both Israel and Mexico. The danger is that the program's short-run success will tempt policymakers to slide into populism by relaxing fiscal discipline while relying on wage and price controls for inflation abatement, as in Argentina and Brazil's heterodox programs. This path will quickly run into domestic capacity and foreign financing constraints, and is likely to leave the country in worse conditions than before the attempted stabilization. Whether well-implemented heterodox adjustment can permanently avoid the output costs of stabilization is less obvious, and remains an issue under debate. Kiguel and Liviatan (1992a) and Végh (1992), for instance, argue that exchange-rate-based stabilization programs, whether orthodox or heterodox, tend to avoid real output costs on impact, only to undergo a recession later. While Kiguel and Liviatan base their view on observations of twelve exchange-rate based stabilizations over three decades, they specifically cite two of the cases examined here—that of Chile during the Southern Cone stabilization of the late 1970s and the recent heterodox experience of Israel. This issue, which has become known as the "boom-recession" cycle associated with exchange-rate-based stabilization, is explored analytically in Chapter 10.

Nine

Inflation and Short-Run Dynamics

SINCE THE monetarist-structuralist controversy of the early 1960s, the nature of the mechanisms underlying the dynamics of inflation has been the subject of a voluminous theoretical and empirical literature in developing countries. Key aspects of the debate in recent years have been the interactions—and the lack of consistency—between fiscal, monetary, and exchange-rate policies; structural factors (such as the degree of capital mobility and the existence of wage and price inertia); credibility problems; and the stance of expectations regarding future policies.

This chapter examines alternative models of the inflationary process and studies the short-run macroeconomic dynamics associated with monetary and exchange-rate policies. The first part begins by contrasting two models of inflation: the "orthodox" or "monetarist" model, which focuses on the interactions between fiscal deficits, money creation, and inflation; and the "new structuralist" model, which emphasizes the links between food bottlenecks, income distribution, and social conflicts over the determination of real wages. We then point out that while these models are traditionally viewed as competing explanations of the inflationary process, they can in fact be combined in a way that casts doubt on the policy prescriptions that would emerge from simple structuralist models. The second part of the chapter focuses on the short- and long-run effects of monetary and exchange-rate policy rules. It begins with a presentation of an optimizing one-good model with imperfect capital mobility, which is then extended to a two-sector, three-good framework. In addition to imperfect capital mobility, the extended model captures a number of structural features that have been shown in previous chapters to play an important macroeconomic role in the developing world (such as nominal wage rigidity and price-setting behavior) and thus provides a useful conceptual framework for the analysis of stabilization policies in developing countries.

9.1 Models of the Inflationary Process

The "orthodox" view of the inflationary process holds that the primary cause of inflation in developing countries is the recourse to money creation by governments faced with limited borrowing options (both domestically and

internationally) for financing large fiscal deficits.[1] By contrast, new structuralists in the tradition of Cardoso (1981) and Taylor (1983, 1991) view
inflation as resulting essentially from the worker-capitalist conflict over the
distribution of income between real wages and profits.

We begin by presenting the orthodox view, highlighting the role of inflationary expectations and the potentially destabilizing role of fiscal rigidities.
We follow by discussing the new structuralist approach to inflation. We then
show how the two models can be merged, by introducing the government
budget constraint in the new structuralist model. An analysis of the effect of
food subsidies on the behavior of inflation in the integrated model highlights
the potentially misleading predictions that may result from the omission of
financing constraints in simple new structuralist models.[2]

9.1.1 Inflation, Money, and Fiscal Deficits

Consider a closed economy with exogenous output. Suppose that the demand for money function takes the Cagan semilogarithmic form used in
analyzing inflationary finance in Chapter 4:

$$m_t = \exp(-\alpha \pi_t^a), \quad \alpha > 0, \tag{1}$$

where $m_t \equiv M_t/P_t$, with M_t representing the base money stock and P_t the
price level. The expected inflation rate is π_t^a. The government cannot issue bonds to the public and finances its primary budget deficit d_t entirely
through seignorage:

$$d_t = \dot{M}_t/P_t = \mu_t m_t, \tag{2}$$

where $\mu_t \equiv \dot{M}_t/M_t$. Combining (1) and (2) implies

$$d_t = \mu_t \exp(-\alpha \pi_t^a), \tag{3}$$

Equation (3) specifies how the primary fiscal deficit affects the equilibrium
rate of growth of the money stock, and hence the equilibrium inflation rate.
However, to the extent that the demand for real money balances is inversely
related to the expected rate of inflation, the possibility of multiple solutions
to (3) arises. As shown below, and in line with our discussion in Chapter
4, the existence of a "seignorage Laffer curve" implies that there are two
steady-state rates of inflation that generate any given amount of seignorage.

Equation (3) is plotted in Figure 9.1, which is adapted from Bruno and
Fischer (1990). Curve D depicts the combinations of μ and π_t^a for which
the primary deficit is constant. Since Equation (3) indicates that $d_t = \mu_t$

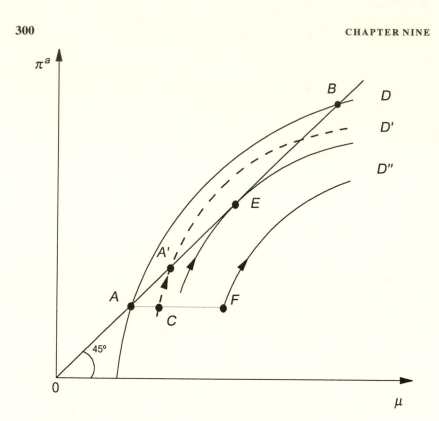

Figure 9.1   Seignorage and Dual Inflation Equilibria
Source: Adapted from Bruno and Fischer (1990, p. 355).

when the expected inflation rate is zero, the deficit is measured by the distance between the origin and the intercept of the D curve on the μ-axis. The government budget constraint is binding at any given moment in time, so that the economy is always located on the D curve.

Differentiating Equation (1) with respect to time yields, since $\dot{m}_t \equiv \dot{M}_t/P_t - m_t\pi_t$,

$$\mu_t - \pi_t = -\alpha\dot{\pi}_t^a, \tag{1'}$$

so that in the steady state

$$\pi = \pi^a = \mu. \tag{4}$$

Equation (4) is represented by the 45° line in Figure 9.1. As depicted in the figure, the D curve and the 45° line intersect twice. There are therefore two potential steady-state positions, that is, two inflation rates at which the primary fiscal deficit is financed through revenue from the inflation tax: a low-inflation equilibrium (point A) and a high-inflation equilibrium (point B). At point A the elasticity of the demand for real money balances is less than unity, while at point B it is greater than unity (Evans and Yarrow, 1981).

Suppose for a moment that the size of the primary deficit is constrained by the amount of revenue that can be generated through money creation. As shown in Chapter 4, the inflation rate that maximizes steady-state seignorage revenue is equal to $\pi^s = 1/\alpha$, and the corresponding level of revenue is given by

$$d^s = \exp(-1)/\alpha.$$

Assume now that the primary deficit that the government wishes to finance is fixed at an arbitrary level $\bar{d}$. Depending on the size of the deficit target, there may be zero, one, or two equilibria. Because the government cannot obtain more than d^s in the long-run equilibrium, there is no steady state if $d > d^s$. For $\bar{d} = d^s$ or $\bar{d} < 0$, there is a unique steady state. For $0 < \bar{d} < d^s$, there are two steady states, and the economy may be "stuck" at the high-inflation equilibrium (point B). To see under what conditions these long-run outcomes obtain, we consider two alternative assumptions about the formation of inflation expectations.

Adaptive Expectations

Consider first the case where inflation expectations are adaptive:

$$\dot{\pi}_t^a = \beta(\pi_t - \pi_t^a), \quad \beta > 0. \tag{5}$$

Combining Equations (1'), (3), and (5) determines—together with an appropriate initial condition—the time path of actual and expected inflation, for a given primary fiscal deficit. From (1') and (5), changes in expected inflation are determined by $\dot{\pi}_t^a = \beta(\mu - \pi_t^a)/(1 - \alpha\beta)$, while the actual rate is $\pi_t = (\mu - \alpha\beta\pi_t^a)/(1 - \alpha\beta)$. With an adaptive expectational scheme, point A is a stable equilibrium while B is unstable, if the speed of adjustment β is small enough ($\beta < 1/\alpha$). Points located to the right of point B lead to a hyperinflation path. The government prints money at an ever-increasing rate, preventing the expected inflation rate from ever coinciding with the actual rate of increase in prices. Although real money balances (the inflation tax base) are reduced at an increasing rate, the pace at which the government is printing money is so rapid that it is still able to finance its deficit.[3]

Suppose that the economy is initially at the stable low-inflation equilibrium (point A), and consider the effect of an increase in the fiscal deficit. Suppose first that the increase is "small," so that curve D shifts to the right to D' but continues to intersect the 45° line twice. The increase in the fiscal deficit thus leads to an instantaneous jump in the rate of money growth—as well as the actual inflation rate—from point A to C, and from then on to a gradual increase in both μ_t and the expected inflation rate from point C to A'. Once expectations begin to adjust, the demand for real money balances starts falling. To compensate for the reduction in the inflation tax base, the government must print money at an accelerated pace, until the new equilibrium is reached. A similar result obtains if the shift in the D curve is such that there exists only one point of intersection with the 45° line (point E). By contrast, if the increase in the fiscal deficit is large, curve D may not intersect the 45° line at all (curve D''). There is thus no steady state, and inflation will keep increasing continually. The economy jumps from point A to point F and follows a hyperinflationary path, moving to the northeast along curve D''.

If bonds can be used as an additional source of financing of the fiscal deficit, dual equilibria will still obtain if the government fixes the interest rate, but a unique steady-state inflation rate is attained when the government sets a nominal anchor for the economy—for instance, by fixing the rate of growth of the nominal money stock.[4] The existence of dual equilibria is thus a consequence of the government's choice of monetary and fiscal policy rules, given the process through which inflationary expectations are formed. This result has implications for the choice of a nominal anchor in disinflation programs, which is discussed in the next chapter.

Perfect Foresight

Consider now the case where inflation expectations are rational, an assumption that can be implemented here by setting $\beta \to \infty$ in (5) and allowing expected and actual prices to jump on impact. In this case, it can be shown that point B is a stable equilibrium and A is unstable. More important, however, because the initial expected rate of inflation can now jump on impact, all points located on curve D are potential short-run equilibria. An increase in the fiscal deficit leads in this setting to an instantaneous jump to a new equilibrium, but there is no guarantee that the economy will be at any particular position on the curve $D'D'$ (at, say, point A'). Inflation, without displaying any sign of instability, may thus be unnecessarily high under perfect foresight.

The above discussion seems to suggest that large budget deficits may lead to hyperinflation only when private agents have adaptive expectations, that is, when they make systematic errors in predicting future inflation. Because the assumption of adaptive expectations is difficult to defend in situations where inflation is high or tends to follow an unstable path, this would seem to make hyperinflation unlikely in the orthodox model. Bruno and Fischer (1990) and Kiguel (1989), however, have shown that large budget deficits may lead to hyperinflation even under perfect foresight, if there is sluggish adjustment toward equilibrium in the money market.

Following Kiguel, assume that the money market adjusts gradually according to

$$\dot{m}_t/m_t = \kappa(\ln m_t^d - \ln m_t), \quad \kappa > 0, \tag{6}$$

where m_t^d denotes desired real balances, given by Equation (1), and κ the speed of adjustment. Equation (6) can equivalently be written as

$$\pi_t = \mu_t - \kappa(\ln m_t^d - \ln m_t), \tag{6'}$$

which indicates that the inflation rate adjusts one-for-one with the rate of growth of the nominal money stock, but adjusts only partially in response to differences between the desired and actual levels of real money balances. The inflation rate is therefore sticky (but not predetermined), while real balances are predetermined at any point in time.

Solving for the logarithm of money demand from Equation (1) and using the identity $\dot{m}_t \equiv \dot{M}_t/P_t - m_t\pi_t$ in Equation (6') yields

$$\dot{m}_t = \frac{\kappa}{(\alpha\kappa - 1)} (\alpha d_t + m_t \ln m_t). \tag{7}$$

Equation (7) is plotted in Figure 9.2 for a value of the deficit equal to d_0 and $\kappa < 1/\alpha$. There are two equilibria, one unstable (point A) and one stable (point B). When the speed of adjustment is very high ($\kappa \to \infty$), Equation (7) becomes

$$\dot{m}_t \cong d_t + \alpha^{-1} m_t \ln m_t,$$

which, for $\dot{m}_t = 0$, gives a curve similar to D in Figure 9.1.

Consider now what happens when the policymaker increases the primary deficit to $d_1 > d_0$. The schedule $[\dot{m}_t = 0]$ moves down, so much so that it may no longer intersect the horizontal axis. Put differently, there may be no stationary value of the inflation rate that ensures adequate revenue from the inflation tax to finance a deficit equal to d_1. In such conditions the behavior of the system will be unstable, characterized by decreasing real money balances and rising rates of inflation. Too large a deficit can therefore lead to a hyperinflationary path, as argued above in the case of adaptive expectations. Under perfect foresight, the potential instability in the inflation process depends crucially on the assumption of sluggish adjustment in the money market. The increase in money growth required to finance a higher deficit creates a temporary excess supply in the money market, which leads to an increase in inflation. The higher inflation rate exerts

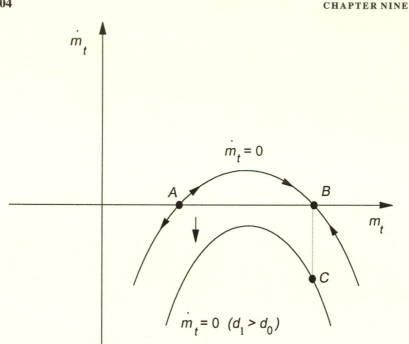

Figure 9.2   Fiscal Deficits and Inflation with Gradual Adjustment of the
Money Market
   Source: Kiguel (1989, p. 152).

two conflicting effects on the equilibrium of the money market. On the one
hand, it reduces the supply of real money balances, which tends to reequili-
brate the market. On the other hand, it leads to a fall in the demand for real
money balances, which tends to amplify the initial disequilibrium. When
the system does not possess a stable long-run equilibrium, the latter effect
dominates the former, and the resulting outcome is accelerating inflation,
with a continuous increase in the rate of expansion of the nominal money
stock.[5] As shown by Kiguel (1989), the possibility that the economy may
follow an unstable inflationary path becomes even more likely if, as a result
of the Olivera-Tanzi effect, discussed in Chapter 4, the erosion in tax revenue results in a positive relation between the primary fiscal deficit and the
inflation rate. The importance of the Tanzi-Olivera effect in hyperinflation
episodes has been emphasized also by Dornbusch (1993).
   To summarize, money financing of fiscal deficits may lead, depending
on the mechanism through which expectations are formed and the speed of
adjustment of the money market, to multiple steady-state equilibria. Governments can therefore find themselves operating at an unnecessarily high

inflation rate. The key message of the analysis, however, is that hyperinflation is an unstable process that emerges as a result of large, unsustainable fiscal deficits financed by money creation. Consequently, an essential feature of stabilization programs in countries undergoing hyperinflation must be a significant fiscal adjustment.

In small, open developing countries, an additional factor that may affect inflation directly in the short run is the exchange rate. A nominal depreciation directly affects the domestic-currency price of import-competing goods and exportables. An indirect effect may also result, as indicated in Chapters 1 and 7, if the cost of imported inputs such as oil and semifinished goods affects[5] pricing decisions directly (see below). Even if the official exchange rate is fixed, fluctuations in the unofficial exchange rate may affect inflation if domestic price setters take into account the behavior of the marginal cost of foreign exchange when setting prices (see Chapter 2). In addition, a depreciation of the exchange rate may also affect inflation by raising nominal wages, through implicit or explicit indexation mechanisms.[6] In such conditions, a real-exchange-rate depreciation is likely to lead to inflationary pressures. The evidence provided by Darrat and Arize (1990), Dornbusch et al. (1990), Jorgensen and Paldam (1986), and Montiel (1989) supports the view that the exchange rate plays an important role in the short-run behavior of inflation in some chronic-inflation countries of Latin America. However, it is worth emphasizing that such evidence is not inconsistent with the presumption that fiscal deficits play a key role in the long run, as argued by the orthodox "fiscal view." For instance, in the results presented by Dornbusch et al. (1990), while almost 46 percent of the variability of inflation in Mexico over the period 1982–87 is accounted for by exchange-rate fluctuations in the short run (against about 12 percent for the fiscal deficit proxy), the proportions change to 40 and 55 percent at a longer horizon. Similarly, for Bolivia during the period 1982–86, the proportions of the variance in inflation accounted for by innovations in the real exchange rate and the fiscal deficit are 36 percent and 31 percent, respectively, in the short run, while in the long run these proportions become 4 percent and 61 percent.

The model developed by Rodríguez (1978) provides a theoretical framework for explaining this type of result. If the fiscal deficit is financed through credit creation by the central bank, as is often the case in developing countries, the monetary expansion will lead to an increase in prices and a progressive erosion of foreign reserves, which will eventually trigger a devaluation if the central bank has limited access to borrowing in international capital markets (see Chapter 6). A devaluation-inflation spiral may develop, in the absence of corrective measures aimed at reducing the deficit. Thus, while the "proximate" cause of inflation may appear to be exchange-rate adjustment, the "ultimate" factor responsible for both inflation and exchange-rate depreciation may stem from fiscal rigidities.

9.1.2 Food Supply, Distribution, and the Wage-Price Cycle

The link between inflation, food supply, and competing claims for the distribution of income is at the heart of the new structuralist approach to inflation. This section presents a modified version of a model developed by Cardoso (1981), which provides a particularly clear formalization of the new structuralist view.

Consider a closed economy producing two goods: an agricultural good, whose production level is denoted Q_A, and a manufactured good, whose production level is Q_I. Food supply in the agricultural sector is given in the short run at $\bar{Q}_A$, while output is demand determined in the industrial sector. The equilibrium conditions in both markets are given by

$$\bar{Q}_A = Q_A^d(\overset{+}{y_t}, \bar{\rho}_t), \qquad \rho_t \equiv P_A(t)/P_I(t),$$

$$Q_I(t) = Q_I^d(\overset{+}{y_t}, \overset{+}{\rho_t}) + \bar{g},$$

where $Q_A^d()$ denotes food demand, which in general depends positively on real factor income y_t and negatively on the relative price of agricultural goods ρ_t. $Q_I^d()$ represents private expenditure on manufactured goods, which depends positively on income and the relative price. $\bar{g}$ measures autonomous government expenditure on industrial goods. Real factor income, measured in terms of industrial goods, is defined as

$$y_t = \rho_t \bar{Q}_A + Q_I(t).$$

Assume, without loss of generality, that the direct effect of changes in ρ_t on demand is zero and let $0 < c < 1$ denote the marginal propensity to consume. Measuring the proportion of consumption spent on agricultural goods by $0 < \delta < 1$, the equilibrium condition of the food market can be written as

$$\rho_t \bar{Q}_A = \delta c y_t = \delta c \left[\rho_t \bar{Q}_A + Q_I(t) \right], \tag{8}$$

while the market-clearing condition for industrial goods is

$$Q_I(t) = (1 - \delta)c \left[\rho_t \bar{Q}_A + Q_I(t) \right] + \bar{g}. \tag{9}$$

To examine the dynamic adjustment process and the behavior of inflation, assume for the moment that prices of industrial goods remain constant and that output in the industrial sector responds gradually to excess demand for manufactured goods:

$$\dot{Q}_I(t) = v\big[(1 - \delta)c(\rho_t \bar{Q}_A + Q_I(t)) + \bar{g} - Q_I(t)\big], \quad v > 0. \quad (10)$$

Similarly, agricultural prices respond gradually to the excess demand for food:

$$\dot{P}_A(t)/P_A(t) = \Theta\big[\delta c(\rho_t \bar{Q}_A + Q_I(t)) - \rho_t \bar{Q}_A\big], \quad \Theta > 0. \quad (11)$$

The rate of change in agricultural prices is thus equal to the rate of change in the relative price, $\dot{\rho}_t/\rho_t$, since prices of industrial goods remain constant.

Equations (10) and (11) constitute a system that determines the dynamic behavior over time of production in the industrial sector and agricultural prices:

$$\begin{bmatrix} \dot{P}_A(t) \\ \dot{Q}_I(t) \end{bmatrix} = \begin{bmatrix} -\Theta(1 - \delta c) & \Theta \delta c \\ v(1 - \delta)c & -v(1 - (1 - \delta)c) \end{bmatrix} \begin{bmatrix} P_A(t) \\ Q_I(t) \end{bmatrix},$$

where, for simplicity, agricultural output and industrial prices are normalized to unity and $\bar{g} = 0$. For global stability, the trace of the coefficient matrix must be negative and its determinant positive.

The equilibrium of the economy is shown in Figure 9.3. The curve $[\dot{P}_A(t) = 0]$, which determines the combinations of industrial output and relative price that maintain equilibrium in the food market, has a positive slope. Points located to the left of this curve are associated with excess supply of food and falling prices, while points located to the right of it indicate excess demand and rising food prices. The curve $[\dot{Q}_I(t) = 0]$ represents the equilibrium condition for the industrial good market. This curve also has a positive slope, which must be steeper than the slope of the $[\dot{P}_A(t) = 0]$ curve to ensure global stability.[7] Points situated to the left of $[\dot{Q}_I(t) = 0]$ indicate excess demand for industrial goods and rising output, while points located to the right of $[\dot{Q}_I(t) = 0]$ indicate an excess supply of manufactured goods and falling output. The steady-state equilibrium of the economy obtains at point E.

Suppose, for instance, that the initial position of the economy is at point A in Figure 9.3, which represents an excess supply of food and an excess demand for manufactured goods. The increase in output in the industrial sector dampens excess demand for manufactured goods while increasing income and the demand for agricultural products—reducing excess supply in that sector. The stability condition ensures that the income effect generated by the increase in industrial output does not exacerbate the initial excess demand in the market for industrial goods. Thus, in this basic framework, food

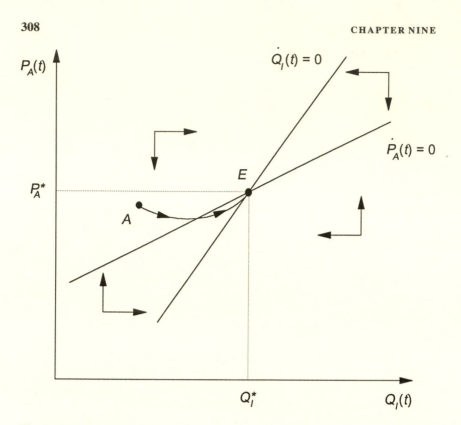

Figure 9.3   Equilibrium in the New Structuralist Model

   Source: Kiguel (1989, p. 152).

prices fall at first and then rise, while industrial output rises continuously over time until the long-run equilibrium is reached. There is no tendency toward instability—because we assumed that industrial prices remain constant and we abstracted from workers' behavior.

    Suppose now that firms in the industrial sector set prices as a fixed mark-up γ over labor costs. Assuming for simplicity that the unit labor requirement for industrial output is normalized to unity, industrial prices are given by

$$P_I(t) = (1 + \gamma)w_t, \quad \gamma > 0. \tag{12}$$

Suppose also that workers have a constant real wage target $\bar{\omega}$, which implies that nominal wages are determined by

$$w_t = \bar{\omega} P_t, \tag{13}$$

where P_t denotes the consumer price index, defined as

$$P_t = P_A(t)^\delta P_I(t)^{1-\delta}, \quad 0 < \delta < 1. \tag{14}$$

Using Equations (12), (13), and (14) yields the "required" relative price, consistent with workers' real wage target:

$$\tilde{\rho} = [(1 + \gamma)\bar{\omega}]^{-1/\delta}. \tag{15}$$

The rate of change of nominal wages is assumed to be determined by the difference between the required price ratio $\tilde{\rho}$ and the actual ratio ρ_t so that, using Equation (12), the rate of change of industrial prices $\pi_I(t)$ is equal to

$$\pi_I(t) = \dot{w}_t/w_t = \kappa(\rho_t - \tilde{\rho}), \quad \kappa > 0, \tag{16}$$

where κ measures the speed of wage adjustment. $\tilde{\rho}$ is thus the relative price at which wage inflation is zero and industrial prices remain constant. Using Equations (11) and (16) in the definition of ρ_t yields

$$\dot{\rho}_t/\rho_t = \Theta[\delta c(\rho_t \bar{Q}_A + Q_I(t)) - \bar{Q}_A] - \kappa(\rho_t - \tilde{\rho}). \tag{17}$$

Figure 9.4 presents a diagrammatic solution of the system consisting of Equations (10), (11), and (17). Curve AA is identical to curve $[\dot{P}_A(t) = 0]$ defined previously, and gives combinations of the relative price and industrial output that ensure continuous equilibrium in the food market. The curves $[\dot{Q}_I(t) = 0]$ and $[\dot{\rho}_t = 0]$ are both upward sloping, with the former having a steeper slope to ensure stability. The slope of the AA curve is by construction also steeper than the slope of the $[\dot{\rho}_t = 0]$ curve. The two curves intersect at point B, where the actual relative price ratio is equal to the required relative price $\tilde{\rho}$ and the food market is in equilibrium. Curves $[\dot{Q}_I(t) = 0]$ and $[\dot{\rho}_t = 0]$ intersect at point E, which determines a value of the relative price $\rho^* > \tilde{\rho}$. Finally, curves $[\dot{Q}_I(t) = 0]$ and AA intersect at point G.

Neither point B, E, nor G represents a long-run equilibrium in this economy. Suppose that the economy is initially at point G, where the food and industrial goods markets are both in equilibrium but real wages are lower than the desired level—or, equivalently, the actual relative price is higher than the required level. Nominal wages therefore increase, raising industrial prices and lowering the relative price of agricultural goods. The negative income effect reduces output in the industrial sector. At point B real wages are at their desired level and the market for food is in equilibrium, but the economy is characterized by excess demand for manufactured goods. Industrial production begins rising, but as the economy moves away from point B

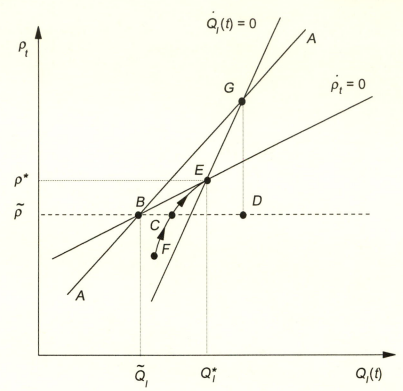

Figure 9.4   The Wage-Price Cycle in the New Structuralist Model
Source: Adapted from Cardoso (1981, p. 275).

(toward, say, point C) the increase in income exerts upward pressure on the relative price of food products.

If the economy is initially in a position such as point F, corresponding to a situation of excess demand in the food market, the upward pressure on agricultural prices is accompanied by a rise in nominal wages, which, in turn, leads to an increase in industrial prices and higher output in that sector. But as long as the excess demand for food remains large relative to the difference between the actual and the desired real wage, nominal wages and thus industrial prices will continue to increase less rapidly than agricultural prices, so that the relative price ρ will rise over time. The upward pressure on the relative price leads to excess demand for manufactured goods, and industrial output rises. The economy therefore moves toward point E, where the curves $[\dot{Q}_I(t) = 0]$ and $[\dot{\rho}_t = 0]$ intersect, and both industrial output and the relative price remain constant. But at that point, excess demand for agricultural products—resulting from the increase in income linked to output expansion in the industrial goods sector—maintains upward pressure on their price. Moreover, since the real wage is lower than desired, both nominal wages and industrial prices will continue to rise. Thus, there is no stable long-run equilibrium in this model because it is overdetermined. The relative price that corresponds to equilibrium in goods markets is inconsistent with the relative price that satisfies workers' claims on income. The outcome may be a self-perpetuating inflationary process, which may be exacerbated if the speed of adjustment of wages to changes in the price ratio increases over time.[8]

A stable, long-run equilibrium can be achieved in the above setting by various government policies. A reduction, for instance, in government spending $\bar{g}$ that is large enough to shift the $[\dot{Q}_I(t) = 0]$ curve to the left—until it intersects the AA and $[\dot{\rho}_t = 0]$ curves at point B—would halt the inflationary spiral, at the cost of lower industrial output. An incomes policy that would bring a reduction in the mark-up coefficient γ could also increase the target relative price $\tilde{\rho}$ toward ρ^* and eliminate the inflationary cycle. Price controls could also prevent capitalists in the industrial sector from raising their prices and maintain the relative share of profits in national income, without necessarily leading to a reduction in output (see the appendix to Chapter 10). Nevertheless, the general implication of the analysis remains that when workers' desired real wage is high relative to the level compatible with long-run equilibrium, inflation stabilization is impossible to achieve without a shift in income distribution.

9.1.3 A Structuralist-Monetarist Model

A crucial and generally implicit assumption in new structuralist models of inflation, including the modified version of Cardoso's model developed above, is that monetary policy fully accommodates changes in the price level. We now present an integrated framework that accounts explicitly for money supply dynamics in the new structuralist model developed above. This extension provides a link with the orthodox approach described earlier and allows us to qualify some of the policy prescriptions commonly advocated by new structuralist economists. The link between prices, money, and fiscal deficits is represented by introducing food subsidies in the model and accounting for the government budget constraint.[9]

In the presence of a subsidy at the rate $0 < s < 1$, the consumer price index is defined as

$$P_t = [(1 - s)P_A(t)]^\delta P_I(t)^{1-\delta}. \tag{14'}$$

Suppose that the government levies a uniform tax on factor income at the rate $0 < \iota < 1$. Its expenditures consist of demand for industrial goods (in quantity $\bar{g}$) and food subsidies. The government budget constraint can be written as

$$\dot{M}_t = P_I(t)\bar{g} + sP_A(t)\bar{Q}_A - \iota[P_A(t)\bar{Q}_A + P_I(t)Q_I(t)],$$

which, in real terms, is equivalent to

$$\dot{m}_t = \bar{g} + (s - \iota)\rho_t\bar{Q}_A - \iota Q_I(t) - \pi_I(t)m_t, \tag{18}$$

where m_t denotes real money balances measured in terms of industrial prices. Assuming that the demand for food products is a positive function of real money balances yields the equilibrium condition of the food market in the presence of food subsidies:

$$(1 - s)\rho_t\bar{Q}_A = \delta c(1 - \iota)[\rho_t\bar{Q}_A + Q_I(t)] + \alpha\delta m_t, \quad 0 < \alpha < 1, \tag{8'}$$

where c is now the propensity to consume out of disposable income. The left-hand side of this expression denotes the postsubsidy value of the supply of food, measured in terms of industrial goods.[10] The last term on the right-hand side measures a real balance effect.

The dynamics of output adjustment in the market for manufactures is now given by

$$\dot{Q}_I(t) = v[c(1 - \delta)(1 - \iota)(\rho_t\bar{Q}_A + Q_I(t)) + \alpha(1 - \delta)m_t + \bar{g} - Q_I(t)]. \tag{10'}$$

Assuming that workers pursue a real wage target as before, the required relative price is now given by

$$\tilde{\rho} = (1 - s)^{-1}[(1 + \gamma)\bar{\omega}]^{-1/\delta}. \tag{15'}$$

After appropriate substitutions, the behavior of the relative price is determined by

$$\dot{\rho}_t/\rho_t = \Theta\left[\frac{\delta c}{1 - s}(\rho\bar{Q}_A + Q_I(t)) + \frac{\alpha}{1 - s}m_t - \rho_t\bar{Q}_A\right] - \kappa(\rho_t - \tilde{\rho}). \tag{17'}$$

Using (16), Equation (18) can be approximated in the vicinity of the initial position (at $t = 0$) by

$$\dot{m}_t \cong \bar{g} + [(s - \iota)\bar{Q}_A - \kappa m_0]\rho_t - \iota Q_I(t) + \kappa(\rho_0 - \tilde{\rho})m_t. \tag{18'}$$

Equations (10'), (17'), and (18') constitute a dynamic system in $Q_I(t)$, ρ_t, and m_t. Instead of analyzing the complete system, let us assume that

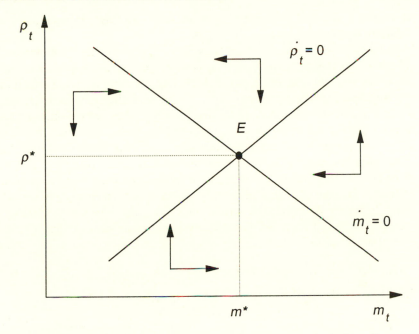

Figure 9.5   Equilibrium with Money and Food Subsidies in the New Structuralist Model

Source: Adapted from Cardoso (1981, p. 275).

output adjustment in the market for industrial goods is instantaneous—that is, $v \rightarrow \infty$. Solving (10') for $Q_I(t)$ with $\dot{Q}_I(t) = 0$ and substituting the result in (17') and (18') thus yields a system of two differential equations in ρ_t and m_t.

A graphical presentation of the equilibrium is shown in Figure 9.5. The locus $[\dot{\rho}_t = 0]$ is positively sloped, since an increase in money holdings raises demand for agricultural and manufactured goods, requiring an increase in the relative price of food to maintain equilibrium. Under the assumption that $(s - \iota)\bar{Q}_A > \kappa m_0$, the locus $[\dot{m}_t = 0]$ is negatively sloped. In this case, global stability is ensured.[11] In this setup, it can be shown that the long-run effect of an increase in the subsidy rate on inflation is ambiguous (see Parkin, 1991; Srinivasan et al., 1989). On the one hand, the increase in subsidy payments increases government spending and reduces the wedge between the actual price ratio and its required level—thus slowing down wage inflation—which tends to raise real money balances. On the other hand, higher activity in the industrial sector raises income tax revenue and reduces the fiscal deficit, exerting a downward pressure on money growth. It can be shown, nevertheless, that if the subsidy rate is high enough initially, then raising it further leads to higher money growth and inflation.

Moreover, if wages are fully flexible, increasing subsidies on food is always inflationary.

The thrust of the preceding analysis is thus that once the link between subsidies, fiscal deficits, and monetary policy is properly taken into account, predictions of new structuralist models that ignore asset accumulation and the government budget constraint may require qualifications. In particular, an increase in subsidies may be inflationary, regardless of the specific assumption made regarding wage formation. More generally, the foregoing discussion suggests that combining orthodox and new structuralist models of inflation may provide new insights into the inflationary process. The emphasis on social conflict and distribution of income may be important in understanding the chronic aspects of inflation in some countries, while accounting for the monetary effects of deficit financing is essential to understanding in almost all cases the transmission mechanism of policy shocks to the inflation rate.

9.2 Dynamics of Monetary and Exchange-Rate Rules

A key aspect of the debate on the choice between money-based and exchange-rate-based stabilization programs is the dynamic path that different policy choices imply for inflation, output, and the current account. We present in this section two optimizing models that allow a rigorous analysis of the dynamics of stabilization policies in developing countries. The usefulness of these models results from their ability to capture some of the salient structural features of developing economies emphasized in previous chapters—particularly the role of imperfect asset substitutability, and nominal wage inertia—and their explicit microeconomic foundations. We begin by considering a one-good framework and then extend the analysis to a two-sector, three-good setting in which we endogenously determine the behavior of inflation and the real exchange rate.[12]

9.2.1 A One-Good Framework

The evidence discussed in Chapter 5 suggests that neither extreme of zero or perfect capital mobility appears to characterize the vast majority of developing countries. More relevant is an intermediate case in which domestic and foreign assets are imperfectly substitutable in private agents' portfolios. In what follows we present an analytical framework that captures this important feature of financial behavior in developing countries.[13]

Consider a small, open economy in which there are three types of agents: households, the government, and the central bank. Domestic production is fixed during the time frame of the analysis, and purchasing power parity holds continuously. All households are identical, and their number is, for simplicity, normalized to unity. Under a regime of predetermined exchange rates, the domestic currency is depreciated at a constant rate by the central bank, whose stock of foreign assets adjusts to equilibrate supply and demand for foreign exchange. Under a regime of flexible exchange rates, foreign reserves of the central bank are constant and the rate of credit growth is predetermined. Households hold three categories of assets in their portfolios: domestic money, foreign bonds, and domestic government bonds. As in the model with zero capital mobility developed in Chapter 4, domestic money bears no interest, but the transactions technology is such that holding money reduces transactions costs. Domestic and foreign bonds are imperfectly substitutable financial assets. The domestic interest rate adjusts to maintain equilibrium in the money market, while (as a result of the small-country assumption) the real rate of return on foreign bonds is determined on world capital markets. The government consumes goods and services, collects lump-sum taxes, and pays interest on its domestic debt. It finances its budget deficit either by issuing domestic bonds, by borrowing from the central bank, or by varying taxes on households.[14]

The household's discounted lifetime utility is given as

$$\int_0^\infty u(c_t)e^{-\alpha t}dt, \quad u(c_t) \equiv \ln c_t, \tag{19}$$

where α denotes the rate of time preference (assumed constant) and c_t consumption. As in Chapter 4, the instantaneous utility function is assumed to be of the logarithmic form and satisfies the usual conditions.

Nominal wealth of the representative household A_t is given by

$$A_t = M_t + B_t + E_t b_t^*, \tag{20}$$

where M_t denotes the nominal money stock, B_t the stock of government bonds, and $E_t b_t^*$ the domestic-currency value of the stock of foreign bonds (with E_t denoting the nominal exchange rate and b_t^* the foreign-currency value of foreign bonds). Letting $m_t \equiv M_t/E_t$ denote real money balances and $b_t \equiv B_t/E_t$ the real stock of government bonds, real wealth can be defined as

$$a_t = m_t + b_t + b_t^*. \tag{20'}$$

The flow budget constraint is given by

$$\dot{a}_t = \bar{y} + i_t b_t + i_t^* b_t^* - \left[1 + v\left(\frac{m_t}{c_t}\right)\right]c_t - \tau_t - (m_t + b_t)\epsilon_t - \gamma(b_t^*)^2/2, \tag{21}$$

where $\bar{y}$ denotes domestic output (assumed exogenous), τ_t the real value of lump-sum taxes, i_t the domestic nominal interest rate, i_t^* the interest rate on foreign bonds, and $\epsilon_t \equiv \dot{E}_t/E_t$ the predetermined rate of depreciation of the exchange rate. As in Chapter 4, the function $v()$ characterizes transactions costs associated with consumption. Holding money is assumed to reduce transactions costs (so that $v' < 0$) but entails diminishing returns ($v'' > 0$). The term $(m_t + b_t)\epsilon_t$ accounts for capital losses on the stocks of money and domestic bonds resulting from changes in the exchange rate. The last term in Equation (21) is used to capture the imperfect substitutability between domestic and foreign bonds. In the context of developing countries, it can be viewed as a measure of the perceived cost associated with a risk of expropriation: the higher the household's holdings of foreign bonds are, the easier it is for the government to identify asset holders (for tax purposes, for instance) and the greater the risk of confiscation. The coefficient γ can be viewed as parameterizing the degree of capital mobility.[15] Capital mobility is higher when the costs associated with holding foreign bonds are lower, so a lower value of γ indicates a higher degree of capital mobility. As shown below, capital mobility is perfect when $\gamma = 0$.

Using (20′), Equation (21) can be written as

$$\dot{a}_t = \rho_t a_t + \bar{y} - \left[1 + v\left(\frac{m_t}{c_t}\right)\right]c_t - i_t m_t - \tau_t + (i_t^* + \epsilon_t - i_t)b_t^* - \gamma b_t^{*2}/2, \quad (21')$$

where $\rho_t = i_t - \epsilon_t$ denotes the domestic real rate of interest.

Households treat ϵ_t, $\bar{y}$, i_t, i_t^*, and τ_t as given and maximize (19) subject to (21′) by choosing a sequence $\{c_t, m_t, b_t, b_t^*\}_{t=0}^{\infty}$. The required optimality conditions are given by

$$1/c_t = \lambda_t \left\{ \left[1 + v\left(\frac{m_t}{c_t}\right)\right] - m_t c_t^{-1} v'\left(\frac{m_t}{c_t}\right) \right\}, \quad (22a)$$

$$-v'\left(\frac{m_t}{c_t}\right) = i_t, \quad (22b)$$

$$b_t^* = (i_t^* + \epsilon_t - i_t)/\gamma, \quad (22c)$$

$$\dot{\lambda}_t = (\alpha - \rho_t)\lambda_t, \quad (22d)$$

and the transversality condition $\lim_{t\to\infty}(a_t e^{-\alpha t}) = 0$. λ_t, the costate variable associated with the flow budget constraint, measures the marginal utility of wealth.

Equation (22a) shows that total consumption is inversely related to marginal transactions costs and the marginal utility of wealth, whose dynamics are described by Equation (22d) as a function of the difference between the rate of time preference and the real domestic interest rate. Equation (22b) indicates that in equilibrium the gain resulting from a reduction in transactions costs associated with higher money holdings must be equal to the nominal interest rate, which measures the opportunity cost of money. Equation (22c) indicates that holdings of foreign bonds depend positively on the differential between the rate of return on foreign assets—adjusted for exchange-rate changes—and the rate of return on domestic assets.[16] When capital mobility is perfect ($\gamma \to 0$), this equation yields the uncovered interest parity condition $i_t = i_t^* + \epsilon_t$. By contrast, when capital mobility is zero (or when γ is very large), holdings of foreign bonds also tend toward zero.[17]

Equation (22b) can be written as

$$m_t = m[i_t]c_t, \quad m' = -1/v'' < 0, \tag{23}$$

which shows that the demand for money depends positively on the level of transactions—as measured by consumption expenditure—and negatively on the domestic nominal interest rate. Substituting Equations (22b) and (23) in (22a) yields

$$1/c_t = \lambda_t \{1 + v[m(i_t)] + i_t m(i_t)\} \equiv \lambda_t \mathbf{p}(\overset{+}{i_t}), \tag{22a'}$$

where $\mathbf{p}()$ denotes the effective price of the consumption good in period t, which depends positively on the nominal interest rate (see Chapter 4). Equation (22a') thus implies that net consumption expenditure is given by

$$c_t = c[\bar{\lambda}_t, \bar{i}_t]. \tag{24}$$

There are no commercial banks in the economy, and the central bank lends only to the government. The nominal money stock is therefore equal to

$$M_t = D_t + E_t R_t, \tag{25}$$

where D_t denotes the stock of domestic credit allocated by the central bank to the government, and R_t the stock of net foreign assets, measured in foreign-currency terms. Changes in the real credit stock $d_t \equiv D_t/E_t$ are given by

$$\dot{d}_t = (\mu_t - \epsilon_t)d_t, \tag{26}$$

where μ_t denotes the rate of growth of the nominal credit stock.

The central bank receives interest on its holdings of foreign assets and its loans to the government.[18] Real profits of the central bank Ω_t are therefore equal to

$$\Omega_t = i^* R_t + \epsilon_t R_t + i_t d_t, \tag{27}$$

where $\epsilon_t R_t$ measures real capital gains on reserves.

The government's revenue sources consist of lump-sum taxes on households, transfers from the central bank, and revenues from the taxation (or confiscation) of foreign assets held by households. It consumes goods and services and pays interest on its domestic debt. It finances its budget deficit by borrowing from the central bank or issuing nontraded bonds.[19] In nominal terms, the flow budget constraint of the government can be written as

$$\dot{B}_t + \dot{D}_t = E_t \bar{g} + i_t B_t + i_t D_t - E_t(\tau_t + \Omega_t + \gamma b_t^{*2}/2),$$

where $\bar{g}$ denotes noninterest government spending, assumed exogenous. In real terms, and using Equation (27), we have

$$\dot{d}_t + \dot{b}_t - \epsilon_t m_t = \bar{g} + \rho_t b_t - i_t^* R_t - \tau_t - \gamma b_t^{*2}/2. \tag{28}$$

Equation (28) indicates that government spending plus net interest payments on the domestic debt, minus lump-sum taxes, confiscation revenue, and interest income on reserves, must be financed by issuance of bonds, an increase in real domestic credit, or seignorage revenue. Solving Equation (28) yields the government's intertemporal budget constraint, which equalizes the present value of government purchases of goods and services to initial holdings of net assets plus the present value of lump-sum taxes subject to the solvency requirement

$$\lim_{t \to \infty} b_t \exp(-\rho_t t) = 0.$$

As discussed in Chapter 4, the solvency constraint rules out indefinite Ponzi games by the government.

Closing the model requires specifying the equilibrium condition for the money market. Equations (23) and (24) imply

$$m_t = m[i_t]c[\lambda_t, i_t],$$

which can be solved for the market-clearing domestic interest rate:

$$i_t = i(\bar{\lambda}_t, \bar{m}_t). \tag{29}$$

Substituting Equation (29) in (24) yields

$$c_t = c(\bar{\lambda}_t, \overset{+}{m}_t). \tag{30}$$

As noted in Chapter 4, an increase in the real money stock raises aggregate consumption since it reduces the domestic interest rate, which stimulates private expenditure. An increase in the marginal value of wealth affects consumption both directly and indirectly. For a given level of the domestic interest rate, it lowers private spending directly. As a result, however, the interest rate falls to maintain money market equilibrium, thus lowering the opportunity cost (or the effective price) of consumption and stimulating spending. It will be assumed that the former effect dominates the latter, so that an increase in the marginal value of wealth reduces private expenditure.

Combining Equations (21'), (25), and (26) yields the consolidated budget constraint of the economy:

$$\dot{R}_t + \dot{b}_t^* = \bar{y} - \bar{g} - \left[1 + v\left(\frac{m_t}{c_t}\right)\right]c_t + i^*(R_t + b_t^*), \tag{31}$$

which determines the behavior over time of the total stock of foreign assets.[20]

Equations (22c), (22d), (26), (28), (29), (30), and (31) describe the evolution of the economy along any perfect-foresight equilibrium path. The system can be rewritten as

$$b_t^* = [i_t^* + \epsilon_t - i(\lambda_t, m_t)]/\gamma, \tag{32a}$$

$$\dot{\lambda}_t = [\alpha - i(\lambda_t, m_t) + \epsilon_t]\lambda_t, \tag{32b}$$

$$\dot{R}_t + \dot{b}_t^* = \bar{y} - \bar{g} + i_t^*(R_t + b_t^*) - c(\lambda_t, m_t), \tag{32c}$$

$$\dot{b}_t + \dot{d}_t = \rho_t b_t + \bar{g} - i_t^* R_t - \tau_t - \epsilon_t m_t, \tag{32d}$$

$$\dot{d}_t = (\mu_t - \epsilon_t)d_t, \tag{32e}$$

$$\dot{m}_t = \dot{d}_t + \dot{R}_t, \tag{32f}$$

where $c() = [1 + v\{m(i())\}]c()$ denotes private consumption expenditure in gross terms, with $c_\lambda < 0$ and $c_m > 0$.[21] Equations (32) represent a differential equation system with six endogenous variables, λ_t, b_t, b_t^*, R_t, d_t, and m_t. It is worth noting that the capital account and the overall balance of payments are defined in terms of changes in the stock of foreign bonds and foreign reserves that occur through time. These definitions do not capture transactions that occur discretely under a regime of predetermined exchange rates, such as those that may be involved in the instantaneous exchange of domestic-currency holdings for foreign bonds. Specifically, although the overall stock of foreign assets in the economy is predetermined, official reserves and the private stock of foreign bonds may jump in response to sudden movements in domestic interest rates. An instantaneous shift in private holdings of foreign bonds is thus associated, under a regime of predetermined exchange rates, with an offsetting movement in the level of foreign reserves held by the central bank.

In what follows, we will assume that the government forgoes the issuance of bonds to finance its deficit ($\dot{b}_t = 0$), and instead borrows from the central bank or varies taxes to balance its budget. Given this assumption, the model can be operated in different modes, depending on the "closure rule" chosen: the rate of devaluation can be treated as predetermined, or the rate of growth of the nominal credit stock can be viewed as predetermined. Regardless of the particular mode chosen, the steady-state solution obtains by setting $\dot{\lambda}_t = \dot{b}_t^* = \dot{R}_t = \dot{d}_t = 0$ in the above system. As can readily be shown from equations (32b) and (32e), in the long-run equilibrium the real domestic interest rate is equal to the rate of time preference, and the rate of domestic credit growth is equal to the devaluation rate. However, alternative closure rules lead to different transitory dynamic paths, as we now show.

9.2.1.1 DEVALUATION RULE

Under a constant rate of devaluation ($\epsilon_t = \epsilon^h$), the rate of growth of the nominal credit stock μ_t is endogenous if taxes cannot be adjusted to finance the fiscal deficit ($\tau_t = \tau_0$). Setting, for simplicity, the constant stock of government bonds and the world interest rate equal to zero, the evolution of the real stock of credit over time is given by

$$\dot{d}_t = \bar{g} - \tau_0 - \epsilon^h m_t,$$

which can be substituted in Equation (32e) to determine μ_t:

$$\mu_t = \epsilon^h + \dot{d}_t/d_t.$$

Since $\dot{m}_t = \dot{d}_t + \dot{R}_t$ from Equation (32f), using the above result and equation (32c) yields

$$\dot{m}_t = \bar{y} - \tau_0 - \epsilon^h m_t - c(\lambda_t, m_t) - \dot{b}_t^*.$$

Since $b_t = \bar{b} = 0$, the stock constraint (20') implies that $m_t = a_t - b_t^*$. Substituting this result in Equation (32a) and taking a linear approximation to $i()$ yields

$$b_t^* = (\epsilon^h - i_\lambda \lambda_t - i_m a_t)/(\gamma - i_m) \equiv H(\overset{+}{\lambda_t}, \overset{+}{a_t}; \overset{+}{\epsilon^h})$$

where $H_a \equiv -i_m/(\gamma - i_m) < 1$. Given this result, we have

$$m_t = a_t - b_t^* = a_t - H(\lambda_t, a_t; \epsilon^h) = h(\overset{-}{\lambda_t}, \overset{+}{a_t}; \overset{-}{\epsilon^h}),$$

where $h_a = \gamma/(\gamma - i_m) < 1$. Substituting this relationship in Equation (32b) and in the above solution for $\dot{m}_t$ yields

$$\dot{\lambda}_t/\lambda_t = \alpha - i[\lambda_t, h(\lambda_t, a_t; \epsilon^h)] + \epsilon^h,$$

$$\dot{a}_t = \dot{m}_t + \dot{b}_t^* = \bar{y} - \tau_0 - \epsilon^h h(\lambda_t, a_t; \epsilon^h) - C(\overset{-}{\lambda_t}, \overset{+}{a_t}; \overset{-}{\epsilon^h}),$$

where $C(\lambda_t, a_t) \equiv c[\lambda_t, h(\lambda_t, a_t; \epsilon^h)]$, $C_\lambda = c_\lambda + c_m h_\lambda$, and $C_a = c_m h_a$.

Taking a linear approximation of these two equations around the initial steady state yields the following system in λ_t and a_t:

$$\begin{bmatrix} \dot{\lambda}_t \\ \dot{a}_t \end{bmatrix} = \begin{bmatrix} -\tilde{\lambda}(i_\lambda + i_m h_\lambda) & -\tilde{\lambda} i_m h_a \\ -\epsilon^h h_\lambda - C_\lambda & -\epsilon^h h_a - C_a \end{bmatrix} \begin{bmatrix} \lambda_t - \tilde{\lambda} \\ a_t - \tilde{a} \end{bmatrix}, \tag{33}$$

where $\tilde{\lambda}$ and $\tilde{a}$ denote steady-state values. The marginal value of wealth λ_t is a forward-looking variable, while total private wealth is predetermined at each moment in time. It can be easily verified that the system (33) is saddlepoint stable and can be solved subject to an initial condition on a_0.[22] A diagrammatic solution of the model is presented in Figure 9.6. The locus $[\dot{\lambda}_t = 0]$ is downward sloping, while the locus $[\dot{a}_t = 0]$ is upward sloping. The saddlepath SS, which has a negative slope, is the unique path leading to the steady-state equilibrium (point E).

Suppose that the economy is initially in a long-run equilibrium position. Consider the effect of a permanent, unanticipated reduction in the devaluation rate from ϵ^h to $\epsilon^s < \epsilon^h$, with no discrete change in the level of the exchange rate. Using the steady-state solutions, it is readily established that a reduction in the devaluation rate raises both $\tilde{\lambda}$ and $\tilde{a}$. From Equations (32a) and (32b), $\tilde{b}^* = (i^* - \alpha)/\gamma$, which is independent of ϵ^h. But since $\tilde{a}$ rises, it must be the case that $\tilde{m}$ rises. Also, from Equation (32b), the real interest rate is equal to the rate of time preference in the steady state and is independent of ϵ^h. Thus, the nominal interest rate, whose initial steady-state value is equal to the rate of time preference plus the devaluation rate, must fall in the same proportion as the devaluation rate. Finally, from (32c), since real wealth rises, gross consumption must also increase in the steady state. But since both real balances and the marginal value of wealth rise, it can be inferred from Equation (30) that the movement in net consumption is ambiguous. To summarize, the steady-state effects of the reduction

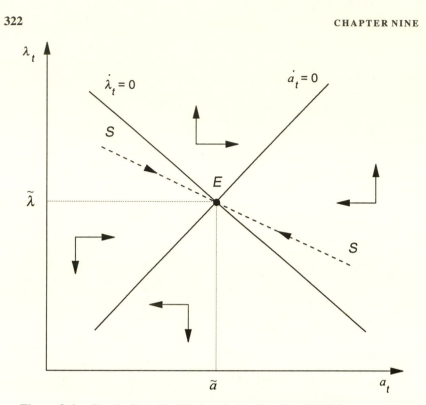

Figure 9.6   Steady-State Equilibrium in the One-Good Model
Source: Adapted from Cardoso (1981, p. 275).

in the devaluation rate are increases in the marginal value of wealth, real money balances, private wealth, and gross consumption (and possibly net consumption); a proportional reduction in the nominal interest rate; and no effect on the real stock of foreign bonds or the real interest rate.

The short-run behavior of the model, as shown by Agénor (1994a), depends on the degree of capital mobility. If capital flows are sufficiently mobile, the impact effect of the reduction in the devaluation rate is a discrete increase in holdings of foreign bonds, as their opportunity cost (the domestic real interest rate) falls on impact—or, equivalently, the nominal interest rate falls by more than the reduction of the devaluation rate. This portfolio shift leads to a fall in real money balances. This instantaneous adjustment takes place through sales of foreign currency assets by the central bank accompanied by a discrete reduction in the domestic money stock. The shift in the composition of assets is such that real private wealth remains constant on impact. At the same time, the marginal value of wealth jumps instantaneously upward to place the economy on the convergent trajectory toward the new steady state. Although the nominal interest rate (and thus the opportunity cost of holding real money balances) falls, the direct effect of the upward jump in the marginal value of wealth on private spending is negative and dominates the expansionary effect resulting from the reduction in the effective price of consumption. The net initial effect on consumption is thus negative.[23] Over time, the nominal interest rate rises to allow the real interest rate to return to its initial steady-state value. The induced increase in the effective price of consumption is not large enough to prevent a gradual increase in private spending, induced by the continuous fall in the marginal value of wealth throughout the transition period. The rise in domestic interest rates leads to capital inflows and a reduction in the stock of foreign bonds toward its initial value. The capital account surplus is large enough to compensate for the current account deficit, leading to an increase in the central bank's holdings of foreign assets and the real money stock over time. The increase in real money balances during the transition period more than compensates for the reduction in foreign bonds, so that total private wealth rises over time. The rate of nominal credit growth falls gradually toward the lower devaluation rate.

In graphical terms, suppose that the economy is initially at point E in Figure 9.7. A permanent, unanticipated reduction in the rate of devaluation shifts both curves $[\dot{\lambda}_t = 0]$ and $[\dot{a}_t = 0]$ to the right, as shown. Since private wealth is predetermined, the marginal utility of wealth jumps upward from point E to point A, located on the new saddlepath $S'S'$, and begins falling afterward. The new steady state is reached at point E'.

9.2.1.2 CREDIT GROWTH RULE

Under a constant-nominal-credit rule ($\mu_t = \mu^h$), foreign reserves of the central bank remain constant ($\dot{R}_t = 0$), and the devaluation/inflation rate is determined endogenously. Setting, for simplicity, the world interest rate and the constant level of reserves equal to zero, Equation (32a) yields

$$\epsilon_t = \epsilon(\overset{-}{\lambda_t}, \overset{-}{d_t}, \overset{+}{b_t^*}; \overset{0}{\mu^h}),$$

which can be substituted out in Equation (32e) to give

$$\dot{d}_t = [\mu^h - \epsilon(\lambda_t, d_t, b_t^*)]d_t. \tag{34}$$

Equation (34) determines changes in the real credit stock. Since $\dot{R}_t = 0$, Equation (32c) can be written as

$$\dot{b}_t^* = \bar{y} - \bar{g} - \mathbf{c}(\lambda_t, d_t), \tag{32c'}$$

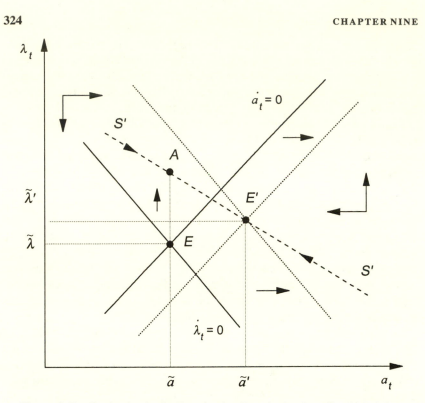

Figure 9.7   Reduction in the Devaluation Rate in the One-Good Model
Source: Adapted from Cardoso (1981, p. 275).

which determines changes in the stock of foreign bonds over time. In contrast to the previous case, therefore, private holdings of foreign assets are predetermined at any point in time. To ensure solvency of the public sector, we assume that lump-sum transfers are continually adjusted to maintain fiscal equilibrium—so that, from Equations (32d) and (32e), $\tau_t = \bar{g} - \mu^h d_t$—in effect allowing us to ignore the government budget constraint.[24]

From Equation (32a), $\gamma b_t^* = \epsilon_t - i_t$. Substituting this result into equation (32b) yields the alternative form $\lambda_t = (\alpha - \gamma b_t^*)\lambda_t$. Using (32c') and (34), the dynamic system driving the economy can now be written as

$$\begin{bmatrix} \dot{\lambda}_t \\ \dot{b}_t^* \\ \dot{d}_t \end{bmatrix} = \begin{bmatrix} 0 & \tilde{\lambda}_\gamma & 0 \\ c_\lambda & 0 & c_d \\ -\tilde{d}\epsilon_\lambda & -\tilde{d}\epsilon_{b^*} & -\tilde{d}\epsilon_d \end{bmatrix} \begin{bmatrix} \lambda_t - \tilde{\lambda} \\ b_t^* - \tilde{b}^* \\ d_t - \tilde{d} \end{bmatrix}, \quad t \geq T. \tag{35}$$

The marginal utility of wealth and the real stock of credit are both jump variables, so to ensure saddlepath stability, system (35) must possess two positive roots and one negative root. In turn, necessary and sufficient conditions for this result are that the determinant of the coefficient matrix in (35) be negative and that its trace be positive. Both conditions are always satisfied since the trace is equal to $-\tilde{d}\epsilon_d > 0$ and the determinant is equal to $-\tilde{\lambda}\tilde{d}\gamma \mathbf{c}_d\epsilon_{b^*} < 0$.

Consider now a reduction in the rate of expansion of the nominal credit stock, from μ^h to $\mu^s < \mu^h$. The real credit stock and thus the rate of depreciation fall on impact. The domestic nominal interest rate must fall proportionately to the reduction in the depreciation rate, implying that the real interest rate *does not* change, in order to keep the real stock of foreign bonds constant on impact. In turn, this requires an upward jump in the marginal value of wealth, which must be large enough to offset the upward pressure on the domestic interest rate resulting from the reduction in the real credit stock. The increase in the marginal value of wealth has a negative effect on consumption, which is, however, fully offset by the positive effect induced by a reduction in the nominal interest rate on the effective price of consumption goods. There are, therefore, no transitional dynamics. The economy jumps immediately to a new steady state, with no effect on consumption, the current account, the stock of foreign bonds, or the real interest rate. The rate of depreciation of the nominal exchange rate falls instantaneously to the level of the lower credit growth rate. The nominal interest rate falls, and is associated with a steady-state increase in real money balances, resulting from a fall in prices.[25]

The thrust of the foregoing discussion, then, is that exchange-rate and monetary rules may lead to very different adjustment paths for the main variables under imperfect capital mobility. Models based on the monetary approach to the balance of payments (such as Calvo and Rodríguez, 1977) typically possess a "dynamic equivalence" property, in the sense that the steady-state solutions and the adjustment paths associated with a monetary rule or an exchange-rate rule are identical.[26] In the model developed here, although either rule can be used to attain a long-run inflation rate target—given the solvency constraint of the public sector—the behavior of the economy during the transition period is completely different.[27] Under a credit growth rule, there is no transitional adjustment as such; the economy jumps immediately to the new steady state. Under an exchange-rate rule, by contrast, there are two types of adjustments: those that occur through time and those that occur instantaneously, in order to maintain portfolio balance. Depending on the constraints that policymakers face in the short run, the nature of the transitional dynamics may determine the adoption of one rule as opposed to the other; the implication of this result for the choice of a nominal anchor in disinflation programs will be examined in the next chapter.

9.2.1.3 DYNAMICS WITH ALTERNATIVE FISCAL POLICY RULES

The adjustment path induced by monetary and exchange-rate policy shocks depends to a large extent on the financing rules that policymakers adopt to close the fiscal deficit. Consider, for instance, a situation in which the government (as before) does not issue bonds, and the central bank sets the rate of growth of nominal credit so as to compensate the government for the loss in value of the real outstanding stock of credit due to inflation ($\mu_t = \epsilon_t$). The government then adjusts lump-sum taxes endogenously to close the fiscal deficit. In this setting, monetary policy and exchange-rate policy cannot be distinguished. This financing rule nevertheless satisfies the transversality condition of the public sector given above and is therefore sustainable. Since the credit rule implies that $\dot{d}_t = 0$, Equation (32d) can be solved for the endogenous level of lump-sum taxes:

$$\tau_t = \bar{g} + \rho_t \bar{b} - (i_t^* + \epsilon_t)R_t - \epsilon_t \bar{d}, \tag{36}$$

where $\bar{b}$ and $\bar{d}$ are the constant levels of domestic bonds and credit. As a result, $\dot{m}_t = \dot{R}_t$, that is, changes in the real money stock reflect only changes in the central bank's net foreign assets. Under an exchange-rate rule, and given Equation (36), the dynamic system driving the economy can be approximated by a linear differential equation system in λ_t and a_t:

$$\begin{bmatrix} \dot{\lambda}_t \\ \dot{a}_t \end{bmatrix} = \begin{bmatrix} -\tilde{\lambda}(i_\lambda + i_m h_\lambda) & -\tilde{\lambda} i_m h_a \\ -(c_\lambda + c_m h_\lambda) & i^* - c_m h_a \end{bmatrix} \begin{bmatrix} \lambda_t - \tilde{\lambda} \\ a_t - \tilde{a} \end{bmatrix}. \tag{37}$$

The system described by (37) is also saddlepoint stable if the determinant of its coefficient matrix is negative, a condition that always holds if the world interest rate is small enough. The short- and long-run dynamics associated with a permanent, unanticipated reduction in the rate of devaluation/credit growth with no discrete change in the level of the exchange rate are qualitatively similar to those described earlier in our discussion of a reduction in the devaluation rate with endogenous credit growth. If the degree of capital mobility is sufficiently high, consumption, nominal and real interest rates, foreign reserves, and private wealth rise continuously during the transition to the new steady state.

Yet another fiscal rule would be to assume that, following an initial policy adjustment, the central bank finances its deficit during a transitory period through bond or money financing, with the promise to switch at a future date to either a lower level of government expenditure or tax financing. This type of rule was examined in Chapter 4 in the context of a closed economy, in our discussion of the "monetarist arithmetic." We will use the model developed above in Chapter 10 to examine (using the fiscal policy rule described by Equation (36)) the behavior of real interest rates in exchange-rate-based programs.

9.2.2 A Three-Good Model with Sticky Wages

We now extend the analysis to consider the case where the economy produces two goods, a home good that is used only for final domestic consumption and an export good, whose output is entirely exported.[28] The capital stock in each sector is fixed, while labor is homogeneous and perfectly mobile. Households and the government consume home goods and an imperfectly substitutable imported good, which is not produced domestically. Producers in the nontraded goods sector set prices as a mark-up over nominal wages, which are set through contracts negotiated with households.

9.2.2.1 HOUSEHOLDS

The consumption decision of households follows a two-stage process. They first determine the optimal level of total consumption given their budget constraint, and then allocate the optimal amount between consumption of home and imported goods.[29]

Under the assumption that labor is supplied inelastically, the representative household's discounted lifetime utility remains as given in Equation (19), and similarly for nominal wealth (Equation (20)). However, since there are now two goods, let P_t denote the domestic price level (defined below), $m_t \equiv M_t/P_t$ real money balances, $b_t \equiv B_t/P_t$ the real stock of government bonds, and $b_t^* \equiv E_t B_t^*/P_t$ the real stock of foreign bonds. Real wealth can thus be defined as

$$a_t = m_t + b_t + b_t^*. \tag{38}$$

Households are subject to an income tax at the rate $0 < \iota < 1$, which is levied on gross income, which consists of net factor income and interest payments. The flow budget constraint is now given by

$$\dot{a}_t = (1 - \iota)(y_t + i_t b_t + i_t^* b_t^*) - \left[1 + \upsilon\left(\frac{m_t}{c_t}\right)\right] c_t$$
$$- \tau_t + \epsilon_t b_t^* - \gamma b_t^{*2}/2 - \pi_t a_t, \tag{39}$$

where y_t denotes net factor income (derived below) and $\pi_t = \dot{P}_t/P_t$ the overall inflation rate. Using (38), Equation (39) can be written as

$$\dot{a}_t = \rho_t a_t + (1 - \iota)y_t - \left[1 + v\left(\frac{m_t}{c_t}\right)\right]c_t - (1 - \iota)i_t m_t$$

$$+ [(1 - \iota)(i_t^* - i_t) + \epsilon_t]b_t^* - \tau_t - \gamma b_t^{*2}/2, \qquad (39')$$

where $\rho_t = (1 - \iota)i_t - \pi_t$ denotes the after-tax domestic real rate of interest.

In the first stage of the consumption decision process, households treat π_t, ϵ_t, y_t, i_t, i_t^*, and τ_t as given and maximize (19) subject to $(39')$ by choosing a sequence $\{c_t, m_t, b_t, b_t^*\}_{t=0}^{\infty}$. The optimality conditions are similar to those derived before:

$$1/c_t = \lambda_t \left\{ \left[1 + v\left(\frac{m_t}{c_t}\right)\right] - m_t c_t^{-1} v'\left(\frac{m_t}{c_t}\right) \right\}, \qquad (40a)$$

$$-v'(\frac{m_t}{c_t}) = (1 - \iota)i_t, \qquad (40b)$$

$$b_t^* = [(1 - \iota)(i_t^* - i_t) + \epsilon_t]/\gamma, \qquad (40c)$$

$$\dot{\lambda}_t = (\alpha - \rho_t)\lambda_t, \qquad (40d)$$

and the transversality condition $\lim_{t \to \infty}(e^{-\alpha t}a_t) = 0$.

After appropriate substitutions, similar to those performed before, gross consumption can be written as

$$\left[1 + v\left(\frac{m_t}{c_t}\right)\right]c_t = \mathbf{c}[\bar{\lambda}_t, (1 - \iota)i_t]. \qquad (41)$$

In the second stage of the consumption decision process, the representative household maximizes a subutility function $v[c_N(t), c_I(t)]$, which is assumed to be homogeneous of degree 1, subject to the static budget constraint

$$P_N(t)c_N(t) + E_t P_I^* c_I(t) = P_t \left[1 + v\left(\frac{m_t}{c_t}\right)\right]c_t, \qquad (42)$$

where $P_N(t)$ denotes the price of the home good, P_I^* the world price of imports—which is constant and set to unity in what follows—$c_N(t)$ net purchases of nontraded goods, and $c_I(t)$ net expenditure on imported goods. The solution to this program yields $v_{c_I}/v_{c_N} = z_t$, where $z_t = E_t/P_N(t)$ is the real exchange rate. This equation indicates, therefore, that the household sets the marginal rate of substitution between home and foreign goods equal to their relative price. Using this condition, together with Equation (42), and assuming that the subutility function is Cobb-Douglas yields the appropriate definition of the domestic consumer price index, P_t:

$$P_t = P_N(t)^\delta E_t^{1-\delta} = E_t z_t^{-\delta}, \quad 0 < \delta < 1, \qquad (43)$$

where δ denotes the share of total spending falling on home goods. Consequently, using Equation (41) yields

$$c_N(t) = \delta P_t c_t / P_N(t) = \delta z_t^{1-\delta} \mathbf{c}[\lambda_t, (1 - \iota)i_t], \qquad (44a)$$

$$c_I(t) = (1 - \delta) P_t c_t / E_t = (1 - \delta) z_t^{-\delta} \mathbf{c}[\lambda_t, (1 - \iota)i_t], \qquad (44b)$$

$$\pi_t = \epsilon_t - \delta \dot{z}_t / z_t. \qquad (44c)$$

9.2.2.2 OUTPUT, PRICES, AND WAGE CONTRACTS

Firms in the home goods sector set prices $P_N(t)$ as a mark-up Θ_t over nominal wages w_t, so that[30]

$$\pi_N(t) = \dot{\Theta}_t / \Theta_t + \dot{w}_t / w_t, \qquad (45)$$

where $\dot{w}_t / w_t$ denotes the rate of growth of nominal wages, and $\pi_N(t)$ denotes the rate of inflation in home good prices.

Output of the home goods sector is determined by the demand side of the market. Using Equation (44a), the equilibrium condition for the home goods market is given by

$$y_N^d(t) = \bar{g}_N + \delta z_t^{1-\delta} \mathbf{c}[\lambda_t, (1 - \iota)i_t], \qquad (46)$$

where $\bar{g}_N$ denotes the exogenous, real level of government spending on home goods. The mark-up rate varies procyclically over time and depends positively on excess demand for home goods:[31]

$$\dot{\Theta}_t / \Theta_t = \xi[y_N^d(t) - \bar{y}_N], \quad \xi > 0, \qquad (47)$$

where $\bar{y}_N$ denotes capacity output.

Technology for the production of the export good is characterized by decreasing returns to labor:

$$y_X(t) = F[n_X(t)], \quad F' > 0, F'' < 0,$$

where y_X denotes output of export goods and n_X the quantity of labor employed in the export sector. Firms maximize real profits $\Pi_X(t)$, given by

$$\Pi_X(t) = y_X(t) - \omega_X(t) n_X(t),$$

where $\omega_t = w_t / P_X(t)$ denotes the real product wage in the export sector, and $P_X(t)$ the domestic price of exports, which, assuming that the exogenous world price is constant and set to unity, is equal to the nominal exchange rate. From the first-order conditions for profit maximization, the supply function can be obtained as

$$y_X(t) = y_X(\omega_t), \quad y_X' < 0, \tag{48}$$

which indicates that output of exportables is inversely related to the product wage.

Using Equations (43) and (48), real factor income y_t, measured in terms of the consumption basket, is given by

$$y_t = z_t^{\delta-1}[y_N(t) + z_t y_X(\omega_t)]. \tag{49}$$

Consistent with our discussion in Chapter 2, nominal wages are assumed sticky, as a result of overlapping labor contracts. Specifically, we assume that nominal wages are set under two alternative contract mechanisms. Under the first scheme, wages are backward looking and depend only on past levels of prices:

$$w_t = \sigma \int_{-\infty}^{t} e^{\sigma(k-t)} P_k \, dk, \quad \sigma > 0,$$

where σ is a discount factor. Differentiating this equation with respect to time yields

$$\dot{w}_t = -\sigma(w_t - P_t). \tag{50}$$

Under the second scheme, wage contracts are assumed to be forward looking and to depend on future prices:

$$w_t = \sigma \int_{t}^{\infty} e^{\sigma(t-k)} P_k \, dk,$$

implying that

$$\dot{w}_t = \sigma(w_t - P_t). \tag{51}$$

Equations (50) and (51) show that changes in the nominal wage under backward- and forward-looking contracts respond in opposite directions to changes in the wage-price differential.[32] Dividing Equations (50) and (51) by w_t, using Equation (43), and noting the definition of the product wage in the export sector yields

$$\dot{w}_t/w_t = -\sigma(1 - z_t^{-\delta}/\omega_t), \tag{50'}$$

$$\dot{w}_t/w_t = \sigma(1 - z_t^{-\delta}/\omega_t). \tag{51'}$$

9.2.2.3 GOVERNMENT AND THE CENTRAL BANK

The nominal money stock is defined as in Equation (25), and the behavior of the real stock of domestic credit is given by (26). The government's revenue sources consist of income taxes and lump-sum taxes on households, transfers from the central bank, and revenue from the confiscation of private foreign bonds. It consumes both home and imported goods, and pays interest on its domestic debt. It finances its budget deficit by borrowing from the central bank and issuing nontraded bonds. In nominal terms, the flow budget constraint of the government can be written as

$$\dot{B}_t + \dot{D}_t = P_N(t)\bar{g}_N + E_t\bar{g}_I + (1 - \iota)i_tB_t - \iota(P_ty_t + i_t^*E_tB_t^*)$$
$$+ i_tD_t - P_t(\tau_t + \Omega_t + \gamma b_t^{*2}/2),$$

where $\bar{g}_I$ denotes government spending on imports and Ω_t real profits of the central bank—defined in a manner similar to Equation (27)—so that, in real terms,

$$\pi_td_t + \dot{b}_t + \dot{d}_t = z_t^{\delta-1}(\bar{g}_N + z_t\bar{g}_I) + \rho_tb_t - \iota(y_t + i_t^*b_t^*)$$
$$- \tau_t - \gamma b_t^{*2}/2 - z_t^{\delta}(i_t^* + \epsilon_t)R_t. \tag{52}$$

Equation (52) indicates that government spending plus net interest payments on the domestic debt minus lump-sum and income taxes, confiscation revenue, and interest income on reserves and foreign bonds must be financed by seignorage revenue, issuance of bonds, or an increase in central bank credit. As indicated above, the government's intertemporal budget constraint can be written in a form that restricts the present value of government purchases of goods and services to be equal to initial holdings of debt plus the present value of total revenue. The solvency requirement for the government is as given previously.

Finally, closing the model requires specifying the equilibrium condition for the money market. This condition is given by

$$d_t + z_t^{\delta}R_t = m[(1 - \iota)i_t]c_t, \tag{53}$$

which can be solved, as before, for the market-clearing domestic interest rate.

9.2.2.4 STEADY-STATE SOLUTION AND DYNAMICS

The model developed above can be used, as done previously, to examine the short- and long-run dynamics associated with monetary and exchange-rate rules, under alternative assumptions about the financing of the fiscal deficit. In the following discussion, rather than going through the exercise of comparing monetary and exchange-rate rules once again, we will focus on the case where the monetary policy rule is set to ensure that the real credit stock remains constant over time.

To begin with, note that differentiating z_t implies

$$\dot{z}_t/z_t = \epsilon_t - \pi_N(t) \tag{54}$$

or, using Equations (45) to (47),

$$\dot{z}_t/z_t = \epsilon_t - \dot{w}_t/w_t - \xi\left\{\bar{g}_N + \delta z_t^{1-\delta}\mathbf{c}[\lambda_t, (1-\iota)i_t] - \bar{y}_N\right\}. \tag{54'}$$

Substituting Equation (50') in (54') implies, with backward-looking wage contracts,

$$\dot{z}_t/z_t = \epsilon_t + \sigma(1 - z_t^{-\delta}/\omega_t) - \xi\left\{\bar{g}_N + \delta z_t^{1-\delta}\mathbf{c}[\lambda_t, (1-\iota)i_t] - \bar{y}_N\right\} \tag{55a}$$

and, with forward-looking contracts,

$$\dot{z}_t/z_t = \epsilon_t - \sigma(1 - z_t^{-\delta}/\omega_t) - \xi\left\{\bar{g}_N + \delta z_t^{1-\delta}\mathbf{c}[\lambda_t, (1-\iota)i_t] - \bar{y}_N\right\}. \tag{55b}$$

Since the central bank sets the rate of growth of nominal credit so as to allow the government to monetize the loss in value of the real outstanding stock of credit due to inflation, $\dot{d}_t = 0$. Assume also that the government forgoes the issuance of bonds to finance its deficit and instead varies lump-sum taxes so as to balance the budget. Equation (52) yields, therefore,

$$\tau_t = z_t^{\delta-1}(\bar{g}_N + z_t\bar{g}_I) - \iota(q_t + i_t^* b_t^*) + \rho_t\bar{b} - (i_t^* + \epsilon_t)z_t^{\delta}R_t - \pi_t\bar{d}, \tag{56}$$

where $\bar{b}$ and $\bar{d}$ denote the constant levels of domestic bonds and credit, which are set to zero in what follows. Substituting Equations (43), (46), (48), and (56) in (39') yields

$$\dot{R}_t + \dot{B}_t^* = y_X(\omega_t) - c_I(t) - \bar{g}_I + i_t^*(R_t + B_t^*), \tag{57}$$

which represents the consolidated budget constraint of the economy.[33] From the equilibrium condition of the money market (Equation (53)), the domestic interest rate is given by

$$i_t = \Phi(\bar{m}_t, \overset{+}{\bar{c}}_t)/(1-\iota). \tag{58}$$

Substituting this result in (41) yields

$$c_t = c(\bar{\lambda}_t, \overset{+}{m}_t), \tag{59}$$

which can be interpreted in a manner similar to equation (30).

Substituting Equation (59) back in (58) implies

$$i_t = \Phi(\bar{\lambda}_t, \bar{m}_t)/(1 - \iota). \tag{58'}$$

Substituting Equations (44b) and (59) in Equation (57) yields

$$\dot{R}_t + \dot{B}_t^* = y_X(\omega_t) - c_I(\bar{\lambda}_t, \overset{+}{m}_t, \bar{z}_t) - \bar{g}_I + i_t^*(R_t + B_t^*). \tag{60}$$

Equations (44b), (53), and (59) show that the net effect of a real-exchange-rate depreciation (a rise in z_t) on consumption of imported goods is, in general, ambiguous. On the one hand, it reduces spending directly since the relative price of foreign goods rises. On the other, it lowers the price level and raises the real money stock, reducing the domestic interest rate and therefore increasing total spending. In the discussion that follows, we will assume that the direct effect dominates the indirect one, so that a depreciation of the real exchange rate reduces purchases of imported goods.

Finally, from the definition of the real product wage in the export sector, we have

$$\dot{\omega}_t/\omega_t = \dot{w}_t/w_t - \epsilon_t = \mp\sigma(1 - z_t^{-\delta}/\omega_t) - \epsilon_t. \tag{61}$$

Depending on whether contracts are backward- or forward-looking, the sign of the expression appearing in parentheses on the right-hand side of Equation (61) is either negative or positive.

Equations (25), (40c), (40d), (44c), (55a) or (55b), (58'), (60), and (61) describe the evolution of the economy along any perfect-foresight equilibrium path. In a more compact form, these equations can be written, assuming a constant foreign interest rate and a constant devaluation rate equal to ϵ^h, as

$$z_t^\delta B_t^* = [(1 - \iota)i^* - \Phi(\lambda_t, m_t) + \epsilon^h)]/\gamma, \tag{62a}$$

$$\dot{\lambda}_t = [\alpha - \Phi(\lambda_t, m_t) + \pi_t]\lambda_t, \tag{62b}$$

$$\dot{\omega}_t/\omega_t = \mp\sigma(1 - z_t^{-\delta}/\omega_t) - \epsilon^h, \tag{62c}$$

$$\dot{z}_t/z_t = \epsilon^h \pm \sigma(1 - z_t^{-\delta}/\omega_t) - \xi[\bar{g}_N + \delta z_t^{1-\delta}\mathbb{C}(\lambda_t, m_t) - \bar{y}_N], \tag{62d}$$

$$\dot{R}_t + \dot{B}_t^* = y_X(\omega_t) - c_I(\lambda_t, m_t, z_t) - \bar{g}_I + i^*(R_t + B_t^*), \tag{62e}$$

$$\pi_t = \epsilon^h - \delta\dot{z}_t/z_t, \tag{62f}$$

$$m_t = \bar{d} + z_t^\delta R_t, \qquad (62g)$$

where $\mathbb{C}(\lambda_t, m_t) = \mathbf{c}[\lambda_t, \Phi(\lambda_t, m_t)]$, and with Equation (56) determining lump-sum taxes residually. As shown by Agénor (1994b), Equations (62) can be further reduced to a dynamic system in the marginal utility of wealth λ_t, the product wage in the export sector ω_t, the real exchange rate z_t, and foreign-currency holdings of the economy, $R_t + b_t^*$.[34] With backward-looking wage contracts the system possesses only one jump variable (λ_t), while with forward-looking contracts it possesses three jump variables $(\lambda_t, \omega_t, \text{and } z_t)$.

A formal derivation and characterization of the perfect-foresight equilibrium path of a linear approximation of the model are provided in Agénor (1994b). We will develop here only the long-run solution of the model. In the steady state, $\dot{\lambda}_t = \dot{z}_t = \dot{\omega}_t = \dot{R}_t = \dot{B}_t^* = 0$. Equation (62b) therefore implies that the after-tax real interest rate is equal to the rate of time preference:

$$(1 - \iota)\tilde{i} - \tilde{\pi} = \alpha, \qquad (63a)$$

where a "$\sim$" is used to denote steady-state values. The market for nontraded goods must be in equilibrium in the steady state, implying from Equations (46) and (62g) that

$$\delta \tilde{z}^{1-\delta} c(\tilde{\lambda}, \tilde{z}^\delta \tilde{R}) = \bar{y}_N - \bar{g}_N. \qquad (63b)$$

This condition implies, using Equation (62d) with $\dot{z}_t = 0$,

$$\tilde{z}^{-\delta}/\tilde{\omega} = 1 \pm \epsilon^h/\sigma. \qquad (63c)$$

From Equations (54) and (62f), the rate of increase in home goods prices and the overall domestic inflation rate must be equal to the devaluation rate $(\tilde{\pi}_N = \tilde{\pi} = \epsilon^h)$. From Equation (62c), since equilibrium in the nontraded goods market implies that $\dot{\Theta}_t = 0$, the rate of growth of nominal wages must also be equal to the rate of devaluation. Substituting Equation (63a) and $\tilde{\pi} = \epsilon^h$ in (62a) yields

$$\tilde{z}^\delta \tilde{B}^* = [(1 - \iota)i^* - \alpha]/\gamma. \qquad (63d)$$

Finally, Equations (62e) and (62g) imply

$$y_X(\tilde{\omega}) - c_I(\tilde{\lambda}, \tilde{z}^\delta \tilde{R}, \tilde{z}) - \bar{g}_I + i^*(\tilde{R} + \tilde{B}^*) = 0. \qquad (63e)$$

Equations (63a)—with $\tilde{\pi} = \epsilon^h$, and $\tilde{i}$ replaced by $\Phi(\tilde{\lambda}, \tilde{z}^\delta \tilde{R})$—and (63b)–(63e) can be solved simultaneously for the steady-state values of

$\tilde{\lambda}$, $\tilde{R}$, $\tilde{B}^*$, $\tilde{z}$, and $\tilde{\omega}$, from which the long-run effects of alternative policy shocks can be assessed. As shown by Agénor (1994b), the effects of a permanent change in the devaluation rate are given, with backward-looking contracts, by[35]

$$\tilde{\lambda} = \lambda(\overset{-}{\epsilon}^h), \qquad \tilde{R} = R(\overset{\pm}{\epsilon}^h), \qquad \tilde{z} = z(\overset{-}{\epsilon}^h),$$
$$\tilde{\omega} = \omega(\overset{-}{\epsilon}^h), \qquad \tilde{B}^* = B^*(\overset{+}{\epsilon}^h), \qquad \tilde{\pi} = \pi(\overset{+}{\epsilon}^h),$$

whereas with forward-looking contracts,

$$\tilde{\lambda} = \lambda(\overset{\pm}{\epsilon}^h), \qquad \tilde{R} = R(\overset{-}{\epsilon}^h), \qquad \tilde{z} = z(\overset{+}{\epsilon}^h),$$
$$\tilde{\omega} = \omega(\overset{+}{\epsilon}^h), \qquad \tilde{B}^* = B^*(\overset{-}{\epsilon}^h), \qquad \tilde{\pi} = \pi(\overset{+}{\epsilon}^h).$$

As shown before, in the long run, regardless of the wage contract mechanism considered, a permanent reduction in the devaluation rate leads to a proportional reduction in overall inflation, the rate of inflation in nontradable prices, and nominal wage growth. It has no effect on the real after-tax interest rate, implying again (from Equation (63a)) that the nominal interest rate falls by the same amount as the inflation rate. For all other variables, however, the mechanism through which wage contracts are formed does affect the long-run outcome. With backward-looking contracts the marginal value of wealth rises, thus dampening consumption and requiring a real exchange-rate depreciation (a fall in the relative price of home goods to maintain equilibrium in the market for nontraded goods). The product wage rises, leading to a fall in output of exportables, and the foreign-currency value of the stock of foreign bonds falls. The net effect on central bank reserves is ambiguous, since both exports and imports (as a result of the increase in the marginal value of wealth and the real depreciation) fall. By contrast, with forward-looking contracts, the net effect of a reduction in the devaluation rate on the marginal value of wealth—and thus total consumption and the demand for imports—is ambiguous. The real exchange rate appreciates—thus raising the real value in domestic-currency terms of holdings of foreign bonds—and the product wage falls, thus raising output of exportable goods. Here central bank holdings of foreign exchange unambiguously increase.

Equations (43) and (63c) yield

$$\tilde{P}/\tilde{w} = 1 \pm \epsilon^h/\sigma \Rightarrow d(\tilde{w}/\tilde{P})/d\epsilon^h \gtrless 0,$$

which indicates that a reduction in the devaluation rate leads to an increase in the real consumption wage $\tilde{w}/\tilde{P}$ under backward-looking contracts, and a fall under forward-looking contracts. The real effects of an exchange-rate-based disinflation policy thus depend critically on the direction of the long-run movement in the real consumption wage.

The two-sector model developed above can be further extended to account for other features deemed relevant for developing countries, such as a positive supply effect of government expenditure (Kimbrough, 1985) or the existence of imported intermediate inputs. Suppose, for instance, that output of nontraded goods is produced using labor n_N and imported intermediate materials J_N according to a fixed-coefficients technology. The production function is thus given by[36]

$$y_N(t) = \min\{n_N(t), \sigma J_N(t)\}, \tag{64}$$

where the parameter $1/\sigma$ measures the amount of intermediate materials that must be combined with a unit of labor to produce a unit of the domestic good. Constant returns to scale prevail in the nontraded goods sector according to Equation (64). Factor demand functions are given by

$$n_N(t) = y_N(t), \qquad J_N(t) = \sigma^{-1} y_N(t).$$

Assuming that the world price of imported inputs is equal to unity, in equilibrium the price of home goods would be given by the zero-profit condition:

$$p_N(t) = w_t + \sigma^{-1} E_t,$$

which implies that $w_t/E_t = z_t - \sigma^{-1}$. If intermediate imports are treated as final tradable goods, modifications of the current account equation are straightforward. Other extensions—such as the introduction of investment and capital accumulation, in line with our discussion in Chapter 3—are also possible, but at the cost of making the model increasingly complex and difficult to solve analytically. A numerical solution remains generally feasible, and we will present in Chapter 11 an example of a large, perfect-foresight model that incorporates some of these features.

This chapter has provided a review of alternative models of the inflationary process and examined the dynamics of monetary and exchange-rate rules. We began by presenting the monetarist and new structuralist models of the inflationary process. The first captures the dynamic relationships among fiscal deficits, monetary financing, and the inflationary process, while the second emphasizes the roles of inelastic food supply, mark-up pricing, and real wage claims in generating an unstable wage-price spiral and general inflation. We then showed that a hybrid model, derived essentially by integrating the government budget constraint and asset accumulation in a standard two-sector new structuralist model, provides a bridge between the two approaches and casts doubts about the policy implications of some simpler models.

We began the second part of the chapter by presenting a one-good optimizing model of a small open economy in which capital mobility is imperfect. Using this framework, we examined the dynamic path of the economy under monetary and exchange-rate rules. An important implication of the analysis is that although both rules may lead to the same inflation target in the long run, the transitional dynamics associated with each of them differ in significant ways. We then extended the analysis to a two-sector, three-good framework with wage contracts (with either backward- or forward-looking price expectations) and mark-up pricing in the nontraded goods sector. Although the extended framework was used to address only the long-run effects of exchange-rate adjustment, we argued that this type of model provides a useful setup for analyzing the short- and long-term implications of a large variety of macroeconomic policy shocks in developing countries.

Ten

Analytical Issues in Disinflation Programs

THE REPEATED failure of disinflation attempts in developing countries, particularly in Latin America, has given rise to a voluminous literature aimed at explaining the mechanisms through which program collapse may occur. While the early literature focused on the role of policy inconsistencies and inertial mechanisms (such as backward-looking implicit or explicit wage indexation, and adaptive inflationary expectations), more recent developments have highlighted the role of credibility and its interactions with expectations regarding the sustainability and political feasibility of government stabilization policies.

This chapter focuses on a selected—but representative—set of issues that have been considered in the recent literature. Section 10.1 focuses on two issues that have drawn much attention in recent discussions on exchange-rate-based stabilization programs: the boom-recession pattern of output (which was discussed in Chapter 8) and the behavior of real interest rates at the inception of such programs. We discuss the various interpretations of these phenomena that have been advanced in the literature, particularly the role of expectations about future government policies, and provide an assessment of alternative views. Section 10.2 examines the role of credibility factors in the formulation and design of stabilization programs. We review alternative mechanisms that have been suggested to enhance the credibility of such programs, including the adoption of a shock therapy approach for "signaling" purposes, the use of multiple nominal anchors, increased central bank independence, and recourse to foreign assistance.

10.1 Two Puzzles in Exchange-Rate-Based Programs

The empirical evidence on stabilization programs reviewed in Chapter 8 indicated that although the use of the exchange rate as a key nominal anchor brought hyperinflation to a halt with a relatively small output cost, success in using the exchange rate has been more limited in chronic-inflation countries. The Southern Cone tablita experiments of the late 1970s, in particular, were associated with a slow reduction in the inflation rate and an appreciation of the real exchange rate. In addition, such programs have often been accompanied by an initial expansion in economic activity, followed by a significant contraction. In the exchange-rate-based stabilization program implemented in Morocco in 1990, an initial expansion followed by a significant slowdown was also discernible. Output grew at an annual rate of more than 10 percent in 1990 (compared with 1.5 percent in 1989) but dropped to 2.4 percent in 1991, −4.1 percent in 1992, and 0.2 percent in 1993. The boom-recession cycle seems to have been observed in both successful and eventually unsuccessful stabilization attempts, and has attracted a lot of interest from development macroeconomists.

The behavior of real interest rates in exchange-rate-based stabilization programs has also been the subject of much debate in recent discussions on macroeconomic adjustment in developing countries. The evidence portrayed in Figures 10.1 and 10.2 suggests that while real interest rates declined at the inception of the program in the Southern Cone "tablita" experiments of the late 1970s, they rose sharply in the heterodox programs of the 1980s implemented in Argentina, Brazil, Israel, and Mexico. In addition, while real interest rates showed a tendency to increase gradually over time in the early experiments, no discernible pattern seems to have emerged in the more recent programs.

This section discusses a variety of analytical models that have attempted to explain the behavior of output and real interest rates in exchange-rate-based stabilization programs. A key aspect of some of these models is the emphasis on the dynamic effects associated with imperfectly credible policy announcements, or more generally the effect of varying expectations about present and future government policies. We begin by examining alternative interpretations of the boom-recession puzzle and then focus on explanations of the behavior of real interest rates.

10.1.1 The Boom-Recession Cycle

The first attempt at explaining the expansion-recession cycle that appears to characterize exchange-rate-based disinflation programs (in particular the tablita experiments) was proposed by Rodríguez (1982). More recently, an alternative explanation was developed by Calvo and Végh (1993a, 1993b). A key feature of the latter approach is its emphasis on the interactions between the lack of credibility (modeled as a temporary policy) and intertemporal substitution effects in the transmission of policy shocks to the real sphere of the economy.[1] We first present the Rodríguez model and then provide a detailed account of the Calvo-Végh "temporariness" model, before evaluating the key features of both models.

10.1.1.1 EXPECTATIONS, REAL INTEREST RATES, AND OUTPUT

The model developed by Rodríguez (1982) to explain the behavior of output in exchange-rate-based programs is based on a small open economy where

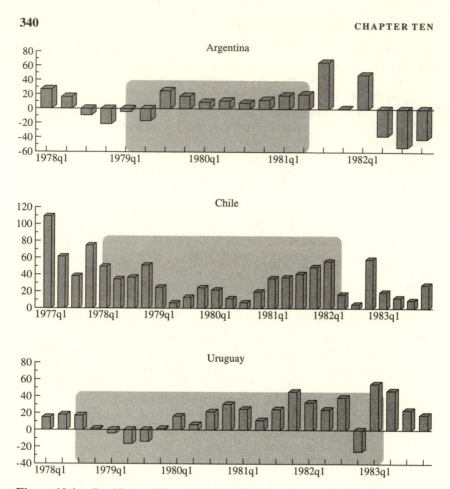

Figure 10.1 Real Interest Rates in the Tablita Experiments (real lending rates, in percent per year)

Source: Végh (1992).

Notes: Real interest rates are calculated by subtracting the one-quarter-ahead inflation rate from the nominal lending rate. Shaded areas indicate periods during which the programs were in place.

the exchange-rate path is preannounced, the money supply is endogenous, expectations follow a backward-looking process, and capital is perfectly mobile internationally.

The basic structure of the model is as follows. The domestic rate of inflation π_t is given by

$$\pi_t = \delta \pi_N(t) + (1 - \delta)\epsilon_t, \quad 0 < \delta < 1, \tag{1}$$

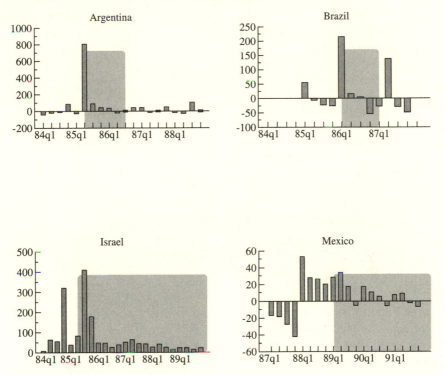

Figure 10.2   Real Interest Rates in Heterodox Experiments (real lending rates, in percent per year)

Source: Végh (1992).

Notes: Real interest rates are calculated by subtracting the one-quarter-ahead inflation rate from the nominal lending rate. Shaded areas indicate periods during which the programs were in place.

where, for simplicity, the rate of increase in world tradable prices is set to zero. Inflation in nontraded goods prices $\pi_N(t)$ depends on the expected behavior of prices in that sector $\pi_N^a(t)$ and excess demand for nontradables $d_N(t)$:

$$\pi_N(t) = \pi_N^a(t) + v'd_N(t), \quad v' > 0. \tag{2}$$

Equations (1) and (2) yield

$$\pi_t = \pi_t^a + vd_N(t), \quad v = \delta v', \tag{3}$$

where $\pi_t^a = \delta \pi_N^a(t) + (1 - \delta)\epsilon_t$. Price expectations are revised using an adaptive process similar to that specified in the first section of Chapter 9 (Equation (5)):

$$\dot{\pi}_t^a = \beta(\pi_t - \pi_t^a), \quad \beta > 0. \tag{4}$$

Aggregate supply is assumed constant at y_0, and aggregate spending d_t varies inversely with the expected real interest rate $\rho_t = i_t - \pi_t^a$, where i_t denotes the nominal interest rate. Excess demand for tradable goods, $d_T(t)$—which is equal to the trade balance deficit—is assumed to depend negatively on the relative price of these goods, defined as $z_t = E_t/P_t$.[2] Excess demand for nontradables is therefore given by

$$d_N = d(\bar{\rho}_t) - y_0 - d_T(\bar{z}_t) = d_N(\overset{+}{z}_t, \bar{\rho}_t). \tag{5}$$

Substituting Equation (5) into (3) yields

$$\pi_t - \pi_t^a = v d_N(z_t, \rho_t), \tag{6}$$

which indicates that unexpected movements in inflation are determined uniquely by excess demand for home goods.

At any moment in time, the real exchange rate z_t is given. Over time, it changes according to

$$\dot{z}_t/z_t = \epsilon_t - \pi_t. \tag{7}$$

Finally, the domestic nominal interest rate i_t is given by the constant world interest rate i^* plus the devaluation rate ϵ_t:

$$i_t = i^* + \epsilon_t. \tag{8}$$

To express the model in a compact form, differentiate the real interest rate with respect to time and use (4) and (6), so that[3]

$$\dot{\rho}_t = -\beta v d_N(z_t, \rho_t). \tag{9}$$

Using Equation (8) and the definition of the real interest rate to substitute out for the expected inflation rate in (6) yields

$$\pi_t = i^* + \epsilon_t - \rho_t + v d_N(z_t, \rho_t). \tag{6'}$$

Finally, substituting Equation (6') in (7) yields

$$\dot{z}_t/z_t = \rho_t - i^* - v d_N(z_t, \rho_t). \tag{10}$$

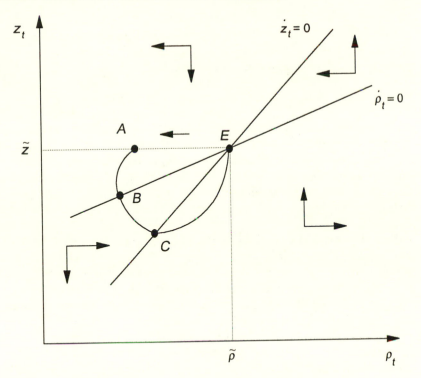

Figure 10.3   Equilibrium and Adjustment in the Rodríguez Model

Equations (9) and (10) constitute a differential equation system in the real interest rate and the real exchange rate. For given levels of these variables, Equation (6') determines the inflation rate.

The steady-state equilibrium of the model is represented in Figure 10.3. The locus $[\dot{\rho}_t = 0]$ is obtained from Equation (9) and determines the combinations of the real interest rate and the real exchange rate for which there is no excess demand in the nontraded goods market $(d_N(t) = 0)$. It has a positive slope since a depreciation in the real exchange rate creates excess demand for home goods, which requires an increase in the real interest rate to restore equilibrium. The locus $[\dot{z}_t = 0]$, which is derived from Equation (10), is also positively sloped and determines the combinations of the real interest rate and the real exchange rate for which the latter variable remains constant. Equations (9) and (10) imply that, in the steady state, the domestic real interest rate must be equal to the world interest rate ($\tilde{\rho} = i^*$), while (6') implies that the long-run inflation rate is equal to the devaluation rate. The system composed of (9) and (10) is (locally) stable if the coefficient matrix defined by

$$A = \begin{bmatrix} -\beta v d_{N\rho} & -\beta v \partial d_{Nz} \\ 1 - v d_{N\rho} & -v \partial d_{Nz} \end{bmatrix}$$

has a positive determinant and a negative trace:

$$\det A = \beta v d_{Nz} > 0, \qquad \text{tr } A = -v(d_{Nz} + \beta d_{N\rho}) < 0.$$

The condition on the determinant of A is always satisfied, but the condition on the trace of A does not necessarily hold. It depends on whether the positive effect of a real-exchange-rate depreciation offsets the negative effect of an increase in the real interest rate on private demand for nontradable goods. Assuming that the condition on tr A holds ensures the (local) stability of the long-run equilibrium of the economy, which obtains at point E in Figure 10.3.

Consider now a reduction in the rate of devaluation from ϵ^h to $\epsilon^s < \epsilon^h$. The results of this experiment are shown in Figure 10.3. The change in the devaluation rate does not affect the position of the curves $[\dot{\rho}_t = 0]$ and $[\dot{z}_t = 0]$, and therefore has no effect on the long-run equilibrium levels of the real exchange rate and the real interest rate. However, the reduction in ϵ_t reduces the real domestic interest rate on impact since, with the expected inflation rate given, it leads to a one-to-one reduction in the nominal interest rate. On impact, the system moves, therefore, from point E to a short-run equilibrium position such as point A, since the real exchange rate is predetermined. The initial fall in the real interest rate generates an excess demand for home goods. The reduction of the devaluation rate tends to reduce prices, but the emergence of excess demand tends to raise them; the net effect on the inflation rate is nevertheless positive, as indicated by Equations (6′) and (8). The actual inflation rate subsequently rises above the expected rate, which also begins to rise gradually. The increase in the expected rate of inflation reduces the real interest rate further over time, leading in the first phase to a gradual process of appreciation of the real exchange rate. In the second phase, however, the excess demand for nontraded goods generated by the fall in the real interest rate begins to dampen the rate of real-exchange-rate appreciation, leading eventually—assuming that the stability conditions given above hold—to an elimination of excess demand. Equilibrium of the nontraded goods market is restored at point B. Nevertheless, the real exchange rate continues to appreciate for a while, because at B the domestic rate of inflation exceeds the rate of devaluation. This leads to an excess supply of nontraded goods, a fall in the expected inflation rate, and a rising real interest rate (movement from B to C). At point C the rate of change of the real exchange rate is zero, but excess supply prevails. Actual and expected inflation continue to fall, leading to a depreciation of the exchange rate (which stimulates the demand for home goods and thus reduces excess supply) and a further rise in the real interest rate. In the long run, therefore, the economy returns to its initial equilibrium position at point E. The new steady-state value of the inflation rate is, by contrast, equal to $\epsilon^s < \epsilon^h$.

The adjustment process following a permanent reduction in the devaluation rate is thus characterized by a period of excess demand, that is, a short-run boom. In the Rodríguez model, the expansion of demand occurs as an inevitable consequence of the assumption of backward-looking expectations. The initial reduction in the devaluation rate leads to a fall in the nominal interest rate and a downward jump in the real interest rate—since the expected inflation rate is a predetermined variable—and hence to an increase in the demand for nontraded goods. This expansion of demand in the home goods sector puts upward pressure on domestic prices. The ensuing appreciation of the real exchange rate dampens the expansion of demand and eventually dominates the initial expansionary effect, leading to a contraction in demand.[4] Thus, for the system to return to its initial equilibrium position, the initial boom must be followed by a demand contraction induced by the progressive appreciation of the real exchange rate in the second phase of the adjustment process, which results from the domestic inflation rate exceeding the devaluation rate.

10.1.1.2 THE "TEMPORARINESS" HYPOTHESIS

In an important series of contributions, Calvo and Végh (1993a, 1993b) have provided an alternative explanation of the boom-recession cycle observed in exchange-rate-based stabilization programs, based on rigorous optimizing foundations and forward-looking expectations. The analytical structure developed by Calvo and Végh is of interest in its own right and, although it represents in several regards a less general framework than the three-good model developed in Chapter 9, is worth considering in detail.[5] As in the Rodríguez model, consider a small open economy producing traded and nontraded goods. The representative household maximizes the discounted lifetime sum of utility, with instantaneous utility separable in both goods:

$$\int_0^\infty [\ln c_T(t) + \ln c_N(t)]e^{-\alpha t}\, dt, \quad \alpha > 0, \tag{11}$$

where $c_N(c_T)$ denotes consumption of nontraded (traded) goods. Households face a cash-in-advance constraint, given by

$$z_t^{-1} c_N(t) + c_T(t) \ge \gamma^{-1} m_t, \quad \gamma > 0, \tag{12}$$

where the real exchange rate is once again defined as $z_t = E_t/P_N(t)$.[6] m_t denotes real money balances measured in terms of traded goods.

Households hold a stock b_t^p of internationally traded bonds, which bears a constant real rate of interest i^* determined on world capital markets. Real financial wealth in terms of traded goods, a_t, is thus $a_t = m_t + b_t^p$. The intertemporal resource constraint faced by the consumer, which equates lifetime resources to lifetime expenditures, is given by

$$a_0 + \int_0^\infty [z_t^{-1} y_N(t) + y_T + \tau_t] e^{-\rho t}\, dt = \int_0^\infty [z_t^{-1} c_N(t) + c_T(t) + i_t m_t] e^{-\rho t}\, dt,$$

(13)

where $y_N(t)$ denotes output of nontraded goods (which is determined below), y_T the exogenous level of output of traded goods, τ_t real transfers from the government, and i_t the domestic nominal interest rate, which, assuming that the uncovered interest parity condition holds, is given by

$$i_t = i^* + \epsilon_t,$$

(14)

where ϵ_t denotes, as before, the devaluation rate.

Households take as given a_0, y_T, $y_N(t)$, τ_t, i_t, and z_t and maximize (11) subject to the cash-in-advance constraint (12)—holding with equality—and the lifetime resource constraint (13) by choosing a sequence $\{c_T(t), c_N(t), m_t\}_{t=0}^\infty$. Assuming that the subjective discount rate α is equal to the world interest rate, the first-order conditions for this optimization problem are given by

$$1/c_T(t) = \lambda(1 + \gamma i_t),$$

(15a)

$$c_N(t) = z_t c_T(t),$$

(15b)

where λ can be interpreted, as before, as the marginal utility of wealth. The interpretation of Equations (15) is similar to that provided in the description of the closed-economy model developed in Chapter 4 and the one-good model described in Section 9.2, with the real effective price of traded goods defined as consisting of their direct, market price (equal to unity) and the opportunity cost of holding γ units of money necessary to carry out the transaction, γi_t.

Output of nontraded goods is demand determined. The rate of change of inflation in the nontraded good sector, $\pi_N(t)$, is assumed to be negatively related to excess demand, which is defined as the difference between actual output (itself determined by the demand side of the market) and its long-run level, $\bar{y}_N$:

$$\dot{\pi}_N(t) = -\Theta[c_N(t) - \bar{y}_N] = \Theta[\bar{y}_N - z_t c_T(t)],$$

(16)

where the second equality follows from Equation (15*b*). The price mechanism specified in Equation (16) follows the model of staggered prices and wages developed by Calvo (1983).[7] It relies on the assumption that firms in the nontraded goods sector determine the prices of their products in a nonsynchronous manner, taking into account the expected future path of demand and of the average price prevailing in the economy. At any moment in time, only a small subset of firms may change their individual prices. The price level is thus a predetermined variable at any given period, but inflation can jump, because it reflects changes in individual prices set by firms. When excess demand develops in the nontraded goods sector, for instance, some firms increase their individual prices, and inflation rises. However, since the subset of firms that have yet to adjust their prices to excess demand diminishes quickly, inflation in home goods prices decreases over time. Hence the change in the home goods inflation rate is inversely related to excess demand for nontraded goods.

As a result of staggered price setting in the nontraded goods sector, the real exchange rate is predetermined in the short run. Differentiating $z_t = E_t/P_N(t)$ with respect to time yields an equation similar to (56) in Chapter 9:

$$\dot{z}_t/z_t = \epsilon_t - \pi_N(t). \tag{17}$$

Closing the model requires a specification of the government's behavior. Under the assumption that the government buys no goods and redeems back to households the interest income on the central bank's net foreign assets and the revenue from money creation, the present value of government transfers is given by

$$\int_0^\infty \tau_t e^{-\alpha t}\, dt = b_0^g + \int_0^\infty (\dot{m}_t + \epsilon_t m_t) e^{-\alpha t}\, dt, \tag{18}$$

where b_0^g denotes the government's initial stock of bonds. Combining equations (13), (14), and (18); defining the total stock of bonds in the economy as $b_t = b_t^p + b_t^g$; and imposing the transversality condition $\lim_{t\to\infty} e^{-\alpha t} b_t = 0$ yields the overall resource constraint:

$$b_0 + y_T/\alpha = \int_0^\infty c_T(t) e^{-\alpha t}\, dt, \tag{19}$$

where b_0 denotes the economy's initial stock of bonds. Equation (19) equates the present value of tradable resources to the present value of purchases of traded goods. Assuming further that transfers are used to compensate households for the depreciation of real money balances yields the economy's current account balance:[8]

$$\dot{b}_t = y_T + i^* b_t - c_T(t). \tag{20}$$

Finally, as in the two-sector framework developed in Chapter 9 and the Rodríguez model described earlier, the overall inflation rate is written as a weighted average of the devaluation rate and the rate of inflation in home goods prices:

$$\pi_t = \delta \pi_N(t) + (1 - \delta)\epsilon_t, \quad 0 < \delta < 1, \tag{21}$$

where the weight δ depends on the share of home goods in total consumption expenditure.

The dynamics of the model are determined by Equations (16), (17), and (20). Because output of traded goods is exogenous and consumption of traded goods depends, from Equation (15a), only on the marginal utility of wealth—which varies over time solely as a result of unexpected shocks[9]—and the domestic interest rate, the system is recursive.[10] For a given path of $c_T(t)$ and ϵ_t, Equations (16) and (17) form the interdependent block, which can be written as

$$\begin{bmatrix} \dot{z}_t \\ \dot{\pi}_N(t) \end{bmatrix} = \begin{bmatrix} 0 & -\tilde{z} \\ -\Theta \tilde{c}_T & 0 \end{bmatrix} \begin{bmatrix} z_t \\ \pi_N(t) \end{bmatrix} + \begin{bmatrix} \tilde{z}\epsilon_t \\ \Theta \bar{y}_N - \tilde{z}c_t(t) \end{bmatrix}. \tag{22}$$

The first row of (22) indicates that, for the real exchange rate to remain constant over time, the rate of inflation in home goods prices must be equal to the devaluation rate. The second row indicates that consumption of non-traded goods must be equal to long-run output for the rate of inflation in home goods prices to remain constant over time. Since $\tilde{c}_T = \bar{y}_N / \tilde{z}$, the determinant of the matrix of coefficients is $-\Theta \bar{y}_N < 0$. The system is therefore saddlepath stable.

Reduction of ϵ_t: Full Credibility

As before, suppose that at time t_0 the government announces an immediate and permanent reduction in the rate of devaluation from an initial value of ϵ^h to $\epsilon^s < \epsilon^h$. The permanent nature of the shock is interpreted by Calvo and Végh as indicating that the announcement carries full credibility, in the sense that private agents are convinced that the devaluation rate will indeed remain at its lower level in the indefinite future.

Through the interest parity condition (Equation (14)), the reduction in the devaluation rate leads to a concomitant fall in the nominal interest rate. Because the exchange-rate adjustment carries full credibility, private agents will expect the nominal interest rate to remain forever at its lower level. Although the reduction in the domestic interest rate is equivalent to a fall in the effective price of consumption, the fact that the exchange-rate adjustment is expected to last forever implies that private agents have no incentives to engage in intertemporal consumption substitution. Since tradable resources do not change, consumption of traded goods remains constant over time. From the system (18), it follows that, since c_T is not affected by permanent changes in the rate of devaluation, a fall in π_N that exactly matches the fall in ϵ_t immediately moves the system to a new steady state. The overall inflation rate of the economy, which is a weighted average of the inflation rate of home goods and that of traded goods (Equation (21)), also falls instantaneously to its new level, ϵ^s. Therefore, a permanent, unanticipated reduction in the devaluation rate—or, in the Calvo-Végh interpretation, a fully credible exchange-rate-based stabilization program—reduces the inflation rate instantaneously at no real costs and is thus superneutral.[11] Moreover, this result holds also if the system starts away from an initial steady-state position.[12]

An important property of the Calvo-Végh model is that the immediate downward jump in inflation and the absence of real effects associated with a reduction in the devaluation rate that is perceived to be permanent occurs despite the existence of staggered price setting by individual forward-looking firms. Price level ridigity does not, by itself, imply stickiness in the inflation rate.[13]

Reduction of ϵ_t: Imperfect Credibility

Consider now the case where the government announces at t_0 a reduction in the devaluation rate, but the public believes that the exchange-rate adjustment will be reversed at some period T in the future. Formally,

$$\begin{cases} \epsilon_t = \epsilon^s & \text{for } t_0 \leq t < T \\ \epsilon_t = \epsilon^h > \epsilon^s & \text{for } t \geq T. \end{cases}$$

Calvo and Végh interpret the belief that the policy is temporary as arising from lack of credibility—an interpretation to which we return below. The dynamic behavior of consumption, the current account, the real exchange rate, and the inflation and real interest rates associated with a temporary exchange-rate policy are illustrated in Figure 10.4. The temporary reduction in the devaluation rate implies, by Equation (14), that the nominal interest rate is lower in the interval $(0, T)$. Consequently, the effective price of traded goods is also lower during the interval $(0, T)$ and consumption of traded goods jumps upward (see Equation (15a)), to a level higher than initial permanent income (given by $y_T + i^*b_0$). However, because the intertemporal resource constraint of the economy (Equation (19)) must be

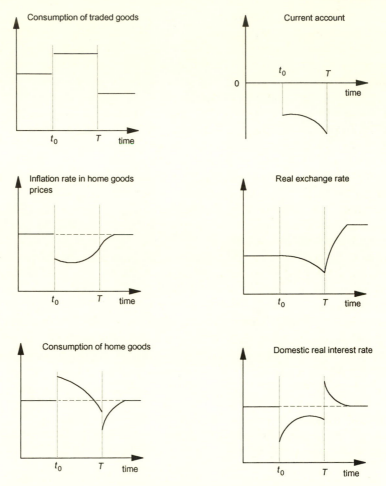

Figure 10.4   Dynamics of the Calvo-Végh "Temporariness" Model with Imperfect Credibility

Source: Calvo and Végh (1993*a*, p. 17).

satisfied for all equilibrium paths, consumption of traded goods must subsequently (for $t \geq T$) fall below initial permanent income and remain forever at that lower level. The upward jump in consumption of traded goods leads on impact to a current account deficit. During the interval $(0, T)$, the deficit continues to increase (despite the fact that consumption of traded goods remains constant) as a result of a reduction over time of interest receipts on foreign bonds. When, at time T, the policy is abandoned, the current account jumps into balance and the stock of foreign bonds remains permanently at a lower level than initially.

The effect of the reduction in the devaluation rate on the path of home goods prices is, on impact, ambiguous. On the one hand, a lower rate of exchange-rate depreciation dampens the rate of inflation in home goods prices. On the other, the increase in aggregate demand tends to raise inflation. The net effect in general is a reduction in the rate of inflation in home goods prices, but by less than the rate of devaluation.[14] After the initial fall, inflation in home goods prices rises continuously, assuming that the horizon T is large enough, in anticipation of the expected resumption of the higher devaluation rate. At time T, the policymaker must decide whether to abandon the program (thus validating the public's expectations) or maintain the devaluation rate at the lower level. If the authorities indeed abandon the program, inflation in home goods prices will continue to increase toward its initial level, as shown in Figure 10.4. If, however, the authorities decide to maintain the lower-devaluation-rate policy, then inflation in home goods prices will jump downward at time T and converge from below toward ϵ^s.

Qualitatively, the overall inflation rate follows the same adjustment path during the interval $(0, T)$ as inflation in home goods prices. The Calvo-Végh model thus predicts that a temporary reduction in the devaluation rate (interpreted as a reflection of a lack of credibility) will lead to inflation inertia. Moreover, the more temporary the exchange-rate policy, or the lower its degree of credibility, the lower the initial fall in the inflation rate.

Because the inflation rate in home goods prices remains systematically above the devaluation rate, the real exchange rate appreciates during the interval $(0, T)$. At time T, regardless of whether the exchange-rate policy is reversed or not, the real exchange rate begins to depreciate. If at that moment the lower-devaluation policy is not abandoned—and if private agents become convinced that it will be adhered to in the indefinite future—inflation in home goods prices falls below the devaluation rate, generating the real depreciation.

The domestic real interest rate, defined as the difference between the nominal interest rate and the rate of inflation in home goods prices, falls on impact, because the rate of inflation in nontraded goods prices drops by less than the devaluation rate and the concomitant fall in the nominal interest rate. It begins rising at first and then falls during the transition, jumping upward when the horizon T is reached, as a result of the jump in the nominal interest rate. Since domestic inflation increases gradually over time, the real interest rate falls monotonically thereafter toward its unchanged steady-state value given by the world interest rate.

Since the relative price of home goods in terms of traded goods cannot change on impact, the increase in the consumption of traded goods leads to a proportional rise in the consumption of home goods (Equation ($15b$)). The gradual appreciation of the real exchange rate leads to a reduction over time of private expenditure on home goods. If the horizon is sufficiently far in the future, a recession may set in well before T is reached. If the horizon is short, output will remain above its full-employment level throughout the transition period. At time T consumption of both traded and nontraded goods jumps downward. After T, the real exchange rate begins to depreciate toward its long-run value, stimulating consumption of home goods. There is, therefore, an initial consumption boom followed later on, possibly before time T is reached, by a contraction. The smaller T is—or, according to the interpretation given above, the lower the credibility of the disinflation policy—the more pronounced are the intertemporal substitution effects, and the larger is the initial rise in the consumption of traded and home goods.

10.1.1.3 AN ASSESSMENT

To a large extent, the explanation of the expansion-recession cycle provided by Rodríguez relies on an arbitrary specification of behavioral functions and expectations formation. Although plausible under certain conditions, the assumption of a backward-looking expectational process appears untenable in the context of economies undergoing a comprehensive macroeconomic adjustment program. As shown by Calvo and Végh (1994), however, Rodríguez's results also obtain if prices are sticky and expectations are forward looking. Nevertheless, the predictions of the Rodríguez model can be substantially altered once behavioral functions are derived from a well-defined microeconomic optimization process, rather than simply postulated. Using an optimizing framework similar in many regards to the one described above, Calvo and Végh (1994) have argued that even in the presence of backward-looking price expectations—as embodied in wage contracts, for instance—a permanent reduction in the devaluation rate may have a contractionary effect, rather than an expansionary effect as predicted by Rodríguez. Essentially, this result obtains because the appreciation of the real exchange rate has an ambiguous effect on output. On the one hand, the real appreciation has a negative impact, since it increases the relative price of home goods. On the other, it stimulates output because it leads to a reduction in the domestic, consumption-based real interest rate.[15] Whether or not the latter effect dominates depends on whether the intertemporal elasticity of substitution (which measures the degree to which agents are willing to shift consumption across periods) is larger than the intratemporal elasticity of substitution between traded and home goods. Hence, the existence of backward-looking expectations may not be sufficient to explain the observed initial expansion in output.

The Calvo-Végh framework provides a conceptually appealing formulation of the major mechanisms at work in the behavior of output in exchange-rate-based disinflation programs. In contrast to Rodríguez, who assumes backward-looking expectations, Calvo and Végh emphasize the

TABLE 10.1
Intertemporal Elasticity of Substitution: Estimates for Developing Countries

Country	Estimate	Source
Argentina	0.2	Reinhart and Végh (1995)
	0.2	Giovannini (1985)
Brazil	0.0	Giovannini (1985)
Chile	0.2	Reinhart and Végh (1995)
	1.6	Arrau (1990)
Israel	2.9	Arrau (1990)
	0.2–1.3	Eckstein and Leiderman (1988)
	0.1	Giovannini (1985)
Mexico	0.2	Reinhart and Végh (1995)
Uruguay	0.5	Reinhart and Végh (1995)
Panel data[a]		Ostry and Reinhart (1992)
Africa	0.4	
Asia	0.8	
Latin America	0.4	
Panel data[b]	0.1	Rossi (1988)

[a] Africa: Egypt, Ghana, Côte d'Ivoire, and Morocco; Asia: Sri Lanka, India, Korea, Pakistan, and Philippines; Latin America: Brazil, Colombia, Costa Rica, and Mexico.

[b] Bolivia, Brazil, Chile, Colombia, Ecuador, Paraguay, Peru, Uruguay, and Venezuela.

role of forward-looking behavior and expectations of future policy reversals. Moreover, the Calvo-Végh framework can be extended to account for uncertainty about the date of the policy reversal—along the lines of Drazen and Helpman (1988, 1990), for instance—and thus may provide an explanation of the volatile behavior of aggregate variables in programs that lack credibility. The U-shaped time profile of inflation predicted by the Calvo-Végh model appears to correspond relatively well to the evidence observed in several exchange-rate-based stabilization attempts that ended in failure (see Chapter 8).

The ability of the Calvo-Végh temporariness hypothesis to explain the boom-recession puzzle depends on the extent to which the degree of intertemporal substitution can explain the large observed changes in private consumption expenditure. However, the available evidence on the intertemporal channel emphasized by Calvo and Végh does not appear to provide strong support for the theory. Table 10.1 summarizes the results of some recent studies that have attempted to estimate the intertemporal elasticity of substitution in developing countries. Early estimates, which were based on a number of restrictive assumptions (in particular, the exclusion of monetary factors), suggest by and large that the intertemporal elasticity of substitution is small and not significantly different from zero.[16] More recent estimates, apart from those obtained by Arrau (1990), suggest that the elasticity is relatively low but nevertheless statistically different from zero.

In principle, even with low intertemporal elasticities of substitution, observed movements in interest rates may be large enough to generate substantial changes in consumption. But while many of the stabilization programs implemented in the mid-1980s (whether ultimately successful or not) were accompanied by a substantial fall in nominal interest rates, the evidence is less compelling with regard to other episodes—particularly the Southern Cone experiments. Reinhart and Végh (1995) have examined this hypothesis using a simulation analysis and have shown that, despite low elasticities, predicted changes in consumption match reasonably well the actual changes in the four heterodox programs implemented in the 1980s (particularly Brazil, Mexico, and Israel), but the accuracy is poor for the tablita experiments. The overall evidence thus does not seem to provide overwhelming support for the view that lack of credibility—modeled as a policy adjustment subject to a future reversal—and intertemporal factors explain output behavior in exchange-rate-based programs.[17]

However, whether the intertemporal elasticity of substitution is small or large may be less important than the above discussion suggests. The results obtained by Calvo and Végh depend also in a crucial manner on the assumption that money and consumption are Pareto-Edgeworth complements. In their framework, the representative household (which faces a constant real rate of interest) attempts to keep the marginal utility of consumption constant over time. To do so, the household must change the path of consumption if the devaluation rate—and therefore the opportunity cost of holding money—is expected to increase at a well-defined future date. The direction of this change depends on whether consumption goods and real money balances are substitutes or complements. If consumption of traded goods and real money balances are Pareto-Edgeworth complements, then private agents will consume more when the nominal interest rate is temporarily lower, leading to a deterioration of the current account. This is the case that Calvo and Végh consider, implicitly, by introducing money through a cash-in-advance requirement. By contrast, if consumption of traded goods and real money balances are Pareto-Edgeworth substitutes, agents will reduce consumption expenditure following a temporary fall in nominal interest rates. A temporary reduction in the devaluation rate leads in this case to a transitory current account surplus, rather than a deficit.[18]

Another difficulty in the Calvo-Végh framework is that the dynamic effects of an imperfectly credible policy depend—in addition to consumer preferences and price-setting rules—critically on the degree of temporariness, that is, the duration of the interval during which the policy is in effect. This feature of the model is a common one in the literature on temporary policy. However, since the period at which the policy is believed to be discontinued is given, credibility is exogenous. As discussed in the next section, a key aspect of credibility is precisely the endogenous interactions between policy decisions, economic outcomes, and the degree of confidence that private agents attach to policymakers' commitment to disinflate.

Finally, two more general points can be made concerning the previous models of the boom-recession cycle. First, instead of modeling exchange-rate policy as a sequence of jumps in the rate of devaluation, an alternative approach would be to consider a gradual reduction in the devaluation rate—an approach that is perhaps more in line with the Southern Cone tablita experiments (see Chapter 8). Obstfeld (1985) has studied the dynamics associated with this type of policy, using an optimizing framework with continuous market clearing and perfect foresight. He emphasizes, as do Calvo and Végh, the importance of intertemporal substitution effects in consumption generated by a gradual and permanent (and thus fully credible) reduction in the devaluation rate. Such a policy increases real money balances, and, if money and consumption are substitutes, consumption rises on impact and falls over time. Initially, the real exchange rate appreciates and a current account deficit emerges. Later on in the program, a real depreciation occurs, and a gradual reduction of the deficit takes place. As before, however, Obstfeld's predictions depend crucially on the treatment of money and consumption in households' utility function.[19] If money and real goods are complements rather than substitutes, the economy's short- and long-run responses to a gradual reduction in the devaluation rate are completely reversed—just as in the Calvo-Végh model.

A more recent analysis of a gradual lowering of the devaluation rate is provided by Roldós (1993), who models money also through a cash-in-advance constraint—an assumption that is functionally equivalent to postulating complementarity between money and consumption in households' utility functions. A gradual, fully credible reduction in the devaluation rate in the model entails, as in Obstfeld's setting, a real exchange-rate appreciation and sustained current account deficits. However, an important feature of the model developed by Roldós is the emphasis on the supply-side effects of exchange-rate policy. An initial boom occurs only when the intertemporal elasticity of substitution in labor supply is larger than that in consumption; it occurs in both production sectors—tradables and nontradables—as real wages fall. The reduction in inflation raises the marginal value of wealth, raising the opportunity cost of leisure and inducing an increase in labor supply in the initial phase of the program. The further reduction over time in the rate of inflation leads to additional increases in labor supply. Contrary to what happens in the Calvo-Végh framework, a recession does not occur later on.[20] The emphasis on intertemporal substitution in labor supply rather than consumption provides a potentially useful interpretation of the recent Mexican stabilization experiment (as well as some other exchange-rate-based experiences reviewed in Chapter 8), which has not been accompanied by an early recession. However, no rigorous testing of this channel has yet been developed, and its empirical importance is therefore unclear.

Finally, neither the Rodríguez nor the Calvo-Végh model of the boom-recession cycle incorporates durable goods, although an anticipated collapse of a stabilization program is likely to have more pronounced real effects in the presence of durable goods. Intuitively, an anticipated increase in the inflation rate and the opportunity cost of purchases immediately would induce an increase in spending on durable goods, an accumulation of inventories by firms, and investment in capital goods (machines and equipment, very often imported from abroad, as argued in Chapter 1), thereby causing a large increase in absorption. Understanding the dynamics of durable goods induced by expectations of relative price changes is thus a critical element in assessing the real effects induced by intertemporal substitution in stabilization programs. Drazen (1990), for instance, has examined the behavior of imports of durable goods in exchange-rate-based disinflation programs. His analysis suggests that a temporary exchange-rate freeze can lead to sharp fluctuations in domestic output and durable goods imports if there is uncertainty about the date at which the freeze will end, and if it is believed to be associated wtih substantial variations in relative prices. Matsuyama (1991) has shown that exchange-rate-based stabilization programs may be subject to "hysteresis" effects in the presence of durable goods.[21] In such conditions, a temporary reduction in the devaluation rate may have a permanent effect, because such a change alters the initial condition for some later moment when the policy is abandoned and the "old" policy is put back in place.[22]

10.1.2 The Behavior of Real Interest Rates

The divergent behavior, as documented in the introduction, of real interest rates in exchange-rate-based stabilization programs implemented during the 1970s and 1980s has received relatively little attention in the literature on macroeconomic adjustment in developing countries. We examine here two alternative models aimed at explaining this apparent puzzle. The first focuses on lack of credibility and the presence of additional nominal anchors, and the second on expectations about future fiscal policy shocks.

10.1.2.1 CREDIBILITY, NOMINAL ANCHORS, AND REAL INTEREST RATES

Models attempting to explain the boom-recession cycle associated with exchange-rate-based programs provide unambiguous predictions regarding the initial movement of real interest rates. In the Rodríguez model, for instance, a permanent, fully credible reduction in the devaluation rate leads to an immediate fall in real interest rates, because price expectations are predetermined at any moment in time. Similarly, in the Calvo-Végh "temporariness" framework described above, an imperfectly credible exchange-rate stabilization leads to an unambiguous fall on impact in the domestic real interest rate. To reconcile their theoretical construct with the diverging pattern observed in the 1970s and 1980s, Calvo and Végh (1993*b*) argue that if money is used as an additional anchor, as a result of the imposition of capital controls or the adoption of a credit target, then real interest rates may rise rather than fall at the inception of an imperfectly credible exchange-rate-based program. If, for instance, capital controls are in place, the money stock becomes predetermined. An increase in domestic money demand associated with a reduction in the devaluation rate requires an accommodating upward adjustment in interest rates. Given that the devaluation rate falls on impact, real interest rates will generally rise.

This line of argument may prove useful for understanding the sharp increase in real interest rates that occurred at the beginning of the Israeli stabilization of the mid-1980s. The restrictive credit policy adopted by the authorities at the inception of the program is widely believed to have been the major factor behind the rise in real interest rates.[23] However, there does not appear to be much evidence suggesting that credit policy was significantly different in the programs implemented in the 1970s and 1980s in Latin America. Capital controls were not apparently intensified at the inception of those programs either.

An issue that has not been fully appreciated in the recent literature relates to the fiscal implications of an exchange-rate-based stabilization program, and the fact that an exchange-rate adjustment is typically only one element of an overall stabilization package comprising trade, financial, and fiscal reforms designed to reduce inflation and improve the current account. An unanticipated reduction in the devaluation rate leads to a deterioration of the financial position of the public sector, through the loss of seignorage and the increase in the real cost of servicing fixed-rate debt issued when nominal interest rates were high (Velasco, 1993). Eventually, the government must correct the fiscal deficit thus created via changes in its policy instruments, such as the rate of growth of domestic credit, lump-sum transfers to private agents, income tax rates, or spending cuts. In a forward-looking world, expectations about the nature of the instruments that the policymakers are likely to implement will have immediate effects on the behavior of real interest rates.[24]

10.1.2.2 EXPECTATIONS, FISCAL ADJUSTMENT, AND REAL INTEREST RATES

We examine here, using the one-good model with imperfect capital mobility developed in Chapter 9, the implications of a two-stage stabilization program for the behavior of real interest rates. We will consider the specification in which lump-sum taxes are endogenously adjusted to finance the budget deficit.

Assume that the economy begins at $t = 0^-$ in a steady state, characterized by a "high" devaluation rate and a "low" income tax rate (on both factor income and interest payments), $0 < \iota^s < 1$. At $t = 0$ the government decides to reduce the devaluation rate from ϵ^h to $\epsilon^s < \epsilon^h$. At the same time that the reduction in the devaluation rate is implemented, the government announces its intention to increase permanently the income tax rate from ι^s to ι^h in the future, at period T or some time after T.[25] The new income tax rate ι^h is common knowledge. However, the public does not entirely believe the policy announcement, and attributes only a given probability $0 \le \sigma \le 1$ that the increase in the income tax rate will be effectively implemented. The coefficient σ can thus be viewed as a measure of the degree of credibility of the fiscal component of the stabilization program. A value of σ close to unity indicates that agents are almost certain that the policy reform will eventually be carried out, while a value of σ close to zero indicates that the public has little confidence in the government's intention to adjust the income tax rate.

The income tax rate that is expected to prevail from $t \ge T$ is thus equal to $\sigma \iota^h + (1 - \sigma)\iota^s$ (which is greater than ι^s as long as σ is positive), and private agents will make their portfolio and consumption decisions accordingly. The dynamics of the economy from $t \ge T$ are now determined by a set of equations similar to Equations (32) in Chapter 9, with Equation (32a) replaced by

$$\gamma b_t^* = \epsilon^h + [1 - (\sigma \iota^h + (1 - \sigma)\iota^s)](i^* - i_t). \tag{23}$$

The solution of the modified system yields a "quasi" steady state, since it is associated with a policy shock that may or may not occur at T or afterward. Once period T is reached, the policy is either implemented or agents start believing it will never be. Uncertainty eventually disappears, and σ becomes unity or zero. Thus, there would normally be a jump in all variables at some moment after period T, after which the economy will begin converging to its "final" steady state. We will here discuss only the quasi steady state, since the focus of attention is the short-run behavior of real interest rates. The solution of the model during the adjustment period $0 < t < T$ is such that the transition that takes place at T is perfectly anticipated.

As shown by Agénor (1994a), the impact effect of a program consisting of an immediate reduction in the rate of devaluation and the announcement of a future tax reform on the marginal value of wealth is in general ambiguous. To understand the short-run dynamics of real interest rates, consider the two polar cases: σ close to zero and σ positive. The case where σ is close to zero corresponds to the case of a permanent, unanticipated reduction in the devaluation rate only at $t = 0$, as described in Chapter 9. Thus (assuming that the degree of capital mobility is relatively high, as indicated earlier), the announcement of a future income tax adjustment that carries little credibility implies that the real after-tax interest rate is likely to fall on impact. By contrast, if σ is close to unity, and if the initial reduction in the devaluation rate is not too large, it can be shown that the real after-tax interest rate will rise on impact. The larger σ is, the larger will be the increase in the after-tax real interest rate.

The thrust of the foregoing analysis is thus that, as long as σ is positive, the net movement in real interest rates at the inception of a two-stage exchange-rate-based stabilization program of the type discussed here is indeterminate. Depending on the degree of confidence in fiscal reform (as well as the degree of capital mobility, the size of the initial exchange-rate adjustment, and the likely increase in the income tax rate), real interest rates may rise or fall. In practice, therefore, movements in real interest rates will reflect not only the type of policies that agents expect the government to implement in the future but also changes in the perceived ability of policymakers to stick to their announcements. An empirical test of the importance of the time profile of fiscal policy as emphasized here is, of course, difficult to implement since expectations of future policy changes are not observed by the econometrician. Nevertheless, the adjustment mechanism described in the foregoing discussion may have played an important role in the contrasting pattern, noted in the introduction to this chapter, in the behavior of real interest rates in the exchange-rate-based stabilization programs implemented in the 1970s and 1980s. As emphasized by many economists, lack of credibility has been a pervasive factor in the short-run dynamics associated with these experiments. However, while most observers have emphasized imperfect credibility of exchange-rate adjustment per se, the analysis developed here has focused on the fiscal dimension of the credibility issue in these programs. In our framework, the initial exchange-rate adjustment is fully credible—in the sense that it is perceived to be permanent. What suffers from a lack of credibility is the announcement of a future tax reform. Our analysis thus suggests that, even when the exchange-rate policy component of an exchange-rate-based stabilization program is fully credible, large fluctuations in real interest rates will be observed in the course of the adjustment process if the degree of confidence in the fiscal policy component of the program varies over time.[26]

10.2 The Role of Credibility in Disinflation Programs

The repeated failure of disinflation programs in developing countries has often been attributed to private agents' lack of confidence in the ability of governments to persevere in reform efforts and to maintain a consistent set of policies over time.[27] Moreover, a tradition of failed stabilization attempts suggests that the credibility problem each new anti-inflation program must confront becomes more severe over time, adding to the downward rigidities that characterize the inflationary process.

The most direct means policymakers can use to publicize their intention to refrain from adopting inflationary policies is, of course, to announce an inflation target. But since the inflation rate is not under the direct control of the authorities, an inflation target not linked to specific policy commitments that can be readily monitored will not be credible to private agents. Establishing the credibility of macroeconomic policies at the outset of a disinflation program is therefore crucial. By altering the formation of price expectations, a credible disinflation policy may substantially reduce the short- and medium-term output and employment costs of restrictive monetary and fiscal policies. For instance, a credible freeze of the exchange rate may reduce anticipations of future inflation, lower nominal interest rates, and consequently dampen the recessionary effect of a restrictive monetary policy. Establishing a reputation for responsible policymaking is particularly important in countries where failed stabilization attempts have created deep-rooted skepticism and a lack of confidence in the willingness or capacity of policymakers to reduce inflation.

The recent literature in macroeconomics has considered a variety of mechanisms aimed at establishing or enhancing policy credibility and the reputation of policymakers. A key feature of the literature is that private agents interact strategically with policymakers and determine their behavior on the basis of their expectations about the likely course of current and future policies (Cukierman, 1992). The purpose of this section is to examine the implications of this literature for the formulation and design of disinflation programs in developing countries. The first part presents an overview of alternative sources of credibility problems. The second part examines alternative mechanisms aimed at alleviating such problems in stabilization programs, including the adoption of a shock therapy approach for signaling purposes, the use of price controls as an additional nominal anchor, increased central bank independence or adherence to a monetary union, and recourse to conditional foreign assistance. The concluding part summarizes the main policy implications of the analysis and provides some final remarks.

10.2.1 Sources of Credibility Problems

A central notion that pervades the recent literature on macroeconomic policy credibility is that when the public lacks confidence in the ability of policymakers to carry out a newly announced stabilization program, disinflation becomes more difficult to achieve. However, "lack of confidence" and "imperfect credibility" have been defined in a variety of ways in the existing literature, depending in part on the issue under consideration. In the context of disinflation programs, the first important aspect of the credibility problem relates to the program itself, specifically, to the policy measures around which it is formulated and the degree to which they are consistent and sustainable. Other relevant aspects, which relate to policymakers' interactions with private agents, emerge as a result of various assumptions concerning the behavior and "characteristics" of those implementing an otherwise consistent program (such as the structure of policy preferences and the reputation of the policymakers themselves), the information structure, and the policy environment.

Internal Inconsistency

First, a credibility problem may emerge when the public perceives that a stabilization program is inconsistent with other policies being pursued simultaneously. A disinflation program that does not include measures to limit the public sector budget deficit will typically lack credibility because private agents will understand its inconsistent nature. The Brazilian Cruzado Plan implemented in 1986, for instance, lost credibility rapidly because private agents quickly realized the inflationary implications of the expansionary fiscal stance the authorities adopted at the outset (see Chapter 8 and Agénor and Taylor, 1993). In addition, inconsistencies in the *overall* formulation of an economic reform program or an inappropriate sequencing of policy measures may hurt the credibility of the stabilization effort, even if the components of the reform program are internally consistent.

Time Inconsistency

Second, the lack of credibility may result from a time inconsistency dilemma faced by policymakers: their optimal ex post strategy may differ from their ex ante strategy. For instance, once nominal wages are set by the private sector, the authorities may find it tempting to disinflate less than they had promised to, in order to generate output gains (Barro and Gordon, 1983). This result obtains because the policymaker is concerned about both inflation and unemployment, and faces an expectations-augmented Phillips curve. The policymaker wants all agents to expect low inflation, in order to exploit a favorable trade-off between inflation and unemployment. But an announcement of a policy of low inflation is not credible. Once expectations are formed, the policymaker has an incentive to renege on the announcement in order to reduce unemployment. Private agents understand the incentive to renege and therefore do not believe the policy announcement in the first place.

A similar time inconsistency problem emerges in a small open economy opting for a fixed-exchange-rate arrangement, as discussed in Chapter 6. By fixing the exchange rate, and therefore the domestic price of tradable goods, the policymaker's aim is to reduce inflationary expectations embodied in prices set in the nontradable sector of the economy. However, price and wage setters understand the policymaker's incentive to deviate from the fixed-exchange-rate announcement and to devalue the currency in order to depreciate the real exchange rate and stimulate output, and therefore will not fully believe the initial announcement.

The policymaker's incentive to inflate need not be based on employment considerations, as in the Barro-Gordon model. It may also arise as a result of the policymaker's desire to reduce the real value of the nominal public debt, or because of seignorage considerations. A simple model that stresses the role of inflation in financing government deficits was developed by Barro (1983).[28] Suppose that the government's objective function takes the form

$$L_t = \Theta S_t - \Phi(\pi_t, \pi_t^a) = \Theta \mu_t m(\pi_t^a) - \exp(\kappa_1 \pi_t + \kappa_2 \pi_t^a), \qquad (24)$$

where all coefficients are defined as positive. μ_t denotes the rate of growth of the nominal money stock, π_t the actual rate of inflation, π_t^a the expected rate of inflation, and $S_t = \mu_t m(\pi_t^a)$ revenue from money creation—that is, seignorage (see Chapter 4), where $m()$ represents money demand. The first term in the loss function (24) represents the benefit the government derives from inflation, which is assumed to be proportional to revenue from money creation. The second term captures two different kinds of costs associated with inflation. The term in π_t reflects menu costs (that is, costs associated with changes in nominal prices) or costs associated with collection lags, resulting from the Olivera-Tanzi effect discussed in Chapter 4. The term in π_t^a reflects the usual distortionary costs of perfectly anticipated inflation.

The demand for real money balances is of the Cagan type and is given by

$$m(\pi_t^a) = \exp(-\alpha \pi_t^a). \qquad (25)$$

Once expectations are set, $m(\pi_t^a)$ is given and the money market equilibrium condition implies that $\pi_t = \mu_t$. The government's problem, then, is to maximize (24) subject to (25) with respect to μ_t.

We now consider two regimes: discretion and rules. Under discretion, the government is unable to convince private agents that it will follow a precise course of action in the future. Since it cannot make a binding commitment, it minimizes Equation (24) subject to (25) with π_t^a given. The solution implied by this behavior is therefore given by

$$\Theta \exp(-\alpha \pi_t^a) - \kappa_1 \exp(\kappa_1 \pi_t + \kappa_2 \pi_t^a) = 0.$$

In equilibrium, $\mu_t = \pi_t = \pi_t^a$, so that the solution is

$$\mu_t^D = \pi_t^D = (\alpha + \kappa_1 + \kappa_2)^{-1} \ln(\Theta/\kappa_1) > 0. \tag{26}$$

The rates of inflation and monetary growth can therefore be higher than the seignorage-maximizing rate $1/\alpha$ derived in Chapter 4, if Θ/κ_1 is large enough.

In the "rules" regime, the government can make a binding—and therefore credible—commitment about its future behavior. It will therefore internalize the effect of its current decisions on future price expectations formed by private agents in choosing its optimal policy. Imposing the equilibrium condition $\pi_t = \pi_t^a$ in the loss function (24), the government's decision problem becomes

$$\max_{\mu_t} L_t = \Theta \mu_t m(\mu_t) - \Phi(\mu_t, \mu_t) \tag{24'}$$

subject to (25). The solution yields, using the approximation $\ln(1 - \alpha\mu_t) \cong -\alpha\mu_t$ for $\alpha\mu_t$ small enough,

$$\mu_t^R = \pi_t^R = (2\alpha + \kappa_1 + \kappa_2)^{-1} \ln[\Theta/(\kappa_1 + \kappa_2)], \tag{27}$$

which can be less than the revenue-maximizing rate $1/\alpha$. It is apparent from Equations (26) and (27) that $\mu_t^D > \mu_t^R$, or that the inflation rate and the rate of monetary expansion are higher under discretion than under rules.[29] The reason is that, under rules, the government internalizes the consequences of its actions on the formation of private agents' expectations. By making a credible commitment to forsaking discretionary actions, the policymaker is able to dampen inflationary expectations and hence achieve a lower inflation rate.

The general implication of models that highlight the time inconsistency dilemma is, therefore, that when policymakers have an ex post incentive to renege on their promises, rational agents will discount announcements of future policy actions or assurances regarding the continuation of present policies. Accordingly, inflation will be difficult to reduce and will instead tend to display persistence over time.

Asymmetric Information

A third source of credibility problems is incomplete or asymmetric information about policymakers themselves: private agents may not be able to assess how serious the incumbents really are about fighting inflation (Barro, 1986). At the outset of a stabilization program, private agents do not entirely believe the authorities' commitment to disinflate, and need time to verify the new policy stance and assess the "true" intentions of policymakers.

Imperfect information of this sort may be particularly prevalent in some developing countries, where policymakers tend to change rapidly, generating confusion about policy objectives and the preferences of the incumbents. Imperfect monitoring abilities prevent private agents from detecting those preferences—unless the policymakers go public. If policymakers have the incentive to do so, they can exploit this informational advantage. The implication is, however, that imperfect monitoring capability reduces the scope for building reputation by policymakers, particularly if private agents learn only gradually, through a backward-induction process (see, for instance, Cukierman, 1992). Without a reputation for being "serious" or "tough," policymakers may find it difficult to dampen inflationary expectations.

Policy Uncertainty and Stochastic Shocks

A fourth source of credibility problems in disinflation programs is the uncertainty surrounding the policy environment and the predictability of policy measures. In a stochastic world, even if a program is coherently formulated and time-consistent—in the sense that policymakers have no incentive to depart ex post from the preannounced policy measures—exogenous shocks large enough to throw the program "off track" may occur (Dornbusch, 1991; Orphanides, 1992a). Under such circumstances, reputable policymakers may not be able to dampen price expectations and bring credibility to a stabilization program, because of the high probability that large shocks will force them to deviate from their targets. Such shocks may be external in nature (such as sharp changes in a country's terms of trade or world interest rates) but may also result from the policy environment itself, especially when the authorities have imperfect control over policy instruments. For instance, the announcement of a fiscal target will not be fully credible if the government does not adequately control the level of government expenditure, if tax revenues are subject to considerable variability, induced by either deterministic or stochastic factors (such as seasonal patterns or abrupt weather changes). Private agents will understand the implications of this lack of control over policy instruments and will accordingly assess the probability that the policy target will not be met.[30] The lower the degree of precision in the manipulation of policy instruments, the more likely it is that private agents will anticipate the possibility of a future collapse of the stabilization effort, and the more rigid downward the inflation rate will usually be. Thus, the lack of policy predictability may create doubts about the sustainability of the reform process and affect the degree of credibility of an otherwise consistent and viable program.

Political Uncertainty

Finally, a credibility problem may emerge when the public perceives that policymakers will be unable to implement their program because its political base may crumble, as may occur when the government is built on a coalition of parties with different ideological orientations or when the government's legitimacy is in doubt. Although private agents may believe in the government's economic objectives and policy intentions, they will also evaluate the political feasibility of potentially painful macroeconomic reforms. The less cohesive political forces are, or the greater the strength of vested interests, the more severe the credibility problem. Moreover, lack of political consensus will often lead agents to expect policy reversals. This uncertainty about future policies, in turn, has drastic implications for the long-term effects of stabilization plans. Strategies believed to be sustainable are likely to elicit both economic and political responses that will reinforce the reform process, while strategies believed to be reversible will have the opposite effect.

In practice, it has proved difficult to provide evidence, even retroactively, regarding the particular type of credibility problem a given program or policymaker faces. Most researchers have worked under the general premise that a credible disinflation program will translate into a change in the process driving a key variable (prices, money demand, nominal wages, or interest rates, for instance), while a program that lacks credibility will often have no discernible effect.[31] Although there has been some substantial methodological progress recently,[32] the paucity of robust quantitative techniques creates serious problems in gauging the practical importance of alternative sources of credibility problems and makes it difficult to devise appropriate policy responses or undertake corrective measures. These practical difficulties, however, make it all the more important to strengthen the design of disinflation programs.

10.2.2 Enhancing the Credibility of Disinflation Programs

A variety of proposals have been made for enhancing credibility in the context of disinflation programs. One line of inquiry has focused on ways to increase the credibility (or, in this case, the consistency) of the reform program itself by devising appropriate contingency clauses. The second and broader line has focused on ways to increase the reputation of the policymakers implementing the program. This subsection deals primarily with the second line of investigation, discussing the conceptual basis of some of these proposals and evaluating their practical policy implications. First, the appropriateness of a shock therapy approach to stabilization as a way to signal the policymakers' "type" to the public and build their reputation is examined. The role of price controls as an additional nominal anchor is then discusssed. Third, institutional reforms, such as an increase in the degree of autonomy of the central bank or adhesion to a monetary union, are evaluated. Finally, the role of external agencies and conditional foreign assistance in alleviating the lack of credibility is examined.[33]

10.2.2.1 SIGNALING AND SUSTAINABILITY

It is often argued that policymakers must make a sharp break with the past to demonstrate their commitment to price stabilization (Rodrik, 1989). This means that the authorities not only must refrain from accommodating inflation at the outset in order to sustain the stabilization effort (and eventually to succeed in controlling inflation), but that they may have to take more drastic measures than they would otherwise choose. Such a course of action may be all the more necessary when a series of unsuccessful attempts has rendered the public highly skeptical about the policymakers' ability and commitment to disinflate, or when the private sector has no yardstick for evaluating policymakers' actions. In such cases, "biting the bullet" by accepting a recession can be perceived by the private sector as a test of the authorities' determination to maintain low inflation (Vickers, 1986). In an economy where inflation is fueled by monetary financing of excessive government spending, an overadjustment in the fiscal sector can also provide an important signal about the authorities' commitment to keep the budget deficit under control. Mexico's drastic fiscal adjustment, from an operational deficit equivalent to 4.5 percent of GDP in 1988 to surpluses of 2.6 percent in 1990 and 3.3 percent in 1992, is widely regarded as an essential element in conveying credibility to the stabilization program initiated at the end of 1987.[34]

However, using overly restrictive monetary and fiscal policies in an attempt to convey signals about the preferences of policymakers to the public may exacerbate the credibility problem, instead of helping to alleviate it. First, excessively harsh policy measures may create expectations that such decisions are not sustainable and will eventually be reversed. As discussed in more detail below, overadjustment (excessive cuts in public spending, for instance) may increase unemployment and undermine political support for painful reforms. Second, if uncertainty about incumbent policymakers relates to their ability to commit themselves to preannounced policies (and not to the authorities' relative concern for output expansion), the optimal behavior may be to partially accommodate inflationary expectations rather than adopt an overly restrictive monetary policy stance (Cukierman and Liviatan, 1991). In effect, when there is a perceived probability that the incumbent government may deviate from its preannounced policy stance, inflationary expectations are subject to an upward bias; since policymakers (whether viewed as "weak" or "strong") dislike recessions, it is optimal for the incumbents to partially accommodate these expectations.[35] Similarly, even in the absence of uncertainty about policymakers themselves, the existence of labor contracts with backward-looking wage indexing clauses may lead to partial accommodation (De Gregorio, 1995). More generally, the signaling argument for a "big bang" approach to stabilization rests on the assumption that the behavior of policymakers depends primarily on their policy preferences, that is, the weight they attach to price stability relative to output. In practice, however, policy decisions are also affected by the state of the economy, which depends in turn on the overall policy stance. To the extent that the output loss associated with a shock therapy approach has an adverse effect on the reelection prospects of the incumbent policymakers, it may weaken credibility by raising the expectation that actual policies will be eventually relaxed (Blanchard, 1985). Even a "tough" policymaker cannot ignore the cost associated with high unemployment, particularly when policies have persistent effects (Drazen and Masson, 1994).

In an environment where reforms create severe short-term costs for large segments of the population, there are temptations to reverse—or at least deviate from—the initial program objectives, particularly when incumbents cannot easily precommit future governments to a specific path of adjustment. Even if price stabilization is in the country's long-run interest, short-sightedness (such as the exclusive concern of the incumbents with their reelection prospects) may induce policymakers to alter or abandon their initial reform program. Moreover, in the context of stabilization plans where fiscal deficits are the root cause of inflation, signaling options may be more limited than is often thought. In such cases, structural fiscal reforms (such as broadening the tax system, privatizing public enterprises, or altering the distribution of public sector wages and salaries to enhance control of government spending) are often called for to make attempts at controlling the fiscal deficit credible. But such reforms cannot be implemented overnight, and can only slowly enhance credibility.

It is the *persistence* over time that matters in establishing the reputation of policymakers, rather than the degree of restrictiveness of the policy measures implemented at the outset of a stabilization program. Macroeconomic adjustment measures that are not regarded as politically and economically sustainable (within the limits imposed by a democratic regime) cannot be credible and may lead to self-fulfilling failure (Buffie, 1994). A critical element in ensuring sustainability is the proper sequencing of stabilization measures in the context of the overall reform effort in an attempt to minimize the distortions that often accompany such programs. For instance, in some cases microeconomic adjustment and institutional changes may need to precede macroeconomic policy reforms to ensure that the overall reform strategy is consistent and to convey credibility to the stabilization package. The proper sequencing of policy actions in the structural and macroeconomic spheres may prove crucial in convincing private agents that stabilization will eventually be achieved. To some extent, ensuring the irreversibility of macroeconomic reforms ensures their sustainability. Sequencing adjustment measures in such a way to make it costly for future policymakers to reverse decisions already undertaken by a reform-minded government enhances the credibility of a disinflation progam.

10.2.2.2 PRICE CONTROLS

The discussion in Chapter 8 indicated that price controls have been used repeatedly (in fact, since the early 1960s) in disinflation programs implemented in developing countries, despite their well-known microeconomic costs.[36] A typical argument provided by policymakers—or their advisors—for the use of price ceilings is the notion that the persistence of inflation results from the existence of lagged wage indexation and backward-looking expectations. The presence of inertial factors means that attempts to combat inflation exclusively through restrictive monetary and fiscal policies will lead to strong recessive effects, which make it impossible for such policies to be continued beyond the short term. More recent theoretical arguments, however, justify the temporary use of price controls as a "transition" mechanism to a low-inflation equilibrium (Bruno and Fischer, 1990), as a coordination device (Dornbusch and Simonsen, 1988), as a way to secure political gains and generate political support (Jonung, 1990), and—most in line with our interest here—as a way to enhance credibility.[37]

The use of price controls (in addition to the money supply or the exchange rate) as a nominal anchor for enhancing credibility has been emphasized by Blejer and Liviatan (1987) and Persson and van Wijnbergen (1993). In Blejer and Liviatan's analysis, the lack of credibility stems from the severe asymmetry of the information available to the public and that held by policymakers. At the outset of a stabilization program, private agents do not entirely believe the authorities' commitment to disinflate, and need time to verify the new policy stance. A price freeze gives policymakers a period during which they can convince the public—by adopting, and sticking to, restrictive monetary and fiscal policies—of the seriousness of their policy targets.[38] Persson and van Wijnbergen provide a game-theoretic analysis of the mechanisms that enable controls to assist in establishing credibility, building on the signaling model developed by Vickers (1986). In their framework, policymakers must signal their willingness to accept a recession in order to gain credibility that they will not resort to inflationary measures or give in to pressure to reverse their policy stance. The temporary use of price and wage controls (in addition to a restrictive monetary policy) allows policymakers to reduce the cost of signaling their commitment to disinflate.

The most frequently cited example of a successful application of price controls is the Israeli stabilization of 1985, during which all nominal variables (including the exchange rate) were frozen (see Chapter 8). In addition to a sharp fiscal contraction (including a cut in subsidies) and an up-front devaluation, the government announced not only a credit freeze but also its intention to maintain the exchange rate fixed, with the understanding that the unions would temporarily suspend COLA clauses and freeze wages for a few months. Agreement on the latter was, in turn, made conditional on the introduction of price ceilings. The tripartite agreement between the government, employers, and trade unions formed the basis for a sharp reduction in inflation. The short-run gains, in terms of a quick reduction in inflation and enhanced government credibility, resulting from the successful application of price controls outweighed the distortions created by the price ceilings.[39]

In addition to the many practical problems associated with the imposition and removal of price controls (such as the enforcement mechanism and the length of the flexibilization stage), the debate on whether price controls improve credibility is far from settled. In the Blejer-Liviatan (1987) framework, for instance, the use of price and wage controls can be counterproductive, since a freeze does not enable the public to learn whether sufficient fiscal restraint has been achieved, that is, whether inflation has really been stopped or has only been temporarily repressed. In fact, controls may lengthen the time required for expectations to adjust to a new equilibrium. In addition, the credibility-enhancing effect of price controls may vanish if policymakers are unwilling or unable to control all prices in the economy, and if forward-looking price setters in the "free," uncontrolled sector understand the incentives to depart from a preannounced price control policy in an attempt to reduce the macroeconomic costs associated with a price freeze (Agénor, 1995a). Paradoxically, the imposition of price controls in such a framework may lead to inflation inertia.

To illustrate this result, consider an economy that produces a large number of homogeneous goods, a proportion of which (such as goods produced by public enterprises) are subject to direct price controls by the policymaker. As discussed in Helpman (1988) and van Wijnbergen (1988), the economy possesses noncompetitive markets and price-setting firms in the "free" sector. The policymaker, who faces an incentive to reduce inflation through the imposition of direct price controls, has an informational advantage over the private sector—due, for instance, to a better monitoring capacity—and sets controlled prices *after* the realization of shocks to the economy. A reduction in the rate of inflation is assumed to increase political support while the deadweight loss from excess demand—resulting from misallocation and resources devoted to nonprice rationing—reduces support, since aggregate real income is reduced. Price ceilings are chosen so as to maximize political support from holding prices down, against the opposition resulting from this deadweight loss. When prices are set below equilibrium, there are incentives for sellers to evade controls, so the policymaker must enforce the ceilings—at a nonprohibitive cost—to make them effective. Firms in the uncontrolled or free sector restrain price increases, beyond the expected increase in controlled prices, to avoid more stringent controls in the future.

Let $p_c(t)$ denote the logarithm of an index of the subset of prices set by the policymaker in period t, and let $\tilde{p}_c(t) \geq p_c(t)$ be the market-clearing equilibrium price, that is, the price that would obtain in the absence of price controls. The deadweight loss D_t due to price ceilings—the loss of (Marshallian) consumer and producer surpluses when excess demand and nonprice rationing result in a misallocation or waste of resources—can be approximated by

$$D_t = \eta[p_c(t) - \tilde{p}_c(t)]^2, \quad \eta > 0, \tag{28}$$

which assumes that the deadweight loss is greater the larger the (squared) deviation between actual and equilibrium prices.[40] The market-clearing equilibrium price is assumed to be determined by

$$\tilde{\pi}_c(t) = \tilde{\pi}_c + v_t, \tag{29}$$

where $\tilde{\pi}_c(t) \equiv \tilde{p}_c(t) - p_c(t-1)$ and v_t denotes a stochastic demand shock, which is assumed to be serially uncorrelated with zero mean and constant variance. The probability distribution from which v_t is drawn is assumed to be common knowledge.

Price setters in the "free" sector set prices $p_n(t)$ so as to protect their relative position and without knowing the realized value of v_t, so that

$$\pi_n(t) \equiv p_n(t) - p_n(t-1) = E_{t-1}\tilde{\pi}_c(t), \tag{30}$$

where $E_{t-1}x_t$ denotes the conditional expectation of x_t based on information available up to the end of time $t - 1$.[41]

Setting $\pi_t \equiv p_t - p_{t-1}$, the rate of change of the domestic price level can be defined by

$$\pi_t = \delta\pi_c(t) + (1 - \delta)\pi_n(t), \quad 0 \leq \delta \leq 1, \tag{31}$$

where δ (assumed given for the moment) denotes the intensity of price controls, that is, the proportion of goods on which the authorities impose price controls.

Whereas agents in the flexible-price sector set prices without knowing the realized value of the demand shock, the policymaker sets controlled prices *after* observing the shock. The policymaker is assumed to use controlled prices to offset some of the effect of v_t on the deadweight loss—for instance, by unexpectedly raising these prices when v_t turns out to be positive.

The policymaker's preferences entail a trade-off between inflation and the deadweight loss resulting from excess demand and price controls. Specifically, the policymaker aims at minimizing the expected loss function

$$L_t = E_t(D_t + \Theta \pi_t^2), \qquad \Theta > 0,$$

or, using (28) and (29),

$$L_t = E_t[\eta(\pi_c(t) - \tilde{\pi}_c - v_t)^2 + \Theta \pi_t^2]. \tag{32}$$

Under discretion, the policymaker chooses a rate of increase of controlled prices such that the difference between political support resulting from a reduction in the inflation rate and political opposition resulting from the deadweight loss is maximized. Formally, $\pi_c(t)$ is chosen in each period so as to minimize (32) subject to (31), without regard to the announced policies, and with private sector expectations taken as given. In the discretionary regime, the rate of change of controlled prices is therefore given by

$$\pi_c(t) = \frac{\eta}{\eta + \delta^2 \Theta} \left\{ \tilde{\pi}_c + v_t - \frac{\delta \Theta (1 - \delta)}{\eta} \tilde{\pi}_n(t) \right\}. \tag{33}$$

Equation (33) indicates that, under discretion, the reaction function of the policymaker calls for setting controlled prices at a level below the equilibrium level—leading to a deadweight loss. The reason for this is, of course, the inflationary cost of an increase in controlled prices. The degree of accommodation of demand shocks is inversely related to the relative inflation-aversion coefficient Θ/η. Also, the higher the (predetermined) level of prices in the free sector, the lower the rate of change of controlled prices.

Consider now the case (referred to as the "commitment" regime in what follows) in which the policymaker adopts a price-setting rule that takes the form[42]

$$\pi_c(t) = \Phi_0 \tilde{\pi}_c + \Phi_1 v_t. \tag{34}$$

The authorities select values of Φ_0 and Φ_1 that minimize the unconditional expectation (32) subject to (34) and, from Equations (30) and (34), $\pi_n(t) = E_{t-1}\pi_c(t) = \Phi_0 \tilde{\pi}_c$. The optimal values can be shown to be[43]

$$\Phi_0 = \eta/(\eta + \Theta), \qquad \Phi_1 = \eta/(\eta + \delta^2 \Theta), \tag{35}$$

where $0 < \Phi_0$ and $\Phi_1 < 1$. A comparison of Equations (33) and (35) shows that under rule (34) the policymaker accommodates demand shocks to the same extent as under discretion, but systematic changes in the equilibrium price are accommodated to a lesser extent. This is because, under commitment, the policymaker can infer the endogenous response of price setters in the free sector through price expectations.

The (ex post) mean value of the inflation rate in the commitment regime is given by

$$E_t \pi_t = \Phi_0 \tilde{\pi}_c + \Phi_1 \delta v_t,$$

and the (unconditional) expected loss is

$$L^C = [\eta(\Phi_1 - 1)^2 + \Theta(\delta \Phi_1)^2]\sigma_v^2 + [\eta(\Phi_0 - 1)^2 + \Theta \Phi_0^2]\tilde{\pi}_c^2, \qquad (36)$$

where σ_v^2 denotes the variance of v_t.

Under discretion, controlled prices are set by (33). Under rational expectations, the optimal solution is such that

$$\pi_n(t) = \kappa \tilde{\pi}_c, \quad 0 < \kappa < 1, \qquad (37a)$$

$$\pi_c(t) = \kappa \tilde{\pi}_c + \lambda v_t, \quad 0 < \lambda < 1, \qquad (37b)$$

where $\lambda \equiv \eta/(\eta + \delta^2 \Theta) = \Phi_1$ and $\kappa = \eta/(\eta + \delta \Theta)$.[44] Under both discretion and commitment, a complete price freeze ($\pi_c(t) \equiv 0$) is optimal when the weight on inflation in the policymaker's loss function is very high, that is, $\Theta \to \infty$.

The (ex post) mean value of the inflation rate under discretion is given by

$$E_t \pi_t = \kappa \tilde{\pi}_c + \lambda \delta v_t,$$

with an (unconditional) expected loss given by

$$L^D = [\eta(\lambda - 1)^2 + \Theta(\lambda \delta)^2]\sigma_v^2 + [\eta(\kappa - 1)^2 + \Theta \kappa^2]\tilde{\pi}_c^2. \qquad (38)$$

A comparison of Equations (38) and (36) shows that, since $\kappa > \Phi_0$, $L^D > L^C$. The nature of this result can be explained as follows. Unless there is a binding arrangement forcing the policymaker to adjust prices so as to maintain equality between supply and demand, there exists a temptation to lower controlled prices below their equilibrium level in order to dampen inflationary expectations and reduce overall inflation. However, once the demand shock is realized, expectations are formed, and prices are set in the rest of the economy, the policymaker has an incentive to raise controlled prices and reduce the deadweight loss—or political cost—associated with the ceilings. Private agents understand this incentive and will expect the authorities to follow the discretionary regime, no matter what regime is announced. As a result, in equilibrium prices in the uncontrolled sector are set at a higher level than they would be if the commitment regime was fully credible—at $\kappa \tilde{\pi}_c$ instead of $\Phi_0 \tilde{\pi}_c$ (Equation (37a)). Inflation is therefore higher under imperfect credibility and entails an additional policy loss.[45]

The above result helps explain why, as shown in Figure 8.1 for Brazil, inflation may remain positive under a partial freeze. The conventional explanation of this phenemonon follows the lines of Paus (1991), who considers Peru's experience during the Emergency Plan implemented in 1985–86. In her view, the attempt to slow down inflation by holding back adjustments in government-determined prices led to a growing deficit of the nonfinancial public sector. The increase in the deficit had an expansionary effect on money supply, which maintained inflationary pressures. The rationale proposed here, by contrast, does not rely on the existence of an accommodative monetary stance. Price setters in the "free" sector understand the incentive that the policymaker has to raise controlled prices after private sector pricing decisions are taken—the reduction in the deadweight loss that ceilings entail. Therefore, they raise prices by more than they would have had they been convinced of the policymaker's commitment to the preannounced price rule. Consequently, the extent of "inflation inertia" results from the lack of credibility of price ceilings, and is in general inversely related to the proportion of prices subject to control.[46,47]

If the policymaker could make a binding commitment to a price-setting rule in the controlled sector, inflation would be lower under a partial freeze. However, unilateral commitments usually lack credibility. Along the lines of our discussion in Chapter 6 on exchange-rate policy, mechanisms that entail reputational forces (and "punishment" strategies) may provide a commitment technology that could alleviate the time inconsistency problem discussed above, and may provide a substitute for a binding agreement.

In practice, price controls have often been used as a substitute for, rather than a complement to, monetary and fiscal adjustment, as in the populist programs described in Chapter 8. While price controls have often been effective in bringing down inflation quickly in the short run, in many cases the initial success has proved difficult to sustain, due to a lack of persistence in macroeconomic policy reforms. Private agents have quickly realized that attempts to legislate prices down would not be very effective, and this has often led to a rapid resurgence of inflation. The evidence reviewed in Chapter 8 suggests that in Argentina, Brazil, and Peru, experiments with stabilization packages involving wage and price controls during the 1980s failed largely because of the policymakers' inability to sustain the fiscal and monetary discipline required to make the short-run drop in inflation sustainable. Under Alan García in Peru, wage and price controls were used as substitutes for, rather than complements to, more orthodox measures. Real wages were allowed to rise substantially, and there was little success in bringing public spending under control. When pressure on prices ultimately forced the relaxation of controls, a new spiral of inflation began. Brazil provides a similar example. As documented in Chapter 8, the authorities implemented in the late 1980s three anti-inflation programs that relied to an important extent on price controls: the Cruzado Plan in 1986, the Bresser Plan in 1987, and the Verano Plan in 1989. However, because the price freeze was not accompanied by adequate macroeconomic policy reforms, the rate of inflation jumped after a brief period of reduced inflation (see Figure 8.1). After the collapse of the Bresser and Verano plans, inflation came back with a vengeance, leading many observers to conclude that the repeated use of price controls had diminished their effectiveness, as economic agents were able to anticipate the price increases that would follow the flexibilization stage.

10.2.2.3 CENTRAL BANK INDEPENDENCE

A possible way for policymakers facing credibility problems to demonstrate their capacity for and unequivocal commitment to reform is to appoint a "conservative" central banker with a well-known dislike for inflation, and whose day-to-day control over monetary policy is relatively free from political pressure or interference from key ministers in the incumbent government (Rogoff, 1985). An independent central bank with a clear and well-publicized mandate to maintain price stability provides an institutional mechanism that may reduce incentives to deviate from rules.

A similar idea, discussed in Chapter 6, is for a high-inflation country to join a monetary union with a fixed-exchange-rate mechanism and surrender the power to conduct an independent monetary policy. By transferring its monetary and exchange-rate policy autonomy to a reputable central bank, a high-inflation country can "borrow" credibility and thus signal its own commitment to price stability, thereby reducing—relative to a purely domestic strategy—the cost of disinflation measured in terms of output and employment losses. In the context of developing countries, where central bank financing of fiscal deficits is often the root cause of inflation, this argument carries considerable weight.[48] Appointment of an independent central banker may remove the temptation to rely on monetary expansion to secure a short-term output gain, reduce the incentive to rely on the inflation tax, and "force" the government to implement fiscal reform. In addition, the political difficulties associated with stabilization programs may be less severe when the policymaking decision process is relatively centralized and insulated from pressures from various interest groups. This argument helps to emphasize the importance of institutional reforms in enhancing the credibility of macroeconomic adjustment programs.

Several recent empirical studies have shown that central bank independence contributes significantly to explaining cross-country variations in the rate of inflation. Countries with central banks enjoying the highest degree of autonomy seem to have the lowest levels and variability of inflation.[49] Institutional reforms aimed at enhancing central bank autonomy have been implemented in a number of countries in the past few years. The 1989 reform in Chile, for instance, grants a large degree of legal independence to the central bank. Legislation granting autonomy to the central bank was enacted in Venezuela in late 1993, and in Pakistan in early 1994. On April 1, 1994, the Central Bank of Mexico became independent.

However, the extent to which policymakers should "tie their hands" by appointing a reputable anti-inflation central banker (or policymaker) to convince the public of their commitment to carrying out a domestic disinflation program remains a subject of controversy. Central bank independence is only one of several institutional devices that can be implemented to ensure price stability and enhance the credibility of macroeconomic policy. Although replacing discretionary actions with a rule-based policy framework implemented by an independent (domestic or foreign) central bank may help reduce the perception of arbitrariness and thereby strengthen confidence in the policymaking process, the signaling effect of such a change in the policy regime may be weak if secrecy prevails in the institution's day-to-day operations. More important, adhering to the rigid rules implemented by a domestic or foreign central bank may lead to suboptimal outcomes (compared with contingent rules) in an economy subject to random shocks. Escape clauses for discretionary actions may be necessary, although extreme care must be taken in defining the conditions under which such clauses should be triggered, in order to avoid negative side effects.[50] Finally, as emphasized by Swinburn and Castello-Branco (1991), central bank independence cannot, by itself, guarantee the credibility of monetary policy. This depends on the overall stance of macroeconomic policy. For instance, if the fiscal policy adopted by the ministry of finance is viewed as inconsistent with the monetary institution's disinflation target, credibility is impossible to achieve, even with an independent central bank.

10.2.2.4 EXTERNAL ENFORCEMENT AND FOREIGN ASSISTANCE

Requests for foreign assistance have traditionally been viewed as the result of a need to generate financial resources and, to a lesser extent, of the existence of cross-conditionality clauses in some bilateral agreements. It has been recognized more recently that credibility problems may also be an important element in explaining why countries engaged in stabilization programs may seek the involvement of foreign institutions and subject themselves to external enforcement. By making foreign assistance conditional on specific policy targets, policymakers may be able to enhance their reputation. An external agent with a reputation for being "tough" can provide a commitment mechanism for enforcing programs, increase private agents' confidence in the intentions of the authorities, and—by increasing, through the threat of sanctions, the cost of deviating from a prespecified inflation target—help reduce inflation (Cukierman and Liviatan, 1992). In a sense, this argument simply extends the conservative banker approach discussed above, and is therefore related to the signaling argument underlying the shock therapy approach to macroeconomic reforms. The difference here is that conditionality wields a threat—no support for restructuring the country's external debt, for instance—that can strengthen the determination of the policymakers to enforce the agreement.[51] An external agency can sustain an effective threat beyond the probable life of a single government, and can also enforce a worse outcome compared with an appointed central banker if the agreement collapses.

Dornbusch and Fischer (1986) have emphasized that, in the pre–World War II stabilization episodes, foreign loans—or the prospect of receiving them—served more as a signal than as an inherent necessity. Typical examples are the loan by the League of Nations to Austria in 1922 and the Polish loan of 1927. Recent formal evidence supports the existence of a credibility factor in explaining why governments relied on foreign enforcement during the stabilization programs implemented in European countries in the 1920s (Santaella, 1993). Regarding recent stabilization episodes, it has been argued that one of the factors that helped to establish quickly the credibility of the 1985 Israeli program was the increase in U.S. foreign aid, which raised the public's confidence in the program in general and, in particular, in the government's ability to peg the exchange rate and successfully withstand possible speculative attacks against the Israeli currency (Cukierman, 1988; Patinkin, 1993).

However, a variety of potential difficulties arise in judging the credibility-enhancing effect of foreign assistance. First, political considerations are often perceived (rightly or wrongly) as playing a critical role in deciding whether particular countries should receive external financial support. As a result, the enforcement mechanism that foreign assistance provides may be insufficient to help domestic private agents assess the policymakers' "type," that is, whether policymakers are genuinely concerned about meeting their disinflation target. Second, by relaxing the economywide budget constraint, such assistance may lead the government to expand its redistributive role, which can exacerbate distortions and endogenously weaken the program (Rodrik, 1989). Third, if the degree of conditionality attached to foreign aid is too tight, uncertainty about external support may rise, leading to delays in stabilization and increasing the likelihood that the program will collapse (Orphanides, 1992b). This scenario may occur, in particular, if foreign capital plays an important role in determining the level of domestic economic activity. To the extent that the conditions attached to foreign assistance appear excessively stringent, inflationary expectations will remain high, depressing aggregate demand and increasing unemployment. In turn, the rise in unemployment may weaken political support and affect the viability of the disinflation effort.

10.2.2.5 SEQUENCING AND POLITICAL SUPPORT

The design and subsequent implementation of a disinflation program require policymakers to make some decisions regarding the distribution of income. In the absence of a broad political consensus in support of the program, such decisions are difficult to make, and the stabilization plan will accordingly be more difficult to implement. For a program to be viable, the size and composition of distributional effects of the macroeconomic reforms must be politically acceptable. The credibility of stabilization programs depends heavily on the degree of political cohesion in the country and the legitimacy and popular support enjoyed by the government.

Political factors play a crucial role in both the shock therapy and gradual approaches to stabilization discussed earlier, in the context of signaling arguments aimed at enhancing credibility. The political trade-off can be summarized in the following terms. On the one hand, drastic measures may help generate credibility in the reform process quickly, particularly when they are implemented during a new administration's "honeymoon" with the public, during which the population is perhaps more willing to accept the costs associated with painful measures. In addition, the initial benefits of sharp adjustment may outweigh the costs that would be associated with the persistence of inflation at a higher level, as well as other social and economic costs that would result from the policy shock. On the other hand, overly costly policy decisions, from a social and economic point of view, run the risk of causing the political consensus to collapse and may lead to a policy reversal at a later stage.

A gradualist strategy may also lack credibility for precisely the same reason that a shock therapy approach may not be credible: future governments may be tempted to adopt discretionary policy reversals. However, the costs in terms of output and employment may be lower with a credible gradual approach than with a shock therapy approach, allowing policymakers to maintain the social and political consensus necessary to sustain the reforms.[52] From the perspective of credibility, circumstances under which a shock therapy approach to stabilization is preferable to a more gradual strategy are therefore likely to vary across countries and over time.

Although broad political support is essential to the sustained success of macroeconomic reforms,[53] it is often difficult to establish a political consensus at the outset of a disinflation program.[54] As argued earlier, in situations where newly elected political leaders enjoy a period of widespread popularity, economic shock treatments have a higher probability of being accepted than prolonged adjustment programs. In general, however, political support tends to dissipate rather quickly if expenditures on basic programs such as education, health, and social services are cut to meet fiscal targets or if unemployment rises in the short term to very high levels. For any given country, the optimal speed of macroeconomic adjustment will depend on a variety of economic and political factors (such as the structure of the economy, the policymaker's preferences, and the degree of political consensus). Although in practice it is extremely difficult to determine the "optimal" pace of reform, it has been argued that two general points need to be taken into account in designing stabilization programs. First, as argued before, it is crucial to sequence macroeconomic and structural reforms in a way that minimizes the short-term drop in output.[55] Second, it may also be important to devise a compensatory scheme for those affected the most, that is, to put in place social safety nets that include (among other options) targeted subsidies on essential food products or cash transfers to vulnerable groups, to protect those least able to absorb the costs of macroeconomic adjustment (low-income families, pensioners, and unemployed workers). The latter appears to be one of the main lessons of the recent literature on the political economy of stabilization programs (Haggard and Kaufman, 1989).[56]

Nevertheless, while equity provides a strong rationale for targeting specific groups in the population, programs that attempt to avoid imposing severe economic costs on those groups deemed vulnerable may not necessarily be more credible (even if the social safety net is cost-effective), because the targeted groups may not be the most politically influential in the country. Targeting specific groups for protection may impose substantial short-term costs on other groups that enjoy greater political power and could undermine the credibility and sustainability of the program as much as—and perhaps more than—ignoring the needs of the vulnerable groups altogether. As argued by Alesina and Drazen (1991), as groups attempt to shift to each other the burden of stabilization, the consequence may be serious delays in the stabilization effort—leading eventually to a complete collapse.

10.2.3 Policy Lessons

Most economists agree that policymakers can speed up the disinflation process and reduce the costs in terms of output by achieving credibility early in the program. Mere pronouncements about monetary and fiscal policies are not credible, because private agents understand that policymakers have obvious incentives to make false announcements and because the public is not likely to pay attention to statements not backed by concrete measures. Policymakers can gain an anti-inflationary reputation only by establishing a track record of consistent low-inflation policies; these, in turn, require the formulation of credible programs. The implementation of a credible disinflation program helps provide an anchor for price expectations, leads to a reduction in the large risk premiums that tend to maintain interest rates at very high levels, and limits the recessionary effects of restrictive monetary and fiscal policies. Although some of the analytical results of the recent macroeconomic literature on credibility are sensitive to particular assumptions (concerning the structure of the economy, the specification of preferences of policymakers and private agents, and the existence of informational asymmetries), and despite the severe limitations of the empirical literature on existing credibility models, some tentative conclusions and broad policy lessons can be drawn from the preceding discussion for the formulation and design of disinflation programs.

The alternative options put forward recently have not created a consensus among economists regarding the optimal way to convey credibility to a disinflation program or to enhance the reputation of policymakers. For instance, it has often been argued that to reduce inflationary expectations effectively in accordance with the disinflationary goal (and thereby facilitate the transition to low inflation), a newly implemented policy must not only appear credible but must be accompanied by clear signals informing the public of the government's actions. In that regard, an overadjustment in the fiscal sector is sometimes viewed as providing an unambiguous signal regarding the policymakers' commitment to continue with stabilization. However, credibly reducing budget deficits often requires the implementation of structural measures to broaden the tax system, privatize state enterprises, and break up monopolies. Such measures take time and have high political costs. In addition, measures that appear too harsh are often perceived as unsustainable.[57] It is the persistence rather than the scope of the initial policy measures that matters. Policy discontinuities represent the most serious obstacle to establishing credibility. Proper sequencing between structural and macroeconomic reforms is also important, as microeconomic and institutional changes often need to precede macroeconomic reforms to ensure success and convey credibility. In particular, although central bank independence does not obviate the need to ensure close coordination among policymakers in a decentralized regime, it helps establish confidence in the goal of price stability.

In a similar vein, it has been argued that because orthodox programs often reduce inflation slowly in chronic-inflation countries, an outcome likely to undermine support for stabilization, imposing price controls at the outset of a program may be beneficial. By reducing inflation quickly, price controls may provide policymakers with "breathing space" before the introduction of additional fiscal and monetary measures aimed at strengthening the stabilization effort. However, the argument does not carry much weight if the freeze is not complete and price setters are forward-looking agents. In addition, countries have typically used price controls as substitutes for fiscal adjustment, leading in many cases to a collapse of the stabilization effort and a resurgence of inflation. Institutional reforms aimed at eliminating inertial mechanisms (such as wage indexation laws and financial indexation provisions) remain essential to breaking persistent inflation in chronic-inflation countries.

To support a stabilization plan, policymakers often have recourse to foreign assistance, through a conditional bilateral agreement between an external agency and the government. Conditional foreign assistance serves two functions. The first is to make credits conditional on the implementation of macroeconomic policy reforms, and the second is to provide a signal about the seriousness of the program and thus lend credibility to policymakers. However, the second dimension may not be operative if political considerations are believed to have played an overwhelmingly important role in the decision to provide foreign aid. The first function can actually reduce credibility if the degree of conditionality is so tight that private agents are led to believe that the authorities cannot meet their policy targets. In terms of its impact on credibility, then, conditionality may not provide an unambiguous mechanism to ensure the success of stabilization programs.

Finally, though many economists believe that stabilization programs should be accompanied by social safety nets aimed at protecting the most vulnerable groups from the effects of macroeconomic reforms, programs that contain such features are not necessarily more credible than others, because the targeted groups may not have much political influence on, say, the reelection prospects of the incumbent.

The public must be clearly informed, at the inception of a stabilization program, that a new economic regime is being introduced. This understanding will help to ensure that the behavior of the private sector will reinforce the reform process, in turn increasing the program's credibility. Policy measures must accordingly be structured to indicate early on that major changes are being introduced. Although signaling a break with past inflationary policies may require a significant tightening in monetary and fiscal policies, emphasis should be put on hard-to-reverse structural actions that clearly demonstrate the direction of the reforms, rather than on excessively stringent macroeconomic policies. Such structural policies should aim at eliminating the principal causes of fiscal imbalances, since the persistence of fiscal deficits makes it less likely that subsequent reforms will be successful. Finally, the fact that stabilization often creates only long-run benefits (which are often discounted by short-sighted agents) means that the prevailing economic conditions should have some bearing on the performance of the strategy. A program that performs well in a number of alternative possible situations seems preferable to one designed for a specific scenario. Consequently, contingencies may need to be considered more systematically in the formulation of disinflation programs. Most important, perhaps, is the need to integrate political factors into the design of stabilization programs. Understanding the endogenous interactions among credibility, macroeconomic policy decisions, and the political environment may be the key challenge that program designers face at the present time.

10.3 Disinflation and Nominal Anchors

The evidence reviewed in Chapter 8 suggested that, in several instances, fixing the exchange rate was a key factor in stopping hyperinflation. Under less extreme circumstances, is the exchange rate to be preferred to, say, a nominal money target? Our discussion in Chapter 9 of the dynamic effects associated with alternative stabilization rules and the foregoing review of sources of credibility problems provide essential elements affecting the choice of a nominal anchor in disinflation programs. We will focus, in particular, on the choice between an exchange rate and a money supply rule, which (as argued in Chapter 8) represent the two major alternative types of orthodox stabilization programs.

The choice among alternative anchors in stabilization programs depends, in general, on four major considerations: the nature of the shocks that are likely to affect the economy during the disinflation process, the degree of controllability of the different policy instruments, the dynamic adjustment path of the economy that the use of such instruments induces, and the intrinsic degree of credibility of the respective choices.[58] These factors are not independent, as the discussion in the previous section suggests.

The role of potential stochastic disturbances in choosing between the exchange rate and the money supply as a nominal anchor has been examined by Fischer (1986) in a model of an open economy with staggered labor contracts. Fischer shows that, in general, the choice between fixing the money stock or the nominal exchange rate depends on the nature and degree of persistence of the shocks that are likely to affect the economy as well as the degree of wage indexation. For instance, when disturbances arise primarily in the real sector, prices tend to be more stable during the disinflation process when the nominal exchange rate is fixed. Under either strategy, however, wage rigidity increases the output cost of disinflation. While Fischer's analysis is based on ex ante indexation, in practice, wage indexation is generally ex post, with the current wage adjusting to past changes in prices.[59] More recently, Fischer (1988) has examined the role of ex post wage indexation in the conduct of disinflation programs based on a reduction of the money stock. Indexation, ex ante or ex post, speeds up the response of the economy to disinflation. In the early stages of the stabilization program, ex post indexation reduces the extent of the recession caused by a permanent, unanticipated reduction in the growth rate of the money stock, but tends to have a long-term recessionary effect. Although Fischer does not examine the implications of ex post indexing for exchange-rate-based disinflation programs, a likely result is that it also increases the long-run output cost in such programs. In any case, however, stochastic shocks are—by definition—difficult to predict in practice, so that basing the choice of a nominal anchor on expected disturbances only may not be an optimal strategy. According to this criterion, unless the variability and the likelihood of occurrence of some category of shocks are deemed very low, a superior approach would probably be to use both anchors.

The extent to which policymakers are able to control their policy instruments can be an important consideration in choosing between monetary and exchange-rate rules. In general, the central bank cannot directly control the money supply, whereas fixing the exchange rate can be done relatively fast and without substantial costs. As argued earlier, the perception by the public of a lack of precision in instrument manipulation may affect the credibility of the disinflation program. On such grounds, then, fixing the exchange rate rather than the money stock may appear preferable. However, policymakers must also be able to convince private agents that they will be able to defend the declared parity. If agents lack confidence in the authorities' ability to do so, speculative attacks will occur, eventually forcing the abandonment of the fixed exchange rate (see Chapter 6). Imposing controls on foreign exchange transactions may not be an appropriate remedy, if rationing in the official market leads to the emergence of a parallel market with a more depreciated rate—since the "signal" that is supposed to be conveyed to price setters by fixing the official exchange rate will be distorted. This problem has, in fact, been a recurrent one in stabilization programs in developing countries.

More important, perhaps, is the fact that the choice of a nominal anchor affects the adjustment path of the economy, and therefore the ultimate outcome of the stabilization program. As illustrated in the one-good model with imperfect capital mobility developed in the previous chapter, the transitory dynamics associated with monetary and exchange-rate rules will usually differ in significant ways. Similarly, in the Calvo-Végh "temporariness" framework described earlier, exchange-rate-based stabilization programs may lead to an initial expansion and a recesssion later on, while money-based programs are characterized invariably by an initial contraction in output. Another example of the importance of considering, in choosing among nominal anchors, the dynamic path induced by alternative policy options is provided by Bruno and Fischer (1990). They consider an extended version of the "orthodox" model of inflation developed in the first section of Chapter 9 and assume that bonds can be used, in addition to money, as a source of financing of the fiscal deficit. Their analysis suggests that dual equilibria exist if the government attempts to fix the real exchange rate, but a unique equilibrium can be attained if the government sets a nominal anchor for the economy—for instance, by fixing the rate of growth of the nominal money stock or the rate of depreciation of the nominal exchange rate. In such conditions, the equilibrium that obtains under perfect foresight is saddlepoint stable, while the inflationary process is globally stable (with slow adaptive expectations) under a fixed nominal rate of exchange depreciation. Similar results obtain from the use of a rule through which the nominal exchange rate is adjusted adaptively to the inflation rate. Thus, by ensuring that policy pursues an appropriate nominal target, the government can avoid the costs of operating at an inflation rate that is higher than the fundamentals require it to be.[60] Lächler (1988) provides yet another example of how the choice of a nominal anchor affects the dynamic path of the economy during adjustment.

The consideration of credibility factors in choosing among alternative nominal anchors is perhaps the most crucial of all, since it interacts with the adjustment path and the degree of controllability of policy instruments. In our discussion of real-interest-rate dynamics, for instance, the degree of credibility of fiscal policy announcements was shown to play a critical role in the short-run behavior of the economy in exchange-rate-based stabilization programs. In the Calvo-Végh framework discussed above, credibility— or the lack thereof—plays an important role in the choice between monetary and exchange-rate targets. In their setup, a key problem that emerges when the exchange rate is used as a nominal anchor is the real appreciation that ensues when the inflation rate in home goods prices is rigid downward— as in the two-sector model with backward-looking wage contracts and mark-up pricing presented in Chapter 9—as a result, in part, of the initial expansion of output that often accompanies these programs. This may immediately weaken the credibility of a policy aimed at fixing the exchange rate, because agents will anticipate future nominal devaluations aimed at realigning relative prices. By contrast, in money-based stabilizations there is an immediate recession, which may weaken endogenously the credibility of the program, if the short-term output and employment cost is high. When the lack of credibility is pervasive, the choice between money and the exchange rate may not matter a great deal; inflation will remain high regardless of the anchor. An exchange-rate rule is, however, more successful in reducing inflation if there is some degree of credibility in the program; in this case, the initial expansion and the upward pressure on the real exchange rate are dampened. Nevertheless, under such a policy regime large intertemporal substitution effects may result, which are conducive to large current account deficits. If policymakers are unable to finance the surge in imports, and rationing ensues in the official market for foreign exchange, fluctuations in the parallel market exchange rate may severely distort the signal that a fixed exchange rate was intended to convey to price setters.

This chapter has provided a review of some analytical issues that arise in disinflation programs. We focused in the first part on two "puzzles" that have characterized exchange-rate-based stabilization programs, namely, the boom-recession pattern of real output and the behavior of real interest rates.

We developed two alternative explanations of output behavior and assessed the capacity of these models (from both empirical and theoretical perspectives) to account for the observed facts. We also presented an explanation of the different pattern of real-interest-rate behavior in the exchange-rate-based programs implemented in the 1970s and those initiated in the 1980s, which relied on private agents' confidence in announcements of future fiscal policies.

We considered a two-stage policy sequence in which the policymaker implements an immediate, permanent reduction in the devaluation rate as the first step in a disinflation program. At the same time, the intention to increase the tax rate on income at some future date is also announced. Private agents, however, do not entirely believe the announcement regarding the fiscal policy component of the program, and attribute a certain probability to the prospect that the authorities will not implement the preannounced increase in income taxes. The behavior of real interest rates at the inception of the program was shown to depend, in particular, on the degree of public confidence (or the degree of credibility) in the policymakers' announcement. When agents believe that the increase in taxes is unlikely to be implemented, domestic real interest rates are likely to fall if the degree of capital mobility is sufficiently high. By contrast, when private agents believe with a high degree of certainty that the increase in the income tax rate will be effectively implemented, real interest rates may rise on impact. Thus, the behavior of real interest rates at the inception of exchange-rate-based stabilization programs may not reflect expectations about the sustainability of the initial exchange-rate adjustment itself, but rather the degree of confidence that private agents attach to the future implementation of the fiscal measures that may be announced in conjunction with the initial set of deflationary policies.

The role of credibility factors in disinflation programs has been the subject of much debate in recent years. We provided a detailed overview of the sources of credibility problems in the second part of the chapter and reviewed recent proposals to enhance the credibility of stabilization programs. We highlighted the role of institutional reforms (such as central bank independence or the removal of backward-looking indexation mechanisms) and the ambiguous nature of prescriptions to "clearly signal" a change in regime. Drastically restrictive policy measures are not necessarily better than more gradual ones, if agents are skeptical about their sustainability, because of their social and political repercussions. Convincing private agents that a government is serious about reform requires more than just applying shock therapy at a moment in time; it requires policy continuity. The perception of possible future reversals is probably the most damaging aspect of the lack of credibility. A proper sequencing of macroeconomic and structural reforms aimed at maintaining domestic political support is essential for ensuring sustainability of the disinflation process.

Finally, we drew on the conclusions of the previous analytical discussions in analyzing the choice among alternative nominal anchors. The choice among anchors is essentially limited to fixing the nominal exchange rate or the money supply, and depends on a variety of considerations: the nature of disturbances that impinge on the economy, the degree of controllability of the different policy instruments, the dynamic adjustment path of the economy that they induce, and their credibility. Fixing the money supply is difficult (since the central bank does not control all elements of the money stock) and typically entails a recession in the short run. The exchange rate is a highly visible price and can be controlled—in the absence of restrictions on trade and capital movements—relatively easily, but generates an initial expansion and a current account deficit, which may either improve or reduce the credibility of the program. Additional anchors, such as price and wage controls, may not work if they suffer from the same type of credibility problems as the instruments they are supposed to complement.

Appendix: Output Effects of Price Controls

We examine here, using a diagrammatic presentation, how differences in market structure and intensity of price controls influence the levels of output following the imposition of price ceilings. The analysis, which follows Helpman (1988), contrasts the effects of price controls on output under competitive and monopolistic markets. We focus on the case where only output prices are controlled, with input prices remaining constant.

Figure 10.5 depicts a single industry under competitive and monopolistic market structures. Panel 1 in the figure describes the competitive industry, with a large number of producers and consumers. MC is the marginal cost or supply curve and D the demand curve of the industry, with the equilibrium price p_E and quantity q_E determined at the intersection of the two curves (point C). Suppose now that the government sets the price at p_c, below the equilibrium price p_E. At the controlled price level, there is excess demand for the good equivalent to AB. The quantity actually transacted in the market is given by the supply function (at point A). Output is thus supply determined in this regime.

Panels 2, 3, and 4 in Figure 10.5 describe a monopolistic industry, where there is only one firm facing a multitude of consumers. In all three panels, the marginal revenue curve MR is below the demand curve D, and equilibrium corresponds to the intersection of the marginal revenue and marginal cost curves, at point E (in contrast to point C under competitive conditions). The equilibrium price p_E corresponds to point B on the demand curve. The three panels illustrate the familiar result that a monopolistic market structure leads to higher prices and lower output levels compared with market

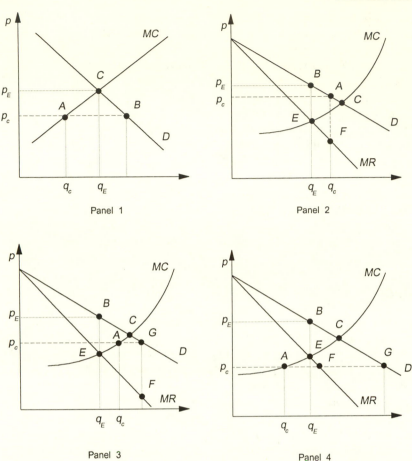

Figure 10.5 Price Controls under Competitive and Monopolistic Markets

competition. However, the panels differ in the intensity of price controls imposed by the government. The implications of such differences are crucial to a proper understanding of the output effects of price controls.

First, consider the case where the controlled price p_c is set at a level below the equilibrium price p_E, but above the equilibrium price that would prevail in a competitive market (panel 2). Under this scenario, the marginal revenue curve becomes horizontal at the level p_c up to point A on the demand curve and then drops to F, coinciding with MR for higher output levels. Profit maximization motives lead the firm to supply the entire amount demanded at the controlled price. This result is valid for all price ceilings above point C and below point B. Hence, price controls lead to an expansion in output.

In the second case, the controlled price is set at a level below the equilibrium price that would prevail under both competitive and monopolistic market structures (panel 3). At the controlled price p_c, the marginal revenue curve becomes horizontal up to point G on the demand curve and then drops to F, coinciding with MR for higher output levels. Output is determined at point A, where the marginal revenue curve intersects the marginal cost curve. Point G represents the quantity demanded at the controlled price. Output is now supply determined and there is excess demand (corresponding to AG), as in the competitive setting. The imposition of price controls also leads to an expansion of output, from q_E to q_c.

In the third case, the controlled price is set at a lower level than under the second case, that is, below the intersection of the marginal revenue and marginal cost curves (panel 4). At the controlled price p_c, point A represents the intersection of the marginal revenue curve (the horizontal line originating at p_c) with the marginal cost curve, while point G corresponds to the quantity demanded. Once again, output is supply determined and there is excess demand in an amount equivalent to AG. However, the imposition of price controls leads now to a fall in output (from q_E to q_c).

Therefore, depending on the intensity of price controls, there are three possible outcomes under a monopolistic market structure. In the first scenario, as long as the price ceiling is above the competitive equilibrium price, there is no excess demand, output is demand determined, and controls lead to an expansion in output. In the second and third scenarios, where the controlled price is set at lower levels, there is excess demand, output is supply determined, and shortages develop. However, while output rises in the second scenario, the third implies a fall in activity. In general, therefore, the output effects of price controls depend on market structure, as well as on the severity of these controls, and on the structure of production costs.

The above results are obtained in a partial-equilibrium setting, where ceilings are imposed only on output prices while input prices are held constant; interactions among markets are also ignored. An equiproportional reduction in all input and output prices for any given industry would leave output unchanged in that industry regardless of market structure.[61] Furthermore, when general equilibrium considerations are introduced, a uniform reduction in prices may affect output through its effects on both aggregate demand and aggregate supply. The effect of price controls on aggregate supply of final output will depend, in general, both on market structure as discussed above and on how much input prices are reduced relative to the price of final output. With regard to aggregate demand, the fall in the general price level may increase real money holdings and stimulate aggregate demand through the real balance effect. To the extent that inflationary expectations are dampened by controls, interest rates will fall and the demand for real money balances will increase. With a given nominal money stock, the increase in money demand will lead to further downward pressure on prices. However, to the extent that price controls reduce expected real income, they may have a negative effect on aggregate demand. Thus, the net effect of an increase in the overall price level on aggregate output may be positive or negative, depending on the initial conditions. In general, the effect of price controls on aggregate output will depend on the size of the competitive sector relative to the monopolistic sector, as well as on the structure of production costs and the extent and intensity of price controls across industries.

The output effects of price controls will also depend on whether parallel goods markets exist. Excess demand in official markets tends to spill over to informal markets, leading to a rise in prices there as well as an increase in output. As argued in the main part of this chapter, if the domestic price level depends on official as well as parallel market prices, the very purpose of controls (a reduction in the rate of inflation) may be defeated by the existence of such markets.

Eleven

Stabilization Policies with Informal Financial Markets

IN countries where informal markets in credit and foreign exchange are large, integrating such markets simultaneously in a consistent macroeconomic framework is an essential step in understanding the process of transmission of economic policy shocks. We presented in Chapter 5 a simplified model, which was used to study the role of monetary policy. The purpose of this chapter is to provide a more comprehensive framework, to account in a more detailed manner for the variety of channels through which prices determined on informal financial markets interact with other macroeconomic variables.

The first part of the chapter presents an analytical framework in which the supply side of the economy is explicitly considered, and discusses—with particular emphasis on leakages between official and unofficial markets, as well as on the behavior of sectoral output—the effects of interest rate liberalization. Although relatively complex in comparison to the framework developed in Chapter 5, the model developed in the first part of this chapter rests nevertheless on a number of simplifying assumptions, regarding in particular the specification of portfolio decisions and the modeling of the demand functions for domestic- and foreign-currency assets. A more detailed macroeconomic model (which incorporates, in addition to informal financial markets, several other important macroeconomic features of developing countries) is developed in the second part. The expanded model is used to examine several types of policy experiments, which have been discussed in previous chapters and have figured prominently in stabilization programs. We consider, in particular, the effects of a change in government spending on home goods, central bank credit to commercial banks, an increase in official lending rates, and a devaluation of the nominal exchange rate.

11.1 An Integrated Analytical Framework

This section develops an integrated model in which controlled official markets for credit and foreign exchange coexist with informal markets, and examines the effects of interest rate liberalization in this setting. In contrast to the analysis developed in Chapter 5, we explicitly model the supply side of the economy and treat expectations as endogenous.[1]

11.1.1 Structure of the Model

Consider a small, open economy in which there are five types of agents: domestic producers, households, commercial banks, the central bank, and the government. The exchange-rate system consists of an official market where the domestic price of foreign currency is fixed at $\bar{E}$ by the central bank. Due to lack of reserves, however, agents are able to settle only a limited proportion of their commercial transactions through the official market. All other foreign-currency operations (trade and capital transactions) are conducted through a quasi-legal parallel market, at a more depreciated exchange rate s_t. Similarly, excess demand for credit by private agents in the official market, which results from the existence of legal ceilings on bank lending rates, is satisfied in an informal loan market, where the interest rate adjusts freely.

Domestic output consists of two goods: a home good, which is consumed only domestically, and an exportable good, whose output is entirely sold abroad. Labor is homogeneous and perfectly mobile across sectors. Households consume three goods, the home good and two imported goods, the first of which is legally imported through official channels, and the second illegally traded through a parallel market. They possess four categories of assets: interest-bearing deposits with the banking system, domestic-currency notes, foreign-currency holdings, and loans extended through the informal credit market. Domestic-currency notes and foreign-currency holdings are imperfectly substitutable, non-interest-bearing assets. The government consumes the home good, collects taxes on legal exports, and provides transfers to households. Commercial banks receive loans from the central bank and provide credit to households and firms producing home goods.[2] In addition to lending to commercial banks, the central bank sets the interest rate that banks charge their customers and allocates foreign exchange to households and the government. Finally, agents are endowed with perfect foresight.

11.1.1.1 PRODUCERS

Firms in both sectors of production use a single input (domestic labor) and maximize profits subject to technological and borrowing constraints. A portion of total production of the export sector is sold illegally, and the rest is repatriated through the official market for foreign exchange. Let σ denote the fraction of total exports earnings repatriated via the parallel market, and $y_X(t)$ total production for export. Assuming that the world price of exports is set to unity, the domestic-currency value of exports channeled through the unofficial market for foreign exchange is given by $\sigma s_t y_X(t)$, while the domestic-currency value of exports repatriated via the official market is $(1 - \sigma)\bar{E} y_X(t)$.[3]

Formally, the representative firm in the export sector chooses the level of output so as to maximize after-tax profits at each point in time, subject to rising marginal labor costs:

$$\max_{y_X} \left\{ (1 - \iota_X)(1 - \sigma)\bar{E} y_X(t) + \sigma s_t y_X(t) - w_t n_X(t) \right\}, \tag{1}$$

subject to

$$n_X(t) = \bar{n}_X y_X(t)^\nu, \quad \nu > 1, \tag{2}$$

where $0 < \iota_X < 1$ measures the ad valorem tax rate on legal exports. Setting $\bar{n}_X \equiv 1$ and maximizing (1) subject to (2) yields

$$y_X^s(t) = [p_X(t)/\nu w_t]^{1/(\nu-1)} \equiv y_X[p_X(\overset{+}{t})/w_t], \tag{3}$$

where $p_X(t) = \sigma s_t + (1 - \iota_X)(1 - \sigma)\bar{E}$ denotes the "effective" price of exports. Equation (3) indicates that a depreciation of the parallel exchange rate, a devaluation of the official exchange rate, or a fall in the wage rate raises total production for exports.

Firms producing the home good must pay wages *before* the sale of output, and therefore borrow to finance their working capital needs. The total cost faced by the representative firm is equal to the wage bill plus the interest payments made on bank and informal market loans needed to pay labor in advance. Formally, the maximization problem faced by the representative firm can be written as

$$\max_{y_N} \left\{ p_N(t)y_N(t) - w_t n_N(t) - i_c L_N^b(t) - i_L(t)L_N^p(t) \right\}, \tag{4}$$

where $p_N(t)$ denotes the price of the home good, i_c the interest rate charged by commercial banks, $i_L(t)$ the interest rate on informal market loans, and $L_N^b(t)$ and $L_N^p(t)$, respectively, loans obtained through the official and unofficial credit markets. Because such loans are in excess demand, firms absorb all loans supplied by commercial banks and therefore treat $L_N^b(t)$ as given in their optimization problem.

Labor costs (in terms of labor units) are given by

$$n_N(t) = \bar{n}_N y_N(t)^\alpha, \quad \alpha > 1, \tag{5}$$

while the firm's financial constraint is given by

$$L_N(t) = L_N^b(t) + L_N^p(t) \geq w_t n_N(t), \tag{6}$$

where $L_N(t)$ denotes total loans received by firms in the home good sector. Constraint (6) will be assumed to be continuously binding, since the only reason for firms to demand loans is to finance labor costs.[4]

Setting $\bar{n}_N \equiv 1$ and maximizing Equation (4) subject to (5) and (6) yields

$$y_N^s(t) = [p_N(t)/\alpha w_t(1 + i_L(t))]^{1/(\alpha-1)} \equiv y_N \left\{ \frac{\overset{+}{p_N}(t)}{w_t[1 + i_L(t)]} \right\}. \quad (7)$$

Equation (7) indicates that supply of home goods is positively related to home goods prices and inversely related to the "effective" cost of labor, $w_t[1 + i_L(t)]$.[5] Substituting Equation (7) in (5) yields the demand for labor, which in turn, using Equation (6), yields the representative firm's total demand for credit:

$$L_N^d(t) = w_t \ell_N^d \left\{ \frac{\overset{+}{p_N}(t)}{w_t[1 + i_L(t)]} \right\}. \quad (8)$$

The financial counterpart to firms' bank and informal market credit is assumed to consist of domestic cash held outside the banking system, $CU_t^N = L_N^d(t)$.[6]

In addition to wages, profits are distributed entirely to households. Using Equations (3) and (7), and using the official exchange rate as the numéraire—that is, the price of the legally imported good, determined by normalizing the world price to unity—net factor income accruing to households is given by

$$y_t = [(1 - \iota_X)(1 - \sigma) + \sigma\rho_t]y_X^s(t) + z_t^{-1}y_N^s(t) \quad (9)$$
$$- i_L(t)[L_N^b(t) + L_N^p(t)]/\bar{E} + (i_L(t) - i_c)L_N^b(t)/\bar{E},$$

where $\rho_t = s_t/\bar{E}$ denotes (1 plus) the parallel market premium and $z_t = \bar{E}/P_N(t)$ the real exchange rate, measured in terms of the official exchange rate. The last term in this expression, $(i_L(t) - i_c)L_N^b(t)/\bar{E}$, measures the real value per unit time of the implicit subsidy to firms producing home goods with access to bank credit.[7]

11.1.1.2 HOUSEHOLDS

Total consumption expenditure by households c_t is proportional to real wealth:

$$c_t = \kappa(\bar{i_d})a_t, \quad \kappa > 0, \quad (10)$$

where i_d denotes the interest rate on bank deposits and $a_t = A_t/\bar{E}$ real financial wealth, defined below. The propensity to consume out of wealth

κ is assumed to vary inversely with the level of the deposit rate, reflecting intertemporal substitution. This formulation captures the effect of interest rates on saving.[8] The composition of consumption expenditure is determined by a fixed allocation rule:[9]

$$c_N(t) = \delta_N \bar{E} c_t / p_N(t) = \delta_N z_t c_t, \quad 0 < \delta_N < 1, \tag{11a}$$

$$c_I(t) = \delta_I c_t, \quad 0 < \delta_I < 1, \tag{11b}$$

$$\tilde{c}_I(t) = (1 - \delta_N - \delta_I)\bar{E} c_t / s_t = \tilde{\delta}_I \rho_t^{-1} c_t, \quad 0 < \tilde{\delta}_I < 1, \tag{11c}$$

where $c_N(t)$ denotes consumption of home goods and $c_I(t)(\tilde{c}_I(t))$ consumption of the legally (illegally) imported good.

Households' nominal financial wealth is defined as

$$A_t = CU_t^p + s_t F_t^p + D_t^p + L_N^p(t) - L_t^p, \tag{12}$$

where CU_t^p denotes domestic-currency notes held by households, F_t^p the foreign-currency value of their holdings of foreign exchange (which are valued at the parallel exchange rate), D_t^p households' deposits in the banking system, and L_t^p loans received from commercial banks. Portfolio allocation is determined in two steps. Overall currency holdings are first determined by a cash-in-advance constraint, which relates consumption expenditure to money balances:

$$cu_t^p + \rho_t F_t^p \geq \alpha^{-1} c_t, \tag{13a}$$

where $cu_t^p = CU_t^p / \bar{E}$, and α denotes the velocity of circulation. The formulation adopted here captures the commonly observed phenomenon of "dollarization," that is, the use of foreign currency in domestic transactions in developing countries (see Chapter 3). The composition of currency holdings depends on the expected rate of depreciation of the parallel exchange rate, $\hat{s}_t$:[10]

$$\frac{\rho_t F_t^p}{cu_t^p + \rho_t F_t^p} = h^F(\hat{s}_t), \quad h^{F\prime} > 0. \tag{13b}$$

Interest-bearing assets are gross substitutes, being positive functions of their own rate of return and negative functions of the rate of return on the alternative asset:[11]

$$D^p / \bar{E} = h^D[\overset{+}{i_d}, \overset{-}{i_L}(t)], \tag{13c}$$

$$L_N^p(t) / \bar{E} = h^L[\overset{-}{i_d}, \overset{+}{i_L}(t)], \tag{13d}$$

where the standard portfolio adding-up constraints are given by

$$\frac{\partial h^D}{\partial i_d} + \frac{\partial h^L}{\partial i_d} = 0, \qquad \frac{\partial h^D}{\partial i_L} + \frac{\partial h^L}{\partial i_L} = 0.$$

Changes in nominal financial wealth are determined by

$$\begin{aligned}
\dot{A}_t &= \bar{E} y_t + \bar{E}[\tau_t - c_I(t)] - s_t \tilde{c}_I(t) - p_N(t) c_N(t) + \dot{s}_t F_t^p \\
&\quad + i_L(t) L_N^p(t) + i_L(t)[(1 - \mu) D_t^p - L_t^p] + [i_L(t) - i_c] L_t^p \qquad (14) \\
&\quad - [(1 - \mu) i_L(t) - i_d] D_t^p,
\end{aligned}$$

where τ_t denotes real transfers from the government and $0 < \mu < 1$ the reserve requirement on bank deposits. Equation (14) relates changes in nominal financial wealth to total factor income (since there are no retained earnings), consumption of home and imported goods, net transfers from the government, capital gains on foreign-currency holdings associated with changes in the parallel exchange rate $\dot{s}_t F_t^p$, interest income from loans to firms $i_L(t) L_N^p(t)$, net interest income from commercial banks (valued at the curb market rate), and the implicit subsidies and taxes associated with the existence of ceilings on official interest rates. The term $(1 - \mu) i_L(t) D_t^p$ measures the interest income that depositors would obtain if official interest rates were not administered, since $(1 - \mu) i_L(t)$ is the interest rate that banks would pay on deposits if there were no restrictions on interest rates (see Equation (18) below). Similarly, the term $i_L(t) L_t^p$ measures interest payments that households would make if commercial banks' lending rates were market related. The term $[i_L(t) - i_c] L_t^p$ measures, therefore, the implicit subsidy to households with access to bank credit, since in general the informal interest rate is higher than the bank lending rate. By contrast, the term $[(1 - \mu) i_L(t) - i_d] D_t^p$ measures the implicit tax on households' deposits associated with interest rate ceilings. The net effect of financial repression is therefore ambiguous and depends on the sign of the last two terms in Equation (14).[12] In general, ceilings on official interest rates will provide a net implicit subsidy if households are sufficiently indebted with respect to the banking system, that is, if the sum of the last two terms of (14) is positive.

11.1.1.3 COMMERCIAL BANKS

Assets of commercial banks consist of credit extended to households (L_t^p) and producers of home goods ($L_N^p(t)$), and reserves held at the central bank, RR_t.[13] Liabilities consist of deposits held by households (D_t^p) and loans received from the central bank ($\bar{L}^{cb}$), which are assumed exogenous. The balance sheet of commercial banks can therefore be written as

$$D_t^p + \bar{L}^{cb} = L_t^p + L_N^b(t) + RR_t. \tag{15}$$

Reserves held at the central bank do not pay interest and are determined by

$$RR_t = \mu D_t^p, \quad 0 < \mu < 1, \tag{16}$$

where μ denotes the required reserve ratio.

The actual level of deposits held by the private sector is demand determined and, from Equation (15), the total supply of credit by commercial banks is therefore $L_b^s(t) = (1 - \mu)D_t^p + \bar{L}^{cb}$. For simplicity, suppose that commercial banks allocate a given proportion $0 < \gamma < 1$ of total credit to households and the rest to firms producing the home good:

$$L_t^p = \gamma L_b^s(t), \qquad L_N^b(t) = (1 - \gamma)L_b^s(t). \tag{17}$$

Loans from the central bank to commercial banks carry an interest rate, which, for convenience, is set equal to the interest rate that commercial banks receive on their loans to the private sector, i_c—itself fixed by the monetary authorities. Banks have no operating costs; assuming that central bank credit is "small" relative to total bank deposits, the zero-profit condition yields

$$i_c \cong i_d/(1 - \mu), \tag{18}$$

which determines the interest rate paid on bank deposits, i_d.[14]

11.1.1.4 THE CENTRAL BANK AND THE GOVERNMENT

The central bank lends to commercial banks but does not lend directly to the private sector. Its balance sheet is given by

$$CU_t + RR_t = \bar{E}R_t + (L_t^g + \bar{L}^{cb}) - \Omega_t, \tag{19}$$

where $CU_t = CU_t^N + CU_t^p$ denotes total currency holdings by private agents, R_t the stock of net foreign assets (which are valued at the official exchange rate), L_t^g loans to the government, and Ω_t the central bank's net worth.[15]

Changes in the central bank's net worth are determined by

$$\dot{\Omega}_t = i^*\bar{E}R_t + i_L(t)(L_t^g + \bar{L}^{cb}) - \bar{E}\tau_t^g - [i_L(t) - i_c](L_t^g + \bar{L}^{cb}), \tag{20}$$

where τ_t^g denotes net transfers to the government budget, i^* represents the rate of interest paid on official foreign reserves, and the last term measures net subsidies from the central bank to the government and commercial banks. Equation (20) assumes that the government pays interest on its internal debt at the rate i_c.

To determine the behavior over time of the central bank's foreign reserves, note that the official current account is given by the difference between legal exports (which represent a fraction $(1 - \sigma)$ of total exports) and legal imports, which are determined by households' spending decisions. Since the domestic-currency price of goods exported or imported through the official market is $\bar{E}$, and since capital transactions are not allowed through the official market, changes in the foreign-currency value of net foreign assets of the central bank are given by

$$\dot{R}_t = (1 - \sigma)y_X(t) + i^*R_t - c_I(t). \tag{21}$$

The unofficial current account, which determines the rate of change of the private stock of foreign currency, is given by

$$\dot{F}_t^p = \sigma y_X(t) - \tilde{c}_I(t). \tag{22}$$

Consider now the behavior of the government. It collects taxes on legal exports and receives transfers from the central bank. It consumes a quantity g_N of home goods, makes transfers to households, and pays interest on its domestic debt. The government budget constraint can therefore be written as

$$\dot{L}_t^g = i_L(t)L_t^g + p_N(t)g_N + \bar{E}(\tau_t - \tau_t^g) - \iota_X\bar{E}(1 - \sigma)y_X(t) - [i_L(t) - i_c]L_t^g, \tag{23}$$

where the last term measures the implicit subsidy provided by controls on official interest rates.

We will assume in the following analysis that the government forgoes the use of credit financing by the central bank ($\dot{L}_t^g = 0$), and instead varies net transfers to households so as to maintain fiscal equilibrium. Equation (23) therefore becomes

$$\tau_t = \iota_X(1 - \sigma)y_X(t) - i_L(t)\bar{L}^g/\bar{E} + (\tau_t^g - z_t^{-1}g_N) + [i_L(t) - i_c]\bar{L}^g/\bar{E}. \tag{24}$$

11.1.1.5 MARKET-CLEARING CONDITIONS

To close the model requires a specification of the equilibrium conditions in the home goods market, the informal credit market, and the money market. As a result of the balance sheet constraints of the different agents in the economy, the last two conditions are not independent. Focusing on the informal credit market implies that the equilibrium conditions are

$$y_N^s(t) = c_N(t) + g_N, \tag{25}$$

$$L_N^p(t) = L_N^d(t) - L_N^b(t). \tag{26}$$

11.1.1.6 THE MODEL IN COMPACT FORM

The first step in solving the model developed above is to put it in a more compact form. To begin with, assume that the central bank maintains its net worth in nominal terms constant at $\bar{\Omega}$ by transferring all its (net) profits to the government, and use the normalization rule $\bar{\Omega} = \bar{L}^g = 0$. Equations (6), (12), (15), and (19) therefore imply that

$$a_t = R_t + \rho_t F_t^p, \tag{27}$$

which indicates that the net worth of the economy—which, given our previous assumptions, is identical to real household wealth—consists only of holdings of foreign currency.

The real wage in terms of the price of the legally imported good is taken as fixed ($w_t = \bar{E}$).[16] The market-clearing equilibrium conditions (25) and (26) therefore become, using Equations (7), (8), (10), (11a), (13c), (13d), (17), and (18),

$$y_N^s[z_t, \bar{i}_L(t)] = \delta_N z_t \kappa(i_d) a_t + g_N, \tag{28}$$

$$h^L( ) = \ell_N^d[z_t, \bar{i}_L(t)] - (1 - \gamma)\{(1 - \mu)h^D( ) + \bar{\iota}^{cb}\}, \tag{29}$$

where $\bar{\iota}^{cb} = \bar{L}^{cb}/\bar{E}$.

Inverting Equation (13b), noting that $\hat{s}_t = \hat{\rho}_t$ and using Equations (10), (13a)—holding with equality—and (27) yields an equation that determines the rate of change of the parallel market premium as a function of holdings of foreign currency, foreign reserves, the level of the premium, and the bank deposit rate:

$$\hat{\rho}_t = \rho[\overset{+}{\hat{\rho}_t}, \ \bar{R}_t, \ \overset{+}{F_t^p}; \ \overset{+}{i_d}]. \tag{30}$$

An increase in the parallel market premium raises the share of foreign-currency holdings in total currency balances, and requires an expected depreciation of the parallel exchange rate to maintain portfolio equilibrium. A similar effect results from an increase in the stock of foreign currency held by households. An increase in foreign reserves held by the central bank raises real wealth and total household expenditure, requiring through the cash-in-advance constraint higher currency holdings. The reduction in the relative share of foreign-currency balances requires a lower expected rate of depreciation of the parallel exchange rate to maintain portfolio equilibrium. An increase in the bank deposit rate lowers consumption expenditure and has the opposite effect.

Using (13) and (27), Equations (28) and (29) can be solved simultaneously to determine the informal interest rate and the real exchange rate that clear the home goods market and the informal loan market:[17]

$$z_t = z(\bar{a}_t; i_d), \qquad i_L(t) = i_L(\overset{+}{\bar{a}}_t; \overset{+}{i}_d).$$ (31)

Equations (31) can be used to examine the short-run, partial-equilibrium effects of changes in the parallel market premium, official and private holdings of foreign-currency assets, and changes in the official deposit rate, on the real exchange rate and the informal interest rate. An increase in the parallel market premium raises real wealth, creating an excess demand for home goods. To maintain equilibrium requires an appreciation of the real exchange rate (that is, a fall in z_t). The ensuing increase in output stimulates the total demand for curb market loans, requiring an increase in the informal interest rate to restore equilibrium. The increase in the cost of credit dampens the expansionary effect of a real-exchange-rate appreciation on output of home goods. If the latter dominates the former, an increase in the parallel market premium has an unambiguously positive effect on output in the home goods sector. An increase in the components of net financial wealth (official reserves or the stock of foreign-currency holdings) has similar effects.

A rise in the deposit rate reduces total consumption and therefore expenditure on nontraded goods, creating a situation of excess supply. Restoring equilibrium now requires a depreciation of the real exchange rate (a rise in z_t) to stimulate consumption and dampen output. In turn, this leads to a reduction in the demand for curb market loans. At the same time, the rise in the deposit rate increases the asset demand for bank deposits and reduces the supply of informal market loans. The net effect on the informal interest rate and the real exchange rate is therefore ambiguous in general. In Equations (31), we assume that the intertemporal effect is not too large, implying that the real exchange rate appreciates and the informal interest rate rises, for a given level of wealth.

With $\dot{\Omega}_t = \bar{L}^g = 0$, Equation (20) yields

$$\tau_t^g = i^* R_t + i_c \bar{l}^{cb},$$ (32)

since $\dot{\bar{E}} = 0$. Substituting Equation (32) in (24) yields

$$\tau_t = \iota_X(1 - \sigma)y_X(t) + i_c \bar{l}^{cb} + (i^* R_t - z_t^{-1} g_N).$$ (33)

Equations (3), (10), (11b), and (21) imply

$$\dot{R}_t = (1 - \sigma)y_X(\rho_t) + i^*R_t - \delta_I\kappa(i_d)a_t, \tag{34}$$

or, using Equation (27),

$$\dot{R}_t = R(\overset{-}{\rho_t}, \overset{-}{R_t}, \overset{-\ p}{F_t}; \overset{+}{i_d}), \tag{34'}$$

where we have assumed that $i^* - \delta_I\kappa < 0$ and $(1 - \sigma)y_X' - \delta_I\kappa\tilde{F}^p > 0$. The first condition holds if the world interest rate is low enough. The second condition indicates that the positive supply effect—on the volume of exports—associated with an increase in the parallel market premium is dominated by the wealth effect, implying that the net impact on changes in official reserves is negative.[18]

From Equations (3), (10), (11c), and (22), the rate of change of the private stock of foreign currency can be written as

$$\dot{F}_t^p = \sigma y_X(\rho_t) - \tilde{\delta}_I\rho_t^{-1}\kappa(i_d)a_t, \tag{35}$$

or, using Equation (27),

$$\dot{F}_t^p = \Phi(\overset{+}{\rho_t}, \overset{-}{R_t}, \overset{-\ p}{F_t}; \overset{+}{i_d}). \tag{35'}$$

Given the form of the expenditure function, the supply effect of an increase in the parallel market premium always dominates the wealth effect on the consumption of illegally imported goods, implying that the net impact of an increase in ρ_t on the rate of accumulation of foreign-currency holdings is positive.[19]

Equations (30), (34'), and (35') determine the dynamic behavior of the parallel market premium ρ_t, net foreign assets of the central bank R_t, and the stock of foreign-currency holdings by households, for given values of i_d.[20] Substituting these solutions into the equilibrium equations (31) and Equation (13a)—holding with equality—determines the solutions for the real exchange rate z_t, the informal interest rate $i_L(t)$, and households' domestic-currency holdings cu_t^p.

11.1.2 Effects of Interest Rate Liberalization

In this subsection we examine the short- and long-run effects of an increase in official interest rates, as proposed by advocates of the McKinnon-Shaw thesis. To simplify the analysis, we examine here only the particular case where there is no surrender requirement on exports ($\sigma = 1$), no imports through legal channels ($\delta_I = 0$), and official reserves bear no interest ($i^* = 0$). The system therefore becomes recursive, with Equations (30) and (35′) determining simultaneously the behavior of the premium and foreign-currency holdings, while Equation (34) implies that $\dot{R}_t = 0$, so that official reserves remain constant over time.[21] Since the dynamic adjustment path of the economy is determined by the long-run solution of the model, we begin with a characterization of the steady-state effects of a rise in bank deposit rates.

The Steady State

The steady-state equilibrium is obtained by setting $\dot{\rho}_t = \dot{F}_t = 0$ in Equations (30) and (35′), implying that

$$\tilde{\rho} = \rho(\overset{-}{i_d}), \qquad \tilde{F} = F(\overset{\pm}{i_d}), \tag{36a}$$

which indicates that although the long-run effect of an increase in the deposit rate on the parallel market premium is unambiguously negative, its effect on the stock of foreign assets is indeterminate. On the one hand, the increase in i_d reduces private expenditure and leads to a higher rate of accumulation of foreign-currency holdings; on the other hand, it lowers the premium and dampens the growth of exports, thus reducing the rate of increase of foreign currency balances.

Substituting the solution values determined by Equations (36a) in Equations (31) yields the steady-state values of the informal interest rate and the real exchange rate:

$$\tilde{i}_L = \tilde{i}_L(\overset{\pm}{i_d}), \qquad \tilde{z} = \tilde{z}(\overset{\pm}{i_d}), \tag{36b}$$

which indicates that the long-run effect of a change in the deposit rate on the informal interest rate and the real exchange rate is ambiguous—in contrast with the partial-equilibrium effect derived earlier. The long-run impact of interest rate liberalization on output in the export sector is negative, whereas the effect on output in the nontraded goods sector is also ambiguous.

To see what happens to the aggregate supply of loans, denoted l^s, note that

$$l^s = h^L(i_d, i_L) + (1 - \mu)h^D(i_d, i_L) + l^{cb},$$

so that

$$\frac{d\tilde{l}^s}{di_d} = \frac{\partial h^L}{\partial i_d} + \left(\frac{\partial h^L}{\partial i_L}\right)\left(\frac{\partial \tilde{i}_L}{\partial i_d}\right) + (1 - \mu)\left[\frac{\partial h^D}{\partial i_d} + \left(\frac{\partial h^D}{\partial i_L}\right)\left(\frac{\partial \tilde{i}_L}{\partial i_d}\right)\right],$$

or equivalently, using the portfolio adding-up constraints:

$$\frac{d\tilde{l}^s}{di_d} = -\mu\left[\frac{\partial h^D}{\partial i_d} + \left(\frac{\partial \tilde{i}_L}{\partial i_d}\right)\left(\frac{\partial h^D}{\partial i_L}\right)\right] < 0.$$

An increase in official deposit rates always reduces the overall supply of credit, given the portfolio structure adopted here.

Transitional Dynamics

Given that official foreign reserves are assumed constant, a graphical presentation of the transitional dynamics can be provided. A linear approximation to Equations (30) and (35′) around the initial steady state is given by

$$\begin{bmatrix} \dot{\rho}_t \\ \dot{F}_t \end{bmatrix} = \begin{bmatrix} \Gamma_\rho & \Gamma_F \\ \Phi_\rho & \Phi_F \end{bmatrix}\begin{bmatrix} \rho_t - \tilde{\rho} \\ F_t - \tilde{F} \end{bmatrix}, \quad \Gamma_\rho, \Gamma_F, \Phi_\rho > 0, \quad \Phi_F < 0. \tag{37}$$

The system described by (37) is locally saddlepoint stable.[22] Given an initial condition on the stock of foreign-currency holdings F_0, an explicit solution can be easily obtained.

The steady-state solution of the model with constant official reserves is depicted in Figure 11.1. The curve $[\dot{F}_t = 0]$ determines the combinations of parallel market premiums and holdings of foreign currency for which the prevailing stock remains constant, while the curve $[\dot{\rho}_t = 0]$ depicts those combinations for which the parallel market premium does not change. The economy's equilibrium path is the unique, nonexplosive path SS with negative slope that passes through the stationary point E. For instance, if the parallel market premium is "too high," households would accumulate foreign exchange at an "excessive" rate—as indicated by the combination of arrows pointing north and east in the figure—and would diverge more and more from the steady state.

The transitional effects associated with an unanticipated, permanent increase in the deposit interest rate are illustrated in Figure 11.2, for the case where the net effect on the long-run level of foreign-currency holdings is negative.[23] Suppose that the economy is initially in a steady-state equilibrium at, say, point E. As a result of the rise in deposit rates, the locus $[\dot{\rho}_t = 0]$ shifts to the left, while the locus $[\dot{F}_t = 0]$ shifts to the right. The parallel market premium jumps downward on impact, from point E to point A, located on the new saddlepath $S'S'$. From there on, the premium starts rising along $S'S'$ and eventually reaches its new steady-state value at E'. The stock of foreign currency falls continuously toward its new equilibrium value. Both the premium and foreign-currency holdings are lower in the new steady state.[24]

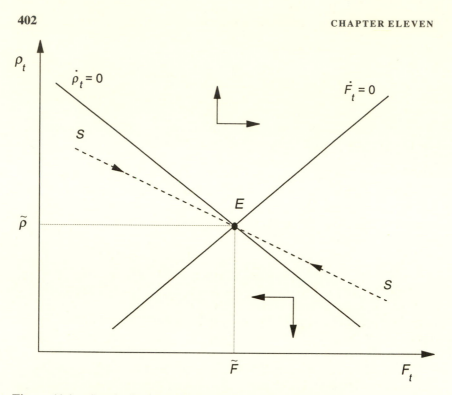

Figure 11.1   Steady-State Equilibrium with Constant Reserves
Source: Agénor (1994e, p. 17a).

The adjustment mechanism can be summarized as follows. The increase in official bank deposits reduces private spending on impact. The initial excess supply for home goods requires a depreciation of the real exchange rate (a rise in z_t) to restore equilibrium. The fall in output in the home goods sector reduces the demand for informal market loans, exerting downward pressure on the informal interest rate. However, the rise in official rates draws funds away from the informal credit market and into the banking system, exerting upward pressure on the curb market interest rate. The net effect is an increase in the informal interest rate. The negative effect of an increase in the cost of borrowing compounds the initial contractionary effect on output in the home goods sector resulting from the real-exchange-rate depreciation. The reduction in the level of transactions creates, through the cash-in-advance constraint, an excess supply for foreign exchange that requires a fall in the parallel market premium on impact to maintain equilibrium. The fall in the premium reduces the supply of exports (which exacerbates the contractionary effect on output) and real wealth, which has a further negative effect on demand for domestic and foreign goods.[25] Over time, the stock of foreign-currency holdings falls, as a result of a lower rate of growth of exports, while the premium rises. If the direct effect of an increase in i_d (on

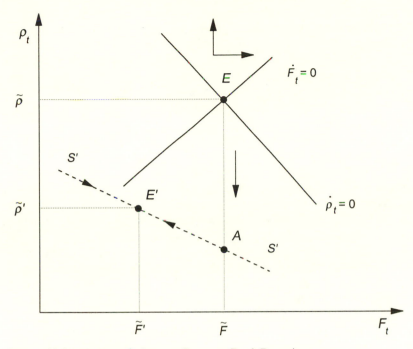

Figure 11.2   Increase in Interest Rates on Bank Deposits

Source: Agénor (1994*e*, p. 18a).

the propensity to spend out of wealth) dominates its net effect on wealth, the demand for home goods will fall over time, leading to a continuous depreciation of the real exchange rate. Since the demand for illegal imports also falls over time, the net effect on foreign-currency holdings during the transition period (as well as in the long run) remains negative. Given our assumptions about the economy's structure and behavioral functions, interest rate liberalization has a contractionary effect on output and employment.

The contractionary effect would not necessarily obtain if it had been assumed here, as in the simplified model developed in Chapter 5, that foreign-currency holdings were determined simultaneously with other asset demand functions, rather than through a cash-in-advance constraint. As shown in the next section, in such a setting the effects of interest rate liberalization depend in important ways on whether bank deposits are closer substitutes than foreign-currency holdings for informal market loans.

11.2 A General Equilibrium Simulation Model

The analytical model presented in the previous section was useful for understanding the supply-side effects of informal financial markets and the role of the real sector in the transmission of macroeconomic policy shocks. However, several simplifying assumptions were imposed on the model to retain tractability. In this section, a more complete macroeconomic framework is described.[26] Because of its complexity, however, the expanded model cannot be solved analytically. We therefore resort to a numerical procedure. We start with a description of the structure of the model and then present the results of alternative policy experiments.

11.2.1 Structure of the Model

As before, we consider a small, open economy with five categories of agents: producers, households, the government, the central bank, and the commercial banks. The economy also produces two goods: a home good, which is used only for final domestic consumption, and an export good, for the sole purpose of exports. The capital stock in each sector remains fixed over the time frame of the analysis, and labor is perfectly mobile across sectors. Households consume home goods as well as an imported final good that is imperfectly substitutable for the home good. Producers also import an intermediate input that is not produced domestically.

The financial system is characterized by the existence of trade and exchange controls, legal ceilings on bank borrowing and lending rates, and the absence of organized markets for securities and equities. As a result, informal credit and foreign exchange markets coexist with official markets. Commercial transactions of the private sector are settled partly in the official market for foreign exchange at a fixed exchange rate, while the rest of the commercial transactions and all capital transactions are settled in the parallel market at a market-clearing exchange rate. Due to the existence of tariffs, foreign exchange controls, and a positive exchange-rate premium, exports are in part smuggled out and imports of final goods are in part smuggled in. Sales of foreign exchange to households for purchases of imports are rationed by the central bank, while foreign-currency sales for imports of intermediate goods by domestic producers and government imports are not subject to restrictions. While interest rates on assets and liabilities of the banking system are fixed by applicable legal norms, the interest rate on curb market loans is determined by prevailing market conditions.

The equations of the model are presented in an appendix to this chapter. In the remainder of this subsection we provide a brief description of the setup of the model.

11.2.1.1 AGGREGATE SUPPLY

Technology for the production of both home and export goods is characterized by a separable, Cobb-Douglas function in capital, labor, and imported intermediate inputs.[27] Under the assumption of profit maximization and perfect competition, a supply equation relating sectoral outputs $y_N(t)$ and $y_X(t)$ to the real product wage in the home goods sector and the relative price of imported inputs can be derived (see, for instance, Islam, 1984). These functions are shown in the appendix as Equations (A1) and (A2), where $P_N(t)$ denotes the price of the home good, $P_X(t)$ the domestic price of exports, $P_J(t)$ the domestic price of imported intermediate goods, and w_t the nominal wage rate.

Under the small-country assumption, the domestic price of intermediate imports is exogenously determined by world prices, while the price of the home good is determined endogenously in the home market. The domestic price of final imports and the domestic price of exports are also determined endogenously, as a result of smuggling activities. Since the foreign export price P_X^* is fixed in the world market, the foreign demand for exports is infinitely elastic and the volume of exports is supply determined. In a manner similar to the specification adopted in the previous section, the domestic supply price of exports is defined as an average of the price of smuggled exports $s_t P_X^*$, weighted by the proportion of smuggled exports σ_t and the after-tax price of official exports $\bar{E}(1 - \iota_X)P_X^*$ (where ι_X measures the tax rate on exports) weighted by the proportion of exports that are legally sold abroad, $1 - \sigma_t$ (Equation (A3)).

Labor contracts last one period and are negotiated one period in advance, so that the wage rate is known by firms at the beginning of the period, that is, before output and home good prices are realized. Nominal wages adjust slowly to their equilibrium value (Equation (A4)). The market-clearing wage w_t^* is derived from the labor-market equilibrium condition, with labor demand in each sector being derived from the first-order conditions for profit maximization (Equation (A5)). $\bar{L}$ denotes the exogenous supply of labor.

The officially recorded gross level of domestic output at factor cost excludes that part of the domestic production for exports that is illegally smuggled out. Net aggregate output at factor cost Z_t is obtained by subtracting real imports of intermediate goods J_t (for which demand functions are derived in both sectors from the first-order conditions for profit maximization, as shown by Equation (A7)) from recorded gross aggregate output (Equation (A6)). P_t denotes the domestic consumer price index, which is used as the numéraire.

The index of domestic consumer prices is defined as a geometric average of the price of the home good and the domestic price of imported consumer goods $P_I(t)$ (Equation (A8)).[28] The domestic-currency price of imported consumer goods depends on the world price of imported goods P_I^* (which is exogenously determined) and on a weighted average of the official and parallel exchange rates (Equation (A9)). The weight on the official exchange rate Φ is related below to the rationing rule followed by the authorities in the official market for foreign exchange.[29]

11.2.1.2 AGGREGATE DEMAND AND DISPOSABLE INCOME

Households hold four categories of assets in their portfolios: domestic-currency notes CU_t, deposits with the banking system D_t^p, foreign-currency-denominated assets F_t^p, and loans extended through the informal credit market. Domestic-currency notes bear no interest and are held only for transactions purposes. Holdings of all assets are financed from agents' net worth or by borrowing through the banking system.[30] Along the lines of the model developed in Chapter 5, bank credit L_t^p and curb market loans are taken to be perfect substitutes in households' portfolios.

Total expenditure by households E_t^p depends positively on real disposable income Z_t^d and real wealth, and negatively on the real interest rate, defined as the difference between the nominal interest rate in the informal credit market $i_L(t)$ and the one-period-ahead expected rate of inflation π_{t+1}^a (Equation (A10)). In turn, real disposable income is defined as the sum of after-tax factor income derived from legally recorded production activities $(1 - \iota)P_t Z_t$, income derived from the smuggling of exports—which is therefore not taxed and is equal to illegal exports in foreign-currency terms, valued at the parallel exchange rate $\sigma_t s_t P_X^* y_X(t)$—and the implicit subsidies and taxes received by households (as creditors and debtors with the banking system) resulting from the existence of interest rate controls (Equation (A11)). Disposable income therefore depends on the level of the financial repression tax, q_t, defined in Equation (A12) and discussed in Chapter 5. With private expenditure given by (A10), demand for the home good is given by the sum of real private expenditure (determined as a fraction of total expenditure) and real government spending on home goods g_N (Equation (A13)).

11.2.1.3 ASSET ACCUMULATION AND FINANCIAL WEALTH

Households' financial wealth A_t is defined as the sum of holdings of domestic-currency notes, bank deposits, bank credit, and foreign exchange (Equation (A14)).[31] The representative household's budget constraint relates flow changes in financial wealth to the portion of disposable income that is not spent (domestic savings), interest income derived from bank deposits and holdings of foreign-currency-denominated assets that are repatriated through the parallel market, interest payments on bank credit, and valuation changes on foreign-currency holdings due to fluctuations in the parallel exchange rate (Equation (A15)).

Desired holdings of foreign-currency-denominated assets (Equation (A16)) are assumed to depend negatively on the interest rate on curb market loans and bank deposits, and positively on the perceived rate of return on foreign interest-bearing assets $i_F(t)$, which depends on the world interest rate i^* and the expected rate of depreciation of the parallel exchange rate

$\hat{s}^a_{t+1}$ (Equation (A17)). Desired holdings of bank deposits, which consist only of interest-bearing deposits, depend positively on the deposit rate and negatively on the interest rate on informal market loans and the rate of return on foreign-currency assets (Equation (A18)). The demand for domestic-currency notes reflects a pure transactions motive, and is based on the assumption that illegal activities require a more intensive use of currency notes than legally recorded ones (Equation (A19)).[32]

11.2.1.4 THE CURRENT ACCOUNT AND THE BALANCE OF PAYMENTS

Since fraudulent trade transactions take place between the economy and the rest of the world, the model distinguishes between the official current account and the unreported current account. Total household demand for imported consumer goods I_t^p is first determined as a constant share of total expenditure (Equation (A20)).[33] However, the central bank satisfies only a fraction Φ of total demand for imported final goods and provides unlimited access to foreign exchange for the government (for final goods imports equal to $P_I^* g_I$) and producers (for imports of intermediate inputs).[34] Total sales of foreign exchange $F_S(t)$ are given by Equation (A21). The officially recorded current account CA_t (which is measured in foreign-currency terms in Equation (A22)) is therefore determined as the difference between the value of recorded exports and interest income on net foreign assets held by the public sector and the central bank, minus total sales of foreign exchange. Since private capital flows through the official foreign exchange market are prohibited, the capital account surplus is equal to the negative value of changes in net holdings of external assets of the public sector ΔF_t^g, which are assumed exogenous. This, together with the reported current account, yields the change in net foreign assets of the central bank ΔR_t (Equation (A23)).

Consider now the unreported current account. Supply of foreign exchange derives from underreported exports. The leakage coefficient σ_t is assumed to depend positively on the exchange-rate ratio $s_t/\bar{E}$ and the export tax rate ι_X (Equation (A24)). The particular functional form adopted here ensures that the higher the tax rate on exports or the higher the premium, the higher will be the underinvoicing share.[35] Demand for foreign exchange by households for final imports not satisfied in the official market spills over to the parallel market. The difference between supply and demand determines the unreported current account, and therefore the rate of change of the private stock of foreign-currency-denominated assets ΔF_t^p (Equation (A25)).

11.2.1.5 THE BANKING SYSTEM

The balance sheet of the commercial banking system is given by Equation (A26). As in the model of the previous section, banks' assets consist of reserves held at the central bank RR_t and credit extended to households, while their liabilities are households' deposits and credit received from the central bank L_t^b. The banks' willingness to accept deposits is infinitely elastic, implying that the actual level of deposits held in the banking system is determined on the demand side of the market. Banks hold no excess reserves but are subject to a required reserve ratio (Equation (A27)). Reserves held at the central bank pay no interest, but credit extended to commercial banks by the monetary authorities carries an interest charge that, for convenience, is set equal to the interest rate banks charge their customers for loans. This rate is controlled by the central bank. The zero-profit condition for the banking system thus determines the interest rate paid on bank deposits, i_d (Equation (A28).

The balance sheet of the central bank equates the monetary base (defined as the sum of currency notes in circulation plus commercial banks' reserves) to the sum of international reserves (valued at the official exchange rate) and the stock of domestic credit extended to the government and commercial banks, minus the central bank's net worth Ω_t (Equation (A29)). Total domestic credit L_t consists of credit to the private sector provided by commercial banks, and credit to the public sector L_t^g and commercial banks L_t^b allocated by the central bank (Equation (A30)). Changes in the central bank's net worth are determined by the difference between interest income on net foreign assets, interest income on lending to commercial banks and the government, valuation changes, and net transfers to the government budget τ_t^g (Equation (A31)).

11.2.1.6 FISCAL DEFICITS AND DOMESTIC CREDIT

The government's revenue sources in the model consist of income taxes on households, taxes on recorded exports, interest income from holdings of foreign-currency-denominated assets, and transfers from the central bank. Spending consists of purchases of both home and imported goods, and interest payments on the domestic public debt. Consequently, the government deficit GD_t is given by Equation (A32). The deficit is financed by borrowing either from the central bank or from world capital markets (Equation (A33)). In the simulation experiments to be reported it is assumed that government expenditure is exogenous and that a ceiling is imposed on foreign financing. Deficits are therefore financed by central bank credit—a typical situation in many developing countries. Equation (A33) therefore determines the evolution of domestic credit to the government.

11.2.1.7 CALIBRATION OF THE MODEL

The model presented above is difficult to estimate, and the strategy adopted by Montiel et al. (1993) is to calibrate it.[36] The parameters used are based

TABLE 11.1
Parameter Values for the Simulation Model

α_L = 0.3	α_N = 0.2	γ = 0.0
δ = 0.8	Φ = 0.2	h_1 = 0.7
h_2 = 0.1	h_3 = −0.5	μ = 0.4
λ_1 = 0.5	λ_2 = 0.6	λ_3 = 0.9
φ_1 = 0.4	φ_2 = 0.7	α_1 = 0.6
α_2 = 1.1	α_3 = 0.5	ν = 0.1
Ψ = 0.0[a]	σ = 0.4	q = 0.25[b]

Source: Monteil et al. (1993, p. 133).
[a]Set to 0.8 for the exchange-rate experiment.
[b]Initial baseline value.

on available econometric estimates where possible, but do not pertain to any particular real-world economy. Rather, they reflect conditions underlying a wide variety of possible systems. This approach can be described as "theoretical simulation," to highlight its complementarity with the solution of small analytical models. Table 11.1 presents the key parameters of the model. The model is solved using the Fair-Taylor iterative technique, which provides a relatively robust solution procedure for models in which agents are endowed with perfect foresight.[37]

11.2.2 Effects of Stabilization Policies

In the model described above, the central bank retains five direct instruments of policy: the level of controlled bank loan interest rates, the required reserve ratio, the amount of credit it extends to the commercial banking system, the proportion of private final imports satisfied in the official foreign exchange market, and the official exchange rate. The fiscal authority determines the income tax rate and the rate of taxation of exports, as well as the levels of spending on home and imported goods. In this subsection we will briefly discuss the results of experiments involving changes in some of these variables. Specifically, we will consider the effects of a 10 percent increase in government spending on home goods, in central bank credit to commercial banks, and in the official lending rate, and of a 10 percent devaluation of the official exchange rate. These shocks represent policy measures that are routinely implemented in developing countries, so understanding their effects and the mechanisms through which they are transmitted in the presence of informal financial markets is central to the design of appropriate macroeconomic policies in countries where such markets are deemed important.

Results of the simulations are reported in Table 11.2, for output of home goods, the domestic price level, the informal interest rate, and the parallel exchange rate.[38] In each case, the policy measure is announced five periods before implementation and carries full credibility. This assumption allows us to consider the dynamic behavior of the economy in the transition period between announcement and effective implementation of the shock.

11.2.2.1 GOVERNMENT SPENDING ON HOME GOODS

Consider first a one-period, fully anticipated 10 percent increase in government spending on home goods, financed by central bank credit. As shown in Table 11.2, the price of home goods begins rising prior to the policy change. Since the nominal wage is maintained at its baseline level, the real product wage unambiguously falls and this, in turn, stimulates supply of home goods. The last effect is rather weak initially, but increases in the period preceding the implementation of the spending shock.

The forthcoming increase in the domestic money supply (associated with the increase in credit-financed government spending) leads to an anticipated future depreciation of the parallel exchange rate and an increase in the expected rate of return on foreign-currency-denominated assets. Agents thus switch away from domestic assets and toward foreign-currency assets before the shock occurs. As a consequence, the parallel exchange rate depreciates, raising the domestic price of imported goods. The rise in the premium induced by the increased demand for foreign exchange reduces the private sector's demand for bank deposits, causing households to shift assets into the informal loan market, leading to a fall in the curb market interest rate. These phenomena exert income and wealth effects that increase private demand prior to the implementation of the fiscal shock. The expected future rise in domestic prices reinforces the drop in the nominal interest rate, causing the real rate of interest to fall initially. In turn, the fall in the real rate further stimulates private expenditure, contributing to the anticipatory increase in domestic prices.

Upon implementation, the rise in government spending is expansionary both directly and through its monetary effects. The increase in the money supply reinforces the direct expansionary impact of the fiscal shock, and operates again through the informal market for foreign exchange, that is, through a sharp increase in the premium. Although the curb interest rate falls when the policy is implemented, the real interest rate actually rises, because the removal of the fiscal stimulus in the next period produces an expected price decline. Thus the transitory nature of the shock diminishes its expansionary effect with forward-looking agents. After the shock is removed, the system returns to its initial equilibrium only gradually, since the monetary effects of the once-and-for-all increase in credit take time to

TABLE 11.2
Simulation Results of Macroeconomic Shocks (percentage deviation from baseline)

	10 Percent Increase in:			
Period	Government Spending on Home Goods	Credit to Commercial Banks	Official Lending Rate	10 Percent Devaluation
	Output (home goods)			
1	0.0	0.0	0.0	0.0
2	0.0	0.0	−0.1	0.0
3	0.1	0.0	−0.1	0.1
4	0.5	0.1	−0.2	0.4
5	2.4	0.2	−0.5	−1.3
10	0.0	0.0	−0.5	−1.4
20	0.0	0.0	−0.1	−1.1
	Price level			
1	0.0	0.1	0.0	0.0
2	0.0	0.1	−0.1	0.1
3	0.1	0.1	−0.2	0.2
4	0.5	0.2	−0.3	0.6
5	2.0	0.3	−0.6	2.7
10	0.1	0.0	−0.6	2.6
20	0.0	0.0	−0.1	2.4
	Curb market rate			
1	0.1	0.3	0.1	0.0
2	0.0	0.1	0.1	0.1
3	−0.1	0.0	0.2	0.1
4	−0.2	−0.2	0.3	0.3
5	−0.4	−7.3	1.4	0.8
10	−0.3	−0.1	2.1	1.7
20	−0.1	−0.1	0.0	2.3
	Parallel exchange rate			
1	0.0	0.1	−0.1	−0.2
2	0.0	0.1	−0.2	−0.2
3	0.0	0.2	−0.4	−0.4
4	0.1	0.4	−0.6	−0.7
5	0.2	0.6	−1.2	−0.8
10	0.1	0.0	−1.1	−1.2
20	0.0	0.0	−0.2	−1.6

Source: Authors' calculations.

dissipate through the balance of payments. Finally, smuggled exports increase the flow of foreign exchange channeled illegally into the economy, but this is more than offset by a rise in smuggled imports, implying that the stock of foreign-currency-denominated assets decreases over time. The portfolio implications of this tend to sustain the initial rise in the curb interest rate, keeping upward pressure on the premium and prolonging the return to the initial steady state.

11.2.2.2 CENTRAL BANK CREDIT TO COMMERCIAL BANKS

A fully anticipated, transitory increase of 10 percent in central bank credit to the commercial banks has effects qualitatively similar to those of the credit-financed increase in government spending examined previously—with the difference that now the increase in credit is removed after one period. During the transition period between announcement and implementation, output and prices rise, the parallel exchange rate depreciates, and the informal interest rate falls. When the increase in central bank credit actually occurs, loans to the private sector by commercial banks expand. As a result, the demand for credit in the informal market falls, and the curb interest rate drops sharply. The reduction in the financial repression tax lowers the implicit subsidy provided by controls on interest rates, therefore reducing disposable income—since households are net debtors—and this has a negative effect on private spending. But the fall in the informal interest rate also reduces the real interest rate, which has a positive effect on private expenditure. The net effect is an expansion of private spending, which stimulates domestic output and raises prices.

The fall in the curb market interest rate gives agents the incentive to switch toward foreign-currency-denominated assets, leading to a sharp spike in the premium. As the stock of foreign assets held by the private sector increases during the transition period, the undoing of the credit expansion leaves the private sector with a portfolio more heavily weighted toward foreign exchange than initially, and the parallel exchange rate appreciates beyond its initial level in the process of restoring portfolio equilibrium. The appreciation of the free exchange rate reduces the propensity to underinvoice exports, increases the flow of foreign exchange channeled through the official market, and reduces the rate of accumulation of foreign-currency-denominated assets.

11.2.2.3 INCREASE IN LENDING RATES

As discussed in Chapter 5 and in the previous section, increases in administered interest rates have been advocated by McKinnon-Shaw followers as a means to attract funds into the organized financial system, thereby enabling banks to increase lending to private agents and foster economic growth. The new structuralist economists have suggested, however, that this policy could in fact reduce the amount of total lending and have an adverse effect on output (see Chapter 5). In the integrated analytical model developed in Section 11.1, we also showed that an increase in official interest rates may be contractionary on impact.

Table 11.2 shows the results of an anticipated, temporary (for five periods only) increase in bank lending rates by one percentage point. A key channel in the transmission mechanism of this shock in the present framework occurs through the portfolio reallocation effects that it induces, as emphasized in Chapter 5. An increase in the bank lending rate also raises the interest rate paid on bank deposits, through the zero-profit condition. The rise in deposit rates leads households to move funds away from both the informal loan market and foreign-currency assets and to increase bank deposits. As a result, the informal interest rate rises when the measure is implemented and the parallel exchange rate appreciates, both on impact and, as is now familiar, when the measure is first announced. As the parallel exchange rate appreciates, the domestic-currency value of financial wealth falls, to an extent that depends on the weight of foreign-currency assets in private portfolios. The reduction in the nominal value of wealth causes a secondary reallocation of portfolios, since the demand for interest-bearing assets is linearly homogeneous in (nonmonetary) financial wealth. Because of this wealth effect, the demand for bank deposits may indeed rise or fall in net terms. Given the behavioral parameters adopted here, the combination of fairly high substitution elasticities between domestic deposits and foreign exchange (that is, the currency substitution setting) and an important share of foreign assets in private portfolios leads to large wealth effects and a reduction in domestic bank deposits at the announcement period, which persists even after bank lending rates are raised.

A variety of factors explain the contractionary effects on output and prices resulting from the rise in lending rates. First, the appreciation of the parallel exchange rate reduces the real value of households' wealth. Second, the exchange-rate appreciation also reduces the producer price for domestic exports. Third, the implicit subsidy provided by financial repression falls, as the increase in deposit rates exceeds the rise in the informal loan market. The latter exerts direct contractionary effects on spending. Consequently, output and domestic prices fall when the measure is implemented, as well as immediately after announcement.

11.2.2.4 DEVALUATION OF THE OFFICIAL EXCHANGE RATE

The controversial aspects of exchange-rate devaluation in developing countries—particularly in relation to short-run movements in real output—

were highlighted in Chapter 7. The discussion of this issue can now be extended by considering a permanent, fully anticipated 10 percent devaluation of the official rate in the presence of informal financial markets.[39]

The results shown in the last column of Table 11.2 indicate that an official devaluation exerts a net contractionary effect on domestic output upon implementation. However, it also has an expansionary effect during the transition period. The channels through which an official parity change affects real output in this model are complex. First, the official devaluation raises the real price of imported inputs, generating a negative supply shock. Second, the devaluation increases the domestic price level directly through its impact on the domestic price of imported goods, thereby increasing the demand for domestic currency. For a given supply, this causes households to shift funds out of deposits, curb market loans, and foreign-currency assets. The result is a higher informal interest rate and an appreciation of the parallel exchange rate.[40] The rise in the informal interest rate has a direct contractionary effect on private spending, as does the reduction in private real wealth brought about by a reduction in the domestic-currency value of foreign assets and higher prices. Moreover, output of the export good falls because the increase in the demand price of exports is dampened by the appreciation in the parallel exchange rate, while the supply price of exports bears the full impact of the increase in the price of imported intermediate goods. At the same time, however, the increase in the informal interest rate raises the implicit financial repression subsidy and thus real private disposable income. This exerts a positive effect on the demand for home goods, as does the switch in expenditure resulting from the real depreciation of the official exchange rate. A positive supply effect also arises from a reduction in the real wage. Given the set of parameters used in the simulation experiments, however, these expansionary effects are outweighed by the contractionary effects.

While the devaluation itself has a net contractionary effect, the anticipation of an official parity change is expansionary. Output rises in the period preceding the enactment of the devaluation because the anticipated increase in prices and parallel-exchange-rate appreciation upon implementation combine to lower the real interest rate. The anticipated appreciation of the parallel exchange rate lowers the rate of return on foreign-currency assets, causing households to increase their lending through the informal credit market, leading to an initial reduction in the informal interest rate. Together with an expected price level increase, this lowers the real interest rate and increases domestic demand in the period preceding the policy shock. Because the induced price level change in this period is much smaller than the price level jump induced by the devaluation in the subsequent period, however, these effects become progressively weaker as one moves backward in time before the devaluation is implemented, and are outweighed at the announcement period by the negative wealth effects resulting from the appreciation of the parallel exchange rate. These results underline, as emphasized in Chapter 7, the importance of a proper account of dynamic features and expectational phenomena in assessing the macroeconomic consequences of exchange-rate adjustment.

———————

The purpose of this chapter has been to examine further the macroeconomic implications of informal markets in credit and foreign exchange. In the first part we presented an analytical model that accounts simultaneously for the existence of both types of parallel markets. In contrast to the model introduced in Chapter 5, the framework developed here provides a detailed treatment of the supply and demand sides of the economy, while accounting explicitly for leakages across official and unofficial markets. The model was used to examine the short- and long-run effects of interest rate liberalization. The analysis confirms that the effect of a rise in bank deposit rates on total lending depends, as emphasized in the recent literature, on the pattern of substitution across assets. In addition, it also suggests that whether a rise in bank deposit rates is contractionary in the short run depends on complex sectoral output effects induced by changes in the parallel market premium, the informal interest rate, and the real exchange rate. In the second part of the chapter, we presented a highly disaggregated simulation model that we calibrated using in part available parameter estimates. The model was used to examine the dynamic effects of several macroeconomic policy measures. The quantitative results help to emphasize the crucial role that informal financial markets may play in the process of transmission of macroeconomic shocks.

Although the analytical and simulation models developed here were relatively complex, they can be developed further in a variety of directions. For instance, as in new structuralist models, the informal credit market was assumed to substitute with equal social efficiency for formal market loans. This assumption may or may not be warranted in practice. In countries where the formal banking system is highly oligopolistic, informal credit markets (which often have limited barriers to entry) may indeed be more competitive and therefore more efficient than official markets. However, in other cases, particularly in low-income developing countries, informal credit markets may be characterized by the existence of quasi-monopolistic structures (Owen and Solis-Fallas, 1989). Exploring the effects of these differences in market structure would further enhance our understanding of the macroeconomic role of informal financial markets.

Appendix: Equations of the Simulation Model

Supply of home goods

$$y_N(t) = e^{(1-\alpha)^{-1}} P_N^\alpha(t) P_J(t)^{-\alpha_J} w_t^{-\alpha_L}, \quad \alpha_L, \alpha_J < 1, \quad \alpha = \alpha_L + \alpha_J < 1$$
$$\tag{A1}$$

Supply of export goods

$$y_X(t) = e^{(1-\alpha)^{-1}} P_X^\alpha(t) P_J(t)^{-\alpha_J} w_t^{-\alpha_L} \tag{A2}$$

Supply price of exports

$$P_X(t) = [s_t \sigma_t + \bar{E}(1 - \iota_X)(1 - \sigma_t)] P_X^*, \quad 0 < \iota_X < 1 \tag{A3}$$

Nominal wage contracts

$$\Delta \log w_t = \Psi(\ln w_t^* - \ln w_{t-1}), \quad 0 \leq \Psi \leq 1 \tag{A4}$$

Market-clearing wage

$$w_t^* = \alpha_L [P_N(t) y_N(t) + P_X(t) y_X(t)] / \bar{L} \tag{A5}$$

Official output at factor cost

$$P_t Z_t = P_N(t) y_N(t) + (1 - \iota_X)(1 - \sigma_t) \bar{E} P_X^* y_X(t) - \bar{E} P_J^* J_t \tag{A6}$$

Demand for imported intermediate inputs

$$J_t = \alpha_J [P_N(t) y_N(t) + P_X(t) y_X(t)] / \bar{E} P_J^* \tag{A7}$$

Domestic price level

$$P_t = P_N(t)^\delta P_I(t)^{1-\delta} \quad 0 < \delta < 1 \tag{A8}$$

Domestic price of final imports

$$P_I(t) = (\bar{E}^\Phi s_t^{1-\Phi}) P_I^* \quad 0 \leq \Phi \leq 1 \tag{A9}$$

Households' expenditure

$$\ln E_t^p = h_1 \ln Z_t^d + h_2 \log(A_{t-1}/P_t) - h_3 [i_L(t) - \pi_{t+1}^a], \quad 0 < h_1 < 1 \tag{A10}$$

Real disposable income

$$P_t Z_t^d = (1 - \iota) P_t Z_t + \sigma_t s_t P_X^* y_X(t) + q_t i_L(t) [L_{t-1}^p - (1 - \mu) D_{t-1}^p] \tag{A11}$$

Financial repression tax

$$q_t = [i_L(t) - i_c(t)]/i_L(t), \quad 0 \le q_t \le 1 \tag{A12}$$

Demand for the home good

$$y_N(t) = g_N + \delta P_t E_t^p / P_N(t) \tag{A13}$$

Financial wealth

$$A_t = CU_t + D_t^p + s_t F_t^p - L_t^p \tag{A14}$$

Households' budget constraint

$$\Delta A_t = P_t(Z_t^d - E_t^p) + i_d D_{t-1}^p + i_F^* s_t F_{t-1}^p - i_c L_{t-1}^p + \Delta s_t F_{t-1}^p \tag{A15}$$

Demand for foreign assets

$$\ln[s_t F_t^p/(A_t - CU_t)] = \lambda_0 - \lambda_1 i_L(t) - \lambda_2 i_d + \lambda_3 i_F(t) \tag{A16}$$

Rate of return on foreign assets

$$i_F(t) \cong i^* + \hat{s}_{t+1}^a \tag{A17}$$

Demand for bank deposits

$$\ln(D_t^p/(A_t - CU_t)] = \alpha_0 - \alpha_1 i_L(t) + \alpha_2 i_d - \alpha_3 i_F(t) \tag{A18}$$

Demand for domestic-currency notes

$$\ln(CU_t/P_t) = \varphi_1 \ln(Z_t) + \varphi_2 \ln[\sigma_t \rho_t P_X(t) y_X(t)/P_t], \quad \varphi_2 > \varphi_1 \tag{A19}$$

Households' demand for final imports

$$I_t^p = (1 - \delta) P_t E_t^p / P_I(t) \tag{A20}$$

Official sales of foreign exchange

$$F_S(t) = P_J^* J_t + P_I^* g_I + \Phi P_I^* I_t^p, \quad 0 \le \Phi \le 1 \tag{A21}$$

Official current account

$$CA_t = (1 - \sigma_t) P_X^* y_X(t) + i_F^*(F_{t-1}^g + R_{t-1}) - F_S(t) \tag{A22}$$

Net foreign assets of the central bank

$$\Delta R_t = CA_t - \Delta F_t^g \tag{A23}$$

Underinvoicing share

$$\sigma_t = 1 - [(1 - \iota_X)/\rho_t]^{\nu}, \quad \rho_t \equiv s_t/\bar{E}, \quad \nu > 1, \quad 0 \le \sigma_t \le 1 \tag{A24}$$

Unreported current account

$$\Delta F_t^p = \sigma_t P_X^* y_X(t) + i_F^* F_{t-1}^p - (1 - \Phi) P_I^* I_t^p \tag{A25}$$

Balance sheet of commercial banks

$$RR_t + L_t^p = D_t^p + L_t^b \tag{A26}$$

Reserve holdings by commercial banks

$$RR_t = \mu D_t^p, \quad 0 \le \mu \le 1 \tag{A27}$$

Interest rate on bank deposits

$$i_c = i_d/(1 - \mu) \tag{A28}$$

Balance sheet of the central bank

$$CU_t + RR_t = \bar{E}R_t + (L_t - L_t^p) - \Omega_t \tag{A29}$$

Total domestic credit

$$L_t = L_t^p + (L_t^b + L_t^g) \tag{A30}$$

Central bank's net worth

$$\Omega_t = \Omega_{t-1} + i_F^* \bar{E}R_{t-1} + i_c(L_{t-1}^b + L_{t-1}^g) + \Delta\bar{E}R_{t-1} - \tau_t^g \tag{A31}$$

Government deficit

$$GD_t = \iota P_t Z_t + i_F^* \bar{E}F_{t-1}^g + \iota_X(1 - \sigma_t)\bar{E}P_X^* y_X(t)$$
$$+ \tau_t^g - [P_N(t)g_N + \bar{E}P_I^* g_I] - i_c L_{t-1}^g \tag{A32}$$

Deficit financing

$$L_t^g = L_{t-1}^g - GD_t + \bar{E}\Delta F_t^g \tag{A33}$$

Part IV

GROWTH, DEBT, AND STRUCTURAL REFORMS

Twelve

Models of Stabilization and Growth

PARTS II and III of this book dealt with issues related to short-run macro-economic management in developing countries. As stated in the introduction, this has been a burgeoning area of research in recent years. Yet it lies outside the scope of traditional development economics, which has been more concerned with growth and structural change. In this part of the book we turn to the interface between short-run macroeconomics and medium-run growth in developing countries, beginning with an overview in this chapter of models whose objective has been to integrate these concerns in an operational and quantifiable framework. In the two subsequent chapters we take up two major policy issues that impinge simultaneously on short-run macro-economics and medium-term growth: external debt and structural reforms.

The central macroeconomic policy challenge faced by many developing countries is how to achieve stabilization and adjustment while minimizing the cost measured in terms of real income. In the past, this tended to refer to reducing inflation and improving the current account while avoiding short-run income losses arising from deficient aggregate demand. More recently, however, the disappointing medium-term growth experience of many developing countries (outside of East Asia) has turned attention to the maintenance or reactivation of the economy's long-run growth momentum. Specifically, rather than simply attempting to avoid the generation of a gap between actual and potential real output during the process of stabilization, macroeconomic policymakers have become increasingly concerned with sustaining or stimulating the underlying growth rate of productive capacity itself.

Of course, growth has always been the primary preoccupation of development economists. Development economics is, after all, about the achievement of desirable levels of economic growth under a particular set of historical circumstances. Typically, however, the generation of capacity growth has been considered in isolation from the issue of stabilization. Growth issues in the traditional literature have often been treated under full-employment assumptions and more often than not in the context of real models. Growth models of this type are considered in Chapter 15, in conjunction with our discussion of the "new growth" literature. What has become of particular interest for both economists and policymakers in the developing world, however, is the interaction among stabilization, adjustment, and growth. In this chapter, therefore, we examine the analytical tools available to address these issues in practical developing-country applications.

Short-run macroeconomic models are identified as such by the assumption that productive capacity is exogenous. In contrast, the study of the interaction between stabilization and growth requires the specification of medium-term models. These models contain two essential features. First, productive capacity is treated as endogenously determined. This requires the specification of production technologies, through either a single aggregate production function or separate sectoral ones. Such functions relate the level of capacity output to the stock of productive factors and total factor productivity. The second feature of medium-term models is a set of relationships that explain the rate of accumulation of productive factors and the rate of change in total factor productivity as functions of the current and expected future values of macroeconomic variables and policy instruments. Equations that explain the rate of accumulation of physical capital, for instance, typically take the form of investment functions (see Chapter 3).

With both features in place, the interaction among stabilization, adjustment, and growth in medium-term models is as follows: Given the predetermined values of total factor productivity and the stock of productive factors, the economy's short-run equilibrium simultaneously determines the levels of output and employment, in addition to the price level, the current account, and the rate of net investment in new productive factors. The rate of net investment in turn determines the stock of productive factors in the next period, which together with updated values of total factor productivity determine the next period's level of productive capacity. Thus, the growth of productive capacity between this period and the next depends on the characteristics of this period's short-run equilibrium, and in particular on the rate of net investment generated in that equilibrium. Medium-term models with dynamics of this type are distinguished from long-run models by their ability to address the short-run problems of stabilization and adjustment simultaneously with the long-run problem of capacity growth.

In this chapter we shall examine four types of macroeconomic models that have long been used in developing countries and that broadly incorporate these features. These include "Bank-Fund" models, "gap" models, macroeconometric models, and computable general equilibrium models. Based on the discussion above, it follows that the success of such models in shedding light on the interactions between stabilization and growth in developing countries depends on three features:

The specification of the determinants of productive capacity.
The description of the forces determining the rate of accumulation of productive assets and total factor productivity.
The quality of the model's description of the economy's short-run equilibrium.

Although all of the models to be examined have been applied frequently in policy formulation in developing nations, we shall argue that all of them are subject to limitations that constrain their usefulness for both policy guidance and analytical work as medium-term models.

12.1 Bank-Fund Models

Among the most parsimonious models aimed at quantifying the effects of stabilization programs and medium-term growth policies are those of the International Monetary Fund and the World Bank. After reviewing the basic features of the model developed by each multilateral institution, we examine the issue of whether the main characteristics of the two approaches can be combined.

12.1.1 The IMF Financial Programming Model

Providing advice to developing countries on macroeconomic policy is an important responsibility of the International Monetary Fund. In addition, the Fund extends financial support to stabilization programs that meet certain criteria: they must be consistent with the principles set out in the institution's articles of agreement and must offer a convincing prospect of repayment. This assistance is conditioned on the borrowing country's compliance with a set of quantitative policy performance criteria drawn up in consultation with the Fund and embodied in a financial (or standby) program. The design of such a program and specification of such criteria rely on a conceptual framework referred to as "financial programming."

The simplest financial programming model is designed to determine the magnitude of domestic credit expansion required to achieve a desired balance-of-payments target under a predetermined exchange rate—the regime that, as argued in Chapter 6, has characteristically been adopted in developing countries.[1] The model is in effect a variant of the monetary approach to the balance of payments (MABP), which, indeed, was pioneered at the Fund.[2] The first equation of the model is the balance sheet identity for the banking system, which equates assets—in the form of credit to the nonbank sector D_t and claims on foreigners R_t—to monetary liabilities M_t:

$$M_t = D_t + E_t R_t, \tag{1}$$

where E_t is the nominal exchange rate. In this relationship, R_t and M_t are endogenous and D_t is an exogenous policy variable under the control of the monetary authorities. The second equation is the definition of velocity v_t as nominal GDP y_t divided by the money stock:

$$v_t = y_t/M_t. \tag{2}$$

In the Fund's version of the MABP, the money market is required to be in flow (but not necessarily stock) equilibrium:

$$\Delta M_t = v_t^{-1} y_t - v_{t-1}^{-1} y_{t-1}. \tag{3}$$

On the assumptions that the nominal exchange rate and velocity are both constant ($E_t = \overline{E}$ and $v_t = v$) and that nominal GDP is exogenous, the model can be solved for the change in the stock of international reserves R_t as a function of v and y_t, as well as of the monetary policy instrument D_t:

$$\overline{E}\Delta R_t = v^{-1}\Delta y_t - \Delta D_t. \tag{4}$$

Alternatively, given a target value for the change in reserves (the balance of payments) and projections for v and y_t, the required expansion in the stock of credit can be derived from

$$\Delta D_t = v^{-1}\Delta y_t - \overline{E}\Delta R_t. \tag{5}$$

As indicated above, in this version of the model nominal output is exogenous. An expanded version, referred to as the "Polak model," makes nominal output endogenous as well (Polak, 1957). We write the balance-of-payments identity as

$$\Delta R_t = X_t - \alpha(y_{t-1} + \Delta y_t) + \Delta F_t, \quad 0 < \alpha < 1. \tag{6}$$

Net exports are taken to have an autonomous component X_t and a component that depends negatively on current nominal income, expressed as last period's value plus the change Δy_t. Net capital inflows ΔF_t are exogenous. With nominal output endogenous and the balance-of-payments identity added, the Polak model consists of two equations in the two unknowns ΔR_t and Δy_t.

The interaction between the money-market equilibrium condition (4) and the balance of payments identity (6) in determining nominal income and the balance of payments is illustrated in Figure 12.1. Equation (4) is depicted as the positively sloped MM locus, while (6) is the negatively sloped locus RR. The equilibrium values of the balance of payments and the change in nominal income are determined by the point of intersection, E. It is easy to show that in this model an increase in the rate of expansion of credit will cause the balance of payments to deteriorate and nominal income to rise, while an increase in exogenous receipts of foreign exchange will improve the balance of payments and raise nominal income. This "Polak" form of the financial programming model can be given a "classical" closure—that is, it

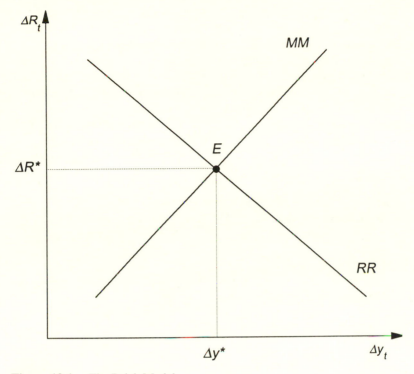

Figure 12.1   The Polak Model

can be solved for the domestic price level, taking real output as exogenous—
or a "Keynesian" closure, in which it is solved for changes in real output,
taking the price level as given.[3]

12.1.2 The World Bank RMSM Model

The IMF financial programming model can be interpreted as a short-run
model of stabilization and adjustment. "Adjustment" in this context refers
to the balance of payments, while "stabilization" refers to the price level in
classical mode and to real output in Keynesian mode. It contains no aggregate production function and does not determine capacity output. By contrast, the World Bank's Revised Minimum Standard Model (RMSM) is a
model of capacity output. RMSM has long been used to generate macroeconomic projections in country economic reports at the Bank. The emphasis in RMSM is on ascertaining whether the domestic and external financing
available to a particular country is adequate to achieve a target for economic
growth.

The key analytical feature of RMSM thus concerns the link between financing and capacity growth. The simplest such link is already contained in the balance-of-payments identity (6). Interpreting y_t as real output, if autonomous net exports are taken to be exogenous ($X_t = \overline{X}$), the economy's growth is determined by the volume of external financing $\Delta F_t - \Delta R_t$.[4] RMSM is then used to calculate the volume of domestic saving required to sustain this increment to output. Assuming a fixed-coefficients Harrod-Domar production function in capital and labor, with capital taken to be the scarce factor, an increase in capacity requires domestic investment I_t of

$$I_t = \sigma \Delta y_t, \tag{7}$$

where σ is the incremental capital/output ratio (ICOR). Letting c_t and S_t denote domestic consumption and saving, respectively, we can use the national income accounting identity

$$I_t = (y_t - c_t) + (\alpha y_t - \overline{X}), \tag{8}$$

and the definition of savings

$$S_t = y_t - c_t, \tag{9}$$

to find the volume of domestic saving required to achieve a given increment to productive capacity:

$$S_t = \overline{X} - \alpha y_{t-1} + (\sigma - \alpha)\Delta y_t. \tag{10}$$

S_t is an increasing function of Δy_t, since σ is a number typically in the neighborhood of 3–4, while α is a fraction. With saving itself linearly related to output in Keynesian fashion,

$$S_t = S_0 + sy_t, \quad 0 < s < 1, \tag{11}$$

the resulting framework can be used to derive the level of autonomous saving required to sustain an increment to capacity output:

$$S_0 = \overline{X} - \alpha y_{t-1} + [\sigma - (\alpha + s)]\Delta y_t. \tag{12}$$

12.1.3 A Simple Bank-Fund Model of Stabilization and Growth

The RMSM consists of Equations (6), (7) to (9), and (11), that is, the four new equations introduced here plus the balance-of-payments identity used earlier. The model can be used in a variety of ways, with the "financing needs" mode described above being the most common. For example, with ΔR_t and Δy_t exogenous (as policy targets), while ΔF_t and S_t are endogenous, the model is solved in "financing needs" mode. With ΔR_t bounded from below, ΔF_t and S_t exogenous, Δy_t endogenous, and (8) setting a minimum value for investment, the model is solved in "two-gap" mode (see below). An alternative application of the RMSM can be combined with the financial programming model to derive a simple Fund-Bank model of adjustment and growth.

Continue to interpret y_t as real output, and suppose that autonomous saving S_0 is exogenous. Then Equation (12) can be solved for the rate of capacity growth Δy_t. Growth of productive capacity is determined in neoclassical fashion by the availability of saving (domestic and foreign, via S_0 and $\overline{X}$) and the productivity of investment, given by σ. This capacity growth rate can be fed into the Polak model given by Equations (4) and (6). Since y_t is now interpreted as real output, and (4) involves nominal income, it must be rewritten as

$$\overline{E}\Delta R_t = v^{-1}\left[(P_{t-1} + \Delta P_t)\Delta y_t + y_{t-1}\Delta P_t\right] - \Delta D_t, \qquad (4')$$

where P_t is the domestic price level. The resulting model can be solved in two ways: if capital inflows are exogenous and the domestic price level is endogenous, (6) yields the balance of payments ΔR_t and (4') the domestic price level. Alternatively, if the domestic price level is exogenous and capital inflows are endogenous, (4') yields the balance of payments and (6) the level of capital inflows.

12.2 "Three-Gap" Models

The "financing gap" method incorporated in the RMSM, which determines feasible output levels from foreign exchange availability, is the most venerable approach to the projection of real output growth in developing countries. "Gap" models, however, are close contenders. Early analyses in this tradition, referred to as "two-gap" models because of their focus on foreign exchange and domestic saving as alternative constraints on growth, date back to Chenery and Strout (1966). More recently, the fiscal dimension of the debt crisis of the 1980s (see Chapter 13) has given rise to a new member of this class of models, dubbed "three-gap" because they add to the previous two constraints a third in the form of a fiscal gap. In this section we describe a three-gap model developed by Bacha (1990).[5]

In Bacha's model, foreign exchange availability is linked directly to the rate of growth of productive capacity and only indirectly to the level of actual real output, in contrast to the "financing needs" approach described above. The ICOR relationship described in Equation (7) is retained, but investment now is assumed to require imported capital goods:

$$Z_t = mI_t, \qquad 0 < m < 1, \tag{13}$$

where Z_t denotes the level of capital goods imports. Let x_t denote the level of exports net of other (noncapital) imports, and J_t the sum of external debt service, transfers, and changes in foreign exchange reserves (previously denoted ΔR_t). Then, from (14) and the balance-of-payments identity, we have

$$I_t = (1/m)[x_t + (\Delta F_t - J_t)]. \tag{14}$$

Suppose that x_t is subject to the upper bound x^*, determined by external demand. Then (15) becomes the inequality

$$I_t \leq (1/m)[x^* + (\Delta F_t - J_t)], \tag{15}$$

which represents the "foreign exchange" constraint on investment, and thus, by Equation (7), on capacity growth.

The "savings" constraint is derived as follows: From the balance-of-payments and national income accounting identities (6) and (8) (suitably modified to incorporate J_t and the modified specification of import demand in the present model), we have

$$I_t = y_t - c_t - g_t - (\Delta F_t - J_t),$$

where g_t denotes government spending. Defining private saving as $S_t^p = y_t - \tau_t - c_t$, where τ_t is government net tax revenue, the previous equation becomes

$$I_t = S_t^p + (\tau_t - g_t) + (\Delta F_t - J_t).$$

Taking private consumption to be exogenous and noting that y_t is bounded above by full-capacity output, it follows that S_t^p is an increasing function of output and is bounded above by private saving at full capacity output, $\tilde{S}^p$. This means that I_t is also bounded from above, so that

$$I_t \leq \tilde{S}^p + (\tau_t - g_t) + (\Delta F_t - J_t), \tag{16}$$

which represents the saving constraint on investment.

Finally, to derive the "fiscal constraint," assume that base money is the only financial asset available for the private sector to hold in this economy, so that the private sector's budget constraint can be written as

$$S_t^p - I_t^p = \Delta H_t / P_t, \tag{17}$$

where I_t^p represents private investment and H_t is the stock of base money. The change in H_t is assumed to be given by

$$\Delta H_t = H(\pi_t, \Theta), \quad 0 < \Theta < 1, \tag{18}$$

where π_t denotes the rate of inflation and Θ the "propensity to hoard," that is, the portion of any increase in income devoted to the accumulation of cash balances. In this case, all foreign capital flows accrue to the government, and the budget constraint of the consolidated public sector can be written as

$$I_t^g = H(\pi_t, \Theta) + (\tau_t - g_t) + (\Delta F_t - J_t), \tag{19}$$

where I_t^g is public investment, which, added to private investment, yields total investment:

$$I_t = I_t^p + I_t^g. \tag{20}$$

The key to deriving the fiscal constraint is the assumption that private and public investment are complements, so that private investment is bounded above by the level of public investment:

$$I_t^p \leq k^* I_t^g, \tag{21}$$

where k^* is the ratio of private to public capital in the composite capital stock. From Equations (19) to (21), the fiscal constraint on total investment takes the form

$$I_t \leq (1 + k^*) [H(\pi_t, \Theta) + (\tau_t - g_t) + (\Delta F_t - J_t)]. \tag{22}$$

This model simultaneously determines the level of output, the current account, the rate of growth of productive capacity, and the rate of inflation. The focus of "gap" models is on the implications for such variables of alternative levels of foreign financing $(\Delta F_t - J_t)$. To illustrate the mechanisms at work, consider Figure 12.2, in which the central endogenous variable I_t is plotted against $(\Delta F_t - J_t)$. Equations (15) and (16) are plotted as the loci FF and SS, representing the foreign exchange and saving constraints, respectively. The slope of SS is unity, as can be verified from Equation (16), while that of FF is $1/m$, which is greater than unity, since m is a fraction. The relative positions of the two curves rely on the assumption that $(1/m)x^* < \tilde{S}^p + (\tau_t - g_t)$. The hatched areas beneath the curves represent the feasible regions for I_t (that is, the values of I_t that satisfy the respective inequalities). If net foreign inflows are $(\Delta F_t - J_t)'$, both constraints are binding and investment is I_t'.

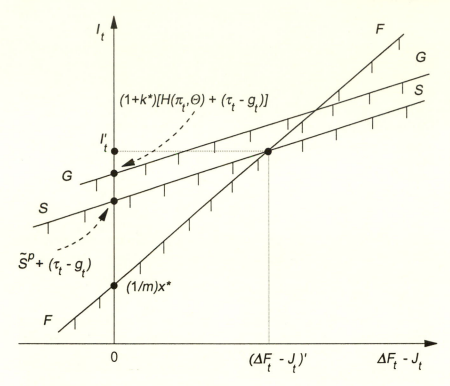

Figure 12.2   The Three-Gap Model

Source: Adapted from Bacha (1990, p. 291).

To the left of $(\Delta F_t - J_t)'$, the foreign exchange constraint binds. Investment (and therefore capacity growth) is determined by foreign exchange availability. Since investment will therefore be less than the level that would satisfy (16) as an equality and since the other components of aggregate demand are fixed, the economy will suffer from Keynesian excess capacity, and actual output will be given by

$$y_t = c_t + (1 - m)I_t^c + x^*, \tag{23}$$

where I_t^c is the actual (constrained) level of investment. If, on the other hand, $(\Delta F_t - J_t)$ exceeds $(\Delta F_t - J_t)'$, the economy will be constrained by domestic saving. Investment will now be determined along SS, and output will be at full capacity. The slack variable in this case is net exports, which are squeezed by domestic demand and are given by

$$x_t = y^* - c_t + (1 - m)I_t^s, \tag{24}$$

where I_t^s denotes the savings-constrained level of investment.

This part of the analysis essentially reproduces the two-gap model of Chenery and Strout. How does the "fiscal gap" fit in? Geometrically, inequality (22) is represented by an area bounded above by a locus (call it GG) with slope $(1 + k^*)$ and vertical intercept $(1 + k^*)[H(\pi_t, \Theta) + (\tau_t - g_t)]$. $(1 + k^*)$ may be greater or less than $1/m$, so GG may be steeper or flatter than FF. Curves GG and SS, on the other hand, have the same slope. Their relative heights, however, depend on the values of π_t and k^*. Although the private sector budget constraint (17) implies that $\tilde{S}^p > H(\pi_t, \Theta)$ as long as I_t^p is positive, the difference between $\tilde{S}^p$ and $H(\pi_t, \Theta)$ decreases with π_t. Thus a larger value of π_t raises the height of GG relative to SS. A larger value of k^* has a similar effect.

There are a number of ways to incorporate the fiscal constraint in the model. The simplest, and most in keeping with the "two gap" analysis, is to treat π_t as an endogenous variable that ensures that (22) holds as an equality. In this case, the role of the fiscal constraint is merely to determine the rate of inflation. Given the value of I_t, Equations (20) and (21) holding as an equality would determine the levels of I_t^p and I_t^g, and given the latter, (22) holding as an equality would determine π_t. Geometrically, the two-gap analysis described above is undisturbed, but endogenous changes in π_t serve to move the GG locus to intersect whichever of the two other loci happens to be binding at a point directly above the relevant value of $(\Delta F_t - J_t)$. An increase in $(\Delta F_t - J_t)$ would in this case not only serve to increase the rate of capacity growth by raising I_t (as in the two-gap approach), but would also reduce the rate of inflation by permitting the government to finance itself externally, rather than through the inflation tax.

Alternatively, if π_t is an exogenous policy variable, GG serves as an independent constraint. If the fiscal constraint does not bind, then k is the slack variable; given I_t and I_t^g, I_t^p is determined, and the actual value of k implied by I_t^p and I_t^g may be smaller than k^*. If the fiscal constraint does bind, then an increase in $(\Delta F_t - J_t)$ will increase capacity growth, because the receipt of foreign financing will result in higher public investment, which in turn will induce more private investment. The actual level of output will rise, through Keynesian demand effects emanating from higher levels of both private and public investment, bringing the economy closer to full capacity utilization, and net exports will fall.

12.3 Macroeconometric Models

The models considered in Section 12.1 rely heavily on accounting identities and are very parsimonious in their use of behavioral parameters. The few parameters used are typically not estimated econometrically, but rather are calculated as simple historical averages or ratios over some recent period.

The models of Section 12.2, by contrast, require a little more behavioral structure, and in applications some of the parameters of three-gap models have been estimated econometrically. Both of these classes of models are easy to use and have the virtue of imposing some discipline on the analysis of the interactions among stabilization, adjustment, and growth in specific country circumstances, but they both omit a substantial amount of economic structure and behavior.

Most important, they are deficient as medium-term models both because of their specification of the determinants of productive capacity as well as of the rate of accumulation of productive factors. In both cases, the production function is of the fixed-coefficients Harrod-Domar type, and neither family of models contains an independent investment function describing the behavior of agents who actually make the decision to accumulate productive factors. In both models investment in physical capital is treated as a residual. The stylized Bank-Fund model treats investment as determined by the available saving, while the three-gap model derives it residually from saving, foreign exchange availability, or the government budget, depending on which is the binding constraint.

In the context of industrial nations, the conventional way of analyzing complicated dynamic macroeconomic phenomena such as those of stabilization, adjustment, and growth is through the use of macroeconometric models. Simulations of such models are often used to explore policy trade-offs in complex dynamic settings. A large number of macroeconometric models have also been estimated in recent years for developing countries, both for individual countries and for groups of countries. While the state of the art is substantially less advanced in the developing-country context than it is for industrial countries, such models may represent an alternative tool for the systematic analysis of the issues posed in this chapter in any particular application. Accordingly, this section provides a brief overview of the structure of "representative" macroeconometric models for developing countries.[6]

12.3.1 Structure of Production

The vast majority of macroeconometric models for developing countries have been built along the lines of the Mundell-Fleming production structure, in spite of several questions (discussed in Chapter 1) regarding its relevance for most developing economies.[7] Thus, the economy is taken to be specialized in the production of a single home good, which is an imperfect substitute for the foreign good. The domestically produced good can be either consumed at home or exported, and domestic residents generally consume both the home good and the foreign good.

12.3.2 Aggregate Supply

The aggregate production function in many macroeconometric models for developing countries takes one of two forms. A family of models dubbed RMSM-X, developed as successors to RMSM at the World Bank, retains the constant ICOR assumption.[8] More commonly, capacity output is specified as a function of capital K_t, labor L_t, and an imported intermediate good J_t:

$$y_t = F(L_t, J_t; K_t), \tag{25}$$

with standard neoclassical properties.[9] Empirically, this function is typically given a Cobb-Douglas or CES form. The capital stock is predetermined in the short run and grows endogenously as the result of net investment. Both the level of total factor productivity and the labor force grow exogenously, and imported intermediate goods are available from the world market in infinitely elastic supply at an exogenous foreign-currency price.[10]

The determination of the domestic-currency price of the home good depends on how the supply side of the economy is modeled in the short run. In the simplest macroeconometric models, the supply side is described along Keynesian fixprice or classical flexprice lines. The simple Keynesian version, however, has no dynamics arising from the expansion of productive capacity, since it takes output to be entirely demand driven. Such models thus assume an explicitly short-run horizon and are not suitable for addressing the issues that concern us in this chapter.[11] In the classical version, continuous full employment is assumed, and output of the home good is determined by the inherited capital stock, the size of the labor force, and the price of the imported intermediate good. More generally, short-run supply behavior is depicted via a variable mark-up price equation. The price of the home good is taken to be determined by unit costs plus a mark-up factor that depends on the rate of capacity utilization in the economy:

$$P_t = P\left[\overset{+}{w}_t, \overset{+}{P^*_j}(t), \overset{+}{y_t/\bar{y}}\right], \tag{26}$$

where w_t is the nominal wage, $\bar{y}$ is the capacity output, and $P^*_j(t)$ is the domestic-currency price of the imported intermediate good.[12] With this specification, the economy's short-run aggregate supply curve is an upward-sloping function of the level of real output, and it is displaced vertically by changes in the nominal wage or in the domestic-currency price of imported inputs.

In Equation (26) the nominal wage and the level of full capacity output are predetermined, while the level of output and the domestic price level are solved out simultaneously. The price of imported intermediate goods, on the other hand, depends only on their exogenous foreign-currency price and the exchange rate. The evolution of full-capacity output has been described above. The behavior of nominal wages is often based on an expectations-augmented Phillips curve:

$$\frac{\Delta w_t}{w_t} = \omega\left[L(y_t, \overset{+}{K}_t, P_t^*)/\overline{L}, \overset{+}{\pi}_t^a\right],\qquad(27)$$

where $\overline{L}$ denotes the labor force, π_t^a the expected inflation rate, and $L(\ )$ actual employment, which is determined from the cost-minimizing decisions of firms.[13] The most common approach to the modeling of expectations formation in macroeconometric models for developing countries has been the use of adaptive expectations.[14]

12.3.3 Aggregate Demand

The demand side of macroeconometric models for developing countries tends to have an *IS-LM* flavor, often with ad hoc adjustments of behavioral relationships to capture specific characteristics of developing economies. On the "*IS*" side, the behavior of private consumption, private investment, exports, and imports is usually motivated by standard textbook considerations, with substantial variation across existing models regarding the specification of consumption and investment. The financial or "*LM*" side of these models is typically problematic, with particular difficulties posed by the modeling of financial repression and capital mobility.

The set of determinants of consumption includes disposable income $y_D(t)$, the real interest rate ρ_t, and some type of real wealth variable $a_t = A_t/P_t$:

$$c_t = c\left[\overset{+}{Y}_D(t), \overset{-}{\rho}_t, \overset{+}{a}_t\right],\quad 0 < c_y < 1.\qquad(28)$$

However, there is no particular consensus on the specification of private consumption behavior, and the specifications range—even within the class of RMSM-X models mentioned previously—from treating consumption as a simple fraction of disposable income (Everaert et al., 1990) to the inclusion, in addition to the variables listed above, of other variables reflecting liquidity constraints and possible Ricardian equivalence effects (Elbadawi and Schmidt-Hebbel, 1991).[15] When wealth is included, the nominal value of private wealth A_t is a predetermined variable that evolves over time in response to private saving, derived from substituting (28) in the private sector's budget constraint.

As suggested at various points in this chapter, the specification of investment behavior is crucial in models of stabilization and growth. Macroeconometric models differ from those discussed previously in their inclusion of an independent investment function.[16] The set of determinants of private investment spending typically includes real output, a cost-of-capital term q_t, and the lagged capital stock:

$$I_t = I(\overset{+}{y}_t, \bar{q}_t, \bar{K}_{t-1}).$$ (29)

However, once again there is wide variation in existing models, even among those of recent vintage, ranging from treating investment as proportional to output at one extreme to including, in addition to the variables listed above, the public capital stock (to capture possible complementarities between private and public capital) and credit-rationing variables at the other extreme.

More generally, the investment functions in macroeconometric models for developing countries suffer from the shortcomings that characterize the literature on investment in the developing world, as described in Chapter 3. Significant features of these investment functions are their omission of forward-looking variables and their failure to account for the likely irreversibility of investment in physical capital. More generally, while the inclusion of independent investment functions is a step forward in these models relative to those examined previously, the actual functions included in macroeconometric models are not well grounded in intertemporal profit-maximizing behavior on the part of firms. Moreover, several structural aspects of potential significance for understanding capital accumulation in developing nations are not adequately dealt with in the investment functions embedded in the macroeconometric models. These include the effect on investment of the existence of an external debt overhang; the role of complementary factors such as infrastructure, human capital, and imported inputs; and the role of financial repression.

Regarding the remaining components of aggregate demand, the treatment of the trade sector tends to be fairly uniform in macroeconometric models for developing countries. Exports are determined by foreign income and the relative price of the home good, while imports depend on the same relative price as well as on domestic real GDP. Some models—see, for instance, Elliott et al. (1986) and Haque et al. (1990)—include a measure of foreign reserve availability in the import demand function, in order to capture the intensity of rationing in the official market for foreign exchange.

The specification of the financial sector—the "*LM*" portion of these *IS-LM* models—is generally fairly rudimentary. The institutional disaggregation typically includes the central bank and the deposit money banks. The central bank's balance sheet is at the heart of the financial sector, with the change in its liabilities (base money) linked to changes in its assets (net foreign assets, changing through the balance of payments, and domestic assets, changing primarily through central bank financing of the fiscal deficit). The demand for money is usually taken to depend on real GDP and a domestic nominal interest rate, which is often treated as endogenous in standard textbook fashion. Careful modeling of financial repression is not commonly found in macroeconometric models, nor is the existence of informal markets.[17] The common treatment of capital mobility leaves foreign interest rates out of domestic asset demand functions, taking capital flows to be exogenous. Yet both the specification of domestic financial markets and their interactions with world capital markets play important roles in the determination of the cost of capital, so the financial sector is crucial to the analysis of the relationship between stabilization and growth.

Thus, while existing macroeconometric models improve on the models of Sections 12.1 and 12.2 by generalizing the production function and including an independent investment function, in many respects they fall short of providing a suitable framework for the analysis of the interactions among stabilization, adjustment, and growth. Most important, neither the aggregate production functions nor the investment functions embedded in existing models reflect important forces influencing capacity growth and the accumulation of productive assets in developing countries, and other features of existing models—such as the production structure, the treatment of expectations, and the specification of the financial system—raise doubts about their ability to capture the effects of stabilization on the endogenous variables that affect accumulation decisions.

12.4 Computable General Equilibrium Models

Conventional macroeconometric models for developing countries such as those described in the previous section tend to exhibit the level of aggregation that is standard for macroeconomic models in general. The individual models mentioned in Section 12.3, for instance, generally contain no more than two domestically produced commodities, and factors of production tend to be aggregated into homogeneous capital, labor, and imported raw materials. An alternative economywide modeling approach for developing countries is the construction of computable general equilibrium (CGE) models. CGE models are essentially applied microeconomic models, designed to study issues such as the effects on resource allocation and income distribution of various types of external shocks or policy interventions.[18]

A key distinction between CGE models and macroeconometric models lies in the level of aggregation assumed for both goods and factors. CGE models are highly disaggregated on both their demand and supply sides. On the supply side, such models tend to contain a large number of distinct production activities and factors of production including, for example, heterogeneous labor and land.[19] The supply of imports is also disaggregated into different types of commodities that can be purchased on the world market, which may differ in their degree of substitutability for domestic goods. Profit-maximizing behavior by firms generates sectoral supply functions for individual domestically produced commodities and demand functions for various types of factors. On the demand side, different types of households are distinguished by the nature of their ownership of factors of production. Utility maximization by individual classes of households generates demand for domestic and foreign goods, as well as supply functions for different types of factors. World demand for domestic goods can exhibit different price elasticities for different goods, permitting the domestic economy to exercise market power over some commodities but not others. Relative price adjustments play a central role in CGE models, but market equilibrium can be completely Walrasian, with relative prices adjusting to clear all markets, or particular markets can fail to clear due to the presence of price rigidities.

A second key distinction between traditional CGE and macroeconometric models concerns their dynamic properties. CGE models are oriented to the solution of period-by-period comparative-statics exercises. They do not solve for a full intertemporal Walrasian equilibrium with intertemporal optimization by households, firms, and government subject to intertemporal budget constraints.[20] Nonetheless, because CGE models are meant to represent actual economies, macroeconomic phenomena of an explicitly intertemporal nature, such as saving and investment, do appear in existing models. However, these phenomena are traditionally modeled in rudimentary fashion. Private households are assumed to save a fixed fraction of their incomes (which may differ across categories of households), public consumption is exogenous, and investment is often either exogenous or determined by the saving rate.

These assumptions have an important implication: with households not spending all of their income each period, and with independent investment and public consumption decisions, CGE models require a period-by-period macroeconomic mechanism to reconcile aggregate saving and investment (in the terminology of the CGE literature, a "closure" rule). Dewatripont and Michel (1987) classify potential closures into four types: Keynesian (real wage adjusts to change aggregate income, permitting saving to equal exogenous investment, but the labor market may not clear), Johansenian (endogenous public or private consumption equates total saving to exogenous investment), Kaldorian (factors are not paid their marginal products), and classical (investment is determined by saving). The sensitivity of numerical results to the particular choice of a closure rule is not always clear, and may vary depending on the issue at hand (see Adelman and Robinson, 1988).

Unfortunately, none of these mechanisms leaves traditional CGE models particularly well suited to the analysis of the links among stabilization, adjustment, and growth. The issue of how the effects of stabilization and adjustment affect the decision to accumulate productive assets cannot be adequately addressed under any of these closures, since all of them have the effect of leaving investment exogenous or equal to saving. Addressing the links between stabilization and growth in the context of a general equilibrium model requires the inclusion of an independent investment function that responds endogenously to current and expected future macroeconomic variables, as in the macroeconometric models of the previous section. Because these intertemporal links are omitted, dynamics in traditional CGE models indeed tend to be too simple to capture the complex interactions among stabilization, adjustment, and growth. The Walrasian problem solved each period is static, with each period's general equilibrium a function of a set of predetermined variables that evolve exogenously over time.

These difficulties with CGE models are obviously not inherent in the methodology, but are simply a reflection of the predominantly microeconomic and single-period comparative-static orientation of traditional CGE models, which encouraged rather simple specifications of macroeconomic phenomena such as saving and investment. In recent years, CGE models have begun to incorporate more sophisticated macroeconomic relationships. Several of the "new structuralist" CGE models in Taylor (1990), as well as the more neoclassical "micro-macro" models patterned after Bourguignon et al. (1992), incorporate traditional macroeconomic relationships—in particular, an independent investment function that depends on a financial variable, giving rise to IS-LM interactions.[21] This modification brings recent CGE models quite close to the "dependent economy" macroeconomic simulation models mentioned in the previous section (see Montiel, 1993b). While these innovations significantly enrich the macro dynamics exhibited by CGE models, the macroeconomics of these models remain relatively simple. In contrast to the static optimizing behavior assumed for within-period sectoral supply and demand functions, dynamic behavior is left rather simple and ad hoc. Intertemporal optimization on the part of either households or firms based on forward-looking expectations remain absent. Thus, while recent CGE models are better equipped than standard macroeconometric models to handle the microeconomic phenomena for which they were designed, such as the effects of trade liberalization on sectoral resource allocation, they do not yet provide a satisfactory vehicle for the study of stabilization and growth.

In summary, none of the medium-term modeling approaches that have been widely used in the developing world is at present able to adequately address the complex dynamic interactions involved in the relationship between stabilization and growth. Progress awaits an improved quantitative understanding of the link between structural policies and total factor productivity, a respecification of sectoral production and investment functions in developing countries to reflect recent developments in our understanding of the determinants of growth as well as the factors affecting capital accumulation, and further progress in short-run development macroeconomics. In the meantime, attempts at integrating short-run stabilization and long-run growth in a coherent medium-term framework will continue to be fraught with difficulties.

Appendix: The Khan-Knight Monetary Disequilibrium Model

A quantitative macroeconomic framework that has been used in various forms by a number of authors to gauge the effects of stabilization policies in developing countries is the "monetary disequilibrium" model developed by Khan and Knight (1981), which is based on the the monetary approach to the balance of payments.[22] In its simplest form, the monetary approach to the balance of payments predicts that, in a small open economy operating under a fixed-exchange-rate regime, a reduction in domestic credit will be completely offset in the long run by international reserve flows that restore the money stock to the level desired by the public. Consequently, this policy would have no lasting effect on deviations of output from its full-capacity level. Nevertheless, during the adjustment process, the reduction in domestic credit is likely to exert effects on prices and lead to substantial variations in output. The size and duration of these effects depend in general on a variety of factors, such as the degree of utilization of productive capacity, the speed of adjustment in foreign assets resulting from changes in the credit stock, the sensitivity of inflation to disequilibria in the money market, and the sensitivity of aggregate demand and its components to changes in real money balances. The Khan-Knight model assumes the existence of a link between fiscal and monetary policies (through the government budget constraint), and explicitly considers the composition of the balance of payments.

A flow chart of the model is provided in Figure 12.3. Changes in money supply are, by definition, equal to changes in credit to the government, changes in credit to the private sector, and variations in international reserves. Changes in credit to the government are linked to fiscal deficits, with foreign financing assumed exogenous. Money demand is related to real income and the expected inflation rate, which is assumed to follow an adaptive process. This formulation follows along the lines of the "conventional" specification discussed in Chapter 3, which assumes that the relevant measure of the opportunity cost of holding money in developing countries is the rate of return on holding real assets.

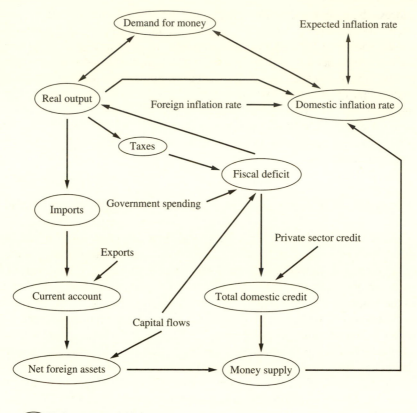

Figure 12.3   Logical Structure of the Khan-Knight Model

In standard fashion, the demand for imports depends on real income and relative prices, while exports are determined by foreign activity and (in some variants of the model) the ratio of export prices (expressed in domestic currency) to domestic prices, which captures the profitability of export production. Changes in net foreign assets are determined by the trade balance plus the services account (which is assumed exogenous) and the change in net external indebtedness of the private and public sectors. The inflation rate is related to the excess supply of real money balances and the rate of inflation abroad, which is measured by the rate of growth of import prices adjusted by the rate of depreciation of the nominal exchange rate. Deviations of output from its full-capacity level respond to excess supply of money balances and (in some versions of the model) the fiscal deficit. Changes in domestic credit result from changes in commercial banks' claims on the private sector and (as indicated above) central bank financing of the government budget deficit.

Tax revenue is a function of economic activity, while public expenditure is treated as exogenous. The specification of the model ensures that in the long run output is at full capacity, equilibrium in the money market prevails, and domestic inflation is determined by foreign inflation. A reduction in domestic credit also has a one-to-one effect on net foreign assets of the central bank in the long run, as predicted by the monetary approach to the balance of payments.

Thirteen

The Debt Overhang, Investment, and Growth

THE SUSPENSION of payments to its foreign bank creditors by Mexico in August 1982 triggered an international debt crisis that dominated macroeconomic policymaking in heavily indebted developing countries for the next decade. The crisis took the form of a sudden and drastic reduction in the scale of voluntary lending to developing nations by bank creditors abroad. Foreign commercial banks had become heavily involved in lending to developing countries during the decade of the 1970s, primarily in the form of syndicated loans at variable interest rates typically expressed in the form of loan-specific spreads over the London Interbank Offered Rate (LIBOR). The crisis led to a period during which many heavily indebted nations in the developing world experienced severely reduced economic growth accompanied by sharp contractions in domestic investment, substantial capital outflows, and, in some cases, greatly increased rates of inflation.

The debt crisis gave rise to a voluminous professional literature treating a wide range of issues, including the causes of the crisis, its macroeconomic consequences for the indebted countries, its likely evolution, and prospects for its resolution. In this chapter we analyze the macroeconomics of developing-country debt. Since the debt literature and the range of topics it covers are so vast, we do not attempt a comprehensive review, but rather present what we regard as a unifying perspective on debt issues by considering external debt as a fiscal problem. This links the topics covered in this chapter with those considered in Chapter 4.[1]

Our approach to the external debt issue is motivated by several observations. Much policy-oriented discussion of the debt problem centered on the question of whether the crisis was one of solvency or one of liquidity. As Kletzer (1988) has observed, however, indebted developing countries were clearly solvent, in the sense that the present value of their prospective resources (as measured by the discounted value of real output flows, for instance) was many times greater than their debt obligations.[2] If these countries were solvent, then, it is necessary to explain why they would have been illiquid, that is, why external creditors would have been unwilling to sustain the pace of lending.

One approach to this question is to distinguish between the ability to pay and the willingness to pay. Thus, while indebted countries may have been solvent (able to pay), the fact of sovereign immunity has the implication that, since legal sanctions to compel payment—of the type that can be ap-

TABLE 13.1

Highly Indebted Countries: Share of Public and Publicly Guaranteed
Debt in Total Debt[a]

	1982			1988		
	Public	Total	Share	Public	Total	Share
Argentina	15.9	27.1	58.6	47.5	49.3	96.4
Bolivia	2.8	3.0	95.7	4.1	4.3	95.9
Brazil	51.7	74.8	69.1	89.9	101.4	88.6
Chile	5.2	14.0	37.5	13.7	16.1	85.3
Colombia	6.0	7.2	83.4	13.8	15.4	90.0
Côte d'Ivoire	5.1	6.2	81.4	7.9	11.6	68.2
Ecuador	3.9	5.5	70.5	9.0	9.1	98.7
Mexico	51.6	59.7	86.4	80.6	86.5	93.1
Morocco	10.2	10.5	97.6	19.4	19.6	99.0
Nigeria	9.1	10.4	87.4	29.3	29.9	98.2
Peru	7.0	8.6	80.7	12.5	13.9	89.8
Philippines	8.9	12.1	73.3	23.0	24.0	95.9
Uruguay	1.7	1.9	89.2	3.0	3.0	97.2
Venezuela	12.4	17.4	71.3	24.6	28.9	85.2
Yugoslavia	5.5	16.3	33.4	14.0	18.6	74.8
Total HICs	196.9	274.8	71.7	392.5	431.9	90.9

Source: World Debt Tables.
[a]Totals are in millions of U.S. dollars; shares are in percent.

plied to domestic debtors—are unavailable against sovereign debtors, debt contracts negotiated with such debtors have to be self-enforcing; that is, debtors must find it in their interest to comply with their payment obligations. In that perspective, the debt crisis can be interpreted as one in which the willingness to pay declined (for a variety of reasons), setting off a recontracting process. Much of the theoretical debt literature has followed this approach, essentially modeling the process of lending to sovereign states. An excellent survey of this literature is provided by Kletzer (1988).

An alternative resolution to the solvency-liquidity problem is based on examining the issue from a more disaggregated perspective. Thus, while the debtor *countries* may have been solvent, debtor *governments* may not have been. The relevance of this perspective is supported by the empirical observation that the overwhelming proportion of the external debt outstanding in the heavily indebted developing countries at the time of the outbreak of the international debt crisis was owed by these countries' public sectors. As Table 13.1 indicates, about three-quarters of the total medium- and long-term gross external debt owed by the highly indebted countries (HICs) as a group in 1982 either represented a direct liability of the public sector or bore a public sector guarantee. This suggests that approaching the crisis from a fiscal perspective may yield insights that would tend to be obscured by treating the debtor country as a single agent—in particular, the crisis can indeed be viewed as one of debtor solvency.

This chapter argues that fiscal factors played a key role in determining the timing, breadth, and macroeconomic implications of the crisis. Moreover, fiscal adjustment has a more fundamental role to play in resolving the macroeconomic problems associated with external debt than would be inferred solely from its contribution to short-run macroeconomic stabilization. Specifically, the longer-term fiscal implications of debt and debt service reduction (DDSR) operations recently undertaken by several HICs under the Brady Plan (see Section 13.3) will be a primary determinant of the success of these operations.

13.1 Origins of the Debt Crisis

The cutoff of the flow of net lending from external creditors to the HICs in the early 1980s reflected a sharp reversal in the perceived ability of the public sectors in these countries to service their debts on market terms; that is, from the perspective of creditors, the public sectors in several of these countries became insolvent. This led to a situation in which economic agents, both foreign and domestic, became reluctant to acquire claims on the economies (not just the public sectors) of the HICs. In turn, this reluctance manifested itself, among other ways, in the cutoff of external private funding.

13.1.1 Public Sector Solvency

As argued in Chapter 4, from the perspective of risk-neutral creditors, the public sector is perceived to be solvent when the present value of its expected future debt service payments, discounted at the safe rate of interest, is equal to the face value of its total debt.[3] Only in this case are the expected returns from lending to the government equal to the opportunity cost of funds, and only in this case, therefore, will both new and existing creditors voluntarily continue to finance the public sector. This condition, as shown in Chapter 4, can be related to the status of the public sector's comprehensive balance sheet. The latter includes not only all currently existing marketable assets and liabilities (which take the form of stocks), but also the present value (discounted at the safe interest rate) of all anticipated future flows of receipts and payment obligations. The capitalized value of the former represents a current asset of the sector, while that of the latter is a current liability. The difference between the value of assets and liabilities, with both defined in this comprehensive fashion, is the public sector's comprehensive net worth. As long as net worth defined in this manner is nonnegative, the government will be solvent, in the sense that the capitalized value of its resources is sufficient to liquidate its liabilities.

In the case of the public sector of a highly indebted country, straightforward manipulation of the sector's budget identity, as in Section 4.2, can be used to show that the resources devoted by the public sector in each period to servicing its debt (both interest and amortization) are equal to the sum of its primary budget surplus and its seignorage revenue. Using the notation of Chapter 4, this can be written as

$$(\rho_t - n_t)\Delta_t - \dot{\Delta}_t = s_t - d_t, \tag{1}$$

where Δ_t denotes total (domestic plus external) public debt, d_t is the primary deficit, and s_t is seignorage revenue, all expressed as ratios to GDP, while ρ_t is the real interest rate at time t and n_t is the rate of growth of real GDP. The solvency condition, given by Equation (21') in Chapter 4, can be written for present purposes as

$$PV(s_t - d_t; \rho_t - n_t, t) \geq \Delta_t, \tag{2}$$

where the effective discount rate is now $\rho_t - n_t$, the difference between the real interest rate and the rate of growth of real GDP.

Given constant values of the ratio of the primary surplus and seignorage to GDP, the preceding result implies that the present value of debt service payments will be infinite whenever the rate of growth of real GDP exceeds the real rate of interest. This is so because receipts from the issue of new debt would always be more than sufficient to service existing debt at the market rate of interest without increasing the debt/GDP ratio. In this case, solvency is guaranteed for any initial finite stock of debt, regardless of the value taken by the sum of the primary surplus and seignorage revenue. In other words, when the rate of growth of real GDP exceeds the real rate of interest, the solvency requirement does not impose a constraint on the future values of the sum of the public sector's primary surplus and seignorage revenue, essentially because the existing debt can be serviced by the sale of new debt, rather than out of the public sector's own resources. On the other hand, when the rate of interest exceeds the rate of growth of real GDP, the proceeds from the sale of new debt at a constant debt/GDP ratio are not sufficient to service the old debt, and the public sector must service the debt using its own resources, that is, by generating sufficiently large primary surpluses and seignorage revenue. The solvency condition described previously determines just how large the magnitudes of the future resources raised by these means must be, and thus acts as a constraint on the present value of future primary surpluses and seignorage revenue.[4]

13.1.2 Application to the Debt Crisis

The immediate trigger for the debt crisis was a reversal in the relationship between the "safe" real interest rate in international capital markets and the rate of growth of real GDP in the HICs (see Sachs, 1989*b*). During most of the decade of the 1970s, the real long-term rate of interest in the industrial countries fell well short of the rate of real GDP growth registered by the HICs as a group, as indicated in Figure 13.1.[5] Under these circumstances the public sectors in these economies could service their existing debt through new borrowing, without the need to generate their own fiscal resources for the purpose. The absence of solvency constraints on fiscal policy in these countries was manifest in large fiscal deficits in many of them during this period (Table 13.2). This suggests that, for a large subset of the HICs, the origin of the crisis is to be found in the public sector. Based on Table 13.2, obvious exceptions are Chile and Venezuela, although Colombia also experienced relatively small fiscal deficits—at least through the end of the 1970s.

At the beginning of the new decade, tight monetary policies in many industrial countries, designed to combat the inflationary consequences of the second oil shock, combined with expansionary fiscal policies in the United States, reversed the relationship between the real interest rate and the rate of growth of the HICs. As shown in Figure 13.1, real long-term interest rates began to rise substantially above the trend real rates of growth registered by these countries. Under these circumstances, servicing the existing debt through new borrowing would have become a Ponzi scheme, in which the debt/GDP ratio would have prospectively risen without bound. Creditors could not be expected to acquiesce in such a scheme, since it would imply that the present value of the net resource transfers that they would receive in return for their new loans would fall short of the face value of such loans. Thus the public sector debtors in the HICs found it necessary to begin to service debt with their own resources. This meant that the previous fiscal performance could not be sustained. A credible fiscal adjustment, offering the prospect of generating sufficient resources via primary surpluses and seignorage revenue to service the large stock of debt that had been accumulated during the previous decade, was called for to maintain the solvency of the public sector borrowers in these countries.

The severity of the adjustment problem confronting the public sector in the HICs was magnified because in many of these countries the public sector had also acquired a substantial amount of domestic debt. Table 13.3 indicates that in several of the highly indebted countries, including the major external debtors (Argentina, Brazil, Mexico, and the Philippines), domestic debt contributed more than 10 percentage points of GDP to the total debt burden of the public sector by 1982. The relationship between the magni-

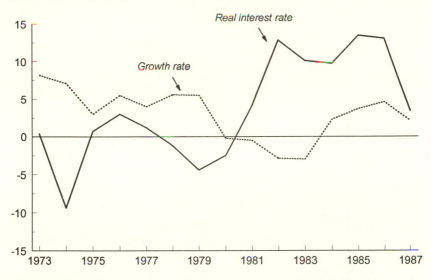

Figure 13.1   Growth and Real Interest Rates in Highly Indebted Developing Countries (annual change, in percent)

Source: Montiel (1992).

TABLE 13.2
Highly Indebted Countries: Public Sector Deficit, 1974–1982
(in percent of GDP)

	1974	*1975*	*1976*	*1977*	*1978*	*1979*	*1980*	*1981*	*1982*	*Average*
Argentina	8.1	15.1	11.7	4.7	6.5	6.5	7.5	13.3	15.1	9.8
Bolivia	−0.7	7.8	10.8	11.5	10.2	8.4	8.7	7.4	5.9	7.8
Brazil	1.0	4.1	5.3	3.9	7.2	13.3	12.2	3.9	5.9	6.3
Chile	5.5	2.1	−4.0	−0.4	−1.3	−4.6	−5.4	−0.3	3.9	−0.5
Colombia	0.9	−0.9	1.9	2.7	1.2	4.0	5.8	6.8	8.9	3.5
Côte d'Ivoire	0.9	2.3	12.4	3.6	8.4	10.3	12.2	11.8	15.9	8.6
Ecuador	−0.8	2.2	3.3	8.3	6.2	2.0	4.6	5.6	6.7	4.2
Mexico	5.9	8.7	8.2	5.4	5.4	6.3	6.8	13.6	16.3	8.5
Morocco	3.9	9.5	18.1	15.8	11.3	10.1	9.0	13.6	9.2	11.2
Peru	6.9	9.8	10.1	9.7	6.1	1.1	4.7	8.4	9.3	7.3
Philippines	—	—	—	—	—	—	—	7.5	6.5	1.6
Venezuela	−20.3	−10.0	−6.3	1.6	3.3	−3.8	−4.4	−3.6	5.6	−4.2

Source: Montiel (1992).

tude of the adjustment burden and the size of the total outstanding gross debt can be given a more precise definition. Let d^* denote the "permanent" primary surplus, that is, a constant value of the primary surplus equal in present value to a given stream of future primary surpluses. Then, from Equation (2), solvency requires that the permanent primary surplus be given by

TABLE 13.3

Highly Indebted Countries: Ratio of Public Debt to GDP

	1976			1982			1988		
	Foreign	Domestic	Total	Foreign	Domestic	Total	Foreign	Domestic	Total
Argentina	21.0	4.8	25.8	52.1	14.0	66.1	55.9	17.4	73.3
Bolivia	56.0	0.0	56.0	102.2	0.0	102.2	104.4	0.0	104.4
Brazil	19.3	8.2	27.5	27.7	16.2	43.9	30.1	18.9	49.0
Chile	45.9	0.6	46.6	61.9	1.6	63.5	79.6	6.8	86.4
Colombia	19.2	1.4	20.6	18.7	1.9	20.6	40.9	10.0	50.9
Côte d'Ivoire	30.2	3.2	33.3	88.1	3.2	91.3	123.5	6.4	129.8
Ecuador	16.9	0.1	17.0	47.9	0.0	47.9	98.1	0.0	98.1
Mexico	22.0	5.1	27.1	37.0	14.9	52.0	51.8	22.4	74.2
Morocco	25.5	21.6	47.1	71.1	23.1	94.2	93.2	31.2	124.4
Nigeria	1.8	1.8	3.6	11.4	12.0	23.4	107.2	20.6	127.8
Peru	40.2	8.8	49.1	34.9	2.4	37.3	76.5	3.1	79.6
Philippines	22.4	17.7	40.1	30.8	16.2	47.0	61.6	26.6	88.2
Uruguay	21.1	4.2	25.3	21.3	5.4	26.7	41.8	23.5	65.3
Venezuela	8.8	0.9	9.7	22.4	4.6	27.1	50.6	7.5	58.1
Yugoslavia	19.2	2.6	21.8	25.9	0.9	26.7	31.1	0.0	31.1

Sources: Guidotti and Kumar (1991) and *World Debt Tables.*

TABLE 13.4

Highly Indebted Countries: Actual and Sustainable Values of the Primary Surplus, 1982 (percent of GDP)

Country	Actual[a]	Sustainable
Argentina	−7.6	7.3
Bolivia	−6.5	8.3
Brazil	−5.5	1.9
Chile	1.9	6.9
Colombia	−3.4	1.0
Côte d'Ivoire	−7.3	6.7
Ecuador	−4.5	1.8
Mexico	−4.7	2.7
Morocco	−8.6	6.3
Nigeria	—	2.2
Peru	−5.2	3.1
Philippines	−4.7	3.6
Uruguay	—	2.6
Venezuela	2.6	1.9
Yugoslavia	—	1.5

Source: Montiel (1992).

[a]For Argentina, Chile, Mexico and Peru these are averages for 1974–82. For the Philippines, the average is for 1981–82 only. All remaining countries use averages for the period 1976–82.

$$d^* = (\rho - n)\Delta_t - (n + \pi)m^*, \qquad (3)$$

where ρ and n are, respectively, the long-term real interest rate and the economy's long-run real growth rate, π the "equilibrium" rate of inflation chosen by policymakers, and m^* the inverse of base money velocity corresponding to the inflation rate π.

Table 13.4 presents estimates of the permanent primary surplus as of 1982 for the fifteen HICs, together with the average level of the primary surplus in each country during the period preceding the outbreak of the debt crisis.[6] The required permanent surplus was in excess of 6 percent of GDP in five cases: Argentina, Bolivia, Chile, Côte d'Ivoire, and Morocco. In the cases of Bolivia, Côte d'Ivoire, and Morocco, this is due to a very large stock of total debt relative to GDP. For Argentina and Chile, it reflects a combination of large debt (in excess of 60 percent of GDP) and slow average growth registered over the period (1968 to 1982) used to estimate the long-run growth rate. Clearly, with the exception of Venezuela, a substantial fiscal adjustment became necessary in all of these countries to preserve public sector solvency when international interest rates rose in the early 1980s.

The debt crisis essentially reflected the market's judgment that the necessary fiscal adjustment was not forthcoming in many of the HICs. Consider what happens when conditions change (in some unspecified manner) such that the solvency condition (2), although previously satisfied, now becomes violated ex ante. Suppose, in particular, that the prospective permanent primary surplus falls short of the value indicated by Equation (3). Under the new conditions, the public sector will be insolvent in an ex ante sense; that is, its comprehensive net worth will be negative. The market, however, will ensure that net worth will not be negative ex post. Adjustment can take several forms. If the prospective fiscal program is unchanged, the public sector may be able to repudiate enough of its domestic debt so as to leave the face value of its remaining total debt equal to what it can expect to service in present value terms under that program.[7] Failing this, the market will simply value the debt at an amount equal to the discounted value of the prospective debt service. Since by assumption this is less than the face value of the debt, the debt will sell at a discount. The discount is precisely the shortfall between the present value of future primary surpluses plus seignorage revenues and the face value of the debt.

When existing debt is selling at a discount, the public sector will be denied fresh funds. To the extent that new loans cannot be credibly assured a senior status relative to existing debt, new credits would immediately be discounted on a par with existing debt. Thus, new lenders would not voluntarily enter the market. While there may be incentives for *existing* creditors to increase their exposure, they would not do so individually (see Krugman, 1988). Thus the absence of fiscal adjustment resulted in the drying up of voluntary lending—that is, the debt crisis.

13.2 Policy Response and Macroeconomic Implications

The foregoing discussion suggests that the substantial discounts that have applied to the external debt of developing countries since the secondary market in these claims arose in the mid-1980s reflect the perception that the degree of fiscal adjustment in response to the reversal in the relationship between the external real interest rate and the long-term growth rate in the indebted countries has indeed not been sufficient to restore the solvency of the public sector in these countries. In principle, the fiscal response can take many forms. In the face of a crisis, adjustment can be postponed as long as a class of creditors can be found who can be induced (or forced) to supply financing. Alternatively, if adjustment is not postponed, primary public sector deficits can be reduced through different types of spending cuts and revenue increases, or debt service can be financed by increased reliance on the inflation tax. Because these alternative responses to the need for fiscal adjustment have very different macroeconomic implications, the macroeconomic consequences of the debt crisis for the debtor countries have largely been a function of the nature of the fiscal response.[8]

As shown in Table 13.5, the net external resource transfer became negative in many of the HICs after the onset of the debt crisis. In view of the fact that the external debt of these countries was largely public, this suggests that the public sectors in the HICs may have begun to service external debt partly out of their own resources. Indeed, as also shown in Table 13.5, increases in primary public sector surpluses were widespread in these countries after 1982. However, as indicated above, this adjustment was insufficient to maintain the solvency of the public sector in most cases. There are at least two reasons for this. First, although the resource transfer became negative in many cases, debt service nevertheless fell short of the contracted amount, so that arrears and reschedulings became common. Second, the financing of the resource transfer may have led to the perception on the part of creditors that even the transfers that were achieved were unsustainable.

In particular, many countries relied on the inflation tax, rather than the primary surplus, to finance debt service payments. Table 13.5 indicates that the rate of inflation accelerated after 1982 in the majority of the heavily indebted countries, particularly those in Latin America (notable Latin American exceptions are Chile and Colombia). Creditors may have been justifiably skeptical that debtors were resigned to living with the associated high levels of inflation forever.[9]

Moreover, to the extent that the primary surplus was indeed increased, the brunt of the adjustment effort was often disproportionately borne by public investment (see Easterly, 1989). Among the heavily indebted countries for which data are available, public investment fell during the 1980s—sometimes drastically—in all but Chile and Colombia (Table 13.5). It is worth noting that, from the perspective of creditors, what matters is the present value of all future primary surpluses, not the value of the surplus in a given year. Reducing public investment will indeed increase the surplus in a given year, but can increase the relevant present value measure only to the extent that the cash rate of return on investment is expected to fall short of the discount rate, that is, to the extent that the potential investment does not meet a market test. While many potential projects in indebted countries undoubtedly fit this description, it remains true that, as long as the canceled investment projects are not pure consumption, the short-run increase in the primary surplus exceeds its permanent increase under this mode of adjustment.

Finally, in several heavily indebted countries, the shortfall in external funding was partly replaced by domestic borrowing. Easterly (1989) documents the importance of this response in the cases of Argentina, Brazil, Chile, Mexico, Morocco, and Yugoslavia. This reliance on domestic

TABLE 13.5
Highly Indebted Countries: Responses to the Debt Crisis, 1976–88

	1976–81	1982	1983	1984	1985	1986	1987	1988
Argentina								
Resource transfer	0.9	4.3	−0.2	−2.6	−1.0	−2.9	−2.0	−2.3
Primary deficit	6.3	8.8	11.7	9.0	3.1	2.4	3.7	5.3
Public investment	11.1	8.1	9.5	7.6	6.8	7.0	7.4	—
Inflation rate[a]	193.4	164.8	343.8	626.7	672.1	90.1	131.3	343.0
Bolivia								
Resource transfer	4.4	−0.7	−2.3	−1.4	−1.7	3.7	1.9	1.4
Primary deficit	8.2	5.4	4.6	3.0	4.9	11.0	9.4	−1.2
Public investment	10.1	6.5	4.6	3.1	3.5	4.7	5.4	—
Inflation rate[a]	19.7	133.3	269.0	1,281.4	11,749.6	276.3	14.6	16.0
Brazil								
Resource transfer	1.3	0.2	0.3	0.9	−2.0	−1.5	−1.8	−2.3
Primary deficit	6.0	2.9	2.1	3.2	8.5	−2.8	−2.7	−4.0
Public investment	10.4	8.7	6.4	6.0	6.2	6.2	6.9	—
Inflation rate[a]	60.9	97.8	142.1	197.0	226.9	145.2	229.7	682.3
Chile								
Resource transfer	−1.1	1.1	4.4	1.9	0.8	−3.1	−3.3	−0.4
Primary deficit	−4.0	3.4	1.7	2.1	−0.3	−0.2	−2.8	−6.8
Public investment	6.2	4.8	4.9	6.3	6.9	7.6	6.9	7.5
Inflation rate[a]	72.0	9.9	27.3	19.9	30.7	19.5	19.9	14.7
Colombia								
Resource transfer	0.7	0.9	1.1	1.7	1.2	2.1	−3.2	−1.4
Primary deficit	2.8	7.3	7.0	4.6	0.9	−2.7	−3.6	−3.4
Public investment	7.2	9.4	8.9	9.0	9.6	8.6	7.9	—
Inflation rate[a]	25.0	24.5	19.8	16.1	24.0	18.9	23.3	28.1
Côte d'Ivoire								
Resource transfer	5.6	6.4	−1.7	−1.6	−4.2	−5.0	—	—
Primary deficit	7.0	9.6	5.2	−4.7	−8.5	−3.6	—	—
Inflation rate[a]	15.4	7.3	5.9	4.3	1.8	7.3	0.4	7.0
Ecuador								
Resource transfer	3.7	−6.2	−2.0	−1.2	−1.8	1.6	0.9	0.2
Primary deficit	3.1	2.2	−3.6	−6.2	−7.0	−0.8	7.2	2.2
Public investment	9.7	9.6	7.9	6.4	6.6	8.6	8.4	—
Inflation rate[a]	12.5	16.3	48.4	31.2	28.0	23.0	29.5	58.2
Mexico								
Resource transfer	2.1	1.5	−3.0	−3.6	−3.7	−4.1	−1.2	−3.1
Primary deficit	4.0	7.7	−4.4	−4.9	−3.9	—	—	—
Public investment	9.5	10.4	7.6	7.1	7.0	6.1	5.4	—
Inflation rate[a]	22.5	58.9	101.8	65.5	57.7	86.2	131.8	114.2
Morocco								
Resource transfer	6.0	5.5	−0.4	3.7	0.5	0.9	1.1	−0.3
Primary deficit	9.3	4.2	6.2	2.6	3.4	0.6	1.2	0.2
Inflation rate[a]	10.2	10.5	6.2	12.4	7.7	8.7	2.7	2.4

Source: Montiel (1992).
[a]Rate of change in consumer prices.

TABLE 13.5 (continued)
Highly Indebted Countries: Responses to the Debt Crisis, 1976–88

	1976–81	1982	1983	1984	1985	1986	1987	1988
Nigeria								
Resource transfer	0.9	2.8	1.0	−1.7	−2.9	−0.9	1.6	−3.2
Primary deficit	0.3	1.0	1.2	1.4	1.6	1.2	1.9	4.5
Public investment	15.4	10.6	8.1	4.3	5.9	7.4	8.0	8.8
Inflation rate[a]	17.1	7.7	23.2	39.6	5.5	5.3	10.3	38.3
Peru								
Resource transfer	1.3	2.4	5.2	4.2	−0.1	0.1	0.5	0.4
Primary deficit	4.0	6.4	8.0	1.8	−2.3	0.0	−0.1	−0.2
Public investment	7.0	10.4	10.4	9.5	7.3	6.3	5.0	—
Inflation rate[a]	55.1	64.4	111.2	110.2	163.4	77.9	85.8	667.0
Philippines								
Resource transfer	2.8	2.6	3.4	0.8	0.7	−1.7	−3.8	−3.8
Primary deficit	0.9	4.2	1.8	−0.0	−1.5	0.3	−2.3	−2.2
Public investment	7.3	7.5	6.4	4.5	3.6	3.2	3.1	3.7
Inflation rate[a]	12.5	10.2	10.0	50.3	23.1	0.8	3.8	8.8
Uruguay								
Resource transfer	0.5	2.2	3.7	−4.2	−3.6	−2.0	−1.8	−2.9
Primary deficit	—	—	—	—	—	—	—	—
Public investment	6.4	7.2	4.1	4.1	3.0	2.9	3.1	—
Inflation rate[a]	53.0	19.0	49.2	55.3	72.2	76.4	63.6	62.2
Venezuela								
Resource transfer	2.4	−1.4	−0.4	−3.5	−3.4	−4.4	−4.9	−2.5
Primary deficit	−3.5	2.9	−3.3	−11.5	−7.7	−3.4	−3.9	−3.8
Public investment	14.4	16.5	14.6	7.7	9.0	12.4	12.6	—
Inflation rate[a]	12.1	9.6	6.3	12.2	11.4	11.5	28.1	29.5
Yugoslavia								
Resource transfer	0.4	−0.4	0.8	−0.9	−1.9	−3.0	−2.7	−2.1
Inflation rate[a]	21.9	31.5	40.2	54.7	72.3	89.8	120.8	194.1

Source: Montiel (1992).
[a]Rate of change in consumer prices.

borrowing partly accounts for the increase reported in Table 13.2 of the share of domestic debt in total public sector debt for these countries between 1982 and 1988. Note that, to the extent that such debt was voluntarily acquired by domestic residents, it must either have been regarded as senior to foreign debt or have been sold at a sufficiently high interest rate in order to offset the immediate discount on its face value (see Dooley, 1986).[10] In either case, the service of this debt aggravates the perceived insolvency of the public sector from the standpoint of external creditors.

When fiscal adjustment is not complete and claims on the public sector sell at a discount under their original face value, how creditors handle their legal claims becomes a matter of considerable importance from a macro-economic point of view. If creditors do not relinquish these claims (that is, if debt is not written down), then the difference between the face value of the debt and its current market value remains as an unresolved claim on the public sector, to be apportioned in an uncertain way among the sector's financial creditors (external and domestic) and domestic agents under the government's jurisdiction. This means, in particular, that further fiscal adjustment, higher levels of inflation tax, or future capital levies cannot be ruled out as a way to deal with this "debt overhang." In this setting, any assets within the reach of the fiscal authority in the indebted country are at risk of future confiscation (that is, through taxation or through a capital levy), and all such assets consequently become impaired (see Sachs, 1989*b*; Dooley, 1986). As a result, investors will demand high rates of return in order to be induced to hold claims—financial or real—on the affected economy. This implies that private investment will be low, domestic market-determined real interest rates will be high and, unless effective capital controls are in place, capital flight can be expected to be substantial.[11]

Table 13.6 suggests that these consequences indeed materialized in the heavily indebted countries in the period following the outbreak of the debt crisis. Since the early 1980s, the HICs have undergone a prolonged period of low private investment coupled with a substantial accumulation of external assets by domestic residents. With the single exception of Colombia, where the slowdown was milder, private investment fell sharply in all the heavily indebted countries for which data were available after 1982. The measure of private capital flight employed in Table 13.6 is the one suggested by the emphasis given here on the fiscal dimension of the debt problem. Taken from Dooley and Stone (1993) and based on Dooley (1988), it treats as flight capital only those private capital outflows that do not remit earnings, thus taking as motivation for the flight of capital the desire to evade prospective domestic taxation. By this measure, only Chile, Ecuador, and Uruguay escaped substantial episodes of capital flight during this period.

13.3 Resolution of the Crisis: The Brady Plan

13.3.1 Outline of the Plan

The distortionary effects of the debt crisis on the domestic economy and its implications for economic growth in the HICs provided international support for an approach to its resolution proposed by former U.S. Treasury Secretary Nicholas Brady in March 1989. Recognizing that existing debt could not be expected to be serviced on its original terms (an expectation embedded in the substantial discounts on developing-country debt trading in the secondary market that began to grow rapidly after 1986), and that the

TABLE 13.6
Highly Indebted Countries: Private Investment and Private External Assets, 1980–88[a]

	1980	1981	1982	1983	1984	1985	1986	1987	1988
Argentina									
Private external assets	14.0	23.2	31.2	31.1	33.9	35.2	33.1	36.7	35.4
Private investment	13.0	9.4	8.9	7.9	6.9	5.5	6.0	6.8	—
Bolivia									
Private external assets	—	—	—	—	—	—	—	—	—
Private investment	7.3	3.8	5.0	2.0	1.6	3.6	4.9	4.9	—
Brazil									
Private external assets	7.2	9.6	5.9	5.8	12.3	8.2	16.7	31.9	23.6
Private investment	14.5	12.0	11.7	9.7	9.5	10.5	12.3	12.8	—
Chile									
Private external assets	1.2	−1.4	−1.3	0.6	−0.7	−0.9	−2.6	−3.2	−6.0
Private investment	15.6	17.5	6.5	4.9	7.3	6.8	7.0	10.0	9.5
Colombia									
Private external assets	0.5	−0.1	−0.4	0.0	1.6	3.0	4.7	6.5	5.9
Private investment	11.4	12.0	11.1	11.0	10.0	9.4	9.3	11.1	—
Ecuador									
Private external assets	3.8	3.0	2.8	3.0	3.8	3.8	4.0	4.1	3.8
Private investment	14.1	11.7	13.0	8.6	9.0	9.5	9.8	14.6	—
Mexico									
Private external assets	16.3	22.9	24.8	35.2	35.3	37.7	42.9	52.3	35.6
Private investment	13.9	14.7	12.7	10.0	10.8	12.2	13.3	13.5	—
Nigeria									
Private external assets	5.2	3.3	0.8	3.4	4.2	8.0	13.1	21.0	22.0
Private investment	—	—	—	—	—	—	—	—	—
Peru									
Private external assets	3.5	2.3	3.6	2.4	2.7	4.2	5.5	6.8	6.4
Private investment	9.7	11.4	11.5	7.9	6.9	6.8	9.3	10.6	—
Philippines									
Private external assets	6.7	7.0	8.7	5.4	4.8	6.7	10.4	10.9	10.1
Private investment	18.4	18.5	18.1	18.8	14.5	11.4	9.7	10.6	12.5
Uruguay									
Private external assets	−0.7	−1.1	−0.9	0.3	0.0	0.5	0.2	0.3	−0.3
Private investment	11.4	10.7	7.9	6.9	5.2	4.5	4.5	5.4	—
Venezuela									
Private external assets	15.2	16.3	15.7	31.9	30.9	30.5	24.8	29.0	23.3
Private investment	13.0	9.8	7.7	4.5	6.6	6.5	6.8	6.6	—

Source: Montiel (1992).

"overhang" of claims over and above the present value of expected future debt service payments was the source of such distortions, the Brady approach involved scaling back such claims by writing down the debt to more realistic levels.

Under the Brady Plan, each participating developing-country debtor government enters into negotiations with its commercial bank creditors to restructure the terms of its obligations. The banks' negotiating committee and the government agree on a "menu" of assets to be offered to individual bank creditors in exchange for existing debt as well as the terms on which the exchange is to take place. After the terms are agreed, each individual bank can decide which of the various assets to accept in exchange for its claims. The menu typically includes a fixed-rate bond issued at par with the existing debt, but paying an interest rate below the rate projected to apply to the existing debt; a variable-rate bond issued at a discount relative to the face value of the existing debt; and a "new money" option permitting the bank to retain its current claims on current terms in exchange for the commitment of a designated amount of new money per dollar of current exposure. The "writedown" element of such deals involves the reduction in face value of the variable-interest bonds, the reduction in debt service on the par-value loans, and the capital loss due to the immediate discount applying to new loans. Typically, the new bonds to be issued in these transactions (referred to as "Brady bonds") carry principal and rolling interest guarantees—the former through the purchase of zero-coupon U.S. Treasury bonds by the debtor to secure the repayment of principal, and through blocked deposits at the New York Federal Reserve Bank to secure the payment of interest for a specified future period of time, renewed as time passes. Funds for these "enhancements" of the quality of bank claims on debtors are supplied either out of the debtor countries' own reserves or through loans from international organizations or individual industrial countries. The latter resources represent the operational support provided to the Brady Plan by the international community.

13.3.2 Macroeconomic Effects: Conceptual Issues

What are the likely macroeconomic implications of the debt and debt service reduction (DDSR) operations carried out through the Brady Plan for the countries undertaking them? To address this issue, it is necessary to draw clear conceptual distinctions among the various mechanisms through which a large stock of public debt can exert macroeconomic effects. Three such mechanisms can be identified.

Let V_t denote the market value of the public sector's external debt. On the simplifying assumption that domestic debt is zero, V_t is the present value of the public sector's expected future primary surpluses plus seignorage revenue:[12,13]

$$V_t = PV(s_t - d_t; \rho_t - n_t, t). \tag{4}$$

The face value of the debt can then be decomposed into the portion that corresponds to its market value and the "shortfall" $\Delta_t - V_t$:

$$\Delta_t = (\Delta_t - V_t) + V_t. \tag{5}$$

Thus $S_t = \Delta_t - V_t$ is the present value of the "unallocated tax burden" (Dooley, 1986) associated with the debt, while V_t corresponds to the portion of the repayment burden that domestic agents expect to bear.

The first channel of transmission operates through V_t. A large value of V_t, regardless of the size of S_t, implies the expectation of substantial future primary surpluses or seignorage revenues. To the extent that these are generated through distortionary taxation or reduced levels of productive public expenditure, the expected rate of return on domestic private asset accumulation will fall and the efficiency of domestic resource allocation will be impaired.[14] This effect is present even when it is confidently expected that the debt will be serviced fully (that is, when $S_t = 0$). In fact, in this case, the effect appears precisely because full debt service is anticipated, but is expected to be achieved through distortionary means. It is worth noting that, in the absence of lump-sum taxes, *any* service of preexisting debt is likely to be achieved through more or less distortionary means.[15] The objective of public policy should be to minimize the distortionary effects associated with a given level of V_t. This is a standard problem in public finance.

When the public sector is not solvent, these effects are attached only to the portion of the debt that is expected to be serviced. The remaining "debt overhang" component does not generate such effects, because the public sector is not expected to raise domestic resources to service it.

The preceding mechanism operates through the present value of the anticipated future debt service associated with a large stock of debt, and would be present even if no debt service payments were currently being made. More generally, it is independent of the time profile of actual debt service payments. The second mechanism depends on the timing of such payments. For a given value of V_t, when the public sector is insolvent (that is, when $S_t > 0$), the cost imposed on the domestic economy of achieving the transfer V_t will be greater the sooner the payments are made. This is so because when the public sector is insolvent, it will be unable to obtain voluntary loans from individual creditors on market terms. In this credit-rationed situation, the intertemporal discount rate used by the public sector will exceed the risk-free market interest rate. Thus any current debt service payments made by the public sector will carry a high intertemporal opportunity cost, that is, will be more costly to the economy (in terms of forgone public investment opportunities or distortionary taxation) than payments of equal present value (discounted at creditors' costs of funds) made later on. This type of liquidity effect arises, then, when insolvency leads to credit rationing and is present even when debt service is financed efficiently (in the least distortionary fashion) by the public sector.

As with the first mechanism described above, these liquidity effects are aggravated when political or other constraints impede the efficient financing of debt service payments. The actual service of the debt requires the mobilization of resources, and this can be achieved in more or less distortionary fashion—for instance, by curtailing inefficient taxes or subsidies on the one hand, versus levying high tax rates on a narrow base on the other. As indicated previously, reliance on inefficient modes of financing negative net resource transfers after 1982, such as the curtailment of public investment and recourse to the inflation tax, may have exerted an independent effect contributing to the harmful macroeconomic consequences of the debt crisis in the form of reduced investment and growth for the majority of the HICs during the 1980s.

A third and conceptually separate mechanism becomes operative when the public sector is insolvent, and is associated with the "debt overhang" component S_t. Unlike V_t, this component of the debt does not exert distortionary macroeconomic effects by increasing the expected value of future taxes; these are already included in V_t. Intuitively, suppose that the government could precommit its future fiscal program, so private agents face no uncertainty about their future tax obligations. In this setting, the level of expected future taxes and the debt overhang are inversely related: the higher the level of expected future taxes, the lower the discount on debt in the secondary market. This is so because higher taxes on domestic residents increase the primary surplus, thereby enhancing the solvency of the public sector. Under these circumstances, a large debt overhang—a substantial discount on debt in the secondary market—suggests precisely that the anticipated future tax burden is low. Implicitly, domestic agents are treated as senior claimants on public sector resources, and the burden of distortionary domestic taxes is eased by "taxing" external creditors.

Instead, the existence of a "shortfall" component of the debt affects the domestic economy through two other channels. The first, analyzed in the extensive literature on the debt overhang, is related to the incentives facing policymakers under such circumstances. A formal model of debt overhang effects on the domestic economy is presented in the appendix to this chapter; the discussion here will be confined to an intuitive description of its predictions. For a given value of expected future debt service V_t, the effects on the domestic economy depend on whether V_t arises from the service of a small stock of debt on contractual terms (so that $\Delta_t = V_t$) or from the expectation that a larger stock of debt will be serviced only partially in some states of nature (so $\Delta_t > V_t$). Specifically, in the presence of a shortfall ($S_t > 0$), the actual value of future debt service is uncertain. Since the resources that creditors will be able to extract from the domestic public sector are likely to increase when domestic macroeconomic outcomes are favorable, creditors will capture some fraction of the payoff to good macroeconomic policies, and this possibility acts as a tax on the returns to such policies, discouraging policymakers from undertaking them. In terms of our notation, the expected value of this tax is already captured in V_t, but the role of $S_t > 0$ is to introduce a distribution for the actual value of future debt service around V_t. The disincentive effect arises from the fact that actual debt service is likely to increase under "good policies," to a maximum of Δ_t.

Some simple calculations suggest, however, that the maximum value of the potential "additional debt overhang tax" on the domestic economy in the aggregate is likely to be small. Letting $\sigma_t = V_t/\Delta_t$ denote the secondary market price of a dollar of debt, and expressing the ratio of the primary surplus plus seignorage to GDP as $s_t - d_t = (\iota_t - g_t)$, where ι_t is the ratio of the present value of net tax revenues plus seignorage to the present value of GDP, and g_t is the ratio of the present value of "exhaustive" (consumption plus investment) public sector spending to the present value of GDP, we can write Equation (4) as

$$\sigma_t\Delta_t = (\iota_t - g_t)y_t, \tag{6}$$

where y_t is the present value of GDP. This can be expressed as

$$g_ty_t + \Delta_t = \iota_ty_t + (1 - \sigma_t)\Delta_t. \tag{7}$$

The left-hand side of this expression represents the present value of the public sector's "uses of funds" (payment obligations), consisting of the present value of its exhaustive spending program and the face value of its debt. The right-hand side represents its "sources of funds," consisting of net taxes (including seignorage) on domestic residents and its "taxation" of creditors, in the form of debt service shortfalls. Given the public sector's payment obligations, an increase in the tax rate ι_t on domestic agents reduces the shortfall $(1 - \sigma_t)$ and vice versa, as previously indicated.

Finally, factoring out y_t from the right-hand side of (7) yields

$$g_ty_t + \Delta_t = \left[\iota_t + (1 - \sigma_t)\frac{\Delta_t}{y_t}\right]y_t. \tag{8}$$

The second term inside the brackets on the right-hand side represents the potential "additional debt overhang tax rate" on domestic residents. It is the

TABLE 13.7
Heavily Indebted Countries: Debt Overhang Tax
Rate (in percent)

	Value of $(\rho - n)$			
	7.00	5.00	3.00	1.00
Argentina	3.09	2.21	1.32	0.44
Bolivia	6.57	4.70	2.82	0.94
Brazil	1.26	0.90	0.54	0.18
Chile	2.40	1.71	1.03	0.34
Côte d'Ivoire	6.65	4.75	2.85	0.95
Ecuador	5.97	4.27	2.56	0.85
Mexico	2.07	1.48	0.89	0.30
Morocco	3.39	2.42	1.45	0.48
Peru	5.09	3.63	2.19	0.73
Philippines	2.20	1.57	0.94	0.31
Uruguay	1.17	0.84	0.50	0.17
Venezuela	2.09	1.49	0.90	0.30

Source: Underlying data were obtained from the
World Bank. Calculations are described in the text.

portion of the public sector's payment obligation that is currently expected
to fall on external creditors. It would do so, however, only if the portion
$(1 - \sigma_t)$ of the debt is forgiven. As long as this "shortfall" remains on the
books, it represents an unallocated tax, and in particular a potential tax on
domestic economic activities. Its size, however, is not large. Using fairly
conservative estimates, including a discount rate of 5 percent (corresponding to $\rho - n$) for GDP, a debt/GDP ratio of 0.6 (see Table 13.2), and a secondary market price of 40 cents on the dollar, yields a representative potential "debt overhang tax" on domestic residents amounting to less than 2
percent of the present value of GDP.

Detailed estimates of this tax for alternative values of $\rho - n$ are presented
in Table 13.7 for all the HICs with available data. These estimates are based
on end-1988 values of the secondary market price σ_t and of the external
debt/GDP ratio. The effective tax rate increases with the real interest rate,
which reduces the present value of future domestic resources, and it decreases with the growth rate of GDP. Even with the relatively high value
of 7 percent for $\rho - n$, however, the tax rate reaches maximum values exceeding 6.5 percent of GDP only for the smaller countries (Bolivia and Côte
d'Ivoire) where the debt/GDP ratio was extremely high and debt was considered at the time to be almost worthless on the secondary market. For the
largest debtors (Brazil and Mexico) the maximum "debt overhang" tax rate
is in the range of 1–2 percent of GDP.

The extent to which a maximum additional loss of this magnitude could provide a serious disincentive for the adoption of otherwise desirable policies is certainly open to question. However, the fact that the maximum additional tax is small by no means rules out disincentive effects on policymakers. Among other things, what ultimately matters is the marginal tax that creditors are able to impose on potential increases in domestic income. While the maximum additional tax may amount to a small fraction of the present value of GDP, it may represent a large fraction of any additions to GDP that could be secured through improved policies.

The existence of a potential additional debt overhang tax may affect not just the incentives facing policymakers, but also those facing private individuals. Would the marginal tax that creditors may impose on the economy in the aggregate—and thus the marginal tax rate that may confront policymakers—discourage the undertaking of new income-producing activities by private individuals? The answer to this question is, probably not. To see why, assume for simplicity that existing domestic economic activity is taxed at a uniform flat rate. New activities are unlikely to be taxed differentially from old ones, and thus can be expected to face the economywide average tax rate. While creditors may extract a high proportion of the economy's increase in income, resulting in a high marginal tax rate as perceived by policymakers, this burden would be borne by new and old private activities alike through an increase in the average tax rate applicable to both. Even with a high marginal tax rate extracted by creditors on increases in domestic income, the change in the economywide average tax rate associated with any single domestic project is likely to prove infinitesimal, and thus would not be internalized by private agents contemplating new activities. It follows that the "additional debt overhang tax" is unlikely to prove a major direct source of disincentive for individual agents. Thus the standard "debt overhang" argument applies to the behavior of policymakers, rather than to that of individual agents.

While the tax rate applicable to new private economic activities may not be made to differ from the economywide average tax rate by the potential "additional debt overhang tax," the future value of this average domestic tax rate will be subject to uncertainty as long as a "shortfall" exists, and uncertainty about future taxes can itself discourage new private economic activities. The figures in Table 13.7 suggest that the range of prospective variation in the average tax rate associated with servicing the "shortfall" may not be large, but these numbers may understate the degree of uncertainty involved for private agents, for several reasons. First, in the event of a breakdown in negotiations with external creditors, the costs of sanctions to the domestic economy may exceed the shortfall. Second, to the extent that a transfer to external creditors is itself financed inefficiently by the public sector, costs to domestic residents will exceed the value of the transfer.

Finally, the uncertainty (at the microeconomic level) associated with tax incidence on individual activities may exceed the uncertainty attached to the average tax rate. This is so because, since the shortfall is not expected to be serviced under the current policy regime, the servicing of this debt may signal a regime switch, involving new taxes, for instance, as part of a fiscal reform. Since the distribution of distortionary taxation in the new tax policy regime would be difficult to foresee, the potential is created for large individual losses, even when the change in the average burden of taxation is not itself large.

The additional uncertainty about future taxes for private domestic agents associated with the shortfall S_t represents a separate channel through which S_t may adversely affect the domestic economy, over and above any disincentive effects on policymakers. In the presence of such uncertainty, irreversible private activities such as investing in physical capital and acquiring claims on the domestic financial system (which may later be subjected to capital controls) are likely to be postponed until the uncertainty is resolved. This effect may account for the behavior of private investment and capital flight in the HICs during the early 1980s.[16] Evidence has now accumulated that uncertainty of this type can deter private economic activities that have an irreversible aspect.[17]

Based on this reasoning, the costs of ex ante public sector insolvency per se (as opposed to those arising from the anticipated servicing of the debt) arise from credit rationing as well as from the distortions introduced into the decisions of both policymakers and individual economic agents by the uncertainty associated with the shortfall (in a present value sense) between the public sector's resources and its obligations.

In this setting DDSR operations, broadly defined to include not just the financial operations associated with debt conversion, but also the full range of macroeconomic conditions attached to Brady Plan–type operations, can make several contributions.

From the point of view of the debtor country, the first and most obvious contribution would be to reduce the present value of anticipated future debt service payments, V_t. This would spare the country not only the burden of effecting the external resource transfer, but also the "secondary burden" associated with distortionary taxation. Since doing so would benefit the residents of the country concerned at the expense of external creditors, DDSR operations of a voluntary nature are unlikely to produce this result. It is possible, indeed, that the fiscal conditions attached to the negotiated adjustment programs that precondition Brady Plan DDSR operations could increase the value of V_t. Note that the effect of the operation on V_t cannot be inferred from secondary market prices alone (since such prices depend on both V_t and the face value of the debt Δ_t) or from the immediate postoperation market value of the debt (since a portion of the payments received by creditors may come from third-party grants or concessional loans). The effect on V_t must be extracted from the postoperation value of the debt (including any up-front payments), net of the grant element (if any) in third-party contributions.

Given V_t, a second potential contribution of DDSR operations would be to restrict the excess "secondary burden" associated with financing the transfer of V_t to the public sector's creditors. This could be accomplished through the fiscal conditions attached to the adjustment program. In particular, such conditions should seek to ensure that the transfer is effected at minimum distortionary cost. No single indicator would suffice to measure the degree of success in this regard, but the relevant broad public finance principles are well known: promotion of a tax system that relies on a broad base as well as low and uniform tax rates, replacement of import quotas by low and uniform tariffs, and protection of public investment programs that meet a market test.

The ultimate goal of DDSR operations should be, of course, to remove the debt overhang, and thus eliminate distortions associated with credit rationing as well as disincentive effects on both policymakers and individual agents. In fact, the most important potential contribution of DDSR operations may be to resolve the allocational issue associated with the "unallocated tax burden" and, to the greatest possible extent, remove this source of uncertainty. In this regard, and based on the reasoning above, a reasonable single indicator of the success of such operations may be the percentage reduction in the shortfall (the secondary market discount times the stock of outstanding debt) that they lead to.

Finally, to the extent that a shortfall is expected to remain at the conclusion of a DDSR operation, the positive effects of the operation from the standpoint of the debtor country will depend on its cash flow implications.

13.3.3 An Overview of Some Early Brady Plan Deals

From the time the Brady Plan was announced in March 1989 to May 1993, a total of twelve developing countries underwent restructuring of their debt to commercial banks under the terms of the plan. The total amount of debt involved in each case, and the total amount of debt reduction achieved, are reported in Table 13.8. Debt reduction was achieved through buybacks (purchases of debt at less than face value), exchanges for bonds at discounted face value but serviced on market terms, and exchanges for bonds at par but with below-market interest rates. Placement of collateral can also be considered an up-front payment of debt. In the case of several small countries

TABLE 13.8
DDSR Operations under the Brady Plan, 1989–93 (in millions of U.S. dollars)

| Country (year) | Debt Reduction | | | Debt Service Reduction | | Prepayments Through Collateralization | Total | Total DDSR/Debt Restructured (percent) | Cost of Debt Reduction |
	Stock of Debt Restructured	Buybacks	Discount Exchange	Principal Collateralized Par Bond	Other Par Bond				
Argentina (1992)	28,066	—	2,420	4,995	—	2,417	9,832	35.0	3,047
Bolivia (1993)	171	78	50	29	—	14	171	100.0	26
Costa Rica (1989)	1,599	991	—	—	101	36	1,128	70.5	196
Guyana (1992)	93	93	—	—	—	—	93	100.0	10
Mexico (1989)	48,231	—	7,191	7,130	—	7,182	21,503	44.6	7,122
Mozambique (1991)	124	124	—	—	—	—	124	100.0	12
Niger (1991)	111	111	—	—	—	—	111	100.0	23
Nigeria (1991)	5,811	3,390	—	651	—	352	4,393	75.6	1,708
Philippines (1989)	1,399	1,399	—	—	—	—	1,399	100.0	670
Philippines (1991)	4,473	1,263	—	569	121	409	2,362	52.8	1,125
Uganda (1993)	152	152	—	—	—	—	152	100.0	18
Uruguay (1991)	1,608	633	—	160	—	95	888	55.2	463
Venezuela (1989)	19,700	1,411	543	2,195	488	1,739	6,376	32.4	2,585

Source: International Monetary Fund, 1993.

(Guyana, Mozambique, Niger, and Uganda), the Brady Plan operations effectively wiped out commercial bank debt, in each case through buybacks. For several larger countries, however, total debt reduction amounted to less than half of the face value of debt. In the rest of the section, we look more closely at the first five Brady Plan deals, none of which involved the complete removal of commercial bank debt.

The first five DDSR deals under the Brady Plan were concluded by Costa Rica, Mexico, the Philippines, Uruguay, and Venezuela.[18] Among the four ways listed above that such operations could have contributed to easing the macroeconomic problems confronting these countries, the extent to which three of them have been accomplished can be directly quantified. These are the change in V_t, the reduction in the shortfall, and the change in the time profile of debt service payments. The extent to which the fiscal conditions attached to the macroeconomic adjustment programs associated with DDSR operations may offer the prospect of reducing the secondary burden arising from the financing of V_t is much more difficult to ascertain. It requires the determination of a fiscal counterfactual in each case, as well as both a detailed examination of the fiscal conditions attached to each program and an assessment of the likely effectiveness of conditionality in bringing these desired outcomes about.

Conceptually, the change in V_t can be measured as the change in the market value of the total external debt plus any up-front cash payments minus "new money" (whether from official or commercial sources) minus grants (or their equivalents, if any) received from third parties.[19] However, several problems arise in applying this definition, two of which are particularly important. First, official debt is not traded in a secondary market, so the effect of DDSR operations on the value of both existing and new official debt requires making an assumption about its seniority status relative to "eligible" commercial bank medium- and long-term debt. Second, the ex ante market price of bank debt cannot be unambiguously observed, since it has to be purged of the effects of the anticipations of the operations. The change in V_t as a result of the DDSR operations in the first five programs negotiated has been estimated by Claessens et al. (1992). Table 13.9 presents their estimates of the increase in V_t for each of the five Brady Plan countries based on the alternative assumptions that official debt is senior and that commercial and official debt are of equal seniority.

The first column of the table assumes that official debt is not subject to country risk, while the second column assumes that official and commercial debt are of equal seniority. Although the differences between the two columns are substantial, suggesting that the estimates are very sensitive to this assumption, these results imply that V_t increased in all cases. While this would not be surprising in the context of strictly voluntary debt exchanges (see Bulow and Rogoff, 1990), the Brady Plan deals contained features

TABLE 13.9
Brady Plan Countries: Changes in V_t from DDSR
Operations (in millions of U.S. dollars)

Country	Official Debt Senior	Equal Seniority
Costa Rica	193	907
Mexico	2,189	8,074
Philippines	451	3,112
Uruguay	53	392
Venezuela	2,444	5,345

Source: Claessens et al. (1992).

intended to avert free-rider problems and to give these operations aspects of concertedness. These outcomes imply, then, that commercial banks have retained a substantial amount of bargaining power.

Regardless of what happens to V_t, the arguments above indicate that the reduction of the shortfall potentially provides an independent benefit to highly indebted countries, by improving the incentive structure facing policymakers and reducing the level of uncertainty for private agents. Since the shortfall is the difference between the face value of the debt and its market value, it can be reduced by reducing Δ_t or increasing V_t. Since effects on V_t have been discussed above, we now consider changes in Δ_t, expressed as a fraction of the original shortfall in the first five Brady Plan countries. This information is presented in Table 13.10. This table is constructed based on the assumption that all external debt is of equal seniority. Thus the total shortfall is calculated by multiplying the total stock of external debt outstanding at the time negotiations on DDSR were undertaken (column 1) by the secondary market discount for medium- and long-term commercial bank

TABLE 13.10
Brady Plan Countries: Debt Reduction in DDSR Operations (in percent of the initial shortfall)

	Debt	Price	Shortfall	Net Debt Reduction	Debt Reduction (percent of shortfall)
Costa Rica	4.8	0.56	2.1	1.0	47.3
Mexico	100.4	0.36	64.3	16.6	25.8
Philippines	29.4	0.46	15.9	0.5	3.1
Uruguay	3.6	0.36	2.3	0.7	30.4
Venezuela	34.8	0.30	24.4	4.3	17.7

Source: Fernández-Arias (1992).

debt prevailing at that time (1 minus the price of debt reported in column 2). Column 4 presents total net debt reduction in each of the five countries as calculated in Fernández-Arias (1992). This is expressed as a proportion of the original shortfall in the final column. Overall, net debt reduction as a percent of the original shortfall was greatest in Costa Rica and was negligible in the Philippines. More importantly, total net debt reduction amounted to a third or less of the original shortfall in four of the five countries.

Combining Table 13.9 with the fourth column of Table 13.10, it is obvious that the early DDSR operations under the Brady Plan had limited aims. In particular, they did not seek the complete elimination of the shortfall. The total shortfall, as given by the third column of Table 13.10, was not eliminated in any of the five countries examined. The extent to which it was reduced by lowering Δ_t, on the one hand, versus increasing V_t, on the other, depends on which of the estimates of the increase in V_t reported in Table 13.9 is used. In view of the limited scale of the operations, it is not surprising that the debt of these countries continued to sell at a discount in the secondary market, and that access to new voluntary credits has been restored only on a limited basis and only in the cases of Mexico and Venezuela.

In this vein, the time profile of debt service payments associated with these operations becomes a relevant concern. Unfortunately, as shown in Fernández-Arias (1992), under reasonable counterfactual assumptions, each of these operations seems to have had adverse liquidity effects over the first four years, with external payments increasing in four of the five countries (the exception being the Philippines) during the first year and decreasing only moderately over the subsequent three years.

In summary, the debt crisis was triggered by a widespread perception that the public sectors in many HICs were rendered effectively insolvent in the changed international environment of the early 1980s by their large stocks of both external and domestic debt as well as by domestic political constraints that impeded credible fiscal adjustment to the new circumstances. The crisis had severe repercussions for investment and growth in the debtor countries, partly because public sector insolvency itself has direct macroeconomic consequences for the domestic economy by creating disincentives to the adoption of appropriate adjustment policies as well as by engendering uncertainty for private agents. In addition to this, however, the drying up of external financing due to insolvency resulted in a liquidity crisis that required some form of fiscal adjustment as a matter of accounting necessity. The actual fiscal response to the liquidity aspects of the crisis—involving increased reliance on domestic financing, the inflation tax, and the curtailment of public investment—was highly inefficient in many countries, leading to capital flight, low investment, and slow growth, while resulting in neither actual nor prospective full debt service, leaving the problem of insolvency in place. The ability of the public sector in many countries to continue to borrow at home after external creditors had pulled out, as well as the extent to which macroeconomic dislocations in the debtor countries were due to direct "debt overhang" effects rather than to the nature of the fiscal response to the liquidity aspects of the crisis, remain matters for future research.[20]

Under the Brady Plan, solutions to the crisis—and removal of its harmful macroeconomic effects—were perceived to involve some combination of writing down the face value of the debt and increasing prospective public sector debt service at minimum distortionary cost to the domestic economy. The early DDSR programs implemented under the Brady Plan represented only partial solutions to the problem, closing without eliminating the gap between the face value of the external debt and the present value of prospective public sector debt service. They did so in part by reducing the former and in part by increasing the latter. Their contribution to easing the immediate liquidity problems of the debtors, however, was not substantial. The most important potential contribution of such programs, then, may have been the reduction, through the policy conditionality associated with resources provided by the international financial institutions, of the secondary burden associated with the internal transfer of resources to the public sector.

Appendix: Incentive Effects of a Debt Overhang

The argument that the existence of a debt overhang creates disincentives for domestic investment in the debtor country, and that debt forgiveness can both stimulate domestic investment and increase the actual payments received by creditors, has been made by a number of economists, but is originally associated with Jeffrey Sachs (1984). It can be summarized with the simple two-period model used in Sachs (1989b). Suppose that the debtor government maximizes the discounted utility $U()$ derived from domestic consumption in each period:

$$U(c_1, c_2) = u(c_1) + \alpha u(c_2),$$ (A1)

where $u()$ is a standard concave utility function, c_t denotes domestic consumption in period t, and $0 < \alpha < 1$ is a discount rate. The country enters the first period with an existing stock of debt, which gives rise to a contractual payment obligation of D_0 during the second period. No debt service payments are due in the first period. Actual payments to the original creditors in the second period are given by R, where $R < D_0$. The actual amount to be paid emerges from negotiations that take place between the government and its original creditors.[21] In the second period the government pays R to its original creditors, plus it services any additional debt it incurs from new creditors in the first period. However, the government cannot agree to pay more than a fraction $0 < \delta < 1$ of the country's second-period income in total debt service. If this constraint becomes binding, all creditors are paid in proportion to their exposure, the implication being that no creditor class (original or new) has seniority.

Under these conditions, the debtor government, acting as a planner, has to decide how much to invest and borrow during the first period, subject to the following constraints:

$$c_1 = F(k_0) + D_1 - I_1, \tag{A2}$$

$$c_2 = F(k_0 + I_1) - (1 + \rho)D_1 - R, \tag{A3}$$

where k_0 is the initial capital stock at the beginning of period 1, I_1 is investment during period 1, D_1 is new borrowing during period 1, ρ is the world risk-free interest rate, and $F()$ is a standard neoclassical production function, with $F' > 0$ and $F'' < 0$. There is also a credit supply constraint to be satisfied by the government, since new loans will be available only if new creditors expect to be fully repaid. Given the existing obligations to the original creditors, this requires

$$(1 + \rho)D_1 < \delta F(k_0 + I_1) - R. \tag{A4}$$

As long as condition (A4) holds, new borrowing D_1 is a choice variable for the government, since funds are available in infinitely elastic supply at the interest rate ρ. If it does not hold, however, the country is unable to borrow at all because new creditors would be unable to receive the market rate of return from lending to this country.[22]

If condition (A4) holds, the first-order conditions for a maximum are

$$-u'(c_1) + \alpha u'(c_2)F'(k_0 + I_1) = 0, \tag{A5a}$$

$$u'(c_1) - \alpha(1 + \rho)u'(c_2) = 0. \tag{A5b}$$

To solve for I_1, substitute (A5b) in (A5a) and simplify. Domestic investment is thus given implicitly by

$$F'(k_0 + I_1) = 1 + \rho. \tag{A6}$$

Substituting Equation (A6) in (A5b) defines first-period borrowing implicitly as a function of R. Intuitively, an increase in R reduces second-period consumption, since it reduces the resources available for consumption in that period. This raises the marginal utility of second-period consumption and thus increases the incentive to postpone consumption. This can be done by reducing first-period borrowing, so D_1 falls. Formally,

$$D_1 = d(R), \qquad -1 < d' = \frac{-\alpha F' u''(c_2)}{u''(c_1) + \alpha(1 + \rho)F' u''(c_2)} < 0. \quad \text{(A7)}$$

Note also that $-1 < (1 + \rho)D_1 < 0$. Thus, while condition (A4) may hold for low values of R, an increase in R reduces the right-hand side of Equation (A4) more than the left-hand side. There will thus be some critical value of R, say R^*, at which condition (A4) will hold as an equality. For $R > R^*$, condition (A4) will be violated. Now suppose that $R = D_0 > R^*$; that is, in the absence of a writedown of the initial debt, the debt service due to the original creditors is such that total debt service in the second period would exceed the amount that the country is willing to pay. In this case, since all creditors would experience a shortfall, new creditors will not enter. Constraints (A2) and (A3) now become

$$c_1 = F(k_0) - I_1, \quad \text{(A8)}$$

$$c_2 = (1 - \delta)F(k_0 + I_1). \quad \text{(A9)}$$

In this credit-rationed regime, the government's only choice is over the level of first-period investment. The first-order condition in this case is given by

$$-u'[F(k_0 + I_1)] + \alpha(1 - \delta)u'[F(k_0 + I_1) - \delta F(k_0 + I_1)]F'(k_0 + I_1) = 0. \quad \text{(A10)}$$

To show that debt forgiveness can increase investment and make both parties better off, let $\tilde{I}_1$ denote the solution to Equation (A10). Total debt service to the original creditors in this case is $\tilde{R} = \delta F(k_0 + \tilde{I}_1)$, which is less than D_0 by assumption. If the original creditors had written down the country's debt obligation to this amount initially, instead of insisting on full payment, constraint (A9) would become

$$c_2 = F(k_0 + I_1) - \tilde{R}, \quad \text{(A9')}$$

with first-order condition:

$$-u'[F(k_0 + I_1)] + \alpha(1 - \delta)u'[F(k_0 + I_1) - \tilde{R}]F'(k_0 + I_1) = 0. \quad \text{(A11)}$$

By substituting $\tilde{R} = \delta F(k_0 + \tilde{I}_1)$ in Equation (A11) and calculating $dI_1/d\delta < 0$, it is easy to show that investment increases when the contractual debt obligation is reduced from D_0 to $\tilde{R}$. The reason is that when contractual debt is not fully serviced, external creditors claim a share of any additional output forthcoming from new investment, essentially imposing a distortionary tax in the form of the fraction δ in (A9), which reduces the incentive for the government to invest. The additional investment increases domestic welfare since, by Equation (A10), $-u'(c_1) + \alpha u'(c_2)F' > 0$ when this expression is evaluated at $\tilde{I}_1$ and $\tilde{R}$, implying that additional investment is welfare enhancing. Thus debt forgiveness increases domestic welfare without harming the original creditors; that is, debt forgiveness is Pareto-improving. With an increase in R to slightly above $\tilde{R}$ (but below D_0), the debtor country could remain better off than in the no-forgiveness condition while increasing the value of debt service to the original creditors over what they would have received without debt forgiveness. In this way, removing the distortionary effect of the debt overhang can make both parties better off.

Fourteen

Trade, Financial, and Exchange-Rate Reforms

GROWING recognition in developing nations of the distortionary effects of government intervention has led in recent years to numerous attempts at liberalizing the domestic financial system, the exchange-rate regime, and international movements of goods and capital. These policies have raised a variety of substantive issues, regarding most notably the appropriate sequencing of reforms, the optimal pace at which liberalization policies should proceed, and the conduct of short-run macroeconomic policy in an economy undergoing extensive structural adjustment. This chapter reviews the recent theoretical and empirical literature on trade, financial, and exchange-rate reforms, with an emphasis on their short- and medium-term macroeconomic implications. The first part of the chapter focuses on the effects of domestic monetary and financial liberalization. We discuss in particular the experience of the Southern Cone countries of Latin America in the late 1970s, which has generated a vast literature over the years. Although a large number of other developing countries have taken steps during the 1980s and early 1990s to deregulate their domestic financial markets, many aspects of the Southern Cone experience have been confronted elsewhere in the developing world, and our discussion is organized so as to draw broad policy lessons.

The unification of dual foreign exchange markets with official and parallel segments is examined in the second part, with particular attention given to the short- and medium-run inflationary effects of such reforms. The third part of the chapter analyzes the macroeconomic effects associated with trade liberalization, focusing on the potential contractionary effect of a reduction in trade barriers on output and employment in the short run. The fourth part discusses the sequencing of alternative types of structural reforms as well as the sequencing of macroeconomic and structural reforms, and examines briefly the role of credibility and political factors in the determination of the optimal pace of reform.

14.1 Monetary and Financial Liberalization

Financial repression was described in Chapter 5 as a policy regime consisting of the imposition of high reserve requirements on banks as well as legal ceilings on their lending and borrowing rates. That description was adequate for the purpose of that chapter, which was to examine how monetary policy works under such a regime. In practice, however, financial repression consists of a broader panoply of legal restrictions on the behavior of banks. In addition to those indicated above, restrictions are imposed on competition in the banking industry and on the composition of bank portfolios. The former take the form of barriers to entry into the banking system and public ownership of banks, while the latter consist of both requirements that banks engage in certain forms of lending, as well as prohibitions from acquiring other types of assets. The former include the imposition of "liquidity ratios," requiring banks to invest a specified share of their portfolios in government instruments, as well as directed lending to specific productive sectors, typically the export sector or agriculture.

Park (1991) draws a useful distinction between monetary reform and financial liberalization in such a context. He defines a monetary reform as an increase in controlled interest rates to near-equilibrium levels, with the remaining set of restrictions on the behavior of banks left in place. By contrast, financial liberalization consists of a much more ambitious set of reforms, directed at removing at least some of the remaining restrictions on bank behavior. Full financial liberalization involves privatization of public financial institutions, the removal of restrictions to entry into banking (including those preventing access by foreign banks), measures aimed at spurring competition in financial markets, the reduction of legal reserve requirements, the elimination of directed lending, and the freeing of official interest rates.

Both monetary reform and various forms of financial liberalization are becoming increasingly common in the developing world. Analytical issues concerning the effects of monetary reform on short-run macroeconomic equilibrium have been addressed in Chapters 5 and 11. This section focuses instead on reviewing the empirical evidence on the effects of monetary reform as a structural policy—that is, a policy designed to enhance medium-term economic growth by promoting the accumulation and efficient use of productive assets—as well as on the lessons that have emerged from the experience of both reform and liberalization in developing countries.

14.1.1 Monetary Reform

The arguments for monetary reform as a structural policy conducive to a higher growth path are due to McKinnon (1973) and Shaw (1973). They can be summarized briefly as follows: In a context in which the saving instruments available in the formal financial system are limited to cash, demand deposits, and time deposits, raising controlled interest rates to near-equilibrium levels may induce an increase in the saving rate as well as a portfolio shift out of inventories, precious metals, foreign exchange, and curb market lending into the formal financial system. The high real interest rates resulting from the reform would actually increase rather than reduce investment in the aggregate, either because the need to accumulate funds to undertake lumpy investments makes money and capital complementary rather than substitute assets (stressed by McKinnon), or because of a "credit availability" effect (the channel emphasized by Shaw). The latter works as follows: When interest rates are at below-equilibrium levels, total investment is limited to the available saving. By increasing total saving and attracting it into the banking system, higher real interest rates would increase investment through enhanced credit availability. Moreover, many high-return projects not previously funded would be undertaken after monetary reform, because banks have scale economies relative to the informal market in collecting and processing information on borrowers. Thus, they are more efficient in channeling funds to high-return investment projects than the informal market. The conclusion is that growth is enhanced both because the increase in saving raises investment and because the quality of investment improves.

According to these arguments, then, raising controlled interest rates should raise the demand for domestic time and saving deposits, which should increase the quantity and improve the quality of domestic investment, in turn increasing the rate of growth. The evidence on these propositions takes two forms. Econometric studies have looked at each of these propositions separately, and sometimes have examined the link between the immediate policy objective (higher real interest rates) and intermediate or ultimate targets in the form of investment and growth. A separate strand of evidence evaluates the experience of countries that have undertaken monetary reforms.

Econometric studies were undertaken on these propositions soon after they were first formulated by McKinnon and Shaw. Vogel and Buser (1976) reasoned that, under financial repression, a higher rate of inflation should reduce private investment, since it would be associated with lower real interest rates. However, they found little evidence of this effect in a sample of sixteen Latin American countries. But at the same time they found that inflation significantly affected the demand for time and saving deposits in these countries, and that the investment level depended positively on the rate of accumulation of time and saving deposits. They interpreted the latter as supportive of the complementarity and credit availability hypotheses. Galbis (1979) also tested McKinnon's direct complementarity hypothesis, in his case by including the rate of investment in money demand functions for nineteen Latin American countries. He found little support for the proposition, since the coefficient of investment was significantly positive in only four of those cases. Like Vogel and Buser, Galbis was unable to find negative effects of inflation on investment levels, either in time series or cross-section investment regressions. In a pooled cross-section–time series sample of twenty developing countries, Lanyi and Saracoglu (1983) found that increases in the real deposit interest rate increased national saving rates and that the real deposit interest rate had a positive and significant coefficient in a regression of the growth rate on the deposit rate.

Fry (1988) undertook a systematic study of the econometric evidence, examining each step in the set of propositions linking monetary reform to economic growth. Using pooled cross-section–time series regressions for several samples of Asian countries, he concluded that the weight of the evidence supported a weak positive effect of real deposit rates on national saving, but a strong positive effect on the demand for money as well as on the supply of credit. Credit supply, in turn, was found to have a strong positive effect on investment, supporting the "credit availability" effect. However, he found no evidence for McKinnon's "complementarity" effect, which he tested by including the investment rate in a money demand function. Finally, Fry found evidence of two types in support of improved quality of investment. First, real deposit rates were positively correlated with the incremental output/capital ratio (ICOR), taken to be a proxy for the efficiency of investment. Second, the real deposit interest rate had a positive effect on growth in a simple regression of one variable on the other. He obtained similar results in a more recent study focusing on a broader set of countries (Fry, 1993).

In most of the studies comprising this literature, the link between real deposit rates and growth has been studied in this simple form. The finding of a positive correlation, however, may be consistent with causation from growth to interest rates, or from a common third factor (such as inflation) to both growth and interest rates. Gelb (1989) explored this issue in more detail, using a cross-section sample of thirty-four developing countries with data from 1965 to 1985. As in other studies, he found that real deposit rates had strong positive effects on both growth and the ICOR, but weaker positive effects on the investment ratio. Moreover, he also found that the inclusion of additional variables weakened the effects of interest rates on investment, but not on ICOR. Overall, he concluded that the efficiency effect on investment, and not the effect on the overall volume of investment, accounted for the positive relationship between real interest rates and growth. He also found that including other measures of distortion weakened the relationship between real interest rates and growth, although it remained positive. Gelb also found that an increase in the real deposit rate increased the share of domestic saving intermediated through the formal financial system, and that this share had a stronger effect on growth than the level of saving itself, which he interpreted as establishing the causal chain between real deposit rates and growth, that is, through more effective intermediation into higher-productivity investment.

Dornbusch and Reynoso (1993), however, have suggested an alternative interpretation of such results. They pointed out that, in a neoclassical growth model, growth of output per capita can be written as

$$\hat{y}_t - n_t = \alpha \left[\left(\frac{I_t}{y_t} \right) \left(\frac{K_{t-1}}{y_t} \right)^{-1} - n_t \right],$$

where y_t is real output, K_t the capital stock, I_t net investment, n_t the rate of growth of the labor force, and α the share of capital. Thus, what matters for contemporaneous growth is the average, not the marginal, efficiency of capital, and this is likely to be improved only very slowly through improved efficiency of investment.[1] Their interpretation of the correlation between real deposit interest rates and growth is that high inflation impedes growth, primarily through distortions induced by uncertainty.

Taking the results of Gelb and the arguments of Dornbusch and Reynoso together leaves the evidence on the effects of monetary reform on growth in an inconclusive state. One interpretation may be that higher real deposit interest rates are unlikely to have strong effects on the saving rate. Both the results cited above and the more detailed evidence reviewed in Chapter 3 are consistent with this conclusion. However, portfolio shifts toward domestic financial instruments are apparently induced by monetary reform. Nevertheless, this may not have a large effect on the volume of investment. There is little evidence in favor of the "complementarity" effect, and while the "credit availability" effect is more strongly supported by the data—in the sense that an increase in the supply of credit, other things equal, is positively correlated with the level of investment (see also Chapter 3)—the absence of a positive relationship between real deposit rates and investment raises the question of whether this correlation should be interpreted as being in support of the "credit availability" channel. Finally, although a positive correlation between real deposit rates and growth seems to be a feature of developing-country data, the interpretation of this relationship is problematic. It may well reflect some contribution of the efficiency effect discussed above, but the real deposit rate may also be serving as a proxy for more general distortions, including the uncertainties associated with high and unstable inflation.

Not surprisingly, the episodic evidence associated with specific-country cases of monetary reform does not provide a clearer verdict, essentially because ceteris paribus conditions do not hold. As an illustration, consider the Korean monetary reform of 1965. As described in McKinnon (1976), nominal deposit and lending rates had been pegged at low levels in Korea prior to the reform, yielding strongly negative real rates in 1963–64. Nominal rates were revised upward, but not freed, in September 1965, and directed credit restrictions were reduced but not eliminated—thus qualifying this episode as a monetary reform rather than a full financial liberalization. Real rates of return rose markedly subsequent to the reform, the ratio of broad money to GDP increased by a factor of 7 between 1964 and 1969, private saving increased, and growth experienced a very strong acceleration. McKinnon interpreted this as supporting the positive effect of monetary reform on growth, through the channels previously mentioned. Giovannini (1985) reached different conclusions. He emphasized that most of the increase in national saving in Korea in the period after 1965 arose in the public sector, due to a fiscal correction. He pointed out further that the measured increase in households' surplus after the reform was a one-shot event concentrated in 1966, and the correlation between the surplus and the real interest rate was negative after that year. He concluded from this that the measured increase in saving may well have been due to the recording of a portfolio shift out of the informal market as a change in saving.

14.1.2 Financial Liberalization

In contrast with the case of monetary reform, the evidence on the effects of financial liberalization is mostly episodic. Even so, a convergence of views has emerged regarding the lessons to be drawn from the experience of developing nations, primarily based on the financial reforms undertaken in the Southern Cone countries of Latin America in the late 1970s. The consensus view is represented by Villanueva and Mirakhor (1990), who argue that success in financial liberalization requires macroeconomic stability and a strong and effective system of bank supervision as preconditions, and that success is more likely if controls on interest rates are removed gradually while these conditions are established.[2] Sri Lanka and Korea are cited as countries that moved to financial liberalization gradually, while the requisite preconditions were put in place. In the absence of these conditions, full financial liberalization is apt to be associated with sharp increases in real interest rates, bankruptcy of financial institutions, and loss of monetary control. Examples of these outcomes are the Southern Cone liberalizations, as well as the experiences of the Philippines and Turkey.

The argument is as follows: Macroeconomic instability increases the variance of and covariance among projects funded by banks. This increases the riskiness of bank portfolios. If deposit insurance is absent or correctly priced, an analysis along the lines of the Stiglitz-Weiss model of credit rationing under informational asymmetries predicts that banks would reduce interest rates and ration credit more severely.[3] With inadequately priced deposit insurance, by contrast, moral hazard will induce banks to raise interest rates to attract deposits and fund high-risk projects, because they in effect face a one-way bet: if the projects pay off, bank owners reap the profits, whereas if they do not, the government foots the bill to pay off depositors, with bank owners risking only their limited capital. This outcome can be avoided when deposit insurance is priced correctly, because doing so forces banks to pay for the higher risk that their portfolio choices impose on the government, causing them to internalize the consequences of their actions. The same result could be ensured by adequate bank supervision, even when deposit insurance is free or inadequately priced.[4]

Villanueva and Mirakhor (1990) cite the contrasting experiences of the Southern Cone countries as well as the Philippines and Turkey, on the one hand, and that of Malaysia, on the other, to illustrate these points. All of these countries moved to full liberalization of interest rates in a very short period. In Argentina, Chile, and Uruguay, rapid removal of interest rate ceilings and credit controls in the mid- to late 1970s[5] was accompanied by the relaxation of bank supervision and the extension of either explicit (Argentina) or implicit (Chile) deposit insurance, all in the context of high inflation and unsatisfactory economic performance. Indeed, the financial liberalization measures were accompanied by innovative macroeconomic stabilization programs in all three countries (see Chapter 8). Previous macroeconomic difficulties implied not just the uncertainties associated with the simultaneous undertaking of stabilization programs, but also that bank portfolios already included an unusual number of bad loans, effectively impairing bank capital and increasing the moral hazard problems created by deposit insurance. In all of the Southern Cone countries, lending rates quickly rose to high real levels, distress borrowing by firms ensued, and bankruptcies became common. In each case, the liberalization and stabilization programs collapsed in the midst of a financial crisis during the early 1980s. The Philippine and Turkish liberalizations in the 1980s were carried out under similar circumstances and in a similar fashion. Not surprisingly, they produced similar results.[6]

The success cases also illustrate the general principles. Although financial liberalization was carried out rapidly in Malaysia beginning in late 1978, the country had a long tradition of macroeconomic stability and banking supervision. The transition to a liberalized financial system proved to be rather smooth, with only a mild increase in real interest rates and no widespread bankruptcies culminating in financial collapse.[7,8] On the other hand, like the Southern Cone countries, Sri Lanka (in 1977) and Korea (in 1981) both undertook liberalization from initial conditions characterized by unsatisfactory macroeconomic performance. However, unlike the Southern Cone countries, both Asian countries moved to remove restrictions on interest rates gradually while pursuing macroeconomic stability and stronger prudential regulation over banks. Greater flexibility (although not full liberalization) was permitted in both countries only after macroeconomic stability was achieved and the supervisory mechanism strengthened.

14.2 Unification of Foreign Exchange Markets

As discussed in previous chapters, attempts at imposing exchange and trade restrictions in developing countries have almost invariably led to the emergence of an illegal market for foreign exchange, whose existence entails a variety of costs—high volatility of exchange rates and prices, creation of incentives to engage in rent-seeking activities or divert export remittances from the official to the parallel market, and loss in tax revenue. Growing recognition of these adverse effects has led policymakers in many developing nations to seek ways to unify the official and parallel markets for foreign exchange.

The process of exchange-rate unification has as its ultimate objective the absorption and legalization of the parallel market for foreign exchange, as well as the elimination of the inefficiencies and market fragmentation associated with a quasi-illegal activity, thereby permitting an efficient allocation of foreign-currency earnings. In practice, unification attempts have often taken the form of adopting (at least for a transitory period) a uniform floating exchange rate.[9] The analytical work in this area has shown that the impact of such a policy shift on the short- and long-run behavior of the exchange rate and inflation is generally ambiguous. We begin by discussing the short-term dynamics of exchange market unification, and then turn to longer-term effects.

14.2.1 Short-Run Dynamics of Unification

The short-run effects of a preannounced future adoption of a unified flexible-exchange-rate arrangement have been examined by Lizondo (1987), Kiguel and Lizondo (1990), and Agénor and Flood (1992). We present here a simple model that allows us to identify the main factors affecting price and exchange-rate dynamics associated with the unification process.[10] After presenting the basic model, we discuss the behavior of the premium and foreign reserves in the pre- and postreform periods.

14.2.1.1 THE PREREFORM DUAL-RATE REGIME

Consider a small open economy operating an informal dual-exchange-rate regime in which an official, pegged exchange rate coexists with a freely determined parallel rate. The official rate applies to current account transactions authorized by the authorities, while the parallel rate is used for capital account transactions and the remainder of current account items. Agents are endowed with perfect foresight and hold domestic- and foreign-currency balances in their portfolios. Domestic output consists of a single exportable good and is taken as exogenous. In each period, exporters surrender a given proportion of their foreign exchange earnings at the official exchange rate, and repatriate the remaining proceeds via the parallel market.

Formally, the model is described by the following log-linear equations, where all parameters are defined as positive:

$$m_t - p_t = -\alpha \dot{s}_t, \tag{1}$$

$$m_t = \Theta R_t + (1 - \Theta)D_t, \quad 0 < \Theta < 1, \tag{2}$$

$$p_t = \delta s_t + (1 - \delta)e_t, \quad 0 < \delta < 1, \tag{3}$$

$$\dot{R}_t = -\Phi(s_t - e_t), \tag{4}$$

$$\dot{D}_t = 0, \tag{5}$$

where m_t denotes the nominal money stock, D_t domestic credit, R_t the stock of net foreign assets held by the central bank, p_t the domestic price level, e_t the official exchange rate, and s_t the parallel exchange rate. All variables are measured in logarithms.

Equation (1) describes money market equilibrium. Equation (2) is a log-linear approximation that defines the domestic money stock as a weighted average of domestic credit and foreign reserves. Equation (3) indicates that the price level depends on the official and parallel exchange rates. This results from the assumption that some commercial transactions are settled in the parallel market, with the price of these imports reflecting the marginal cost of foreign exchange—that is, the parallel rate. The purchasing-power parity assumption holds, therefore, at a composite exchange rate, and the foreign price level has been set to unity (so that its logarithm is zero) for simplicity.[11] Equation (4) describes the behavior of net foreign assets. The negative effect of the premium—defined as the difference between the official and the parallel exchange rates—on the behavior of reserves results from its impact on underinvoicing of exports. The higher the parallel exchange rate is relative to the official rate, the greater will be the incentive to falsify export invoices and to divert export proceeds to the unofficial market.[12] Finally, Equation (5) indicates that the stock of credit is constant over time.

In the prereform dual-exchange-rate system, the forward-looking parallel rate s_t and the predetermined level of official reserves R_t are endogenous variables while the official exchange rate e_t is assumed set at $\bar{e}$ by the authorities. In the postreform, unified flexible-rate regime, by contrast, $s_t = e_t = \epsilon_t$ and reserves remain constant. We now examine the behavior of endogenous variables across the two regimes.

Setting $D_t = \bar{D}$ and solving (1)–(5) yields

$$\begin{bmatrix} \dot{s}_t \\ \dot{R}_t \end{bmatrix} = \begin{bmatrix} \delta/\alpha & -\Theta/\alpha \\ -\Phi & 0 \end{bmatrix} \begin{bmatrix} s_t \\ R_t \end{bmatrix} + \begin{bmatrix} -(1-\Theta)\bar{D}/\alpha + (1-\delta)\bar{e}/\alpha \\ \Phi\bar{e} \end{bmatrix}. \quad (6)$$

System (6) is saddlepoint stable, with one negative root (denoted by ρ_1) and one positive root, ρ_2.[13] Solving for the particular solutions yields

$$s_t = s^* + C_1 \exp(\rho_1 t) + C_2 \exp(\rho_2 t), \quad (7a)$$

$$R_t = R^* + \kappa_1 C_1 \exp(\rho_1 t) + \kappa_2 C_2 \exp(\rho_2 t), \quad \kappa_1 > 0, \quad \kappa_2 < 0, \quad (7b)$$

where C_1 and C_2 are as yet undetermined coefficients, and $s^* = \bar{e}$ and $R^* = [\bar{e} - (1-\Theta)\bar{D}]/\Theta \geq 0$ denote the steady-state values of the parallel rate and foreign exchange reserves.

Let us first suppose that the existing dual-rate system is expected to last forever. Stability would then require setting $C_2 = 0$ in the solutions (7a) and (7b). Using an initial condition on reserves $\bar{R}_0$ thus allows the determination of C_1. The economy's equilibrium path in this scenario is the unique nonexplosive path SS (which passes through the stationary point E) depicted in Figure 14.1. For a positive (negative) premium, reserves are falling (increasing), as indicated by the arrows pointing west (east) in the figure. The saddlepath SS has a positive slope (equal to $-\rho_1\Phi$) and is flatter than the curve $[\dot{s}_t = 0]$.[14]

If the policymakers announce their intention to switch to a floating-rate arrangement at a well-defined date in the future, forward-looking agents will anticipate the abandonment of the dual-rate system. In that case, the coefficient C_2 will not be zero. Instead, as shown below, coefficients C_1 and C_2 will be determined so as to satisfy the constraints imposed by a perfectly anticipated transition to the postreform regime.

14.2.1.2 THE POSTREFORM FLEXIBLE-RATE REGIME

Let $T > 0$ denote the future transition date announced at period $t = 0$, that is, the initial instant at which the policymakers intend to switch to the flexible-rate regime. In the postreform flexible-rate system $\epsilon_t = e_t = s_t$, a condition that yields, from Equation (4), $\dot{R}_t = 0$. Therefore, reserves remain constant beyond $t \geq T$ at, say, the level R_T^+. Under these assumptions, the unified flexible exchange rate is determined by

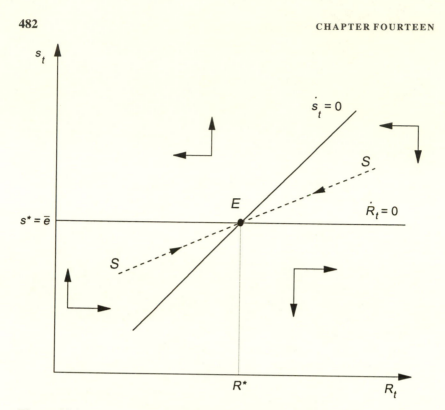

Figure 14.1   Steady-State Equilibrium Prior to Reform

$$\alpha\dot{\epsilon}_t - \epsilon_t = -m_T^+, \quad t \ge T, \tag{8}$$

where

$$m_T^+ = \Theta R_T^+ + (1 - \Theta)\bar{D}, \quad t \ge T. \tag{9}$$

Equation (8) is a linear differential equation in ϵ_t, whose solution is

$$\epsilon_t = C\exp(t/\alpha) + m_T^+, \quad t \ge T. \tag{10}$$

Ruling out speculative bubbles requires setting $C = 0$. The exchange rate in effect at the instant the economy switches to a unified floating-rate regime is therefore

$$\epsilon_T^+ = m_T^+, \quad t \ge T, \tag{11}$$

which depends on the reform date, since it is linearly related to the terminal stock of reserves at T. The relationship between reserves and the unified exchange rate at time T defines a "terminal curve," denoted CC in the analysis that follows, whose slope is equal to Θ.[15]

14.2.1.3 DYNAMICS IN ANTICIPATION OF REFORM

We now examine how reserves and the premium will evolve when agents perfectly anticipate the transition from a dual-rate regime to a flexible system. Essentially, this requires establishing conditions that "connect" the two regimes. In the present model, there are two such requirements: an initial condition on reserves, and a price continuity condition, which prevents a jump in the parallel exchange rate at the moment the reform is implemented:

$$R_0 = \bar{R}_0, \qquad s_T = \epsilon_T^+ \qquad \text{for } t \geq T. \tag{12}$$

Conditions (12) allow us to determine the constants C_1 and C_2 in the solutions for reserves and the parallel exchange rate obtained for the dual-rate regime (Equations 7). Setting $t = 0$ in Equation (7b), $t = T$ in Equations (7a) and (7b), and using (11) and (12) yields

$$\kappa_1 C_1 + \kappa_2 C_2 = \bar{R}_0 - R^*, \tag{13a}$$

$$R^* + \kappa_1 C_1 \exp(\rho_1 T) + \kappa_2 C_2 \exp(\rho_2 T)$$
$$= s^* + C_1 \exp(\rho_1 T) + C_2 \exp(\rho_2 T). \tag{13b}$$

Solving this system yields

$$C_1 = [(1 - \kappa_2) \exp(\rho_2 T)(\bar{R}_0 - R^*) - \kappa_2(R^* - \bar{e})]/\Delta, \tag{14a}$$

$$C_2 = [\kappa_1(R^* - \bar{e}) - (1 - \kappa_1) \exp(\rho_1 T)(\bar{R}_0 - R^*)]/\Delta, \tag{14b}$$

where $\Delta = \kappa_1(1 - \kappa_2) \exp(\rho_2 T) - \kappa_2(1 - \kappa_1) \exp(\rho_1 T)$.

Substituting Equations (14) in Equations (7) yields the solutions for the parallel exchange rate and foreign reserves prior to reform, that is, for $0 \leq t < T$. As shown by Equations (14), these solutions depend on the relation between the initial value of reserves $\bar{R}_0$ and its steady-state value in the (permanent) dual-rate regime R^*, as well as the initial level of domestic credit, since $R^* - \bar{e} = -(1 - \Theta)(\bar{D} - \bar{e})/\Theta$. A realistic case for developing countries is an initial situation in which a positive premium exists up to an instant before the future reform is announced, that is, where $s_0 > \bar{e} = s^*$. From Equations (7), it can be verified that such a condition is satisfied for $\bar{R}_0 > R^*$.

Assuming that this condition holds, two cases must be considered, depending on the initial positions of the saddlepath SS and the terminal curve

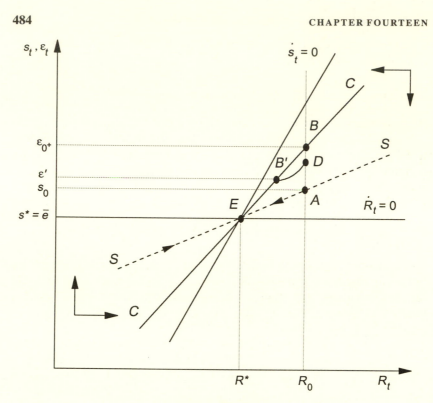

Figure 14.2   Dynamics upon Unification: Case I

CC. Figure 14.2 illustrates the case where CC is steeper than SS.[16] In such a situation, $\bar{e} < s_0 < \epsilon_T^+$. An announcement at $t = 0^+$ of a future reform at T leads to an immediate depreciation of the parallel exchange rate—relative to its previously anticipated path—and a gradual fall in reserves.

The dynamic behavior in anticipation of reform in this scenario is illustrated in Figure 14.2. As assumed above, the economy before the reform announcement is such that $\bar{R}_0 > R^*$ (corresponding to a positive premium) and is located on a point such as A on the saddlepath SS. The position of the steady-state equilibrium in the postunification regime depends on the length of the transition date T. Consider first the case where the reform occurs "overnight," that is, where $T \to 0^+$. Upon announcement, the economy moves immediately to its postreform steady state. The parallel exchange rate jumps from point A to point B (located on CC), with no change in the initial—and therefore final—stock of reserves, and a unified exchange rate equal to ϵ_{0^+}.

Consider now the case where T is positive. At the moment the future reform is announced, the parallel exchange rate depreciates instantaneously (jumping to a point such as D) and appreciates continuously

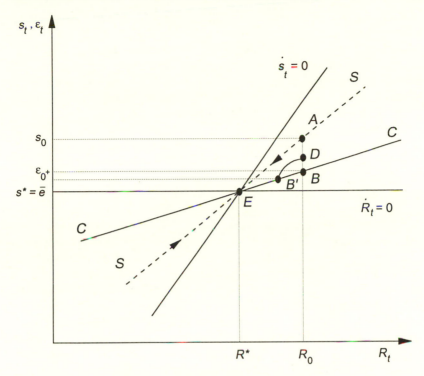

Figure 14.3 Dynamics upon Unification: Case II

during the transition period toward point B' on curve CC, which is reached—without further jumps—at the moment the reform is implemented, T. The unified exchange rate is equal to ϵ', which is more appreciated than ϵ_{0+}. Finally, if the exchange-rate reform is announced to occur in the very distant future—that is, for $T \to \infty$—the announcement will have no effect on the path of the parallel exchange rate and reserves. The economy will remain at the initial position A upon announcement, and then move along the original saddlepath SS toward point E.[17] There are therefore three possible paths associated with unification when the terminal curve CC is steeper than SS. While reserves fall continuously, the parallel market exchange can either jump instantaneously to a more depreciated equilibrium level, appreciate continuously following an initial depreciation, or appreciate continuously with no initial jump toward the unified exchange rate. In the second scenario, the unified exchange rate may be above or below the initial parallel exchange rate, depending on the length of the transition period and the parameter values.

Consider now the case where the terminal curve CC is flatter than the initial saddlepath SS. This case, which is illustrated in Figure 14.3, corresponds to $s_0 > \epsilon_T^+ > \bar{e}$. If the reform occurs overnight, the parallel exchange rate will appreciate immediately and jump from point A to point B located on CC. If the reform is preannounced, the initial downward jump is from point A to a point such as D, followed by a movement along the unstable trajectory DB' during the transition period. In this scenario, thus, the transition process is characterized by falling reserves and a continuous appreciation of the parallel exchange rate—with or without an initial downward jump, depending on the length of the transition period.

In summary, the short-run behavior of the parallel exchange rate in anticipation of reform depends on the state of expectations about the timing of reform, the initial position of the economy, the length of the transition period between announcement and implementation of reform, and the macroeconomic policy stance that agents expect policymakers to adopt in the postreform regime. If the unification attempt is fully anticipated, agents will, in order to avoid capital losses, adjust their portfolios toward foreign-currency-denominated assets if the uniform floating exchange rate is expected to be more depreciated than the existing parallel rate, and toward domestic-currency-denominated assets if it is expected to be more appreciated. As a result of this portfolio adjustment, the parallel market rate will depreciate or appreciate immediately (at the moment the unification attempt is announced or when expectations are formed), in the latter case toward the level asset holders expect the postunification floating rate to be. After the initial jump, and if the reform is known to take place in the near future, the parallel market rate will steadily depreciate or appreciate toward the unified exchange rate during the transition to unification.[18]

The reason for the jump in the parallel exchange rate upon announcement of the reform is as follows. If the unified exchange rate associated with an overnight reform is, for instance, more depreciated than the initial level of the parallel exchange rate and the official exchange rate, agents realize that the future reform may imply a depreciation of the official exchange rate, a rise in prices, and therefore a reduction in real money balances. Under perfect foresight, these future effects are reflected immediately in the expected—and actual—rate of depreciation of the parallel rate, leading agents to reduce their demand for the domestic currency. But since the initial money stock is constant (reserves cannot jump at $t = 0$), equilibrium in the money market can be maintained only if an immediate rise in prices occurs—or only if the parallel exchange rate depreciates.

In practice, the date at which the reform will take place in the future may not be perfectly known. Asset holders may also be uncertain about the type of exchange-rate regime the authorities would adopt following a reform attempt. For instance, instead of assuming that the authorities will adopt a unified floating-exchange-rate system, they could envisage a transition to a uniform fixed-exchange-rate regime. A likely outcome of the introduction of uncertainty about the reform date or the nature of the post-transition regime is that expectations of reform would cause a jump in the parallel exchange rate at the moment the reform is implemented, as well as volatile exchange-rate movements prior to transition if this type of uncertainty varies over time. In such conditions, it may be particularly difficult to interpret short-run movements in the parallel exchange rate. Erratic fluctuations in exchange rates induced by uncertainty about the reform date or the postunification regime may distort portfolio decisions and have an adverse inflationary effect.

14.2.2 Longer-Run Effects of Unification

The longer-run macroeconomic effects of exchange market unification depend essentially on the fiscal implications of exchange-rate reform, as emphasized by Pinto (1989, 1991a). Pinto's analysis is based on a model whose basic characteristics are similar to the short-run model developed above. In addition, however, he explicitly models government behavior and assumes that rationing occurs in the official market for foreign exchange. In Pinto's framework, the government buys imported goods and uses the foreign exchange surrendered by exporters to pay for them. Excess foreign exchange is resold to the private sector at the official exchange rate. Thus, reserves remain constant over time and the dynamics of money supply are determined by credit policy.

Production for exports, which takes place under a constant-returns-to-scale technology, is partly smuggled out and partly sold through the official market. As a result, the parallel market premium acts as an implicit tax on exports taking place through official channels. Since exporters face rising marginal costs to smuggling, the allocation of output between the official and the parallel markets is determined by equating marginal returns. Pinto shows that in equilibrium the proportion of smuggled exports is positively related to the parallel market premium.

Private agents spend a fixed fraction of their wealth on imported consumption goods. The government finances its deficit by credit from the central bank:

$$\dot{D}_t = \bar{e}(\bar{g} - \tau_t),\tag{15}$$

where $\bar{e}$ denotes the official exchange rate, $\bar{g}$ government imports, and τ_t conventional taxes. Equation (15) implies that

$$\dot{m}_t = (\bar{g} - \tau_t) - \epsilon m_t,\tag{16}$$

where m_t measures the real money stock in terms of the official exchange rate and ϵ is the constant rate of official depreciation. Equation (16) indicates that in the steady state ($\dot{m}_t = 0$) the budget deficit is financed by the inflation tax ϵm^*.

To identify the steady-state revenue from the implicit tax on exports requires moving from the "recorded" deficit measured in terms of the official exchange rate (Equation (15)) to the "true" deficit measured in terms of the parallel exchange rate. Let ρ denote (1 plus) the parallel market premium. The "true" long-run capital loss incurred by the private sector as a result of the inflation tax is $\epsilon m^*/\rho^*$. Similarly, while officially recorded taxes are equal to $\bar{e}\tau$, the real tax burden is equal to τ/ρ^*. If the long-run value of the premium is positive ($\rho^* \geq 1$), the "true" fiscal burden imposed by the inflation tax and conventional taxes is lower than the recorded one. But since real government spending does not depend on the premium, the difference between the "recorded" and the "true" tax burdens is the implicit tax on exports, $\bar{g} - \tau/\rho^* - m^*\epsilon/\rho^*$. Since $\bar{g} - \tau = m^*\epsilon$, this expression is equal to $\bar{g}(1 - 1/\rho^*)$. Equivalently, the steady-state government budget constraint can be written as

$$\bar{g} = \tau + m^*\epsilon = \rho^*\left(\frac{\tau}{\rho^*} + \frac{m^*\epsilon}{\rho^*}\right) = \bar{g}\left(1 - \frac{1}{\rho^*}\right) + \frac{\tau}{\rho^*} + \frac{m^*\epsilon}{\rho^*}, \qquad (17)$$

which explicitly shows how the implicit tax on exports serves to finance goverment expenditure. If the elasticity of the demand for domestic money is less than unity, there exists a trade-off between the inflation tax rate and the premium for a given level of the fiscal deficit. Put differently, a decline in the implicit tax on exports must be compensated by an increase in the inflation (devaluation) rate. By unifying, the government loses the tax revenue implicit in the premium, $\bar{g}(1 - 1/\rho^*)$. The larger the implicit tax on exports prior to reform, the larger the jump in inflation upon unification, since the policymakers attempt to compensate for a fall in revenue by an increase in monetary financing of the fiscal deficit and a higher tax on domestic money holdings.

Pinto's emphasis on the trade-off between the premium and inflation in the unification process remains largely valid if the assumption that agents are subject to rationing in the official market for foreign exchange is replaced by the hypothesis that the official market clears through changes in foreign reserves (Lizondo, 1991a).[19] However, while the emphasis on the implicit taxation of exports appears warranted in view of the experience of some developing countries, Pinto's analysis neglects another important source of implicit tax or subsidy that is associated with informal dual-exchange-rate regimes. As emphasized by Agénor and Ucer (1994), taxes on imports are an important source of revenue for developing countries, notably in sub-Saharan Africa. In many countries, the official rather than the parallel market exchange rate (which, as indicated in Chapter 2, is often highly correlated with domestic prices) is used for customs valuation purposes. The use of the official exchange rate for the valuation of imports for duty purposes provides an implicit subsidy to importers. To the extent that the subsidies provided through this channel are large relative to the revenue generated from the implicit tax on exports, the net long-run effect of exchange market unification may be a fall (rather than an increase) in the domestic inflation rate. Indeed, the evidence reported by Agénor and Ucer (1994) seems to suggest that prior to unification significant net quasi-fiscal losses were registered in many countries operating informal currency markets.

14.2.3 Evidence on Unification Attempts

The experience of developing countries with exchange market unification has attracted a great deal of attention recently. Much interest has focused on the experience of sub-Saharan African countries in the mid-1980s.[20] While some of these countries chose to follow a gradual path to unification, most of them opted for an "overnight" approach, which involved floating the official exchange rate and simultaneously removing foreign exchange controls. In Ghana, for instance, unification took the form of large but widely spaced devaluations over almost four years (April 1983–March 1987), with an "overnight" float occurring at the last stage, and was accompanied by reductions in the fiscal deficit. By contrast, in Nigeria the currency was floated overnight, in September 1986.

The experience of sub-Saharan African countries indicates first that, in some countries—particularly Sierra Leone and Zambia, where a floating arrangement was implemented in July 1986 and September 1985, respectively—exchange-rate unification led to a surge in inflation. Second, the evidence suggests that the parallel market premium rose substantially in the months preceding the unification attempt and fell sharply upon implementation of reform. The unified floating exchange rate that emerged immediately after the reform took place was in some cases very close to the prereform parallel rate—implying that the drop in the premium resulted essentially from a sharp depreciation of the official exchange rate. This was the case most notably in Nigeria. However, despite a sharp drop on impact, a significant premium reemerged subsequently in some countries—most notably Ghana, Sierra Leone, Somalia, and Zambia.

Other countries that have recently unified their foreign exchange markets by adopting a floating-exchange-rate arrangement include Egypt (early 1991), Guyana (March 1990), India (March 1993), Iran (March 1993), Jamaica (September 1991), Madagascar (May 1994), Peru (August 1990), Sri Lanka (August 1990), Trinidad and Tobago (April 1993), and Venezuela (March 1989).[21] Prior to floating, these countries had widespread trade and exchange restrictions—such as surrender requirements on exports, import licensing procedures, and prohibitions on specific goods. These restrictions led to substantial diversion of foreign exchange to the parallel market, creating in some cases severe balance-of-payments problems. In Jamaica, for instance, the current account deficit in relation to exports reached almost 30 percent in 1989, compared with a surplus the year before. The ratio of official reserves to imports fell from 12 percent in 1988 to less than 7 percent in 1989.

The experience of Jamaica, Guyana, and Sri Lanka is particularly revealing. In addition to balance-of-payments difficulties, the prereform period was marked by rising inflation in all three countries. In Jamaica the inflation rate (measured in terms of the consumer price index) rose from 8 percent in 1988 to 13 percent in 1989 and 22 percent in 1990. In Sri Lanka inflation rose from 8 percent in 1987 to an average of 13 percent in 1988–89 and 21 percent in 1990. The parallel market premium also displayed a rising trend in these countries: it rose from 18 percent in 1987 to 22 percent in 1988 and 28 percent in 1989 in Jamaica. In Guyana the premium increased from about 50 percent in 1989 to 130 percent in 1990. In Sri Lanka the exchange-rate differential jumped from 2 percent in 1987 to an average of 25 percent in the ensuing three years.

In all three countries the adoption of a floating-exchange-rate system was accompanied by a substantial relaxation of trade and capital account restrictions. The system introduced by Jamaica was a full-fledged floating interbank arrangement, while Guyana and Sri Lanka adopted a more gradual approach to implementing a floating-rate regime. Their approach consisted of either excluding certain types of transactions from the interbank market (Guyana) or restricting the margins of fluctuations of the exchange rate (Sri Lanka). After the reform was implemented, the parallel market premium dropped considerably, to an average of 40 percent in Guyana, 7 percent in Jamaica, and 1 percent in Sri Lanka, during the subsequent year. However, the import/reserves ratio recovered sharply only in Guyana. The overall balance of payments deteriorated in all three cases. There was also a noticeable acceleration of inflation in Guyana and Jamaica, while the inflation rate fell considerably in Sri Lanka. In the former cases, a sharp acceleration of money growth occurred at the same time, from 21 percent in 1990 to more than 50 percent in 1991 in Jamaica, and from 50 percent in 1989 to an average of 80 percent in 1990–91 in Guyana.

The analytical models presented above provide a formal basis for interpreting the empirical evidence on the short-run behavior of inflation and the premium observed during the unification process. The inflationary burst observed in some cases may result not from the elimination of the quasi-fiscal revenue derived from the implicit tax on exports (as emphasized by Pinto,

1991), but rather from the inability of policymakers to control the primary budget deficit (namely, government spending) and the rate of expansion of the money supply (Agénor and Ucer, 1994). This was probably the case in several unification experiments attempted in sub-Saharan African countries. The increase in the premium in the periods prior to reform can be interpreted as being, in part, the result of expectations about the timing of the reform process, as well as about the size and direction of movements in the official and parallel exchange rates upon implementation. As argued earlier, faced with a possibility of a future depreciation of the parallel exchange rate, for instance, asset holders would tend to reallocate their portfolio away from domestic-currency-denominated assets, causing the parallel rate to depreciate immediately and the premium to rise. The fact that the parallel market exchange rate in some cases did not undergo a large "jump" at the moment the reform was implemented is consistent with the intuition that the timing of reform was predicted with a relatively high degree of accuracy by private agents. At the time of implementation, only the official exchange rate adjusts in a discrete fashion, because most of the effects of the change in the exchange-rate regime have already been discounted through the parallel market by forward-looking agents. Finally, the reemergence of a significant premium subsequent to reform occurred in countries where money growth was not kept under control, foreign exchange controls were retained or reintroduced, and inflation rose substantially.

14.3 Macroeconomic Effects of Trade Reforms

Recognition of the adverse effects of import substitution strategies has led an increasing number of developing countries to adopt commercial policies conducive to a more liberal external trade regime.[22] A reduction in trade barriers (such as tariffs and import quotas) fosters an adjustment in relative prices and a reallocation of resources toward the sector producing exportables. In the long term, successful trade liberalization leads to an expansion of exports and a contraction of activity in import-competing industries, as well as an overall transfer of resources from sectors producing nontradables toward those producing tradables.

While trade reforms aim at improving the allocation of resources in the long run, macroeconomic management is concerned with the short-term determination of output, inflation, and the balance of payments. Despite this difference in focus, the conduct of macroeconomic policy interacts in significant ways with the design of trade reforms. The adoption of more liberal commercial policies, such as a reduction in nominal protection, typically entails short-run output and employment costs, which may hinder the attainment of macroeconomic objectives or impose severe constraints on the

TABLE 14.1
Trade Liberalization and Employment (in thousands of persons)

Episode	Year Before Reform	Average over Reform Period	Year after Reform
Argentina (1967–70)	1,836	1,847	1,914
Argentina (1976–80)	1,863	2,099	2,132
Brazil (1965–73)	1,780	2,182	3,397
Chile (1974–81)	515	487	351
Korea (1978–79)	2,000	2,196	2,099
Peru (1979–80)	675	717	736
Philippines (1960–65)	1,456	1,647	1,825
Philippines (1970–74)	2,056	2,313	2,596
Singapore (1968–73)	61	139	210
Sri Lanka (1968–70)	74	108	97
Sri Lanka (1977–79)	112	134	155
Turkey (1970–73)	485	551	651
Turkey (1980–84)	799	829	—

Source: Papageorgiou et al. (1990, p. 37).
Notes: Data refer to employment in the manufacturing sector only.

manipulation of macroeconomic policy instruments. In this section, we examine the macroeconomic effects of trade reforms. We begin by reviewing briefly some recent evidence on trade liberalization. We then analyze, using a simple macroeconomic model, the output and employment effects of commercial policy reforms.[23]

14.3.1 Trade Reforms: Some Recent Evidence

An extensive study of trade liberalization in nineteen countries, during thirty-six distinct episodes of reform undertaken in developing countries between World War II and 1984, was recently completed by the World Bank (Papageorgiou et al., 1990). The study suggests that despite major differences in the historical circumstances under which the reform attempts were implemented, successful liberalization episodes have been characterized by their comprehensive nature, the systematic elimination of quantitative restrictions on imports, political stability, prudent macroeconomic policies (limited fiscal deficits), the maintenance of restrictions on capital movements until trade reforms were sufficiently advanced, and a significant initial depreciation (followed by relative stability afterward) of the real exchange rate. Moreover, there appears to be no strong evidence suggesting that liberalization was associated with sharp reductions in employment and a short-run contraction in output. Table 14.1, for instance, shows that with the exception of Chile, employment in the manufacturing sector did not fall during the year in which the reform was implemented, and in many cases grew relatively strongly in the subsequent year.[24] The balance of payments also improved significantly in most cases, as the growth of exports outpaced the increase in imports.

Since the mid-1980s, far-reaching trade reforms have been implemented in the developing world. Prior to reform, extensive barriers to trade (high tariffs, quantitative restrictions on imports, and extensive controls on foreign exchange transactions) were in place in most of these nations. A particularly interesting set of episodes took place in Latin America and the Caribbean.[25] Partly in relation to different macroeconomic conditions, the extent and timing of reforms differed significantly across these countries. In Peru, for instance, where the trade regime prior to reform was severely distorted, reform was extensive. Import policy reform consisted of dismantling non-tariff barriers such as quantitative restrictions and foreign exchange controls, and eliminating widespread exemptions. Export policy reform involved a reduction or elimination of price and quantitative barriers to exports, and the introduction or improvement of incentives for export promotion and diversification.

Indicators of trade regime before and after the most recent reforms are shown in Table 14.2 for fifteen Latin American and Caribbean countries. Average tariff rates (or rates of nominal protection) were reduced dramatically, particularly in Brazil, Costa Rica, and Colombia.[26] The number of tariff rates in Brazil was reduced from eighteen prior to reform (in 1990) to nine by the end of 1993. In Colombia, the number of tariff rates fell from twenty-two in 1990 to four in 1992. The dispersion of tariffs was also substantially reduced, particularly in Colombia, Costa Rica, and Ecuador. The degree of openness increased significantly, as a result of an expansion of both exports and imports in real terms. This is all the more remarkable since many of the reforms that took place in Latin America were introduced in a difficult macroeconomic context: high inflation, sluggish economic activity, balance-of-payments difficulties, and scarce foreign exchange reserves. In Bolivia, for instance, the inflation rate stood at more than 1,000 percent per annum, and in Brazil at more than 200 percent, in the first year of reform. Nevertheless, almost all the episodes of trade reform referred to in the table were preceded by, or associated with, a significant depreciation of the real exchange rate.[27] Figure 14.4 for Chile, for instance, shows the continuous real depreciation and the strong expansion of export volumes that took place in the aftermath of the recent round of trade liberalization. Thus, the evidence provided by the recent experience of Latin American and Caribbean countries regarding the crucial role played by an initial or concomitant depreciation of the real exchange rate corroborates the

TABLE 14.2
Indicators of Trade Regimes Before and After Reform

Country	Average Tariff[a] (in percent)		Tariff Range (in percent)		Openness[b]	
	Before	After	Before	After	Before	After
Argentina	42	15	15–115	5–22	38.6	54.3
Bolivia	12	8	—	5–10	57.5	83.9
Brazil	51	21	0–105	0–65	21.1	25.3
Chile	35	11	35	11	44.9	56.3
Colombia	61	12	0–220	5–20	28.2	32.7
Costa Rica	53	15	0–1,400	5–20	58.7	78.9
Ecuador	37	18	0–338	2–25	48.7	50.8
Guatemala	50	15	5–90	5–20	31.3	35.6
Honduras	41	15	5–90	5–20	62.8	61.8
Jamaica	—	20	—	0–45	105.5	163.5
Mexico	24	13	0–100	0–20	22.6	34.3
Paraguay	—	16	—	3–86	51.0	63.1
Peru	—	17	0–120	5–25	30.4	41.6
Uruguay	32	18	10–55	12–24	38.0	45.1
Venezuela	37	19	0–135	0–50	49.3	53.3

Source: Alam and Rajapatirana (1993).
[a]Average unweighted legal tariff rates, in percent.
[b]Ratio of imports plus exports over GDP.
Notes: "Before" corresponds to the prereform year and "after" to the postreform year. The prereform year is 1984 for Chile; 1985 for Bolivia, Costa Rica, Guatemala, Honduras, and Mexico; 1987 for Brazil and Uruguay; 1986 for Argentina; 1988 for Paraguay and Peru; and 1989 for Ecuador and Venezuela. The postreform year refers to 1990 for Mexico; 1991 for Argentina, Bolivia, Chile, Jamaica, Paraguay, and Venezuela; and 1992 for all other countries.

comprehensive review provided by Papageorgiou et al. (1990) and the results of a more recent World Bank project summarized by Corden (1993).

14.3.2 Trade Liberalization, Wage Rigidity, and Employment

Although one of the main conclusions of the comprehensive study summarized by Papageorgiou et al. (1990) is that the short-term output and employment costs of trade liberalization reform appear to be less dramatic than commonly thought, there are a variety of potential channels through which such reforms may lead to contractionary effects in the short run. To the extent that such costs may have an adverse effect on the sustainability of the adjustment process, leading possibly to sudden policy reversals or the

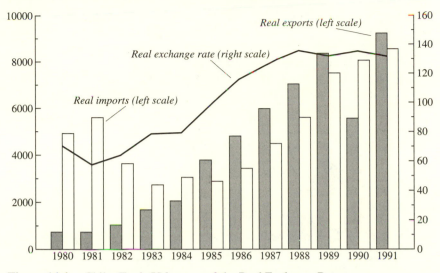

Figure 14.4   Chile: Trade Volumes and the Real Exchange Rate

complete abandonment of the reform effort, it is important to understand the mechanisms through which such effects might operate. In what follows we use a macroeconomic model developed by Buffie (1984*b*) to study the output and employment effects of trade liberalization. The model provides a fairly detailed treatment of the production side of the economy, and is therefore particularly suited to examining the real effects of trade reform. A key implication of the model is that trade reform (which often includes measures aimed at depreciating the real exchange rate) raises the relative price of imported inputs and, if wages are not perfectly flexible, can lead to a contraction in output.

14.3.2.1 THE ANALYTICAL FRAMEWORK

Consider an economy that produces tradable and nontradable goods using three factors of production: capital, labor, and an intermediate input, which is not produced domestically. The capital stock is sector-specific and fixed within the time frame of the analysis. For simplicity, imported inputs are not subject to tariffs and their domestic price P_J is equal to the nominal exchange rate E. The world price of traded goods is fixed on world markets, and the domestic price is given by

$$P_T = (1 + \alpha)E, \tag{18}$$

where $\alpha > 0$ is a coefficient that measures the extent to which import tariffs and export subsidies have raised the domestic price of the tradable good above its world market level.

Assuming that each sector's output is produced by competititve firms operating with a constant-returns-to-scale technology, the sectoral factor demands can be written as

$$L_h = y_h[L_h(t), J_h(t), \bar{K}_h]C_w^h[w_t, \rho_h(t), E], \tag{19a}$$

$$\bar{K}_h = y_h[L_h(t), J_h(t), \bar{K}_h]C_\rho^h[w_t, \rho_h(t), E], \tag{19b}$$

$$J_h = y_h[L_h(t), J_h(t), \bar{K}_h]C_E^h[w_t, \rho_h(t), E], \tag{19c}$$

where $h = N, T$ refers to production sectors, y_h is sector h's output, C^h is sector h's unit cost function, w is the nominal wage, and $\rho_h(t)$ is the rental rate on capital in sector h.[28] Let $P_h(t)$ denote final prices in sector h. The zero-profit condition yields

$$P_h(t) = w_t C_w^h + \rho_h(t)C_\rho^h + EC_E^h. \tag{20}$$

Equations (19) and (20) can be solved for the output and factor demand levels and the rental rate of capital, as a function of the nominal wage, the price of imported inputs (the nominal exchange rate), and the price of final goods.

Households consume both categories of goods and hold only domestic money in their portfolios. Assuming homothetic preferences and a utility function separable in goods and money, relative sectoral demand functions can be defined as homogeneous functions of degree zero in prices:

$$D_h(t)/A_t = d_h[P_N(t), P_T], \quad 0 \le d_h \le 1, \tag{21}$$

where A_t, aggregate nominal expenditure, is defined by

$$A_t = P_N(t)y_N^s(t) + P_T y_T^s(t) - EJ_t - (\bar{M} - M_t^d), \tag{22}$$

where J_t denotes total imports of intermediate goods. Equation (22) indicates that aggregate expenditure is equal to the difference between net factor income and hoarding, which depends on the difference between actual $(\bar{M})$ and desired (M^d) money balances.[29] In turn, desired balances are assumed to depend on net factor income:

$$M^d = P_N(t)y_N^s(t) + P_T y_T^s(t) - EJ_t. \tag{23}$$

Nominal wages are indexed to the price level, which is defined as a geometrically weighted average of prices of traded and nontraded goods:

$$w_t = \bar{w}[P_N^\delta(t)E^{1-\delta}]^\gamma, \quad \bar{w} > 0, \quad 0 < \delta, \gamma < 1, \tag{24}$$

Finally, the market-clearing condition for the nontraded goods market can be written as

$$y_N^s(t) = A_t d_N[P_N(t), P_T], \tag{25}$$

which determines the price of nontraded goods. Logarithmically differentiating Equations (21)–(23) and simplifying yields, in terms of rates of change,

$$\hat{L}_h(t) = \hat{\rho}_h(t)\Theta_K^h(\sigma_{LK}^h - \sigma_{KK}^h) + \epsilon\Theta_J^h(\sigma_{LJ}^h - \sigma_{KJ}^h) + \hat{w}_t\Theta_L^h(\sigma_{LL}^h - \sigma_{LK}^h), \tag{26}$$

where Θ_n^h denotes the share of factor n in sector h's total production costs, and σ_{nm} the partial elasticity of substitution between factors n and m. ϵ denotes the devaluation rate.

Using (20) to substitute out for $\hat{\rho}_h(t)$ in (26) and rearranging yields (for details, see Buffie, 1984b):

$$\hat{L}_h(t) = \mathbf{L}_h[\overset{+}{\pi}_h(t), \overset{\pm}{\epsilon}, \overset{-}{\hat{w}_t}], \tag{27a}$$

$$\hat{J}_h(t) = \mathbf{J}_h[\overset{+}{\pi}_h(t), \overset{-}{\epsilon}, \overset{\pm}{\hat{w}_t}]. \tag{27b}$$

The partial derivatives given above are functions of the elasticities of substitution between factors. The sign of the cross-price terms is a priori indeterminate, due to the usual possible divergence between output and substitution effects. Because the factor demand functions are homogeneous of degree zero, the sum of all partial derivatives in each equation is equal to zero.

From Equation (24), the rate of change of nominal wages is given by

$$\hat{w} = \gamma[\delta\pi_N(t) + (1 - \delta)\pi_T]. \tag{28}$$

Equations (22)–(25), (27), and (28) can be solved simultaneously for $\hat{L}_h(t)$, $\hat{J}_h(t)$, $\hat{w}_t$, and $\pi_N(t)$ as a function of π_T or ϵ. Because in general the solutions are fairly complicated, we will focus on two particular cases.

14.3.2.2 FIXED NOMINAL WAGES

Suppose that nominal wages are fixed ($\gamma = 0$) and that, for simplicity, imported inputs are used only in the tradables sector.[30] Trade liberalization is modeled as a lowering of import tariffs and export subsidies coupled with a nominal devaluation. The package is assumed to be designed in such a way that the reduction in tariffs is less than the rate of devaluation, implying an increase in the domestic price of tradables—and thus of imported inputs.

If nominal wages are fixed, the effect of the trade reform program on employment in the traded goods sector is indeterminate. On the one hand, the net devaluation leads to a fall in the product wage, which stimulates the demand for labor. On the other hand, however, liberalization also leads to an increase in the relative price of imported inputs. Whether the net effect is positive or negative depends on the pattern of substitution across factors and the effect on gross output. If the production function in the traded goods sector is separable between primary factors and imported inputs, the condition that determines whether employment in the traded goods sector rises or falls is given by

$$\pi_T - \epsilon\,\vartheta_{JT} \gtrless 0, \tag{29}$$

where ϑ_{JT} denotes the share of imported inputs in production costs in the tradables sector. However, if the production function is *not* separable and capital and imported inputs are better substitutes than labor and imported inputs, condition (29) is not sufficient to guarantee an increase in labor demand and employment.

The condition for employment to rise following trade liberalization is that the expansionary, expenditure-switching effect dominates the "hoarding effect" induced by the relative price change and the expenditure-reducing effect induced by the negative income effect (itself resulting from the relative price change), as well as the potential fall in employment in the traded goods sector. If the (compensated) cross-price elasticity of demand for nontraded goods is large enough, the net effect of liberalization is an expansion of employment in the nontraded goods sector. If, by contrast, the cross-price elasticity of the demand for nontraded goods is small, the net effect of trade reform on employment is likely to be negative. Thus, the overall effect of liberalization on employment is generally ambiguous in an economy with immobile capital in the short run and nominal wage rigidity.

14.3.2.3 FLEXIBLE WAGES

Assume now that wages are free to adjust to changes in prices, and that only the traded goods sector uses imported intermediate inputs. Then the effects of trade liberalization become even more uncertain than with nominal wage rigidity. The product wage in the traded goods sector may rise, thus further reducing the demand for labor in that sector. In the nontraded goods sector, to the extent that the negative income effect associated with lower employment in the traded goods sector and the possible increase in the product wage compensate for the expenditure-switching effect of liberalization, employment may also fall. In this two-sector framework, therefore, an overall decline in the real consumer wage—that is, a fall in the nominal wage divided by the consumer price index—may be associated with increased unemployment in the economy. The simulation experiments performed by Buffie (1984*b*) for reform packages involving various degrees of tariff cuts and devaluations, and for various degrees of wage indexation and elasticities of substitution between factors, suggest that, in a large number of plausible cases, contractionary effects on employment may be large enough to offset the expansionary effects. Real wage rigidity, in particular, increases considerably the short-run contraction in employment that is associated with trade liberalization, unless there is a very high degree of substitutability between labor and imported inputs.

Although the evidence so far available does not suggest that trade reforms have had a large adverse effect on employment in the short run, the above discussion indicates that the interactions between the process of wage formation and the structure of production activities may well lead to undesirable macroeconomic outcomes. It is important to note that even if trade liberalization entails short-run adjustment costs, it may still be beneficial in the long run, since elasticities of substitution between production inputs are generally higher than in the short run. It is nevertheless important to weigh carefully potential short-run costs and devise the reform process so as to minimize them. We will examine in the next section the implication of this general principle for the sustainability and the optimal pace of reform, taking into account political factors and the need to maintain credibility in the adjustment process.

14.4 Sequencing and Speed of Reforms

While the focus of the foregoing discussion has been largely on the short- and medium-term macroeconomic effects of specific reforms (in the domestic financial system and the exchange and trade regimes), the determination of the appropriate pace of reform and the sequential order of specific policies that policymakers should follow when implementing comprehensive reform programs also raise important practical and conceptual questions. We begin this section by examining issues raised by the sequencing of reforms, focusing on the extent to which the success of reform programs depends on the order of liberalization. We then discuss the determination of the appropriate pace of reform in the presence of adjustment costs, and discuss the role of credibility and sustainability in this context.

14.4.1 Sequencing of Reforms

The existence of adjustment costs and political or administrative constraints usually prevents the most desirable approach to reform: the simultaneous removal of all distortions.[31] Determining the appropriate sequencing of policy reforms is thus an inescapable practical issue for policymakers, and may have a considerable bearing on the success of any adjustment program. The sequencing question normally involves several dimensions: first, the timing of liberalization of the domestic financial market and the capital account of the balance of payments; second, the opening of the trade and capital accounts; and third, the sequencing of macroeconomic adjustment programs and structural reforms.

14.4.1.1 FINANCIAL REFORM AND THE OPENING OF THE CAPITAL ACCOUNT

A large consensus exists among development macroeconomists that the domestic financial system must be liberalized—by freeing up domestic interest rates, increasing reliance on indirect instruments for the purposes of monetary control, and strengthening domestic financial institutions and markets, along the lines discussed in the first part of this chapter—before opening the capital account of the balance of payments. If real domestic interest rates are maintained by government fiat much below world levels, the removal of capital controls will lead to sustained capital outflows and eventually to a balance-of-payments crisis. Uncertainty about the sustainability of reform, which may be particularly acute in the first stages of a liberalization program, may exacerbate the degree of volatility of capital movements and worsen the crisis. This is one of the main lessons drawn from the experience of the Southern Cone countries during the turbulent period covering the end of the 1970s and the beginning of the 1980s (Hanson, 1992).[32]

More generally, opening the capital account without macroeconomic stability may lead to large capital outflows, increasing the opportunity for currency substitution. The reduction in the inflation tax base resulting from the substitution of foreign assets for domestic-currency holdings may lead to an inflation burst if fiscal rigidities prevent adjustment of the primary deficit.[33] If instead governments choose to initially increase external borrowing, private agents will understand that the adverse effect of higher external debt on the solvency of the public sector will eventually force a fiscal adjustment, an inflation burst, or a "debt crisis" along the lines discussed in Chapters 4 and

13. A high likelihood that domestic-currency assets may be taxed explicitly or implicitly will accelerate capital flight.[34]

14.4.1.2 CAPITAL AND CURRENT ACCOUNT LIBERALIZATION

The debate on the appropriate sequencing of trade and capital account liberalization was stimulated to a large extent by the experience of Asian countries (most notably Korea and Indonesia) in the 1960s, and the reform programs implemented by the Southern Cone countries of Latin America in the late 1970s.[35] Among the latter group of nations, Argentina and Uruguay opened their capital account before removing impediments to trade transactions. Chile, by contrast, reduced barriers to international trade before lifting capital controls. In the 1960s Korea also opened its trade account before relaxing controls on capital movements, while Indonesia reduced trade barriers and simultaneously eliminated most controls on capital movements.

Opening the capital account prior to liberalizing the external trade regime is not, in general, a desirable reform strategy. If (as argued earlier) the domestic financial system is liberalized prior to the removal of capital controls, massive capital inflows are likely to occur, leading to a buildup of reserves and, if not sterilized, fostering monetary expansion, domestic inflation, and a sustained appreciation of the real exchange rate.[36] However, as argued above, a successful liberalization of the trade account generally requires a real *depreciation* of the domestic currency to offset the adverse effect of cuts in tariff protection on the balance of payments, and thus stimulate exports and dampen imports.[37] The real appreciation that tends to be associated with the removal of capital controls is likely, on the contrary, to reduce profitability in export industries and have an adverse effect on the reallocation of resources, thereby lengthening—or even derailing—the adjustment process. Even if trade and capital account reforms are implemented simultaneously, the slow response of the real sector to changes in relative prices in the short run and the relatively faster response of capital flows means that the net outcome is likely to be an appreciation of the real exchange rate.[38] Opening the current account first is thus desirable, followed by gradual opening of the capital account. Edwards (1984) and McKinnon (1973, 1993) have been the major advocates of the view that tariffs should be reduced prior to lifting capital controls.[39]

Another line of argument supporting the Edwards-McKinnon view rests on the potential output effects of the sequencing of trade and capital account liberalization. As argued by Rodrik (1987), for instance, trade liberalization may have a contractionary effect in the short run if it is preceded or accompanied by capital account liberalization. The mechanism emphasized by

Rodrik is the effect of trade reform on the real interest rate. In the absence of restrictions on capital movements, trade liberalization amounts to a rise in the consumption rate of interest if the future price of traded goods is expected to fall relative to its current level. Intertemporal substitution leads private agents to react by switching spending from the present to the future. With unused production capacity and demand-determined output, the result is a contraction in activity and an increase in unemployment. In a medium-term context, Krueger (1985) has argued that liberalizing capital movements in a country where the capital/labor ratio is low reduces the rate of return to capital, the rate of accumulation, and therefore long-term growth. Opening the current account first may stimulate output sufficiently to compensate for this negative effect.

An important issue that has arisen in the debate on the sequencing of trade and capital account reforms—an issue of relevance for all the literature dealing with the sequencing of policy reforms—relates to the role of intertemporal considerations, and the effect of various types of distortions prior to reform. Several authors—see Edwards (1989a), Khan and Zahler (1985), and Edwards and van Wijnbergen (1986)—have attempted to take into account these features. Not surprisingly, the case for the "current account first, capital account next" sequence is not as clear-cut as described above, and depends on the type and degree of initial distortions. Nevertheless, it has been shown that opening the capital account first may not be optimal in many circumstances. Edwards and van Wijnbergen (1986), for instance, have shown that relaxing capital controls in the presence of tariffs amplifies existing distortions, while the reverse sequence is generally neutral or may even be positive.

Intertemporal effects can also result from the lack of credibility in one or several components of the sequencing strategy leading to capital and current account liberalization. This aspect has been emphasized most forcefully by Calvo (1987a, 1989). His analysis suggests that if a given reform is not credible to private agents, adopting other liberalization measures may actually reduce welfare. For instance, liberalizing the capital account at a time when the public believes that a reduction in tariffs will be reversed in the future will lead private agents to use capital inflows to finance large imports of goods, particularly durable goods. Lack of credibility thus plays the role of an intertemporal distortion. The capital account should not be liberalized before agents have achieved a sufficient degree of confidence in the sustainability of the trade liberalization program. Thus, credibility affects not only the speed of reform (as discussed below) but also the optimal sequencing strategy.

A significant omission in the sequencing debate is the fact that, as documented in Chapter 5, capital mobility in developing countries may be higher than what is suggested by the intensity of legal restrictions, because agents use alternative, unofficial channels to transfer funds to and from the rest of the world. The de facto opening of the capital account means that removing legal restrictions on capital controls may not have much effect on the portfolio structure of private agents—assuming that the perceived risk involved in transacting through unofficial channels is not too high—and that the surge in capital inflows through official channels may simply be reflecting a diversion of flows that were formerly transiting through illegal (but tolerated) channels. Similarly, to the extent that a large portion of external trade is carried through unofficial illegal channels, the removal of tariffs is likely to affect mostly the distribution of transactions between official and unofficial markets. In such conditions, the question of the appropriate order of sequencing becomes essentially that of determining the real efficiency gains that the economy would achieve under alternative strategies by legalizing previously illegal activities.

14.4.1.3 MACROECONOMIC STABILIZATION AND STRUCTURAL ADJUSTMENT

The empirical evidence discussed earlier suggests that successful trade reforms must, in general, be preceded or accompanied by a depreciation of the real exchange rate. Real devaluations ensure the sustainability of the liberalization process by dampening the excess demand for importables that the removal of tariffs induces. While the real exchange rate is not itself a policy variable, it can be influenced by nominal devaluations and restrictive demand policies. Thus, exchange-rate adjustment constitutes a key element of a trade liberalization program. This is precisely the mechanism we used to formalize trade reform in our previous discussion focusing on the short-run output and employment effects of commercial policies.

Stabilization is generally viewed as a precondition for the implementation of a full-fledged trade liberalization program. Three arguments are conventionally advanced to defend this proposition (see Mussa, 1987; Rodrik, 1995). First, macroeconomic instability—which typically translates into high and variable inflation rates—distorts the signals transmitted by changes in relative prices brought by trade reforms. Second, to the extent that trade liberalization takes the form of substantial tariff reductions and may have an adverse effect on tax revenue, large initial macroeconomic imbalances may severely constrain the scope of measures that can be taken and the pace of tariff reductions. Third, the real devaluation that accompanies liberalization is often brought about by large nominal devaluations, which may exacerbate inflation if monetary and fiscal policies are not tight enough. Moreover, devaluations affect the role of the exchange rate as a nominal anchor and may damage the credibility of the stabilization effort. The latter consideration is largely a reflection of the trade-off discussed in Chapter 6 between inflation stabilization and the expansion of output.

While the adverse effect of macroeconomic instability can hardly be denied, the argument that the decline in revenue from tariffs and export taxes induced by trade liberalization may complicate short-run macroeconomic management because of its impact on the fiscal deficit is not as clear-cut as is often thought. On the one hand, it is correct that in many developing countries taxes on trade are an important source of government revenue (see Table 1.7). The reduction in revenue in these cases may indeed lead to increased money financing and higher inflation. On the other hand, however, trade liberalization may also lead to an increase in output and domestic revenue, even in the short run. First, the removal of quantitative restrictions on imports and the output effect may be such that the increase in the tax base (the volume of imports) more than compensates for the reduction in tariff rates, bringing an overall increase in revenue. Second, reducing tariff rates when they are already very high reduces incentives for smuggling, underinvoicing, and engaging in rent-seeking activities (such as lobbying for import exemptions), to such an extent that tax revenue may rise, as the Laffer curve would predict. In fact, Greenaway and Milner (1991) find no significant relationship between trade reform and the amount of revenue collected from taxes on external trade in developing countries.

Nevertheless, in some countries the fiscal objective may be relatively important in the early stages of the liberalization process, and may affect the pace and extent of tariff reform. In cases where concern over the fiscal impact of trade reform is important, tariff reductions should proceed in steps, through implementation of gradual reductions in the overall level and structure of tariffs, following the pace of progress in expanding the domestic revenue base. As alternative domestic revenue sources develop over time, the relative importance of the fiscal objective will diminish, allowing an acceleration in the pace of trade reform and the removal of tariffs (Falvey and Kim, 1992). Thus, the pace of trade reform in the early stages may be constrained by the scope for fiscal adjustment.

An important element in the timing of trade and macroeconomic reforms is the role of credibility factors. As discussed at length in Chapter 10, the credibility of a disinflation program may be damaged if appropriate structural measures are not implemented prior to the adoption of a restrictive monetary and fiscal stance. Likewise, implementing tariff reforms without much confidence in macroeconomic management will create doubts about the overall sustainability of the reform process.[40] The fact that trade reforms require, as pointed out earlier, a real-exchange-rate depreciation is often regarded as a source of conflict from a credibility point of view. When the real depreciation is brought about by a nominal devaluation, the increase in the price of tradables will usually translate into a temporary rise in inflation, which may confuse agents about the policymakers' commitment to macroeconomic stability. However, the trade-off involved in the use of nominal devaluations may not be as acute as it appears. In particular, Rodrik (1995) has argued that in countries where the source of nominal wage rigidity is a lack of confidence in the macroeconomic policy stance, a credible commitment to a fixed exchange rate is likely to attenuate, rather than exacerbate, the potential conflict between trade liberalization (which requires a real devaluation) and exchange-rate stability—which is necessary for the exchange rate to play its role as a nominal anchor for domestic price setters.

In practice, however, two issues arise. First, the lack of fiscal reform does not seem to explain liberalization failures in some developing countries, particularly those of the Southern Cone. Fernández (1985), for instance, has argued that the liberalization program implemented in Chile in the early 1980s did not avert a financial crisis, even though the central government budget moved into surplus at the beginning of the program. Second, in practice, trade reforms have been implemented in conjunction with macroeconomic stabilization programs rather than after stabilization has been achieved. Bolivia and Mexico (as documented by Ten Kate, 1992) are two recent examples. Thus the question of determining the appropriate timing between structural reforms and macroeconomic adjustment may be to some extent moot. Ensuring the success of trade reforms requires maintaining a supportive macroeconomic environment (tight monetary and fiscal policies), not only at the inception of the program but also in a continuous fashion, to ensure that the associated real depreciation is not eroded by upward pressure on domestic prices. As emphasized in Chapter 10, consistency between macroeconomic policy measures and trade (or, more generally, structural) reforms is essential to foster credibility and ensure success of the *overall* reform program.

14.4.2 Adjustment Costs, Credibility, and the Speed of Reform

The long-standing debate about gradual versus overnight policy reform was reviewed in Chapter 10, in the context of our discussion on the credibility of stabilization programs. Issues similar to those discussed there also arise in the context of structural reforms. Trade liberalization, for instance, has strong effects on income distribution, because it affects industries differentially. Social conflicts can be exacerbated if there are more "losers" than "winners," depending on the power structure and the relative strength of sectoral lobbies. Reform may have a large output cost in the short run because, for instance, the reallocation of resources across sectors takes time and is limited by the degree of intersectoral labor mobility—which is itself related to the need for workers to acquire different skills.

A particularly large increase in unemployment in the short run may affect endogenously the credibility of reform and weaken political support, forcing the authorities to abandon the liberalization process. Thus, if the political pressure imposed by "losers" as a result of a sudden removal of protection is believed to be strong enough to stop or reverse the reform effort, a government may want to liberalize gradually. More generally, a gradual liberalization program may be the optimal response in a context where policymakers aim at minimizing adjustment costs—or, equivalently, maximizing the probability of sustaining the reform effort.[41] At the same time, however, doubts will be created about the commitment to reform if the adjustment process is too slow. This outcome may encourage political forces opposing liberalization. Providing sustained external assistance, by allowing policymakers to maintain the momentum of the reform effort, may be of crucial importance in such circumstances.

Over the past few years a large number of developing countries have adopted policies aimed at liberalizing their domestic financial systems, as well as regulations concerning external transactions in goods, foreign exchange, and capital movements. This chapter has provided an overview of the main policy issues involved in implementing such reforms, with an emphasis on their short- and medium-term macroeconomic aspects.

It was argued that financial reform can take the limited form of raising controlled interest rates closer to market-clearing levels (which we referred to as monetary reform) or the more comprehensive form of the removal of the panoply of restrictions imposed on the financial system. The weight of the evidence does not support the view that the former enhances economic growth by increasing the *volume* of domestic saving and investment; whether it may do so by improving the *efficiency* of capital formation is an unresolved issue that will be taken up again in the next chapter. More thorough financial reform must be undertaken with care. In the presence of an explicit or implicit deposit guarantee, complete financial liberalization with inadequate bank supervision may encourage excessive risk taking on the part of domestic financial institutions and lead to financial crises, particularly if the macroeconomic environment is unstable.

Our analysis of the unification of foreign exchange markets indicated that the behavior of official and parallel exchange rates, inflation, and budget deficits in the periods leading to and the periods following the unification process depends in important ways on the formation of expectations and the perceived policy stance in the short run, as well as the structure of budget deficits in the medium run. The parallel market premium represents an implicit tax on exports repatriated through official channels, since governments in developing countries are typically net buyers of foreign exchange from the private sector. For a given fiscal deficit, and assuming that the inflation elasticity of money demand is less than unity, there exists a trade-off between the premium and inflation, which represents a tax on domestic-currency balances. The unification process, which entails the loss of the implicit tax on exports, may therefore result in a substantial (and permanent) rise in the rate of inflation and the rate of depreciation of the exchange rate, if the authorities attempt to compensate for a fall in revenue by an increase in monetary financing. However, governments also provide an implicit subsidy to importers by taxing imports at the official, rather than the parallel, exchange rate. The net effect on inflation is thus in general ambiguous. More generally, exchange market liberalization eliminates not only the incentives to divert foreign exchange from the official to the parallel market, but also distortions associated with rent-seeking activities—such as the bribing of government officials to secure access to foreign exchange, or customs officers to evade tariffs—thus raising the efficiency of economic transactions.

Trade reforms (essentially, the reduction of import tariffs and the elimination of import quotas) have been relatively successful in many developing countries. Although the evidence reviewed here does not seem to indicate that the short-run output and employment costs have been large, we argued that a contractionary effect may occur in certain circumstances and should not be dismissed as a mere curiosity. The degree of real wage rigidity and the pattern of substitution across inputs in the production process were shown to provide two essential elements for understanding how real costs can arise in the short term. In particular, a high degree of real wage rigidity raises the short-run employment cost of trade liberalization. In addition, the lack of labor mobility in the short run may exacerbate the increase in unemployment that may result from the removal of nominal protection to import-competing industries. Thus, ensuring flexibility of the labor market may be a precondition for a successful liberalization program (Edwards, 1989a).

The consensus view on the sequencing of external accounts is that current account liberalization should precede the removal of capital controls. Capital inflows that may be associated with the relaxation of restrictions on capital transactions may lead to an appreciation of the real exchange rate, which in turn may have an adverse effect—likely to be exacerbated in the presence of imported inputs in the production process—on profitability in export industries. Although in general the optimal ordering of liberalization policies depends also on the type and size of distortions prior to reform, in practice the "current account first, capital account next" sequence has remained a fairly robust proposition.

The argument that the scope for trade liberalization through tariff reductions may be limited by their adverse effects on fiscal deficits does not seem to be well supported by the available evidence. More importantly, while many economists have recognized that the success of structural reforms requires macroeconomic stabilization, the extent to which stabilization itself depends on the credibility of structural adjustment has not always been well appreciated. When these interactions are taken into account, the whole debate regarding the determination of the appropriate sequencing between

structural reforms and macroeconomic adjustment may well have been mis-
guided. Finally, we argued that the pace of reform depends on adjustment
costs (related to structural features such as the degree of intersectoral labor
mobility) and the existence of a political consensus, which affect endogenously the degree of credibility of the adjustment program. A well-designed
liberalization program must account for, in addition to direct economic
costs, the indirect effects arising from the potential loss of credibility and
the collapse in the consensus for reform.

Part V

ENDOGENOUS GROWTH, POLITICAL ECONOMY,
AND LABOR MARKETS

Fifteen

Human Capital, Financial Intermediation, and Growth

THE wide dispersion of output growth rates across countries is a well-documented economic fact. Countries that at one time had similar levels of per-capita income have subsequently followed very divergent patterns, with some seemingly caught in an "underdevelopment trap," or long-term stagnation, and others able to sustain high growth rates. The contrast between the postwar experiences of the developing countries of Asia and Africa is particularly striking in this regard. In 1960 average real per-capita incomes in Asian and African countries were roughly similar. Thirty years later, income per capita had more than tripled in Asia while it had risen only moderately in Africa.[1] During the past two decades alone, real output grew more than 6 percent per annum in Asia, compared with an average of 2.8 percent in Africa and 3.7 percent for Latin America (Table 15.1). Per-capita income declined in all developing regions during the 1980s except in Asia, where it grew by nearly 5 percent a year. Within regions, significant disparities also exist. In 1950 real per-capita income in Costa Rica was half that of Argentina. By 1990 per-capita income in Costa Rica had more than tripled, while Argentina's only doubled. Botswana maintained an average growth rate of 5 percent a year during the 1970s and 1980s, while for Africa as a whole the average growth rate was 2.8 percent.

Traditional neoclassical approaches, which attribute growth to exogenous technological progress, are incapable of explaining the wide disparities in the pace of economic growth across countries. In the past few years considerable efforts have been devoted to understanding the sources of growth and explaining the divergent patterns observed across countries. This research has highlighted the existence of a variety of "endogenous" mechanisms that foster economic growth, and has suggested new roles for public policy.[2] This literature has expanded at a rapid pace, and it is impossible within the context of this book to provide a comprehensive overview of the different approaches that have been developed.[3] We review in this chapter some of the salient features of the "new growth" literature, with particular attention to developments emphasizing the role of human capital and financial intermediation in the growth process. The first part of the chapter provides a brief review of the neoclassical growth model and examines the available evidence, based on the methodology derived from the neoclassical approach, on the sources of growth in developing countries. The second part provides an analytical overview of the recent literature whose main focus has been the role of human capital and financial factors in the

TABLE 15.1

Developing Countries: Growth Performance (annual percentage changes)

	1971–92	1971–81	1982–92
All Developing Countries			
Real GDP	4.8	5.6	4.0
Real per-capita GDP	2.4	3.1	1.7
By Region			
Africa			
Real GDP	2.8	3.7	1.9
Real per-capita GDP	—	0.9	−0.9
Asia			
Real GDP	6.3	5.9	6.7
Real per-capita GDP	4.4	4.0	4.8
Middle East and Europe			
Real GDP	4.4	6.0	2.9
Real per-capita GDP	1.0	2.6	−0.6
Western Hemisphere			
Real GDP	3.7	5.9	1.6
Real per-capita GDP	1.3	3.2	−0.5
By Composition of Exports			
Fuel exporters			
Real GDP	4.2	6.1	2.3
Real per-capita GDP	1.1	2.8	−0.6
Nonfuel exporters			
Real GDP	5.1	5.5	4.7
Real per-capita GDP	2.9	3.3	2.6
By Financial Criteria			
Net creditors			
Real GDP	5.1	6.7	3.5
Real per-capita GDP	1.1	2.8	−0.5
Net debtors			
Real GDP	4.8	5.5	4.1
Real per-capita GDP	2.5	3.2	1.9

Source: International Monetary Fund, *World Economic Outlook* (May 1993, p. 44).

Notes: Data refer to ninety countries accounting for 95 percent of developing-country output. Aggregates are weighted averages, with weights based on PPP valuation of country GDPs.

growth process. The third part reviews the recent econometric evidence on the determinants of growth and highlights some of the methodological issues confronting many of the available studies. The concluding part of the chapter provides an interim assessment of the recent literature and suggests some areas of investigation that may prove fruitful for understanding growth mechanisms in developing countries.

15.1 The Neoclassical Growth Model

The neoclassical growth model was developed by Solow (1956) and Swan (1956). It is built upon an aggregate, constant-returns-to-scale production function that combines labor and capital (with diminishing marginal returns) in the production of a composite good. Savings are assumed to be a fixed fraction of output, and technology improves at an exogenous rate. Assuming that the production function is Cobb-Douglas, output per capita y_t is given by

$$y_t = A_t k_t^{1-\sigma}, \quad 0 < \sigma < 1, \tag{1}$$

where k_t denotes the capital/labor ratio and A_t measures the level of technology. Capital accumulation is given by

$$\dot{k}_t = s y_t - \delta k_t, \quad 0 < s, \quad \delta < 1, \tag{2}$$

where s denotes the propensity to save and δ the rate of depreciation of physical capital. Equation (2) incorporates the equilibrium condition of the goods market or, equivalently, the equality between investment I_t and saving, $I_t = s y_t$.

Solow showed that if population and technology grow at a constant rate, the steady-state values of output per effective worker and the capital/effective labor ratio are also constant and proportional to the rate of (labor-augmenting) technological change. Although the saving rate has no effect in the long run on the growth rate per capita, it affects (positively) the *level* of per-capita income in the steady state.[4] In addition, the model implies that countries with similar production technologies as well as comparable saving and population growth rates should converge to similar steady-state levels of per-capita income. This convergence property means that poor countries starting with a relatively low standard of living and a lower capital/labor ratio will grow faster during the transition as they catch up with the rich countries, but ultimately both groups will arrive at the same level of per-capita income.[5]

The neoclassical growth model led to the "sources-of-growth" approach, a popular empirical methodology aimed at analyzing the determinants of changes in output. The approach uses an aggregate production function to decompose growth into "contributions" from different sources, namely, the growth rates of factor inputs weighted by their competitive factor shares (the "contribution" of factors), plus a residual. This residual is often labeled "technical progress," but it is more adequately described as the difference between the growth of output and a weighted sum of the growth of inputs, that is, the growth in total factor productivity.

Formally, assume that the production function takes the form $y_t = A_t F(K_t, L_t)$.[6] In terms of percentage changes, we have

$$\mathbf{g} \equiv \frac{\dot{y}_t}{y_t} = \frac{\dot{A}_t}{A_t} + A_t F_K \frac{\dot{K}_t}{y_t} + A_t F_L \frac{\dot{L}_t}{y_t} = \mathbf{g}_A + \alpha_K \mathbf{g}_K + \alpha_L \mathbf{g}_L, \qquad (3)$$

where $\alpha_J = F_h h_t / y_t$ (for $h = K, L$) denotes the elasticity of output with respect to input h. $\mathbf{g}_A$ is the rate of growth of total factor productivity and is derived as a residual. Under conditions of competitive equilibrium, factors are paid their marginal products. The coefficient $\alpha_L(\alpha_K)$ is thus equal to the share of labor (capital) income in total output. In the presence of constant returns to scale, the sum of all share coefficients must be equal to unity. With a Cobb-Douglas production technology as described in Equation (1), assuming that factors of production are paid their marginal products implies that $\alpha_K = 1 - \alpha_L$, and that labor's share corresponds to the parameter σ.

A large number of studies based on the sources-of-growth methodology have been conducted in industrial and developing nations over the years. Chenery (1986) reviewed many of the studies conducted in the 1960s and 1970s; a subset of his results is presented in Table 15.2. The table presents the decomposition of growth, including estimates of factor shares, for a group of developing countries. The data show that estimates of the capital share vary considerably across countries, ranging from 26 percent for Honduras to more than 60 percent for Singapore. The average (unweighted) estimate derived from the studies compiled by Chenery indicates, however, that the capital share is about 40 percent, compared with about 30 percent for industrial countries, which indicates that the production function exhibits significantly diminishing marginal returns to capital. The data presented in the table also suggest that the effect of capital accumulation on growth varies substantially across countries, apparently playing a limited role in Ecuador and a much more significant one in Turkey, for instance. On average, nevertheless, growth in the capital stock appears to have a limited effect on output growth during the periods covered. Most countries, by contrast, have a high growth rate of labor input. The contribution of total factor productivity to growth also varies substantially across countries, being small in countries such as Venezuela and significant in Ecuador, Korea, Taiwan, and the Philippines, where it accounts roughly for half of total growth. The

TABLE 15.2
Productivity and Growth in Developing Countries (average annual percentage change)

| Country | Period | Growth Rate | | | Factor Share[a] | | Residual[b] |
		Output	Capital	Labor	Capital	Labor	
Argentina	1960–74	4.1	3.8	2.2	—	—	17.1
Brazil	1960–74	6.8	3.1	2.8	—	—	21.9
Chile	1960–74	4.4	4.2	1.9	—	—	27.3
Colombia	1960–74	5.6	3.9	2.8	—	—	37.5
Ecuador	1950–62	4.7	2.8	3.4	38.0	62.0	46.2
Honduras	1950–62	4.5	3.7	2.9	26.0	74.0	31.0
Korea	1960–73	9.7	6.6	5.0	36.7	63.3	42.3
Mexico	1960–74	5.6	3.9	2.8	—	—	37.5
Philippines	1947–65	5.8	—	—	—	—	43.5
Singapore	1972–80	8.0	9.5	5.5	61.1	38.9	−0.1
Taiwan	1955–60	5.2	2.7	1.8	40.0	60.0	59.5
Turkey	1963–75	6.4	6.8	1.0	55.0	45.0	34.8
Venezuela	1960–74	5.1	4.5	3.3	—	—	11.8

Source: Adapted from Chenery (1986, pp. 20–21).

[a]In percent.

[b]In proportion of output growth.

average contribution of the residual, however, appears to be substantially less than in developed countries.

A more recent study using the sources-of-growth methodology is that of Elías (1992), who examines the growth process in seven Latin American countries (Argentina, Brazil, Chile, Colombia, Mexico, Peru, and Venezuela) over the period 1940–85. His study considers different kinds of labor and capital inputs, and he defines a gross and quality component for each of them. In the case of labor, the gross component is the arithmetic sum of employment across characteristics (such as education, sex, and age), whereas for capital it is the arithmetic sum of different categories of capital. The quality component of each input is established by considering their diverse characteristics.[7] The quality component thus captures changes in the composition of factors of production over time.

The results obtained by Elías for the period 1940–80 are summarized in Table 15.3. Output growth averaged 5.3 percent in annual terms for the group as a whole. The quality of labor rose on average by 1.4 percent, and the quantity of labor by 2 percent. Although the quality of capital apparently fell by 0.4 percent, its quantity grew at more than 4 percent annually. Given the average labor share of 40 percent, labor contributed 1.3 percent to the average growth rate. Capital's overall contribution amounted to 2.5 percent. Technological progress therefore accounted for 1.5 percent of the

TABLE 15.3
Productivity and Growth in Latin America, 1940–80 (average annual percentage change)

	Output Growth Rate	Capital		Labor		Total Factor Productivity
		Quantity	Total Contribution	Quantity	Total Contribution	
Latin America[a]	5.3	5.1	2.5	2.6	1.3	1.5
Argentina	3.6	3.1	1.6	1.9	1.0	1.1
Brazil	6.4	6.5	3.3	2.6	1.3	1.9
Chile	3.8	2.6	1.3	2.0	1.0	1.5
Colombia	4.8	4.1	2.1	3.1	1.6	1.2
Mexico	6.3	5.1	2.6	2.9	1.5	2.3
Peru	4.2	5.7	2.9	2.7	1.4	0.0
Venezuela	5.2	5.9	3.0	3.5	1.8	0.5
Japan	5.2	7.9	2.4	1.3	0.9	1.9
United States	3.6	3.2	0.8	1.7	1.3	1.6

Source: Adapted from Elías (1992, p. 160).
[a] Average for all seven countries listed below.

TABLE 15.4

Developing Countries: Decomposition of Trend Output Growth
(average annual percentage change)

	1971–92	1971–81	1982–91
All Developing Countries			
Trend GDP	5.2	6.0	4.2
Capital contribution	2.5	3.1	2.0
Labor contribution	1.3	1.6	1.3
Total factor productivity	1.3	1.3	1.0
By Region			
Africa			
Trend GDP	3.4	4.5	2.3
Capital contribution	1.9	2.9	1.0
Labor contribution	1.3	1.4	1.5
Total factor productivity	0.2	0.2	−0.2
Asia			
Trend GDP	6.5	6.2	6.8
Capital contribution	2.8	2.9	2.9
Labor contribution	1.1	1.4	1.1
Total factor productivity	2.6	1.9	2.9
Middle East and Europe			
Trend GDP	5.0	6.5	3.3
Capital contribution	3.3	4.6	2.1
Labor contribution	1.6	1.9	1.6
Total factor productivity	—	—	−0.4
Western Hemisphere			
Trend GDP	4.0	6.2	1.6
Capital contribution	1.9	3.0	1.0
Labor contribution	1.5	2.0	1.3
Total factor productivity	0.5	1.3	−0.7

Source: International Monetary Fund, *World Economic Outlook* (May 1993, p. 48).

Notes: Trend output is defined as a three-year moving average of real GDP. For coverage, see the notes to Table 15.1.

rate of growth. Thus, for the group as a whole, capital made the highest contribution to output growth (47 percent), while the contribution of labor was roughly similar to that of total factor productivity. Capital made a greater contribution to growth both because of its quantity and because of its share. By contrast, the quality of labor played a more important role in the growth of the labor input.

Evidence for a broader group of developing countries is presented in Table 15.4, which shows the decomposition of trend or potential output growth

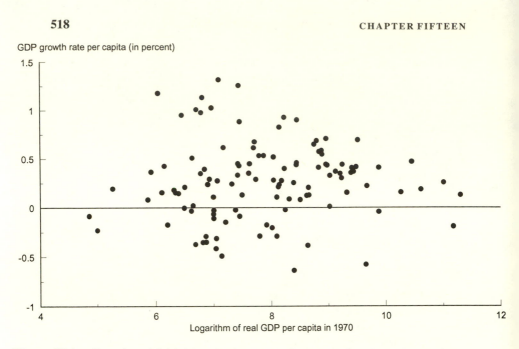

Figure 15.1   Growth and Initial Per-Capita Income in Developing Countries (period averages over 1970–90)

Source: Khan and Kumar (1993).

for developing countries during the 1970s and 1980s. The data suggest that, overall, the contribution of capital to potential output growth was the most important and that total factor productivity accounted for about the same share as labor in its contribution to growth. These results are similar to those obtained by Elías (1992). There are, however, sharp differences across regions. Total factor productivity accounts for only a negligible share of growth in Africa and the Middle East, but provides a substantial contribution to growth (more than twice as much as labor and almost on a par with capital's contribution) in Asia.

15.2 Endogenous Growth Theories: A Brief Overview

In the neoclassical growth model reviewed above, capital exhibits diminishing marginal returns in the production process. This feature of the model prevents it from providing an explanation for the wide variations across countries in either per capita income or growth rates, and for the fact that poor countries do not seem to grow faster than rich ones (Figure 15.1).[8] In addition, output growth is independent of the saving rate and is determined only by demographic factors (the rate of population growth) and the rate of technological progress. But since population growth and technological change are assumed exogenous, the model does not explain the mechanisms that generate steady-state growth, and therefore does not allow an evaluation of the mechanisms through which government policies can potentially influence the growth process. The new growth literature addresses these limitations of the neoclassical model by proposing a variety of channels through which steady-state growth arises endogenously. We begin by discussing the role of externalities and the assumption of constant returns to scale in the new theories, and we then focus on the role of human capital accumulation and the interactions between economic growth and financial development.

15.2.1 Externalities and Increasing Returns

Two broad approaches have been followed in the new growth literature to relax the assumption of diminishing returns to capital imposed in the basic neoclassical growth model. The first consists of viewing all production inputs as some form of reproducible capital, including not only physical capital (as emphasized in the basic neoclassical framework), but other types as well, especially human capital (Lucas, 1988) or the "state of knowledge" (Romer, 1986). A simple growth model along these lines is the so-called AK model proposed by Rebelo (1991), which results from setting $\sigma = 0$ in Equation (1):

$$y_t = Ak_t, \tag{4}$$

where k_t is now interpreted as a broad measure of capital—a composite measure of the physical and human capital stock. The production function is thus linear and exhibits constant returns to scale, but does not yield diminishing returns to capital. Using the capital accumulation equation (2), steady-state growth per capita can be shown to be equal to

$$\mathbf{g} = sA - \delta, \tag{5}$$

which implies that the growth rate is positive (for $sA > \delta$) and that the level of income per capita rises without bound. An important implication of the AK model is thus that, in contrast to the neoclassical model, an increase in the saving rate permanently raises the growth rate per capita. In addition—and again in contrast with the neoclassical growth model, which predicts that poor countries should grow faster than rich countries—the AK model implies that poor nations whose production process is characterized by the same degree of technological sophistication as other nations always grow at the same rate as rich countries, regardless of the initial level of income.

The *AK* model thus does *not* predict convergence even if countries share the same technology and are characterized by the same pattern of saving, a result that seems to accord well with the empirical evidence.

The *AK* model has proved very popular in the endogenous growth literature and has been extended in various directions. Rebelo (1991), for instance, has examined the implications of considering separately the production of consumption goods, physical capital, and human capital goods. His analysis demonstrates, in particular, that endogenous steady-state growth obtains if a "core" of capital goods is produced according to a constant-returns-to-scale technology and without the use of nonreproducible factors. Put differently, to obtain positive growth requires only that there exist a subset of capital goods whose production takes place under constant returns to scale and does not require the use of nonreproducible inputs.

The second approach to generating growth endogenously consists of introducing spillover effects or externalities in the growth process. The presence of externalities implies that if, say, one firm doubles its inputs, the productivity of the inputs of other firms will also increase. Introducing spillover effects leads to a relaxation of the assumption of diminishing returns to capital.[9] In most models externalities take the form of general technological knowledge that is available to all firms, which use it to develop new methods of production. An exception to this specification is Lucas (1988), where externalities take the form of public learning, which increases the stock of human capital and affects the productivity of all factors of production.[10] Another exception is Barro (1990), who introduces externalities associated with public investment.

The presence of externalities is closely associated with the existence of increasing returns to scale in the production function. However, an important implication of the above description is that in models exhibiting spillover effects and externalities, sustained growth does not result from the existence of external effects, but rather from the assumption of constant returns to scale in all production inputs that can be accumulated. As emphasized by Rebelo (1991), increasing returns are thus neither necessary nor sufficient to generate endogenous growth.

15.2.2 Human Capital and Knowledge

One particular source of externalities that has been emphasized in the recent growth literature is the accumulation of human capital and its effect on the productivity of the economy. Lucas (1988) provides one of the best-known attempts to incorporate the spillover effects of human capital accumulation, in a model built upon the idea that individual workers are more productive, regardless of their skill level, if other workers have more human capital.

A simplified presentation of Lucas's model is as follows.[11] Human capital is accumulated through explicit "production": a part of individuals' working time is devoted to accumulation of skills. Formally, let k_t denote physical capital per worker and h_t human capital per worker or, more generally, "knowledge" capital. The production process is described by

$$y_t = A k_t^{\sigma} [u h_t]^{1-\sigma}, \quad 0 < u < 1, \tag{6}$$

where u denotes the fraction of time that individuals devote to producing goods. As before, the growth of physical capital depends on the saving rate ($I_t = s y_t$), while the growth rate of human capital is determined by the amount of time devoted to its production:

$$\dot{h}_t / h_t = \alpha(1 - u), \quad \alpha > 0. \tag{7}$$

In this economy the long-run growth rate of both capital and output per worker is $\alpha(1 - u)$, the rate of human capital growth, and the ratio of physical to human capital converges to a constant. In the long run, the level of income is proportional to the economy's initial stock of human capital. In this particular formulation, the saving rate has no effect on the growth rate.

The important implication of the external effect captured in the model presented by Lucas (1988) is that under a purely competitive equilibrium its presence leads to an underinvestment in human capital because private agents do not take into account the external benefits of human capital accumulation. The equilibrium growth rate is thus smaller than the optimal growth rate, due to the existence of externalities. Because the equilibrium growth rate depends on the rate of investment in human capital, the externality implies that growth would be higher with more investment in human capital. This leads to the conclusion that government policies (subsidies) are necessary to increase the equilibrium growth rate up to the level of the optimal growth rate. A government subsidy to human capital formation or schooling could potentially result in a substantial increase in the rate of economic growth.[12]

An alternative approach to assessing the role played by external effects in the growth process is proposed by Romer (1986). In his framework the source of the externality is the stock of knowledge rather than an aggregate stock of human capital. Knowledge is produced by individuals, but since newly produced knowledge can be, at best, only partially and temporarily kept secret, the production of goods and services depends not only on private knowledge but also on the aggregate stock of knowledge.[13] Firms or individuals only partially reap the rewards from the production of knowledge, and so a market equilibrium results in an underinvestment in knowledge accumulation. To the extent that knowledge can be related to the level of technology, Romer's framework can be viewed as an attempt to determine endogenously the rate of technological progress. In subsequent work, Romer (1990) also explains endogenously the decision to invest in technological change, using a model based on a distinction between a research sector and the rest of the economy. In that framework, firms cannot appropriate all the benefits of knowledge production, implying that the social rate of return exceeds the private rate of return to certain forms of capital accumulation. A tax and subsidy scheme can thus be utilized to raise the rate of growth.

15.2.3 Effects of Financial Intermediation

Development economists have long emphasized the importance of financial development for economic growth. But while the early literature recognized this link—see McKinnon (1973), Shaw (1973), and the discussion in Chapter 14—a rigorous formulation of the interactions between financial factors and growth has begun to take shape only recently, in the context of the new generation of endogenous growth theories.

A simple way to introduce financial factors in a growth model is, following Pagano (1993), to assume that a fraction $1 - \mu$ of saving is "lost" as a result of financial disintermediation activities:

$$\mu s y_t = I_t, \quad 0 < \mu < 1. \tag{8}$$

Assuming that the production technology is described by constant returns to scale to capital as in Rebelo's model, the steady-state growth rate per capita is now equal to

$$\mathbf{g} = s\mu A - \delta. \tag{9}$$

Equation (9) provides a convenient framework for discussing the different channels through which financial development can affect economic growth. First, financial development may raise the saving rate, s. Second, it may raise A, the marginal productivity of the capital stock. Third, it may lead to an increase in the proportion of saving allocated to investment (or, equivalently, an increase in μ), a phenomenon that—in the spirit of McKinnon (1973), who emphasized the use of cash and bank deposits as a channel for capital accumulation by credit-constrained enterprises—we may call the "conduit" effect.

15.2.3.1 EFFECTS ON THE SAVING RATE

While the early development literature emphasized the existence of an unambiguously positive effect of financial development on the saving rate, the new growth literature has shown that the direction of this effect is not consistent. The development of financial markets offers households the possibility of diversifying their portfolios and increases their borrowing options—affecting, therefore, the proportion of agents subject to liquidity constraints, which may in turn affect the saving rate (Jappelli and Pagano, 1994). Financial development also tends to reduce the overall level, and to modify the structure, of interest rates, the latter by reducing the spread between the rate paid by borrowers (typically firms) and that paid to lenders (households). Although these factors are bound to affect saving behavior, in each case the effect is ambiguous. For instance, an increase in the overall level of interest rates may have a positive or negative effect on the saving rate. The net effect depends, in particular, on banks' and portfolio holders' attitude toward risk.[14]

The ambiguous effect of financial intermediation on the saving rate may be compounded when all partial effects associated with financial development are taken into account. For instance, Bencivenga and Smith (1991) demonstrate that the direct effect of the emergence of banking activities may be a reduction in the saving rate. However, as emphasized in the previous chapter, if at the same time the positive impact of financial development on the productivity of capital and the efficiency of investment is taken into account (see the following discussion), the net effect on growth may well be positive.

15.2.3.2 EFFECTS ON THE ALLOCATION OF CAPITAL

A key function of financial intermediaries is the efficient allocation of resources to investment projects that provide the highest marginal return to capital. In the above framework, financial intermediation increases the average productivity of capital A (and thus the growth rate) in two ways: by collecting, processing, and evaluating the relevant information on alternative investment projects; and by inducing entrepreneurs, through their risk-sharing function, to invest in riskier but more productive technologies.

The link between the informational role of financial intermediation and productivity growth has been emphasized by Greenwood and Jovanovich (1990). In their model, capital may be invested in a safe, low-yield technology or a risky, high-yield one. The return to the risky technology is affected by two types of shocks: an aggregate shock, which affects all projects alike, and a project-specific shock. Unlike individual entrepreneurs, financial intermediaries with their large portfolios can identify the aggregate productivity shock, and thus induce their customers to select the technology that is most appropriate for the current realization of the shock. The more efficient allocation of resources channeled through financial intermediaries raises the productivity of capital and thus the growth rate of the economy.

   Another critical function of financial intermediation is that it enables entrepreneurs to pool risks (Pagano, 1993). This "insurance" function results
from the fact that financial intermediaries allow investors to share the unin-
surable risk (resulting from, say, liquidity shocks) and the diversifiable risk
deriving from the variability of the rates of return on alternative assets. The
possibility of risk sharing affects saving behavior (as discussed above) as
well as investment decisions. In the absence of banks, households can guard
against idiosyncratic liquidity shocks only by investing in productive assets
that can be promptly liquidated, thus frequently forgoing investments that
are more productive but also more illiquid. This inefficiency can be considerably reduced by banks, which pool the liquidity risk of depositors and
invest most of their funds in more illiquid and more productive projects.
This effect is captured in an endogenous growth framework by Bencivenga
and Smith (1991). They show that banks increase the productivity of investment both by directing funds to illiquid, high-yield technology and by
reducing the investment waste due to premature liquidation. As in Greenwood and Jovanovich (1990), the productivity gain leads to a higher growth
rate.[15]

15.2.3.3 THE "CONDUIT" EFFECT, FINANCIAL REPRESSION, AND GROWTH

Financial intermediation operates as a tax—at the rate μ in Equation (9)—in
the transformation of saving into investment. Financial intermediation thus
has a growth-deterring effect because intermediaries appropriate a share
of private saving. To a large extent, the costs associated with financial intermediation represent payments (such as fees and commissions) that are
received by intermediaries in return for their services. An important issue
in developing countries, however, may be that such absorption of resources
results from explicit and implicit taxation—such as high rates of reserve requirements, as discussed in Chapter 5—and by excessive regulations, which
lead to higher costs and therefore inefficient intermediation activities.[16] As
emphasized in Chapter 14, to the extent that reforms of the financial system
lead to a reduction in the cost and inefficiencies associated with the intermediation process (that is, leading to a rise in μ), the result will be an increase
in the growth rate.
   The role of financial repression in the context of growth models has received much attention recently. As discussed in Chapter 5, financial repression is to a large extent a fiscal phenomenon. In countries where collecting
conventional taxes is costly, governments often choose to repress their financial systems to increase revenue, even though they recognize the detrimental growth effects of such policies. Roubini and Sala-i-Martin (1995) have
emphasized this view, in a model in which inflation is viewed as a proxy
for financial repression.[17] In addition, constraints on bank portfolio choices

may reduce the volume and productivity of investment—by reducing the volume of funds channeled to deposit-taking financial intermediaries and causing a less efficient distribution of any given volume of such funds—thus impeding growth (Courakis, 1984). We present here a simplified version of a model developed by De Gregorio (1993) that captures the link between inflation—which depends inversely on the degree of efficiency of the tax system—and growth.

Consider a closed economy consisting of households, firms, and the government. Households hold no money but hold an indexed bond issued by the government.[18] Capital is the only input in the production process, which takes place under constant returns to scale. Firms hold money because it reduces transactions costs associated with purchases of new equipment. Capital mobility is precluded, so that domestic investment must equal domestic saving. Inflation is, for the moment, assumed exogenous.

The representative household maximizes the present value of utility stream

$$\int_0^\infty \frac{c_t^{1-\sigma}}{1-\sigma} e^{-\alpha t} dt, \quad 0 < \sigma < 1, \tag{10}$$

subject to the flow budget constraint

$$\dot{b}_t = (1 - \iota)(y_t + \rho b_t) - c_t - \tau_t, \tag{11}$$

where $1/\sigma$ denotes the elasticity of intertemporal substitution, b_t the real stock of government indexed bonds, $0 < \iota < 1$ the income tax rate, ρ the real rate of return on bonds, y_t total factor income, and τ_t net lump-sum taxes paid by households. For simplicity, income taxes are levied at the same rate on all components of gross income.

Maximization of (10) subject to (11) yields

$$\dot{c}_t/c_t = \sigma^{-1}[(1 - \iota)\rho - \alpha]. \tag{12}$$

As in the *AK* model discussed earlier, production is assumed to exhibit constant returns to scale:

$$y_t = Ak_t. \tag{13}$$

Firms require money to purchase new capital goods. The (gross) cost of investing I_t units is thus equal to $I_t[1 + v(m_t/I_t)]$, where m_t denotes firms' real money holdings. The properties of the function $v()$ that characterize the transactions technology are similar to those described in Chapters 4 and 9 ($v' < 0, v'' > 0$). The representative firm maximizes the present discounted value of its cash flow, net of the opportunity cost of its holdings of money balances. The latter is given by $(\rho + \pi_t)m_t$, where π_t is the inflation rate. Thus the firm maximizes

$$\int_0^\infty \left[Ak_t - \left\{ 1 + v\left(\frac{m_t}{I_t}\right) \right\} I_t - (\rho + \pi_t)m_t - \dot{m}_t \right] e^{-\rho t} dt, \qquad (14)$$

subject to $\dot{k}_t = I_t$. The solution yields

$$-v'\left(\frac{m_t}{I_t}\right) = \rho + \pi_t \Rightarrow m_t = m(\rho + \pi_t)I_t, \quad m' = -1/v'' < 0, \quad (15a)$$

$$\dot{q}_t/q_t = \rho - (A/q_t), \qquad (15b)$$

$$q_t = 1 + v\left(\frac{m_t}{I_t}\right) - \frac{m_t}{I_t}v'\left(\frac{m_t}{I_t}\right), \qquad (15c)$$

where q_t denotes the shadow price of capital (see Abel, 1990). Equation (15a) defines the firm's demand for money. Since cash flows are not subject to direct taxation, the opportunity cost of holding money is given by the sum of the before-tax real interest rate plus the inflation rate. The arbitrage equation (15b) can be solved (after imposing the relevant transversality condition) to show that the shadow price of capital is equal to the present discounted value of the marginal product of capital. Equation (15c) indicates that q_t exceeds unity (the price of the composite good) because of the existence of transactions costs incurred in buying a new unit of capital.

Substituting Equation (15a) in (15c) yields

$$q_t = 1 + v[m(\rho + \pi_t)] + (\rho + \pi_t)m(\rho + \pi_t) \equiv q(\rho + \pi_t), \quad q' > 0, \qquad (16)$$

which indicates that q_t is constant—at, say, $\tilde{q}$—if the inflation rate is constant. From Equation (15b), the real interest rate is in this case equal to

$$\tilde{\rho} = A/\tilde{q}. \qquad (17)$$

The government budget constraint is given by

$$\dot{m}_t + \dot{b}_t = g_t - \iota y_t - \tau_t - \pi_t m_t. \qquad (18)$$

where g_t denotes public expenditure, which is taken to be a constant fraction of output. In what follows we also assume that the government forgoes the use of bonds to finance its deficit ($\dot{b}_t = 0$), and instead adjusts lump-sum taxes continuously to maintain fiscal equilibrium.

The aggregate resource constraint of the economy is given by

$$y_t = c_t + \left\{ 1 + v\left(\frac{m_t}{I_t}\right) \right\} I_t + g_t. \tag{19}$$

Using the above system of equations, it can be established that consumption, output, and capital grow at a constant rate in the steady state, which is equal to[19]

$$\mathbf{g} = \sigma^{-1}[(1 - \iota)\tilde{\rho} - \alpha], \tag{20}$$

which is also the rate of growth of real money balances. The model has no transitional dynamics; that is, the economy grows continuously at the rate given by Equation (20).

This model generates an inverse relationship between output growth and the rate of inflation, as can be verified from Equations (16), (17), and (20). This relationship is due to the negative effect of inflation on the profitability of investment. A higher rate of inflation raises the "effective" price of capital goods, which (in addition to its market price) incorporates the opportunity cost of holding money to facilitate purchases of capital goods. The increase in transactions costs raises the shadow value of installed capital, dampens investment, and reduces the growth rate.[20]

To the extent that inflation is viewed as a proxy for financial repression (as in Roubini and Sala-i-Martin, 1995), the negative effect of inflation on growth may reflect distortions stemming from financial markets rather than the usual direct distortionary effects of inflation. An alternative, and perhaps more general, interpretation is to view inflation directly as a tax, which is determined, as discussed in Chapter 4, by the government so as to maximize seignorage revenue (given an expenditure or deficit target) subject to the constraint that conventional taxes are subject to rising marginal collection costs.[21] If that interpretation is correct, an inefficient tax system may be the main factor explaining the correlation between high inflation rates and low growth rates.

15.3 Empirical Evidence and Assessment

The renewed interest in growth theory has led in the past few years to a flurry of econometric studies aimed at examining the determinants of growth. These studies have typically been conducted using large cross-section data sets. In this section we provide a selective review of the most significant results. Before we do so, however, reviewing the descriptive evidence may be useful. Table 15.5 presents the major characteristics of high-, medium-,

TABLE 15.5

Developing Countries: Growth Characteristics (in percent per year, unless otherwise indicated)

	1971–92	1971–81	1982–92
All Developing Countries			
Real GDP growth	5.0	5.7	4.2
Real per-capita GDP growth	2.7	3.3	2.0
Total fixed investment	21.7	21.7	21.7
Public investment	12.1	11.9	12.4
Private investment	9.6	9.8	9.3
Total saving	22.6	23.1	22.1
Government final consumption	11.9	11.5	12.3
Export volume growth	6.9	6.8	7.0
Incremental capital/output ratio	3.2	3.2	3.7
High-Growth Countries			
Real GDP growth	7.0	7.1	6.9
Real per-capita GDP growth	5.0	5.1	4.8
Total fixed investment	23.8	22.2	25.6
Public investment	11.8	10.8	12.8
Private investment	12.0	11.3	12.8
Total saving	27.3	26.5	28.1
Government final consumption	11.9	11.4	12.4
Export volume growth	9.1	8.8	9.4
Incremental capital/output ratio	2.5	2.4	2.9
Medium-Growth Countries			
Real GDP growth	4.1	5.3	2.8
Real per-capita GDP growth	1.5	2.5	0.5
Total fixed investment	20.5	21.3	19.6
Public investment	12.7	12.9	12.6
Private investment	7.7	8.4	7.0
Total saving	20.0	20.9	19.0
Government final consumption	11.5	11.3	11.8
Export volume growth	5.8	6.0	5.7
Incremental capital/output ratio	3.4	3.6	3.7
Low-Growth Countries			
Real GDP growth	1.8	3.0	0.6
Real per-capita GDP growth	−0.5	0.7	−1.6
Total fixed investment	19.6	21.7	17.4
Public investment	11.0	11.6	10.2
Private investment	8.7	10.1	7.1
Total saving	18.0	20.6	15.1
Government final consumption	13.2	12.9	13.5
Export volume growth	3.2	2.7	3.7
Incremental capital/output ratio	4.9	4.6	6.6

Source: International Monetary Fund, *World Economic Outlook* (May 1993, p. 47).

Notes: For coverage, see notes to Table 15.1. The high-growth group consists of the top third of countries that achieved the highest growth rate during 1971–72, and so on.

and low-growth developing countries using annual data for the past two decades.[22] The data suggest that fast-growing economies have substantially higher saving and investment rates, more efficient investment as measured by the incremental capital/output ratio, and a higher rate of export growth than medium- and slow-growing economies. At the same time, the size of the government, as measured by the share of public final consumption in output, does not seem to vary substantially across the different groups of countries.

The bulk of the recent empirical literature on growth has focused on estimating cross-country regressions in search of a set of stable relations among the various variables suggested by the recent theories. This literature has been plagued, however, by a series of methodological problems. One of the major difficulties is that the data necessary to adequately test the predictions of the new models of growth do not exist or are difficult to construct. In some cases the quality of the data is also inadequate. From an econometric standpoint, many studies suffer from an inappropriate treatment of measurement and specification errors, and lack of appreciation of the potential for bidirectional causality.

Levine and Renelt (1992) have provided a careful examination of the degree of robustness of some of the most recent cross-country growth regressions. Three major findings emerge from their analysis. Investment rates (for both physical and human capital) are positively and significantly correlated with average growth rates across a wide variety of samples and specification. Figure 15.2, which shows the correlation between investment rates and growth in Latin America over a thirty-five-year period, is suggestive of this relation. Trade, or the degree of openness measured either by the export-to-output ratio or the import-to-output ratio, is also closely related to growth and investment. However, the close correlation between trade variables and investment makes it difficult to identify their separate effects on growth. The correlation of other variables with growth (such as fiscal policy, inflation, the primary and secondary school enrollment rates, the rate of increase in total population, and the initial level of income) does not appear to be very robust.

More recent studies have corroborated the findings of Levine and Renelt, while others have provided stronger evidence on specific variables. Studies that highlight the importance of the degree of openness and, more generally, an outward orientation for growth are those of Alam (1991), Dollar (1992), Edwards (1993b), Khan and Kumar (1993), Knight et al. (1993), and Lee (1993). Trade distortions, in these studies, have a negative effect on growth.[23] The stock of human capital and foreign direct investment have a positive but generally weak direct effect on per-capita output growth. Regarding the role of financial variables and inflation on growth, the recent evidence is highly supportive. King and Levine (1993) show a robust

Investment (percent of GDP)

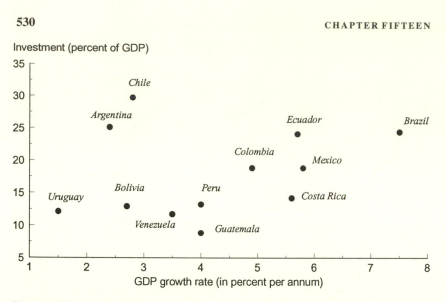

Figure 15.2 Investment and Growth in Latin America (period averages over 1950–85)

Source: De Gregorio (1992).

correlation between the degree of financial development and growth, investment, and the efficiency of capital.[24] Fischer (1993) establishes a negative association between growth, inflation, and fiscal deficits in a large group of countries, while De Gregorio (1992, 1993a) finds evidence of a negative relationship between the level of inflation (an indicator of tax system inefficiency rather than financial repression, as argued earlier), the variability of inflation (an indicator of macroeconomic stability), and growth in Latin America. Although the study by Nelson and Singh (1994) shows no significant effect of fiscal deficits on growth in developing countries during the the 1970s and 1980s, private investment appears to have played a very significant and positive role. Finally, Roubini and Sala-i-Martin (1992) find that growth appears to be negatively correlated with the bank reserve ratio, a more adequate proxy (in view of our discussion in Chapter 5) for financial repression.

Recent studies have also emphasized the differential effect of public and private investment on growth. As discussed in Chapter 3, public investment in infrastructure, to the extent that it proves complementary to private investment, can increase the marginal product of private capital—thereby raising the economy's growth rate (Barro, 1990). This is a particularly important link in developing countries. By contrast, if public production activities compete with private initiative, there may be substitution or crowding-out effects that may lead to adverse effects on growth.[25] Using a sample of ninety-five developing nations over the period 1970–90, Khan and Kumar (1993) have shown that the effects of private and public investment on growth differ significantly, with private investment being consistently more productive than public investment. Knight et al. (1993) and Nelson and Singh (1994) also show that the level of public investment in infrastructure has had a significant effect on growth, particularly during the 1980s.

The topic of economic growth has been the subject of renewed interest in the past few years. This chapter has provided an overview of conventional and more recent theories of economic growth. Traditional neoclassical theory views economic growth as a result of exogenous technological progress. By contrast, the recent literature highlights the existence of a variety of channels through which steady-state growth may emerge endogenously.

The new growth theories have brought significant advances in our understanding of the growth process. They have stressed the importance of invention, human capital accumulation, the development of new technologies, and financial intermediation as important determinants of economic growth. The empirical evidence reviewed here suggests indeed that countries that grow faster devote a larger share of output to investment (in physical as well as human capital), have lower inflation and a more stable macroeconomic environment, and are more open than slow-growing countries.

A general implication of recent theories is that countries that save and invest more will grow faster in the long run. Public policies aimed at encouraging saving, particularly those designed to enhance the efficiency of financial intermediation, may have a sustained effect on per-capita income. Although it is too early to measure how successful recent attempts have been at explaining the diversity of growth experiences across countries—the available evidence is not yet conclusive in many regards, and does not allow discrimination among alternative models—and what and how policies should be designed to influence the rate of growth, some tentative conclusions emerge. Macroeconomic stability and the removal of structural distortions, particularly in the financial sector, foster economic growth by improving the incentives to save and invest, as well as the efficiency of investment. The evidence that outward-oriented countries seem to grow more rapidly than others also seems relatively robust.

At a broader level, the experience of East Asian countries provides several lessons on the range of policies that are conducive to rapid growth and development. Although sustained private investment (induced by high levels of domestic financial saving) and rapidly growing human capital (fostered by increased public spending on primary and secondary education) were the principal engines of growth, a series of other factors directly or indirectly played a significant role in what has become known as the "East Asian miracle" (World Bank, 1993). Prudent macroeconomic management, rapid growth and productivity improvement in the agricultural sector, selective government interventions in the industrial sphere and in the functioning of financial markets—such as the adoption of low real interest rates and directed-credit programs in the early stages of economic growth—a reliable legal framework, changes in the incentive structure of the trade regime, public investment in infrastructure, openness to foreign technology, limited price distortions, and the ability to adapt policies to changing circumstances, all contributed to faster and more efficient accumulation of private capital and higher productivity growth in East Asia (World Bank, 1993). Although the nature and extent of public sector involvement in the growth process in East Asia remain controversial (see, for instance, Sachs, 1987), there seems to be general agreement that government intervention aimed at removing obstacles to market mechanisms or other sources of market failures is not harmful to growth.

At the analytical level, several themes of particular relevance to developing countries warrant further investigation. A key issue, as emphasized by Pagano (1993), is how to explain endogenously the degree of financial development and its evolution over time. The role of income distribution, production infrastructure, and political stability are also areas that deserve careful consideration. In developing nations, inadequate infrastructure (in particular, electricity and water supply, the transportation network, and telephone services) is often a critical impediment to growth and may account for a substantial part of the low factor productivity that has often been observed. There exists, therefore, a potential for government action through not only the provision of education but also the provision of infrastructure services. Finally, the role of informal activities in fostering economic growth has received only scant attention.[26] As argued repeatedly in previous chapters, financial repression typically leads to the emergence of informal credit markets which, although perhaps less efficient than their official counterparts, have helped alleviate the impact of such restrictions. Excessive taxation also tends to drive economic activities underground. Examining the role of informal financial, labor, and product markets in a medium- and long-run context may provide valuable insights into the growth process in developing countries.

Sixteen

The Political Economy of Stabilization and Adjustment

> The reemergence of political economy as a discernible field, with a significant, integrated, and mathematically rigorous literature, represents the reintegration into a refined paradigm of those features of reality that economists discarded in order to facilitate theorizing. (Ordeshook, 1990, p. 10).

Recent developments in mainstream macroeconomics have emphasized the role of political factors in the determination of government policy decisions.[1] Such decisions are viewed as the outcome of collective actions resulting, through political institutions, from a process of aggregation of individual policy preferences. In representative democracies, one mechanism through which such preferences are conveyed to policymakers is the electoral process. The focus on presidential elections and macroeconomic outcomes has generated, in industrial countries, an extensive literature on the "political business cycle."

Recent research on stabilization and structural adjustment programs in developing countries has also emphasized the role of political factors in the outcome of policy reforms. This growing literature has provided much insight regarding the factors that explain the level and instability of inflation, the setting of macroeconomic policy instruments, and the adoption and collapse of disinflation programs and structural reforms. The first part of this chapter reviews the general approach followed in this literature. The second and third parts focus, respectively, on analytical models and empirical evidence on elections-induced business cycles in developing countries.

16.1 Politics, Economic Policy, and Adjustment

Much attention in the analysis of stabilization and structural adjustment programs in developing countries has focused on the political incentives and institutional constraints faced by policymakers. The rationale for such scrutiny has been clearly expressed by Bates (1990, p. 44):

> We must look to the political incentives that shape politicians' economic choices; for ... politicians are not perfect agents of economic interests but rather have distinctive political incentives of their own. We must therefore understand the nature

of the political problems politicians try to solve when making economic policy. We must also look at the ideologies that motivate their interventions. If politicians do take the initiative, we must turn our attention from the economic forces that demand political intervention to the political forces that supply it.

Two areas in which the role of political factors has been emphasized recently are the decision to adopt (and sometimes abandon) structural adjustment programs, and the effect of political instability on inflation and budget deficits.[2]

16.1.1 The Political Economy of Structural Adjustment

Stabilization and adjustment policies, regardless of their medium- and long-run beneficial effects for the country as a whole, entail the imposition of short-term costs and have important social, political, and distributional implications.[3] Policies typically advocated in the context of structural adjustment programs (such as public sector reform, devaluation, elimination of marketing boards, or reduction of food subsidies) may threaten the constituencies that political leaders rely on. Privatization of public enterprises, for instance, usually entails the loss of jobs—or rent-creating positions—at times when unemployment may already be high. Real-exchange-rate adjustment through a nominal devaluation may raise food prices and the cost of imports dramatically, creating hardship for low-income urban households. Increases in agricultural producer prices may also raise the cost of food to urban workers, at least in the short term. A key issue in the political economy of structural adjustment programs has therefore been to determine how these shocks can be absorbed, and which ones different types of governments may have difficulty coping with. Without a proper understanding of the political consequences of structural reforms, the potential alienation of important constituencies may jeopardize the adjustment process at its inception and lead to a return to the "status quo" (Haggard and Kaufman, 1989).

Typically, governments attempt to control economic outcomes in order to create or maintain political support. Politicians rationally advocate government intervention because the imposition of market regulations may facilitate the construction of political organizations. Rulers try to institutionalize their regimes by establishing webs of patron-client relations to garner the support necessary for them to remain in power (Bates, 1990). Leaders reward loyal political followers or those deemed important for their continued tenure in office by direct state intervention in the economy (such as subsidies,[4] privileged access to public enterprises, and selective allocation of licenses for foreign trade), which ensures that resources flow to these groups.

Intervention of this sort typically leads to systems where goods are allocated through state coercion, a process that inhibits the market from conveying information through price signals. Viewed from this perspective, disastrous economic policies can be seen as "arrangements" by which potential political instability is reduced (Bates, 1990).

By contrast, economic reforms entail significant political changes that may weaken the power structure of existing leaders to an unacceptable level. Bates (1990) has emphasized that structural adjustment creates a volatile political climate in which the threat of even minor disruptions must be taken seriously. A group with close ties to a given leadership may experience a "status reversal" during structural adjustment because its privileged access to public resources may be lost. For instance, raising taxes may eventually be beneficial to growth and employment (if the additional revenue is productively invested) but can also lead to the loss of political support. Similarly, once prices are liberalized, subsidies on foodstuffs or other basic commodities of the urban population can no longer be used to prevent civilian disturbances. But the urban population is important if incumbents want to retain control of the cities and stay in power. Regimes that depend on a combination of coercion and patronage to remain in power become more repressive when undergoing structural adjustment, compared to constitutionally elected governments. Indeed, given that there may be no way to continue previously established clientelistic networks in the new environment, leaders may have no choice but to repress some of their former supporters in order to maintain stability. Therefore, the real repression that results from structural adjustment may not be from quelling food riots when austerity packages are first instituted, but from the elimination of some of the noncoercive measures that governments could previously use to keep potentially threatening groups under control.[5]

The central message of the recent literature is that structural adjustment also implies changes in the political system, which may involve a shift not only in the relative power structure but also in the mechanism through which leaders relate to their constituencies. Structural adjustment takes time, and although it may ultimately promote economic growth and improve the well-being of all groups, it implies short-run costs. Adjustment programs, whether efficiency or welfare focused, will fail if they do not recognize the interdependence of efficiency, welfare, and political feasibility.[6] Without a proper understanding of the political logic of structural adjustment, it is difficult to understand why long-term reform programs may become unattractive to political leaders beyond a certain point—the so-called adjustment fatigue phenomenon—even if short-term costs are absorbed. Programs therefore not only must be designed to fit particular economic conditions, but must also take into account the political structure.

16.1.2 Political Instability, Inflation, and Fiscal Deficits

The role of political factors in the determination of inflation and the size of budget deficits in developing countries has been the focus of much recent attention. Haggard (1991) and Haggard and Kaufman (1990), for instance, have argued that Argentina, Brazil, Uruguay, and Chile (before Pinochet) show patterns of inflation that are correlated with political events, generally combining two or three of the political mechanisms expected to erode stable macroeconomic management: strong labor movements linked to polarized political parties, severe tenure insecurities, and a propensity toward government with strongly redistributive orientations. In the case of Argentina, the failure to stabilize in the face of endemic inflation has gone hand in hand with continued political polarization and instability, and the failure of any group to consolidate its power effectively (Dornbusch and dePablo, 1989).

The relationship between political instability and budget deficits has been examined by Edwards and Tabellini (1991) and Roubini (1991). Both studies argue that governments composed of large, short-lived, and unstable coalitions of political parties are associated with large budget deficits. Roubini (1991), in particular, shows that budget deficits in developing countries are heavily influenced by the degree of political instability (measured by an index of political cohesion and stability in the government, and the probability of military coups) as well as public finance considerations—with no apparent direct effect of elections.[7]

16.2 Political Stabilization Cycles

A dominant theme in the political economy literature in developing countries has been the fragility of political power, despite recent moves in several countries toward democratic systems, and the means that politicians attempt to use to secure reelection. Ames (1987, pp. 98–99), for instance, writes:

> Latin American executives ... rarely attain the security and autonomy of their counterparts in industrialized nations. If an executive represents a civilian-competitive regime, the chances of his party electing its successor are slim, and the possibility of implementing a policy package significantly improving those chances is equally poor. When competitively elected leaders face midterm elections, the cost of the political process itself distorts budgets and adds to inflationary pressures.

As argued earlier, contractionary policies designed to reduce inflation impose substantial political costs, particularly when their economic benefits are small and slow to emerge. When an incumbent faces reelection, there is a temptation to manipulate policy instruments for electoral gains—a strategy conducive to the emergence of political business cycles. Generally speaking, a political business cycle refers to policy-induced fluctuations in macroeconomic aggregates (such as output, unemployment, and the inflation rate) that are synchronized with the timing of major elections. Early models viewed these cycles as resulting essentially from a deliberate attempt by incumbent governments to manipulate the economy for electoral gains. Elected officials—or, more generally, the political parties that support politicians in office—have been described as being essentially concerned with maximizing their reelection prospects.[8] These early models of political business cycles were, however, based on several restrictive assumptions, most notably the assumption of an "irrational" electorate. By contrast, more recent analytical approaches have incorporated the assumption of rational and forward-looking voters and have emphasized the role of informational asymmetries among agents. These models yield predictions similar to those of the early literature, but emphasize the synchronization between the timing of elections and cycles in policy instruments, rather than cycles in macroeconomic outcomes. In this section alternative theories of the political business cycle and their implications for macroeconomic policy instruments are examined. The analysis considers first traditional, "opportunistic" models, and then focuses on more recent, "equilibrium" models with informational asymmetries.

16.2.1 "Opportunistic" Models

Opportunistic models of political business cycles assume that politicians care only about remaining in office. We begin by examining the "traditional" model, which emphasizes the inflation-unemployment trade-off in a closed economy. We then develop a framework that highlights the role of exchange-rate policy and the trade-off between inflation and competitiveness.

16.2.1.1 ELECTIONS, INFLATION, AND UNEMPLOYMENT

The seminal opportunistic model of political business cycles was developed by Nordhaus (1975). The model relies essentially on an expectations-augmented Phillips curve and backward-looking expectations. Voters have a distribution of preferences that depends on inflation and unemployment. Assume that elections occur every T periods, with T fixed over time for simplicity. The aggregate voting function, which relates the probability of reelection of the incumbent to economic outcomes, is given by

$$V_0(T) = -\int_0^T (u_t^2/2 + \Theta \pi_t) e^{\rho t} \, dt, \quad \Theta > 0, \tag{1}$$

where u_t denotes the unemployment rate, π_t the inflation rate, ρ the rate of "memory loss" by voters, and Θ the weight attached to inflation relative to unemployment.[9] For simplicity, the actual inflation rate is assumed to enter linearly in the voting function, and the "desired" inflation rate (related, for instance, to seignorage considerations) is assumed to be zero. The expectations-augmented Phillips curve is given by

$$\pi_t = \delta_0 - \delta_1 u_t + \pi_t^a, \tag{2}$$

where π_t^a denotes the expected inflation rate. The assumption of backward-looking expectations, or inertia in voters' preferences, is captured by specifying an adaptive expectational process:

$$\dot{\pi}_t^a = \alpha(\pi_t - \pi_t^a), \quad \alpha > 0. \tag{3}$$

The incumbent government maximizes (1) subject to the inflation-unemployment trade-off (2) and the formation of expectations (3). Substituting Equation (2) in (1), the decision problem can be written as

$$\max V_0(T) = -\int_0^T [u_t^2/2 + \Theta(\delta_0 - \delta_1 u_t + \pi_t^a)]e^{\rho t} \, dt, \tag{4}$$

subject to (3). The Hamiltonian is defined as

$$H(u_t, \pi_t^a, \lambda_t, t) = -[u_t^2/2 + \Theta(\delta_0 - \delta_1 u_t + \pi_t^a)]e^{\rho t} + \lambda_t \alpha(\delta_0 - \delta_1 u_t), \tag{5}$$

where λ_t is the costate variable, which can be interpreted as measuring the marginal electoral gain resulting from a reduction in the expected inflation rate. Necessary conditions for an interior optimum are given by[10]

$$\partial H/\partial u_t = 0 \rightarrow u_t = \delta_1(\Theta - \alpha\lambda_t)e^{-\rho t}, \tag{6a}$$

$$\dot{\lambda}_t = -\partial H/\partial \pi_t^a \rightarrow \lambda_t = \Theta e^{\rho t}, \tag{6b}$$

$$\lambda_T = 0, \tag{6c}$$

subject to, from (2) and (3),

$$\dot{\pi}_t^a = \alpha(\delta_0 - \delta_1 u_t). \tag{6d}$$

The terminal condition (6c) indicates that at time T there is no further electoral gain from reducing the inflation rate.[11] The solution of the differential equations (6b) and (6d) subject to (6a), the terminal condition (6c), and an initial condition on the inflation rate π_0^a, is

$$u_t = \left(\frac{\Theta\delta_1}{\rho}\right)[\rho - \alpha + \alpha e^{-\rho(t-T)}], \tag{7a}$$

$$\pi_t^a = \pi_0^a + \alpha\left[\delta_0 - \frac{\delta_1^2\Theta(\rho - \alpha)}{\rho}\right]t - \left(\frac{\alpha\delta_1}{\rho}\right)^2 \Theta e^{\rho T}(1 - e^{-\rho t}), \tag{7b}$$

$$\lambda_t = \Theta(e^{\rho t} - e^{\rho T})/\rho. \tag{7c}$$

Equations (2) and (7) determine the behavior of inflation and unemployment in the course of an election cycle.[12] Unemployment and inflation fall smoothly in the periods leading to elections (since it is best to reduce these variables at the end of the cycle, so as to exert the maximum impact on voters) and rise sharply after the electoral outcome. Thus, over several electoral cycles, inflation and unemployment display a sawtooth pattern.[13] Assuming that the unemployment rate is inversely related to the level of aggregate demand, the prediction of the model is thus that the incumbent will increase government spending (and therefore aggregate demand) in the periods leading to the election in order to exploit the short-term Phillips curve. Following the elections, a contraction in spending will occur so as to reduce inflation—a policy that at the same time leads to a recession and a rise in unemployment.[14]

16.2.1.2 ELECTIONS AND DEVALUATION CYCLES

A particularly interesting area in which to look for policy instrument cycles synchronized with electoral cycles in developing countries is exchange-rate policy. In what follows we develop a simple political economy model of devaluation with backward-looking contracts.[15] Consider a small, open economy producing nontraded and traded goods. Let π_t denote the inflation rate, defined as

$$\pi_t = \delta\pi_N(t) + (1 - \delta)\epsilon_t, \quad 0 < \delta < 1, \tag{8}$$

where $\pi_N(t)$ is the rate of inflation in nontradable prices and ϵ_t the rate of devaluation of the nominal exchange rate. For simplicity, we assume that world inflation is zero. Increases in nontradable prices are determined by the rate of growth of nominal wages, $\pi_N(t) = \omega_t$. In turn, the rate of growth of nominal wages is set in a manner similar to the backward-looking contract mechanism discussed in Chapter 9, and thus depends only on past inflation rates:

$$\omega_t = \mu\int_{-\infty}^{t} e^{\mu(k-t)}\pi_k\,dk, \quad \mu > 0, \tag{9}$$

where μ is a discount factor. Differentiating (9) with respect to time yields

$$\dot{\omega}_t = -\mu(\omega_t - \pi_t). \tag{10}$$

The incumbent government maximizes the aggregate voting function subject to the equilibrium pricing equation and the equation determining the behavior of wages. The incumbent sets the devaluation rate so as to maximize votes on election eve. Elections take place every T periods. Popularity is inversely related to the difference between the rate of growth of real output (which depends on the rate of change of the real exchange rate, $\epsilon_t - \pi_N(t)$) and its trend growth rate, as well as inflation.[16] Setting trend output growth to zero, the government's objective is thus to maximize the voting function

$$V_0(T) = -\int_0^T e^{\rho t}\{[\epsilon_t - \pi_N(t)]^2/2 + \Theta \pi_t^2/2\} dt, \tag{11}$$

where Θ denotes the relative weight the incumbent attaches to inflation relative to output, and ρ is again the rate of memory loss. Using Equation (8) and $\pi_N(t) = \omega_t$, the decision problem becomes

$$\max -\int_0^T e^{\rho t}\{(\epsilon_t - \omega_t)^2/2 + \Theta[\delta \omega_t + (1 - \delta)\epsilon_t]_t^2/2\} dt, \tag{12}$$

subject to, from (8) and (10),

$$\dot{\omega}_t = -\kappa(\omega_t - \epsilon_t), \quad \kappa \equiv \mu(1 - \delta) \tag{13}$$

and an initial condition on ω_0. Forming the Hamiltonian of the system and denoting by λ_t the costate variable (which measures the marginal electoral gain resulting from a reduction in the rate of growth of wages), necessary (and, from concavity, sufficient) conditions for an optimum are given by

$$\frac{\partial H}{\partial \epsilon_t} = [1 + \Theta(1 - \delta)^2]\epsilon_t - [1 - \Theta\delta(1 - \delta)]\omega_t + \kappa\lambda_t = 0, \tag{14a}$$

$$\dot{\lambda}_t = -\rho - \frac{\partial H}{\partial \omega_t}$$

$$= [1 - \Theta\delta(1 - \delta)]\epsilon_t - (1 + \Theta\delta^2)\omega_t + (\kappa - \rho)\lambda_t, \tag{14b}$$

$$\lambda_T = 0, \tag{14c}$$

subject to (13) and the initial condition $\omega_0 = \bar{\omega}_0$. The transversality condition (14c) indicates that at time T there is no further electoral gain from reducing the rate of growth of nominal wages. Combining Equations (14a) and (14c) yields

$$\epsilon_T = \frac{1}{1 + \Theta(1 - \delta)^2}[1 - \Theta\delta(1 - \delta)]\omega_T \leq \omega_T. \tag{15}$$

Taking the time derivative of Equation (14a) and using (13), (14a), and (14b) yields the following first-order linear differential equation system in ϵ_t and ω_t:

$$\begin{bmatrix} \dot{\epsilon}_t \\ \dot{\omega}_t \end{bmatrix} = \begin{bmatrix} \kappa - \rho & -\alpha \\ \kappa & -\kappa \end{bmatrix}\begin{bmatrix} \epsilon_t \\ \omega_t \end{bmatrix}, \tag{16}$$

where $\alpha = [1 + \Theta(1 - \delta)^2]^{-1}[(\kappa - \rho)\{1 - \Theta\delta(1 - \delta)\} - \kappa\Theta\delta] \lesseqgtr 0$. We assume here that $\kappa > \rho$.

Equation (16) can be solved subject to a given condition on the rate of change of nominal wages and the terminal condition (15). A necessary and sufficient condition for saddlepath stability to obtain is that the determinant of the matrix of coefficients appearing in (16) be negative.[17] If α is negative, this condition is always satisfied. If α is positive, we need $\alpha/(\kappa - \rho) < 1$, a condition that is interpreted graphically below. Assuming that this condition holds, the complete solution to (16) is given by

$$\omega_t = \tilde{\omega} + C_1 \exp(\nu_1 t) + C_2 \exp(\nu_2 t), \tag{17a}$$

$$\epsilon_t = \tilde{\epsilon} + \left[\frac{(\kappa - \rho) - \nu_1}{\alpha}\right]C_1 \exp(\nu_1 t)$$

$$+ \left[\frac{(\kappa - \rho) - \nu_2}{\alpha}\right]C_2 \exp(\nu_2 t), \tag{17b}$$

where $\nu_1 < 0$ and $\nu_2 > 0$ are the roots of the system and $(\tilde{\omega}, \tilde{\epsilon})$ the steady-state solutions. Given that world inflation is zero, both steady-state values are also zero. To ensure the existence of a stationary cycle requires setting $\tilde{\omega}_0 = \omega_T$ in the above expressions. Using the terminal condition (15), Equations (17) can then be solved for the constant terms C_1 and C_2.

The behavior of the devaluation rate and the rate of change of nominal wages during the electoral cycle is represented in Figure 16.1 for $\alpha > 0$, and in Figure 16.2 for $\alpha < 0$. Curves $[\dot{\epsilon}_t = 0]$ and $[\dot{\omega}_t = 0]$ represent combinations of ϵ_t and ω_t for which the devaluation rate and the rate of change of nominal wages, respectively, remain constant. The saddlepath stability condition provided earlier requires that the $[\dot{\omega}_t = 0]$ curve be steeper (in absolute value) than the $[\dot{\epsilon}_t = 0]$ curve. In both figures, the saddlepath is denoted SS. It has a positive slope for $\alpha > 0$ and a negative slope for $\alpha < 0$.

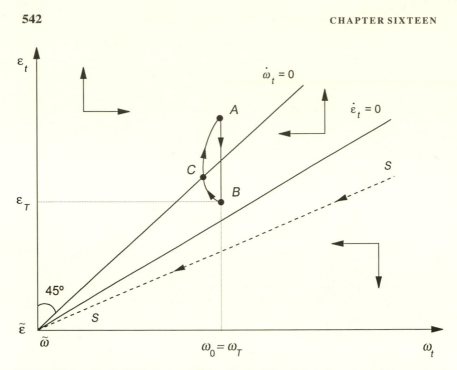

Figure 16.1   The Electoral Devaluation Cycle, Case I: $\alpha > 0$

The path of the devaluation rate during an electoral cycle is depicted in both figures by the sequence ABC. Immediately after assuming office, the incumbent lowers the devaluation rate, which jumps from point A to point B.[18] The inflation rate also jumps downward, and output falls. Since contracts are backward looking, wages cannot change instantaneously. In the periods leading to the electoral contest, with output becoming increasingly important in the eyes of voters, the devaluation rate is increased at an increasing rate. Wages initially fall—up to point C, located on the $[\dot{\omega}_t = 0]$ curve—to catch up with the initial downward jump in the devaluation rate, and then begin to rise. The economy eventually returns to point A, which is reached an instant before period T, and a new cycle starts again. Note that at T, as indicated by Equation (15), the rate of devaluation is maintained below the rate of change in nominal wages. The intuitive interpretation of this result is that a government concerned with its reelection prospects will tend to stimulate output until the last moment before the electoral contest takes place.

The predictions of the opportunistic model of devaluation cycles presented above are therefore qualitatively similar to those predicted by the original Nordhaus model: In the periods leading to the election, the government will increase the rate of depreciation of the nominal exchange rate so

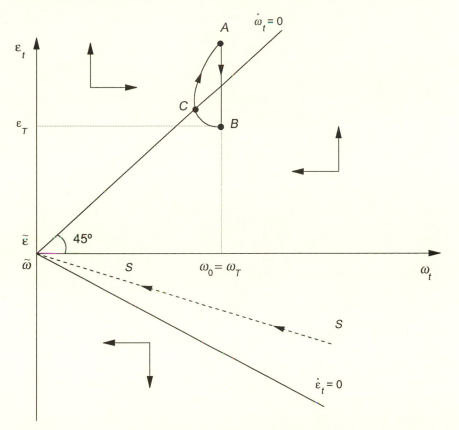

Figure 16.2   The Electoral Devaluation Cycle, Case II: $\alpha < 0$

as to depreciate the real exchange rate and stimulate output. Following the elections, a sharp appreciation of the nominal exchange rate will occur so as to reduce the rate of increase in prices. A recession will consequently occur in the aftermath of the election. However, an important difference (to which we will return below) is that in the opportunistic model of devaluation cycles inertial factors are not a reflection of backward-looking expectations by voters (as in the original Nordhaus model), but rather the consequence of institutional wage-setting mechanisms.

16.2.2 Models with Informational Asymmetries

Recent research on politico-economic models explains political business cycles on the basis of two key assumptions: First, voters are rational and forward looking, and second, they are imperfectly informed about the incumbent government's policy preferences and objectives. Both assumptions play an important role in generating electoral cycles in the new theories. In the Nordhaus model described earlier, assuming that voters are rational and forward looking implies that they will evaluate candidates for office on the basis of their expected *future* performance. The implications of the assumption of perfect foresight can formally be evaluated by setting $\alpha \to \infty$ in the solution equations $(7a)$–$(7c)$. This implies, under usual stability conditions, that there will be no "cycle" as such. By itself, therefore, the rationality of expectations in opportunistic models of the Nordhaus type negates the existence of a political business cycle, since agents can "see" beyond the election date the policy shift required to reduce inflation.

In addition to the assumption of rational expectations, recent developments in the theory of political business cycles have emphasized the existence of informational asymmetries between policymakers and voters. The most important models in this class, which rely on a game-theoretic framework, are those of Rogoff and Sibert (1988) and Rogoff (1990).[19] In these models, governments are also opportunistic, in the sense that they are concerned about their reelection prospects, but there is a critical informational asymmetry: voters do not know precisely the "type" of the incumbent (that is, the level of "competence" of the government, defined as its efficiency in reducing "waste" in fiscal decisions and in providing public goods), a characteristic that, to the incumbent, is perfect information. The incumbent government therefore has an incentive to "signal" its competence—since voters rationally prefer more, rather than less, competent policymakers—by manipulating government spending (or, more generally, tax rates, public utility prices, and so on) before elections. An electoral cycle in government expenditures results, therefore, from an informational asymmetry about the incumbent government's competency in the provision of public goods.[20] Inflationary effects of an expansionary policy are felt after a lag, and therefore occur only after the election has taken place. In addition, in Rogoff's (1990) model, the increase in government spending for signaling purposes may take the form of a preelectoral increase in "consumption" expenditures or highly "visible" transfers—which immediately affect disposable income—and a reduction in "capital" expenditure—which affects individual welfare only with lags. Therefore, spending cycles may also take the form of distortions in the composition of public expenditures. In this type of model, voters judge the performance of the incumbent government by looking at current and past macroeconomic outcomes; they are therefore backward looking, as in Nordhaus-type opportunistic models.

The common implication of both traditional and recent "rational" political business cycle models is, consequently, the existence of systematic manipulation of policy instruments before elections—in particular, government expenditure.[21] An important difference between opportunistic and "rational" approaches is, however, that the type of budgetary cycles occurring, for instance, in Rogoff's (1990) model need not occur systematically in every election. This result is particularly useful in understanding the lack of robust statistical evidence often observed in empirical analyses, as discussed below. Another important difference is that the "rational" electoral cycle will be reflected in the pattern of policy instruments—but not necessarily in the behavior of output, inflation, or unemployment.

This brief review of "old" and "new" theories of the political business cycle leads to several important considerations. First, in developing countries where governments are elected through a democratic process, incumbents may face the same type of incentives for reelection as their counterparts in industrial countries. Thus, at least in principle, the same type of political business cycle phenomenon should be operative. Second, the inertial factor in opportunistic models may result not from backward-looking expectations per se, but (as explicitly recognized in our model of devaluation cycles) from the nature of labor contracts or other forms of market rigidities, such as sticky prices or inertia in trade flows (van der Ploeg, 1989). In such conditions, even if the private sector is forward looking and rationally anticipates future economic and political events, a vote-maximizing strategy by the incumbent might still lead to political business cycles. Finally, although in the opportunistic models examined here the ideological orientation of political parties—as well as incumbent governments—matters for the setting of economic policy only through its possible effects on relative weights attached to policy targets in the objective function, recent efforts have attempted to consider a situation where incumbent governments are concerned not only with reelection prospects but also with their ideological commitment (see Nordhaus, 1989). This line of research may be particularly relevant when it is not possible to identify parties with specific ideological preferences.

16.3 Elections-Induced Economic Cycles: The Evidence

Empirical attempts aimed at determining the existence of systematic politically induced cycles in macroeconomic outcomes and policy instruments—in developed as well as developing countries—have yielded, at best, mixed results. In this section we review some of the empirical evidence available for the developing world and provide our own econometric estimates. Our analysis focuses on the effect of presidential electoral cycles on government spending in three Latin American countries: Colombia, Costa Rica, and Venezuela.

16.3.1 Informal Evidence

Although regular electoral cycles are not the norm in developing countries,[22] there are several examples of institutionalized multiparty systems with stable presidential electoral cycles in these countries, particularly in Latin America: Chile (before and after Pinochet), Colombia, Costa Rica, Mexico, and Venezuela.[23] Costa Rica and Venezuela represent good examples of a liberal, representative, and constitutional democracy in Latin America. Colombia has been a democracy for most of the 160 years since its independence, and has been a two-party system since about the 1840s. The Conservative and Liberal parties have alternated in power for most of that time. Since 1886 the country has had a strong executive power directed by a president who is elected for four years in direct national elections. In 1958 the leaders of the two major parties agreed to establish a mechanism that would ensure presidential alternation between them. The agreement specified that the presidency would alternate every four years, and that the highest positions in the cabinet and public agencies would be shared among nominees of the two parties. The arrangement lasted almost twenty years; its legacy is believed to persist even now in many aspects of government and public administration (Whitehead, 1990). Costa Rica has also enjoyed a stable electoral system for a long time. As in Colombia, presidential elections occur every four years. Venezuela is the oldest and one of the most stable democracies in South America. The system has displayed, since 1958, considerable institutional continuity. In four consecutive elections the opposition party defeated and replaced the incumbent government (1968, 1973, 1978, and 1983). In Mexico the president can serve only for one six-year term, although the same party has remained in power for several decades.

Political scientists have provided many descriptive accounts of the effect of elections on macroeconomic policy in this group of countries. Whitehead (1990), for instance, has argued that in Mexico central government spending follows a cyclical pattern—rising in the first budget of a new president, falling for the next couple of years, and then rising again in the rush to complete projects before the term's end. In this cycle, austerity measures tend to occur in year 1 of each presidency (1971, 1977, and 1983, for instance), to the extent that the new president adopts politically unpopular measures to "purge" previous excesses. In the second and third years of the presidency, new spending initiatives are launched to bring patronage and popularity to the new incumbent: 1972–73, 1977–78, and 1984–85 saw programs of economic reactivation—weaker in the third case because of the debt crisis, but noticeable nonetheless. The last year of the presidency often has a disorderly character, resulting from the lack of control over expenditures.

Haggard and Kaufman (1990) have argued that Chile provides probably one of the clearest cases of a well-defined elections-induced economic cycle. In four of the Chilean episodes that they consider (1953–55, 1958–59, 1962–64, and 1968–70), surges in inflation at the end of a presidential term could be traced to expansionary programs instituted as the new president took office. Since these programs were launched in recessionary conditions, they were initially successful in stimulating growth without having much effect on inflation. By the second half of each administration, however, the expansion began to strain the limits of existing production capacities. With upcoming elections, incumbent governments accommodated inflationary demands from organized labor and business interests. Each president would thus leave office in the context of stagflation, and the cycle would begin again under his successor. Two of these cycles involved populist governments, and in the last two episodes the party system became increasingly polarized as well. Haggard and Kaufman have also argued that in Uruguay, the inflation bursts of 1968 and 1973 were preceded by large increases in public sector wages and fiscal deficits implemented by incumbent governments during the electoral campaigns of 1967 and 1971.

16.3.2 Econometric Evidence

Formal econometric models aimed at testing the existence of politico-economic cycles in developing countries are recent and have focused largely on determining cycles in macroeconomic policy instruments—in particular government spending—rather than cycles in output, inflation, and unemployment.[24] A key assumption in these studies is that—in line with the opportunistic model reviewed earlier—an expansionary fiscal policy, in the form of an increase in transfers, subsidies, or other components of government spending, results from the desire of politicians to expand output and generate political support in preelection periods.[25]

Ames (1987) provides one of the first attempts in this direction, focusing on the case of seventeen Latin American countries between 1947 and 1982. His empirical analysis provides some support for the assumption that governments tend to alter the composition of government spending so as to capture electoral gains.[26] Karnik (1990) provides econometric results supporting the assumption that government spending in India has been sensitive to the electoral cycle. More recently, Edwards (1994) has provided a quantitative analysis of political business cycles for Chile over the period 1952–73. An important innovation in Edwards's approach is that it accounts not only for presidential elections but also for parliamentary elections. He also combines ideological motivation and reelection concerns in his regression model, and finds evidence supporting both.

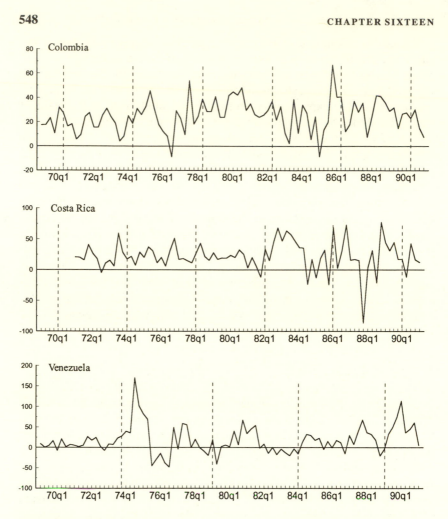

Figure 16.3   Government Spending and the Electoral Cycle in Latin America (annual percentage changes)

16.3.2.1 ELECTORAL CYCLES AND GOVERNMENT EXPENDITURE

To further enhance our understanding of the effect of political factors on the setting of policy instruments, we provide our own econometric tests of a model of public expenditure behavior for a group of countries that has not so far been studied systematically—Colombia, Costa Rica, and Venezuela. As indicated earlier, these countries have maintained constitutional regimes with a regular, institutionalized electoral cycle. The key assumption, as outlined above, is that an expansionary fiscal policy (taking, for instance, the form of an increase in transfers or subsidies) may result from the desire of politicians to expand output and generate political support in preelection periods. As an alternative measure of total government spending, the behavior of net domestic credit to the government is also examined. Finally, we turn our attention to changes in the composition of public spending in order to determine whether, as suggested by Rogoff (1990), some components of expenditure tend to follow a more pronounced electoral cycle.

The rate of growth of public spending in Colombia, Costa Rica, and Venezuela is shown in Figure 16.3, together with presidential election dates during the period 1970–90.[27] A priori, no clear pattern seems to emerge. This is not surprising, however, considering the variety of economic factors that, together with possible political considerations, may influence the short-term behavior of public expenditure. To account for such factors requires the specification of a formal econometric framework.

A good point of departure for formulating a politico-economic model of government expenditure can be found in the work of Ames (1987). Following Ames, we develop a model that links movements in central government public expenditure to political and economic factors. Specifically, we consider a framework in which fluctuations in total spending depend on the timing of elections, and the behavior of potential budgetary resources. The rate of growth of central government spending at time t, $\Delta \ln G_t$, is assumed to depend on the following series of variables:

The rate of change of government expenditure at the preceding period, $\Delta \ln G_{t-1}$, which accounts for "administrative constraints" and may reflect the tendency of bureaucrats to continually expand public spending.

The rate of change of fiscal revenue at the preceding period, $\Delta \ln T_{t-1}$, which accounts for a "resource constraint" on government outlay plans.

The rate of change of net foreign assets during the preceding period, $\Delta \ln R_{t-1}$, which accounts for the "foreign exchange constraint" the government may face, if public spending has a high import component.

A dummy variable, IMF, which takes a value of 1 for all quarters during which the country has an arrangement with the International Monetary Fund, and 0 otherwise. Introducing this variable is meant to capture the idea that Fund programs almost always call for fiscal restraint, as part of the conditionality required for assistance.

A series of electoral dummies, tot_elec, and $elec_{-k}$, for $k = 0, \ldots, 4$. The first dummy takes a value of 1 in the current and four previous quarters of the election. The second set of dummy variables is used to identify separately the effect of each quarter preceding the election date.

The first three variables should have a positive effect on the rate of growth of spending, while the existence of a Fund program should be associated with declines in public spending. If, before elections, spending rises as incumbents try to ensure electoral success, the last set of dummies should also have a positive and statistically significant effect.

TABLE 16.1
Estimation Results: Government Expenditure: 1972q1–1990q4

	Colombia		Costa Rica		Venezuela	
	(1)	(2)	(1)	(2)	(1)	(2)
Constant	0.187	0.160	0.351	0.354	0.155	0.161
	(2.209)	(1.716)	(4.587)	(3.925)	(2.226)	(1.884)
$\Delta \ln G_{t-1}$	0.029	0.061	0.441	0.519	0.125	0.107
	(0.054)	(0.110)	(0.463)	(0.847)	(0.764)	(0.542)
$\Delta \ln T_{t-1}$	0.195	0.179	0.061	0.091	0.458	0.461
	(1.516)	(1.354)	(0.351)	(0.517)	(3.786)	(3.499)
$\Delta \ln R_{t-1}$	0.007	0.005	0.032	0.027	0.189	0.192
	(0.138)	(0.098)	(0.525)	(0.462)	(2.408)	(2.297)
IMF	−0.015	−0.017	0.036	0.051	−0.005	−0.007
	(−0.769)	(−0.803)	(1.021)	(1.429)	(−0.138)	(−0.168)
tot_elec	0.004	—	0.044	—	−0.019	—
	(0.287)		(1.087)		(−0.836)	
elec	—	0.059	—	0.121	—	0.031
		(0.895)		(0.757)		(0.238)
$elec_{-1}$	—	−0.059	—	0.125	—	−0.149
		(−0.838)		(0.813)		(−0.907)
$elec_{-2}$	—	0.031	—	−0.061	—	0.096
		(0.453)		(−0.380)		(0.572)
$elec_{-3}$	—	−0.039	—	0.135	—	−0.007
		(−0.553)		(1.187)		(−0.045)
$elec_{-4}$	—	0.071	—	−0.087	—	−0.101
		(1.138)		(−0.764)		(−0.768)
R^2	0.756	0.763	0.710	0.734	0.541	0.552
σ	0.116	0.117	0.213	0.208	0.198	0.203
$\eta(4)$	0.657	0.541	1.539	1.229	2.274	1.729
arch(4)	0.579	0.624	0.156	0.025	0.697	0.451
F	—	0.365	—	1.391	—	0.397
Chow	0.317	0.190	2.127	1.203	1.113	0.978

Source: Authors' calculations.

Estimation results for the model are presented in Table 16.1.[28] The lagged value of government spending is not significant in any of the regressions, nor is the IMF dummy (the variable has, in fact, the wrong sign for Costa Rica). Tax revenues have a significant positive effect for Venezuela and (to a lesser extent) for Colombia. Net foreign assets have a positive effect on spending only in Venezuela. The electoral dummies, whether for the previous year as a whole (given in the first column for each country) or for individual quarters (second column), are not significant. These results do not, therefore, provide much evidence of an electoral cycle in government expenditure.[29]

16.3.2.2 DETERMINANTS OF DOMESTIC CREDIT TO THE GOVERNMENT

A second approach to testing for an electoral cycle in government spending is to use the rate of growth of net domestic credit to the central government, $\Delta \ln L_t$, as an indicator of public outlays. This approach rests on several assumptions. First, with a given fiscal revenue capacity and limited borrowing options, changes in expenditure are often financed by domestic credit. Second, the central bank may be—as is often the case in developing countries—largely dependent on the executive power and may not be able to resist government pressure to monetize budget deficits. Finally, an additional argument for using domestic credit to the government as an alternative and "broader" measure of public spending relates to the possibility that the incumbent government may use "extrabudgetary" spending—a fairly common practice in developing countries. Such outlays would not typically be recorded in budgetary statistics as such, but the change in domestic credit to the government might capture them.

Estimation results when the rate of change of domestic credit to the government is used as the dependent variable, and with the same set of regressors as before, are presented in Table 16.2. Overall, the coefficient of determination is not high, but the other diagnostic tests indicate a somewhat plausible specification, although the Lagrange multiplier test suggests persistent autocorrelation of residuals for Venezuela. The lagged value of credit growth is significant in almost all cases. Taxes and foreign reserves, by contrast, are not significant. The *IMF* dummy has the correct sign and is significant at the 10 percent level for Costa Rica. The overall electoral dummy is significant only for Colombia. The quarterly dummies are all significant at the 5 percent level for at least a quarter in all cases: the fourth quarter for Colombia, and the second quarter for Costa Rica and Venezuela. The results therefore provide limited support for the assumption that expenditures respond to the electoral cycle.

16.3.2.3 ELECTIONS AND THE COMPOSITION OF PUBLIC EXPENDITURE

The econometric results reported in Tables 16.1 and 16.2 do not allow a distinction between the classical, opportunistic budgetary cycle and the equilibrium political budgetary cycle. As discussed above, however, in addition to predicting elections-induced cycles in government policy

TABLE 16.2
Estimation Results: Domestic Credit to the Government: 1972q1–1990q4

	Colombia		Costa Rica		Venezuela	
	(1)	*(2)*	*(1)*	*(2)*	*(1)*	*(2)*
Constant	−0.576	−0.246	0.036	0.336	−0.045	1.203
	(−0.659)	(−1.405)	(0.255)	(2.674)	(−0.486)	(0.637)
$\Delta \ln L_{t-1}$	0.556	0.438	0.503	0.426	0.029	0.536
	(1.710)	(1.863)	(1.916)	(3.891)	(0.251)	(2.265)
$\Delta \ln T_{t-1}$	−0.553	0.939	0.214	0.281	0.064	0.348
	(−0.604)	(1.021)	(0.715)	(1.190)	(0.235)	(1.207)
$\Delta \ln R_{t-1}$	1.306	0.567	−0.037	−0.047	0.037	0.001
	(1.227)	(0.723)	(−0.431)	(−0.745)	(0.121)	(0.002)
IMF	0.056	0.012	−0.045	−0.141	0.032	0.016
	(0.118)	(0.051)	(−1.026)	(−1.723)	(0.118)	(0.112)
tot_elec	0.925	—	−0.045	—	−0.136	—
	(2.529)		(−1.026)		(−0.781)	
elec	—	0.211	—	−0.004	—	0.075
		(0.453)		(−0.021)		(0.209)
elec$_{-1}$	—	0.303	—	0.483	—	0.943
		(0.685)		(2.598)		(2.057)
elec$_{-2}$	—	0.145	—	−0.051	—	−1.092
		(0.336)		(−0.284)		(−0.941)
elec$_{-3}$	—	−0.364	—	−0.054	—	0.041
		(−0.733)		(−0.295)		(0.109)
elec$_{-4}$	—	1.147	—	−0.102	—	0.283
		(2.578)		(−0.521)		(0.779)
R^2	0.351	0.319	0.263	0.307	0.014	0.241
σ	0.658	0.579	0.343	0.349	0.645	0.567
$\eta(4)$	0.209	0.918	0.536	0.625	2.168	1.193
arch(4)	0.254	2.119	0.289	0.509	0.569	0.506
F	—	1.695	—	1.441	—	2.543
Chow	0.723	0.927	0.497	1.712	0.013	0.107

Source: Authors' calculations.

instruments, Rogoff's (1990) analysis provides a further testable implication: incumbent governments tend to bias preelection spending policy toward current expenditures (such as transfers) and away from public investment. Little evidence is available on this type of effect in developing countries. In one of the few studies that we are aware of, Ames (1987) has argued

TABLE 16.3
Estimation Results: Wages and Transfers: 1972–90

	Colombia	Costa Rica	Venezuela
Constant	3.892	−0.069	0.427
	(2.239)	(−0.086)	(0.643)
$\Delta \ln s_{t-1}$	0.116	1.014	0.901
	(0.293)	(5.497)	(5.921)
$\Delta \ln y_t$	−0.009	−0.001	−0.004
	(−0.778)	(−0.059)	(−0.073)
elec	0.005	0.002	−0.016
	(0.117)	(0.095)	(−0.998)
R^2	0.123	0.723	0.765
$\hat{\sigma}$	0.049	0.027	0.027
$\eta(1)$	3.107	0.349	1.297
arch(1)	0.088	0.391	0.285
Chow	0.261	0.035	0.256
Estimation Period	1978–89	1974–90	1971–89

Source: Authors' calculations.
Notes: The diagnostic tests used in the table are defined in footnote 28. Estimation is performed on annual data. Numbers in parentheses denote t statistics. Chow denotes the value of the predictive Chow test for one-period-ahead predictions (that is, 1989 for Colombia and Venezuela, and 1990 for Costa Rica).

that in Costa Rica the share of government wages and salaries in total expenditures rose before every election—except the election of 1965. We now examine this issue for the three countries considered above.

Table 16.3 reports estimation results of an econometric model that relates the logarithm of the share of wages, salaries, and transfers in total government spending, $\ln s_t$, to its one-period lagged value (a measure of inertia), $\ln s_{t-1}$; the current rate of economic growth (which captures cyclical effects on the composition of expenditure), $\Delta \ln y_t$; and a dummy value, elec, that takes the value 1 in the year in which presidential elections take place and 0 otherwise.[30] The results show that the specification appears reasonable for Costa Rica and Venezuela, but not for Colombia; the diagnostic tests indicate evidence of serial correlation in the residuals in the latter case. The rate of growth of output is not significant in any equation, although it has the expected negative sign. The estimates also suggest no significant effect of the electoral dummy variable on the composition of public spending.

The results can be summarized as follows. The assumption that government spending responds to the reelection concerns of incumbents does not appear to hold. When the dependent variable is net credit to the government, some statistical evidence of a positive effect of the electoral cycle seems to exist. However, such evidence on spending cycles is not very strong. Finally, there does not appear to be any systematic shift in the composition of public expenditures in the periods preceding presidential elections. The inconclusive nature of our results is in accord with the recent study of Alesina et al. (1993), who do not find much evidence in favor of an electoral cycle in government spending in developed countries. The conclusions reached here might perhaps be interpreted in a similar way: the lack of robust statistical results may reflect the fact that governments do not manipulate spending systematically, but only when election outcomes appear highly uncertain for the incumbent seeking reappointment.

An alternative explanation may follow along the lines suggested by Ames (1987), who argues that while incumbents in the pluralist regimes of advanced industrial countries may indeed attempt to maximize their chances of reelection by synchronizing economic policy decisions with the election cycle (that is, by stimulating output and reducing unemployment in the periods preceding the vote), in developing countries governments often spend to recruit and retain followers. The concern of political leaders for their own survival is not necessarily greatest just before elections. Claims faced by governments from constituency pressures go beyond the cyclical demands imposed by elections. There need not be, therefore, any systematic link between elections and macroeconomic policy cycles.

Before we pass a definitive judgment, however, the type of empirical analysis developed here should be extended in various directions. First, alternative measures of government spending, including, for instance, spending by semipublic enterprises, could be used.[31] Second, a "popularity index" could be introduced in the equation in order to examine the effect that changes in popularity may have on a government's propensity to manipulate policy instruments. However, opinion polls on political issues are rare in developing countries, and this extension may prove particularly difficult.[32] Third, the role of midterm parliamentary elections on the behavior of aggregate government spending should also be examined, as done by Edwards (1994). Fourth, there are important institutional factors that must be taken into account, notably the degree of independence of the central bank and the structure of the budgetary process. Fifth, it may be worth investigating "partisan" effects that appear, for industrial democracies, to have played an important role in the behavior of macroeconomic policy instruments.[33]

———————

The recent literature on the political economy of stabilization programs and structural adjustment has identified a variety of channels through which formal characteristics of the political system affect macroeconomic management. Although the available evidence does not appear to provide strong support for the view that policy instruments and macroeconomic outcomes in developing countries respond systematically to the political objectives of incumbents, it is widely accepted that economic outcomes reflect choices constrained by political institutions, and economic reforms have long-term political consequences. Preelectoral manipulation of government policy instruments may occur, but not necessarily in a systematic manner because of the existence of noncontingent constraints. An important implication of the analysis is the necessity to evaluate ex ante the political feasibility of stabilization plans. As emphasized in Chapter 10, the political context in which stabilization plans and structural adjustment programs are implemented must be taken into account in the design of these programs to ensure sustainability of the reform effort. Identifying the best ways to do so, and at the same time maintaining the feasibility and overall consistency of the program, remains a major challenge for economists and policymakers.

Seventeen

Macroeconomic Adjustment with Segmented Labor Markets

THE NATURE and extent of labor market segmentation in developing countries have been subjects of much discussion over the years, particularly in the context of urbanization policy and migration between rural and urban areas. As indicated in Chapter 2, Harris and Todaro (1970) showed in a seminal contribution that the existence of a binding minimum wage in the urban sector can lead, even if the rural labor market is competitive, to a persistent wage differential between the rural and urban sectors and to the emergence of unemployment in equilibrium. Moreover, expansion of labor demand or real wage restraint in the urban sector may not restore full employment and may even increase unemployment.

Much recent work has focused on the role of labor market segmentation in the context of trade and structural reform.[1] However, the implications of various types of dualism or segmentation of labor markets for the short-run determination of output and employment in an open developing economy have not received much attention in the existing literature. This chapter discusses some of these implications, focusing in particular on the role of imperfect labor mobility for the effectiveness of macroeconomic policy shocks.[2] Section 17.1 presents a partial-equilibrium framework. A dynamic, general equilibrium model with homogeneous labor but imperfect mobility across sectors is developed in Section 17.2. This model is used in Section 17.3 to analyze the short- and long-run effects of a permanent reduction in government spending on nontraded goods. Section 17.4 extends the discussion to account for minimum wage legislation and labor heterogeneity.

17.1 A Partial-Equilibrium Framework

The importance of accounting for market segmentation and the degree of wage flexibility for a proper understanding of the effects of macroeconomic shocks on unemployment can be illustrated with a simple graphical analysis. Consider a small open economy producing traded and nontraded goods using only labor, the supply of which is given. The determination of wages and employment under four different assumptions regarding labor market adjustment is shown in Figure 17.1. In all four panels the horizontal axis measures total labor available to the economy, $O_T O_N$. The vertical axis

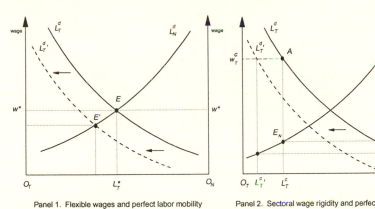

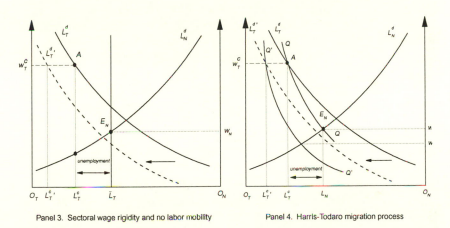

Figure 17.1   Labor Mobility, Sectoral Wage Rigidity, and Adjustment

measures the wage rate in the economy, which is either uniform across sectors or sector specific. The demand for labor in the traded (nontraded) goods sector is represented by the downward-sloping curve L_T^d (L_N^d). Consider first panel 1, which is based on the assumption that wages are perfectly flexible and labor perfectly mobile across sectors. The initial equilibrium position of the labor market obtains at point E, where the economywide wage rate is equal to w^*, labor employed in the traded goods sector is $O_T L_T^*$, and labor used in the production of nontraded goods is $L_T^* O_N$.

In panels 2, 3, and 4 the wage rate in the traded goods sector is fixed at w_T^c (above the economywide, market-clearing wage) while wages in the nontraded goods sector remain flexible.[3] The panels differ in the underlying assumptions regarding the degree of intersectoral labor mobility. In panel 2, labor can move freely across sectors, as in panel 1. Perfect labor mobility, together with wage flexibility in the nontraded goods sector, prevents the emergence of unemployment. The initial equilibrium obtains at point A in the traded goods sector, corresponding to an employment level of $O_T L_T^c$, and at point E_N in the nontraded goods sector, with wages equal to w_N and employment to $L_T^c O_N$. In panel 3 labor is completely immobile within the time frame of the analysis. The labor force in the traded goods sector is equal to $O_T \bar{L}_T$, while the supply of labor in the nontraded goods sector is measured by $\bar{L}_T O_N$. Since sectoral labor supply is completely inelastic and wages cannot adjust in the traded goods sector, unemployment will typically emerge in that sector. The situation depicted in panel 3 indicates that employment in the traded goods sector is equal to $O_T L_T^c$ and unemployment to $L_T^c \bar{L}_T$. Finally, panel 4 is an adaptation of the Harris-Todaro labor allocation mechanism, which assumes that equilibrium obtains when the wage rate in the nontraded goods sector is equal to the expected wage in the traded goods sector. The downward-sloping locus QQ is a rectangular hyperbola along which this equality holds, and is known as the Harris-Todaro curve (Corden and Findlay, 1975).[4] The intersection of the L_N^d curve with QQ determines the wage rate and the employment level in the nontraded goods sector, while the intersection of the L_T^d curve with the horizontal line drawn at w_T^c determines employment in the traded goods sector. The initial equilibrium is therefore also characterized by unemployment, which is equal to $L_T^c L_N$.

Suppose that the demand for labor in the traded goods sector falls, as a result of a macroeconomic shock—a reduction, say, in sectoral autonomous demand—shifting the curve L_T^d to the left.[5] If wages are perfectly flexible and labor perfectly mobile across sectors, adjustment of the labor market leads to a fall in the overall wage rate in the economy and a reallocation of labor across sectors, leading the economy to a new equilibrium (point E' in panel 1) with full employment.

Consider now what happens in the presence of a sector-specific wage rigidity. If labor is perfectly mobile across sectors, the demand shock leads only to a reallocation of the labor force and a fall in wages in the nontraded goods sector (panel 2). However, if workers cannot move across sectors, the reduction in demand leads to an increase in unemployment in the traded goods sector, with no effect on wages and employment in the nontraded goods sector (panel 3). With a labor allocation mechanism of the Harris-Todaro type, the demand shock reduces employment in the traded goods sector, as in the preceding case. However, the effect on the unemployment rate is now ambiguous. This is because the QQ curve shifts to the left following the shift in L_T^d since the fall in employment reduces the likelihood of being hired and, therefore, the expected wage in the traded goods sector. This implies that more workers would elect to seek employment in the nontraded goods sector, bidding wages down. Employment therefore increases in the nontraded goods sector, while wages fall. However, despite the re-allocation of labor across sectors, in equilibrium unemployment may well increase in the traded goods sector. The thrust of the analysis, therefore, is that it is critically important to assess correctly the key features of the labor market in order to evaluate the implications of macroeconomic shocks on wages, employment, and the unemployment rate in the economy.[6] We now turn to a formal, general equilibrium analysis of these issues.

17.2 A Macroeconomic Model with Segmented Labor Markets

Consider a small open economy in which there are three types of agents: producers, households, and the government. All firms and households are identical. The official exchange rate is fixed. The economy produces two goods, a nontraded good used only for final domestic consumption and a traded good whose price is determined on world markets. The capital stock in each sector is fixed during the time frame of the analysis. Labor is homogeneous and imperfectly mobile across sectors. The labor market consists of two sectors: a primary segment, corresponding to the traded goods sector, where employment and wages are determined by firms; and a secondary segment, corresponding to the nontraded goods sector, where employment is determined by the interactions of supply and demand. Whereas wages in the secondary market are fully flexible, efficiency considerations lead firms in the primary segment of the market to offer a premium over the wage that prevails in the secondary sector.[7] Firms in the traded goods sector make their employment decisions first. Although workers who are not hired in the traded goods sector could be absorbed in the nontraded goods sector, imperfect labor mobility prevents an instantaneous reallocation of the labor force. Households consume both traded and nontraded goods, supply labor inelastically, and hold a traded bond, whose constant rate of return is determined on world markets. The government collects lump-sum taxes and consumes nontraded goods. It finances its budget deficit by varying taxes on households. Finally, wage and employment expectations are assumed to depend on prevailing conditions in the labor market.

17.2.1 Output and the Labor Market

With the world price of traded goods set to unity, the domestic price of traded goods is given by $P_T(t) = \bar{E}$, where $\bar{E}$ denotes the nominal exchange rate. The production technology in the traded goods sector is given by

$$Q_T(t) = Q_T[e_t L_T(t)], \quad Q_T' > 0, \quad Q_T'' < 0, \quad (1)$$

where Q_T denotes output, L_T employment measured in natural units, and e_t effort. Production takes place under decreasing returns to labor. The effort function takes the form

$$e_t = 1 - \Lambda \left\{ \frac{\omega_N(t)}{\omega_T(t)} \right\}^{\gamma}, \quad \gamma > 0, \tag{2}$$

where $\omega_T(t) \equiv w_T(t)/\bar{E}$ denotes the product wage in the traded goods sector, $\omega_N(t) \equiv w_N(t)/\bar{E}$ the real wage in the nontraded goods sector, measured in terms of traded goods, w_T (w_N) the nominal wage in the traded (nontraded) goods sector, and $0 < \Lambda < 1$. Equation (2) indicates that effort is related positively to the real wage in the traded goods sector and negatively to the real wage in the nontraded goods sector, which measures the opportunity cost of effort. For $\omega_T(t) = \omega_N(t)$, the minimum level of effort is $1 - \Lambda$, and given $\omega_N(t)$, effort is concave in $\omega_T(t)$. For simplicity, we set $\Lambda = 1$ in the discussion that follows.[8]

The representative firm in the traded goods sector maximizes its real profits, given by

$$\Pi_T = Q_T(t) - \omega_T(t)L_T(t),$$

with respect to $\omega_T(t)$ and L_T, for $\omega_N(t)$ given.[9] The first-order conditions for this optimization problem are

$$\omega_T(t)/e_t = Q_T', \qquad 1/e_{\omega_T}[.] = Q_T', \tag{3}$$

which imply

$$e_{\omega_T}[.]\omega_T(t) = e_t. \tag{4}$$

Equation (4) indicates that in equilibrium the elasticity of effort with respect to the product wage is unity. It generalizes the Solow condition (see Layard et al., 1991) to a two-sector economy and can be solved for the real efficiency wage in the traded goods sector, for a given value of the secondary sector wage. Using Equation (2), Equation (4) yields

$$\omega_T(t) = \delta \omega_N(t), \quad \delta \equiv (1 + \gamma)^{1/\gamma} > 1, \tag{5}$$

which indicates that the efficiency wage is always higher than the opportunity cost of effort. A graphical determination of the efficiency wage is shown in Figure 17.2.

Substituting the optimal value of $\omega_T(t)$ from Equation (5) in Equation (2) and the result in Equation (3) determines the equilibrium effort level and the demand for labor in the traded goods sector, L_T^d:

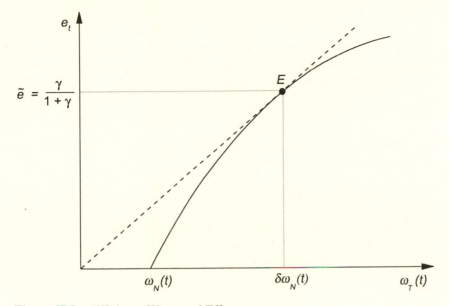

Figure 17.2   Efficiency Wages and Effort

$$L_T^d(t) = \frac{1}{e[.]}Q_T'^{-1}\{\omega_T(t)/e[.]\} \equiv L_T^d[\omega_N(t)], \quad L_T^{d\,'} < 0. \qquad (6)$$

An increase in the real wage in the nontraded goods sector reduces the demand for labor in the traded goods sector. A rise in $\omega_N(t)$ increases the real efficiency wage in the traded goods sector more than proportionately, thus raising effort. However, the increased effort is not sufficient to dampen the negative, direct effect of the increase in the real efficiency wage on labor demand. In addition, the increase in effort leads to a direct reduction in labor demand in order to keep constant the marginal product of labor, measured in efficiency units. As a result of both effects, labor demand falls with an increase in $\omega_N(t)$.

Substituting Equations (2), (5) and (6) in (1) yields

$$Q_T(t) = \mathbb{Q}_T[\omega_N(t)], \quad \mathbb{Q}_T' < 0, \qquad (7)$$

which indicates that an increase in the real wage in the nontraded goods sector reduces output of traded goods.

Production in the nontraded goods sector is determined by

$$Q_N(t) = Q_N[L_N(t)], \quad Q_N' > 0, \quad Q_N'' < 0, \qquad (8)$$

and real profits (in terms of traded goods) are given by

$$\Pi_N = z_t^{-1}Q_N(t) - \omega_N(t)L_N(t),$$

where $z_t = \bar{E}/P_N(t)$ denotes the real exchange rate, and $P_N(t)$ the domestic price of nontraded goods. Profit maximization yields the familiar equality between marginal revenue and marginal cost:

$$\omega_N(t) = z_t^{-1}Q_N'[L_N(t)], \tag{9}$$

from which labor demand can be derived as $L_N^d(t) = Q_N'^{-1}[z_t\omega_N(t)]$. Substituting this result in (8) implies

$$Q_N(t) = \mathbb{Q}_N[z_t\omega_N(t)], \quad \mathbb{Q}_N' < 0, \tag{10}$$

where $z_t\omega_N(t)$ measures the product wage in the nontraded goods sector. From Equations (7) and (10), real factor income, measured in terms of the price of traded goods, is given by

$$q_t = z_t^{-1}\mathbb{Q}_N[z_t\omega_N(t)] + \mathbb{Q}_T[\omega_N(t)]. \tag{11}$$

The determination of the equilibrium wage in the nontraded goods sector is discussed below.

17.2.2 Consumption and the Market for Nontraded Goods

Households supply a fixed quantity of labor $\bar{L}$ inelastically and consume traded and nontraded goods. Consumption of both categories of goods depends on the real exchange rate and the stock of assets:

$$c_T(t) = c_T(\overset{+}{\bar{z}_t}, \overset{+}{b_t}), \qquad c_N(t) = c_N(\overset{+}{z_t}, \overset{+}{b_t}), \tag{12}$$

where $c_N(t)$ denotes consumption of nontraded goods, $c_T(t)$ consumption of traded goods, and b_t the real stock of traded bonds. The flow budget constraint of the household is given by

$$\dot{b}_t = i^*b_t + q_t - z_t^{-1}c_N(t) - c_T(t) - \tau_t, \tag{13}$$

where τ_t denotes real lump-sum taxes (measured in terms of traded goods) and i^* the constant world interest rate.

Using Equations (10) and (12), the equilibrium condition of the market for nontraded goods can be written as

$$\mathbb{Q}_N[z_t\omega_N(t)] = c_N(z_t, b_t) + g_N, \tag{14}$$

where g_N denotes government spending on nontraded goods. Equation (14) can be solved for the real exchange rate, for given values of $\omega_N(t)$ and b_t.

17.2.3 The Government

The government maintains spending on nontraded goods at a constant level in real terms, and adjusts lump-sum taxes to balance the budget:

$$\tau_t = z_t^{-1} g_N. \tag{15}$$

17.2.4 Labor Market Adjustment

The process through which the labor market operates in this economy is as follows. Available workers first queue up to seek employment in the primary segment of the labor market. Firms in the primary market determine the real efficiency wage and hire randomly from the queue—since labor is homogeneous, firms treat workers symmetrically—up to the point where their demand for labor is satisfied. Although workers who cannot find a job in the traded goods sector could apply for work in the nontraded goods sector, reallocation of the labor force cannot occur instantaneously—as a result, for instance, of large relocation or congestion costs. Imperfect labor mobility implies, therefore, that the distribution of the work force across sectors is predetermined at any moment in time, and that unemployment will emerge, in equilibrium, in the traded goods sector of the economy.

Formally, let $\bar{L}$ be total labor supply in the economy. The equilibrium condition that equates supply and demand for workers in the secondary market is given by

$$\bar{L} - L_T^s(t) = L_N^d[z_t \omega_N(t)], \tag{16}$$

where $L_T^s(t)$ denotes the supply of labor in the traded goods sector. For a given value of the real exchange rate, Equation (16) can be solved for the equilibrium value of $\omega_N(t)$:

$$\omega_N(t) = \omega_N[\bar{z}_t, \overset{+}{L_T^s}(t)]. \tag{17}$$

A real depreciation lowers the real wage in the nontraded goods sector (measured in terms of traded goods) because on impact a real depreciation raises the product wage in that sector, exerting a negative effect on labor demand, which puts downward pressure on the market-clearing wage. An increase in the size of the labor force in the traded goods sector raises the real wage in the nontraded goods sector, since it lowers the effective supply of labor in the secondary segment of the labor market.

The mechanism through which workers migrate across sectors follows the formulation of Harris and Todaro (1970) and relates movements of labor to the expected differential between sectoral wages (see Chapter 2). The expected wage in the traded goods sector is equal to the going wage weighted by the probability of being hired. Since hiring is random, this probability can be approximated by the prevailing employment ratio. The expected wage in the nontraded goods sector is simply the going wage, since the probability of finding employment is unity in that sector. Thus, the supply of labor in the traded goods sector evolves over time according to

$$\dot{L}_T^s(t) = \kappa \left[\frac{\omega_T(t) L_T^d(t)}{L_T^s(t)} - \omega_N(t) \right], \quad \kappa > 0, \tag{18}$$

where κ denotes the speed of adjustment.

17.3 Government Spending, Real Wages, and Employment

Before we examine the short- and long-run properties of the model, we will express it in a more compact form. Substituting the market-clearing wage from Equation (17) in the equilibrium condition of the nontraded goods market (Equation (14)) yields

$$\mathbb{Q}_N[z_t \omega_N(z_t, L_T^s(t))] \equiv q_N[\bar{z}_t, \bar{L}_T^s(t)] = c_N(z_t, b_t) + g_N, \tag{19}$$

from which it can be established that the net effect of a real depreciation on output of nontraded goods is negative.

Solving Equation (19) yields the equilibrium solution for the real exchange rate:

$$z_t = z[\bar{b}_t, \bar{L}_T^s(t); \bar{g}_N]. \tag{20}$$

An increase in the stock of bonds raises private spending on nontraded goods, and requires an appreciation of the real exchange rate to maintain equilibrium. An increase in government spending on nontraded goods has a similar effect. An increase in labor supply in the traded goods sector raises the real wage in the nontraded goods sector, dampening production, and requiring again a real appreciation to eliminate excess demand for nontraded goods.

Substituting the market-clearing wage (Equation (17)) in Equation (7) and using (20) yields the supply function of traded goods:

$$Q_T^s(t) = q_T[\bar{b}_t, \bar{L}_T^s(t); \bar{g}_N],\qquad(21)$$

which indicates that an increase in the stock of foreign bonds, or an increase in public spending on nontraded goods, by inducing a real appreciation, raises the real wage in the nontraded goods sector and reduces output of traded goods. An increase in labor supply in the traded goods sector also has an adverse effect on output of traded goods, as a result of its indirect, negative effect on output of nontraded goods and the real exchange rate, as well as through its direct effect on wages in the secondary segment of the labor market.

Substituting Equations (11), (12), (14), (15), (20), and (21) in Equation (13) yields

$$\dot{b}_t = i^* b_t + q_T[b_t, L_T^s(t); g_N] - c_T[\overset{+}{b}_t, \overset{+}{L}_T^s(t); \overset{+}{g}_N],\qquad(22)$$

which determines the rate of accumulation of foreign bonds.

Finally, substituting the wage premium equation (5), using the solution of the market-clearing wage as a function of the real exchange rate (Equation (17)), and substituting out the equilibrium solution (20) in (18) yields

$$\dot{L}_T^s(t) = \kappa L_T[\bar{\omega}_N(t)] = \kappa L_T[\bar{b}_t, \bar{L}_T^s(t); \bar{g}_N].\qquad(23)$$

An increase in $\omega_N(t)$ raises the return on working in the nontraded goods sector. At the same time, it raises the efficiency wage in the traded goods sector, lowers employment in that sector, and thus reduces the probability of being employed in the primary segment of the market, given the size of the labor force. Thus, the net effect of an increase in the wage in the nontraded goods sector on expected earnings in alternative employment opportunities is unambiguously negative.

Equations (22) and (23) determine the behavior of foreign assets and the size of the work force in the traded goods sector over time, while Equation (20) determines the equilibrium level of the real exchange rate. A linear approximation around the steady state to Equations (22) and (23) yields

$$\begin{bmatrix} \dot{b}_t \\ \dot{L}_T^s(t) \end{bmatrix} = \begin{bmatrix} a_{11} & a_{12} \\ \kappa(\partial L_T/\partial b) & \kappa(\partial L_T/\partial L_T^s) \end{bmatrix} \begin{bmatrix} b_t - \tilde{b} \\ L_T^s(t) - \tilde{L}_T^s \end{bmatrix},\qquad(24)$$

where $\tilde{b}$ and $\tilde{L}_T^s < \bar{L}$ denote the steady-state solutions of the system, and the coefficients a_{11} and a_{12} are given by

$$a_{11} = i^* + \left(\frac{\partial q_T}{\partial b}\right) - \left(\frac{\partial c_T}{\partial b}\right) < 0, \qquad a_{12} = \left(\frac{\partial q_T}{\partial L_T^s}\right) - \left(\frac{\partial c_T}{\partial L_T^s}\right) < 0,$$

where we have assumed that i^* is small enough.

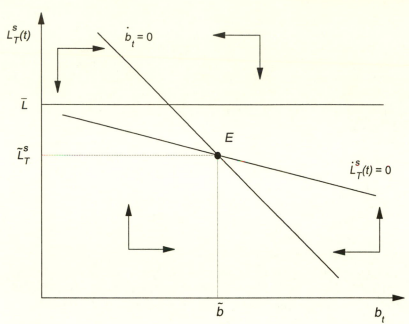

Figure 17.3   Steady-State Equilibrium with Relative Wage Rigidity

The system described by (24) is globally stable if the determinant of the coefficient matrix is positive, and if its trace is negative. While the second condition always holds, the first requires a restriction that can be interpreted graphically. The locus $[\dot{b}_t = 0]$ in Figure 17.3 gives the combinations $(b_t, L_T^s(t))$ for which the stock of foreign assets remains constant, while the locus $[\dot{L}_T^s(t) = 0]$ depicts the combinations of b_t and $L_T^s(t)$ for which labor supply in the traded goods sector does not change over time. The stability condition requires, as shown in the figure, that the $[\dot{b}_t = 0]$ curve be steeper than the $[\dot{L}_T^s(t) = 0]$ curve. The steady-state equilibrium obtains at point E.

Equations (5) and (18) imply that the steady-state unemployment rate in the traded goods sector, $\tilde{u}_T$, is given by

$$\tilde{u}_T = (\delta - 1)/\delta > 0, \tag{25}$$

which indicates that, since $\delta > 1$, the long-run unemployment rate does not depend on aggregate demand policies and is always positive.

Consider now a permanent reduction at $t = 0$ in government spending on nontraded goods. Using Equations (22) and (23), it can be shown that the reduction in g_N has in general an ambiguous effect on the steady-state values of the labor force in the traded goods sector, as well as the stock of foreign bonds. Figure 17.4 illustrates the case where the change in g_N raises

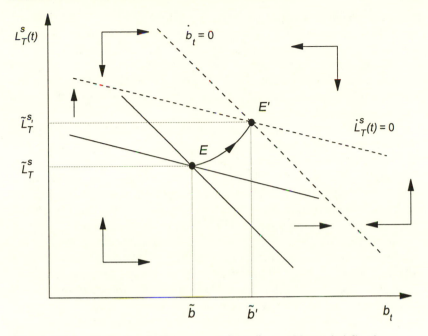

Figure 17.4 Reduction in Government Spending on Nontraded Goods

both variables in the long run. Assuming that the economy is initially located in a steady-state equilibrium (at point E), the adjustment process takes the economy monotonically toward point E'. During the transition, the real exchange rate appreciates, and real wages in both sectors rise continuously. Unemployment may or may not increase in the short run. But it must increase (fall) during the transition if it falls (rises) initially, since its steady-state value does not change.

17.4 Labor Heterogeneity, Minimum Wages and Unemployment

The analysis of segmented labor markets developed above has been extended in several directions by Agénor and Aizenman (1994). They examine the implications of fiscal and labor market policies on output, wages, and unemployment in a general equilibrium model of a small, open developing economy with a large informal sector, a heterogeneous work force, and labor market segmentation—induced not only by firms' optimizing behavior (as emphasized in the foregoing discussion) but also as a result of labor market legislation. The production structure assumes that while production in the formal sector consists of traded goods and uses skilled and unskilled labor, output in the informal sector consists solely of nontraded goods and is produced using only unskilled labor. In a manner similar to that described above, firms in the formal sector set the wage rate for skilled labor so as to minimize labor cost per efficiency unit. Skilled workers' effort depends positively on their wage relative to the wage paid in the informal sector, which measures the opportunity cost of effort. Unskilled workers employed in the formal sector earn a legally fixed minimum wage, while wages of unskilled workers in the informal sector are fully flexible. In equilibrium, as a result of efficiency considerations, a noncompetitive wage differential emerges across skill categories.

Under the assumption of perfect labor mobility across sectors, Agénor and Aizenman show that a permanent, unanticipated reduction in government spending on nontraded goods leads in the long run to a depreciation of the real exchange rate, a fall in the market-clearing wage for unskilled labor, an increase in the production of traded goods, and a lower stock of net foreign assets held by the private sector. A permanent, unanticipated reduction in the minimum wage for unskilled workers is also shown to increase output and the demand for labor in the formal sector. Hence, in a two-sector economy in which the minimum wage is binding only in the formal sector and wages in one segment of the labor market are competitively determined, efficiency wage considerations do not appear to alter the neoclassical presumption: a reduction in the minimum wage improves competitiveness and expands the formal sector at the expense of the informal sector.

Agénor and Aizenman also consider the implications of direct income taxation and unemployment benefits for skilled workers in the formal sector. They begin by assuming that the unemployment benefit scheme consists of paying a constant real wage to the unemployed and show that, under fairly general conditions, an "unemployment Laffer curve" relating the minimum wage and the income tax rate emerges. If the economy operates on the "correct" portion of the Laffer curve, a reduction in the level of unemployment compensation raises the level of employment of skilled workers—thus leading to an expansion of the relative size of the formal sector. If, alternatively, the unemployment benefit scheme is assumed to link the level of compensation to the minimum wage for unskilled workers and the after-tax wage for skilled workers, a reduction in the unemployment benefit rate is also likely to lead to an expansion of output, effort, and employment in the formal sector—at a rate proportional to the difference between the increase in effort and the fall in the premium associated with skilled workers' wage.

Finally, Agénor and Aizenman consider the case where unskilled workers face a decision to migrate from the informal sector to the formal sector. They derive the incentive structure on the basis of which workers form their decision along the lines of the Harris-Todaro mechanism described earlier. The analysis suggests that, in the long run, the unemployment rate of unskilled workers (measured in terms of the total work force with low qualifications) varies inversely with the market-clearing wage for unskilled labor, but that a change in the minimum wage for unskilled labor in the formal sector has an ambiguous effect. An important prediction of the analysis is the absence of a strong correlation between output fluctuations and unemployment in the short run, if the speed of labor reallocation across sectors is relatively high. As noted in Chapter 2, this prediction appears to be consistent with the available evidence for developing countries.

The purpose of this chapter has been to examine the implications of efficiency considerations and imperfect labor mobility for the short-run dynamics associated with macroeconomic policy shocks. Given the almost complete absence of empirical evidence on these issues in developing countries, the approach we followed was essentially conceptual. After presenting a simple graphical analysis showing the role of labor mobility and partial wage rigidity in the adjustment of the labor market, we developed a two-sector model of a small open economy with segmented labor markets. The model assumes that while firms in the traded goods sector determine both wages and employment, wages in the nontraded goods sector are determined by the equilibrium condition between supply and demand. In addition, labor productivity in the traded goods sector was taken to depend on the attractiveness of opportunities— measured by real wages—that workers face inside and outside the sector. The equilibrium solution of the model indicated that firms in the traded goods sector always set the real wage above the level that prevails in the nontraded goods sector. Even in the face of persistent sectoral unemployment, firms in the traded goods sector would not reduce wages because to do so would reduce productivity. We examined the short- and long-run effect of a permanent reduction in government expenditure on output, employment, and wages. The analysis showed that, in particular, the long-run level of unemployment in the traded goods sector cannot be altered by aggregate demand policies.

We then considered briefly several additional issues that arise in the analysis of segmented labor markets. We examined, in particular, the case of an economy with a large informal sector, a heterogeneous work force, minimum wage legislation, and unemployment benefits. Beyond the specific results discussed here, a general lesson can be derived from the analysis. The issues of labor market segmentation (resulting either from firms' optimizing behavior or legally imposed wage restrictions, as discussed above, or from the existence of trade unions) and sectoral labor mobility deserve careful attention in discussions related to short-run macroeconomic adjustment in developing countries. Shocks that lead to labor reallocation across sectors and large changes in wage dispersion may have important aggregate effects that should be accounted for in the design of macroeconomic programs. Identifying the alternative opportunities available to workers is also essential for understanding the interactions between different segments of the labor market and the ultimate effects of macroeconomic policy shocks on employment and the unemployment rate.

Epilogue

THE PAST two decades have witnessed the development of a variety of analytical approaches aimed at understanding better the macroeconomic issues faced by developing countries. This book has attempted to provide a coherent presentation of some of these developments. Although in many regards the principles, methods, and models used in the recent literature apply to both developed and developing nations, the main theme throughout the book is that structural differences between the two groups of countries require focusing on different behavioral features of private agents, and may change altogether the way development macroeconomists should approach particular issues. Of course, structural characteristics are not immutable; features deemed important from a macroeconomic point of view today may be less relevant tomorrow. As liberalization and structural reforms continue in developing countries, some of the issues discussed in this book may be less relevant in a few years. However, development is hardly a linear process. Understanding the distortionary effects of government-induced restrictions, for instance, remains a worthy endeavor, since it may allow policymakers to better appreciate the costs of policy reversals. Rather than summarizing the policy lessons drawn in the previous chapters, we present in this epilogue some final reflections and suggestions for future research in development macroeconomics.

Although our treatment of macroeconomic issues has often been relatively technical, the policy relevance of the models discussed in the previous chapters has been repeatedly emphasized. This has led, at times, to the use of models with postulated behavioral functions, although we have tried in several instances—particularly in our discussion of the dynamics of monetary and exchange-rate rules—to provide explicit microfoundations for these functions. The search for "first principles" is far from being of a purely academic and aesthetic nature; using functional forms with a shaky microeconomic basis may not only invalidate the analytical predictions of the model, but may also lead to incorrect policy advice. For instance, in our discussion of models of speculative attacks and balance-of-payments crises, it appeared that it is not only the elasticity of money demand that determines the shape and effects of such crises, but also the degree of intertemporal substitution—a phenomenon that is hard to isolate without a model with proper microfoundations. Likewise, in our discussion of the boom-recession cycle associated with exchange-rate-based stabilization programs, we indicated that the predictions obtained with arbitrary demand functions and those derived from an optimizing framework are substantially different.

The use of dynamic optimizing models with explicit microeconomic foundations is likely to become the standard methodological approach in development macroeconomics—as is already the case in industrial country macroeconomics. Modeling choices and analytical tractability may well impose restrictions on the specification of these models, conditioning to some extent the outcomes. An essential requirement, however, is to go beyond representative agent models and account for heterogeneity across agents. For instance, liquidity-constrained agents do not behave in the same way as agents that do not face such constraints. Thus, an important challenge to development macroeconomists today is to model not only market imperfections and institutional idiosyncracies of actual economies, but also heterogeneities across agents, in order to enhance the usefulness of their analysis to policymakers.

Beyond this general methodological point, there are several areas, some of which have been discussed to some extent in the previous chapters, that warrant further investigation. In particular, the issues discussed in the last part of the book raise important theoretical and empirical questions that remain unanswered. For instance, although our discussion of macroeconomic adjustment with segmented labor markets accounted for important features of developing economies (the heterogeneity of the labor force and the existence of a large informal sector), we considered only a situation where labor mobility across skill categories was hampered by a variety of costs (notably, relocation or congestion costs). An important issue on which little was said relates to the mechanisms through which workers acquire skills over time. Likewise, the role of the informal financial sector—in particular, the role of informal credit markets—has been largely neglected in the "new growth" theories, but may represent an essential element for understanding the growth process in developing countries.

We have examined in various places the links between politics and macroeconomics. We argued that the interactions among political factors, the behavior of economic agents, and the setting of policy instruments played a crucial role in the determination of the degree of credibility of stabilization programs, and we presented some evidence on the effects of electoral cycles on the behavior of domestic credit and government spending in some developing countries. Similarly, we have shown how the setting of exchange-rate policy may respond to the incumbent government's concern with its reelection prospects. Yet much more analytical and empirical work is needed in this area. For instance, the decision to impose price controls, which is difficult to justify on the basis of purely economic arguments, is probably very responsive to policymakers' desire to secure their positions in office or improve the likelihood that they will be reelected. Understanding the political motivations of policymakers is essential for formulating sustainable macroeconomic adjustment programs.

Another area that has been discussed in much detail relates to the role of distributional issues and their effect on macroeconomic outcomes in the short and medium term.[1] Our discussion of the new structuralist model of inflation has helped to emphasize the important role that such considerations may play in the design of a disinflation program. Any shift in relative prices is bound to affect profitability and the distribution of income across sectors and economic groups. Resistance to these changes by various groups in society may exacerbate social conflicts and political instability, affecting the outcome of policy reforms. A meaningful analysis of distributional issues requires relaxing the assumption of representative agents that underlies most of the optimizing models presented in this book. Here again, progress requires focusing on the modeling of heterogeneities across agents.

There are also issues that have not been discussed at all in this book, such as the role of stock markets in the transmission mechanism of macroeconomic shocks. The phenomenal growth of these markets in several developing countries over the past few years, particularly in Asia and Latin America, raises important questions for the conduct of monetary policy, domestic financial reform, and the choice of an exchange-rate regime.[2] Being forward looking in nature, these markets are likely to play an important role in the transmission of actual and future policy changes, similar to that played by informal financial markets.

Finally, we have refrained from discussing issues pertaining to reforming socialist countries of Eastern Europe and the former Soviet Union. In many regards, these countries have common structural features with developing countries. In other regards, however, there are important structural differences that must be taken into account in discussing macroeconomic policy. After all, this is precisely the view that we adopted at the introduction to this book in arguing that macroeconomic analysis of developing countries is different from standard industrial country macroeconomics. For instance, the particular relation between firms and commercial banks in socialist economies in transition—a legacy of the communist regimes—alters substantially the nature of the debate on the conduct of monetary policy. Although many of the policy lessons derived in the previous chapters may appear to be applicable to these countries, a deeper attempt at integrating their particular features may invalidate some of these propositions.

Despite our emphasis on the analytical basis of macroeconomic policy, we have attempted to review the available empirical evidence on a large number of issues. Although considerable progress has been achieved in the past few years, the empirical literature is still far from satisfactory in several key areas. For instance, the empirical evidence on the dynamics of real and nominal wages (particularly in the context of disinflation programs) remains limited. Isolating and measuring the effects of political factors on the setting of macroeconomic policy instruments has also not commanded the attention it deserves. Techniques for assessing the credibility of macro-economic reform programs are not well advanced, although some progress has recently been registered in this area. Recent developments in econometrics have provided a large array of new methods for empirical analysis, and their continuous application to the macroeconomic problems faced by developing countries is an essential aspect of future research in this area. The interaction between theoretical constructs and empirical results is, as in most other areas of economics, a key element for future progress.

Applying theoretical results to real-world settings is a difficult task and requires taking carefully into account individual-country circumstances. Experience suggests that this somewhat obvious point cannot be stressed too much. Proponents of economic reform who ignore structural and institutional constraints can do so only at the cost of repeated failures. Our hope is that the analytical elements provided in this book will assist policymakers and their advisors in designing more sensible macroeconomic adjustment programs.

Notes

Introduction and Overview

1. Many of the issues that were raised at the time are still the focus of considerable interest among economists and are discussed in various parts of this book.

2. For instance, two of the most popular textbooks in the field of economic development, those of Gillis et al. (1992) and Todaro (1994), devote only a few pages to short-run macroeconomic issues.

3. To a large extent, this is also the case for recent books attempting to focus on development macroeconomics, such as Cook and Kirkpatrick (1990) and Ross (1991). Although some of these books provide ample factual information on developing economies, from an analytical point of view they hardly go beyond simple open-economy models developed for an industrial-country setting.

4. The recent literature in macroeconomics has recognized the shortcomings of this approach and the need to introduce two or more kinds of agents, such as liquidity-constrained versus non-liquidity-constrained agents. See Kirman (1992), who argues that representative-agent models provide only "pseudo microfoundations" to macroeconomic behavioral equations, Greenwald and Stiglitz (1987) and Stiglitz (1992).

Chapter 1
Scope of Development Macroeconomics

1. Actually, although high inflation is more prevalent in developing nations than among industrial countries, it has been much more common in Latin America than in other parts of the developing world.

2. See Kay (1989) for a discussion of the historical background of the structuralist school.

3. A similar list of common characteristics of structuralist models is offered by Lustig (1992).

4. The role of distributional conflict in fostering macroeconomic instability has indeed recently begun to be emphasized in the growth literature. See, for example, Persson and Tabellini (1994).

5. This group consists of the major industrial countries. Its members are Canada, France, Germany, Italy, Japan, the United Kingdom, and the United States.

6. In 1971 the share of such primary commodities in the exports of low- and middle-income countries amounted to about three-fourths. Both figures are from the World Bank (1993).

7. There is, however, continuous debate on whether there has been a secular deterioration in primary-commodity prices relative to prices of manufactured goods—the so-called Prebisch-Singer thesis. For alternative views on this issue, see Bleaney and Greenaway (1993b), Cuddington (1992), and Reinhart and Wickham (1994).

8. See Cavallo (1981) and van Wijnbergen (1985) for evidence on the empirical importance of the costs of financing working capital in Argentina and Korea, respectively.

9. Recently, however, it is a surge in capital inflows that has complicated the conduct of macroeconomic policy in many Latin American countries, as well as several Asian nations.

Chapter 2
Aggregate Accounts, Production, and Market Structure

1. Of course, in many macromodels it is desirable to disaggregate deposits into demand and time deposits, since demand functions for these assets differ in general. For the purpose at hand, though, this distinction is unimportant, since both types of deposits are assets of the private nonfinancial sector and liabilities of the banking system.

2. We shall assume that there is a fixed stock of these, given by $\bar{H}$, so that whereas the price of such hedges can vary over time, their quantity cannot.

3. Note that financial saving does not include the acquisition of inflation hedges. This is because their stock is fixed and they are held only by the nonfinancial private sector, so they cannot be acquired from agents outside the sector.

4. To avoid cumbersome double subscripts, time subscripts on interest rates have been omitted.

5. L_t^{bg} denotes *net* credit to the public sector from the central bank. As such, it is the sum of public sector bonds held by the central bank plus bank credit in the form of, say, overdrafts, minus public sector deposits.

6. The minus sign is introduced here because we shall adopt, for uniformity, the convention that the symbol F denotes a net claim on the rest of the world.

7. A detailed discussion of quasi-fiscal deficits is provided in Chapter 4.

8. See Mundell (1963) and Fleming (1962). The Mundell-Fleming model is presented in all standard texts on open-economy macroeconomics. For a particularly thorough description, see Frenkel and Razin (1987).

9. See Dornbusch (1980) for a description of the Mundell-Fleming model under flexible exchange rates.

10. That is, if $x_t = x(z_t, \ldots)$ and $m_t = m(z_t, a_t, \ldots)$ represent the behavior of real exports and real imports, respectively, so that $b_t = x_t - z_t m_t$, assuming $b_z > 0$ requires, at an initial value of $b_t = 0$, that $\eta_{xz} + \eta_{mz} - 1 > 0$, where η_{xz} and η_{mz} are elasticities.

11. Given the solution for z_t, Equation (39) determines the real wage in terms of importables, ω_t.

12. The magnitude of the shift is given by $dz_t/d\omega_t = -z_t/(\omega_t + b_z)$, so the proportional shift is $(dz_t/d\omega_t)(\omega_t/z_t) = -\omega_t/(\omega_t + b_z)$.

13. For a given value of ω_t, there is a unique value of z_t that satisfies Equation (39), so this equation holds only at a single point along KK, say at F. Along KK to the northwest of F labor demand falls short of labor supply, and to the southeast of F labor demand exceeds supply.

14. As with the previous model, real absorption is taken as exogenous here for expository purposes. For a fully specified dependent-economy model, see Buiter (1988).

15. Both slopes are calculated around initial values $z_t = \omega_t = 1$.

16. The term "Dutch disease" arose out of concern about deindustrialization in the Netherlands as a result of North Sea oil discoveries. A comprehensive survey of the literature on this issue is provided by Corden (1984).

17. See, for instance, Edwards (1988), who emphasizes the role of labor reallocation across sectors.

18. In some countries, the formal sector is not entirely confined to urban areas; wage earners bound by explicit contracts may also be employed in agriculture.

19. Rosenzweig (1988) suggests that the proportion of the labor force in wage employment is positively correlated with the urbanization rate, the size of the public sector, and the share of manufacturing, construction, and mining in aggregate output.

20. Most estimates are derived from labor force surveys and, less frequently, general censuses of population. The International Labor Office, from which most of the data discussed here were obtained, has devoted considerable effort to establishing adequate measures of unemployment in developing countries.

21. Labor unions, for instance, have long been viewed as the main culprits in explanations of wage rigidity in Latin America. The recent wave of institutional reforms in some countries—most notably Argentina, Chile, and Mexico—has greatly reduced their bargaining power and ability to impose wage settlements on employers.

22. See Blanchard and Fischer (1989, pp. 523–25). Carmichael et al. (1985) provide a detailed discussion of wage indexation rules in an open-economy context. Most of the analytical literature assumes the existence of ex ante indexation. In practice, wage indexation is generally ex post, with the current wage adjusting to past changes in prices. Fischer (1988) examines the role of ex post wage indexation in the conduct of disinflation programs.

23. For instance, the theory of "inertial inflation" developed by Arida and Lara-Resende (1985) ascribes inflation inertia to contract indexation.

24. Condon et al. (1990) and Corbo (1985a) estimate a standard Phillips curve, which relates the rate of growth of nominal wages to output deviations from trend (a measure of the excess demand for labor) and the expected inflation rate. The evidence in favor of Phillips curve relationships in developing countries is, however, relatively scarce. See Nugent and Glezakos (1982) for an early discussion.

25. There is now a voluminous literature on developed countries that views involuntary unemployment as the result of efficiency wages. See Blanchard and Fischer (1989) and Layard et al. (1991).

26. The discussion on informal credit and foreign-currency markets here is based to a large extent on Agénor (1992) and Montiel et al. (1993), to which the reader is referred for more details.

27. High informal interest rates tend to reflect the informational advantage of moneylenders and the limited alternatives available to borrowers, but they do not necessarily include pure rents that accrue to moneylenders. See Montiel et al. (1993, pp. 22–25).

28. Trade restrictions may have been the critical factor in low-income countries, while capital controls may have been the predominant cause in middle-income countries. There is, however, no firm empirical evidence to support this conjecture.

29. The imposition of a tariff itself creates incentives for smuggling but does not create incentives for the emergence of a parallel currency market (Bhagwati and Hansen, 1973). Such a market will usually emerge only if foreign exchange controls are in place. But in the particular case where the sale or purchase of legal foreign exchange requires legal trade, the existence of a positive tariff will be sufficient to induce both illegal trade activities and foreign-currency transactions (Pitt, 1984). For a general-equilibrium analysis of the interactions between parallel markets in goods and foreign exchange, see Agénor (1995b) and Azam and Besley (1989).

30. Capital controls in developing countries have been justified with a variety of arguments. As discussed in detail by Mathieson and Rojas-Suárez (1993), three important considerations have been (1) to limit the disruptive effect on trade of exchange-rate instability brought about by volatile capital movements and to prevent balance-of-payments crises, (2) to maintain a high degree of financing of domestic investment by domestic saving, and (3) to prevent an erosion of the domestic (implicit and explicit) tax base. The first consideration is discussed in Chapter 6 and the others are discussed in Chapter 5, together with the evidence on the effectiveness of capital controls in developing countries.

31. The figure also indicates that the premium has been at times substantially negative in some countries, a somewhat surprising fact since exchange restrictions in the official market relate typically to the purchase of foreign currency and not to the sale. See Montiel et al. (1993, pp. 30–31) for elaborations on this point.

32. Government officials may also allow—or be involved in—diversion of foreign exchange from the official to the parallel market in return for bribes and favors.

33. Smuggling may take place with regard to illegal or prohibited goods. Cocaine exports, for instance, are considered to account for a large share of the unofficial inflow of U.S. dollars in some Latin American countries. In Brazil, illegal trade (gold and coffee exports, in particular) is believed to account for a large share of foreign currency inflows in the parallel market.

34. The extent to which traders engage in fake invoicing is typically measured by partner country trade-data comparisons. For instance, the scale of underinvoicing of exports can be assessed by examining the ratio of exports to major partner countries, as shown by domestic data, to the corresponding imports as recorded in partner-country data. When this ratio is less than unity, the evidence points to underinvoicing of exports. Such comparisons require adjusting the trade data for transport costs, timing of transactions, and classification of transactions.

35. The welfare implications of parallel currency markets have been discussed by a variety of authors. See, for instance, Feenstra (1985) and Greenwood and Kimbrough (1987), who focus on trade-related controls. Stockman and Hernández (1988) provide a more general discussion of the welfare effects of exchange and capital controls.

Chapter 3
Behavioral Functions

1. See Deaton (1992) for an extensive review of recent research on consumption. The presentation that follows abstracts from demographic factors, such as dependency rates. Nicola Rossi (1989) develops and tests an analytical framework that

links dependency rates, consumption, and saving rates in developing countries. See also Collins (1991).

2. If allotted to the present, lifetime utility would rise by u'; if allotted to the next period, it would yield $(1 + \rho)$ units of future consumption and thus $(1 + \rho)u'(c_{t+1})$ units of future utility, worth $[(1 + \rho)/(1 + \alpha)]u'(c_{t+1})$ today.

3. As is well known, greater uncertainty need not imply higher saving in the model described here. In the presence of uncertainty, the household maximizes expected utility, and the Euler equation sets the marginal utility of current consumption equal to the *expected* value of the marginal utility of saving. The effect of uncertainty on current consumption will depend on the source of the uncertainty and the properties of the instantaneous utility function. If uncertainty concerns future income, for instance, a precautionary saving motive will exist only if marginal utility is convex (see Gersovitz, 1988).

4. Contrary results were found for a panel of ten developing countries by Schmidt-Hebbel et al. (1992), who concluded that current, rather than trend, income explained household consumption-saving decisions for these countries. Other results in the same study, however, were consistent with consumption-smoothing behavior.

5. In addition, both Gan and Soon (1994) and Zuehlke and Payne (1989)—whose study focuses on Brazil, India, Korea, and Mexico—reject the rational expectations version of the permanent income hypothesis, which in recent years has been popular in industrial countries (see Abel, 1990).

6. However, this evidence is not unambiguous. The direction of causality between saving rates and per-capita income growth may run either way. Moreover, if life-cycle saving accounts for these results, then in fast-growing countries the age-consumption profile should be relatively more tilted toward the young than in slow-growing countries. Yet, as Deaton (1989) shows, this does not appear to have been the case in a sample of several developing countries for which such data were available.

7. Veidyanathan (1993), using a group of almost sixty countries and annual data covering three decades, also finds that consumers in the developing world are subject to liquidity and borrowing constraints.

8. See Chapter 14. The case for liberalization does not rest only on this argument, however, since whether saving increases or not, liberalization may affect the efficiency with which a given level of saving is allocated among potential investment opportunities.

9. A recent survey is provided by Balassa (1990); for a review of the early evidence, see Mikesell and Zinser (1973). Empirical work on saving behavior in developing countries, and particularly on the relation between saving and interest rates, has been handicapped by severe limitations of data. Saving data, as a rule, are calculated as a residual item, either by taking the difference between gross national product and consumption expenditure or by subtracting the current account deficit (less net factor income from abroad) from gross domestic investment. In either case, the data on aggregate saving can be subject to substantial measurement errors. Furthermore, since nominal interest rates are often regulated, they tend to exhibit little or no variation for extended periods.

10. Such findings are not limited to Asia. McDonald (1983), using time series data, found negative interest rate effects on consumption in ten of twelve Latin

American countries, while Leite and Makonen (1986) derived similar results for six African countries. In both cases estimated interest effects were small.

11. See, for instance, the models described in Chapter 12.

12. See Bleaney and Greenaway (1993a), and Servén and Solimano (1993a). As discussed in Chapter 13, the collapse of investment was particularly marked in the highly indebted countries of Latin America.

13. Servén and Solimano (1993b) provide an overview of specification issues that arise in the formulation of investment functions in developing nations.

14. The relationships between investment, the real cost of capital, and the real exchange rate are also analyzed by Cardoso (1993) and Faini and de Melo (1992). This issue is further examined in Chapter 7, in the context of our review of the contractionary effects of devaluation.

15. See, for instance, Sachs (1989a). Borensztein (1990) has argued, however, that credit rationing on international capital markets may have a more detrimental effect on domestic investment than the debt overhang, even in highly indebted countries.

16. To the extent that public sector projects are financed through concessional foreign lending, of course, the resources available to the private sector are not reduced.

17. Alesina and Tabellini (1989), for instance, have examined analytically the effect of political uncertainty on investment and capital flight in developing countries. Their analysis shows that the possibility of electing a government prone to tax capital and productive activities leads to a substitution of productive domestic investments in favor of consumption and capital flight, leading to a reduction of domestic output.

18. The investment rule in the presence of irreversibility and uncertainty requires that expected profits be no less than the user cost of capital plus the opportunity cost of exercising the option to invest. This option has value because by delaying the decision, the investor can choose not to invest in future states of nature where it has become apparent that profits will be low; the expected future return from the investment therefore tends to be higher with delay than without. The option has no value if investment decisions can be reversed, since divestment can take place in low-profit states.

19. That is, whether the firm is monopolistically or perfectly competitive, or whether it faces a binding sales constraint.

20. Sundararajan and Thakur (1980) found the coefficient of the public sector capital stock in the private investment equation to be statistically insignificant in both of the countries (India and Korea) they studied. The coefficient measuring the relationship between public and private investment was statistically significant only in one country (Greece) out of the five studied by Wai and Wong (1982).

21. The complementarity between public and private investment has important implications for growth and employment when adjustment measures aimed at reducing the fiscal deficit take the form of severe cuts in public expenditure on infrastructure. Buffie (1992) has argued that this link may explain the protracted recession that has been associated with adjustment programs in highly indebted Latin American countries, in the aftermath of the debt crisis.

22. The evidence is not highly supportive, because such effects are attributed to insolvency, not to a large debt stock as such (see Chapter 13).

23. Some early studies attempted to use a proxy for the market-clearing interest rate. Wong (1977), for instance, used an index of credit restraint, defined as the natural logarithm of the ratio of domestic credit to output.

24. As shown by Goldfeld and Sichel (1990), an equation like (8) can be derived as the solution of an optimization problem in which agents minimize the loss resulting from a disequilibrium between actual and desired money balances, given the existence of adjustment costs. We assume here that the adjustment of the demand for money toward its equilibrium value occurs in real rather than nominal terms.

25. Goldfeld and Sichel (1990) provide a comprehensive review of econometric issues that arise in the estimation of money demand models.

26. Another implication of recent techniques is that they clarify the conditions under which the practice of renormalizing the money demand function using the inflation rate as the dependent variable, determined by the excess growth of nominal balances over real money demand, is a valid procedure (see, for instance, Darrat and Arize, 1990).

27. The term "dollarization" is also used in many Latin American countries. As suggested by Calvo and Végh (1992), this term should be taken to refer to the use of foreign currency as a unit of account and store of value, whereas "currency substitution" should be used to refer to a stage where, beyond dollarization, foreign money is also used as a medium of exchange.

28. An additional factor that may help explain the increase in currency substitution relates to technological advances in communication and financial management, which have substantially reduced the cost of transferring funds across country borders.

29. Poloz (1986) has developed an analytical framework in which currency substitution emerges as the result of a precautionary motive for holding cash balances.

30. See Dodsworth et al. (1987) for an early discussion of the evolution of domestic foreign-currency bank deposits in developing countries.

31. These data are defined as "cross-border bank deposits of nonbanks by residence of depositor" and are derived from reports on the geographic distribution of the foreign assets and liabilities of deposit banks prepared by the authorities of a large number of international banking centers.

32. We will discuss in the following chapters the implications of dollarization and currency substitution for fiscal, monetary, and exchange-rate management in developing countries.

33. Note that a switch from foreign-currency deposits held in the domestic banking system to deposits held abroad would also have an adverse effect on domestic credit and other macroeconomic variables in the short run and the long run. Rodríguez (1993) discusses the macroeconomic effects associated with a change in the location of foreign deposits.

34. For a detailed list of references, see Agénor and Khan (1992), Calvo and Végh (1992), and Giovannini and Turtleboom (1994), who also discuss the evidence pertaining to industrial countries.

35. Phylaktis and Taylor do not find strong evidence in favor of currency substitution. This result is not particularly surprising, since their sample consists only of high-inflation countries. In such conditions the dominant factor in the determination of money demand is often just the expected inflation rate, which may be highly correlated with exchange-rate movements.

36. Agénor and Lennblad (1992) derive Equation (9) explicitly from an optimizing framework; see also Rogers (1990). An alternative specification is used by Márquez (1987), who directly specifies a constant elasticity of substitution utility function in domestic and foreign money balances.

37. A more recent study based on cointegration techniques was done by Kamin and Ericsson (1993), who attempt to explain why the degree of dollarization in Argentina has not fallen during the early 1990s, despite a drastic reduction in inflation.

38. The importance of accounting for U.S. dollars in circulation in studies of currency substitution is illustrated by the commonly held view that up to 80 percent of the stock of U.S. bank notes could be circulating outside the United States.

39. Agénor and Khan (1992) also compare the forward-looking model with a conventional, partial adjustment model. Comparison of the alternative models is performed on the basis of tests on properties of residuals, forecasting capabilities, and nonnested tests. The results indicate that the forward-looking rational-expectations model outperforms the standard currency substitution model.

40. Hoover (1988) provides a particularly lucid review of the debate on policy ineffectiveness. For a critical evaluation of the rational-expectations hypothesis, see Pesaran (1988). It should be noted that despite some well-known conceptual shortcomings of the Muthian concept of rational expectations, it has been widely adopted and used in contemporary macroeconomics.

41. He argued that a reasonable rule of thumb based on his results was that 10 percent of unanticipated money growth caused a 1 percent deviation of output from trend.

42. Cozier (1986) provides another study that focuses on a more diversified group of countries. His analysis is based on a model of a completely specialized economy, producing one good for export and importing all consumption goods—assumptions that, as discussed in Chapter 2, are fairly restrictive.

43. This point is demonstrated by Montiel (1991a), who uses a framework that extends the "dependent-economy" model developed by Blejer and Fernández (1980).

44. The evidence discussed in Chapter 5 indeed suggests that international capital mobility, although not perfect, may be quite high in many developing countries.

Chapter 4
Fiscal Deficits, Public Solvency, and the Macroeconomy

1. We thus focus on the stabilization aspects of fiscal policy and public finance, and abstract from allocative and distributional issues (see Goode, 1984).

2. Our presentation of the balance sheet of the public sector abstracts from assets such as natural resources and publicly owned capital—components that may, in practice, be important in some countries. Buiter (1983) has argued that the exclusion of such assets and liabilities may give a misleading estimate of the government's net worth, as well as its present and future financial constraints. We also exclude from public resources the cash income derived from the public sector capital stock, as well as sales of public sector assets as a source of financing of the budget deficit. Given the level of generality of our presentation, ignoring these components seems justified.

3. See also Shahin (1992).

4. The importance of nontax revenue in the Middle Eastern countries is explained largely by the importance of direct revenues from oil, while in other developing regions it results essentially from the state's involvement in industrial activities or the marketing of agricultural products.

5. For a conceptual analysis of the implications of foreign aid on fiscal policy, see Kimbrough (1986).

6. See Equation (14) of Chapter 2.

7. If we assume that only the government borrows abroad, the change in foreign reserves of the central bank is given by the balance-of-payments identity

$$\dot{R}_t = TB_t - i^*(F_t^g - R_t) + \dot{F}_t^g,$$

where TB_t denotes net exports, or the trade balance. Substituting this equation in (5) yields, with $\dot{M}_t = \dot{B}_t = 0$:

$$TB_t = P_t(g_t - \tau_t) + i_t B_t,$$

which relates the fiscal deficit and the trade balance.

8. The most general concept of public sector deficit is the change in the government's net worth, which equals the expected present value of all taxes, including seignorage revenue (to be discussed), plus the net value of current assets (including natural resources and fixed capital), less the current value of all noncontingent and contingent liabilities (Buiter, 1983). However, few attempts have been made to use this concept in practice.

9. With zero world inflation, if the economy produces only one good and purchasing power parity holds in absolute and relative terms—so that $E_t = P_t$ and $\epsilon_t = \pi_t$, where $\epsilon_t \equiv \dot{E}_t/E_t$ denotes the devaluation rate—and if uncovered interest parity holds continuously (that is, $i_t = i_t^* + \epsilon_t$), Equation (6c) simplifies to

$$d_t \equiv \tau_t - g_t - (i_t - \pi_t)\left[\left(\frac{B_t}{P_t}\right) + F_t^*\right].$$

10. An overview of measurement problems that arise in assessing the size of fiscal deficits is provided by Blejer and Cheasty (1991).

11. Implicit taxes on foreign exchange transactions are levied when exporters must surrender foreign-currency proceeds at prices lower than some importers can buy it from the central bank. The opposite also occurs frequently: central banks may subsidize certain sectors by selling foreign exchange at rates below the rate paid to exporters. In a broader economic sense, the "tax" levied or the "subsidy" provided can be measured in unit terms by the parallel market premium, when a well-functioning informal market for foreign exchange exists. As mentioned in Chapter 2 and discussed later in Chapter 14, the existence of such taxes has important implications for the unification of foreign-exchange markets.

12. Quoted by Dornbusch (1993, p. 19).

13. Many macroeconomists use the terms "seignorage" and "inflation tax" interchangeably. As shown by Equation (6'), this is a rather regrettable habit.

14. Evidence for the 1970s is presented by Cukierman, et al. (1992).

15. See Auernheimer (1974) for an explicit account of transitional effects in the determination of the optimal inflation rate.

16. See Calvo and Végh (1992) for a more detailed discussion of these issues.

17. Olivera (1967), in an attempt to provide an explanation of chronic inflation in Latin America in the 1960s, argued that as a result of fiscal lags nominal revenues are fixed in the short run, so that their real value falls with inflation. Aghevli and Khan (1978) and Dutton (1971) were also among the first economists to emphasize the tax-inflation nexus.

18. An alternative to Tanzi's formulation would be to assume that conventional taxes are given by $\text{Tax}(\pi^s) = \text{Tax}(0)e^{-n\pi^s}$.

19. In the simulations reported in Table 4.2 the inflation rate is assumed to be directly controllable by the monetary authority; that is, the feedback effect from money creation to prices is taken to be instantaneous. In practice this assumption may not be warranted and may bias the results considerably.

20. Dixit (1991) has argued that, in general, it is not only the optimal level of the inflation tax that is affected by the presence of collection lags, but the whole tax structure. In such conditions the collection costs associated with alternative, conventional taxes, rather than the revenue yielded by the different taxes, may become a critical consideration. In particular, the presence of lags may raise the excess burden of income taxes, warranting greater reliance on the inflation tax than would be the case in the absence of collection lags. See, however, Mourmouras and Tijerina (1994) for an evaluation of Dixit's conjecture.

21. Dornbusch and Fischer (1993) and Dornbusch et al. (1990) adopt the conventional view that the revenue motive does not explain high inflation in developing countries. It should be noted, however, that based on the recent evidence provided by Phylaktis and Taylor (1992, 1993) for the Taiwanese hyperinflation of 1945–49 as well as for some recent episodes of high inflation in Latin America (Argentina, Bolivia, Brazil, Chile, and Peru), the assumption that the average inflation rate that prevailed during the 1970s and 1980s was equal to the revenue-maximizing rate $1/\alpha$ cannot be rejected.

22. Along the same lines, Fishlow and Friedman (1994) have shown that a high degree of income tax evasion (which typically increases with the rate of growth of prices) will raise the inflation rate required to fund a given level of the fiscal deficit.

23. If purchasing power parity holds (so that $z_t \equiv 1$) and uncovered interest parity prevails, Equation (16) becomes

$$\frac{\dot{M}_t}{P_t y_t} + \dot{b}_t + \dot{f}_t^* = g_t - \tau_t + (\rho_t - n_t)(b_t + f_t^*),$$

where $\rho_t = i_t - \pi_t$ denotes the real interest rate. We will, however, focus in what follows on the more general formulation (16).

24. The condition $\rho_t > n_t$ is the requirement that the economy be dynamically efficient in closed-economy macroeconomics (see Blanchard and Fischer, 1989, pp. 103–4). Although the real interest rate may remain below the growth rate for substantial periods of time in fast-growing economies (such as the newly industrialized countries of Asia), this cannot be the case indefinitely.

25. See Spaventa (1987). In addition, rules that appear sustainable in a perfect-foresight world may not be feasible in a stochastic environment, as shown by Bohn (1990).

26. Anand and van Wijnbergen (1989) provide a detailed description of the methodological issues involved in deriving deficit levels that are consistent with

internal and external debt strategies, an inflation target, and alternative exchange-rate arrangements.

27. Equation (23) is derived by decomposing national saving, S_t (as defined in Chapter 2), into its private and public components, denoted by S_t^p and S_t^g, respectively, and rearranging terms.

28. See Leiderman and Blejer (1988), Haliassos and Tobin (1990), and Seater (1993) for extensive discussions of the conditions under which debt neutrality fails to hold. Barro (1989) offers a more sympathetic view.

29. The studies reviewed by Easterly and Schmidt-Hebbel (1994) are part of a large World Bank research project attempting to examine the macroeconomic implications of fiscal deficits. The countries included in the project (Argentina, Chile, Colombia, Côte d'Ivoire, Ghana, Morocco, Mexico, Pakistan, Thailand, and Zimbabwe) represent a fairly wide range of developing-country macroeconomic experiences and structural characteristics.

30. The analytical framework used by Sargent and Wallace is based on an overlapping generations model with a number of restrictive assumptions. Liviatan's formulation is more general. It should also be noted that the question addressed by Sargent and Wallace was the anticipation of a once-and-for-all increase in the level of the nominal money stock, rather than in the rate of money growth, as is done here.

31. See Fernández (1991a) for an analysis of the Sargent-Wallace monetarist arithmetic with an endogenous real interest rate.

32. Liviatan derives (26) from an explicit optimization setup. The condition $\alpha = (1 - \iota)\rho$ ensures a stationary solution for consumption. Note that the interest elasticity of real money balances is equal to unity; see Drazen (1985) for the general case.

33. The assumption that there exists an upper bound on the stock of real bonds b_T^+ that private agents are willing to hold seems to ignore that the stock of domestic debt can tend to infinity without violating the government's solvency constraint, as long as all interest income received by the public can be taxed away in a lump-sum fashion (McCallum, 1984). However, if lump-sum taxation is not feasible, bond financing of fiscal deficits and debt accumulation cannot continue indefinitely (Erbas, 1989). To the extent that private agents perceive correctly the constraints that the government faces, they will also anticipate any attempt to stabilize the level of public debt in the future.

34. However, as shown by Liviatan (1986), the constancy of real money balances on impact does not necessarily hold under more general conditions, particularly if money and real goods are either substitutes or complements, or if consumption is highly sensitive to changes in the real interest rate.

35. The assumption of a nonzero population growth rate is necessary to avoid degenerate dynamics in the present case.

36. By a chain of reasoning similar to that developed above, it can be shown that we must also have $\dot{m}_t = 0$ for $t \geq T$. Thus the second stage of the monetary experiment must correspond to a steady state.

37. See also Drazen and Helpman (1990). Kawai and Maccini use a Blanchard-Yaari framework in which households have uncertain lifetimes (see Blanchard and Fischer, 1989, pp. 115–26). Their analysis also has important implications for the correlation between deficits and real interest rates, which are discussed next.

38. As shown in the next chapter, the assumption of zero capital mobility is not well founded empirically. It is, however, a convenient simplification here and will be relaxed when we discuss stabilization policy in Chapter 9, using essentially an extension of the present framework.

39. Namely, the function is strictly concave and satisfies the Inada conditions $u'(0) \to \infty$, $u'(\infty) \to 0$. An alternative and more general specification would be to assume that the instantaneous utility function is of the constant relative risk aversion variety:

$$u(c_t) \equiv c_t^{1-\sigma}/(1 - \sigma), \quad \sigma > 0,$$

where $1/\sigma$ measures the intertemporal elasticity of substitution; see Blanchard and Fischer (1989, pp. 43–44). The case considered here is equivalent to assuming $\sigma = 1$.

40. Put differently, the representative household must purchase the gross amount $[1 + v(m_t/c_t)]c_t$ in order to consume the net amount c_t. This formulation has been used by, among others, Kimbrough (1992). Alternatively, money could be introduced directly in the utility function—as in Liviatan (1984) or Obstfeld (1985), for instance—or through a Clower-type cash-in-advance constraint, as for instance in Calvo (1986). Feenstra (1986) examines the conditions under which these approaches are equivalent to explicitly considering liquidity costs in the representative household's budget constraint.

41. See, for instance, Beavis and Dobbs (1990) for a discussion of the solution procedure for this type of optimization problem.

42. The net effect of a change in the real money stock on gross consumption is, in general, ambiguous. On the one hand, an increase in real money balances raises net consumption (by reducing the nominal interest rate), while on the other (for a given level of expenditure) it reduces transactions costs. We assume, however, that the net effect is positive.

43. Solving Equation (45) for c_t and Equation (46) for λ_t yields

$$c_t = c(\overset{+}{\rho_t}, \overset{+}{R_t}), \qquad \lambda_t = \lambda(\bar{c}_t, \bar{\rho}_t),$$

which can be combined to yield $\lambda_t = \lambda[c(\rho_t, R_t), \rho_t] \equiv h(\bar{\rho}_t, \bar{R}_t)$.

Differentiating the last Equation with respect to time and substituting it together with Equations (44c) and (50) in the resulting equation yields

$$\dot{\rho}_t = h_\rho^{-1}[\alpha - (1 - \iota)\rho_t]h(\rho_t, R_t) + h_\rho^{-1}h_R c(\overset{+}{\rho_t}, \overset{+}{R_t}) - h_\rho^{-1}h_R(\bar{y} - \bar{g}).$$

The second dynamic Equation is given by substituting Equation (51') in Equation (50).

44. The subjective probability that monetization will be used in the future is assumed exogenous in the Kawai-Maccini framework. In a different setting, Masson (1985) relates this probability to the size of the deficit relative to output.

45. This result was highlighted by new structuralist economists—see, for instance, Taylor (1983) and van Wijnbergen (1982)—in their discussion of the stagflationary effects of monetary policy. See Chapter 11 for a more detailed discussion of this issue.

46. Fischer and Easterly (1990) argue that this was the case during the 1980s in Bangladesh.

47. The assumption of Ricardian equivalence—the independence of private consumption and investment from the government's mix of borrowing and tax financing—reviewed earlier implies the absence of any relation between fiscal deficits and the current account. With debt neutrality, deficit reductions brought about through tax increases would lead to an equal reduction in private saving, leaving the current account unchanged. Likewise, permanent cuts in public spending would merely result in an equal increase in private consumption and have no effect on the current account balance. However, it was shown earlier that the evidence supporting the debt neutrality proposition is weak.

48. Intertemporal effects may also alter the impact of government spending on the real exchange rate, as shown in a more general context by Frenkel and Razin (1992, Chapter 11).

49. The results of Khan and Kumar show a positive impact of fiscal deficits on current account imbalances when the regression is run for the 1970s only, with no significant effect appearing for the 1980s. However, the stock of external debt appears to be highly significant in the 1980s. These results may reflect the fact that fiscal deficits were financed mainly by current account deficits in the 1970s, which then fueled a large buildup of external debt.

50. In addition to financing constraints, government behavior in developing countries may be subject to political constraints on expenditure and taxation options (see Chapter 16).

Chapter 5
Financial Markets, Capital Mobility, and Monetary Policy

1. Papademos and Modigliani (1983) provide a comprehensive macro-economic framework that integrates most types of assets found in the financial systems of industrial countries.

2. By contrast, the role of bank credit in corporate capital structure varies considerably across industrial countries. According to recent estimates provided by the Bank for International Settlements (*Annual Report,* June 1994), at the end of 1992, while bank credit amounted to about 30 percent of total indebtedness of private non-financial corporations in Canada and the United States, it reached 63 percent in the United Kingdom, 68 percent in Italy, 74 percent in Japan, and well above 80 percent in France and Germany.

3. Liquidity requirements specify that banks must hold specific types of government securities, in amounts proportional to their deposit liabilities, over and above required reserves.

4. See Mathieson and Rojas-Suárez (1993) for a general review of the evidence on the effectiveness of capital controls. Section 5.4 focuses on the case of developing countries.

5. Since financial repression creates an economic rent for favored borrowers, a secondary efficiency loss arises from the rent-seeking activities stimulated by the existence of such rents.

6. Bencivenga and Smith (1992) and Roubini and Sala-i-Martin (1995) examine the determination of the optimal degree of financial repression in a growth context. The latter study, however, treats inflation as a proxy for financial repression, an assumption that is not very useful for our purpose here.

7. Brock (1989) shows how the asset demand equations (1) can be derived from a simple optimization problem in which cash balances and deposits provide liquidity services that reduce transactions costs.

8. McKinnon and Mathieson (1981) discuss the case where the policymaker's objective is to minimize the inflation rate (instead of maximizing inflation tax revenue) with respect to the required reserve ratio.

9. Effective reserve ratios in Table 5.1 are calculated by subtracting line 14a in the IMF *International Financial Statistics* (*IFS*) from line 14 and dividing by the sum of lines 34 and 35, minus line 14a. Seignorage is calculated by dividing changes in line 14 by line 99b. The currency component is from line 14a divided by 99b, while the reserve component is from line $(14 - 14a)$ divided by line 99b.

10. Aizenman (1986) models capital controls in the context of a dual-exchange-rate regime under which controls generate a wedge between the exchange rates applied for current and capital account transactions. Capital controls can also be modeled as a surrender requirement on some categories of exports at a more appreciated exchange rate.

11. The interpretation of the world interest rate as a measure of the "true" cost of funds is appropriate only if the country under consideration does not face quantity rationing in international capital markets. While this assumption may be a valid one for some of the countries included in the sample considered by Giovannini and de Melo, it may not be a reliable approximation for some others.

12. In addition, Giovannini and de Melo found that there appears to be a positive relation between the rate of inflation and revenue from financial repression and capital controls.

13. This situation is referred to as one in which uncovered parity holds.

14. The "peso problem" refers to a situation in which a nonzero probability of a future parity change produces a forward discount on the domestic currency (Krasker, 1980). See also Chapter 6.

15. On ARMA and ARCH models in econometrics, see Harvey (1990).

16. Granger causality tests have also been used to gauge directly the relationship between domestic credit and foreign reserves. Kamas (1986), for instance, finds bidirectional causality between these two variables for Mexico and Venezuela—a result that suggests both successful sterilization and a significant offsetting effect.

17. It is worth noting that, in some of his more recent writings, McKinnon (1993) emphasizes the effect of interest rates on the efficiency, rather than the level, of investment. See Chapter 15 for further discussion.

18. Kapur (1976) has suggested that, in addition to raising investment in fixed capital, the increased availability of credit would provide banks with the opportunity to increase financing of working capital, a situation that can also lead to a higher growth rate. Burkett and Vogel (1992) and Mathieson (1980) provide other extensions of the McKinnon-Shaw approach that capture the dependence of firms on credit to finance their purchases or working capital.

19. For simplicity, we assume that banks do not hold excess reserves. van Wijnbergen (1983b) considers the case where banks choose between free reserves and loans depending on the inflation rate and the bank lending rate.

20. Note that excess demand in the official market materializes in the informal credit market only if the perceived costs of engaging in informal activities are not

prohibitive. As shown by Frenkel (1990) in the case of parallel currency markets, the existence of such costs can lead to a substantially different relation between excess demand in the official market and "effective" demand in the informal market. For simplicity, we abstract from these complications here.

21. Although there are three distinct assets in the system, banks' supply of credit is perfectly elastic. Thus the excess demand for deposits is identically zero, and Walras's law applies only to the two remaining assets.

22. This result would not hold if, in addition to being a function of the real informal market rate, aggregate demand was also a function of real wealth (as in the integrated model developed in Chapter 11) because of induced effects on the parallel market premium.

23. Of course, if commercial banks are not subject to reserve requirements and if the portfolio shift comes out of the informal credit market only ($h_d^C = 0$), the change in the bank deposit rate will have no effect on output. By contrast, if the central bank imposes a 100 percent reserve requirement ($\mu = 1$) on bank deposits, output will contract.

24. The model can be extended to consider also what happens when the central bank allows commercial banks to raise their lending rate, i_c. In the framework used here, lending rates have no impact on the demand for credit, since official bank credit is extended at below-market interest rates. A change in lending rates, however, changes the "scarcity rent" that accrues to firms who benefit from privileged access to the official credit market for a given level of credit. If banks can hold excess reserves, an increase in the lending rate may induce them to reduce these reserves and raise their loans to firms. This increase may have an expansionary effect.

25. Owen and Solis-Fallas (1989) have criticized the Taylor–van Wijnbergen efficiency argument, citing the existence of quasi-monopolistic structures in informal credit markets. Although this argument may be valid for low-income developing countries, it may lose some of its relevance in a semi-industrialized context. For further discussion of this point, see Kapur (1992) and Liang (1988).

26. Other attempts to integrate informal currency markets include computable general equilibrium models, the monetary approach (which highlights the role of money market disequilibriums in determining the behavior of parallel exchange rates), and models of two-tier exchange-rate systems that incorporate intermarket leakages. The last category of models yields predictions that are qualitatively similar to those derived from currency substitution models. See Montiel et al. (1993) for a more detailed discussion of these alternative approaches.

27. An increase in the parallel market premium raises the domestic price of the imported good (direct effect) but lowers the smuggling ratio, because demand falls.

28. Such models have been developed by Edwards (1989b), Kamin (1993), Kharas and Pinto (1989), Kiguel and Lizondo (1990), Lizondo (1987, 1991a), and Pinto (1989, 1991a). The analytical formulation used by Dornbusch et al. (1983) may not be adequate for countries with underdeveloped financial systems. Moreover, the process of currency substitution has gained importance in developing countries over the past few years, as discussed in Chapter 3.

29. Frenkel (1990) develops a partial equilibrium framework in which he explicitly derives the demand curve for foreign exchange in the parallel market. See also Nowak (1984).

30. An increase in the parallel market rate, given the official exchange rate, increases the share of exports channeled through the unofficial market for foreign currency via underinvoicing or smuggling, and thus increases the flow supply of foreign exchange. Conversely, import demand will fall, as will the share of imports channeled through the parallel market (as a result of overinvoicing or smuggling), which will in turn decrease the flow demand for foreign currency.

31. Kamin also shows that Nowak's (1984) result, according to which an official devaluation will be associated with an appreciation of the parallel exchange rate, depends critically on the assumption that the central bank does not accumulate foreign-currency assets.

32. The J-curve phenomenon refers to a situation in which a change in the real exchange rate (induced by an official devaluation, for instance) leads first to a deterioration of the trade balance and subsequently to a gradual improvement. A common explanation of this phenomenon is based on the view that at the time a relative price change occurs, goods in transit and under contract have already been purchased, and the completion of these transactions dominates short-term changes in the trade balance. Over time, as trade elasticities increase, the trade balance begins to improve. The evidence obtained by Bahmani-Oskooee and Malixi (1992), however, does not provide much support for J-curve effects in developing countries.

33. In addition to its impact on the propensity to underinvoice exports, an increase in the premium—without an equivalent increase in domestic prices—may generate a positive wealth effect on aggregate demand, which may cause further deterioration of the current account of the balance of payments.

34. Agénor (1994d) provides a framework that characterizes the "devaluation cycle" generated by speculative changes in the parallel market premium.

35. The analytical framework is taken from Montiel (1991b) and Montiel et al. (1993, pp. 84–108). The version of the model described in this section takes expectations as exogenous and ignores leakages from the official to the informal market for foreign exchange. A more detailed conceptual framework integrating informal markets is developed in Chapter 11.

36. In recent years, many developing countries have begun to adopt indirect, market-based monetary management procedures. Primary auctions of government and central bank securities have been conducted in Costa Rica, Indonesia, Kenya, Korea, Mexico, Pakistan, Sri Lanka, Malaysia, and the Philippines, as well as other countries. However, only Mexico has moved to genuine open-market operations in the secondary market as a key instrument of monetary policy. Most other countries continue to rely mainly on the type of direct policy tools analyzed here—with the possible exception of Malaysia, where government deposits are a key monetary policy instrument.

37. Alternatively, F_t^P could be interpreted more broadly as an asset with a flexible, market-determined domestic currency price that is traded in organized markets by well-informed agents. In this guise, it could represent gold or land, as well as foreign exchange.

38. Money (in the form of bank deposits) is assumed to be held strictly for transactions purposes, so the level of real financial wealth enters as a scale variable to satisfy adding-up constraints in the demand functions for curb market loans and foreign exchange, but not for deposits.

39. This is actually an approximation to the true present value of the subsidy, which depends on the entire stream of future interest rates and credit. This approximation is valid only under the assumption of static expectations.

40. This assumes, of course, that foreign exchange reserves do not pay interest.

41. Sales at the official rate may be inadvertent. For example, the case of "leakages" from the official to the parallel market arising from export underinvoicing or import overinvoicing can be treated as a sale of foreign exchange to the parallel market at the official rate. Models incorporating such leakages are presented in Agénor (1995b) and Bhandari and Végh (1990).

42. The model is solved under the perfect-foresight assumption in Montiel (1991b) and Montiel et al. (1993, pp. 102–8).

43. As discussed in Section 5.4, this analysis is familiar from the new structuralist literature.

44. Note that the presence of a direct McKinnon-Shaw effect of i_d on consumption would add a negative interest rate effect on aggregate demand, contributing to the ambiguity of the outcome.

45. If the foreign exchange is sold at the official rate, this will be partly offset by a positive wealth effect on the asset demand for loans due to the windfall reaped by households, rendering the effect on the informal interest rate ambiguous. If sales are at the free exchange rate, however, this effect is absent, and the loan interest rate unambiguously rises.

Chapter 6
Exchange-Rate Management I: Credibility and Crises

1. We do not examine here the practical considerations involved in assessing the appropriateness, timing, and size of a parity change. See, for instance, the contributions in Dornbusch and Helmers (1988).

2. For some countries in Table 6.2, the nature of the exchange-rate regime changed during this period. In such cases, countries are classified according to the form of arrangement that dominated the period.

3. The CFA Franc Zone consists of two separate groups of sub-Saharan African countries and the Comoros. The first group includes the seven members of the West African Monetary Union (Benin, Burkina Faso, Côte d'Ivoire, Mali, Niger, Senegal, and Togo), whose central bank (the BCEAO) has responsibility for conducting a common monetary policy. The second group consists of the six members of another common central bank, the BEAC (Cameroon, the Central African Republic, Chad, the Congo, Equatorial Guinea, and Gabon). Each of the two groups and the Comoros maintain separate currencies: the franc de la Communauté Financière Africaine for the countries of the West African Monetary Union, the franc de la Coopération Financière en Afrique Centrale for the BEAC countries, and the Comorian franc for the Comoros. The currencies of the two groups and the Comoros, however, are commonly referred to as the CFA franc.

4. For a further discussion, see Aghevli et al. (1991).

5. In addition to the reasons adduced in the previous section, some countries may have opted for more flexible arrangements in order to "disguise" the depreciation of the domestic currency, enabling governments to avoid the political costs of announced devaluations.

6. These arguments relate, in particular, to the role of exchange-rate stability in the promotion of trade flows and foreign investment. See Aghevli et al. (1991) for a recent review of the literature on the choice of an exchange-rate regime.

7. This literature has developed to a large extent from Barro and Gordon's (1983) seminal work on monetary policy, which emphasizes the interdependence between the behavior of private, forward-looking agents and centralized policymakers. In this context, credibility issues emerge because of an incentive for policymakers to pursue a strategic advantage and seek short-run gains by reneging on previously announced policies, leading to time inconsistency problems. For a survey of this literature, see Cukierman (1992).

8. Credibility issues are further discussed in Chapter 10, in the context of disinflation programs.

9. The analysis that follows draws on Agénor (1994c).

10. Without this assumption, there would be no incentive for the authorities to adjust the exchange rate. Price stickiness may result from a variety of factors. The existence of "menu costs," for instance, may prevent agents from revising nontradable prices immediately following a nominal exchange-rate adjustment.

11. Note that, in this one-period setup, the real-exchange-rate target could be expressed equivalently in *level* form; the rate of change formulation used here is simply easier to work with analytically.

12. Note that Equation (4) would not be independent of Θ if the cost of deviations from the real-exchange-rate target in the loss function (2) were quadratic. Note also that the policymaker may be concerned not only with competitiveness of the tradable sector, but also with the beneficial effects of an appreciation of the real exchange rate. For instance, a real appreciation could benefit the economy by lowering the cost of imported intermediate goods. Such concerns may be captured by adding a weight to the exchange-rate target in (2).

13. However, the government would be subject to a credibility problem, yielding as outcome the discretionary equilibrium, if it merely announces a fixed exchange rate. For the new equilibrium to emerge, the commitment must be perceived as binding. We assume that this can be achieved for the moment, and will return to this issue later.

14. However, if the effect of the demand shock on nontradable prices is large enough, the loss under precommitment can exceed that obtained under discretion, that is, $\bar{L}^g > \tilde{L}^g$.

15. For positive demand shocks, the loss under cheating will always be less than that obtained under discretion ($\ddot{L}^g < \tilde{L}^g$), whatever the value of d_N.

16. The figure assumes that $\alpha/\lambda > \delta(1 - \delta)\Phi d_N$, which ensures that $\bar{\epsilon} > 0$.

17. Note that this is an argument for a zero rate of crawl under a predetermined exchange rate, not an argument for a predetermined rate in lieu of a flexible one.

18. An increase in the degree of "openness" (as measured by a fall in δ) reduces the temptation to devalue, since it increases the effect of exchange-rate changes on overall inflation, and thus increases the punishment. The net effect on exchange-rate credibility of an increase in openness is therefore unambiguously positive.

19. A more detailed discussion of these issues is provided in Agénor (1994c).

20. In Barro's (1986) framework, reputation is explicitly defined in probabilistic terms. However, his model has the unattractive feature of involving a phase of

randomizing strategy by the policymaker. See Rogoff (1989) for a discussion of Barro's analysis.

21. However, whether these monetary zones can be considered optimal remains a controversial issue. See, for instance, Boughton (1993) for a discussion of the optimality of the CFA Franc Zone.

22. The foreign country is assumed not to face time inconsistency problems.

23. A case in point is the Bretton Woods system. The properties of monetary policy rules combining discretionary and state-contingent mechanisms have been discussed by Flood and Isard (1989).

24. Minimizing Equations (2) and (3) with $d_N = \Theta = 0$ with respect to π_N and ϵ, respectively, and substituting for π_N in the first equation yields $\epsilon = \kappa - \upsilon\epsilon^a - \Omega\pi_T^*$. Taking the conditional expectation of this equation and solving for ϵ^a yields Equation (21).

25. Strictly speaking, it is the unconditional expectation of the rate of foreign inflation (rather than $\bar{\pi}_T^*$) that determines the anticipated rate of devaluation in the purely discretionary regime. The difference, however, is small if c is large and can be abstracted from for simplicity.

26. Equation (22) is obtained by substituting Equation (21) in the equation for ϵ derived previously, $\epsilon = \kappa - \upsilon\epsilon^a - \Omega\pi_T^*$.

27. This section draws to a large extent on Agénor and Flood (1994).

28. Since capital is perfectly mobile, the stock of foreign reserves can jump discontinuously as private agents readjust their portfolios in response to current or anticipated shocks.

29. In general, the exchange-rate solution can be derived—assuming no bubbles—by using the forward expansion of Equation (30),

$$e_t = (\gamma/\alpha)\int_t^\infty e^{(t-k)/\alpha}[D_k + (1-\gamma)\bar{R} - \delta]\,dk,$$

or by using Equation (27),

$$e_t = (\gamma/\alpha)\int_t^\infty e^{(t-k)/\alpha}[D_t + (k-t)\mu + (1-\gamma)\bar{R} - \delta]\,dk,$$

which expresses the shadow floating exchange rate as the "present discounted value" of future fundamentals. Integrating this expression by parts yields Equation (36).

30. Note also that the larger the initial proportion of domestic credit in the money stock (the higher γ), the sooner the collapse. γ, however, appears in our reduced form as an artifact of log-linearization, and is used in the model mainly to convert the exogenous credit growth rate to a money supply growth rate.

31. R_t is discontinuous at time t_c. It is positive as approached from below and jumps down to its critical level $\bar{R}$ at t_c.

32. Recall that R denotes the logarithm of the stock of foreign reserves, so it is simply an accounting convention to set $\bar{R} = 0$.

33. This analysis can be easily extended to consider the case where the precollapse regime is a crawling peg arrangement. See, for instance, Connolly and Taylor (1984).

34. Note that the new fixed exchange rate, to be viable, must be greater than (that is, more depreciated) or equal to the rate that would have prevailed had there been a permanent postcrisis float.

35. As before, this is implied by the absence of arbitrage profits, which rules out anticipated discrete changes in the exchange rate.

36. The last term in Equation (41) represents a "speculative bubble" component, which was ruled out from the solution (33) by imposing the transversality condition $C = 0$. Imposing the terminal condition $\bar{e}_H = e_{t_c+T}$ now requires $C \neq 0$.

37. Formally, since $\kappa_0 = \alpha\gamma\mu$ and $\kappa_1 = 1$, these restrictions are given by

$$\bar{e} = \alpha\gamma\mu + \gamma(D_0 + \mu t_c) + C\exp(t_c/\alpha),$$
$$\bar{e}_H = \alpha\gamma\mu + \gamma[D_0 + \mu(t_c + T)] + C\exp[(t_c + T)/\alpha].$$

Direct manipulation of these equations yields the solutions for C and t_c given in Equations (42a) and (42b).

38. Note that Equations (42) yield a solution for the collapse time that is equivalent to (37) with $\bar{R} = 0$ and for $\tau \to \infty$, since $\Omega \to 0$ and $(1 - \gamma)R_0 = \bar{e}_0 - \gamma D_0$.

39. If $\bar{e}_H$ is high enough, it is possible that $t_c \leq 0$. In this case, the speculative attack occurs at the moment speculators learn that the fixed-exchange-rate cannot be defended indefinitely.

40. Other models focusing on real exchange-rate effects of an anticipated collapse include those of Claessens (1991), Connolly and Taylor (1984), and Calvo (1987a).

41. A formulation of wage contracts similar to the one proposed by Willman is used in the two-sector optimizing framework developed in Chapter 9.

42. The relation between speculative attacks and the solvency of the public sector in an economy with interest-bearing debt has also been examined by Ize and Ortíz (1987).

43. In developing countries capital controls have often been of a permanent nature; see, for instance, Edwards (1989b) for Latin American countries. Temporary controls have typically been used in industrial countries, notably in Europe.

44. There have been many applications of the stochastic model of exchange-rate crises. See, in particular, Cumby and van Wijnbergen (1989) for Argentina, and Blanco and Garber (1986), Connolly and Fernández (1987), and Goldberg (1994) for Mexico.

45. In fact, the imposition of capital controls may even "backfire" by bringing forward the collapse of the fixed exchange rate if the measure is anticipated well in advance by private agents. Similarly, foreign borrowing may precipitate an exchange-rate crisis if the associated increase in the cost of servicing the public debt raises the rate of growth of domestic credit.

Chapter 7
Exchange-Rate Management II: Contractionary Devaluation and Real-Exchange-Rate Rules

1. A good example of a country that has followed this type of rule in a more or less systematic fashion is Jordan since 1990. In Latin America, Brazil and Colombia have also adopted real-exchange-rate rules at times since the early 1960s.

2. The analysis in Section 7.1 draws heavily from Agénor (1991) and Lizondo and Montiel (1989). Section 7.2 is based on Montiel and Ostry (1991).

3. Although Equation (1) is an ad hoc specification of aggregate consumption behavior, it mimics closely the consumption behavior implied by an optimizing model—that is, one in which intertemporal utility is additively separable, the rate of time preference is constant, and instantaneous utility is of the constant relative risk aversion family.

4. Implicitly, therefore, we are assuming that the consumers' utility function is of the Cobb-Douglas form. See Chapter 9.

5. This result will continue to hold, after allowing for quantity responses on the part of imports and exports, as long as the price elasticity of demand for imports is not too large. It can readily be demonstrated in a model in which traded goods are differentiated into exportables and importables, as in Khan and Montiel (1987).

6. As explained in Chapter 4, we assume here that the government does not borrow directly from the public.

7. If such debt were in fact owed by the private sector, of course, F^g would not appear in identity (7).

8. It was argued in Chapter 3 that this is the empirically relevant case for most developing countries.

9. As indicated in Chapter 3, holdings of foreign assets by residents of several highly indebted developing countries may indeed be quite substantial.

10. The signs of the partial derivatives with respect to $w_t/\bar{E}$, $w_t/P_N(t)$, and z_t in Equations (11) assume that factors of production are complementary in the sense that an increase in the use of one factor increases the marginal productivity of the other factors.

11. As indicated in Chapter 5, the assumption of imperfect substitutability seems empirically relevant for a large number of developing countries.

12. The following analysis could equivalently be conducted in the context of the money market.

13. To derive this result, express z^a as a function of e^a and $(z_t - z^a)$ as a function of $(\bar{e} - e^a)$ in Equation (19), and assume that the condition $dz^a/de^a \leq d(z_t - z^a)/d(e - e^a)$ holds.

14. The change in w_t can be obtained by differentiating Equation (19) with respect to e^a or $(\bar{e} - e^a)$, imposing $dz^a/de^a < 1$ or $d(z_t - z^a)/d(\bar{e} - e^a) < 1$. The change in the price of traded goods is unity, whereas that for nontraded goods can be obtained from the definition of the real exchange rate, which implies, using logarithms, that $p_N(t) = \bar{e} - z_t$.

15. A negative interest rate effect on loan demand is included by analogy with the households' transactions demand for money but is not necessary for the following analysis. Both loan demand and the cost of holding loans in Equation (24) should depend on the expected *real* interest rate measured in terms of nontraded goods. Because we are treating expected inflation as exogenous, however, the expected inflation component of the real interest rate is suppressed here for notational convenience.

16. For given values of i_t, $\omega_N(t)n_N(t)$, and $z_t J_N(t)$, the smaller their elasticities with respect to the interest rate, the larger the upward displacement of the output supply curves caused by an increase in i_t. Also, larger values of the partial derivatives with respect to real labor costs and the real cost of imported inputs will magnify these upward supply shifts.

17. The working capital–supply function nexus was discussed in Chapter 5 and is further examined in Chapter 11.

18. Kamin shows, for instance, that the reduction in trade deficits that often follows devaluations is attributable to sharp increases in exports rather than decreases in imports, a result that seems to contradict the conventional "short-term elasticity pessimism" found in much of the literature. An explanation of this puzzle, based on an analysis of under-/overinvoicing of trade flows, is provided in Kamin (1993) and was discussed in Chapter 5.

19. It should be emphasized, however, that most authors have considered the case of a *nominal* devaluation rather than a *real* change in the exchange rate, as is done by Agénor. Although empirical evidence provided by Cooper (1971), Kamin (1988), Himarios (1989), and Edwards (1989b) shows that large nominal devaluations have in general been associated with a significant (and, in some cases, lasting) real-exchange-rate depreciation, in a theoretical context the distinction is crucial. The nominal exchange rate can be treated as exogenous in a fixed-parity regime, but the real exchange rate is endogenous.

20. As a consequence, the negative-output impact of an anticipated depreciation of the real exchange rate is larger, in absolute terms, than the expansionary effect of an unanticipated depreciation.

21. The reason is that, with Taylor-type wage contracts, newly negotiated wages respond to output fluctuations anticipated over the life of the contract.

22. In Equation (28), units have been chosen so that all prices are equal to unity initially.

23. The domestic inflation rate π_t can be expressed as $\epsilon_t - \delta \hat{z}_t$ under the assumption that foreign inflation is zero, where $-\delta \hat{z}_t$ measures the contribution to aggregate inflation of the rate of change of the price of nontraded goods, which represent a fraction δ of the consumption basket. Under fixed exchange rates, $\epsilon_t = 0$, and $\pi_t = -\delta \hat{z}_t$, which is also zero in the steady state with a constant real exchange rate. Under real-exchange-rate targeting, by contrast, $\hat{z}_t$ becomes zero and ϵ_t needs to be replaced by π_t in Equation (28).

24. It is assumed that the marginal propensity to save remains positive even after allowing for the loss of interest income caused by the instantaneous portfolio shift into money that is produced by an increase in household income.

25. The fact that $y_N^s{}' < 0$ can be rigorously shown by substituting into the output supply function the equilibrium real wage as a function of the terms of trade.

26. Montiel and Ostry (1992) examine how capital controls can make tight credit policy more effective in reducing inflation. The effects of other types of shocks under real-exchange-rate targeting are examined by Lizondo (1993), in a model where domestic and foreign assets are imperfect substitutes. The role of temporary policy shocks is discussed by Calvo et al. (1994), who also examine empirically the experience of Brazil, Chile, and Colombia.

Chapter 8
An Overview of Stabilization Programs

1. The role of terms-of-trade changes is evident in the frequency with which the years 1974 and 1979–80 appear in Table 8.1, particularly among oil-exporting

countries in the Middle East, Nigeria, and Indonesia. Short periods of political instability also played a role in Indonesia in 1967–68, the Philippines in 1984, El Salvador in 1986, and several other countries.

2. Analytical issues associated with stabilization are taken up in Chapters 9 and 10.

3. A description of various experiences is contained in Dornbusch and Edwards (1991). The discussion in this section is based on Dornbusch and Edwards (1990), where the particular experiences of Chile under Allende (1970–1973) and Peru under García (1986–1989) are discussed in detail. On Peru, see also Pastor (1992) and Cáceres and Paredes (1991).

4. That is, buying foreign exchange high from exporters and selling it low to importers. See Section 4.1 for a discussion of the fiscal aspects of central bank losses.

5. In fact, stabilization programs supported by the use of IMF resources have usually been of this type. Such programs have historically featured a fiscal objective and a domestic credit target, based on a projection (but not necessarily a target) for money supply growth. See Chapter 12 for a more complete discussion.

6. The Mexican episode is described in Section 8.4; for Brazil, see Kiguel and Liviatan (1988). The experience of these countries is indeed consistent with evidence on the macroeconomic effects of IMF–supported stabilization programs: the current account improves, growth slows, and effects on inflation are not clear-cut. See Goldstein and Montiel (1986), Khan (1990), and Killick et al. (1992).

7. The account in this section is based on Sachs (1986). See also Pastor (1992).

8. Sachs (1986) estimates that changes in the parallel market exchange rate accounted for as much as 90 percent of the changes in the consumer price index in the period preceding stabilization. See also Morales (1986).

9. For a review of the monetary approach to the balance of payments, see Frenkel and Mussa (1985), Kreinin and Officer (1978), and Wilford (1986).

10. The experience of the Southern Cone countries during the late 1970s has generated a voluminous interpretive literature. See Foxley (1983) and Ramos (1986) for an early overview. For more recent retrospective accounts summarizing alternative views on the Southern Cone experience, see Corbo and de Melo (1989) and Solimano (1990).

11. The account that follows is based on Hanson and de Melo (1985), as well as Corbo and de Melo (1987).

12. Public investment (associated with a major dam project) contributed to this outcome, as did the easing in 1974 and final removal in 1977 of restrictions on capital goods imports as part of the trade liberalization program.

13. The Argentine program is analyzed in Fernández (1985), on which the discussion that follows is based.

14. The Alfonsín and Sarney governments in Argentina and Brazil, respectively, had both recently replaced long-standing military regimes, and the National Unity government in Israel was formed to deal with a political crisis in the occupied territories. While the Salinas government in Mexico did not signify a discontinuity in the political structure, it clearly represented a major break with the economic policies pursued by past governments.

15. Overviews of the experience with heterodox stabilization in developing countries are provided by Knight et al. (1986) and Blejer and Cheasty (1988).

16. The exchange rate was devalued by 18 percent and gasoline prices were raised by 12 percent in the week before the program was announced.

17. This was achieved by depreciating the peso for the purposes of such contracts by a monthly rate of 29 percent in the months following the implementation of the program.

18. Deposit and lending rates were regulated. The rate on thirty-day deposits was capped at 4 percent per month, while the ceiling on the lending rate was 6 percent.

19. Chapter 10 provides a theoretical explanation for inflation persistence under price controls, based on credibility factors.

20. The latter would, of course, decrease the base for the inflation tax (see Chapter 4).

21. Unfortunately, effective indexation in Israel did not extend to the tax system, and this contributed to a collapse in real tax revenue in early 1984 as inflation accelerated. This phenomenon is emphasized by Cukierman (1988).

22. These "package deals" consisted of a series of tripartite agreements among the government, the labor federation, and employers' organizations concluded between November 1984 and July 1985. They involved price freezes and stipulated wage increases. Since the currency was devalued rapidly during that period, key relative prices were changed in the direction indicated.

23. As indicated in Table 8.10, tax receipts increased markedly during the first two quarters of 1985.

24. Reference is made to a "new" shekel because a new currency was introduced in August 1985, at the rate of 1,500 old shekels per new shekel. However, this change in currency involved nothing more than a change in numéraire.

25. In spite of the initial wage increase, the devaluation and increases in subsidized prices led to a 20 percent reduction in real wages on impact (Cukierman, 1988).

26. Liviatan (1988a) has suggested that inflation in Israel might not quite have stabilized at the OECD rate only because the shekel was pegged to the dollar, which was depreciating against the currencies of major industrial countries. Of course, this also helped to prevent real trade–weighted appreciation of the shekel.

27. Annualized rates are given in Table 8.10.

28. See Liviatan (1988a). The commodities with traditionally controlled prices included basic foodstuffs, government services, and those produced by public monopolies.

29. Real private consumption increased by 14 percent in 1986 and by a further 7 percent in 1987. Competing explanations have been offered for this phenomenon. Calvo (1987a) and Calvo and Végh (1993a) suggest that reductions in nominal interest rates stimulate the consumption of liquidity services, which are complementary to other goods and services through a cash-in-advance mechanism. Liviatan (1988a) mentions the possibility that Ricardian equivalence held in Israel, so that the increase in private consumption simply replaced public consumption. Finally, the increase in aggregate private consumption may respond to a redistribution of income within the private sector toward wage earners. See Chapter 10 for further discussion of the pattern of consumption and output in stabilization programs.

30. Of course, recording Israel's disappointing growth performance during this period does not require its attribution to the stabilization program, since many other

events were taking place in the country at the same time—notably, the Palestinian *intifada* in the occupied territories.

31. These included reductions in tax withholding designed to facilitate the indexation of tax liabilities and a shift in the tax burden on financial assets from assets that did not maintain their real values during high inflation to those that served as inflation hedges (see Blejer and Cheasty, 1988).

32. Rapid growth of the narrow money stock (M1) was expected under a successful program as the economy remonetized. However, M4 included indexed assets, the demand for which should have fallen as part of the portfolio shift to M1.

33. Modiano (1988) reports such shortages in the case of milk, meat, and new cars ocurring as early as March 1986.

34. According to Modiano (1988), automobile prices increased by 80 percent, cigarettes by up to 120 percent, and beverages by 100 percent. Public sector prices were adjusted upward as well.

35. From December 1979 to December 1982, Mexican external debt more than doubled, increasing from $40 billion to $91 billion.

Chapter 9
Inflation and Short-Run Dynamics

1. The evidence reviewed in Chapter 4 showed that in the short run the link between inflation and fiscal deficits is rather tenuous. As discussed in that chapter, in the medium term the relation appears to hold reasonably well, in part because it is less distorted by short-term changes in the financing mix and expectational effects. For some additional, direct evidence on the long-run relationship between money growth and price increases in high-inflation developing countries, see Shirvani and Wilbratte (1994).

2. To simplify the presentation, we consider throughout this section a closed economy. Extending the results to an open economy, although not a trivial matter, would not affect qualitatively the most salient conclusions derived here.

3. When the speed of adjustment of expectations is very high, the low-inflation equilibrium becomes unstable while the high-inflation equilibrium becomes stable. As noted by Bruno and Fischer (1990), if the speed of adjustment of expectations rises with the rate of inflation, both equilibria may be stable.

4. See Bruno and Fischer (1990). As shown by Lee and Ratti (1993), dual equilibria may still emerge with regard to other variables of the economy, such as the levels of real money balances, real bond holdings, and real interest rates.

5. Since $\dot{m}_t = d_t - \pi_t m_t$, seignorage is constant along the unstable path. At the stationary equilibrium where $\dot{m}_t = 0$, seignorage equals the inflation tax.

6. In turn, the initial depreciation of the exchange rate may result from an external shock, such as a deterioration in the terms of trade or a sudden increase in external debt payments. Dornbusch (1993) has argued that in Argentina in the early 1980s, for instance, deteriorating terms of trade aggravated the external debt shock and forced a depreciation of the real exchange rate.

7. Formally, the slopes of the $[\dot{P}_A(t) = 0]$ and $[\dot{Q}_I(t) = 0]$ curves are given by, respectively,

$$\left.\frac{dP_A}{dQ_I}\right|_{\dot{P}_A=0} = \frac{\delta c}{1-\delta c}, \qquad \left.\frac{dP_A}{dQ_I}\right|_{\dot{Q}_I=0} = \frac{1-(1-\delta)c}{(1-\delta)c}.$$

Calculating the determinant of the coefficient matrix given previously establishes that the relationship between the slopes indicated in the text is sufficient for global stability, since the condition on the trace of the coefficient matrix always holds.

8. In an extension of her analysis to an open economy, Cardoso (1981) argues that a devaluation of the real exchange rate has only a temporary effect on the trade balance but may generate a wage-price cycle similar to the one described here.

9. The analysis follows Parkin (1991) and Srinivasan et al. (1989). For an analysis of food subsidies and inflation in a conventional new structuralist framework, see Taylor (1979, pp. 73–83).

10. We assume in the following analysis that $s < 1 - \delta(1 - \iota)c$, to ensure that, for a given level of industrial output, a rise in the relative price of food reduces excess demand for agricultural goods.

11. If $(s - \iota)\bar{Q}_A > \kappa m_0$, stability requires that the slope of the $[\dot{m}_t = 0]$ curve be steeper than that of the $[\dot{p} = 0]$ curve.

12. Informal financial markets, which were shown in Chapters 3 and 5 to play a critical role in the transmission process of monetary policy in settings where such markets are sizable, are abstracted from here—in part because of the analytical complexities that such markets introduce (see Chapter 11). We thus omit them to retain tractability.

13. The model developed here is adapted from Agénor (1994a) and represents an extension of the model with zero capital mobility developed in Chapter 4 to analyze the relationship between fiscal deficits, policy expectations, and real interest rates.

14. The assumption that the government may finance its fiscal deficit in part by issuing bonds may not be appropriate for most developing countries (see Chapter 5). It is, however, relevant for several upper-middle-income countries of Latin American and Asia. In any case, we do not focus on bond financing here.

15. This specification has been used in a different context by Turnovsky (1985), who also provided a different rationale.

16. The stock treatment of the capital account adopted here differs substantially from the flow formulation used by various authors, such as Kiguel (1987), in nonoptimizing macroeconomic models.

17. Turnovsky (1985) discusses the restrictions that must be imposed on the rate of time preference α to ensure that steady-state consumption is stationary under perfect capital mobility, and that the real interest rate is independent of the foreign interest rate under zero capital mobility. The case where γ is large corresponds to the model used in Chapter 4 to analyze the effect of fiscal deficits on real interest rates.

18. For simplicity, we assume that the interest rate paid by the government on central bank loans is equal to the market rate of interest on domestic bonds.

19. We thus exclude the possibility that the government may borrow abroad. This assumption may be particularly adequate for the smallest developing countries, which have only limited access to international capital markets.

20. Notice that the quadratic term in Equation (21′) does not appear in (31), since it cancels out from using (28). Agénor (1994a) provides a more general treatment of the confiscation risk.

21. As in Chapter 4, although it is in general ambiguous, the net effect of a change in real money balances on gross consumption is assumed to be positive.

22. The determinant of the coefficient matrix is given by

$$\Delta \equiv \tilde{\lambda}[(i_\lambda + i_m h_\lambda)(\epsilon^h h_a \mathbb{C}_a) - i_m h_a(\epsilon^h h_\lambda + \mathbb{C}_\lambda)].$$

Since $-(\epsilon^h h_\lambda + \mathbb{C}_\lambda) > 0$ and $-(\epsilon^h h_a + \mathbb{C}_a) < 0$, the second term in the expression in brackets is always negative. Also, $h_\lambda = i_\lambda/(\gamma - i_m)$, so that $i_\lambda + i_m h_\lambda = [i_\lambda(\gamma - i_m) + i_m i_\lambda]/(\gamma - i_m) < 0$. Therefore, $\Delta < 0$.

23. Put differently, consumption falls, as shown in Equation (30), as a result of both an increase in the marginal value of wealth and a reduction in real money balances.

24. Given that the nominal credit stock grows at a predetermined rate, the solution for the level of the exchange rate obtains once the path of the real credit stock is known.

25. Turnovsky (1985) obtains qualitatively similar results.

26. The monetary approach to the balance of payments is discussed in more detail in Chapter 12.

27. Auernheimer (1987), Kiguel (1987), and Velasco (1993) also develop models in which the adjustment path depends on the prevailing policy rule. In particular, Kiguel develops a model with an endogenous real sector and imperfect capital mobility and shows how the path of the real exchange rate varies under alternative policy rules. Velasco (who assumes zero capital mobility) argues that the rise in real interest rates during the transition to the steady state determines the sustainable size of the primary (noninterest) fiscal deficit, leading to nonequivalence also in the long run.

28. All other assumptions of the one-good model—particularly regarding the structure of private portfolios—are maintained in the present framework, which follows Agénor (1994b). For simplicity and clarity, we abstract from the existence of an import-competing sector. Such an extension would, however, be useful for analyzing terms-of-trade shocks, as discussed in Chapter 2. See Khan and Montiel (1987).

29. Precise conditions for the two-stage budgeting process of the type considered here to be well defined are given in Deaton and Muellbauer (1980).

30. If firms in the nontraded goods sector maximize profits and if the production technology is characterized by constant returns to scale, "pure" mark-up pricing (that is, a constant mark-up rate) would prevail. With a more general production process, however, prices would also depend on (excess) aggregate demand for home goods, as for instance in Buffie (1985), Dornbusch (1982), and Calvo and Végh (1994). A discussion of mark-up pricing in a monopolistic competition framework is provided by Blanchard (1986).

31. There is little evidence on the degree of cyclicality of mark-up rates in developing countries. The econometric evidence seems, in fact, to support the "pure" mark-up hypothesis, with no role attached to excess demand (see, for instance, Parkin, 1991). In the following analysis we will indeed assume that ξ, although positive, is small.

32. Equations (50) and (51) are adapted from Willman (1988). The forward-looking case is conceptually close to Calvo's (1983) overlapping-contract formulation.

w_t in Equation (51) can be interpreted as the nominal wage stipulated in new contracts as well as those renewed at time t. Assuming that wage contracts are negotiated directly between producers and individual employees, w_t can be viewed as measuring the marginal cost of labor and is thus the relevant price that producers incorporate in their price-setting decisions. However, in contrast to Calvo's formulation, in which the domestic price level is a weighted average of past contract wages (and is thus predetermined at any moment in time), in the present formulation home goods prices—and therefore the real exchange rate—can jump on impact.

33. Integrating Equation (57) yields, as before, the economy's intertemporal budget constraint, which requires that the current level of foreign assets be equal to the discounted stream of the excess of domestic absorption of imported goods over future production of exports.

34. Note that in this model, if the mark-up remains constant over time (so that $\xi = 0$), the nominal wage becomes equal to the price of nontraded goods (setting $\Theta = 1$) and the real product wage in the export sector becomes equal to the inverse of the real exchange rate. One of the dynamic equations driving these variables therefore becomes redundant. In addition, the system becomes recursive: Equation (32d), say, could be solved separately for the real exchange rate, which would thus depend only on changes in the nominal devaluation rate.

35. These results are obtained under the assumption that the sensitivity of the mark-up rate to changes in excess demand for nontraded goods is relatively small, as indicated above.

36. A similar formulation is adopted by Obstfeld (1986b).

Chapter 10
Analytical Issues in Disinflation Programs

1. The role of intertemporal substitution in consumption—simply put, that agents are sensitive to changes in the relative price of consuming now rather than later—was also emphasized by Obstfeld (1985), whose contribution is discussed later.

2. Note that the relative price in Rodríguez's model is *not* the real exchange rate, since the price index P_t is a weighted average of the prices of traded and nontraded goods. However, this has no substantial effect on the results, and we will refer to z_t as the real exchange rate here.

3. In deriving Equation (9), the devaluation rate is assumed constant over time, so that, by (8), the domestic nominal interest rate is constant as well.

4. Dornbusch (1982) obtains a similar result in a model with sticky prices and rational expectations, which suggests that the assumption of adaptive expectations may not be the key element explaining the boom-recession pattern in the Rodríguez model (see the following discussion). Note that if prices are flexible, the real exchange rate can appreciate on impact, so that the initial net output effect of the reduction of the devaluation rate may be ambiguous. This is essentially the result obtained by Fischer (1986) in a model with rational expectations and staggered contracts.

5. The Calvo-Végh framework represents, in many regards, an extension of the cash-in-advance model presented by Calvo (1986). We refrain in what follows from discussing the role of currency substitution in their framework despite the

importance of this feature in many developing countries, as noted in Chapter 3. See Calvo and Végh (1993a).

6. As before, the foreign-currency price of the traded good is set to unity for simplicity.

7. Calvo's formulation has been extended to account for partial wage indexation by Ambler and Cardia (1992).

8. The household's flow budget constraint is given by

$$\dot{m}_t + \dot{b}_t^p = z_t^{-1}[y_N(t) - c_N(t)] + y_T + i^* b_t^p - \tau_t - c_T(t) - \epsilon_t m_t,$$

while the government's flow constraint is

$$\dot{m}_t - \dot{b}_t^g = \tau_t - i^* b_t^g - \epsilon_t m_t.$$

Setting $\tau_t = \epsilon_t m_t$ in the above equation yields $\dot{m}_t = \dot{b}_t^g - i^* b_t^g$. Substituting these results in the consumer's flow constraint and setting $c_N(t) = y_N(t)$ yields Equation (20).

9. From the intertemporal budget constraint and the optimality conditions, the equilibrium shadow price of wealth can be derived as a function of predetermined or exogenous variables only.

10. The assumption that output of traded goods is exogenous may appear far-fetched, given that the real exchange rate is endogenous. However, it may be justified by low trade elasticities in the short run. Endogenizing y_T would break the recursiveness of the model.

11. In the presence of currency substitution, however, a permanent reduction in the devaluation rate has a real effect on impact. As shown by Calvo and Végh (1993a), it leads to a substitution away from foreign-currency holdings and to a positive wealth effect that stimulates consumption expenditure and output. The inflation rate in home goods prices can also rise on impact. The model cannot, however, predict a subsequent recession in that case.

12. This would not be the case if the rate of time preference was assumed endogenous (regardless of whether the instantaneous utility function is separable in consumption and real money balances), as implied by Obstfeld's (1981) analysis. The increase in real money balances associated with a permanent reduction in the devaluation rate would in this case raise the level of instantaneous utility and make private agents more impatient. The increase in consumption would lead to a current account deficit.

13. In a substantially different framework that emphasizes staggered price and wage setting, Ball (1994) has also shown that under full credibility a fast disinflation (a large reduction in the rate of money growth) causes a boom rather than a recession. In Ball's model, as is the case here, the inflation rate is free to jump in spite of price level inertia.

14. In the absence of the aggregate demand effect, inflation in home goods prices would fall by the same proportion as the rate of devaluation, as occurs with a permanent shock. The overall inflation rate would also fall one-to-one with the devaluation rate.

15. While the real interest rate determines the level of aggregate demand in the Rodríguez model, it determines only its rate of growth in the formulation of Calvo and Végh (1994).

16. A limitation of existing studies attempting to estimate intertemporal elasticities of substitution is the absence of a distinction between durable and nondurable goods. This is likely to bias econometric estimates against the temporariness hypothesis.

17. Calvo and Végh (1993a) have shown that, in addition to the intertemporal channel, lower nominal interest rates—induced by a reduction in the devaluation rate—can also lead to higher consumption if households face liquidity constraints such that cash is needed to meet interest payments. Such constraints affect consumption both by further reducing the effective price of goods consumed and by lowering the consumption-based real interest rate. There is, however, no clear evidence supporting this effect.

18. This limitation of the Calvo-Végh temporariness framework is essentially similar to that highlighted by Calvo (1986) and Obstfeld (1985), in a different context.

19. In Obstfeld's analysis, the consumer's utility function belongs to the constant-relative-risk-aversion class and is defined by

$$
u(c_t, m_t) = \begin{cases} \dfrac{1}{1 - \rho}[c_t^\gamma m_t^{1-\gamma}]^{1-\rho} & \text{if } \rho < 1 \text{ or } \rho > 1 \\ \gamma \ln c_t + (1 - \gamma) \ln m_t & \text{if } \rho = 1. \end{cases}
$$

where $0 < \gamma < 1$ and the elasticity of intertemporal substitution σ is equal to $1/\rho$. This formulation implies that the intratemporal elasticity of substitution between consumption and money is equal to unity. When $\rho < 1$, consumption and money are Edgeworth-Pareto complements (that is, $u_{cm} > 0$), while when $\rho > 1$ they are substitutes ($u_{cm} < 0$).

20. This is not surprising since Roldós considers only the case where the adjustment of the devaluation rate is fully credible, or permanent.

21. A dynamic system is said to exhibit hysteresis if the steady state depends on initial conditions.

22. The fact that the steady state may depend on initial conditions in optimizing models with infinite-lived agents and a constant discount rate has not been discussed in much detail in the existing literature. In particular, its implications for the evaluation of temporary shocks have received relatively little consideration (see Turnovsky and Sen, 1991). Note that in models where the equality between the discount rate and the world interest rate is dropped (as, for instance, in Obstfeld, 1981) hysteresis would generally not emerge.

23. See Chapter 8 and Patinkin (1993). The restrictive credit stance was brought about by an increase in the discount rate and the level of reserve requirements on bank deposits, and the tightening of restrictions on short-term capital flows.

24. The link between anticipations about future policies and current policy outcomes was emphasized in Chapter 4, in our discussion of the short-term links between fiscal deficits, inflation, and the current account.

25. Since lump-sum taxes are endogenously adjusted to equilibrate the budget, there is no intrinsic rationale in the present model for justifying the use of distortionary taxation from the point of view of public finance. However, the decision to raise the income tax rate may rest on distributional considerations being pursued simultaneously with the stabilization objective, or because a tax hike is viewed as

having a "signaling" effect regarding the policymakers' commitment to reform and adjustment.

26. The variability of real interest rates may also result from uncertainty regarding the date at which the disinflation effort is expected to collapse. This result would follow from those established by Drazen and Helpman (1988, 1990).

27. The lack of policy credibility as a source of inflation persistence has been emphasized by various authors, including Blejer and Liviatan (1987), Dornbusch (1991), Sargent (1983), van Wijnbergen (1988), and Végh (1992). As discussed above, lack of credibility is also a key determinant of the short- and long-run dynamics associated with stabilization programs.

28. The formulation used in the subsequent analysis is adapted from Cukierman (1992). Similar models have been developed by Bruno (1991) and Kiguel and Liviatan (1994). Heymann and Sanguinetti (1994) consider explicitly the role of government spending and the Olivera-Tanzi effect in the determination of the optimal discretionary inflation rate.

29. It can also be shown that $L(\pi_t^D) - L(\pi_t^R) > 0$, which indicates that the rules regime is Pareto-superior to the discretionary regime.

30. In a sense, the lack of credibility results from the inability of policymakers to precommit to particular actions in response to different states of the environment. Although, in principle, fully contingent mechanisms might eliminate this source of credibility problem, in practice they are hard to formulate.

31. This assertion does not necessarily hold. In exchange-rate-based stabilization programs, as argued by Calvo and Végh (1993b) and Végh (1992), lack of credibility may translate initially into large real effects, rather than a sharp reduction in inflation.

32. See Agénor and Taylor (1993), Baxter (1985), and Rojas (1990).

33. The discussion throughout focuses on countries where policymakers must deal with high inflation, rather than hyperinflation. Kiguel and Liviatan (1992b) have argued that credibility is easier to establish in the latter case. In chronic-inflation countries, where inertial mechanisms—such as staggered contracts, and implicit or explicit indexation—are well developed, the public tends to view disinflation programs as postponable, thus reducing their credibility. By contrast, the very nature of hyperinflation often leads private agents to believe that the process is not sustainable.

34. The imposition of price controls and the appointment of a "conservative" central banker (options to be discussed further) have also been advocated as signaling mechanisms. Only the use of orthodox policy instruments for signaling purposes is considered for the present.

35. In addition, when the perceived characteristics (that is, policy preferences) of policymakers differ widely across the different "types," signaling may simply not be the optimal strategy (Andersen, 1989). Even if such characteristics are not too dissimilar, signaling in Vickers's (1986) framework may still not be optimal. This applies particularly when policymakers heavily discount future gains and do not find it worthwhile to bear the immediate costs of a sharper disinflation policy (see Chapter 6).

36. Depending on market structure, however, price controls may lead to an expansion in output in the short run, as emphasized by Helpman (1988). See the appendix to this chapter for a discussion of this result.

37. Kiguel and Liviatan (1992b), for instance, have argued that in high-inflation economies, staggered price setting is not the prime cause of persistence. In such economies, contracts are of a very short duration and are highly synchronized. Inertia, in their view, stems mainly from credibility and coordination problems.

38. By bringing the rate of inflation down quickly, price and wage controls lead to an improvement in the fiscal deficit in real terms (as a result of a reverse Olivera-Tanzi effect), adding credibility to the fiscal component of adjustment.

39. Bruno (1991) has argued that the freeze of all nominal variables, other than the exchange rate, was short-lived and that significant changes in relative prices took place only a few months after the initial shock—primarily a real wage increase and a real appreciation. Yet the authorities were successful in maintaining a lower inflation rate, suggesting that the signaling of serious intentions and precommitment by the government constituted the most important benefit of the synchronized freeze in the early stage of the stabilization effort.

40. This type of measure, however, provides only a lower bound on the dead-weight loss because it assumes that quantities produced at controlled prices are obtained by the consumers who value them most, and because it excludes the cost of resources devoted to nonprice rationing.

41. The information set up to $t - 1$ is common to the policymaker and the private sector and is assumed to include all relevant data on the policymaker's incentives and constraints.

42. In a linear-quadratic setting such as the one considered here, the optimal rule will also be linear as in (34).

43. Note that the choice of the policy rule is assumed to be made before the realization of the demand shock, although the actual level of controlled prices is set after observing v_t.

44. Note that $\pi_n(t)$ in (37a) differs from $\pi_c(t)$ in (37b) only by the last term, since demand shocks cannot be anticipated by price setters in the flexible price sector. They fully take into account the systematic component of the price controls policy, which implies that the policymaker's objective of reducing the deadweight loss creates only inflation and no real gains.

45. This result assumes that the rule followed in the commitment regime is the outcome of an optimization process. If the authorities adopt an ad hoc rule—of the type $\pi_c(t) = 0$, for instance—there will be no reason, in general, for the private sector to suspect that the authorities will depart from it, since the optimization process, from which the incentive to renege stems, has been eschewed. The outcome of this is thus unclear and may not yield any definite ranking between "commitment" and "discretionary" regimes. However, since the policymaker has chosen a policy arbitrarily, private agents will eventually realize that there is nothing preventing the choice of a different policy in an equally arbitrary way in the future.

46. As a result, $\partial(L^D - L^C)/\partial\delta < 0$. Note that, from Equations (35) and (37), under a complete freeze $\delta = 1$ and $\Phi_0 = \kappa$, so that the discretionary and commitment regimes yield the same outcome. This follows trivially from the fact that with comprehensive ceilings the inflationary bias of a discretionary regime disappears.

47. Agénor (1995a) shows, in addition, that the intensity of price controls can be chosen so as to minimize the loss associated with a discretionary monetary policy. But this results in the effective imposition of price ceilings only if the cost of

enforcing them is not too high, or if the weight attached to price distortions in the policymaker's loss function is sufficiently small.

48. The evidence presented by Cukierman (1992) suggests that there has been a substantial degree of accommodation of inflation in the behavior of central bank credit in developing countries, compared with industrial countries.

49. See, for instance, Alesina and Summers (1993) and Cukierman (1992). Central bank independence in empirical studies is measured in terms of a variety of factors, including the appointment mechanisms for the governor and the board of directors, the turnover of central bank governors, the approval mechanism for conducting monetary policy (the extent to which the central bank is free from involvement from the government or parliament), statutory requirements of the central bank regarding its basic aim and financing of the budget deficit (including whether or not interest rates are levied on deficit financing), and the existence of a ceiling on total government borrowing from the central bank.

50. See Lohmann (1992) and the discussion in Chapter 6.

51. Foreign assistance is usually contingent on a series of actions that must take place before loans are disbursed, in order to gauge the policymakers' commitment to macroeconomic reforms.

52. In principle, the cost associated with maintaining austerity over a prolonged period under a gradual approach may be as high as the short-term cost associated with a shock therapy approach if output recovers rapidly in the aftermath of stabilization. In practice, however, future benefits are often heavily discounted by private agents, in a sense forcing policymakers to focus on short-run costs.

53. Patinkin (1993), for instance, emphasizes the crucial role played by the "national-unity government" formed in September 1984 in the success of the Israeli stabilization program of 1985.

54. However, as argued by Drazen and Grilli (1993), periods of very high inflation—or, more generally, periods of severe economic crises, as emphasized by Williamson and Haggard (1994)—create incentives for the resolution of social conflict and thus facilitate the introduction of economic reforms. By contrast, policies aimed at reducing the cost of inflation (such as widespread indexation mechanisms) may raise the inflation rate and lead to delays in the adoption of reforms.

55. Obviously, if policymakers are not prepared to accept any short-term contraction in output and employment—because of, say, electoral reasons—credibility will be impossible to achieve.

56. As argued by Haggard (1991, p. 248), "Compensating losers... may prove less costly than political opposition that undermines programs." Of course, the design of the safety net program itself is important. Expenditures associated with these mechanisms should not prevent macroeconomic stabilization.

57. In a sense, attempting to establish credibility via signaling is a "razor's edge" problem: measures that are not "bold" enough will not do, but measures perceived to be excessively harsh will generate expectations of future reversals.

58. An additional factor that needs to be accounted for in discussing the choice among nominal anchors in developing countries is the existence of currency substitution. This issue is discussed at length by Calvo and Végh (1992), who suggest that the existence of a high degree of currency substitution may lead to the adoption of an exchange-rate rule.

59. As a result, the real wage tends to rise when the inflation rate is reduced—for instance, at the beginning of a disinflation program. See Simonsen (1983).

60. However, as argued by Lee and Ratti (1993), this may occur at a higher interest rate level than necessary, with a potentially adverse output effect.

61. The foregoing analysis would nevertheless remain valid as long as output prices were lowered more than input prices.

Chapter 11
Stabilization Policies with Informal Financial Markets

1. The analysis that follows draws on Agénor (1994e), who provides a more elaborate version of the model developed here.

2. The assumption that commercial banks lend only to firms engaged in the production of home goods is made for simplicity only. The analysis could be easily extended to the case where all firms borrow from commercial banks.

3. For simplicity, σ is treated as constant and $1 - \sigma$ can be interpreted as a surrender requirement on export proceeds imposed by the central bank. For models in which the leakage coefficient is endogenous, see Agénor (1995b) and Kamin (1993).

4. Rojas-Suárez (1987) models credit constraints in a conceptually similar manner. For an alternative approach, see Bruno (1979). In general, firms need working capital for the duration of the production process (including the time required to sell their final products) to finance not only labor costs but also the build-up of inventories of finished and intermediate goods, as well as raw materials.

5. Note that although firms have (limited) access to credit through commercial banks at below-market interest rates, it is the marginal cost of funds (the informal interest rate) that matters and that appears in Equation (7).

6. Assuming instead that firms hold deposits with commercial banks would not qualitatively alter the results to be derived.

7. The last two terms could have been written more simply as $-i_L(t)L_N^p(t)/\bar{E} - i_c L_N^b(t)/\bar{E}$. We chose to write them in the form (9) to make the financial repression subsidy explicit. The subsidy to creditors associated with financial repression was introduced and discussed in Chapter 5.

8. The real, rather than the nominal, interest rate should appear in (10). Our formulation simplifies considerably the presentation. We also assume that the degree of intertemporal substitution in consumption is determined by the bank deposit rate—or as shown below, the bank lending rate—although the marginal cost of funds is equal to the informal interest rate. Since our purpose is to analyze the effects of easing interest rate ceilings, this assumption captures the McKinnon-Shaw effect.

9. As indicated in Chapter 9, the allocation of consumption expenditure according to a fixed percentage rule is optimal if the underlying utility function is Cobb-Douglas.

10. If domestic and foreign currencies are perfect substitutes as means of exchange (as indicated in Equation (13a)), the expectation of a positive rate of depreciation would imply a corner solution—zero holdings of domestic currency. To exclude this case, we implicitly assume that the rate of return on foreign-currency

holdings is highly variable, enabling us to specify in a nontrivial manner the desired composition of currency balances. Agénor (1994e) provides a more general treatment.

11. Note that the income elasticity of the demand functions for interest-bearing assets is equal to zero. For simplicity, the asset demand functions are written in "absolute" form.

12. Note that the sum of the last three terms is equal to actual net interest income received by households from banks, $i_d D_t^p - i_c L_t^p$.

13. For simplicity, it is assumed that banks hold no excess reserves. The analysis could easily be extended in that direction, following, for instance, van Wijnbergen (1983a).

14. Note that, since $\mu > 0$, in general $i_d < i_c$.

15. The importance of a proper accounting of central bank net worth was emphasized in Chapter 2.

16. Assuming that wages are indexed also on home goods prices would not affect the thrust of the following analysis, but would make export volumes a function of the real exchange rate—in addition to the premium (see Agénor, 1994e). What is important here is that nominal wages do not fully reflect contemporaneous changes in *parallel* market prices—that is, the parallel exchange rate. This is typically the case in developing countries not facing a situation of hyperinflation (see Chapter 8), because formal indexation is often linked to the behavior of officially measured prices.

17. Imposing stability of the dynamic system in z and i_L associated with Equations (28) and (29)—so that an excess supply of goods leads to a real depreciation, and an excess demand for loans to a rise in the informal interest rate—ensures that the determinant of the matrix of coefficients of (28)–(29) in z and i_L is unambiguously negative. We also assume that the intertemporal effect of a change in the deposit rate is not too large.

18. This assumption is less restrictive than it appears at first. This is because the coefficient σ, which is treated as constant here, is normally a positive function of the premium, as shown by Agénor (1995b) and Kamin (1993). The evidence provided by Kamin also supports the assumption of an inverse relationship between the level of the premium and foreign reserves.

19. Thus, $\sigma y_X' + \tilde{\delta}_I \kappa(\tilde{R}/\tilde{\rho}^2) > 0$. Note that the condition given above, $(1 - \sigma)y_X' - \delta_I \kappa \tilde{F}^p < 0$, implies a lower bound on the surrender requirement rate $1 - \sigma$, given by

$$1 \geq \sigma \geq \max\left\{1 - \frac{\delta_I}{y_X'}\kappa \tilde{F}^p, 0\right\}.$$

20. In general, these solutions depend also on government spending on home goods g_N, the real stock of credit from the central bank to commercial banks $\bar{I}^{cb}$, and the reserve requirement coefficient, μ. These terms are omitted because we only focus in what follows on changes in deposit rates.

21. This type of "rationing rule" in the official market for foreign exchange has been examined in a model with parallel currency markets by Kharas and Pinto (1989).

22. The determinant of the system is $\Gamma_\rho \Phi_F - \Gamma_F \Phi_\rho < 0$, implying that the two roots are of opposite sign.

23. It is straighforward to extend the analysis to consider the effects of a preannounced increase in the official deposit rate.

24. If, on the contrary, the long-run effect of an increase in i_d on the stock of foreign cash balances were assumed positive, the parallel market premium would also jump downward on impact but would continue to fall toward the new steady state.

25. The increase in deposit rates also increases central bank income (from loans to commercial banks) and government transfers, dampening the negative wealth effect.

26. Montiel et al. (1993) provide more details on the structure of the model as well as the simulation results.

27. The assumption of Cobb-Douglas production functions is rather restrictive. As noted in Chapter 7 in our review of the contractionary devaluation controversy, a more general specification of the production technology may be important for understanding the supply-side effects of policy shocks.

28. The price index and the consumption and import behavioral equations that follow reflect the assumption that the instantaneous utility function for consumption of the private sector is of the Cobb-Douglas type.

29. Market prices of imported goods depend on the marginal cost of foreign exchange. Thus, an equation such as (A9) would hold when certain categories of goods can be imported freely at the official exchange rate, while others cannot. If all imported goods are rationed, Φ would be zero.

30. Foreign borrowing of private agents that is repatriated (as it would be) through the parallel exchange market does not affect the model, since only net private holdings of foreign-currency-denominated assets matter.

31. Note that foreign-currency holdings are valued at the parallel market exchange rate. Note also that since loans in the informal credit market are transacted between households and firms, they cancel out in the definition of private sector wealth.

32. The familiar adding-up constraints on the interest-bearing components of wealth bear on the parameters of Equations (A16) and (A18) only, and not on (A19). Consequently, in the former equations, only interest-bearing financial wealth appears as the scale variable.

33. This specification implies that the quantity of final goods imported through the official market depends on relative price changes, while the *share* of such goods in total private consumption does not.

34. Note that this formulation implies a well-defined link between the rationing scheme and the determination of the domestic price of imports.

35. As discussed in Section 11.1, the magnitude of these effects can in general be expected to be inversely related to the perceived implicit and explicit costs of engaging in illegal transactions and to the degree of enforcement of exchange restrictions. The functional form adopted here assumes that there exist rising costs associated with illegal activities (such as a higher probability of being caught). Note also that our specification implies that even if the parallel market premium is zero, the existence of an export tax would still provide an incentive to underinvoice.

36. Mansur and Whalley (1984) provide a perceptive discussion of the pros and cons of calibration versus estimation procedures, in the context of computable general equilibrium models (see Chapter 12).

37. In adopting this procedure, some key parameters were subjected to sensitivity analysis, in order to determine the robustness of observed patterns in the behavior of the model. However, sensitivity analysis cannot "prove" in any sense that the chosen parameter values are "true" values, nor that the conclusions derived are completely general. See Montiel et al. (1993) for a detailed discussion of the simulation procedure and the parameter set.

38. The nominal wage is maintained at its market-clearing, base-run level in the first three experiments, allowing us to focus on the mechanisms of transmission to the real sector other than wage flexibility as such. For the exchange-rate experiment, wages are assumed to adjust rapidly to their new equilibrium level. Finally, in the initial steady state, it is assumed that financial repression provides a net subsidy to households (rather than imposing a tax), implying that the experiments take into account the existence of a "quasi-fiscal" deficit—that is, an excess of expenditure over income in the financial public sector—a common phenomenon in many developing countries (see Chapter 4).

39. Devaluation profits are assumed to be retained by the central bank, rather than transferred to the government. Also, as mentioned earlier, wages are assumed to adjust relatively quickly—but not instantly—to their new equilibrium level. As a result, a mechanism frequently cited through which devaluation may adversely affect real output (that is, automatic wage indexation to price level movements) is absent.

40. The parallel market premium therefore falls as a result of both the devaluation of the official exchange rate and the appreciation of the free exchange rate.

Chapter 12
Models of Stabilization and Growth

1. The description of financial programming models that follows is based on Khan et al. (1990).

2. See International Monetary Fund (1987). For a review of the monetary approach, see Frenkel and Mussa (1985), Kreinin and Officer (1978), and Wilford (1986). The main prediction of the monetary approach is discussed in the appendix to this chapter.

3. For further discussion, see Khan et al. (1990).

4. Alternatively, given a target increment to output, Equation (6) can be used to derive that requisite volume of external financing $\Delta F_t - \Delta R_t$.

5. Taylor (1991, Chapter 8) develops an alternative approach. A useful survey of gap models is provided by Taylor (1994).

6. For a critical survey of the literature and references to different types of macroeconomic models for developing countries, see Montiel (1993b), on which this section is based. Econometric models for developing countries have actually generally been of two types. The text discusses what might be described as "open-economy $IS\text{-}LM$ aggregate supply" models. An entirely different class of models, termed "monetary disequilibrium" models in Montiel (1993b), is not discussed here,

because these models do not in general treat capacity growth and capital accumulation as endogenous variables. The prototype "monetary disequilibrium" model, by Khan and Knight (1981), is described in the appendix to this chapter.

7. Exceptions are rare, although many Mundell-Fleming models for developing countries do contain a traditional export sector that is effectively treated as an enclave. For applied developing-country "dependent economy" models, see Adams and Adams (1990), Haque et al. (1994), and Montiel (1993*a*).

8. See the models by Servén and Solimano (1990*b*) for Chile, Everaert et al. (1990) for Turkey, and Elbadawi and Schmidt-Hebbel (1991) for Zimbabwe.

9. See, for example, Kwack (1986), Easterly and Kongsamut (1991), and Vines and Warr (1993).

10. Note that the aggregate production function described here does not include the public capital stock as a separate argument, does not reflect phenomena required to generate "endogenous" steady-state growth (as discussed in Chapter 15), and does not permit total factor productivity to respond to current policies. There are some exceptions to the omission of the public capital stock; see, for instance, Easterly and Kongsamut (1991) and Haque et al. (1994).

11. Vial (1989) presents a survey of models of this type in use in Latin America as of the late 1980s.

12. Price equations of this form are incorporated in the econometric models developed for several Latin American and Caribbean countries by the joint UNDP/ILPES modeling project (see García, 1986). Such a specification was also estimated by Elliott et al. (1986) for Kenya, and underlies the reduced-form price equations estimated by Conway (1987) for Turkey, and by Vines and Warr (1993) for Thailand.

13. The specification of the price-wage block described here is used, for instance, in models for Korea by Elliot et al. (1986) and for Chile by Condon et al. (1990). See also the models of Chile and Venezuela described by Vial (1989).

14. There are several recent exceptions to this rule. Applied developing-country macroeconomic models using rational expectations are surveyed in Montiel (1993*b*).

15. Both Elliot et al. (1986) and Vines and Warr (1993), for example, model consumption as a function of disposable income and the lagged real money stock. Haque et al. (1990) include both interest rates and disposable income in their consumption function, but omit a wealth variable.

16. There are exceptions, however, for example, the "positive" closure of Servén and Solimano's (1990*b*) RMSM-X model for Chile derives investment as residually equal to savings.

17. Again, there are exceptions. The informal credit market plays an important role in van Wijnbergen's (1985) model for Korea, and Agénor (1990*b*) develops a macroeconometric model with a parallel market for foreign exchange and estimates it for a pooled time series–cross section sample of developing countries.

18. For recent surveys of the literature on CGE models, see Bandara (1991) and Decaluwé and Martens (1988).

19. A CGE model for Venezuela by Bourguignon et al. (1983), for example, contained sixty-five different production activities.

20. See Dewatripont and Michel (1987) for an evaluation of the role of intertemporal optimization in CGE models.

21. For a discussion of these recent models, see Robinson (1991).

22. See the references provided in Montiel (1993*b*). Other applications of the monetary disequilibrium model include Blejer (1977), Keller (1980), Lipschitz (1984), Sassanpour and Sheen (1984), and Sundararajan (1986).

Chapter 13
The Debt Overhang, Investment, and Growth

1. The link between the debt crisis, inflation, and fiscal deficits in highly in-debted countries has also been stressed by a variety of authors, including Cardoso (1992), Cardoso and Fishlow (1990), Cooper (1991), Dornbusch (1993), and Reisen (1989).

2. We present evidence on this issue in the second part of Section 13.3 (notably Table 13.7).

3. The term "safe rate of interest" refers to the rate of interest applicable to assets that are free of default risk, such as Treasury bills.

4. See Cohen (1994) for a detailed discussion of the roles of the real interest rate and the growth rate in imposing a solvency constraint on sovereign borrowers.

5. The real interest rate depicted in Figure 13.1 is the annual average of the monthly series of real *ex post* annual yields on 30-year U.S. government bonds (line 61 in the IMF's *International Financial Statistics*), deflated by the U.S. wholesale price index. The average growth rates for the HICs are from the IMF *World Economic Outlook*.

6. For the purpose of these calculations, the "equilibrium" inflation rate is taken to be the lowest sustained rate of inflation experienced by these countries during 1968–82, and the estimate of base money velocity was derived from that associated with these rates of inflation.

7. This could take the form of a once-and-for-all capital levy. The repudiation option is available only for domestic debt, of course, since the domestic government has no legal means to compel external creditors to surrender their claims.

8. See Easterly (1989), for instance.

9. Further, as discussed in Chapter 4, a number of mechanisms exist through which the yield of the inflation tax may be eroded over time.

10. In many countries, however, the acquisition of domestic debt may have been in-voluntary, in the form of required reserves held by private financial institutions. In this case, of course, the degree of fiscal "adjustment" is understated, since such reserve requirements amount to disguised taxation of the financial system (see Chapter 5).

11. The scope for effective capital controls in developing countries is open to question. The evidence discussed in Chapter 5 suggests that such controls have been largely ineffective.

12. The role of domestic debt in the analysis that follows depends on whether external debt or domestic debt is treated as senior to the other. If domestic debt were senior, then the present value of expected payments to domestic creditors would have to be subtracted from the right-hand side of Equation (4). If both types of debt were of equal seniority, then the right-hand side of (4) would be multiplied by the share of external debt in total debt. As it stands, (4) is equivalent to treating external debt as senior. To avoid the straightforward, but tiresome, consideration of each of these cases, we simply assume that domestic debt is nonexistent.

13. No attempt is made here to explain why the public sector chooses to repay—that is, why V_t is not zero. The debt literature contains extensive discussion of this issue, involving sanctions available to external creditors permitting them to appropriate a share of domestic income (see Sachs, 1984; Kletzer, 1988). It is assumed that, to the extent that such sanctions fall on the private sector, the political system ensures that they are internalized by the government.

14. As noted in Chapter 4, the observation that an increase in the stock of public sector debt implies future distortionary taxation is a common argument against Ricardian equivalence.

15. Note, in passing, that these arguments do not imply that all public debt accumulation is harmful to growth. To the extent that public borrowing finances investment that meets a market test, or is used for public consumption smoothing in response to a transitory negative income shock, the means to service the debt will be available in the future without the necessity of increasing the distortionary burden of taxation.

16. However, to attribute all of these dislocations to the "uncertainty effect" would probably be an overstatement, because it would fail to account for the possible role of the type of fiscal adjustment undertaken by the HICs after 1982. As suggested previously, the mode of fiscal adjustment may have played an independent role in generating unfavorable macroeconomic outcomes. Untangling the direct debt overhang effects on the economies of the highly indebted countries from the indirect effects transmitted through the type of fiscal adjustment remains an unfinished research task.

17. For the effects of potential taxation on capital flight from developing countries, see Dooley (1988). An analysis of the negative effects of uncertainty on private investment in developing countries is presented by Rodrik (1991); see also Chapter 3.

18. See Claessens et al. (1992) for details of the individual deals. On Mexico's deal, see also Claessens and van Wijnbergen (1993).

19. Note that, when measured in this way, an up-front payment made out of the country's own resources would have no effect on V_t, because the market value of the debt would fall by the amount of the payment. This reflects a reduction in the resources available for debt service in the future.

20. As indicated previously, the extent to which domestic financing can be viewed as the result of voluntary market transactions is unclear.

21. Such negotiations are not explained by the model. Indeed, its purpose is to evaluate the consequences of alternative values of R for both parties.

22. Recall that such creditors cannot be senior, and so would be repaid $\{\delta F(k_0 + I_1)/[(1 + \rho)D_1 + R]\}(1 + \rho)D_1 < (1 + \rho)D_1$, if (A4) is violated.

Chapter 14
Trade, Financial, and Exchange-Rate Reforms

1. This argument relies on the use of the standard neoclassical production function. The new endogenous growth literature has provided examples of production technologies, such as the "AK" function described in the next chapter, for which this argument would lose its force, because the marginal and average products of

capital are equal. However, the empirical relevance of these alternatives to the standard neoclassical specification remains an unsettled issue.

2. See also Galbis (1993), Leite and Sundararajan (1990), and Sundararajan and Baliño (1991). Galbis dubs this convergence of views the "Washington consensus," since it has emerged from the experience of the international lending institutions in promoting financial reforms.

3. See Jaffee and Stiglitz (1990) for a detailed discussion of the Stiglitz-Weiss model. In a recent extension of their analysis, Stiglitz and Weiss (1992) have shown that even if lenders can vary simultaneously collateral requirements and interest rates charged to loan applicants, credit rationing is still an equilibrium outcome in the presence of adverse selection and incentive problems.

4. This outcome would be avoided by supervision through the imposition of loan-loss reserves and capital adequacy standards, which increase the potential losses of shareholders when banks undertake risky loans.

5. Chile began its liberalization process in 1974, Argentina in 1975, and Uruguay in 1976.

6. For a discussion of the financial liberalization experience of Turkey, with particular emphasis on the role of market structure and competition in the banking industry, see Denizer (1994).

7. The need for policymakers to follow a gradual program of financial liberalization in order to limit the risk of widespread bankruptcies was emphasized by Mathieson (1980).

8. As pointed out by Cho (1986) in a discussion of the Stiglitz-Weiss model, interest rate liberalization does not completely eliminate credit rationing because at sufficiently high interest rates the additional risk may cause banks' expected profits to be lower. The problem may be compounded by the fact that firms may have no alternative opportunity to raise capital resources for investment. Hence, Cho suggests that the development of stock markets should be fostered along with the liberalization of the financial system. A potential difficulty with Cho's conclusions is that stock markets are not widely used as primary sources of capital in developing countries, just as in industrial countries (see Chapter 5). However, the recent evidence provided by the International Finance Corporation suggests that in countries such as Korea, Mexico, Thailand, and Turkey, equity funds (as a share of net investment expenditures) may have exceeded debt finance or internally generated funds during the 1980s.

9. Although, in theory, unification can also take the form of adopting a uniform fixed exchange rate at the outset or a crawling peg regime—with changes in net foreign assets clearing the official market—few developing countries have followed these options in recent years.

10. The model is based on assumptions very similar to those underlying portfolio models of informal currency markets, discussed in Chapter 2. It is developed in more detail in Agénor and Flood (1992), who also discuss the real implications of exchange-rate reforms. Agénor and Ucer (1994) analyze the case where the postreform regime is a managed floating arrangement.

11. Alternatively, the coefficient δ can be viewed as an approximation to the share of transactions settled illegally in the parallel market relative to total trade transactions. The value of δ resulting from the interpretation given in the text is likely to be closer to unity than the value obtained with this alternative view.

12. A more general model of reserve changes would involve including a positive term (Ω, say) in Equation (5), which would capture the central bank's policy regarding assignment of transactions between markets. The higher the proportion of exports—and the lower the proportion of imports—legally assigned to the official market, the higher Ω would be. Such a formulation would imply a positive premium in the steady state derived below.

13. The determinant of the coefficient matrix is $-\Phi\Theta/\alpha < 0$.

14. An increase in the interest elasticity α rotates the curves [$\dot{s}_t = 0$] and SS clockwise. An increase in $\bar{D}$ shifts the curve $\dot{s}_t = 0$ to the left and moves point E horizontally also to the left. A rise in the propensity to underinvoice Φ translates into a clockwise rotation of SS. Finally, a devaluation of the official exchange rate leads to an upward shift of the [$\dot{R}_t = 0$] curve and a rightward shift of the [$\dot{s}_t = 0$] curve. In the long run, a devaluation leads to an equiproportional depreciation of the parallel exchange rate and an increase in reserves.

15. The use of the terminal curve CC in the Agénor-Flood unification model was suggested by Lai and Chang (1994).

16. Note that here the CC curve (whose slope is equal to Θ) cannot be steeper than the [$\dot{s}_t = 0$] curve (whose slope is equal to Θ/δ), since by assumption $\delta < 1$. In the more general setup discussed by Agénor and Flood (1992), however, this possibility exists and affects the short-run dynamics of the system.

17. To show these results formally, set $T \to \infty$ in Equations (14). Similarly, setting $T \to 0$ in these equations yields $s_0 \to \epsilon_T^+$ and $R_0 \to \bar{R}_0$.

18. In the more general framework developed by Agénor and Flood (1992), the parallel exchange rate may also, during the transition period, appreciate first and then depreciate in a second phase.

19. A seemingly controversial aspect of Pinto's analysis may be his assumption of a positive premium in the steady state. This property does not emerge in the short-run model developed previously, nor does it hold in the optimizing framework developed by Bhandari and Végh (1990). However, Agénor (1995b) has shown that the Bhandari-Végh result is *not* a natural implication of optimizing models once illegal imports, in addition to underinvoicing of exports, are introduced in the analysis. Intuitively, this is because the requirement of equilibrium in the unreported current account (which determines the rate of change of foreign-currency holdings) does not necessarily imply the absence of an exchange-rate differential. The premium is, consequently, equal to zero only in particular circumstances.

20. These countries include Gambia, Ghana, Nigeria, Sierra Leone, Somalia, Zaire, and Zambia. These experiences are examined by Agénor (1992), Ghei and Kiguel (1992), Roberts (1989), and Pinto (1989, 1991b).

21. See Agénor and Ucer (1994) and Kiguel and O'Connell (1994) for a review of several of these experiences.

22. The adverse effects of import substitution policies have been well documented in the trade and development literature: an industrial structure heavily dependent on imported intermediates and capital goods, slow export growth and recurrent balance-of-payments difficulties, and severe allocative distortions. See, for instance, Bruton (1989).

23. We do not discuss here in a systematic manner the welfare implications of trade liberalization. See Edwards and van Wijnbergen (1986), Kähkönen (1987),

Rodrik (1987), and Ostry (1991). Rodrik, in particular, examines the welfare effects of trade reform in a model where, as in the framework to be developed here, price and wage rigidities lead to Keynesian unemployment.

24. Edwards (1993) has argued that the negative employment effect that has been associated with trade liberalization in Chile may have resulted from the segmented nature of the labor market, which has impeded short-run adjustment.

25. Also of interest are the recent experiences of Bangladesh, Egypt (where trade reform began in 1986), and Ghana, where reform began in 1983. In the last two countries, trade liberalization has followed a very gradual path.

26. The data shown in Table 14.2 refer only to changes in legal taxes. They underestimate the true extent of import liberalization, since they do not account for the widespread elimination of surcharges and other quantitative restrictions.

27. For details, see Alam and Rajapatirana (1993). Peru, where the real exchange rate appreciated despite a substantial depreciation of the nominal exchange rate, represents the only exception. One factor underlying the real appreciation of Peru's currency is the large inflow of capital attracted by the relatively high interest rates induced by tight monetary policy (see Pastor, 1992).

28. Obtaining the results displayed in Equations (19) requires using Shephard's lemma, according to which the cost-minimizing input demand functions are given by the partial derivatives of the cost function with respect to the relevant prices. See Buffie (1984b).

29. For a detailed discussion of the hoarding function and its use in open-economy macroeconomics, see Dornbusch and Mussa (1975) and Frenkel and Mussa (1985).

30. As shown by Buffie (1984b), the introduction of imported inputs in the non-tradables sector does not affect the qualitative nature of the analysis.

31. As argued by Edwards (1984), overnight liberalization may also be suboptimal as a result of efficiency considerations.

32. The financial reform implemented in Indonesia in the early 1980s occurred after opening of the capital account. Prudent macroeconomic management, however, prevented destabilizing effects from speculative capital flows (Hanna, 1994).

33. Brock (1984) has argued, however, that opening the capital account does not necessarily lead to a reduction in inflation tax revenue. For instance, higher reserve requirements on bank deposits held by nonresidents may help compensate for a reduction in the inflation tax base (domestic-currency holdings) induced by a higher degree of substitution between domestic and foreign currencies.

34. In turn, if capital flight negatively affects the rate of capital accumulation, capital market liberalization may have an adverse effect on welfare in the presence of increasing returns to scale in the production process (Song, 1993).

35. A comprehensive discussion of the sequencing debate in light of the experience of the Southern Cone countries is provided by Edwards (1984, 1989a). For more recent overviews, see Falvey and Kim (1992), Galbis (1994), and Hanson (1992).

36. If the country undergoing liberalization has limited access to international financial markets or if credibility in the reform process is low (because of perceptions of future policy reversals), opening the capital account may lead to capital flight rather than capital inflows, which would be limited by the increased risk of repatriation. Sustained capital outflows would lead to a depreciation of the real exchange

rate, whose effect on trade flows may not be large enough to avoid continuous reserves losses, and eventually a balance-of-payments crisis if monetary policy is not tightened (see Park, 1994). This outcome would thus inhibit the trade liberalization process. In practice, however, the more common experience in developing nations following the removal of restrictions on capital flows has been an appreciation of the real exchange rate.

37. Without a real depreciation, the surge in imports would lead to a deterioration of the current account, which may generate protracted balance-of-payments difficulties or pressure to reimpose tariffs, thus affecting the credibility of the liberalization program.

38. The econometric evidence provided by Morandé (1988, 1992) supports the view that capital inflows have been the main causal factor behind the appreciation of the Chilean Peso in the late 1970s. See also McNelis and Schmidt-Hebbel (1993).

39. See also Khan and Zahler (1983, 1985).

40. In turn, lack of credibility about the sustainability of trade reform may have an adverse effect on private saving and investment. Aizenman (1992) dicusses the signaling role that capital outlays may play in a framework where the risk of policy reversal translates into uncertainty about future tariffs.

41. Froot (1988) examines the effect of credibility factors on the optimal speed of trade reform, while Mussa (1986) discusses the role of adjustment costs on the optimal pace of liberalization.

Chapter 15
Human Capital, Financial Intermediation, and Growth

1. Among the "Four Tigers" (Hong Kong, South Korea, Singapore, and Taiwan) alone, real income per capita increased more than fourfold between 1960 and 1990.

2. The revival of growth theory can be largely attributed to the influential contributions of Lucas (1988), Grossman and Helpman (1991), and Romer (1986).

3. Barro and Sala-i-Martin (1995) provide an extensive overview of the new economics of growth.

4. Changes in the saving rate also affect the rate of growth in the short run. But in the long run, a rise in the saving rate leads only to a proportional increase in the capital/output ratio.

5. This implication of the neoclassical growth model holds regardless of whether countries are closed or open to international trade. The model also predicts that convergence may occur more rapidly if countries are open and have full access to international capital markets. The relative scarcity of capital and the lower capital/labor ratio in poor countries entails a higher rate of return to capital, leading to capital inflows, accelerated capital accumulation, and higher growth. But if a country can only borrow to finance part of its capital (for instance, if investment in human capital must be financed by domestic savings), the open-economy version of the neoclassical growth model yields essentially the same convergence rate as the closed-economy model. See Barro and Sala-i-Martin (1995).

6. Technical progress is thus assumed to be "Hicks neutral," in the sense that it raises the output achievable with a given combination of capital and labor without affecting their relative marginal products.

7. The rate of change of the quality of labor is determined as the weighted sum of the changes in the share of each characteristic considered for the composition of the labor force. The weights are the ratio of the unit wage of each kind of labor to the average wage rate for the whole labor force. A similar procedure is used to derive the rate of change of the quality component of the capital stock.

8. The neoclassical growth model predicts only "conditional" convergence, that is, a tendency for per-capita income to converge across countries only after controlling for the determinants of the steady-state level of income—production technology, and saving and population growth rates. The absence of a significant correlation between the growth rate of per-capita income and the level of income at a base period (as shown in Figure 15.1) cannot, therefore, be construed as evidence against the convergence hypothesis. In fact, recent work has found significant evidence in support for conditional convergence. See Barro and Sala-i-Martin (1994), Khan and Kumar (1993), Knight et al. (1993), and Mankiw et al. (1992).

9. A critical difference between this class of models and those based on reproducible capital is that the existence of externalities often results in suboptimality of the competitive equilibrium, creating the scope for welfare-improving government intervention. See the subsequent discussion of the Lucas model.

10. A taxonomic presentation of the alternative approaches aimed at incorporating externalities and increasing returns to scale in the growth literature is provided by Verspagen (1992). He also discusses various approaches to modeling the innovation process, among others the "quality ladder" concept of Grossman and Helpman (1991).

11. Lucas's (1988) original formulation is cast in an optimizing framework in which private agents determine their consumption path by maximizing their utility subject to an intertemporal resource constraint. The main point of his analysis, however, can be made by assuming a constant saving rate, as in Lucas (1993).

12. Lucas (1988) also develops a second model that assumes a different structure of technological change. In this alternative framework all human capital accumulation occurs through on-the-job training, or learning by doing, rather than through the time allocated by workers to this accumulation. Thus, it is the time devoted directly to production activities that determines the rate of growth.

13. The existence of knowledge externalities poses the question of whether there is an incentive to produce innovation. Romer assumes that firms or individuals engaged in the production of knowledge enjoy some degree of monopoly power (through, say, patent protection) that ensures temporary appropriability.

14. The evidence reviewed in Chapter 3 on saving in developing countries suggests that the link between interest rates and saving rates is, at best, tenuous. It is worth noting that in his more recent writings, McKinnon (1993) seems to adopt the view that the positive effect of high real interest rates on growth stems from the improved efficiency of investment, rather than higher saving rates. See also Fry (1993) and Polak (1989).

15. Alternatively, consumers' liquidity risk can be shared via a stock market. In the model developed by Greenwood and Jovanovic (1990), for instance, the stock market allows agents to reduce rate-of-return risk by fostering portfolio diversification.

16. Note that even if the rents or implicit taxes extracted by financial intermediaries and the government were spent on investment rather than consumption, the

absorption of resources may still have an adverse effect on growth—particularly if the productivity of capital in the private sector is higher than elsewhere.

17. As argued in Chapter 5, however, this assumption may not be valid since in general the inflation tax and the financial repression tax may be substitutable taxation instruments. An alternative proxy for financial repression, used by Easterly (1993), for instance, is the real interest rate, calculated using official nominal interest rates. An adequate measure of financial repression, as suggested in Chapter 5, should account for the interest rate differential between the official and the informal credit markets.

18. The assumption that households hold no money is made for simplicity only. As shown by De Gregorio, in the setup considered here households' behavior with respect to inflation has no effect on the growth rate. In fact, if only consumers faced transactions costs, the marginal productivity of capital and thus the real rate of interest would not depend on the inflation rate, and there would be no effect of inflation on growth.

19. See De Gregorio (1993) for details. To ensure positive growth, we assume that $(1 - \iota)\tilde{\rho} > \alpha$.

20. De Gregorio (1993) also develops a framework in which inflation affects the efficiency, rather than the level, of investment.

21. De Gregorio (1993) adopts the latter view. He also argues that, at least in the case of Latin America, there appears to be little correlation between financial intermediation and inflation.

22. The incremental capital/output ratio shown in Table 15.5 is defined as the change in the capital stock relative to the change in output.

23. The parallel market premium has been used in a number of studies as an indicator of structural distortions, particularly in the trade and financial areas (see, for instance, Easterly, 1993). Results are often highly significant but, as noted by Levine and Renelt, the precise channels through which the premium may affect growth are usually not specified.

24. The financial indicators used by King and Levine include the size of the formal financial sector relative to output, the importance of banks relative to the central bank, the ratio of credit allocated to firms relative to output, and the share of total credit allocated to firms.

25. The effect of public investment on private investment and growth depends also on the form of taxation used to finance it (Cashin, 1995). For instance, if capital expenditure by the public sector is financed by an increase in direct taxes and a reduction in private saving, the net effect on growth may be negative despite a positive effect on the marginal productivity of capital.

26. van Wijnbergen (1983a, 1983b) is one of the few authors who discusses the role of informal credit markets in a growth context. Obviously, his analysis did not benefit from the most recent advances in the economics of growth.

Chapter 16
The Political Economy of Stabilization and Adjustment

1. See, for instance, Alesina (1991) and Whitehead (1990). The effect of political factors on public policy decisions has long been the central issue in the "public

choice" literature, particularly in the analysis of rent-seeking behavior. The focus on macroeconomic issues is, however, more recent.

2. See Frey and Eichenberger (1994), and Roemer and Radelet (1991). The role of elections per se is examined subsequently.

3. See Bates (1990), Corden (1990), Nelson (1990), Nelson and Waterbury (1988), and Haggard and Kaufman (1989, 1990). We examined in Chapter 10 the relation between income distribution, political instability, and the credibility of stabilization programs.

4. Governments often set food prices below the "true" market price in order to subsidize urban workers, who may be politically important to the regime.

5. Nelson and Waterbury (1988) examine political factors leading to the success or failure of adjustment efforts by nineteen governments in thirteen countries in the 1980s (Argentina, Brazil, Colombia, Costa Rica, Chile, the Dominican Republic, Jamaica, Mexico, Peru, the Philippines, Ghana, Nigeria, and Zambia).

6. Edwards and Santaella (1993) provide evidence that political instability weakens a government's capacity to implement successful adjustment. See also Williamson and Haggard (1994).

7. It should be emphasized, however, that empirical correlations between political and economic instability do not establish unidirectional causality.

8. Nordhaus (1975) provides the first systematic analysis of this type of cycle. See Alesina (1991) and Nordhaus (1989) for recent surveys of this literature.

9. ρ is a backward-looking, not a forward-looking, rate of discount and corresponds to the rate at which past performance is discounted by voters.

10. From concavity, these conditions are also sufficient.

11. Technically, (6c) holds because there is no endpoint condition on the expected inflation rate. See, for instance, Beavis and Dobbs (1990, Chapter 7).

12. Note that from Equation (7a), $\dot{u}_t = -\alpha\delta_1\Theta e^{-\rho(t-T)}$. Unemployment falls, therefore, from an initial level (obtained by setting $t = 0$ in Equation (7a)) of $u_0 = (\Theta\delta_1/\rho)[\rho - \alpha + \alpha e^{\rho T}]$, to $u_T = \Theta\delta_1$. But since, from Equation (2), the natural rate (obtained by setting $\pi = \pi^a$) is given by δ_0/δ_1, the level of unemployment at the end of the electoral cycle will differ in general from the natural rate, implying instability in the inflation rate.

13. The slope of the time profile of inflation and unemployment is steeper the higher is ρ, and flattens out for $\rho \to 0$, as the incumbent gives less and less weight to the effect of future inflation on the current decision of voters.

14. It is important to keep in mind that the nature of the cycles depends critically on the structure of voters' preferences. In Nordhaus's model, rather than expanding the economy before an election, the incumbent may follow an anti-inflationary policy (that is, a restrictive fiscal policy) if inflation is perceived by voters as the most pressing economic issue. See, for instance, Neck (1991).

15. The model is, in many regards, similar to that used to examine the credibility of exchange-rate regimes in Chapter 6. For an alternative model, see van der Ploeg (1989), who emphasizes the role of J-curve effects.

16. Thus, as before, the "desired" inflation rate is assumed to be zero.

17. The requirement that the system be saddlepath stable ensures that if the length of the electoral cycle tends toward infinity, the system would evolve along a unique path toward the equilibrium values of the devaluation rate and nominal wage growth.

18. The jump in the devaluation rate is finite because of the existence of a positive cost of inflation in the aggregate voting function (parameter Θ), which implies that it would be suboptimal to induce an arbitrarily large exchange-rate adjustment at any time during the electoral cycle, as this would carry a correspondingly large cost to voters. But note that the initial downward jump is not large enough to put the economy onto the saddlepath SS. This occurs only if $T \to \infty$, in which case the economy jumps immediately to its steady-state position.

19. See also Cukierman and Meltzer (1989), who claim that the asymmetry of information between voters and the government results from imperfect monitoring of shocks affecting the economy. Terrones (1989) extends Rogoff's (1990) analysis to account for endogenous election dates.

20. Note that if there is monetary financing, an expenditure cycle will also be associated with a monetary cycle.

21. Recent theories do not, in fact, provide precise predictions regarding whether a preelectoral fiscal expansion will occur through a reduction in taxes or an increase in government outlays.

22. For instance, Ames (1987, p. 12) notes that between 1945 and 1982, administrations in Latin America ended their terms with elections in 82 instances and with military coups in 51 cases.

23. For a discussion of Latin American political systems, see Diamond and Linz (1989).

24. For industrial countries, see Alesina et al. (1993), who consider a sample of eighteen economies. They show that, although there is little evidence of preelectoral effects on output and unemployment, there is some evidence of a "political budget cycle" (or "loose" fiscal policy) prior to elections, as well as a monetary cycle.

25. A rationale for focusing on public expenditure is to assume that, because of rigidities and various lags in the tax system, tax rates cannot be adjusted instantaneously. Alternatively, it can be argued that due to a high degree of tax evasion, changes in tax rates do not have much effect on agents' behavior. In either case, tax rates cannot be manipulated for short-run electoral gains.

26. In addition to examining the hypothesis that incumbent governments respond to approaching elections by increasing real outlays, Ames also tests the assumption that newly elected governments reward their followers, and therefore increase public spending, after taking office. His attempts to establish the second assumption did not prove very successful. In fact, Ames shows that spending actually *declined* after elections—as predicted by the opportunistic model.

27. Elections occur in May every four years starting in 1970 in Colombia, and in February of the same year for Costa Rica. In Venezuela elections occur in December every five years, starting in 1973.

28. For a definition of the test statistics used in Tables 16.1 and 16.2, see Harvey (1990). In all tables, R^2 denotes the coefficient of determination, σ the estimated standard error of the regression, $\eta(4)$ the Lagrange multiplier test statistic for serial correlation in the residuals of order up to 4, and $arch(4)$ the Engle test statistic for autoregressive conditional heteroscedasticity of order up to 4. *Chow* denotes the Chow predictive failure test statistic, over the period 1989q1 to 1990q4. Numbers in parentheses denote t statistics. A "—" indicates that the parameter is zero or is not defined. Seasonal dummies were included in all regressions but are not reported.

29. Note that since the data cannot distinguish expenditure appropriations and the actual implementation of public spending decisions, an increase in expenditures may well appear to occur *after* the elections. There is, however, no such evidence here.

30. Estimation was also performed with the lagged value of *elec* and the lagged value of $\Delta \ln y$, but the results obtained were similar to those reported here.

31. Alternatively, it might be useful to consider government spending inclusive and exclusive of interest payments on the public debt. However, there is no a priori reason to believe that certain components of expenditure—such as interest payments—may not be altered, or delayed, when the government is essentially concerned with its reelection prospects.

32. For an attempt to measure government popularity in developing countries, see Karnik (1990).

33. See Alesina et al. (1993). Partisanship effects are not, however, particularly relevant when coalitional forces play an important role in the electoral process. For the three Latin American countries considered above, for instance, it is difficult to identify clear ideological shifts from "left" to "right," because of the populist tendencies of incumbent governments.

Chapter 17
Macroeconomic Adjustment with Segmented Labor Markets

1. Edwards (1988), for instance, examines the relationships between terms-of-trade disturbances, tariffs, and the labor market, under alternative assumptions about wage formation and labor mobility.

2. Demekas (1990) has provided one of the first studies attempting to examine the implications of labor market segmentation in a general equilibrium framework. The analysis that follows draws, in part, on the models developed by Agénor and Aizenman (1994) and Agénor and Santaella (1994).

3. The source of wage rigidity in the traded goods sector is deliberately left unspecified at this stage. A common rationale is the existence of a government-imposed minimum wage, which typically covers only the manufacturing sector. A different interpretation is provided in the general equilibrium model presented below.

4. As indicated in Chapter 2, the expected wage in the traded goods sector is defined as the product of the actual wage in that sector times the probability of being hired, which is measured by the employment ratio: $w_T(L_T^d/O_T\bar{L}_T)$. The equilibrium condition of the Harris-Todaro model implies, therefore, that $w_N(O_T\bar{L}_T) = w_T L_T^d$. Since L_T^d is a decreasing function of w_T in general, the preceding condition defines the rectangular hyperbola QQ. The requirement that wage rates be equal to the marginal product of labor for $w_T = w_T^c$ is met only at points A and E_N on the QQ curve.

5. This partial-equilibrium analysis abstracts from induced effects of the aggregate demand shock on relative prices, income, and wealth, and assumes that the position of the demand curve for labor in the nontraded goods sector does not change.

6. Note that the existence of unemployment in the situation depicted in panel 3 may be only a short-run phenomenon, if labor can adjust over time, so that the long-run outcome might be similar to that which obtains in panel 2.

7. There is a voluminous literature on developed countries that treats unemployment as the consequence of efficiency wages. See Haley (1990) and Layard et al. (1991). The introduction of efficiency considerations here implies that it is the wage *ratio* that remains constant over time rather than, as in the Harris-Todaro framework, the absolute wage in one sector.

8. The effort function given in Equation (2) is derived from explicit microeconomic considerations by Agénor and Aizenman (1994), taking into account shirking behavior and monitoring costs. As shown by Agénor and Santaella (1994), a relative wage equation similar to (5), which follows, would emerge in the presence of a trade union in the traded goods sector, with bargaining occuring on the level of wages.

9. We assume also for simplicity that firms in the traded goods sector observe wages in the nontraded goods sector before making their own wage decisions.

Epilogue

1. The relationship between income inequality and economic growth has been the subject of an extensive literature in development economics. Recent evidence suggests the existence of a positive correlation between growth and a reduction in income inequality (Persson and Tabellini, 1994), particularly in East Asian countries (World Bank, 1993). Larraín and Vergara (1993) suggest that investment may be the channel that links income inequality and growth. A more equitable distribution of income reduces social conflict, thus reducing uncertainty and creating a more stable environment for investment.

2. According to data compiled by the International Finance Corporation, the combined capitalization of equity markets in developing countries (the market value of the equity of firms quoted on the stock markets) rose almost tenfold between 1983 and 1993. The increase in market capitalization of traded equities was particularly marked in Latin America (Argentina, Brazil, Chile, and Mexico) and Asia (India, Korea, Malaysia, Taiwan, Thailand, and the Philippines).

References

Abel, Andrew B. 1990. "Consumption and Investment." In *Handbook of Monetary Economics*. Vol. II, edited by Benjamin Friedman and Frank H. Hahn. Amsterdam: North Holland.

Adams, Charles, and Claire Hughes Adams. 1990. *Scenario and Forecast Adjustment Model for Developing Countries*. Staff Studies for the World Economic Outlook, International Monetary Fund. Washington, D.C.: IMF.

Adams, Charles, and Daniel gros. 1986. "The Consequences of Real Exchange Rate Rules for Inflation." *IMF Staff Papers* 33 (September): 439–76.

Adelman, Irma, and Sherman Robinson. 1988. "Macroeconomic Adjustment and Income Distribution." *Journal of Development Economics* 29 (July): 23–44.

Agénor, Pierre-Richard. 1990a. "Output and Unanticipated Credit with Imported Goods and a Foreign Exchange Constraint." *Journal of Quantitative Economics* 6 (July): 367–82.

———. 1990b. "Stabilization Policies in Developing Countries with a Parallel Market for Foreign Exchange: A Formal Framework." *IMF Staff Papers* 37 (September): 560–92.

———. 1991. "Output, Devaluation, and the Real Exchange Rate in Developing Countries." *Weltwirschaftliches Archives* 127 (March): 18–41.

———. 1992. *Parallel Currency Markets in Developing Countries: Theory, Evidence, and Policy Implications*. Essay in International Finance no. 188, Princeton University.

———. 1994a. *The Behavior of Real Interest Rates in Exchange Rate-Based Stabilization Programs*. Working Paper no. 94/75, International Monetary Fund (June).

———. 1994b. "Wage Contracts, Capital Mobility and Macroeconomic Policy." Unpublished. International Monetary Fund (July).

———. 1994c. "Credibility and Exchange Rate Management in Developing Countries." *Journal of Development Economics* 45 (August): 1–16.

———. 1994d. "Exchange Restrictions and Devaluation Crises." *International Review of Economics and Finance* 3 (December): 361–72.

———. 1994e. The Macroeconomics of Informal Financial Markets. Unpublished. International Monetary Fund (December).

———. 1995a. "Credibility Effects of Price Controls in Disinflation Programs." *Journal of Macroeconomics* 17 (Winter): 161–171.

———. 1995b. "Illegal Trade, Devaluation and Exchange Rate Dynamics." *Journal of International Trade and Economic Development* 4 (March):1–15.

Agénor, Pierre-Richard, and Joshua Aizenman. 1994. *Macroeconomic Adjustment with Segmented Labor Markets*. Working Paper no. 4769, National Bureau of Economic Research (June).

Agénor, Pierre-Richard, and Robert P. Flood. 1992. "Unification of Foreign Exchange Markets." *IMF Staff Papers* 39 (December): 923–47.

———. 1994. "Macroeconomic Policy, Speculative Attacks and Balance of Payments Crises." In *The Handbook of International Macroeconomics,* edited by Frederick van der Ploeg. Oxford: Basil Blackwell.

Agénor, Pierre-Richard, and Mohsin S. Khan. 1992. *Foreign Currency Deposits and the Demand for Money in Developing Countries.* Working Paper no. 92/1. International Monetary Fund (January). (Forthcoming, *Journal of Development Economics.*)

Agénor, Pierre-Richard, and Anna Lennblad. 1992. *Inflation and Monetary Reform.* Working Paper no. 92/60, International Monetary Fund (May).

Agénor, Pierre-Richard, and Julio A. Santaella. 1994. "Efficiency Wages, Disinflation, and Labor Mobility." Unpublished. International Monetary Fund (August).

Agénor, Pierre-Richard, and Mark P. Taylor. 1993. "Analyzing Credibility in High-Inflation Economies." *Economic Journal* 103 (March): 329–36.

Agénor, Pierre-Richard, and Murat E. Ucer. 1994. "Exchange Market Reform, Inflation, and Fiscal Deficits." Unpublished. International Monetary Fund (November).

Aghevli, Bijan B. 1977. "Inflationary Finance and Growth." *Journal of Political Economy* 85 (December): 1295–309.

Aghevli, Bijan B., James M. Boughton, Peter J. Montiel, Delano Villanueva, and Geoffrey Woglom. 1990. *The Role of National Savings in the World Economy.* Occasional Paper no. 67, International Monetary Fund (March). Washington, D.C.: IMF.

Aghevli, Bijan B., and Mohsin S. Khan. 1978. "Government Deficits and the Inflationary Process in Developing Countries." *IMF Staff Papers* 25 (September): 383–416.

Aghevli, Bijan B., Mohsin S. Khan, and Peter J. Montiel. 1991. *Exchange Rate Policy in Developing Countries: Some Analytical Issues.* Occasional Paper no. 78, International Monetary Fund (March). Washington, D.C.: IMF.

Ahumada, Hildegard. 1992. "A Dynamic Model of the Demand for Currency: Argentina, 1977–1988." *Journal of Policy Modeling* 14 (June): 335–61.

Aizenman, Joshua. 1986. "On the Complementarity of Commercial Policy, Capital Controls, and Inflation Tax." *Canadian Journal of Economics* 19 (February): 114–33.

———. 1987. "Inflation, Tariffs and Tax Enforcement Costs." *Journal of International Economic Integration* 2 (Autumn): 12–28.

———. 1992. "Trade Reforms, Credibility, and Development." *Journal of Development Economics* 39 (July): 163–87.

Aizenman, Joshua, and Nancy P. Marion. 1993. "Macroeconomic Uncertainty and Private Investment." *Economics Letters* 41 (February): 207–10.

Alam, Asad, and Sarath Rajapatirana. 1993. *Trade Policy Reform in Latin America and the Caribbean in the 1980s.* PRE Working Paper no. 1104, World Bank (February).

Alam, M. Shahid. 1991. "Trade Orientation and Macroeconomic Performance in LDCs: An Empirical Study." *Economic Development and Cultural Change* 39 (July): 839–48.

Alberro, José. 1981. "The Lucas Hypothesis and the Phillips Curve: Further International Evidence." *Journal of Monetary Economics* 11 (March): 239–50.

Alesina, Alberto. 1991. "Macroeconomics and Politics." In *Macroeconomics Annual,* edited by Stanley Fischer. Cambridge, Mass.: National Bureau of Economic Research.

Alesina, Alberto, Gerald D. Cohen, and Nouriel Roubini. 1993. "Electoral Business Cycle in Industrial Democracies." *European Journal of Political Economy* 9 (March): 1–23.

Alesina, Alberto, and Allan Drazen. 1991. "Why Are Stabilizations Delayed?" *American Economic Review* 81 (December): 1170–88.

Alesina, Alberto, and Lawrence H. Summers. 1993. "Central Bank Independence and Macroeconomic Performance." *Journal of Money, Credit, and Banking* 25 (May): 151–62.

Alesina, Alberto, and Guido Tabellini. 1989. "External Debt, Capital Flight, and Political Risk." *Journal of International Economics* 27 (November): 199–220.

Alexander, Sidney S. 1952. "Effects of a Devaluation on a Trade Balance." *IMF Staff Papers* 2 (April): 263–78.

Ambler, Steve, and Emanuela Cardia. 1992. "Optimal Anti-Inflation Programs in Semi-Industrialized Economies: Orthodox versus Heterodox Policies." *Journal of Development Economics* 38 (January): 41–61.

Ames, Barry. 1987. *Political Survival: Politicians and Public Policy in Latin America.* Berkeley: University of California Press.

Anand, Ritu, and Sweder van Wijnbergen. 1989. "Inflation and the Financing of Government Expenditure: An Introductory Analysis with an Application to Turkey." *World Bank Economic Review* 3 (March): 17–38.

Andersen, Torben M. 1989. "Credibility of Policy Announcements—The Output and Inflation Costs of Disinflationary Policies." *European Economic Review* 33 (January): 13–30.

Arida, Persio, and Andre Lara-Resende. 1985. "Inertial Inflation and Monetary Reform: Brazil." In *Inflation and Indexation,* edited by John Williamson. Washington, D.C.: Institute for International Economics.

Arrau, Patricio. 1990. *Intertemporal Substitution in a Monetary Framework: Evidence from Two Latin American Countries.* PRE Working Paper no. 549, World Bank (December).

Arrau, Patricio, José De Gregorio, Carmen Reinhart, and Peter Wickham. 1995. "The Demand for Money in Developing Countries: Assessing the Role of Financial Innovation." *Journal of Development Economics* 46 (April): 317–40.

Asilis, Carlos M., Patrick Honohan, and Paul D. McNelis. 1993. "Money Demand during Hyperinflation and Stabilization: Bolivia." *Economic Inquiry* 31 (April): 262–73.

Auernheimer, Leonardo. 1974. "The Honest Government's Guide to the Revenue from the Creation of Money." *Journal of Political Economy* 92 (May): 598–606.

———. 1987. "On the Outcome of Inconsistent Programs under Exchange Rate and Monetary Rules." *Journal of Monetary Economics* 19 (March): 279–305.

Azam, Jean-Paul, and Timothy Besley. 1989. "General Equilibrium with Parallel Markets for Goods and Foreign Exchange." *World Development* 17 (December): 1921–30.

Bacchetta, Philippe. 1990. "Temporary Capital Controls in a Balance-of-Payments Crisis." *Journal of International Money and Finance* 9 (March): 246–57.

Bacha, Edmar L. 1990. "A Three-Gap Model of Foreign Transfers and the GDP Growth Rate in Developing Countries." *Journal of Development Economics* 32 (April): 279–96.

Bahmani-Oskooee, Mohsen, and Margaret Malixi. 1992. "More Evidence on the J Curve from LDCs." *Journal of Policy Modeling* 14 (October): 641–53.

Bailey, Martin J. 1956. "The Welfare Cost of Inflationary Finance." *Journal of Political Economy* 64 (April): 93–110.

Balassa, Bela. 1990. "The Effects of Interest Rates on Savings in Developing Countries." *Banca Nazionale del Lavoro Quarterly Review* 60 (March): 101–18.

Ball, Laurence. 1994. "Credible Disinflation with Staggered Price-Setting." *American Economic Review* 84 (March): 282–89.

Bandara, Jayatilleke S. 1991. "Computable General Equilibrium Models for Development Policy Analysis in LDCs." *Journal of Economic Surveys* 5 (January): 3–69.

Barbone, Luca, and Francisco Rivera-Batiz. 1987. "Foreign Capital and the Contractionary Impact of Currency Devaluation, with an Application to Jamaica." *Journal of Development Economics* 26 (June): 1–15.

Barro, Robert J. 1974. "Are Government Bonds Net Wealth?" *Journal of Political Economy* 82 (November): 1095–117.

——. 1978. "Unanticipated Money, Output, and the Price Level in the United States." *Journal of Political Economy* 86 (June): 549–80.

——. 1979. "Money and Output in Mexico, Colombia and Brazil." In *Short-term Macroeconomic Policy in Latin America,* edited by Jere Berhman and James A. Hanson. Cambridge, Mass.: Ballinger.

——. 1983. "Inflationary Finance under Discretion and Rules." *Canadian Journal of Economics* 16 (February): 1–16.

——. 1986. "Reputation in a Model of Monetary Policy with Incomplete Information." *Journal of Monetary Economics* 17 (March): 3–20.

——. 1989. "The Ricardian Approach to Budget Deficits." *Journal of Economic Perspectives* 3 (March): 37–54.

——. 1990. "Government Spending in a Simple Model of Endogenous Growth." *Journal of Political Economy* 98 (Supplement): 103–25.

Barro, Robert J., and David B. Gordon. 1983. "A Positive Theory of Monetary Policy in a Natural Rate Model." *Journal of Political Economy* 91 (August): 589–610.

Barro, Robert J., and Xavier Sala-i-Martin. 1995. *Economic Growth.* New York: McGraw-Hill.

Bates, Robert. 1990. "Macropolitical Economy in the Field of Development." In *Perspectives on Political Economy,* edited by James E. Alt and Kenneth A. Shepsle. Cambridge: Cambridge University Press.

Baxter, Marianne. 1985. "The Role of Expectations in Stabilization Policy." *Journal of Monetary Economics* 15 (May): 343–62.

Beavis, Brian, and Ian Dobbs. 1990. *Optimization and Stability Theory for Economic Analysis.* Cambridge: Cambridge University Press.

Bencivenga, Valerie R., and Bruce D. Smith. 1991. "Financial Intermediation and Endogenous Growth." *Review of Economic Studies* 58 (April): 195–209.

——. 1992. "Deficits, Inflation, and the Banking System in Developing Countries." *Oxford Economic Papers* 44 (October): 767–90.

Bevan, David, Paul Collier, and Jan W. Gunning. 1993. "Trade Shocks in Developing Countries: Consequences and Policy Responses." *European Economic Review* 37 (April): 557–65.

Bhagwati, Jagdish N., and Bent Hansen. 1973. "A Theoretical Analysis of Smuggling." *Quarterly Journal of Economics* 87 (May): 172–87.

Bhalla, Surjit. 1980. "The Measurement of Permanent Income and Its Application to Saving Behavior." *Journal of Political Economy* 88 (August): 722–43.

Bhandari, Jagdeep S., and Carlos A. Végh. 1990. "Dual Exchange Markets under Incomplete Separation: An Optimizing Model." *IMF Staff Papers* 37 (March): 146–67.

Bini Smaghi, Lorenzo. 1982. *Independent Monetary Policy and Capital Mobility in LDCs: The Case of Malaysia, 1978–81.* Working Paper no. 82/72, International Monetary Fund (November).

Blanchard, Olivier J. 1983. "Price Asynchronization and Price Level Inertia." In *Inflation, Debt and Indexation*, edited by Rudiger Dornbusch and Mario H. Simonsen. Cambridge, Mass.: MIT Press.

———. 1985. "Credibility, Disinflation, and Gradualism." *Economic Letters* 17 (March): 211–17.

———. 1986. "The Wage Price Spiral." *Quarterly Journal of Economics* 101 (August): 543–65.

Blanchard, Olivier J., and Stanley Fischer. 1989. *Lectures on Macroeconomics.* Cambridge, Mass.: MIT Press.

Blanco, Herminio, and Peter M. Garber. 1986. "Recurrent Devaluation and Speculative Attacks on the Mexican Peso." *Journal of Political Economy* 94 (February): 148–66.

Bleaney, Michael, and David Greenaway. 1993*a*. "Adjustment to External Balance and Investment Slumps in Developing Countries." *European Economic Review* 37 (April): 577–85.

———. 1993*b*. "Long-Run Trends in the Relative Price of Primary Commodities and in the Terms of Trade of Developing Countries." *Oxford Economic Papers* 45 (July): 349–63.

Blejer, Mario I. 1977. "The Short-Run Dynamics of Prices and the Balance of Payments." *American Economic Review* 67 (June): 419–28.

———. 1978. "Black-Market Exchange Rate Expectations and the Domestic Demand for Money: Some Empirical Evidence." *Journal of Monetary Economics* 4 (November): 767–73.

Blejer, Mario I., and Adrienne Cheasty. 1988. "High Inflation, Heterodox Stabilization and Fiscal Policy." *World Development* 16 (September): 867–81.

———. 1991. "The Measurement of Fiscal Deficits: Analytical and Methodological Issues." *Journal of Economic Literature* 29 (December): 1644–78.

Blejer, Mario I., and Roque B. Fernández. 1980. "The Effects of Unanticipated Money Growth on Prices and on Output and Its Composition in a Fixed-Exchange-Rate Open Economy." *Canadian Journal of Economics* 13 (March): 82–95.

Blejer, Mario I., and Mohsin S. Khan. 1984. "Private Investment in Developing Countries." *IMF Staff Papers* 31 (June): 379–403.

Blejer, Mario I., and Nissan Liviatan. 1987. "Fighting Hyperinflation: Stabilization Strategies in Argentina and Israel." *IMF Staff Papers* 34 (September): 409–38.

Bohn, Henning. 1990. "Sustainability of Budget Deficits with Lump-Sum and with Income-Based Taxation." *Journal of Money, Credit, and Banking* 23 (August): 580–604.

Borensztein, Eduardo. 1990. "Debt Overhang, Credit Rationing and Investment." *Journal of Development Economics* 32 (April): 315–35.

Boschen, John F., and John L. Newman. 1989. "Monetary Effects on the Real Interest Rate in an Open Economy: Evidence from the Indexed Argentine Bond Market." *Journal of International Money and Finance* 8 (June): 201–17.

Boughton, James M. 1993. "The Economics of the CFA Franc Zone." In *Policy Issues in the Operation of Currency Unions,* edited by Paul R. Masson and Mark P. Taylor. Cambridge: Cambridge University Press.

Bourguignon, Francois, William H. Branson, and Jaime De Melo. 1992. "Adjustment and Income Distribution: A Micro-Macro Model for Counterfactual Analysis." *Journal of Development Economics* 38 (January): 17–39.

Bourguignon, Francois, Gilles Michel, and Dominique Miqueu. 1983. "Short-Run Rigidities and Long-Run Adjustments in a Computable General Equilibrium Model of Income Distribution and Development." *Journal of Development Economics* 13 (August): 21–43.

Branson, William H. 1986. "Stabilization, Stagflation, and Investment Incentives: The Case of Kenya 1979–80." In *Economic Adjustment and Exchange Rates in Developing Countries,* edited by Sebastián Edwards and Liaqat Ahamed. Chicago: University of Chicago Press.

Brock, Philip L. 1984. "Inflationary Finance in an Open Economy." *Journal of Monetary Economics* 14 (July): 37–53.

———. 1989. "Reserve Requirements and the Inflation Tax." *Journal of Money, Credit, and Banking* 21 (February): 106–21.

Bruno, Michael. 1979. "Stabilization and Stagflation in a Semi-Industrialized Economy." In *International Economic Policy: Theory and Evidence,* edited by Rudiger Dornbusch and Jacob A. Frenkel. Baltimore: Johns Hopkins University Press.

———. 1991. *High Inflation and the Nominal Anchors of an Open Economy.* Essay in International Finance no. 183, Princeton University.

Bruno, Michael, and Stanley Fischer. 1990. "Seignorage, Operating Rules, and the High Inflation Trap." *Quarterly Journal of Economics* 105 (May): 353–74.

Bruno, Michael, and Sylvia Piterman. 1987. *Israel's Stabilization: A Two-Year Review.* Publication no. 2398, National Bureau of Economic Research (October).

Bruton, Henry. 1989. "Import Substitution." In *Handbook of Development Economics.* Vol. II, edited by Hollis B. Chenery and T. N. Srinivasan. Amsterdam: North Holland.

Buffie, Edward F. 1984a. "Financial Repression, the New Structuralists, and Stabilization Policy in the Semi-Industrialized Economies." *Journal of Development Economics* 14 (April): 305–22.

———. 1984b. "The Macroeconomics of Trade Liberalization." *Journal of International Economics* 17 (August): 121–37.

———. 1985. "Price-Output Dynamics, Capital Inflows, and Real Appreciation." *Oxford Economic Papers* 37 (December): 529–51.

———. 1986a. "Devaluation and Imported Inputs: The Large Economy Case." *International Economic Review* 27 (February): 123–40.

———. 1986b. "Devaluation, Investment and Growth in LDCs." *Journal of Development Economics* 20 (March): 361–79.

———. 1989. "Imported Inputs, Real Wage Rigidity and Devaluation in the Small Open Economy." *European Economic Review* 33 (September): 1345–61.

———. 1992. "Short- and Long-Run Effects of Fiscal Policy." *World Bank Economic Review* 6 (May): 331–51.

———. 1994. "Public Sector Layoffs, Credibility, and the Dynamics of Inflation in a Simple Macromodel." Unpublished. Indiana University (February).

Buiter, Willem H. 1983. "Measurement of the Public Sector Deficit and Its Implications for Policy Evaluation and Design." *IMF Staff Papers* 30 (June): 306–49.

———. 1985. "A Guide to Public Sector Debt and Deficits." *Economic Policy* 1 (November): 13–80.

———. 1987. "Borrowing to Defend the Exchange Rate and the Timing of and Magnitude of Speculative Attacks." *Journal of International Economics* 23 (November): 221–39.

———. 1988. "Structural and Stabilization Aspects of Fiscal and Financial Policy in the Dependent Economy." *Oxford Economic Papers* 40 (June): 220–45.

———. 1989. "Some Thoughts on the Role of Fiscal Policy in Stabilization and Structural Adjustment in Developing Countries." In *Principles of Budgetary and Financial Policy,* edited by Willem H. Buiter. Cambridge, Mass.: MIT Press.

Buiter, Willem H., and Urjit R. Patel. 1992. "Debt, Deficits and Inflation: An Application to the Public Finances of India." *Journal of Public Economics* 47 (March): 171–205.

Bulow, Jeremy, and Kenneth Rogoff. 1990. "Cleaning up Third World Debt Without Getting Taken to the Cleaners." *Journal of Economic Perspectives* 4 (February): 31–42.

Burgess, Robin, and Nicholas Stern. 1993. "Taxation and Development." *Journal of Economic Literature* 31 (June): 762–830.

Burkett, Paul, and Robert C. Vogel. 1992. "Financial Assets, Inflation Hedges, and Capital Utilization in Developing Countries." *Quarterly Journal of Economics* 107 (May): 773–84.

Burton, David. 1983. "Devaluation, Long-Term Contracts, and Rational Expectations." *European Economic Review* 23 (September): 19–32.

Cáceres, Armando, and Carlos Paredes. 1991. "The Management of Economic Policy, 1985–1989." In *Peru's Path to Recovery,* edited by Carlos Paredes and Jeffrey Sachs, Washington, D.C.: Brookings Institution.

Calomiris, Charles W., and Ian Domowitz. 1989. "Asset Substitutions, Money Demand, and the Inflation Process in Brazil." *Journal of Money, Credit, and Banking* 21 (February): 78–89.

Calvo, Guillermo A. 1983. "Staggered Contracts and Exchange Rate Policy." In *Exchange Rates and International Macroeconomics,* edited by Jacob A. Frenkel. Chicago: University of Chicago Press.

———. 1985. "Currency Substitution and the Real Exchange Rate: The Utility Maximizing Approach." *Journal of International Money and Finance* 4 (June): 175–88.

———. 1986. "Temporary Stabilization: Predetermined Exchange Rates." *Journal of Political Economy* 94 (December): 1319–29.

———. 1987a. "Balance of Payments Crises in a Cash-in-Advance Economy." *Journal of Money, Credit, and Banking* 19 (February): 19–32.

——. 1987b. "On the Cost of Temporary Policy." *Journal of Development Economics* 27 (October): 245–62.

——. 1989. "Incredible Reforms." In *Debt, Stabilization and Development,* edited by Guillermo A. Calvo, Ronald Firdlap, Pentti Kouri, and Jorge Braga de Macedo. Oxford: Basil Blackwell.

——. 1991. "Temporary Stabilization Policy: The Case of Flexible Prices and Exchange Rates." *Journal of Economic Dynamics and Control* 15 (January): 197–213.

Calvo, Guillermo A., Leonardo Leiderman, and Carmen M. Reinhart. 1993. "Capital Inflows and Real Exchange Rate Appreciation in Latin America: The Role of External Factors." *IMF Staff Papers* 40 (March): 108–51.

Calvo, Guillermo A., Carmen M. Reinhart, and Carlos A. Végh. 1994. "Targeting the Real Exchange Rate: Theory and Evidence". *Journal of Development Economics* 47 (June): 97–133.

Calvo, Guillermo A., and Carlos A. Rodríguez. 1977. "A Model of Exchange Rate Determination under Currency Substitution and Rational Expectations." *Journal of Political Economy* 85 (June): 617–25.

Calvo, Guillermo A., and Carlos A. Végh. 1992. *Currency Substitution in Developing Countries.* Working Paper no. 92/40, International Monetary Fund (June).

——. 1993a. "Credibility and the Dynamics of Stabilization Policy: A Basic Framework." In *Advances in Econometrics,* edited by Christopher A. Sims. Cambridge: Cambridge University Press.

——. 1993b. "Exchange Rate–Based Stabilization under Imperfect Credibility." In *Open Economy Macroeconomics,* edited by Helmut Frisch and Andreas Worgotter. New York: St. Martin's Press.

——. 1994. "Stabilization Dynamics and Backward-Looking Contracts." *Journal of Development Economics* 43 (February): 59–84.

Canarella, Giorgio, and Stephen K. Pollard. 1989. "Unanticipated Monetary Growth, Output, and the Price Level in Latin America." *Journal of Development Economics* 30 (April): 345–58.

Canavese, Alfredo J., and Guido Di Tella. 1988. "Inflation Stabilization or Hyperinflation Avoidance: The Case of the Austral Plan in Argentina, 1985–87." In *Inflation Stabilization,* edited by Michael Bruno, Guido Di Tella, Rudiger Dornbusch, and Stanley Fischer. Cambridge, Mass.: MIT Press.

Cardoso, Eliana. 1981. "Food Supply and Inflation." *Journal of Development Economics* 8 (June): 269–84.

——. 1992. "Deficit Finance and Monetary Dynamics in Brazil and Mexico." *Journal of Development Economics* 37 (November): 173–97.

——. 1993. "Private Investment in Latin America." *Economic Development and Cultural Change* 41 (July): 833–48.

Cardoso, Eliana, and Rudiger Dornbusch. 1987. "Brazil's Tropical Plan." *American Economic Review* 77 (May): 288–92.

Cardoso, Eliana, and Albert Fishlow. 1990. "The Macroeconomics of Brazilian External Debt." In *Developing Country Debt and Economic Performance.* Vol. 2, edited by Jeffrey Sachs. Chicago: University of Chicago Press.

Cardoso, Eliana, and Ann Helwege. 1992. *Latin America's Economy: Diversity, Trends and Conflicts.* Cambridge, Mass.: MIT Press.

Carmichael, Jeffrey, Jerome Fahrer, and John Hawkins. 1985. "Some Macro-economic Implications of Wage Indexation: A Survey." In *Inflation and Unemployment—Theory, Experience and Policymaking,* edited by Victor E. Argy and John W. Neville. London: G. Allen and Unwin.

Cashin, Paul. 1995. "Government Spending, Taxes, and Economic Growth." *IMF Staff Papers* 42 (June): 237–69.

Cavallo, Domingo. 1981. "Stagflationary Effects of Monetarist Stabilization Policies in Economies with Persistent Inflation." In *Development in an Inflationary World,* edited by June Flanders and Assaf Razin. New York: Academic Press.

Chandravarkar, Anand. 1987. *The Informal Financial Sector in Developing Countries: Analysis, Evidence, and Policy Implications.* SEACEN Occasional Paper no. 2 (August) (Kuala Lumpur, Malaysia).

Chenery, Hollis B. 1986. "Growth and Transformation." In *Industrialization and Growth,* edited by Hollis B. Chenery, Sherman Robinson, and Moshe Syrquin. Oxford: Oxford University Press.

Chenery, Hollis B., and Alan Strout. 1966. "Foreign Assistance and Economic Development." *American Economic Review* 56 (September): 679–733.

Cho, Yoon Je. 1986. "Inefficiencies from Financial Liberalization in the Absence of Well-Functioning Equity Markets." *Journal of Money, Credit, and Banking* 18 (May): 191–99.

Chopra, Ajit. 1985. "The Speed of Adjustment of the Inflation Rate in Developing Countries: A Study of Inertia." *IMF Staff Papers* 32 (December): 693–733.

Chopra, Ajit, and Peter J. Montiel. 1986. "Output and Unanticipated Money with Imported Intermediate Goods and Foreign Exchange Rationing." *IMF Staff Papers* 33 (December): 697–721.

Choudhary, Munir A., and Amar K. Parai. 1991. "Anticipated Monetary Policy and Real Output: Evidence from Latin American Countries." *Applied Economics* 23 (April): 579–86.

Choudhry, Nurun N. 1991. "Collection Lags, Fiscal Revenue and Inflationary Financing: Empirical Evidence and Analysis." Working Paper no. 91/41, International Monetary Fund (April).

Claessens, Stijn. 1991. "Balance of Payments Crises in an Optimal Portfolio Model." *European Economic Review* 35 (January): 81–101.

Claessens, Stijn, Ishac Diwan, and Eduardo Fernández-Arias. 1992. *Recent Experience with Commercial Bank Debt Reduction.* PRE Working Paper no. 995, World Bank (October).

Claessens, Stijn, and Sweder van Wijnbergen. 1993. "Secondary Market Prices and Mexico's Brady Deal." *Quarterly Journal of Economics* 108 (November): 965–82.

Cohen, Daniel. 1993. "Low Investment and Large LDC Debt in the 1980's." *American Economic Review* 83 (June): 437–49.

———. 1994. "Growth and External Debt." In *The Handbook of International Macroeconomics,* edited by Frederick van der Ploeg. Oxford: Basil Blackwell.

Collins, Susan M. 1991. "Saving Behavior in Ten Developing Countries." In *National Saving and Economic Performance,* edited by B. Douglas Bernhein and John B. Shoven. Chicago: University of Chicago Press.

Condon, Timothy, Vittorio Corbo, and Jaime de Melo. 1990. "Exchange-Rate Based Disinflation, Wage Rigidity, and Capital Inflows." *Journal of Development Economics* 32 (January): 113–31.

Connolly, Michael B. 1986. "The Speculative Attack on the Peso and the Real Exchange Rate: Argentina, 1979–81." *Journal of International Money and Finance* 5 (March): 117–30.

Connolly, Michael B., and Arturo Fernández. 1987. "Speculation Against the Pre-Announced Exchange Rate in Mexico: January 1983 to June 1985." In *Economic Reform and Stabilization in Latin America,* edited by Michael Connolly and Claudio González-Vega. New York: Praeger.

Connolly, Michael B., and Dean Taylor. 1984. "The Exact Timing of the Collapse of an Exchange Rate Regime and Its Impact on the Relative Price of Traded Goods." *Journal of Money, Credit, and Banking* 16 (May): 194–207.

Conway, Patrick. 1987. *Economic Shocks and Structural Adjustment: Turkey after 1973.* Amsterdam: North Holland.

Cook, Paul, and Colin Kirkpatrick. 1990. *Macroeconomics for Developing Countries.* London: Harvester Wheatsheaf.

Cooper, Richard N. 1971. "Currency Devaluation in Developing Countries." Essay in International Finance no. 86, Princeton University.

———. 1991. *Economic Stabilization in Developing Countries.* San Francisco: ICS Press.

Corbo, Vittorio. 1985a. "International Prices, Wages and Inflation in an Open Economy: A Chilean Model." *Review of Economics and Statistics* 67 (June): 564–73.

———. 1985b. "Reforms and Macroeconomic Adjustment in Chile during 1974–84." *World Development* 13 (August): 893–916.

Corbo, Vittorio, and Jaime de Melo. 1987. "Lessons from the Southern Cone Policy Reforms." *World Bank Research Observer* 2 (July): 111–42.

———. 1989. "External Shocks and Policy Reforms in the Southern Cone: A Reassessment." In *Debt, Stabilization and Development,* edited by Guillermo A. Calvo, Ronald Findlay, Pentti Kouri, and Jorge Braga de Macedo. Oxford: Basil Blackwell.

Corbo, Vittorio, and Paul D. McNellis. 1989. "The Pricing of Manufactured Goods during Trade Liberalization: Evidence from Chile, Israel and Korea." *Review of Economics and Statistics* 71 (August): 491–99.

Corbo, Vittorio, and Klaus Schmidt-Hebbel. 1991. "Public Policies and Saving in Developing Countries." *Journal of Development Economics* 36 (July): 89–115.

Corden, W. Max. 1984. "Booming Sector and Dutch Disease Economics: Survey and Consolidation." *Oxford Economic Papers* 36 (November): 359–80.

———. 1989. "The Relevance for Developing Countries of Recent Developments in Macroeconomic Theory." In *Debt, Stabilization and Development,* edited by Guillermo A. Calvo, Ronald Findlay, Pentti Kouri, and Jorge Braga de Macedo. Oxford: Basil Blackwell.

———. 1990. "Macroeconomic Adjustment in Developing Countries." In *Public Policy and Economic Development,* edited by Maurice Scott and Deepak Lal. Oxford: Clarendon Press.

———. 1993. "Exchange Rate Policies for Developing Countries." *Economic Journal* 103 (January): 198–207.

Corden, W. Max, and Ronald Findlay. 1975. "Urban Unemployment, Intersectoral Capital Mobility and Development Policy." *Economica* 42 (February): 59–78.

Courakis, Anthony S. 1984. "Constraints on Bank Choices and Financial Repression in Less Developed Countries." *Oxford Bulletin of Economics and Statistics* 46 (November): 341–70.

Cox, W. Michael. 1983. "Government Revenue from Deficit Finance." *Canadian Journal of Economics* 16 (May): 264–74.

Cozier, Barry V. 1986. "A Model of Output Fluctuations in a Small, Specialized Economy." *Journal of Money, Credit, and Banking* 18 (May): 179–90.

Cuddington, John. 1986. *Capital Flight: Estimates, Issues and Explanations.* Study in International Finance no. 58, Princeton University.

———. 1992. "Long-Run Trends in 26 Primary Commodity Prices." *Journal of Development Economics* 39 (October): 207–27.

Cukierman, Alex. 1988. "The End of the High Israeli Inflation: An Experiment in Heterodox Stabilization." In *Inflation Stabilization,* edited by Michael Bruno, Guido DiTella, Rudiger Dornbusch, and Stanley Fischer. Cambridge, Mass.: MIT Press.

———. 1992. *Central Bank Strategy, Credibility, and Independence.* Cambridge, Mass.: MIT Press.

Cukierman, Alex, Sebastián Edwards, and Guido Tabellini. 1992. "Seignorage and Political Instability." *American Economic Review* 82 (June): 537–55.

Cukierman, Alex, and Nissan Liviatan. 1991. "Optimal Accommodation by Strong Policymakers under Incomplete Information." *Journal of Monetary Economics* 27 (February): 99–127.

———. 1992. "Dynamics of Optimal Gradual Stabilizations." *World Bank Economic Review* 6 (September): 439–58.

Cukierman, Alex, and Allan Meltzer. 1989. "A Political Theory of Government Debt and Deficits in a Neo-Ricardian Framework." *American Economic Review* 79 (September): 713–32.

Cumby, Robert E., and Maurice Obstfeld. 1983. "Capital Mobility and the Scope for Sterilization: Mexico in the 1970s." In *Financial Policies and the World Capital Market,* edited by Pedro A. Armella, Rudiger Dornbusch, and Maurice Obstfeld. Chicago: University of Chicago Press.

Cumby, Robert E., and Sweder van Wijnbergen. 1989. "Financial Policy and Speculative Runs with a Crawling Peg: Argentina 1979–1981." *Journal of International Economics* 27 (August): 111–27.

Darrat, Ali F., and Augustine C. Arize. 1990. "Domestic and International Sources of Inflation in Developing Countries." *International Economic Journal* 4 (Winter): 55–69.

Deaton, Angus S. 1989. "Saving in Developing Countries: Theory and Review." In *World Bank Economic Review,* Proceedings of the World Bank Annual Conference on Development Economics. Washington, D.C.: World Bank.

———. 1992. *Understanding Consumption.* Oxford: Oxford University Press.

Deaton, Angus, and John Muellbauer. 1980. *Economics and Consumer Behavior.* Cambridge: Cambridge University Press.

Decaluwé, Bernard, and André Martens. "CGE Modeling and Developing Economies: A Concise Empirical Survey of 73 Applications to 26 Countries." *Journal of Policy Modeling* 10 (December): 529–68.

De Gregorio, José. 1992. "Economic Growth in Latin America." *Journal of Development Economics* 39 (July): 59–84.

———. 1993. "Inflation, Taxation, and Long-Run Growth." *Journal of Monetary Economics* 31 (June): 271–98.

———. 1995. "Policy Accommodation and Gradual Stabilizations." *Journal of Money, Credit, and Banking.* 27 (August): 727–41.

Dellas, Harris, and Alan C. Stockman. 1993. "Self-Fulfilling Expectations, Speculative Attacks, and Capital Controls." *Journal of Money, Credit, and Banking* 25 (November): 721–30.

Demekas, Dimitri G. 1990. "Labor Market Segmentation in a Two-Sector Model of an Open Economy." *IMF Staff Papers* 37 (December): 849–64.

Denizer, Cevdet. 1994. "The Effects of Financial Liberalization and New Bank Entry on Market Structure and Competition in Turkey." Unpublished. World Bank (June).

Deutsch, Joseph, and Ben-Zion Zilberfarb. 1994. "Inflation Variability and Money Demand in Developing Countries." *International Review of Economics and Finance* 3 (March): 57–72.

Dewatripont, Mathias, and Gilles Michel. 1987. "On Closure Rules, Homogeneity, and Dynamics in Applied General Equilibrium Models." *Journal of Development Economics* 26 (June): 65–76.

Diamond, Larry, and Juan J. Linz. 1989. "Politics, Society, and Democracy in Latin America." In *Democracy in Developing Countries,* edited by Larry Diamond, Juan J. Linz, and Seymour M. Lipset. Boulder, Colo.: L. Rienner.

Díaz Alejandro, Carlos F. 1963. "A Note on the Impact of Devaluation and the Redistributive Effect." *Journal of Political Economy* 71 (December): 577–80.

———. 1965. *Exchange Rate Devaluation in a Semi-Industrialized Country.* Cambridge, Mass.: MIT Press.

Dixit, Avinash. 1991. "The Optimal Mix of Inflationary Finance and Commodity Taxation with Collection Lags." *IMF Staff Papers* 38 (September): 643–54.

Dodsworth, John R., Mohamed El-Erian, and D. Hammann. 1987. *Foreign Currency Deposits in Developing Countries—Origins and Economic Implications.* Working Paper no. 87/12, International Monetary Fund (March).

Dollar, David. 1992. "Outward-Oriented Developing Economies Really Do Grow More Rapidly: Evidence from 95 LDCs, 1976–1985." *Economic Development and Cultural Change* 40 (April): 523–44.

Domowitz, Ian, and Ibrahim Elbadawi. 1987. "An Error-Correction Approach to Money Demand: The Case of Sudan." *Journal of Development Economics* 26 (August): 257–75.

Donovan, Donal J. 1981. "Real Responses Associated with Exchange Rate Action in Selected Upper Credit Tranche Stabilization Programs." *IMF Staff Papers* 28 (December): 698–727.

———. 1982. "Macroeconomic Performance and Adjustment under Fund-Supported Programs." *IMF Staff Papers* 29 (June): 171–203.

Dooley, Michael. 1986. *An Analysis of the Debt Crisis.* Working Paper no. 86/14, International Monetary Fund (December).

———. 1988. "Capital Flight: A Response to Differences in Financial Risk." *IMF Staff Papers* 35 (September): 422–36.

Dooley, Michael, Jeffrey Frankel, and Donald Mathieson. 1987. "International Capital Mobility: What Do Saving Investment Correlations Tell Us?" *IMF Staff Papers* 34 (September): 503–30.

Dooley, Michael, and Peter Isard. 1980. "Capital Controls, Political Risk, and Deviations from Interest Parity." *Journal of Political Economy* 88 (April): 370–84.

Dooley, Michael, and Mark R. Stone. 1993. "Endogenous Creditor Seniority and External Debt Values." *IMF Staff Papers* 40 (June): 395–413.

Dornbusch, Rudiger. 1980. *Open-Economy Macroeconomics.* New York: Basic Books.

———. 1982. "PPP Exchange-Rate Rules and Macroeconomic Stability." *Journal of Political Economy* 90 (February): 158–65.

———. 1991. "Credibility and Stabilization." *Quarterly Journal of Economics* 106 (August): 837–50.

———. 1993. "Lessons from Experiences with High Inflation." In *Stabilization, Debt, and Reform,* collected papers, Prentice Hall (Englewood Cliffs, New Jersey: 1993).

Dornbusch, Rudiger, Daniel V. Dantas, Clarice Pechman, Roberto Rocha, and Demetri Simoes. 1983. "The Black Market for Dollars in Brazil." *Quarterly Journal of Economics* 98 (February): 25–40.

Dornbusch, Rudiger, and Juan Carlos de Pablo. 1989. "Debt and Macroeconomic Instability in Argentina." In *Developing Country Debt and the World Economy,* edited by Jeffrey D. Sachs. Chicago: University of Chicago Press.

Dornbusch, Rudiger, and Sebastián Edwards. 1990. "Macroeconomic Populism." *Journal of Development Economics* 32 (April): 247–77.

———. eds. 1991. *The Macroeconomics of Populism in Latin America.* Chicago: University of Chicago Press.

Dornbusch, Rudiger, and Stanley Fischer. 1986. "Stopping Hyperinflations, Past and Present." *Weltwirtschaftliches Archives* 122 (1): 1–47.

———. 1993. "Moderate Inflation." *World Bank Economic Review* 7 (January): 1–44.

Dornbusch, Rudiger, and F. Leslie Helmers, eds. 1988. *The Open Economy: Tools for Policymakers in Developing Countries.* New York: Oxford University Press.

Dornbusch, Rudiger, and Michael Mussa. 1975. "Consumption, Real Balances and the Hoarding Function." *International Economic Review* 16 (June): 415–21.

Dornbusch, Rudiger, and Alejandro Reynoso. 1993. "Financial Factors and Economic Development." In *Policymaking in the Open Economy,* edited by Rudiger Dornbusch. New York: Oxford University Press.

Dornbusch, Rudiger, and Mario H. Simonsen. 1988. "Inflation Stabilization: The Role of Incomes Policy and Monetization." In *Exchange Rates and Inflation,* edited by Rudiger Dornbusch. Cambridge, Mass.: MIT Press.

Dornbusch, Rudiger, Federico Sturzenegger, and Holger Wolf. 1990. "Extreme Inflation: Dynamics and Stabilization." *Brookings Papers on Economic Activity* 1 (March): 1–84.

Doroodian, Khosrow. 1993. "Macroeconomic Performance and Adjustment under Policies Commonly Supported by the International Monetary Fund." *Economic Development and Cultural Change* 41 (July): 849–64.

Dowla, Asif, and Abdur Chowdhury. 1991. "Money, Credit, and Real Output in the Developing Economies." Unpublished. Department of Economics, Marquette University.

Drazen, Allan H. 1985. "Tight Money and Inflation: Further Results." *Journal of Monetary Economics* 15 (January): 113–20.

———. 1990. "Can Exchange Rate Freezes Induce Business Cycles?" Unpublished. University of Maryland (November).

Drazen, Allan H., and Vittorio Grilli. 1993. "The Benefits of Crises for Economic Reforms." *American Economic Review* 83 (June): 598–607.

Drazen, Allan H., and Elhanan Helpman. 1988. "Stabilization Policy with Exchange Rate Management under Uncertainty." In *Economic Effects of the Government Budget,* edited by Elhanan Helpman, Assaf Razin, and Efraim Sadka. Cambridge, Mass.: MIT Press.

———. 1990. "Inflationary Consequences of Anticipated Macroeconomic Policies." *Review of Economic Studies* 57 (January): 147–66.

Drazen, Allan H., and Paul R. Masson. 1994. "Credibility of Policies versus Credibility of Policymakers." *Quarterly Journal of Economics* 109 (August): 735–54.

Dutton, Dean S. 1971. "A Model of Self-Generating Inflation: The Argentine Case." *Journal of Money, Credit, and Banking* 3 (May): 245–62.

Easterly, William. 1989. "Fiscal Adjustment and Deficit Financing during the Debt Crisis." In *Dealing with the Debt Crisis,* edited by Ishrat Husain and Ishac Diwan. Washington, D.C.: World Bank.

———. 1993. "How Much Do Distortions Affect Growth?" *Journal of Monetary Economics* 32 (November): 187–212.

Easterly, William, and Piyabha Kongsamut. 1991. "A Macroeconomic Model for Colombia." Unpublished. World Bank (August).

Easterly, William, and Klaus Schmidt-Hebbel. 1994. "Fiscal Adjustment and Macroeconomic Performance: A Synthesis." In *Public Sector Deficits and Macroeconomic Performance,* edited by William Easterly, Carlos A. Rodríguez, and Klaus Schmidt-Hebbel. Oxford: Oxford University Press.

Eckstein, Zvi, and Leonardo Leiderman. 1988. Estimating Intertemporal Models of Consumption and Money Holdings and Their Implications for Seignorage and Inflation. Working Paper no. 4-88, Tel-Aviv University (April).

Edwards, Sebastián. 1983. "The Short-Run Relation Between Growth and Inflation in Latin America." *American Economic Review* 73 (June): 477–82.

———. 1984. *The Order of Liberalization of the External Sector in Developing Countries.* Essay in International Finance no. 156, Princeton University.

———. 1986. "Are Devaluations Contractionary?" *Review of Economics and Statistics,* 68 (August): 501–8.

———. 1988. "Terms of Trade, Tariffs and Labor Market Adjustment in Developing Countries." *World Bank Economic Review* 2 (May): 165–85.

———. 1989a. *On the Sequencing of Structural Reforms.* Working Paper no. 3138, National Bureau of Economic Research (October).

———. 1989b. *Real Exchange Rates, Devaluation and Adjustment: Exchange Rate Policies in Developing Countries.* Cambridge, Mass.: MIT Press.

———. 1993. "Openness, Trade Liberalization, and Growth in Developing Countries." *Journal of Economic Literature* 31 (September): 1358–93.

———. 1994. "The Political Economy of Inflation and Stabilization in Developing Countries." *Economic Development and Cultural Change* 42 (January): 235–66.

Edwards, Sebastián, and Mohsin S. Khan. 1985. "Interest Rate Determination in Developing Countries: A Conceptual Framework." *IMF Staff Papers* 32 (September): 377–403.

Edwards, Sebastián, and Peter J. Montiel. 1989. "Devaluation Crises and the Macroeconomic Consequences of Postponed Adjustment in Developing Countries." *IMF Staff Papers* 36 (December): 875–904.

Edwards, Sebastián, and Julio A. Santaella. 1993. "Devaluation Controversies in the Developing Countries: Lessons from the Bretton Woods Era." In *A Retrospective on the Bretton Woods System,* edited by Michael D. Bordo and Barry Eichengreen. Chicago: University of Chicago Press.

Edwards, Sebastián, and Guido Tabellini. 1991. "Explaining Fiscal Policies and Inflation in Developing Countries." *Journal of International Money and Finance* 10 (Supplement, March): 16–48.

Edwards, Sebastián, and Sweder van Wijnbergen. 1986. "The Welfare Effects of Trade and Capital Market Liberalization." *International Economic Review* 27 (February): 141–48.

Elbadawi, Ibrahim A., and Klaus Schmidt-Hebbel. 1991. *Macroeconomic Structure and Policy in Zimbabwe: Analysis and Empirical Model (1965–88).* PRE Working Paper no. 771, World Bank (September).

El-Erian, Mohamed. 1988. "Currency Substitution in Egypt and the Yemen Arab Republic." *IMF Staff Papers* 35 (March): 85–103.

Elías, Victor J. 1992. *Sources of Growth: A Study of Seven Latin American Countries.* San Francisco: ICS Press.

Elliott, James, Sung Y. Kwack, and George Tavlas. 1986. "An Econometric Model of the Kenyan Economy." *Economic Modeling* 3 (January): 2–30.

Erbas, S. Nuri. 1989. "The Limits on Bond Financing of Government Deficits under Optimal Fiscal Policy." *Journal of Macroeconomics* 11 (Fall): 589–98.

Evans, J. L., and George K. Yarrow. 1981. "Some Implications of Alternative Expectations Hypotheses in the Monetary Analysis of Hyperinflations." *Oxford Economic Papers* 33 (March): 61–80.

Everaert, Luc, Fernando García-Pinto, and Jaime Ventura. 1990. "A RMSM-X Model for Turkey." PRE Working Paper no. 486, World Bank (August).

Faini, Ricardo, and Jaime de Melo. 1992. "Adjustment, Investment and the Real Exchange Rate in Developing Countries." In *Reviving Private Investment in Developing Countries,* edited by Ajay Chhibber, Mansoor Dailami, and Nemat Shafik. Amsterdam: North Holland.

Fair, Ray C. 1987. "International Evidence on the Demand for Money." *Review of Economics and Statistics* 69 (August): 437–80.

Falvey, Rod, and Cha Dong Kim. 1992. "Timing and Sequencing Issues in Trade Liberalisation." *Economic Journal* 102 (July): 908–24.

Faruqee, Hamid. 1991. "Dynamic Capital Mobility in Pacific Basin Developing Countries: Estimation and Policy Implications." Working Paper no. 91/115, International Monetary Fund (November).

Feenstra, Robert C. 1985. "Anticipated Devaluation, Currency Flight and Direct Trade Controls in a Monetary Economy." *American Economic Review* 75 (June): 386–401.

———. 1986. "Functional Equivalence Between Liquidity Costs and the Utility of Money." *Journal of Monetary Economics* 17 (March): 271–91.

Feldstein, Martin, and Charles Horioka. 1980. "Domestic Saving and International Capital Flows." *Economic Journal* 90 (June): 314–29.

Fernández, Roque B. 1985. "The Expectations Management Approach to Stabilization in Argentina 1976–82." *World Development* 13 (August): 871–92.

———. 1991. "Exchange Rate Policy in Countries with Hyperinflation: The Case of Argentina." In *Exchange Rate Policies in Developing and Post-Socialist Countries,* edited by Emil-Maria Claassen. San Francisco: ICS Press.

Fernández-Arias, Eduardo. 1992. "Costs and Benefits of Debt and Debt Service Reduction." Unpublished. World Bank (March).

Fischer, Stanley. 1983. "Seignorage and Fixed Exchange Rates: An Optimal Inflation Tax Analysis." In *Financial Policies and the World Capital Market,* edited by Pedro Aspe Armella, Rudiger Dornbusch, and Maurice Obstfeld. Chicago: University of Chicago Press.

———. 1986. "Exchange Rate versus Money Targets in Disinflation." In *Indexing, Inflation, and Economic Policy,* edited by Stanley Fischer. Cambridge, Mass.: MIT Press.

———. 1987. "The Israeli Stabilization Program, 1985–1986." *American Economic Review* 77 (May): 275–78.

———. 1988. "Real Balances, the Exchange Rate and Indexation: Real Variables in Disinflation." *Quarterly Journal of Economics* 103 (March): 27–49.

———. 1993. "The Role of Macroeconomic Factors in Growth." *Journal of Monetary Economics* 32 (December): 485–512.

Fischer, Stanley, and William Easterly. 1990. "The Economics of the Government Budget Constraint." *World Bank Research Observer* 5 (July): 127–42.

Fishlow, Albert, and Jorge Friedman. 1994. "Tax Evasion, Inflation and Stabilization." *Journal of Development Economics* 43 (February): 105–23.

Fishlow, Albert, and Samuel Morley. 1987. "Debts, Deficits and Destabilization: The Perversity of High Interest Rates." *Journal of Development Economics* 27 (October): 227–44.

Fitzgerald, E. V. K., Karel Jansen, and Rob Vos. 1994. "External Constraints on Private Investment Decisions in Developing Countries." In *Trade, Aid, and Development,* edited by Jan Willem Gunning, Henk Kox, Wouter Tims, and Ynto de Wit. New York: St. Martin's Press.

Fleming, J. Marcus. 1962. "Domestic Financial Policies under Fixed and under Floating Exchange Rates." *IMF Staff Papers* 9 (March): 369–80.

Flood, Robert P., and Peter M. Garber. 1984. "Collapsing Exchange Rate Regimes: Some Linear Examples." *Journal of International Economics* 17 (August): 1–13.

Flood, Robert P., and Peter Isard. 1989. "Monetary Policy Strategies." *IMF Staff Papers* 36 (December): 612–32.

Foxley, Alejandro. 1983. *Latin American Experiments in Neoconservative Economics.* Los Angeles: University of California Press.

Frenkel, Jacob A., and Richard M. Levich. 1975. "Covered Interest Arbitrage: Unexploited Profits?" *Journal of Political Economy* 83 (April): 323–38.

Frenkel, Jacob A., and Michael L. Mussa. 1985. "Asset Markets, Exchange Rates and the Balance of Payments." In *Handbook of International Economics.* Vol. II, edited by Ronald W. Jones and Peter B. Kenen. Amsterdam: North Holland.

Frenkel, Jacob A., and Assaf Razin. 1987. "The Mundell-Fleming Model a Quarter Century Later: A Unified Exposition." *IMF Staff Papers* 34 (December): 567–620.

———. 1992. *Fiscal Policies and the World Economy.* 2nd ed. Cambridge, Mass.: MIT Press.

Frenkel, Jacob A., and Carlos A. Rodríguez. 1982. "Exchange Rate Dynamics and the Overshooting Hypothesis." *IMF Staff Papers* 29 (March): 1–30.

Frenkel, Michael. 1990. "Exchange Rate Dynamics in Black Markets." *Journal of Economics* 51 (May): 159–76.

Frey, Bruno S., and Reiner Eichenberger. 1994. "The Political Economy of Stabilization Programmes in Developing Countries." *European Journal of Political Economy* 10 (May): 169–90.

Froot, Kenneth A. 1988. "Credibility, Real Interest Rates, and the Optimal Speed of Trade Liberalization." *Journal of International Economics* 25 (August): 71–93.

Fry, Maxwell J. 1988. *Money, Interest and Banking in Economic Development.* Baltimore: Johns Hopkins University Press.

———. 1993. "Financial Repression and Economic Growth." Working Paper no. 93-07, University of Birmingham (July).

Galbis, Vicente. 1979. "Money, Investment, and Growth in Latin America, 1961–73." *Economic Development and Cultural Change* 27 (April): 423–43.

———. 1993. *High Real Interest Rates under Financial Liberalization: Is There a Problem?* Working Paper no. 93/7, International Monetary Fund (January).

———. 1994. "Sequencing of Financial Sector Reforms: A Review." Working Paper no. 94/101, International Monetary Fund (September).

Gan, Wee-Beng, and Lee-Ying Soon. 1994. "Rational Expectations, Saving and Anticipated Changes in Income: Evidence from Malaysia and Singapore." *Journal of Macroeconomics* 16 (Winter): 157–70.

García, Eduardo. 1986. "Modelos neo-Keynesianons para América Latina." Unpublished. Latin American and Caribbean Institute for Economic and Social Planning (ILPES), RLA/86/29 (July).

Gelb, Alan. 1989. *Financial Policies, Growth, and Efficiency.* Working Paper WPS 202, World Bank (June).

Gersovitz, Mark. 1988. "Saving and Development." In *Handbook of Development Economics,* edited by Hollis B. Chenery and T. N. Srinivasan. Amsterdam: North Holland.

Giavazzi, Francesco, and Marco Pagano. 1988. "The Advantage of Tying One's Hands: EMS Discipline and Central Bank Credibility." *European Economic Review* 32 (June): 1055–82.

Gillis, Malcolm, Dwight H. Perkins, Michael Roemer, and Donald R. Snodgrass. 1992. *Economics of Development.* 3rd ed. New York: W. W. Norton.

Giovannini, Alberto. 1985. "Saving and the Real Interest Rate in LDCs." *Journal of Development Economics* 18 (August): 197–217.

Giovannini, Alberto, and Martha de Melo. 1993. "Government Revenue from Financial Repression." *American Economic Review* 83 (August): 953–63.

Giovannini, Alberto, and Bart Turtelboom. 1994. "Currency Substitution." In *The Handbook of International Macroeconomics,* edited by Frederick van der Ploeg. Oxford: Basil Blackwell.

Goldberg, Linda S. 1994. "Predicting Exchange Rate Crises: Mexico Revisited." *Journal of International Economics* 34 (May):413–30.

Goldfeld, Stephen M., and Edward D. Sichel. 1990. "The Demand for Money." In *Handbook of Monetary Economics*. Vol. I, edited by Benjamin Friedman and Frank H. Hahn. Amsterdam: North Holland.

Goldstein, Morris. 1986. "Global Effects of Fund-Supported Adjustment Programs." Occasional Paper no. 42, International Monetary Fund (March).

Goldstein, Morris, and Peter J. Montiel. 1986. "Evaluating Fund Stabilization Programs with Multicountry Data: Some Methodological Pitfalls." *IMF Staff Papers* 33 (June): 304–44.

Goode, Richard. 1984. *Government Finance in Developing Countries*. Washington, D.C.: Brookings Institution.

Greenaway, David, and Chris Milner. 1991. "Fiscal Dependence on Trade Taxes and Trade Policy Reform." *Journal of Development Studies* 27 (April): 96–132.

Greene, Joshua, and Delano Villanueva. 1991. "Private Investment in Developing Countries." *IMF Staff Papers* 38 (March): 33–58.

Greenwood, Jeremy, and Boyan Jovanovic. 1990. "Financial Development, Growth, and the Distribution of Income." *Journal of Political Economy* 98 (October): 1076–107.

Greenwood, Jeremy, and Kent P. Kimbrough. 1987. "Foreign Exchange Controls in a Black Market Economy." *Journal of Development Economics* 26 (June): 129–43.

Grossman, Gene M., and Elhanan Helpman. 1991. *Innovation and Growth in the World Economy*. Cambridge, Mass.: MIT Press.

Grosse, Robert. 1992. "Colombia's Black Market in Foreign Exchange." *World Development* 20 (August): 1193–1207.

Guidotti, Pablo E., and Manmohan S. Kumar. 1991. *Domestic Public Debt of Externally Indebted Countries*. Occasional Paper no. 80, International Monetary Fund (June). Washington, D.C.: IMF.

Guidotti, Pablo E., and Carlos A. Rodríguez. 1992. "Dollarization in Latin America." *IMF Staff Papers* 39 (September): 518–44.

Gupta, Kanhaya L. 1987. "Aggregate Savings, Financial Intermediation, and the Interest Rate." *Review of Economics and Statistics* 69 (May): 303–11.

Gylfason, Thorvaldur. 1987. "Credit Policy and Economic Activity in Developing Countries with IMF Stabilization Programs." Study in International Finance no. 60, Princeton University (August).

Gylfason, Thorvaldur, and Ole Risager. 1984. "Does Devaluation Improve the Current Account?" *European Economic Review* 25 (June): 37–64.

Gylfason, Thorvaldur, and Marian Radetzki. 1991. "Does Devaluation Make Sense in the Least Developed Countries?" *Economic Development and Cultural Change* 40 (October): 1–25.

Gylfason, Thorvaldur, and Michael Schmid. 1983. "Does Devaluation Cause Stagflation?" *Canadian Journal of Economics* 16 (November): 641–54.

Haan, Jakob de, and Dick Zelhorst. 1990. "The Impact of Government Deficits on Money Growth in Developing Countries." *Journal of International Money and Finance* 9 (December): 455–69.

Haggard, Stephan. 1991. "Inflation and Stabilization." In *Politics and Policy Making in Developing Countries*, edited by Gerald E. Meier. San Francisco: ICS Press.

Haggard, Stephan, and Robert Kaufman. 1989. "The Politics of Stabilization and Structural Adjustment." In *Developing Country Debt and the World Economy,* edited by Jeffrey D. Sachs. Chicago: University of Chicago Press.

———. 1990. "The Political Economy of Inflation and Stabilization in Middle-Income Countries." PRE Working Paper no. 444, World Bank (June).

Haley, James. 1990. "Theoretical Foundations for Sticky Wages." *Journal of Economic Surveys* 4 (April): 115–55.

Haliasos, Michael, and James Tobin. 1990. "The Macroeconomics of Government Finance." In *Handbook of Monetary Economics.* Vol. II, edited by Benjamin M. Friedman and Frank H. Hahn. Amsterdam: North Holland.

Hanna, Donald. 1994. "Indonesian Experience with Financial Sector Reform." Discussion Paper no. 237, World Bank (May).

Hanson, James A. 1980. "The Short-Run Relation Between Growth and Inflation in Latin America." *American Economic Review* 70 (December): 972–89.

———. 1983. "Contractionary Devaluation, Substitution in Production and Consumption, and the Role of the Labor Market." *Journal of International Economics* 14 (February): 179–89.

———. 1985. "Inflation and Imported Input Prices in Some Inflationary Latin American Economies." *Journal of Development Economics* 18 (August): 395–410.

———. 1992. "Opening the Capital Account: A Survey of Issues and Results." Working Paper WPS no. 901, World Bank (May).

Hanson, James A., and Jaime de Melo. 1985. "External Shocks, Financial Reforms, and Stabilization Attempts in Uruguay during 1974–83." *World Development* 13 (August): 917–40.

Haque, Nadeem U. 1988. "Fiscal Policy and Private Sector Saving Behavior in Developing Economies." *IMF Staff Papers* 35 (June): 316–35.

Haque, Nadeem U., Assim Husain, and Peter J. Montiel. 1994. "An Empirical 'Dependent Economy' Model for Pakistan." *World Development* 22 (October): 1585–97.

Haque, Nadeem U., Kajal Lahiri, and Peter J. Montiel. 1990. "A Macroeconometric Model for Developing Countries." *IMF Staff Papers* 37 (September): 537–59.

Haque, Nadeem U., and Peter J. Montiel. 1989. "Consumption in Developing Countries: Test for Liquidity Constraints and Finite Horizons." *Review of Economics and Statistics* 71 (August): 408–15.

———. 1991. "Capital Mobility in Developing Countries: Some Empirical Tests." *World Development* 19 (October): 1391–98.

———. 1994. "The Macroeconomics of Public Sector Deficits: The Case of Pakistan." In *Public Sector Deficits and Macroeconomic Performance,* edited by William Easterly, Carlos A. Rodríguez, and Klaus Schmidt-Hebbel. Oxford: Oxford University Press.

Harberger, Arnold C. 1963. "The Dynamics of Inflation in Chile." In *Measurement in Economics,* edited by Carl F. Christ. Stanford, Calif.: Stanford University Press.

Harris, John, and Michael P. Todaro. 1970. "Migration, Unemployment and Development: A Two-Sector Analysis." *American Economic Review* 60 (March): 126–43.

Harvey, Andrew C. 1990. *The Econometric Analysis of Time Series.* 2nd ed. London: P. Allan.

Helpman, Elhanan. 1988. "Macroeconomic Effects of Price Controls: The Role of Market Structure." *Economic Journal* 98 (June): 340–54.

Hentschel, Jesko. 1992. *Imports and Growth in Highly Indebted Countries*. Berlin: Springer-Verlag.

Heymann, Daniel. 1989. "From Sharp Disinflation to Hyper and Back: The Argentine Experience, 1985–89." Unpublished. CEPAL (November).

Heymann, Daniel, and Pablo Sanguinetti. 1994. "Fiscal Inconsistencies and High Inflation." *Journal of Development Economics* 43 (February): 85–104.

Himarios, Daniel. 1989. "Do Devaluations Improve the Trade Balance? The Evidence Revisited." *Economic Inquiry* 27 (January): 143–68.

Hoffman, Dennis L., and Chakib Tahiri. 1994. "Money Demand in Morocco: Estimating Long-Run Elasticities for a Developing Country." *Oxford Bulletin of Economics and Statistics* 56 (August): 305–24.

Hoover, Kevin D. 1988. *The New Classical Macroeconomics*. Oxford: Basil Blackwell.

Horn, Henrik, and Torsten Persson. 1988. "Exchange Rate Policy, Wage Formation, and Credibility." *European Economic Review* 32 (October): 1621–36.

Horton, Susan, Ravi Kanbur, and Dipak Mazumdar. 1994. "Overview." In *Labor Markets in an Era of Adjustment*. Washington, D.C.: World Bank.

International Monetary Fund. 1987. *Theoretical Aspects of the Design of Fund-Supported Programs*. Occasional Paper no. 55, International Monetary Fund (September). Washington, D.C.: IMF.

Islam, Shafiqul. 1984. "Devaluation, Stabilization Policies and the Developing Countries." *Journal of Development Economics* 14 (January): 37–60.

Ize, Alain, and Guillermo Ortiz. 1987. "Fiscal Rigidities, Public Debt, and Capital Flight." *IMF Staff Papers* 34 (June): 311–32.

Jaffee, Dwight, and Joseph Stiglitz. 1990. "Credit Rationing." In *Handbook of Monetary Economics*. Vol. II, edited by Benjamin M. Friedman and Frank H. Hahn. Amsterdam: North Holland.

Jappelli, Tullio, and Marco Pagano. 1994. "Saving, Growth, and Liquidity Constraints." *Quarterly Journal of Economics* 109 (February): 83–110.

Jonung, Lars. 1990. *The Political Economy of Price Controls*. Brookfield, Vt.: E. Gower.

Jorgensen, Steen L., and Martin Paldam. 1986. *Exchange Rates and Domestic Inflation: A Study of Price/Wage Inflation in Eight Latin American Countries, 1946–85*. Working Paper no. 10, Aarhus University.

Jung, W. S. 1985. "Output-Inflation Tradeoffs in Industrial and Developing Countries." *Journal of Macroeconomics* 7 (Winter): 101–14.

Kähkönen, Juha. 1987. "Liberalization Policies and Welfare in a Financially Repressed Economy." *IMF Staff Papers* 34 (September): 531–47.

Kamas, Linda. 1986. "The Balance of Payments Offset to Monetary Policy: Monetarist, Portfolio Balance, and Keynesian Estimates for Mexico and Venezuela." *Journal of Money, Credit, and Banking* 18 (November): 467–81.

———. 1992. "Devaluation, National Output and the Trade Balance: Some Evidence from Colombia." *Weltwirtschaftliches Archives* 128 (3): 425–44.

Kamin, Steven B. 1988. "Devaluation, External Balance and Macroeconomic Performance: A Look at the Numbers." Study in International Finance no. 62, Princeton University (August).

——. 1993. "Devaluation, Exchange Controls, and Black Markets for Foreign Exchange in Developing Countries." *Journal of Development Economics* 40 (February): 151–69.

Kamin, Steven B., and Neil R. Ericsson. 1993. Dollarization in Argentina. Working Paper no. 460, International Finance Division, Federal Reserve Board (November).

Kapur, Basant. 1976. "Alternative Stabilization Policies for Less Developed Economies." *Journal of Political Economy* 84 (August): 777–95.

——. 1992. "Formal and Informal Financial Markets, and the Neo-Structuralist Critique of the Financial Liberalization Strategy in Less Developed Countries." *Journal of Development Economics* 38 (January): 63–77.

Karnik, Ajit V. 1990. "Elections and Government Expenditures: The Indian Evidence." *Journal of Quantitative Economics* 6 (January): 203–12.

Karras, Georgios. 1994. "Government Spending and Private Consumption: Some International Evidence." *Journal of Money, Credit, and Banking* 26 (February): 9–22.

Kawai, Masahiro, and Louis J. Maccini. 1990. "Fiscal Policy, Anticipated Switches in Methods of Finance, and the Effects on the Economy." *International Economic Review* 31 (November): 913–34.

——. 1991. *The Effects of Anticipated Switches in Budget-Deficit Financing Methods in a Small Open Economy.* Working Paper no. 91–35, University of British Columbia (September).

Kay, Cristobal. 1989. *Latin American Theories of Development and Underdevelopment.* London: P. Routledge.

Khan, Mohsin S. 1980. "Monetary Shocks and the Dynamics of Inflation." *IMF Staff Papers* 27 (June): 250–84.

——. 1990. "Evaluating the Effects of IMF-Supported Adjustment Programmes: A Survey." In *International Finance and the Less Developed Countries,* edited by Kate Phylaktis and Mahmood Pradham. New York: St. Martin's Press.

Khan, Mohsin S., and Malcolm D. Knight. 1981. "Stabilization Programs in Developing Countries: A Formal Framework." *IMF Staff Papers* 28 (March): 1–53.

Khan, Mohsin S., and Manmohan S. Kumar. 1993. *Public and Private Investment and the Convergence of Per Capita Incomes in Developing Countries.* Working Paper no. 93/51, International Monetary Fund (June).

——. 1994. "Determinants of the Current Account in Developing Countries, 1970–1990." Unpublished. International Monetary Fund (March).

Khan, Mohsin S., and J. Saul Lizondo. 1987. "Devaluation, Fiscal Deficits, and the Real Exchange Rate." *World Bank Economic Review* 1 (January): 357–74.

Khan, Mohsin S., and Peter J. Montiel. 1987. "Real Exchange Rate Dynamics in a Small Primary-Exporter Country." *IMF Staff Papers* 34 (December): 687–710.

Khan, Mohsin S., Peter J. Montiel, and Nadeem U. Haque. 1990. "Adjustment with Growth: Relating the Analytical Approaches of the IMF and the World Bank." *Journal of Development Economics* 32 (January): 155–79.

Khan, Mohsin S., and C. Luis Ramírez-Rojas. 1986. "Currency Substitution and Government Revenue from Inflation." *Revista de Análisis Económico* 1 (June): 79–88.

Khan, Mohsin S., and Roberto Zahler. 1983. "The Macroeconomic Effects of Changes in Barriers to Trade and Capital Flows." *IMF Staff Papers* 30 (June): 223–82.

———. 1985. "Trade and Financial Liberalization Given External Shocks and Inconsistent Domestic Policies." *IMF Staff Papers* 32 (March): 22–55.

Kharas, Homi, and Brian Pinto. 1989. "Exchange Rate Rules, Black Market Premia and Fiscal Deficits: The Bolivian Hyperinflation." *Review of Economic Studies* 56 (July): 435–47.

Khor, Hoe E., and Liliana Rojas-Suárez. 1991. "Interest Rates in Mexico." *IMF Staff Papers* 38 (December): 850–71.

Kiguel, Miguel A. 1987. "The Non-Dynamic Equivalence of Monetary and Exchange Rate Rules under Imperfect Capital Mobility and Rational Expectations." *Journal of International Money and Finance* 6 (June): 207–14.

———. 1989. "Budget Deficits, Stability and the Dynamics of Hyperinflation." *Journal of Money, Credit, and Banking* 21 (May): 148–57.

Kiguel, Miguel A., and Nissan Liviatan. 1988. "Inflationary Rigidities and Orthodox Stabilization Policies: Lessons from Latin America." *World Bank Economic Review* 2 (September): 273–98.

———. 1991. "The Inflation-Stabilization Cycles in Argentina and Brazil." In *Lessons of Economic Stabilization and Its Aftermath,* edited by Michael Bruno, Stanley Fischer, Elhanan Helpman, Nissan Liviatan, and Leora Meridor. Cambridge, Mass.: MIT Press.

———. 1992a. "The Business Cycle Associated with Exchange Rate Based Stabilization." *World Bank Economic Review* 6 (May): 279–305.

———. 1992b. "When Do Heterodox Stabilization Programs Work? Lessons from Experience." *World Bank Research Observer* 7 (January): 35–57.

———. 1994. "A Policy-Game Approach to the High Inflation Equilibrium." *Journal of Development Economics* 45 (October): 135–40.

Kiguel, Miguel A., and J. Saul Lizondo. 1990. "Adoption and Abandonment of Dual Exchange Rate Systems." *Revista de Analisis Económico* 5 (March): 3–23.

Kiguel, Miguel A., and Stephen A. O'Connell. 1994. "Parallel Exchange Rates in Developing Countries: Lessons from Eight Case Studies." Policy Research Working Paper no. 1265, World Bank (March).

Killick, Tony, Moazzam Malik, and Marcus Manuel. 1992. "What Can We Know about the Effects of IMF Programmes?" *World Economy* 15 (September): 599–632.

Kimbrough, Kent P. 1985. "An Examination of the Effects of Government Purchases in an Open Economy." *Journal of International Money and Finance* 4 (March): 113–33.

———. 1986. "Foreign Aid and Optimal Fiscal Policy." *Canadian Journal of Economics* 19 (February): 35–61.

———. 1992. "Speculative Attacks: The Roles of Intertemporal Substitution and the Interest Elasticity of the Demand for Money." *Journal of Macroeconomics* 14 (Fall): 689–710.

King, Robert G., and Ross Levine. 1993. "Finance and Growth: Schumpeter Might Be Right." *Quarterly Journal of Economics* 108 (August): 717–37.

Kirman, Alan P. 1992. "Whom or What Does the Representative Individual Represent?" *Journal of Economic Perspectives* 6 (Spring): 117–36.

Kletzer, Kenneth. 1988. "External Borrowing by LDCs: A Survey of Some Theoretical Issues." In *The State of Development Economics,* edited by Gustav Ranis and Paul T. Schultz. New York: Basil Blackwell.

Knight, Malcolm, Norman Loayza, and Delano Villanueva. 1993. "Testing the Neoclassical Theory of Economic Growth." *IMF Staff Papers* 40 (September): 512–41.

Knight, Peter T., F. Desmond McCarthy, and Sweder van Wijnbergen. 1986. "Escaping Hyperinflation." *Finance and Development* 23 (December): 14–17.

Krasker, William S. 1980. "The 'Peso Problem' in Testing the Efficiency of Forward Exchange Rate Markets." *Journal of Monetary Economics* 6 (March): 269–76.

Kreinin, Mordechai, and Lawrence H. Officer. 1978. *The Monetary Approach to the Balance of Payments: A Survey.* Study in International Finance no. 43, Princeton University (November).

Krueger, Ann O. 1985. "How to Liberalize a Small, Open Economy." In *The Economics of the Caribbean Basin,* edited by Michael Connolly and John McDermott. New York: Praeger.

Krugman, Paul. 1979. "A Model of Balance of Payments Crises." *Journal of Money, Credit, and Banking* 11 (August): 311–25.

———. 1988. "Financing vs. Forgiving a Debt Overhang." *Journal of Development Economics* 29 (November): 253–68.

Krugman, Paul, and Lance Taylor. 1978. "Contractionary Effects of Devaluation." *Journal of International Economics* 8 (August): 445–56.

Kwack, Sung Y. 1986. "Policy Analysis with a Macroeconomic Model of Korea." *Economic Modeling* 3 (July): 175–96.

Lächler, Ulrich, 1988. "Credibility and the Dynamics of Disinflation in Open Economies." *Journal of Development Economics* 28 (May): 285–307.

Lahiri, Ashok K. 1989. "Dynamics of Asian Savings: The Role of Growth and Age Structure." *IMF Staff Papers* 36 (March): 228–61.

Lai, Ching-Chong, and Wen-Ya Chang. 1994. "Unification of Foreign Exchange Markets: A Comment." *IMF Staff Papers* 41 (March): 163–70.

Lanyi, Anthony, and Rüsdü Saracoglu. 1983. *Interest Rate Policies in Developing Countries.* Occasional Paper no. 22, International Monetary Fund (October).

Larraín, Felipe, and Rodrigo Vergara. 1993. "Investment and Macroeconomic Adjustment: The Case of East Asia." In *Striving for Growth after Adjustment,* edited by Luis Servén and Andrés Solimano. Washington, D.C.: World Bank.

Layard, Richard, Stephen Nickell, and Richard Jackman. 1991. *Unemployment.* Oxford: Oxford University Press.

Lee, Jong-Wha. 1993. "International Trade, Distortions, and Long-Run Economic Growth." *IMF Staff Papers* 40 (June): 299–328.

Lee, Kiseok, and Ronald A. Ratti. 1993. "On Seignorage, Operating Rules, and Dual Equilibria." *Quarterly Journal of Economics* 108 (May): 543–50.

Leff, Nathaniel H., and Kazuo Sato. 1988. "Estimating Investment and Savings Functions for Developing Countries." *International Economic Journal* 2 (September): 1–18.

Le Fort, Guillermo R. 1988. "The Relative Price of Nontraded Goods, Absorption, and Exchange Rate Policy in Chile, 1974–82." *IMF Staff Papers* 35 (June): 336–70.

Leiderman, Leonardo, and Mario I. Blejer. 1988. "Modeling and Testing Ricardian Equivalence." *IMF Staff Papers* 35 (March): 1–35.

Leiderman, Leonardo, and Assaf Razin. 1988. "Testing Ricardian Neutrality with an Intertemporal Stochastic Model." *Journal of Money, Credit, and Banking* 20 (February): 1–21.

Leite, Sérgio P., and Dawit Makonen. 1986. "Saving and Interest Rates in the BCEA Countries: An Empirical Analysis." *Savings and Development* 10 (July): 219–31.

Leite, Sérgio P., and Ved Sundararajan. 1990. "Issues in Interest Rate Management and Liberalization." *IMF Staff Papers* 37 (December): 735–52.

Levine, Ross, and David Renelt. 1992. "A Sensitivity Analysis of Cross-Country Growth Regressions." *American Economic Review* 82 (September): 942–63.

Liang, Ming-Yih. 1988. "A Note On Financial Dualism and Interest Rate Policies: A Loanable Funds Approach." *International Economic Review* 29 (August): 539–49.

Lipschitz, Leslie. 1984. "Domestic Credit and Exchange Rates in Developing Countries: Some Policy Experiments with Korean Data." *IMF Staff Papers* 31 (December): 595–635.

Liviatan, Nissan. 1984. "Tight Money and Inflation." *Journal of Monetary Economics* 13 (January): 5–15.

———. 1986. "The Tight Money Paradox—An Alternative View." *Journal of Macroeconomics* 8 (Winter): 105–12.

———. 1988a. *Israel's Stabilization Program.* PRE Working Paper no. 91, World Bank (September).

———. 1988b. "On the Interaction between Monetary and Fiscal Policies under Perfect Foresight." *Oxford Economic Papers* 40 (March): 193–203.

Lizondo, J. Saul. 1983. "Interest Differential and Covered Interest Arbitrage." In *Financial Policies and the World Capital Market,* edited by Pedro Aspe Armella, Rudiger Dornbusch, and Maurice Obstfeld. Chicago: University of Chicago Press.

———. 1987. "Unification of Dual Exchange Markets." *Journal of International Economics* 22 (February): 57–77.

———. 1991a. "Alternative Dual Exchange Market Regimes." *IMF Staff Papers* 38 (September): 560–81.

———. 1991b. "Real Exchange Rate Targets, Nominal Exchange Rate Policies, and Inflation." *Revista de Análisis Económico* 6 (June): 5–21.

———. 1993. "Real Exchange Rate Targeting under Imperfect Asset Substitutability." *IMF Staff Papers* 40 (December): 829–51.

Lizondo, J. Saul, and Peter J. Montiel. 1989. "Contractionary Devaluation in Developing Countries: An Analytical Overview." *IMF Staff Papers* 36 (March): 182–227.

Lohmann, Susan. 1992. "Optimal Commitment in Monetary Policy: Credibility versus Flexibility." *American Economic Review* 82 (March): 273–86.

Lucas, Robert E., Jr. 1973. "Some International Evidence on Output-Inflation Trade-offs." *American Economic Review* 63 (June): 326–34.

———. 1976. "Econometric Policy Evaluation: A Critique." In *The Phillips Curve and Labor Markets,* edited by Karl Brunner and Allan H. Meltzer. Carnegie-

Rochester Conference Series on Public Policy, Vol. 1. Amsterdam: North-Holland.

———. 1988. "On the Mechanics of Economic Development." *Journal of Monetary Economics* 22 (January): 3–42.

———. 1993. "Making A Miracle." *Econometrica* 61 (March): 251–72.

Lustig, Nora. 1992. "From Structuralism to Neostructuralism: The Search for a Heterodox Paradigm." In *The Latin American Development Debate,* edited by Patricio Meller. Boulder, Colo.: Westview Press.

Macedo, Jorge Braga de. 1987. "Currency Inconvertibility, Trade Taxes and Smuggling." *Journal of Development Economics* 27 (October): 109–25.

Mankiw, N. Gregory, David Romer, and David N. Weil. 1992. "A Contribution to the Empirics of Economic Growth." *Quarterly Journal of Economics* 107 (May): 407–37.

Mansur, Ahsan, and John Whalley. 1984. "Numerical Specification of Applied General Equilibrium Models: Estimation, Calibration, and Data." In *Applied General Equilibrium Analysis,* edited by Herbert E. Scarf and John B. Shoven. New York: Cambridge University Press.

Marquez, Jaime. 1987. "Money Demand in Open Economies: A Currency Substitution Model for Venezuela." *Journal of International Money and Finance* 6 (June): 167–78.

Masson, Paul R. 1985. "The Sustainability of Fiscal Deficits." *IMF Staff Papers* 32 (August): 577–605.

Mathieson, Donald. 1980. "Financial Reform and Stabilization Policy in a Developing Economy." *Journal of Development Economics* 7 (September): 359–95.

Mathieson, Donald, and Liliana Rojas-Suárez. 1993. "Liberalization of the Capital Account: Experiences and Issues." Occasional Paper no. 103, International Monetary Fund (March).

Matsuyama, Kiminori. 1991. "On Exchange-Rate Stabilization." *Journal of Economic Dynamics and Control* 15 (January): 7–26.

McCallum, Bennett T. 1984. "Are Bond-Financed Deficits Inflationary? A Ricardian Analysis." *Journal of Political Economy* 92 (February): 123–35.

McDonald, Donogh. 1983. *The Determinants of Saving Behavior in Latin America.* Working Paper no. 83/26, International Monetary Fund (April).

McKinnon, Ronald I. 1973. *Money and Capital in Economic Development.* Washington, D.C.: Brookings Institution.

———. 1976. "Saving Propensities and the Korean Monetary Reform in Retrospect." In *Finance in Growth and Development,* edited by Ronald McKinnon. New York: Marcel Dekker.

———. 1993. *The Order of Economic Liberalization.* 2nd ed. Baltimore: Johns Hopkins University Press.

McKinnon, Ronald I., and Donald J. Mathieson. *How to Manage a Repressed Economy.* Essay in International Finance no. 145, Princeton University (December).

McNelis, Paul D., and Klaus Schmidt-Hebbel. 1993. "Financial Liberalization and Adjustment." *Journal of International Money and Finance* 12 (June): 249–77.

Meller, Patricio, and Andrés Solimano. 1987. "A Simple Macro Model for a Small Open Economy Facing a Binding External Constraint." *Journal of Development Economics* 26 (June): 25–35.

Melvin, Michael. 1988. "The Dollarization of Latin America as a Market-Enforced Monetary Reform: Evidence and Implications." *Economic Development and Cultural Change* 36 (April): 543–58.

Melvin, Michael, and Jerry Ladman. 1991. "Coca Dollars and the Dollarization of South America." *Journal of Money, Credit, and Banking* 23 (November): 752–63.

Michaely, Michael. 1954. "A Geometric Analysis of Black Market Behavior." *American Economic Review* 44 (September): 627–37.

Mikesell, Raymond F., and James E. Zinser. 1973. "The Nature of the Savings Function in Developing Countries: A Survey of the Theoretical and Empirical Literature." *Journal of Economic Literature* 11 (March): 1–26.

Mirakhor, Abbas, and Peter J. Montiel. 1987. *Import Intensity of Output Growth in Developing Countries, 1970–85.* Staff Studies for the World Economic Outlook, International Monetary Fund. Washington, D.C.: IMF.

Modiano, Eduardo M. 1988. "The Cruzado First Attempt: The Brazilian Stabilization Program of February 1986." In *Inflation Stabilization,* edited by Michael Bruno, Guido Di Tella, Rudiger Dornbusch, and Stanley Fischer. Cambridge, Mass.: MIT Press.

Montiel, Peter J. 1986. "Long-Run Equilibrium in a Keynesian Model of a Small Open Economy." *IMF Staff Papers* 33 (March): 685–708.

———. 1987. "Output and Unanticipated Money in the 'Dependent Economy' Model." *IMF Staff Papers* 34 (June): 228–59.

———. 1989. "Empirical Analysis of High-Inflation Episodes in Argentina, Brazil and Israel." *IMF Staff Papers* 36 (September): 527–49.

———. 1991*a.* "Money versus Credit in the Determination of Output for Small Open Economies." *Open Economies Review* 2 (May): 203–10.

———. 1991*b.* "The Transmission Mechanism for Monetary Policy in Developing Countries." *IMF Staff Papers* 38 (March): 83–108.

———. 1992. "Fiscal Aspects of Developing-Country Debt Problems and DDSR Operations: A Conceptual Framework." Unpublished. World Bank (August).

———. 1993. "A Macroeconomic Simulation Model for India." Unpublished. World Bank (February).

———. 1994. "Capital Mobility in Developing Countries: Some Measurement Issues and Empirical Estimates." *World Bank Economic Review* 8 (September): 311–50.

Montiel, Peter J., Pierre-Richard Agénor, and Nadeem U. Haque. 1993. *Informal Financial Markets in Developing Countries.* Oxford: Basil Blackwell.

Montiel, Peter J., and Jonathan Ostry. 1991. "Macroeconomic Implications of Real Exchange Rate Targeting in Developing Countries." *IMF Staff Papers* 38 (December): 872–900.

———. 1992. "Real Exchange Rate Targeting under Capital Controls." *IMF Staff Papers* 39 (March): 58–78.

Morales, Juan Antonio. 1986. "Estabilización y Nueva Política Económica en Bolivia." Unpublished. Economic Commission for Latin America and the Caribbean (October).

Morandé, Felipe G. 1988. "Domestic Currency Appreciation and Foreign Capital Inflows: What Comes First?" *Journal of International Money and Finance* 7 (December): 448–66.

————. 1992. "Dynamics of Real Asset Prices, the Real Exchange Rate, and Foreign Capital Inflows: Chile, 1976–1989." *Journal of Development Economics* 39 (July): 111–39.

Mourmouras, Alex, and José A. Tijerina. 1994. "Collection Lags and the Optimal Inflation Tax." *IMF Staff Papers* 41 (March): 30–54.

Mundell, Robert A. 1963. "Capital Mobility and Stabilization Policy under Fixed and Flexible Exchange Rates." *Canadian Journal of Economics and Political Science* 29 (November): 475–85.

Musgrove, Phillip. 1979. "Permanent Household Income and Consumption in Urban South America." *American Economic Review* 69 (June): 355–68.

Mussa, Michael. 1986. "The Adjustment Process and the Timing of Trade Liberalization." In *Economic Liberalization in Developing Countries,* edited by Armeane M. Choksi and Demetris Papageorgiou. Oxford: Basil Blackwell.

————. 1987. "Macroeconomic Policy and Trade Liberalization: Some Guidelines." *World Bank Research Observer* 2 (January): 61–77.

Neck, Reinhard. 1991. "The Political Business Cycle under a Quadratic Objective Function." *European Journal of Political Economy* 7 (4): 439–67.

Nelson, Joan M. 1990. "The Politics of Economic Adjustment in Developing Nations." In *Economic Crisis and Policy Choice,* edited by Joan M. Nelson. Princeton, N.J.: Princeton University Press.

Nelson, Joan M., and John Waterbury. 1988. *Fragile Coalitions: The Politics of Economic Adjustment.* New Brunswick: Transaction Books.

Nelson, Michael A., and Ram D. Singh. 1994. "The Deficit-Growth Connection: Some Recent Evidence from Developing Countries." *Economic Development and Cultural Change* 43 (October): 167–91.

Nordhaus, William. 1975. "The Political Business Cycle." *Review of Economic Studies* 42 (April): 169–90.

————. 1989. "Alternative Models of Political Business Cycles." *Brookings Papers in Economic Activity* 1 (March): 1–68.

Nowak, Michael. 1984. "Quantitative Controls and Unofficial Markets in Foreign Exchange: A Formal Framework." *IMF Staff Papers* 31 (June): 406–31.

Nugent, Jeffrey B., and Constantine Glezakos. 1982. "Phillips Curves in Developing Countries: The Latin American Case." *Economic Development and Cultural Change* 30 (January): 321–34.

Obstfeld, Maurice. 1981. "Capital Mobility and Devaluation in an Optimizing Model with Rational Expectations." *American Economic Review* 71 (May): 217–21.

————. 1984. "Balance of Payments Crises and Devaluation." *Journal of Money, Credit, and Banking* 16 (May): 208–17.

————. 1985. "The Capital Inflows Problem Revisited: A Stylized Model of Southern Cone Disinflation." *Review of Economic Studies* 52 (October): 605–25.

————. 1986. "Capital Flows, the Current Account, and the Real Exchange Rate: Consequences of Liberalization and Stabilization." In *Economic Adjustment and Exchange Rates in Developing Countries,* edited by Liaqat Ahmed and Sebastián Edwards. Chicago: University of Chicago Press.

————. 1986c. "Speculative Attacks and the External Constraint in a Maximizing Model of the Balance of Payments." *Canadian Journal of Economics* 19 (March): 1–22.

Olivera, Julio H. 1967. "Money, Prices and Fiscal Lags: A Note on the Dynamics of Inflation." *Banca Nazionale del Lavoro Quarterly Review* 20 (September): 258–67.

Ordeshook, Peter C. 1990. "The Emerging Discipline of Political Economy." In *Perspectives on Political Economy,* edited by James E. Alt and Kenneth A. Shepsle. Cambridge: Cambridge University Press.

Orphanides, Athanasios. 1992*a*. "Credibility and Reputation in Stabilization." Unpublished. Federal Reserve Board (May).

———. 1992*b*. *The Timing of Stabilizations.* Working Paper no. 194, Federal Reserve Board (April).

Ortíz, Guillermo. 1983. "Currency Substitution in Mexico: The Dollarization Problem." *Journal of Money, Credit, and Banking* 15 (May): 174–85.

Oshikoya, Temitope W. 1994. "Macroeconomic Determinants of Domestic Private Investment in Africa." *Economic Development and Cultural Change* 42 (April): 573–96.

Ostry, Jonathan D. 1991. "Trade Liberalization in Developing Countries." *IMF Staff Papers* 38 (September): 447–79.

Ostry, Jonathan D., and Carment M. Reinhart. 1992. "Private Saving and Terms of Trade Shocks: Evidence from Developing Countries." *IMF Staff Papers* 39 (September): 495–517.

Owen, Dorian P., and Otton Solis-Fallas. 1989. "Unorganized Money Markets and 'Unproductive' Assets in the New Structuralist Critique of Financial Liberalization." *Journal of Development Economics* 31 (October): 341–55.

Pagano, Marco. 1993. "Financial Markets and Growth: An Overview." *European Economic Review* 37 (April): 613–22.

Papademos, Lucas, and Franco Modigliani. 1983. "Inflation, Financial and Fiscal Structure, and the Monetary Mechanism." *European Economic Review* 21 (March): 203–50.

Papageorgiou, Demetris, Armeane M. Choksi, and Michael Michaely. 1990. *Liberalizing Foreign Trade in Developing Countries.* Washington, D.C.: World Bank.

Park, Daekeun. 1994. "Foreign Exchange Liberalization and the Viability of a Fixed Exchange Rate Regime." *Journal of International Economics* 36 (February): 99–116.

Park, Yung Chul. 1991. "Financial Repression and Liberalization." In *Liberalization in the Process of Economic Development,* edited by Lawrence B. Krause and Kim Kihwan. Berkeley: University of California Press.

Parkin, Vincent. 1991. *Chronic Inflation in an Industrializing Economy: The Brazilian Inflation.* Cambridge: Cambridge University Press.

Pastor, Manuel, Jr. 1992. *Inflation, Stabilization, and Debt: Macroeconomic Experiments in Peru and Bolivia.* Boulder, Colo.: Westview Press.

Patinkin, Don. 1993. "Israel's Stabilization Program of 1985, or Some Simple Truths of Monetary Theory." *Journal of Economic Perspectives* 7 (March): 103–28.

Paus, Eva. 1991. "Adjustment and Development in Latin America: The Failure of Peruvian Orthodoxy." *World Development* 19 (May): 411–34.

Pazos, Felipe. 1972. *Chronic Inflation in Latin America.* New York: Praeger.

Persson, Torsten, and Guido Tabellini. 1994. "Is Inequality Harmful for Growth?" *American Economic Review* 84 (June): 600–621.

Persson, Torsten, and Sweder van Wijnbergen. 1993. "Signalling, Wage Controls, and Monetary Disinflation Policy." *Economic Journal* 103 (January): 79–97.

Pesaran, Hashem. 1988. *The Limits to Rational Expectations.* Oxford: Basil Blackwell.

Pfeffermann, Guy, and Andrea Madarassy. 1993. *Trends in Private Investment in Developing Countries 1993.* IFC Discussion Paper no. 16, World Bank.

Phelps, Edmund S. 1973. "Inflation in a Theory of Public Finance." *Swedish Journal of Economics* 75 (March): 67–82.

Phylaktis, Kate. 1988. "Capital Controls: The Case of Argentina." *Journal of International Money and Finance* 7 (September): 303–20.

———. 1991. "The Black Market for Dollars in Chile." *Journal of Development Economics* 37 (November): 155–72.

Phylaktis, Kate, and Mark P. Taylor. 1992. "Monetary Dynamics of Sustained High Inflation: Taiwan, 1945–1949." *Southern Economic Journal* 58 (January): 610–22.

———. 1993. "Money Demand, the Cagan Model, and the Inflation Tax: Some Latin American Evidence." *Review of Economics and Statistics* 75 (February): 32–37.

Pindyck, Robert. 1991. "Irreversibility, Uncertainty, and Investment." *Journal of Economic Literature* 29 (September): 1110–48.

Pinto, Brian. 1989. "Black Market Premia, Exchange Rate Unification and Inflation in Sub-Saharan Africa." *World Bank Economic Review* 3 (September): 321–38.

———. 1991a. "Black Markets for Foreign Exchange, Real Exchange Rates and Inflation." *Journal of International Economics* 30 (March): 121–35.

———. 1991b. "Unification of Official and Black Market Exchange Rates in Sub-Saharan Africa." In *Exchange Rate Policies in Developing and Post-Socialist Countries,* edited by Emil-Maria Claassen. San Francisco: ICS Press.

Pitt, Mark. 1984. "Smuggling and the Black Market for Foreign Exchange." *Journal of International Economics* 16 (June): 243–57.

Polak, Jacques J. 1957. "Monetary Analysis of Income Formation and Payments Problems." *IMF Staff Papers* 6 (November): 1–50.

———. 1989. *Financial Policies and Development.* Organisation for Economic Cooperation and Development, Development Centre, Paris.

Poloz, Stephen S. 1986. "Currency Substitution and the Precautionary Demand for Money." *Journal of International Money and Finance* 5 (March): 115–24.

Ram, Rati. 1984. "Further International Evidence on Output-Inflation Tradeoffs." *Canadian Journal of Economics* 17 (August): 523–40.

Rama, Martín. 1993. "Empirical Investment Equations in Developing Countries." In *Striving for Growth after Adjustment,* edited by Luis Servén and Andrés Solimano. Washington, D.C.: World Bank.

Ramírez, Miguel D. 1994. "Public and Private Investment in Mexico, 1950–90: An Empirical Analysis." *Southern Economic Journal* 61 (July): 1–17.

Ramírez-Rojas, C. Luis. 1985. "Currency Substitution in Argentina, Mexico, and Uruguay." *IMF Staff Papers* 32 (December): 629–67.

Ramos, Juan. 1986. *Neoconservative Economics in the Southern Cone of Latin America, 1973–83.* Baltimore: Johns Hopkins University Press.

Rebelo, Sergio. 1991. "Long-Run Policy Analysis and Long-Run Growth." *Journal of Political Economy* 99 (June): 500–521.

Reinhart, Carmen M., and Vincent R. Reinhart. 1991. "Output Fluctuations and Monetary Shocks." *IMF Staff Papers* 38 (December): 705–35.

Reinhart, Carmen M., and Carlos A. Végh. 1995. "Nominal Interest Rates, Consumption Booms, and Lack of Credibility." *Journal of Development Economics* 46 (April): 357–78.

Reinhart, Carmen M., and Peter Wickham. 1994. "Commodity Prices: Cyclical Weakness or Secular Decline?" *IMF Staff Papers* 41 (June): 175–213.

Reisen, Helmut. 1989. "Public Debt, External Competitiveness, and Fiscal Discipline in Developing Countries." Study in International Finance no. 66, Princeton University (November).

Reisen, Helmut, and Helene Yeches. 1993. "Time-Varying Estimates on the Openness of the Capital Account in Korea and Taiwan." *Journal of Development Economics* 41 (August): 285–305.

Rennhack, Robert, and Guillermo Mondino. 1988. *Capital Mobility and Monetary Policy in Colombia.* Working Paper no. 88/77, International Monetary Fund (August).

Risager, Ole. 1988. "Devaluation, Profitability and Investment." *Scandinavian Journal of Economics* 90 (June): 125–40.

Roberts, John. 1989. "Liberalizing Foreign-Exchange Rates in Sub-Saharan Africa." *Development Policy Review* 7 (June): 115–42.

Robinson, David J., Yangho Byeon, and Ranjit Teja. 1991. "Thailand: Adjusting to Success—Current Policy Issues." Occasional Paper no. 85, International Monetary Fund (August).

Robinson, David J., and Peter Stella. 1993. "Amalgamating Central Bank and Fiscal Deficits." In *How to Measure the Fiscal Deficit: Analytical and Methodological Issues,* edited by Mario I. Blejer and Adrienne Cheasty. Washington, D.C.: International Monetary Fund.

Robinson, Sherman. 1991. "Macroeconomics, Financial Variables, and Computable General Equilibrium Models." *World Development* 19 (November): 1509–25.

Roca, Santiago, and Rodrigo Priale. 1987. "Devaluation, Inflationary Expectations and Stabilisation in Peru." *Journal of Economic Studies* 14: 5–33.

Rodríguez, Carlos A. 1978. "A Stylized Model of the Devaluation-Inflation Spiral." *IMF Staff Papers* 25 (March): 76–89.

———. 1982. "The Argentine Stabilization Plan of December 20th." *World Development* 10 (September): 801–11.

———. 1991. *The Macroeconomics of the Public Sector Deficit: The Case of Argentina.* Working Paper WPS no. 632, World Bank (March).

———. 1993. "Money and Credit under Currency Substitution." *IMF Staff Papers* 40 (June): 414–26.

Rodríguez, Miguel A. 1991. "Public Sector Behavior in Venezuela: 1970–85." In *The Public Sector and the Latin American Debt Crisis,* edited by Felipe Larraín and Marcelo Selowsky. San Francisco: ICS Press.

Rodrik, Dani. 1987. "Trade and Capital Account Liberalization in a Keynesian Economy." *Journal of International Economics* 23 (August): 113–29.

———. 1989. "Credibility of Trade Reforms—A Policymaker's Guide." *World Economy* 12 (March): 1–16.

———. 1991. "Policy Uncertainty and Private Investment in Developing Countries." *Journal of Development Economics* 36 (October): 229–42.

———. 1995. "Trade Liberalization and Disinflation." in Understanding Interdependence, ed. by Peter B. Kenen. Princeton University Press. Princeton, N.J.

Roemer, Michael, and Steven C. Radelet. 1991. "Macroeconomic Reform in Developing Countries." In *Reforming Economic Systems in Developing Countries,* edited by Dwight H. Perkins and Michael Roemer. Cambridge, Mass.: Harvard University Press.

Rogers, John H. 1990. "Foreign Inflation Transmission under Flexible Exchange Rates and Currency Substitution." *Journal of Money, Credit, and Banking* 22 (May): 195–206.

Rogoff, Kenneth A. 1985. "The Optimal Degree of Commitment to an Intermediate Monetary Target." *Quarterly Journal of Economics* 100 (November): 1169–89.

———. 1989. "Reputational Constraints on Monetary Policy." In *Modern Business Cycle Theory,* edited by Robert J. Barro. Cambridge, Mass.: Harvard University Press.

———. 1990. "Equilibrium Political Budget Cycles." *American Economic Review* 80 (March): 21–36.

Rogoff, Kenneth A., and Anne Sibert. 1988. "Elections and Macroeconomic Policy Cycles." *Review of Economic Studies* 60 (January): 1–16.

Rojas, Patricio. 1990. "Credibility, Stabilization and Trade Liberalization in Mexico." Unpublished. Massachussetts Institute of Technology.

Rojas-Suárez, Liliana. 1987. "Devaluation and Monetary Policy in Developing Countries: A General Equilibrium Model for Economies Facing Financial Constraints." *IMF Staff Papers* 34 (September): 439–70.

———. 1990. "Risk and Capital Flight in Developing Countries." Working Paper no. 90/64, International Monetary Fund (July).

Roldós, Jorge. 1993. *On Credible Disinflation.* Working Paper no. 93/90, International Monetary Fund (November).

Romer, Paul. 1986. "Increasing Returns and Long-Run Growth." *Journal of Political Economy* 94 (October): 1002–37.

———. 1990. "Endogenous Technological Change." *Journal of Political Economy* 98 (October): s71–s102.

Rosenzweig, Mark. 1988. "Labour Markets in Low-Income Countries." In *Handbook of Development Economics.* Vol. I, edited by Hollis Chenery and T. N. Srinivasan. Amsterdam: North Holland.

Ross, Anthony C. 1991. *Economic Stabilization for Developing Countries.* Brookfield, Vt.: Edward Elgar.

Rossi, José W. 1989. "The Demand for Money in Brazil: What Happened in the 1980s." *Journal of Development Economics* 31 (October): 357–67.

Rossi, Nicola. 1988. "Government Spending, the Real Interest Rate, and the Behavior of Liquidity-Constrained Consumers in Developing Countries." *IMF Staff Papers* 35 (March): 104–40.

———. 1989. "Dependency Rates and Private Savings Behavior in Developing Countries." *IMF Staff Papers* 36 (March): 166–81.

Roubini, Nouriel. 1991. "Economic and Political Determinants of Budget Deficits in Developing Countries." *Journal of International Money and Finance* 10 (Supplement, March) 49–72.

Roubini, Nouriel, and Xavier Sala-i-Martin. 1992. "Financial Repression and Economic Growth." *Journal of Development Economics* 39 (July): 5–30.

———. 1995. "A Growth Model of Inflation, Tax Evasion and Financial Repression." *Journal of Monetary Economics* 35 (April): 275–301.

Sachs, Jeffrey. 1984. "Theoretical Issues in International Borrowing." Study in International Finance no. 54, Princeton University (July).

———. 1986. *The Bolivian Hyperinflation and Stabilization.* Working Paper no. 2073, National Bureau of Economic Research (November).

———. 1987. "Trade and Exchange Rate Policies in Growth-Oriented Adjustment Programs." In *Growth-Oriented Adjustment Programs,* edited by Vittorio Corbo, Morris Goldstein, and Mohsin S. Khan. Washington, D.C.: International Monetary Fund.

———. 1989a. "The Debt Overhang of Developing Countries." In *Debt, Stabilization and Development,* edited by Guillermo A. Calvo, Ronald Findlay, Pentti Kouri, and Jorge Braga de Macedo. Oxford: Basil Blackwell.

———. 1989b. "Introduction." In *Developing Country Debt and the World Economy,* edited by Jeffrey Sachs. Chicago: University of Chicago Press.

Salter, Walter E. 1959. "Internal and External Balance: The Role of Price and Expenditure Effects." *Economic Record* 35 (August): 226–38.

Santaella, Julio. 1993. "Stabilization Programs and External Enforcement." *IMF Staff Papers* 40 (September): 584–621.

Sargent, Thomas J. 1983. "Stopping Moderate Inflations: The Methods of Poincaré and Thatcher." In *Inflation, Debt and Indexation,* edited by Rudiger Dornbusch and Mario H. Simonsen. Cambridge, Mass.: MIT Press.

Sargent, Thomas J., and Neil Wallace. 1981. "Some Unpleasant Monetarist Arithmetic." *Federal Reserve Bank of Minneapolis Quarterly Review* 5 (Fall): 1–17.

Sassanpour, Cyrus, and Jeffrey Sheen. 1984. "An Empirical Analysis of the Effects of Monetary Disequilibria in Open Economies." *Journal of Monetary Economics* (Amsterdam) 13 (January): 127–63.

Savastano, Miguel A. 1992. "The Pattern of Currency Substitution in Latin America: An Overview." *Revista de Análisis Económico* 7 (June): 29–72.

Schmid, Michael. 1982. "Stagflationary Effects of a Devaluation in a Monetary Model with Imported Intermediate Goods." *Jahrbucher fur Nationalokonomie und Statistik* 197 (March): 107–29.

Schmidt-Hebbel, Klaus, and Tobias Muller. 1992. "Private Investment under Macroeconomic Adjustment in Morocco." In *Reviving Private Investment in Developing Countries,* edited by Ajay Chhibber, Mansoor Dailami, and Nemat Shafik. Amsterdam: North Holland.

Schmidt-Hebbel, Klaus, Steven B. Webb, and Giancarlo Corsetti. 1992. "Household Saving in Developing Countries." *World Bank Economic Review* 6 (September): 529–47.

Seater, John. 1993. "Ricardian Equivalence." *Journal of Economic Literature* 31 (March): 142–90.

Servén, Luis. 1990a. *A RMSM-X for Chile.* PRE Working Paper no. 508, World Bank (September):

———. 1990b. *Anticipated Real Exchange Rate Changes and the Dynamics of Investment.* PRE Working Paper no. 562, World Bank (December).

Servén, Luis, and Andrés Solimano. 1993a. "Economic Adjustment and Investment Performance in Developing Countries: The Experience of the 1980s." In *Striving for Growth after Adjustment,* edited by Luis Servén and Andrés Solimano. Washington, D.C.: World Bank.

———. 1993*b*. "Private Investment and Macroeconomic Adjustment: A Survey." In *Striving for Growth after Adjustment,* edited by Luis Servén and Andrés Solimano. Washington, D.C.: World Bank.

Shafik, Nemat. 1992. "Modeling Private Investment in Egypt." *Journal of Development Economics* 39 (October): 263–77.

Shahin, Wassim N. 1992. *Money Supply and Deficit Financing in Economic Development.* Westport, Conn.: Greenwood.

Shaw, Edward S. 1973. *Financial Deepening in Economic Development.* New York: Oxford University Press.

Sheehey, Edmund J. 1986. "Unanticipated Inflation, Devaluation and Output in Latin America." *World Development* 14 (May): 665–71.

Shirvani, Hassan, and Barry Wilbratte. 1994. "Money and Inflation: International Evidence Based on Cointegration Theory." *International Economic Journal* 8 (March): 11–21.

Simonsen, Mario H. 1983. "Indexation: Current Theory and the Brazilian Experience." In *Inflation, Debt and Indexation,* edited by Rudiger Dornbusch and Mario H. Simonsen. Cambridge, Mass.: MIT Press.

Sjaastad, Larry A. 1983. "Failure of Economic Liberalization in the Southern Cone of Latin America." *World Economy* 6 (March): 5–26.

Solimano, Andrés. 1986. "Contractionary Devaluation in the Southern Cone: The Case of Chile." *Journal of Development Economics* 23 (September): 135–51.

———. 1990. "Inflation and the Costs of Stabilization." *World Bank Research Observer* 5 (July): 167–85.

Solow, Robert M. 1956. "A Contribution to the Theory of Economic Growth." *Quarterly Journal of Economics* 50 (February): 65–94.

Song, E. Young. 1993. "Increasing Returns and the Optimality of Open Capital Markets in a Small Growing Economy." *International Economic Review* 34 (August): 705–13.

Spaventa, Luigi. 1987. "The Growth of Public Debt." *IMF Staff Papers* 34 (June): 374–99.

Srinivasan, T. G., Vincent Parkin, and David Vines. 1989. *Food Subsidies and Inflation in Developing Countries: A Bridge between Structuralism and Monetarism.* Working Paper no. 334, Centre for Economic Policy Research (August).

Stiglitz, Joseph E. 1974. "Alternative Theories of Wage Determination and Unemployment in LDCs: The Labor Turnover Model." *Quarterly Journal of Economics* 98 (May): 194–227.

———. 1982. "Alternative Theories of Wage Determination and Unemployment: The Efficiency Wage Model." In *The Theory and Experience of Economic Development,* edited by Mark Gersovitz, Carlos F. Diaz-Alejandro, Gustav Ranis, and Mark R. Rosenzweig. London: Allen and Unwin.

———. 1992. "Alternative Approaches to Macroeconomics: Methodological Issues and the New Keynesian Economics." In *Macroeconomics: A Survey of Research Strategies,* edited by Alessandro Vercelli and Nicola Dimitri. Oxford: Oxford University Press.

Stiglitz, Joseph E., and Andrew Weiss. 1992. "Asymmetric Information in Credit Markets and Its Implications for Macroeconomics." *Oxford Economic Papers* 44 (October): 694–724.

Stockman, Alan C. 1989. "The Cash-in-Advance Constraint in International Economics." In *Finance Constraints and the Theory of Money,* edited by S. C. Tsiang and Meier Kohn. Orlando, Fla.: Academic Press.

Stockman, Alan C., and Alejandro D. Hernández. 1988. "Exchange Controls, Capital Controls, and International Financial Markets." *American Economic Review* 78 (June): 362–74.

Summers, Lawrence H. 1988. "Tax Policy and International Competitiveness." In *International Aspects of Fiscal Policy,* edited by Jacob A. Frenkel. Chicago: University of Chicago Press.

Sundararajan, Ved. 1986. "Exchange Rate versus Credit Policy: Analysis with a Monetary Model of Trade and Inflation for India." *Journal of Development Economics* 20 (January): 75–105.

Sundararajan, Ved, and Tomás J. Baliño. 1991. "Issues in Recent Banking Crises." In *Banking Crises: Cases and Issues,* edited by Ved Sundararajan and Tomás J. Baliño. Washington, D.C.: International Monetary Fund.

Sundararajan, Ved, and Subhash Thakur. 1980. "Public Investment, Crowding Out, and Growth: A Dynamic Model Applied to India and Korea." *IMF Staff Papers* 27 (December): 814–55.

Swan, Trevor W. 1956. "Economic Growth and Capital Accumulation." *Economic Record* 32 (November): 334–61.

———. 1960. "Economic Control in a Dependent Economy." *Economic Record* 36 (March): 51–66.

Swinburn, Mark, and Marta Castello-Blanco. 1991. "Central Bank Independence and Central Bank Functions." In *The Evolving Role of Central Banks,* edited by Patrick Downes and Reza Vaez-Zadeh. Washington, D.C.: International Monetary Fund.

Tanzi, Vito. 1978. "Inflation, Real Tax Revenue, and the Case for Inflationary Finance: Theory with an Application to Argentina." *IMF Staff Papers* 25 (September): 417–51.

———. 1988. "Lags in Tax Collection and the Case for Inflationary Finance: Theory with Simulations." In *Fiscal Policy, Stabilization, and Growth in Developing Countries,* edited by Mario I. Blejer and Ke-young Chu. Washington, D.C.: International Monetary Fund.

Taylor, John B. 1980. "Aggregate Dynamics and Staggered Contracts." *Journal of Political Economy* 88 (February): 1–23.

Taylor, Lance. 1979. *Macro Models for Developing Countries.* New York: McGraw-Hill.

———. 1983. *Structuralist Macroeconomics.* New York: Basic Books.

———. 1990. *Socially Relevant Policy Analysis.* Cambridge, Mass.: MIT Press.

———. 1991. *Income Distribution, Inflation and Growth.* Cambridge, Mass.: MIT Press.

———. 1994. "Gap Models." *Journal of Development Economics* 45 (October): 17–34.

Ten Kate, Adriaan. 1992. "Trade Liberalization and Economic Stabilization in Mexico: Lessons of Experience." *World Development* 20 (May): 659–72.

Terrones, Marco E. 1989. *Macroeconomic Policy Cycles under Alternative Electoral Structures.* Working Paper no. 8905, University of Western Ontario (April).

Todaro, Michael P. 1994. *Economic Development.* 5th ed. White Plains, N.Y.: Longman.

Tseng, Wanda S., and Richard Corker. 1991. *Financial Liberalization, Money Demand, and Monetary Policy in Asian Countries.* Occasional Paper no. 84, International Monetary Fund.

Turnham, David. 1993. *Employment and Development: A New Review of Evidence.* OECD Development Centre, Paris.

Turnovsky, Stephen J. 1981. "The Effects of Devaluation and Foreign Price Disturbances under Rational Expectations." *Journal of International Economics* 11 (February): 33–60.

——. 1985. "Domestic and Foreign Disturbances in an Optimizing Model of Exchange Rate Determination." *Journal of International Money and Finance* 1 (March): 151–71.

Turnovsky, Stephen J., and Partha Sen. 1991. "Fiscal Policy, Capital Accumulation, and Debt in an Open Economy." *Oxford Economic Papers* 43 (January): 1–24.

van der Ploeg, Frederick. 1989. "The Political Economy of Overvaluation." *Economic Journal* 99 (September): 850–55.

van Wijnbergen, Sweder. 1982. "Stagflationary Effects of Monetary Stabilization Policies." *Journal of Development Economics* 10 (April): 133–69.

——. 1983a. "Credit Policy, Inflation and Growth in a Financially Repressed Economy." *Journal of Development Economics* 13 (August): 45–65.

——. 1983b. "Interest Rate Management in LDCs." *Journal of Monetary Economics* 12 (September): 433–52.

——. 1985. "Macro-Economic Effects of Changes in Bank Interest Rates: Simulation Results for South Korea." *Journal of Development Economics* 18 (August): 541–54.

——. 1986. "Exchange Rate Management and Stabilization Policies in Developing Countries." *Journal of Development Economics* 23 (October): 227–47.

——. 1988. "Monopolistic Competition, Credibility and the Output Costs of Disinflationary Programs." *Journal of Development Economics* 29 (November): 375–98.

——. 1991. "Fiscal Deficits, Exchange Rate Crises, and Inflation." *Review of Economic Studies* 58 (January): 81–92.

Veidyanathan, Geetha. 1993. "Consumption, Liquidity Constraints and Economic Development." *Journal of Macroeconomics* 15 (Summer): 591–610.

Végh, Carlos A. 1989a. "The Optimal Inflation Tax in the Presence of Currency Substitution." *Journal of Monetary Economics* 24 (July): 139–46.

——. 1989b. "Government Spending and Inflationary Finance." *IMF Staff Papers* 46 (September): 657–77.

——. 1992. "Stopping High Inflation: An Analytical Overview." *IMF Staff Papers* 39 (September): 626–95.

Velasco, Andrés. 1987. "Financial Crises and Balance of Payments Crises—A Simple Model of the Southern Cone Experience." *Journal of Development Economics* 17 (October): 263–83.

——. 1993. "Real Interest Rates and Government Debt during Stabilization." *Journal of Money, Credit, and Banking* 25 (May): 251–72.

Verspagen, Bart. 1992. "Endogenous Innovation in Neo-Classical Growth Models: A Survey." *Journal of Macroeconomics* 14 (Fall): 631–62.

Vial, Joaquím. 1989. *Macroeconomic Models for Policy Analysis in Latin America.* Technical Note no. 127, CIEPLAN (March).

Vickers, John. 1986. "Signalling in a Model of Monetary Policy with Incomplete Information." *Oxford Economic Papers* 38 (November): 443–55.

Villanueva, Delano, and Abbas Mirakhor. 1990. "Strategies for Financial Reforms." *IMF Staff Papers* 37 (September): 509–36.

Vines, David, and Peter G. Warr. 1993. "Macroeconomic Adjustment in Thailand: An Econometric Dissection." Unpublished. Center for Economic Policy Research (April).

Vogel, Robert C., and Stephen A. Buser. 1976. "Inflation, Financial Repression, and Capital Formation in Latin America." In *Money and Finance in Growth and Development,* edited by Ronald I. McKinnon. New York: Marcel Dekker.

Wai, U. Tun, and Chorn-Huey Wong. 1982. "Determinants of Private Investment in Developing Countries." *Journal of Development Studies* 19 (October): 19–36.

Whitehead, Laurence. 1990. "Political Explanations of Macroeconomic Management: A Survey." Unpublished. Nuffield College, Oxford.

Wilford, Walton T. 1986. "The Monetary Approach to Balance of Payments and Developing Nations: A Review of the Literature." In *The Monetary Approach to International Adjustment,* edited by Bluford H. Putnam and D. Sykes Wilford. New York: Preager.

Williams, Michael A., and Michael G. Baumann. 1986. "International Evidence on Output-Inflation Tradeoffs: A Bootstrap Analysis." *Economic Letters* 21 (February): 149–53.

Williamson, John, and Stephan Haggard. 1994. "The Political Conditions for Economic Reform." In *The Political Economy of Economic Reform,* edited by John Williamson. Washington, D.C.: Institute for International Economics.

Willman, Alpo. 1988. "The Collapse of the Fixed Exchange Rate Regime with Sticky Wages and Imperfect Substitutability between Domestic and Foreign Bonds." *European Economic Review* 32 (November): 1817–38.

Wolpin, Kenneth I. 1982. "A New Test of the Permanent Income Hypothesis: The Impact of Weather on the Income and Consumption of Farm Households in India." *International Economic Review* 23 (October): 583–94.

Wong, Chorn-Huey. 1977. "Demand for Money in Developing Countries: Some Theoretical and Empirical Results." *Journal of Monetary Economics* 3 (January): 59–86.

Wong, David Y. 1990. "What Do Saving-Investment Relationships Tell Us about International Capital Mobility?" *Journal of International Money and Finance* 9 (March): 60–74.

World Bank. 1993. *The East Asian Miracle.* New York: Oxford University Press.

Zuehlke, Thomas W., and James E. Payne. 1989. "Tests of the Rational Expectations–Permanent Income Hypothesis for Developing Economies." *Journal of Macroeconomics* 11 (Summer): 423–33.

Index of Names

A

Abel, Andrew B., 81, 579
Adams, Charles, 255, 612
Adams, Claire Hughes, 612
Adelman, Irma, 437
Agénor, Pierre-Richard, 64,
    93, 95, 101, 202, 217,
    251, 254, 322, 334, 335,
    358, 361, 369, 479, 488,
    489, 491, 567, 568, 577,
    578, 581, 582, 590, 591,
    592, 593, 594, 596, 600,
    601, 605, 606, 608,
    609, 612, 615, 616,
    623, 624
Aghevli, Bijan B., 77, 120, 584,
    591, 592
Ahumada, Hildegard, 88
Aizenman, Joshua, 64, 86, 121,
    158, 567, 568, 588, 618,
    623, 624
Alam, Asad, 617
Alam, M. Shahid, 529
Alberro, José, 97
Alesina, Alberto, 378, 554,
    580, 607, 620, 621, 622,
    623
Alexander, Sydney S., 221, 228,
    229, 233
Ambler, Steve, 603
Ames, Barry, 536, 547, 549, 552,
    554, 622
Anand, Ritu, 584
Andersen, Torben M., 605
Arida, Persio, 577
Arize, Augustine C., 305
Arrau, Patricio, 87, 89, 353
Asilis, Carlos, 88

Auernheimer, Leonardo, 120,
    583, 601
Azam, Jean-Paul, 578

B

Bacchetta, Philippe, 217
Bacha, Edmar C., 427
Bahmani-Oskooee, Mohsen, 590
Bailey, Martin J., 120
Balassa, Bela, 579
Baliño, Tomás J., 615
Ball, Laurence, 603
Bandara, Jayatilleke S., 612
Barro, Robert J., 76, 97, 98,
    99, 127, 200, 361, 362,
    363, 520, 530, 585, 592,
    618, 619
Bates, Robert, 533, 534, 535, 621
Baumann, Michael G., 98
Baxter, Marianne, 605
Beavis, Brian, 586, 621
Bencivenga, Valerie R., 523,
    524, 587
Besley, Timothy, 578
Bevan, David, 78
Bhagwati, Jagdish N., 578
Bhalla, Surjit, 77
Bhandari, Jagdeep S., 591, 616
Bini Smaghi, Lorenzo, 165
Blanchard, Olivier J., 59, 78, 114,
    242, 246, 367, 577, 584,
    585, 586, 601
Blanco, Herminio, 594
Bleaney, Michael, 85, 86, 575, 580
Blejer, Mario I., 85, 94, 109, 110,
    111, 368, 369, 582, 583,
    584, 597, 599, 605, 613

Bohn, Henning, 584
Borensztein, Eduardo, 580
Boschen, John F., 165
Boughton, James, 593
Bourguignon, François, 438, 612
Branson, William H., 236, 237,
        252, 253, 254
Brock, Philip L., 115, 154, 588,
        617
Bruno, Michael, 299, 302, 368,
        382, 599, 605, 606, 608
Bruton, Henry, 616
Buffie, Edward F., 233, 236, 239,
        367, 495, 497, 499, 501,
        536, 580, 617
Buiter, Willem H., 124, 125, 216,
        576, 582, 583, 601
Bulow, Jeremy, 465
Burgess, Robin, 106
Burkett, Paul, 588
Burton, David, 239
Buser, Stephen A., 474

C

Cáceres, Armando, 597
Calomiris, Charles W., 95
Calvo, Guillermo A., 95, 160, 325,
        339, 345, 347, 348, 349,
        351, 352, 353, 354, 355,
        356, 357, 382, 383, 502,
        581, 583, 586, 594, 596,
        598, 601, 602, 603, 604,
        605, 607
Canarella, Giorgio, 100
Canavese, Alfredo J., 284
Cardia, Emanuela, 603
Cardoso, Eliana, 14, 85, 86, 291,
        293, 299, 306, 311, 580,
        600, 613
Carmichael, Jeffrey, 577
Cashin, Paul, 620
Castello-Branco, Marta, 375

Cavallo, Domingo, 169, 575
Chandravarkar, Anand, 66
Chang, Wen-Ya, 616
Cheasty, Adrienne, 109, 110, 111,
        583, 597, 599
Chenery, Hollis B., 427, 514
Chhibber, Ajay, 84
Cho, Yoon Je, 615
Chopra, Ajit, 100, 101
Choudhary, Munir A., 100
Chowdhury, Abdur, 165
Claessens, Stijn, 218, 465,
        594, 614
Cohen, Daniel, 86, 613
Collins, Susan M., 579
Condon, Timothy, 62, 577, 612
Connolly, Michael B., 219,
        593, 594
Conway, Patrick, 612
Cook, Paul, 575
Cooper, Richard N., 229, 248,
        596, 613
Corbo, Vittorio, 62, 79, 128, 276,
        577, 597
Corden, W. Max, 96, 101, 494,
        558, 577
Corker, Richard, 89
Courakis, Anthony S., 525
Cox, W. Michael, 115
Cozier, Barry V., 582
Cuddington, John, 161, 575
Cukierman, Alex, 121, 360, 364,
        366, 376, 583, 592, 598,
        605, 607, 622
Cumby, Robert E., 165, 219, 594

D

Dailami, Mansoor, 84
Darrat, Ali F., 305
Deaton, Angus S., 76, 79, 578,
        579, 601
Decaluwé, Bernard, 612

De Gregorio, José, 120, 367, 525,
    530, 620
Dellas, Harris, 217
Demekas, Dimitri G., 623
de Melo, Jaime, 580, 597
de Melo, Martha, 157, 158, 588
Denizer, Cevdet, 615
de Pablo, Juan, 536
Deutsch, Joseph, 89
Dewatripont, Mathias, 437, 612
Diamond, Larry, 622
Díaz Alejandro, Carlos F., 228,
    229, 248
Di Tella, Guido, 284
Dixit, Avinash, 584
Dobbs, Ian, 586, 621
Dodsworth, John R., 581
Dollar, David, 529
Domowitz, Ian, 88, 95
Donovan, Donal J., 250
Dooley, Michael, 161, 162, 166,
    454, 457, 614
Dornbusch, Rudiger, 60, 176,
    255, 291, 293, 304, 305,
    364, 368, 376, 476, 536,
    576, 583, 584, 589, 591,
    597, 599, 601, 602, 605,
    613, 617
Doroodian, Khosrow, 250
Dowla, Asif, 165
Drazen, Allan H., 130, 218,
    356, 367, 378, 585,
    605, 607
Dutton, Dean S., 584

E

Easterly, William, 119, 126,
    138, 148, 451, 585, 586,
    612, 613
Edwards, Sebastián, 162, 180, 218,
    230, 231, 233, 249, 251,
    252, 502, 507, 529, 547,

    554, 577, 589, 594,
    596, 597, 617, 620,
    621, 623
Eichenberger, Reiner, 621
Elbadawi, Ibrahim, 88, 434, 612
El-Erian, Mohamed, 95
Elías, Victor J., 515, 518
Elliott, James, 435, 612
Erbas, S. Nuri, 585
Ericsson, Neil R., 95, 582
Evans, J. L., 301
Everaert, Luc, 434, 612

F

Faini, Ricardo, 580
Fair, Ray C., 87, 409
Falvey, Rod, 504, 617
Faruqee, Hamid, 164
Feenstra, Robert C., 10, 578, 586
Feldstein, Martin, 166
Fernández, Arturo, 594
Fernández, Roque B., 505, 582,
    585, 597
Fernández-Arias, Eduardo,
    467
Findlay, Ronald, 558
Fischer, Stanley, 59, 78, 114, 115,
    126, 242, 246, 286, 299,
    302, 368, 376, 381, 382,
    530, 577, 584, 585, 586,
    599, 602
Fishlow, Albert, 138, 584, 613
Fitzgerald, E. V. K., 86
Fleming, J. Marcus, 576
Flood, Robert P., 209, 217, 479,
    593, 615, 616
Foxley, Alejandro, 597
Frenkel, Jacob A., 161, 576, 587,
    597, 611, 617
Frenkel, Michael, 589
Frey, Bruno S., 621
Friedman, Jorge, 584

Froot, Kenneth A., 618
Fry, Maxwell J., 77, 79, 475, 619

G

Galbis, Vicente, 474, 475, 615, 617
Gan, Wee-Beng, 77, 579
Garber, Peter M., 209, 594
García, Eduardo, 612
Gelb, Alan, 475, 476
Gersovitz, Mark, 76, 579
Ghei, Nita, 616
Giavazzi, Francesco, 204
Gillis, Malcolm, 575
Giovannini, Alberto, 80, 157, 158,
     581, 588
Glezakos, Constantine, 577
Goldberg, Linda S., 220, 594
Goldfeld, Stephen M., 581
Goldstein, Morris, 18, 254, 597
Goode, Richard, 120, 582
Gordon, David B., 200, 361, 362,
     592
Greenaway, David, 85, 86, 504,
     575, 580
Greene, Joshua, 86
Greenwald, Bruce, 575
Greenwood, Jeremy, 523, 524,
     578, 619
Grilli, Vittorio, 607
Gros, Daniel, 255
Grosse, Robert, 68
Grossman, Gene M., 618, 619
Guidotti, Pablo E., 138
Gylfason, Thorvaldur, 231,
     232, 233, 250, 251, 252,
     253, 254

H

Haan, Jakob de, 128
Haggard, Stephan, 378, 536, 547,
     607, 621

Haley, James, 624
Haliasos, Michael, 585
Hanna, Donald, 617
Hansen, Bent, 578
Hanson, James A., 99, 233, 251,
     500, 597, 617
Haque, Nadeem U., 78, 79, 124,
     127, 128, 163, 435, 612
Harberger, Arnold C., 13
Harris, John, 63, 556, 558,
     564, 568
Harvey, Andrew C., 87, 88,
     588, 622
Helmers, F. Leslie, 591
Helpman, Elhanan, 130, 218, 369,
     385, 585, 605, 618, 619
Helwege, Ann, 14
Hernández, Alejandro D., 578
Heymann, Daniel, 286, 605
Himarios, Daniel, 596
Hoffman, Dennis L., 87
Hoover, Kevin D., 96, 582
Horioka, Charles, 166
Horn, Henrik, 200
Horton, Susan, 23, 61

I

International Monetary Fund,
     611
Isard, Peter, 162, 593
Islam, Shafiqul, 233, 405
Ize, Alain, 594

J

Jaffee, Dwight, 615
Jappelli, Tullio, 523
Jonung, Lars, 368
Jorgensen, Steen L., 305
Jovanovich, Boyan, 523, 524,
     619
Jung, W. S., 98

K

Kähkönen, Juha, 616
Kamas, Linda, 165, 252, 253, 588
Kamin, Steven B., 95, 177, 179,
    180, 249, 250, 252, 582,
    589, 590, 596, 608
Kapur, Basant, 588, 589
Karnik, Ajit V., 547, 623
Karras, Georgios, 80
Kaufman, Robert, 378, 536,
    547, 621
Kawai, Masahiro, 137, 146, 148,
    585, 586
Kay, Cristobal, 575
Keller, Peter, 613
Khan, Mohsin S., 85, 87, 93,
    95, 115, 147, 148, 162,
    250, 254, 439, 502, 529,
    530, 581, 582, 584, 587,
    595, 597, 601, 611, 612,
    618, 619
Kharas, Homi, 589, 609
Khor, Hoe E., 162
Kiguel, Miguel A., 297, 302, 303,
    304, 479, 589, 597, 600,
    601, 605, 606, 616
Killick, Tony, 249, 597
Kim, Cha Dong, 504, 617
Kimbrough, Kent P., 215, 216, 336,
    578, 583, 586
King, Robert G., 529, 620
Kirkpatrick, Colin, 575
Kirman, Alan P., 575
Kletzer, Kenneth, 442, 443, 614
Knight, Malcolm D., 439, 529,
    531, 612, 619
Knight, Peter T., 597
Kongsamut, Piyabha, 612
Krasker, William S., 218, 588
Kreinin, Mordechai, 165, 597, 611
Krueger, Ann O., 502
Krugman, Paul R., 207, 221, 226,
    228, 230, 450

Kumar, Manmohan S., 138, 148,
    529, 530, 587, 619
Kwack, Sung Y., 612

L

Lächler, Ulrich, 383
Ladman, Jerry, 68
Lahiri, Ashok K., 78
Lai, Ching-Chong, 616
Lanyi, Anthony, 475
Lara-Resende, Andre, 577
Larraín, Felipe, 86, 624
Layard, Richard, 62, 577, 624
Lee, Jong-Wha, 529
Lee, Kiseok, 599, 608
Leff, Nathaniel H., 85
Le Fort, Guillermo R., 62
Leiderman, Leonardo, 78, 585
Leite, Sérgio P., 580, 615
Lennblad, Anna, 582
Levich, Richard M., 161
Levine, Ross, 529, 620
Liang, Ming-Yih, 589
Linz, Juan J., 622
Lipschitz, Leslie, 613
Liviatan, Nissan, 130, 136, 137,
    287, 297, 366, 368, 369,
    376, 585, 586, 597, 598,
    605, 606
Lizondo, J. Saul, 147, 161, 228,
    255, 259, 479, 488, 589,
    594, 596
Lohmann, Susan, 607
Lucas, Robert E., Jr., 9, 97, 100,
    519, 520, 521, 618, 619
Lustig, Nora, 575

M

Maccini, Louis J., 137, 146, 148,
    585, 586

Macedo, Jorge Braga de, 174, 176
Madarassy, Andrea, 22
Makonen, Dawit, 530
Malixi, Margaret, 590
Mankiw, N. Gregory, 619
Mansur, Ahsan, 611
Marion, Nancy, 86
Márquez, Jaime, 582
Martens, André, 612
Masson, Paul R., 367, 586
Mathieson, Donald J., 578, 587, 588, 615
Matsuyama, Kiminori, 356
McCallum, Bennet T., 585
McDonald, Donogh, 80, 579
McKinnon, Ronald I., 152, 169, 473, 474, 475, 476, 477, 501, 522, 588, 619
McNelis, Paul D., 618
Meller, Patricio, 252
Meltzer, Allan H., 622
Melvin, Michael, 68, 95
Michaely, Michael, 174
Michel, Gilles, 437, 612
Mikesell, Raymond F., 579
Milner, Chris, 504
Mirakhor, Abbas, 22, 477, 478
Modiano, Eduardo M., 599
Modigliani, Franco, 587
Mondino, Guillermo, 165
Montiel, Peter J., 22, 65, 66, 78, 79, 101, 124, 127, 128, 147, 160, 163, 165, 166, 180, 218, 228, 237, 239, 254, 255, 305, 408, 438, 577, 578, 582, 589, 590, 591, 594, 595, 596, 597, 601, 610, 611, 612, 613
Morales, Juan Antonio, 597
Morandé, Felipe G., 618
Morley, Samuel, 138
Mourmouras, Alex, 584
Muellbauer, John, 601

Muller, Tobias, 86
Mundell, Robert A., 576
Musgrove, Phillip, 77
Mussa, Michael L., 503, 597, 611, 617, 618

N

Neck, Reinhard, 621
Nelson, Joan M., 621
Nelson, Michael A., 530, 531
Newman, John L., 165
Nordhaus, William, 537, 542, 543, 544, 545, 621
Nowak, Michael, 589, 590
Nugent, Jeffrey B., 577

O

Obstfeld, Maurice, 165, 213, 216, 355, 586, 602, 603, 604
O'Connell, Stephen A., 616
Officer, Lawrence H., 165, 597, 611
Olivera, Julio H., 116, 584
Ordeshook, Peter C., 533
Orphanides, Athanasios, 364, 376
Ortíz, Guillermo, 95, 594
Oshikoya, Temitope W., 85, 86
Ostry, Jonathan D., 255, 586, 594, 617
Owen, Dorian P., 415, 589

P

Pagano, Marco, 204, 522, 523, 524, 532
Paldam, Martin, 305
Papademos, Lucas, 587
Papageorgiou, Demetris, 492, 494
Parai, Amar K., 100
Paredes, Carlos, 597

Park, Daekeun, 618
Park, Yung Chul, 473
Parkin, Vincent, 60, 313, 600, 601
Pastor, Manuel, Jr., 597, 617
Patel, Urjit R., 124
Patinkin, Don, 376, 604, 607
Paus, Eva, 373
Payne, James E., 579
Pazos, Felipe, 265
Persson, Torsten, 200, 368,
    575, 624
Pesaran, Hashem, 582
Pfefferman, Guy, 22
Phelps, Edmund S., 112
Phylaktis, Kate, 94, 162, 581, 584
Pindyck, Robert, 84
Pinto, Brian, 487, 490, 589,
    609, 616
Pitt, Mark, 174, 578
Polak, Jacques J., 619
Pollard, Stephen K., 100
Poloz, Stephen S., 581
Prebisch, Raúl, 14
Priale, Rodrigo, 253

R

Radelet, Steven C., 621
Radetzki, Marian, 233, 253
Rajapatirana, Sarath, 617
Ram, Rati, 98
Rama, Martín, 84, 85
Ramírez, Miguel D., 85
Ramirez-Rojas, C. Luis, 94, 115
Ramos, Juan, 597
Ratti, Ronald A., 599, 608
Razin, Assaf, 78, 576, 586
Rebelo, Sergio, 519, 520, 522
Reinhart, Carmen M., 62, 87,
    354, 575
Reinhart, Vincent R., 62
Reisen, Helmut, 163, 613

Renelt, David, 529
Rennhack, Robert, 165
Reynoso, Alejandro, 476
Risager, Ole, 231, 232, 236, 237,
    252, 253
Roberts, John, 70, 616
Robinson, David J., 111, 163
Robinson, Sherman, 437, 612
Roca, Santiago, 253
Rodríguez, Carlos A., 115, 147,
    305, 325, 339, 345, 348,
    352, 356, 581, 602, 603
Rodrik, Dani, 86, 366, 376, 502,
    503, 505, 614, 617
Roemer, Michael, 621
Rogers, John H., 582
Rogoff, Kenneth A., 201, 204, 374,
    465, 544, 545, 549, 552,
    593, 622
Rojas, Patricio, 605
Rojas-Suárez, Liliana, 160, 161,
    162, 578, 587, 608
Roldós, Jorge, 355
Romer, Paul, 519, 521, 522,
    618, 619
Rosenzweig, M., 56, 63, 577
Ross, Anthony C., 575
Rossi, José W., 87
Rossi, Nicola, 79, 80, 578
Roubini, Nouriel, 524, 527, 530,
    536, 587

S

Sachs, Jeffrey, 273, 446, 454, 468,
    532, 580, 597, 614
Sala-i-Martin, Xavier, 524, 527,
    530, 587, 618, 619
Salter, Walter E., 48
Sanguinetti, Pablo, 605
Santaella, Julio A., 376, 621,
    623, 624

Saracoglu, Rüsdü, 475
Sargent, Thomas J., 130, 585, 605
Sassanpour, Cyrus, 613
Sato, Kazuo, 85
Savastano, Miguel A., 95
Schmid, Michael, 233, 251,
    252, 254
Schmidt-Hebbel, Klaus, 77, 79,
    80, 86, 119, 128, 138, 148,
    434, 579, 585, 612, 618
Seater, John, 127, 585
Sen, Partha, 604
Servén, Luis, 82, 83, 580, 612
Shafik, Nemat, 85
Shahin, Wassim N., 128, 582
Shaw, Edward S., 152, 169, 473,
    474, 522
Sheehey, Edmund J., 100, 251
Sheen, Jeffrey, 613
Shirvani, Hassan, 599
Sibert, Anne, 544
Sichel, Edward D., 581
Simonsen, Mario H., 60, 291,
    368, 608
Singh, Ram D., 530, 531
Sjaastad, Larry, 13
Smith, Bruce D., 523, 524, 587
Solimano, Andrés, 252, 253, 580,
    597, 612
Solis-Fallas, Otton, 415, 589
Solow, Robert M., 513
Song, E. Young, 617
Soon, Lee-Ying, 77, 579
Spaventa, Luigi, 584
Srinivasan, T. G., 313, 600
Stella, Peter, 111
Stern, Nicholas H., 106
Stiglitz, Joseph E., 63, 575, 615
Stockman, Alan C., 10, 217, 578
Stone, Mark R., 454
Strout, Alan, 427
Summers, Lawrence H., 166, 607
Sundararajan, Ved, 85, 580,
    613, 615

Swan, Trevor, 48, 513
Swinburn, Mark, 375

T

Tabellini, Guido, 536, 575,
    580, 624
Tahiri, Chakib, 87
Tanzi, Vito, 116, 117, 118, 120
Taylor, Dean, 593, 594
Taylor, John B., 96, 255, 409
Taylor, Lance, 3, 14, 62, 168, 169,
    221, 226, 228, 230, 246,
    299, 438, 586, 600, 611
Taylor, Mark P., 94, 361, 581,
    584, 605
Ten Kate, Adriaan, 505
Terrones, Marco E., 622
Thakur, Subhash, 85, 580
Tijerina, José A., 584
Tobin, James, 585
Todaro, Michael P., 63, 556, 558,
    564, 568, 575
Tseng, Wanda S., 89
Turnham, David, 57
Turnovsky, Stephen J., 239, 600,
    601, 604
Turtelboom, Bart, 581

U

Ucer, Murat E., 488, 489, 491, 615

V

van der Ploeg, Frederick, 545, 621
van Wijnbergen, Sweder, 62,
    88, 168, 169, 173, 217,
    219, 231, 232, 236, 237,
    239, 246, 368, 369, 502,
    575, 584, 586, 588, 594,
    605, 609

Végh, Carlos A., 87, 95, 115, 121,
    158, 297, 339, 345, 348,
    349, 351, 352, 353, 354,
    355, 356, 357, 382, 383,
    581, 583, 591, 598, 601,
    602, 603, 604, 605, 607,
    612, 614, 616, 620
Veidyanathan, Geetha, 127,
    128, 579
Velasco, Andrés, 219, 357, 601
Vergara, Rodrigo, 86, 624
Verspagen, Bart, 619
Vial, Joaquím, 612
Vickers, John, 202, 366, 368, 605
Villanueva, Delano, 86, 477, 478
Vines, David, 612
Vogel, Robert C., 474, 475, 588

W

Wai, U. Tun, 85, 580
Wallace, Neil, 130, 585
Warr, Peter G., 612
Waterbury, John, 621
Weiss, Andrew, 615
Whalley, John, 611

Whitehead, Laurence,
    546, 620
Wickham, Peter, 575
Wilbrate, Barry, 599
Wilford, Walton T., 597, 611
Williams, Michael A., 98
Williamson, John, 607, 621
Willman, Alpo, 214, 215, 601
Wolpin, Kenneth I., 77
Wong, Chorn-Huey, 85, 580, 581
Wong, David Y., 166
World Bank, 531, 532, 575, 624

Y

Yarrow, George K., 301
Yeches, Helene, 163

Z

Zahler, Roberto, 502, 618
Zelhorst, Dick, 128
Zilberfarb, Ben-Zion, 89
Zinser, James E., 579
Zuehlke, Thomas W., 579

Index of Subjects

A

accelerator, 81, 82, 85
accounting framework, 38–44
adjustable peg. *See* crawling peg
aggregate demand, 84, 97–99,
    185, 189, 224, 230, 232,
    236, 603
AK model, 519–20, 525, 614
Argentina, 214, 215, 219, 280–81,
    282–86
asset accumulation, 39–43, 140,
    147, 257, 315–16, 319,
    327–28, 337, 346, 348,
    394, 406–7, 562
asset market equilibrium, 170–71,
    181, 393–94

B

balance of payments
  absorption approach to,
    228–29, 233
  crises, 93, 189, 207–20, 578
  monetary approach to, 275,
    278, 423, 439, 441, 589,
    597, 611
Bank-Fund models, 423–27
Barro-Gordon model, 200,
    361–62, 592
Bolivia, 272–75
boom-recession cycle, 297,
    339–56, 571
Brady Plan, 33, 296, 454–67
Brazil, 214, 219, 290–93,
    373–74
budget constraint
  consolidated, 43, 347, 527

private sector, 39, 130–31,
    170, 181–82, 315, 327–28,
    346, 428–29, 525, 562,
    603
public sector, 40–42, 106–8,
    110, 122, 125, 131–34,
    149, 183, 216, 311–12,
    324, 347, 429, 526,
    563, 603

C

Cagan model, 114, 299, 362
  and hyperinflation,
    299–306
capital account liberalization,
    500–503, 507
capital accumulation. *See*
    investment
capital controls, 67, 153–54,
    157–59, 162, 180, 188, 203,
    207, 217, 222, 357,
    501–3, 577, 578, 587, 588,
    594, 613
capital flight, 33, 67, 69–70,
    160–61, 281, 454, 500–501,
    580, 617
capital inflows, 296, 576, 618
capital mobility
  degree of, 22, 101, 159, 164,
    188, 256, 314–17, 326,
    358, 503, 525, 582, 586,
    600, 601
  empirical evidence on, 159–67
  and informal credit markets, 163
  and macro models, 140
capital stock, 234–36, 245

capital stock (continued)
  and investment, 235–36,
    426, 435
cash balance effect, 233–34
cash-in-advance constraint, 10,
    345, 354–55, 586, 602
Cavallo-Patman effect, 169, 247
central bank, 40–41, 107, 317–18,
    331, 374–75, 395–96,
    408, 412
  independence, 374–75, 379
CES production function, 243,
    245, 433
CFA Franc Zone, 192–93, 591,
    593
Chile, 203, 214, 219, 267–69,
    271–72, 275–76, 547
Cobb-Douglas
  production function, 243–45,
    254, 404, 433, 513–14,
    610
  utility function, 256, 328,
    608, 610
collection costs, 120–21, 157–58
collection lags, 116–20
commercial banks, 42–43, 170–71,
    394–95, 407–8, 412
commodity prices, 18–19, 78
complementarity hypothesis,
    474–76
computable general equilibrium
    models, 436–38
consumption, 73–81
  and finite horizons, 75, 78–79,
    127–28
  and income, 75
  and interest rates, 80, 579–80,
    619
  public, 75, 80–81
  and wealth, 182, 233–34, 392
costate variable, 141, 316
crawling peg, 19–20, 191–92,
    593, 615

credibility
  of disinflation programs,
    359–80, 503
  of exchange-rate policy,
    195–207, 221, 348–52
  of trade reform, 502,
    504–5
credit availability effect,
    474–76
credit rationing, 26, 29, 82, 102,
    435, 580, 615
curb market loans. See informal
    credit markets
currency substitution, 70, 89–95,
    102, 115, 177, 187, 393,
    581, 582, 603, 607
  and portfolio approach, 176–80,
    393, 589
currency union. See monetary
    union
current account
  deficit, 43–44, 126–27, 147–49,
    177–79, 203, 214–15, 217,
    250, 253, 257, 350, 383,
    407, 583, 587
  liberalization. See trade
    liberalization

D

DDSR operations. See debt
    reduction
debt
  crisis, 120, 124, 147, 149, 293,
    442–54, 500
  external, 20–21, 33, 231–32,
    234, 442–71, 587
  internal, 108, 110, 137–38,
    451, 453
  overhang, 83, 86, 435,
    454, 458–61, 468–71,
    580

debt (continued)
  reduction, 444, 456–67
dependent-economy model, 49–52,
    53, 72, 101, 224–25, 241,
    576, 582
devaluation
  contractionary effects of,
      224–55, 501
  crisis, 189
  cycle, 590
  effects of, 82–83, 177–80,
      224–55, 320–23, 344–45,
      348–52, 596
  and electoral cycles, 539–43
discount rate, 123, 445
disinflation. *See* inflation and
    stabilization
dollarization. *See* currency
    substitution
durable goods, 87, 356
Dutch disease, 54–55, 577
dynamic equivalence property,
    325

E

efficiency wages, 64, 560–61,
    577, 624
effort function, 560, 624
elasticity of substitution, 243, 245,
    253, 497, 499
endogenous growth theories,
    518–32
escape clause, 205–6
Euler equation, 74, 79–80, 579
exchange controls, 67–68, 276,
    280, 382, 404
exchange rate
  fixed, 45, 191–94, 207–10,
      213, 221
  floating/flexible, 19, 191–93,
      207–10, 213, 221, 480–89
  official, 33, 191, 413–15, 479–81

parallel, 70, 175–80, 383, 391,
    479–91, 590
real, 45, 49–52, 147–48, 185,
    196, 199–200, 204, 206,
    214–15, 220, 224,
    255–62, 343–45, 351,
    392, 398, 501, 506–7, 540,
    543, 562, 567, 596, 600,
    603, 617–18
rules, 32, 191, 198–200
exchange-rate-based programs,
    275–82, 338–59, 381–83
expectations
  adaptive, 301–2, 342, 434, 538
  rational. *See* perfect foresight
  static, 185, 591
expenditure-switching effects,
    253

F

Fair-Taylor iterative technique, 409
financial intermediation, 169,
    173, 619
financial liberalization, 472,
    477–79, 500–503
financial programming, 423–25
financial repression, 23, 26, 76,
    85, 152–59, 180, 193, 394,
    473–74, 524, 527, 530, 532,
    587, 588, 611, 620
  tax, 153, 158–59, 182, 185–86,
      188, 620
fiscal constraint, 428–29
fiscal deficit, 42, 108–11,
    122–24, 126–49, 203,
    299–306, 366, 445–50,
    487–89, 491, 506, 536
fiscal rigidities, 500
food subsidies, 311–14, 621
food supply, 306–11, 336
foreign currency deposits,
    90–93, 581

foreign exchange
  demand for, 69–70, 89
  rationing, 29, 68, 82, 382, 383,
      405, 435, 609
  reserves, 142
  supply of, 68–69
Fund. *See* International Monetary
  Fund

G

government
  budget constraint. *See* budget
      constraint, public sector
  debt. *See* debt, internal
  regulations, 34, 56, 67–68,
      87, 109
gradualism, 266, 377–78, 505–6
growth
  and financial intermediation,
      522–27, 529–30
  and fiscal deficits, 530
  and human capital, 520–22, 529
  and income distribution,
      532, 624
  with increasing returns, 520
  and inflation, 525–27

H

Harris-Todaro locus, 558, 568
Harris-Todaro migration model, 63,
  558, 564
heterodox programs, 32, 266,
  282–96
high-inflation equilibrium, 301
hyperinflation
  experiences with, 269–70,
      272–75
  models of, 299–306, 605
hysteresis, 356, 604

I

implicit tax on exports, 488–90,
  506
import substitution, 616
imported inputs, 4, 15, 22–23, 82,
  101, 224, 227–28, 235–37,
  241, 243–46, 252–53, 336,
  404–5, 433, 495–99, 592
imports of capital goods, 82–83,
  236, 428
Inada conditions, 586
income distribution, 228–30, 248,
  299, 311, 573, 624
inflation, 31–32
  chronic, 265, 276
  and electoral cycles, 537–39
  and exchange rates, 305–6
  expectations of, 62, 88, 129–30,
      301–4, 434
  and fiscal deficits, 128–37,
      299–306, 536
  and growth, 525–27
  hedge, 67, 69
  inertial, 577
  new structuralist model of,
      306–14, 573
  and policy announcements,
      129–30
  and price controls, 33, 268,
      368–74
  revenue-maximizing rate of,
      112–19, 149, 363
  and seignorage, 111–16, 134,
      147, 156–57, 362–63
  and stabilization, 32, 195,
      265–97, 503–5
  tax, 67, 70, 106, 112–21,
      154–59, 188, 193, 255,
      257, 259, 431, 451, 500,
      527, 584, 598, 599, 617,
      620
  and tight money, 130–37

and time inconsistency, 120,
  361–63
informal credit markets
  implications of, 33, 88, 147,
    168–74, 180–88,
    389–415, 532
  structure of, 65–67
informal loan markets. *See*
  informal credit markets
informal markets, 33, 64–71, 77,
  389–415
interest parity, 161–64, 208, 256,
  346, 584
interest rate ceilings, 390, 406, 473
interest rates
  and complementarity hypothesis,
    474–76
  and devaluation, 237–40
  in exchange-rate-based
    programs, 339–52,
    356–59
  and expectations, 139–46, 342,
    357–59
  and fiscal deficits, 123–24,
    137–46, 149
  in informal credit markets,
    33, 392–94, 398–403,
    410–15
  and intertemporal substitution,
    349–52, 355, 392–93
  and investment, 102
  liberalization, 399–403, 412–13,
    473–77
  and monetary policy, 130–37
  and money demand, 87–88,
    94–95, 131, 141, 154,
    215, 436
  and savings, 79–80
International Monetary Fund,
  249–50, 549
intertemporal budget constraint,
  121–25, 216, 318, 349,
  602, 603

intertemporal elasticity of
  substitution, 80, 215,
  353–55, 571, 586, 604
investment
  and credit rationing, 30, 82, 85
  determinants of, 81–86, 426,
    428, 435
  and foreign exchange rationing,
    82, 85
  and growth, 513–32
  and interest rates, 474
  and the real exchange rate,
    82–83
  and saving balance, 44, 126
  and saving correlation, 166
Israel, 286–90, 368–69

J

J curve, 179, 590, 621
Jamaica, 490

K

Keynes-Kalecki effect, 62
Khan-Knight monetary model,
  439–41
Korea, 476–77, 478

L

labor contracts, 62, 215, 242, 366
labor market(s)
  functioning of, 45–48, 50–52,
    55–56
  segmentation, 34, 62–64, 72,
    556–69, 572, 617
Laffer curve, 114, 117, 119, 299,
  504, 568
liquidity constraints, 78–79, 102,
  127–28, 572, 575, 579, 604

Lucas critique, 9
Lucas supply function, 96–102

M

macroeconomic instability, 31–32,
        68, 84, 86, 503–4, 531,
        575
mark-up pricing, 62, 168, 308,
        311, 329, 336–37, 383, 433,
        601, 602
Marshall-Lerner condition, 45, 253
McKinnon-Shaw
    model of financial repression,
        152–53
    and new structuralists, 169–74
    policy prescriptions, 169, 399,
        473–77
Mexico, 108, 159, 214, 220,
        293–96, 546
minimum wages, 568
monetarist model of inflation,
        298–306
monetarists vs. new structuralists,
        3, 13–14
monetary autonomy, 165–66
monetary policy
    dynamics effects of, 180–88
    and exchange-rate dynamics,
        180–88
    instruments, 180, 320, 323,
        409
    and interest rates, 130–37
    and parallel market exchange
        rates, 180–88
monetary reform, 473–77
monetary union, 203–7, 221
money demand, 87–95, 119, 126,
        129, 131, 141, 215, 362,
        436, 439, 581
money-based programs, 270–75
Mundell-Fleming model, 18,
        44–48, 50, 432, 576, 612

N

neoclassical growth model,
        513, 518
new structuralist
    methodology, 3, 14–15
    model of informal loan markets,
        168–74
nominal anchors, 356, 381–83
nontraded goods, 48–49, 53, 147,
        225–27, 232, 346
no-Ponzi game condition. *See*
        solvency constraint

O

offset coefficient, 165
Okun's law, 59, 64
Olivera-Tanzi effect, 116–19,
        230–32, 283, 304,
        362, 605
orthodox macroeconomics, 13

P

parallel market premium, 68–69,
        71, 179–80, 184, 218, 219,
        392, 397–98, 404, 483, 491,
        506, 611, 620
parallel markets for foreign
        exchange
    models of, 180–88
    structure of, 67–72
perfect foresight, 127, 197,
        208–9, 221, 302–4, 501,
        544, 584
permanent income hypothesis,
        77, 579
Peru, 269–70, 373
peso problem, 161, 218, 588
Phillips curve, 98, 242, 434,
        537–38, 577
Polak model, 424–25, 427

policy ineffectiveness
    proposition, 96
policy trade-off, 71, 155
political business cycles, 536–54
political feasibility, 535
populism, 267–70
portfolio
    allocation, 393
    balance approach, 176–80
PPP-based exchange-rate rule. *See*
    real-exchange-rate targeting
Prebisch-Singer thesis, 575
price
    controls, 268, 278, 285–86, 291,
        293, 295, 365, 368–74,
        385–88, 572, 605
    level inertia, 347, 349
    variability, 70–71, 89
price-setting rules. *See* mark-up
    pricing
private capital formation. *See*
    investment
public sector
    consumption, 80–81
    expenditure, 26–28, 144–46,
        232, 548–54, 564–67, 587
    investment, 22, 82, 83–86, 147,
        435, 530, 580, 620
    revenue, 28–29, 230–32
purchasing power parity, 140, 223,
    275, 480, 584

Q

quasi-fiscal deficit, 41, 110–11,
    148, 283, 489–90, 611

R

rate of time preference, 140, 315
real-exchange-rate targeting,
    255–62, 596

rent-seeking activities, 70, 504,
    507, 587
required reserves, 115, 154–57,
    170, 183, 187, 589
Ricardian equivalence, 75, 127–28,
    231, 598
RMSM model, 425–27
RMSM-X model, 433–36, 612
Rodríguez model, 339–45,
    348, 352

S

saddlepath, 144–46, 321, 323,
    348, 401, 481, 483, 485,
    541, 622
saving
    "hump," 76–77
    and investment, 473–77
    precautionary, 76
    private, 73–80
seignorage
    and fiscal deficits, 106, 122–25,
        148, 445
    and inflation, 70, 147, 299–305,
        362–63
sequencing of reforms, 377–78,
    499–508
shock therapy approach, 266,
    377–78
smuggling
    and exports, 68, 174–76, 390,
        405–6, 480, 487–89, 578
    real trade models of, 174–75
Solow condition, 560
Solow-Swan growth model. *See*
    neoclassical growth model
solvency constraint, 121–25, 130,
    149, 216, 318, 325, 444–49
sources-of-growth approach,
    513–18
Southern Cone experiments. *See*
    tablita experiments

speculative attacks. *See* balance of
    payments crises
speculative bubble, 594
stabilization programs
    in developing countries, 503–5
    in the Southern Cone. *See* tablita
        experiments
Stiglitz-Weiss model, 477, 615
stock markets, 573, 615, 619, 624
structuralist-monetarist model,
    311–14

T

tablita experiments, 275–81,
    338–39, 354–55, 477–78,
    597
temporariness hypothesis,
    345–56, 382
terms of trade, 45, 49, 52, 78, 86,
    256, 596
    changes in, 47–48, 53–54, 260,
        596, 599, 601
three-gap model, 427–31
time inconsistency
    in exchange-rate policy,
        195–200, 220, 361–62
    in monetary policy, 120, 361–63,
        592
Tobin's *q*, 82
trade
    balance, 215, 248
    liberalization, 33, 275, 278,
        491–99, 501–7
trade unions, 56, 577, 624
traded goods, 49, 225–27, 229
transactions costs, 10, 140, 142,
    316, 525
transversality condition, 123–24,
    141, 316, 328, 347,
    540, 594
two-gap model, 427, 431

U

uncertainty
    political, 32, 121, 273, 364–65,
        536, 580
    about reform date, 486–87, 605
unemployment, 57, 568
    benefits, 64, 568
    and inflation, 537–39
    and real wages, 61–62, 497–99
    in segmented labor markets,
        556–59, 566
    and wage rigidity, 507, 556–59
unification of foreign exchange
        markets, 71, 479–91,
        506–7
Uruguay, 276–80
user cost of capital, 82, 85, 435
utility function
    Cobb-Douglas, 595
    constant relative risk aversion,
        586, 595, 604
    instantaneous, 140, 345, 579,
        586, 595, 603
    logarithmic, 140, 315, 345

W

wage contracts, 62, 96, 215, 255,
    329–30, 405, 539–40, 596,
    601–2
wage formation, 23, 308, 329–30,
    543, 556–57
wage indexation, 60–62, 237,
    242, 253, 329–30, 381, 603,
    609
wage inertia, 23, 55, 60–62
wages
    nominal, 62, 229, 240–43,
        308–11, 329–30, 433,
        497–99, 539, 541–43,
        609, 611

real, 61–62, 229, 237, 242,
    308–11, 335, 498–99
relative, 560
wealth accumulation. *See* asset
    accumulation

wealth effect, 233–34
welfare, 578
working capital, 15, 23, 168, 224,
    239–40, 246–48, 253, 391,
    575, 588, 596